Special Edition

USING
JAVASCRIPT

Special Edition

USING
JAVASCRIPT

Written by Mark C. Reynolds with

Ray Daly • Rick Darnell • Bill Dortch
Mona Everett • Scott J. Walter • Andrew Wooldridge

Special Edition Using JavaScript

Library of Congress Catalog No.: 96-68041

ISBN: 0-7897-0789-6

98 97 96   6 5 4 3 2 1

Interpretation of the printing code: the rightmost double-digit number is the year of the book's printing; the rightmost single-digit number, the number of the book's printing. For example, a printing code of 96-1 shows that the first printing of the book occurred in 1996.

Credits

PRESIDENT
Roland Elgey

PUBLISHER
Joseph B. Wikert

PUBLISHING DIRECTOR
Jim Minatel

EDITORIAL SERVICES DIRECTOR
Elizabeth Keaffaber

MANAGING EDITOR
Sandy Doell

DIRECTOR OF MARKETING
Lynn E. Zingraf

SENIOR SERIES EDITOR
Chris Nelson

ACQUISITIONS EDITOR
Doshia Stewart

PRODUCT DIRECTOR
Mark Cierzniak

PRODUCTION EDITORS
Kelli M. Brooks
Jeff Riley

EDITORS
Tom Cirtin
Chuck Hutchinson
Theresa Mathias

ASSISTANT PRODUCT MARKETING MANAGER
Kim Margolius

SOFTWARE SPECIALISTS
Dr. Donald Doherty
Oran J. Sands

TECHNICAL EDITORS
Dr. Donald Doherty
Stephen Feather
Faisal Jawdat
Chris Means
Joe Risse
Doug Welch
Martin Wyatt

TECHNICAL SPECIALIST
Nadeem Muhammad

OPERATIONS COORDINATOR
Patricia J. Brooks

EDITORIAL ASSISTANT
Andrea Duvall

ACQUISITIONS ASSISTANTS
Jane K. Brownlow
Andrea Duvall
Lisa Farley

BOOK DESIGNER
Ruth Harvey

COVER DESIGNERS
Dan Armstrong
Ruth Harvey

PRODUCTION TEAM
Brian Buschkill, Chad Dressler,
Trey Frank, Jason Hand, Sonja Hart,
Damon Jordan, Daryl Kessler,
Stephanie Layton, Michelle Lee,
Clint Lahnen, Julie Quinn,
Kaylene Riemen, Laura Robbins,
Bobbi Satterfield

INDEXER
Tim Griffin

Composed in *Century Old Style* and *Franklin Gothic* by Que Corporation.

About the Authors

Mark C. Reynolds has wide-ranging interests in network programming, UNIX internals, and computer animation. He holds an M.S. degree in mathematics from M.I.T. He has edited and translated a number of works of mathematics, including Stanislaus Ulam's posthumous collection of essays, "Science, Computers and People: From the Tree of Mathematics."

He is Contributing Editor for *Web Developer* magazine, and co-author of Que's hugely successful title, *Client/Server Programming with RPC and DCE*. Currently, Mark is a consultant for Adaptive Optics Associates, Inc. (a unit of United Technologies Corporation), where he works on device drivers, image processing, Java, Tcl, and computer special effects. He is also an avid rock climber and mountaineer. Mark can be reached at **mark@aoa.aoainc.com**.

Ray Daly started the world's first consumer software mail order company in 1978, and a year later he started the first software store in the world. With the store came a customer support BBS, followed later by a fiction BBS called Story Board.

His current online activities include www.onsports.com, "Sponsor/Sponsored Site of the Day," e-mail services including the Capitals mailing list at mailcall.com, Web pages for his family (Janine, Juno, and Red), HTMLjive™, and customer dependent consulting.

Rick Darnell is a midwest native currently living with his wife and two daughters in Missoula, Montana. He began his career in print at a small weekly newspaper after graduating from Kansas State University with a degree in broadcasting. While spending time as a freelance journalist and writer, Rick has seen the full gamut of personal computers since starting out with a Radio Shack Model I in the late 1970's. When not in front of his computer, he serves as a volunteer firefighter and member of a regional hazardous materials response team.

Dr. Donald Doherty is a brain scientist and a computer expert. His research into signal processing in both brains and computers keeps him pushing technology to its fullest capacity. Don enjoys sharing some of his adventures through writing about computers and the Internet.

Bill Dortch has developed software professionally for nearly 20 years. In 1995 he founded hIdaho Design, a Web site design company focused on highly interactive, multimedia site development. Prior to starting hD, Bill was Principal Software Architect at Frye Computer Systems, a leading supplier of network management software. Bill's products have been both commercially and critically successful, and have won many awards, including *LAN Magazine's* Product of the Year, Editor's Choice from *PC Magazine*, *Infoworld*, and *PC Week*, and many others.

A former Boston resident, Bill now lives in Northern Idaho with his cat, Lucky. He can be reached at **http://www.hidaho.com** or **bdortch@hidaho.com**.

Mona Everett, Ph.D., is a biochemist turned programmer. She works as a senior scientific software development specialist for Computer Data Systems, Inc., and is currently working on developing front-end access for a large medical epidemiological database. She is expert in Window's Delphi and Visual Basic as well as Mac's HyperCard.

JavaScript is the most recent addition to her programming repertoire. In addition, she can program in C or Pascal for either platform. Because she has taught for many years, she is particularly interested in educational and other software that enables people to use computers and communicate comfortably. You can contact her at **everett@txdirect.net** or check out her Morphic Molecules pages at **http://www.txdirect.net/users/everett**.

Scott J. Walter "cut his teeth" in computers on an Apple II (no plus) when he was in the seventh grade. By the time he reached senior high, he was working as an assistant to the computer science teacher and programming in BASIC, FORTRAN, Pascal, and assembly language. He was hired by a Minnesota-based software publisher in 1986, and has been developing retail software ever since. In that time, he has built and directed research and development departments at two companies; taught Pascal, C, C++, Windows, and Macintosh programming at the individual and small-business levels; co-authored (and continues to host the Web site for) *The Complete Idiot's Guide to JavaScript*; and had the time to invent a recipe for "Cajun-Italian Spaghetti Sauce" with his brother, Matthew.

Scott's current penchants are for Java, JavaScript, VBScript, ActiveX, UNIX, Windows, C++, Delphi, and other budding development technologies. He is currently a "consultant at large" in the Minneapolis area, and invites you to contact him via e-mail at **sjwalter@winternet.com** or through his home page at **http://www.winternet.com/~sjwalter/**.

Andrew Wooldridge is assistant Webmaster at Wells Fargo Bank, a pioneer in online banking and Internet services since 1989. Prior to joining Wells Fargo, he was Webmaster of Global Village Communications. Andrew started the HTML Writer's Guild, and has created the popular JavaScript Index at **http://www.c2.org/~andreww/javascript/**, which receives 40,000 hits per month.

Acknowledgments

The people at Que deserve a large measure of praise for their patience, perseverance, and hard work. I would especially like to thank Doshia Stewart and Kelli Brooks for their ongoing support, guidance, and impressive organizational skills. Many other people at Que have also worked very hard on this book, and are to be congratulated on the outcome.

This book would not have been possible without the strenuous efforts and prodigious technical knowledge of the entire writing team. I am very grateful for their individual contributions, each of which was indispensable.

Mark C. Reynolds

To my wife, who supported me through the whole thing.

Andrew Wooldridge

Dedications

To HB and PMcG, who give life meaning.

Mark C. Reynolds

To my new baby Jesse Andrew.

Andrew Wooldridge

We'd Like To Hear from You!

As part of our continuing effort to produce books of the highest possible quality, Que would like to hear your comments. To stay competitive, we *really* want you, as a computer book reader and user, to let us know what you like or dislike most about this book or other Que products.

You can mail comments, ideas, or suggestions for improving future editions to the address below, or send us a fax at (317) 581-4663. Our staff and authors are available for questions and comments through our Internet site, at **http://www.mcp.com/que**, and Macmillan Computer Publishing also has a forum on CompuServe (type **GO QUEBOOKS** at any prompt).

In addition to exploring our forum, please feel free to contact me personally to discuss your opinions of this book: I'm **mcierzniak.que.mcp.com** on the Internet, and **76245,476** on CompuServe.

Thanks in advance—your comments will help us to continue publishing the best books available on new computer technologies in today's market.

Mark Cierzniak
Product Director
Que Corporation
201 W. 103rd Street
Indianapolis, Indiana 46290
USA

NOTE Although we cannot provide general technical support, we're happy to help you resolve problems you encounter related to our books, disks, or other products. If you need such assistance, please contact our Tech Support department at 800-545-5914 ext. 3833.

To order other Que or Macmillan Computer Publishing books or products, please call our Customer Service department at 800-835-3202 ext. 666.

Contents at a Glance

VI | Appendixes

Table of Contents

Introduction

Five years ago the Internet was mostly the province of academics and programmers, and the World Wide Web was an obscure idea in the minds of a few researchers. Today both are experiencing explosive growth and unparalleled interest. Web pages are being created at an astonishing rate. The fundamental challenge of Web page development is that while it is easy to create a Web page, it is more difficult to create an attractive and exciting one.

HTML, the markup language that describes the appearance of a page, is easy to learn, and requires no background in programming. HTML has undergone several revisions in order to meet the expanding needs of Web page authors. However, there are limits to what can be achieved inside HTML. The Java programming language was introduced to dramatically extend the Web developer's set of tools, but is still more complex than HTML. Java is very easy to learn; however, like most programming languages, it isn't easy to master. JavaScript bridges this gap. ■

JavaScript offers the Web page author a new level of sophistication without requiring him to become a programmer. JavaScript brings dynamic and powerful capabilities to Web pages, yet JavaScript is no more difficult to learn than HTML. JavaScript can be used to solve common problems, such as validating forms input, and can also be used to create dramatic and visually appealing content, which would be impossible with HTML. The goal of this book is to completely explore JavaScript, from the mundane to the extraordinary. It is designed as an introduction, a reference, and a continuous source of ideas, so that you may continually improve the Web pages that you create.

Who Should Use This Book?

JavaScript is a very new language—even newer than Java. Despite its newness it has attracted great attention because of its expressive power. This book is directed at anyone who wishes to master that power in order to create more attractive, dynamic, and interesting Web pages.

No programming knowledge is required to benefit from this book, but some knowledge of HTML and Web page authoring is assumed. No prior experience with JavaScript is required, either. This book is designed to be inclusive, and provide information to all JavaScript users, from complete beginners to established experts. If you create Web pages and wish to enliven and enhance them, this book adds JavaScript to your toolbox. If you have already learned JavaScript and wish to go further and break through to complete mastery, this book gives you the information to do so.

How This Book Is Organized

The organization of this book is based on a modular approach to learning JavaScript. The intent is to provide material suitable for all levels of knowledge, from the complete beginner to the advanced JavaScript programmer. To this end the book has five sections.

Part I, "JavaScript the Language," introduces the JavaScript language. The complete syntax and semantics of the language are thoroughly described, with particular attention paid to the close correspondence between HTML elements and JavaScript objects. Chapter 1, "What Is JavaScript?" discusses JavaScript's overall role in the development of Web pages. Chapter 2, "JavaScript: The Language," gives the syntax of JavaScript. This leads directly into a description of the relationship between events on a Web page and JavaScript, in chapter 3, "Events and JavaScript." This is followed by an introduction to the all-important topic of JavaScript objects in chapter 4, "JavaScript Objects."

Part II, "JavaScript Objects," is a greatly expanded presentation of the JavaScript object model that begins in chapter 4 of part I. JavaScript objects can be classified as built-in objects or HTML objects. Built-in objects are thoroughly described in chapter 5, "Built-In JavaScript Objects," while chapters 6 through 8 focus on HTML objects. Validation of HTML forms is the subject of chapter 6; each form element is also a JavaScript object. Navigation objects, such as links and anchors, are then described in chapter 7, while chapter 8 presents the top-level objects associated with the Web browser itself. Part II concludes with a thorough treatment of user-defined objects in chapter 9.

One of the tremendous advantages of a scripting language such as JavaScript is its capability to integrate diverse technologies on a single Web page. Part III is devoted to examining such technologies. Chapter 10 deals with plug-ins, which are becoming increasingly abundant and useful on the World Wide Web. The Java programming language has received massive attention, and is quite similar to JavaScript in structure. Chapter 11 provides a thorough introduction to Java, while chapter 12 focuses on the critical topic of Web page animation using Java. Finally, chapter 13 presents the Visual Basic scripting language in brief, and also looks at its plug-in technology, OLE controls.

Part IV brings the user the most advanced material available on creating special effects using JavaScript. Controlling Web page appearance, producing spectacular visual effects, and fine-tuning user interaction are the subjects of in-depth treatment in chapters 14 through 16. Each chapter contains at least one fully worked example that can be used immediately. JavaScript server technology is reviewed in chapter 17, while various development tools for JavaScript are covered in chapter 18. Part IV concludes with an in-depth look at Web page development using the innovative frames technology in chapter 19.

The fifth part of this book is devoted to Learning from the Pros. This part contains advanced solutions to common, yet difficult problems. Several innovative techniques are described here, as well as pointers on how to enliven any JavaScript Web page. Chapters 20 through 22 describe site outlines in JavaScript, conversion from standard HTML to frames, and a JavaScript online order system.

The book concludes with a series of reference appendixes that summarize critical information presented in the main body of the text. A glossary of common JavaScript terms is given, along with a capsule description of all major JavaScript resources. A language summary is provided, as well as a list of known bugs in the current implementation of JavaScript (version 2.0.1). Future enhancements are also discussed in brief.

How to Use This Book

If you are completely new to JavaScript then you should begin with an in-depth study of the introductory language materials of part I. This should be followed by the more thorough treatment of JavaScript objects in part II. From that point on any chapter or section can be consulted, based on your own particular interest. It should be noted that later chapters are generally more advanced than earlier ones, however.

If you are already familiar with JavaScript then you are encouraged to explore this book in a goal-oriented manner. The alternative technologies discussed in part III may well be new to you, even if you are an experienced Web professional. Finally, parts IV and V should have something new and informative for everyone, as they are intended to help you stretch the limits of JavaScript technology.

Conventions Used in This Book

Que has more than a decade of experience writing and developing the most successful computer books available. With that experience, we've learned what special features help readers the most. Look for these special features throughout the book to enhance your learning experience.

The following font conventions are used in this book to help make reading it easier.

- *Italic type* is used to introduce new terms.
- Screen messages, code listings, and command samples appear in monospace type.
- Code that you are instructed to type appears in **monospace bold type**.

 T I P Tips present short advice on a quick or often overlooked procedures. These include shortcuts.

N O T E Notes present interesting or useful information that isn't necessarily essential to the discussion. A note provides additional information that may help you avoid problems or offers advice that relates to the topic.

CAUTION

Cautions look like this and warn you about potential problems that a procedure may cause, unexpected results, or mistakes to avoid.

 This icon indicates you can also find the related information on the enclosed CD-ROM. ●

JavaScript the Language

What Is JavaScript?

by Ray Daly

Remember the thrill of visiting your first Web page and clicking your first hyperlink to another site? The excitement of surfing from California to Maine, from Australia to Finland? This interactive nature of the Web attracts millions of people to the Web every day.

With JavaScript, new dynamic elements let you go beyond the simple click and wait. Users will not just read your pages but also interact with them. Your pages come alive for any user, even with the slowest Internet connection. Users will get quick responses because the interaction does not need to involve the server but can take place in their browser.

This interaction can change your pages into an application. Put together a few buttons, a text box, and some code to produce a calculator. Or an editor. Or a game. Or the "killer" JavaScript application that everyone wants. Users will save your JavaScript enhanced pages to use your application again and again.

JavaScript on the Web

See the vairous ways JavaScript is making more dynamic Web sites. Some are so good, you'll save them to use over and over again.

See how simple JavaScript pages can be

You will see easy-to-implement code that lets you add entirely new features to your Web site.

JavaScript pages can also be complex

With JavaScript you can have interaction between frames and multiple windows. It's not just for gadgets.

Learn the difference between JavaScript and Java

Though the two languages share the same first name, they are very different. Don't mistake them for being the same.

Scripts make great applications

There is no firm definition of a scripting language. An examination of several can provide some insights to where you can go with JavaScript.

JavaScript is a programming language that allows scripting of events, objects, and actions to create Internet applications. ∎

Live Content on the WWW

In building Web pages, you present information to your audience. The design and layout should entice them to explore your site. Your hyperlinks provide several predefined, but different, paths to see your information.

With JavaScript, your pages come alive! Your pages respond to the requests of your audience beyond a simple click here or there. Many more interactive elements are now available for exciting design and layout. Your users are no longer just readers. People will interact with your documents, not just read them. Your users can now interact with forms, change the look and feel of your Web documents, and use multiple windows.

Forms Explode with Information

With JavaScript, forms are a consideration in nearly every page you design. Text fields and textareas can dynamically change in response to user responses. Your audience will look for buttons, selections, radio buttons, and checkboxes. Your pages will change at their touch. The following examples show you how JavaScript makes forms come alive:

- ■ *Calculators*—Where is that calculator when you need it? On your page (see fig. 1.1). Beyond simple arithmetic, you can do conversions in hexadecimal, calories, metric, and more. Expand the form and you have the unlimited world of spreadsheets—for example, simple tax forms, grade-point averages, and survey analysis.

- ■ *Display time*. What time is it? It's easy to show in a basic text box (see fig. 1.2). Or how about the time anywhere in the world? Add in a little math and show users the elapsed time. Different math produces a countdown time. A little different code and you have a population explosion or national debt counter.

FIG. 1.1
Calculator built in to a Web page with JavaScript.

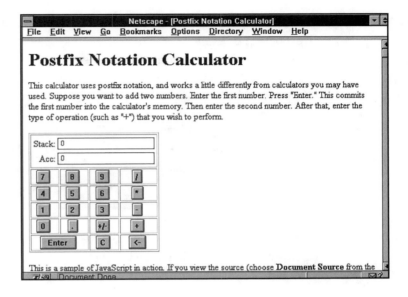

FIG. 1.2
JavaScript time displays usually show you the local time.

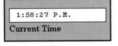

■ *Feedback status.* As you build JavaScript applications, there will be a lot going on. Your code will have loops, increment variables, and track user inputs.

■ *Let the users in on what's going on.* Provide feedback with a numeric counter (see fig. 1.3). Say it "graphically" with a bar graph made of ASCII characters and show a status literally.

FIG. 1.3
Text boxes can feed back status of applications to users numerically, with ASCII graphics, or verbally, in text boxes.

■ *Verification*. With user input, you usually want to verify the validity of the response. For example, if you want the response to be a number between 1 and 10, JavaScript can verify that the user's response falls in that range. If not, the code can notify the user and ask again for the input (see fig. 1.4). Once verified, the result is submitted to the server.

FIG. 1.4
Provide your users with instant feedback without waiting for a response from the server.

■ *Entertainment*. Everyone wants to have fun—even when learning. You can convey your information as an interactive game or even as a joke (see figs. 1.5 and 1.6). The source code is very simple (see listing 1.1).

FIG. 1.5
Punchline: now you see the joke without the punchline revealed.

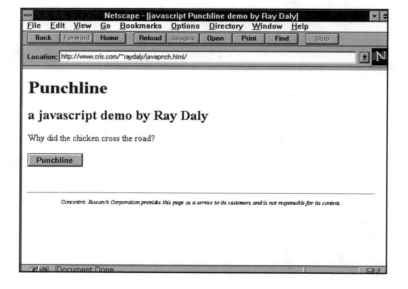

FIG. 1.6
Here's the punchline, hidden until you are ready to see it.

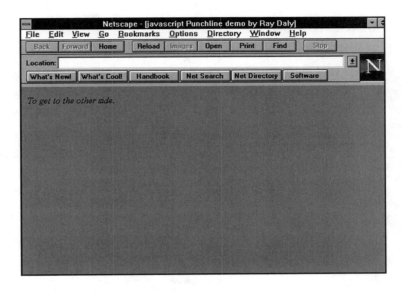

The source code in listing 1.1 is easy to modify to tell your own jokes on the Web without giving away the punchline.

On the CD

Listing 1.1   javapnch.htm   Code for JavaScript Punchline

```
<HTML>
<HEAD>
<TITLE>javascript Punchline demo by Ray Daly</TITLE>
<SCRIPT LANGUAGE="LiveScript">
<!-- hide this script from some browsers
function Punchline () {
   document.write ("<BODY BGcolor=#00EE00><P>
   ➥<I>To get to the other side.</P></I>") ;
}
//  hidden ray.daly@mailcall.com 12/16/95-->
</SCRIPT>
</HEAD>
<BODY>
<H1>Punchline</H1>
<H2>a javascript Punchline demo by Ray Daly</H2>
<P>Why did the chicken cross the road?</P>
<FORM>
<P><INPUT TYPE="button"  VALUE="Punchline" onClick=Punchline()>
</P>
</FORM>
</BODY>
</HTML>
```

Look and Feel Is An Option

All of the elements inside the window of a browser are available in JavaScript. You can dynamically change some of these elements. Or you can examine the elements of one document and use that information to create a different document. The following are some examples of changing the look and feel of documents:

- *Change colors.* Ever get to a page where the colors nearly make you go blind? Give your users a choice of several color combinations of backgrounds and text colors. As your application displays documents, use your users' colors (see fig. 1.7).

TIP There are too many colors for a user to choose. Don't make them experiment; let them select from some good combinations you have already tested.

FIG. 1.7
Sample of menu where you can change the background color.

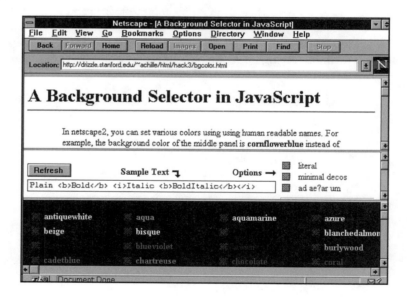

- *Change links.* Normally, users click hyperlinks and off they go to the site you specified as the URL for the hyperlink. With JavaScript, this link can change based on user responses. If a user indicates a preference to baseball over football, your code can change the hyperlink to point to the Yankees instead of the Cowboys.

■ *Reformat Pages.* Since JavaScript can examine all of the elements of a document, you can read a document in one frame and completely reformat it in another.

An example is HTML Analysis (see fig. 1.8). In the control panel at the bottom of the window, you specify a URL that is displayed in the left frame. The right panel is generated from the code activated by the REDO button. This code reads the HTML code of the left document and creates an entirely new document that lists all of the hyperlinks. This new document is displayed in the right frame.

Listing 1.2 shows the frames for HTML Analysis.

On the CD

Listing 1.2   hanalysi.htm   Frames for HTML Analysis

```
<HTML>
<HEAD>
<TITLE>HTML Analysis by Ray Daly</TITLE></HEAD>
<FRAMESET ROWS="80,300,*">
      <FRAME SRC="hanalys1.htm" NAME="control">
      <FRAME SRC="" NAME="displayhere">
      <FRAME SRC="" NAME="analysis">
<FRAME SRC="guide.htm" NAME="guide">
</FRAMESET>
</HTML>
```

Listing 1.3 shows the code for HTML Analysis.

Listing 1.3   hanalys1.htm   Code for HTML Analysis

```
<HTML>
<HEAD>
<TITLE>hanalys1.htm: part of hanalysi.htm</TITLE>
<SCRIPT Lanuguage="JavaScript">
function doit() {
   for (i = 0; i <parent.displayhere.document.links.length; i++) {
     parent.analysis.document.write (parent.displayhere.document.links[i]
     ➥ + "<BR>")
   }
}</SCRIPT></HEAD>
<BODY>
<A HREF="http://www.cris.com/~raydaly/htmljive.html" TARGET="displayhere">
Get a page.</A>
<FORM><INPUT TYPE="button" VALUE="Probe it" onClick="doit()"></FORM>
</BODY>
</HTML>
```

CAUTION

The HTML Analysis application is not stable on all platforms. Make sure the URL is completely loaded prior to doing the analysis.

FIG. 1.8
The URL specified in the top frame is displayed in the second frame. The third frame shows only the links from that page. Such tools are a great way to make certain pages on your site meet your standards.

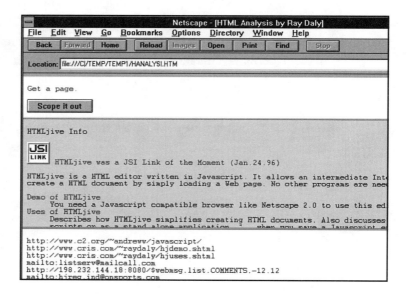

 You can reformat pages for dramatic results. Instead of showing the entire document in a large frame, bring the source document into an extremely small frame. Then display your reformatted document in the much larger frame. If the frame with your source is small enough, your users won't even know what the original looked like.

■ *Tools for analysis.* Analyzing tools are a very interesting derivative of reformatting documents. Instead of displaying a reformatted document, analyzing tools provide an analysis of a document. Tools could check such simple things as word counts, link counts, or other statistics. Code could even be written to show the tree structure of all of the objects in a document. Or you could write code to verify that pages meet the criteria for your corporate site.

Multiple Windows and Frames

Netscape introduced frames and JavaScript with Navigator 2.0. You will probably also find yourself using another popular feature: opening multiple windows for browsing the Web. Microsoft Internet Explorer 3.0 also supports JavaScript, frames, and multiple windows. Add some JavaScript behind these new features and the browser becomes a kaleidoscope on the WWW. No longer are you limited to browsing one page at a time. Now you can view multiple documents and see a multifaceted view of the Internet world. The following list examines using multiple windows and frames:

- *Alert, confirm, and prompt dialog boxes*. JavaScript has its own built-in dialog boxes you can use in your design. Alert users to take caution (see fig. 1.9), confirm an action with an okay or cancel response (see fig. 1.10), or prompt for a text input (see fig. 1.11).

FIG. 1.9
Alert box notifies the user, but provide no choices.

FIG. 1.10
Confirm box notifies the user and allows him to cancel the action.

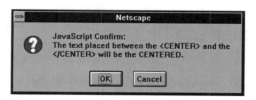

FIG. 1.11
Prompt box lets the user type a response to your code.

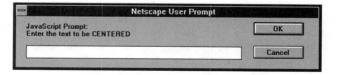

- *Control windows*. Beyond the built-in dialog boxes, you can create your own controls with custom windows. Populate them with buttons, text boxes, or icons to control the results in your other windows.

■ *Navigation windows.* Have two, three, or more windows all opened simultaneously. As the user navigates from one, the others display various screens of information. For example, each window might pull in a live image from a different point around the globe as selected by the user. Internet Tri-Eye provides live views from around the world (see fig. 1.12).

FIG. 1.12
Internet Tri-Eye is an example of a multi-window application and a control panel. Selections in one frame produce results in other frames.

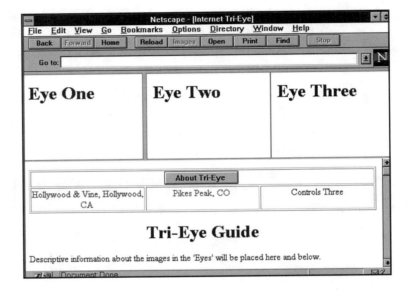

Interact with Other Live Objects

Sun Microsystems and Netscape Communications introduced JavaScript. An additional 28 leading computer companies, including AOL, AT&T, Borland, Digital Equipment Corporation, Hewlett-Packard Corporation, and Oracle Corporation endorsed JavaScript. Microsoft supports JavaScript in Internet Explorer 3.0. These companies support JavaScript because it is an open standard object language. Several companies will introduce products that incorporate JavaScript. This will allow even more interaction. The following products support JavaScript:

■ *Netscape's LiveWire.* LiveWire is a visual development environment for creating Internet applications. This new product provides enhancements to a server including JavaScript. The same language that you use to make your pages come alive on the browser can be used to respond to requests at the server. Instead of writing CGI scripts in Perl, C, or some other language, use JavaScript.

■ *Plug-ins*. Plug-ins are software that work with Netscape's Navigator. Third-party publishers such as Adobe, MacroMedia, Borland, and many others produce these applications. This software will allow viewing of other file formats, multimedia presentations, and specialized functions.

N O T E For more information on plug-ins, visit this site: **http://home.netscape.com/ comprod/products/navigator/version_2.0/plugins/**. ■

The number of plug-ins for browsers is expected to grow astronomically. As these applications become more sophisticated, they are expected to use JavaScript as their scripting language. In addition, many of these publishers will allow JavaScript in the browser to interact with their plug-ins. The objects in this software will be available or exposed to JavaScript.

N O T E Microsoft is actively promoting its scripting language VBScript. The primary function of this language is to interact with and create external applications. Because this language is a subset of Microsoft's Visual Basic and works with ActiveX controls, it is expected to have a substantial impact. ■

Netscape Navigator 2.0 supports a new functionality-enhancing feature that provides inline support for a huge range of Live Objects. With Live Objects, developers can deliver rich multimedia content through Internet sites, allowing users to seamlessly view that content with plug-ins such as Adobe Acrobat, Apple QuickTime, and Macromedia Shockwave for Director in the client window—all without launching any external helper applications.

■ *New Internet Products*. Given the scope of the companies behind JavaScript, you can expect to see some very specialized Internet products. Many of these products will use JavaScript for customizing.

Role of Scripting

There is no definitive definition of a scripting language. Sometimes the term is used to make a distinction from compiled languages. However, some languages like C or C++ can be used for scripting as well as full applications. The term scripting is also used because a language will react to, control, or "script" a series of events. Even macro languages built into PC applications like spreadsheets, databases, word processors, and multimedia applications are now often called scripting languages.

The purpose of most scripting languages is to extend the capabilities of applications. Just as the authors of this book cannot imagine every creative use you will make of JavaScript, software authors cannot imagine every possible use of their applications. To make their products more versatile, they add a scripting language. With JavaScript you have a scripting language to use your imagination on the Web.

Current uses of scripting languages may give you an insight of the potential for JavaScript. You probably know that macros are built in to many PC applications. Apple's HyperCard contains a very powerful scripting feature. Perl is a scripting language used in many CGI scripts you use on the Web.

PC Macros Become Scripts

Traditionally, a macro feature was added to PC software to allow a simple series of commands to be executed with a single keystroke. With great fanfare publishers introduced this feature as a way to reduce repetitive tasks and save time. For example, a word processor's simple macro might change the entire style of a document.

Over time the macro feature of various applications became complex scripting languages. As scripts became longer and nontrivial, they extended the software beyond its normal purpose. New and creative combinations of commands made the software the basis for entirely new applications—for example, a set of word processing scripts for maintaining a small mailing list.

These scripting languages in software are so sophisticated that they are the subject of college courses. Many universities now require courses in spreadsheet scripting for accounting and business students. Art majors are learning scripting procedures for high-end graphics and multimedia packages. Legal courses include using scripts to create documents. And computer science majors have a variety of courses involving scripting languages.

A defining factor of this type of scripting language is that they only work with applications. Scripts in word processors add word processing features. Scripts in spreadsheets add spreadsheet features. These scripts do not go beyond the nature of the software, but they use the existing commands of the software. In our example, the mailing list script still works with words, the standard element of the word processor. This becomes a limitation on the usefulness of this script.

With the popularity of program suites like Microsoft Office, Lotus SmartSuites, and Perfect Office, PC publishers have started making the same scripting language work with more than one application. (Some would say that, at this point, macro languages become scripting languages.) Not only is the same language used in each application, the script language helps the applications work together. Microsoft expanded the role of Visual Basic to work with Microsoft Access and Excel. Lotus has developed LiveBasic for its product suite.

With the PC environment, the role of scripting languages is serious business. It's the subject of college courses and often used to build nontrivial applications.

N O T E Historically, scripting has made several "killer applications." These are applications, that define a whole new category of software, significantly expand the market, and provide a primary reason for people to use a computer. The first successful spreadsheet was VisiCalc, which disappeared with the success of Lotus 1-2-3. The latter had scripting. There were many different database applications on the market before Ashton-Tate's dBase, but this product was programmable with a scripting language.

Scripting gave these applications a competitive edge. First, it was a feature that could be used to sell the product. Second, people actually started to use the feature and create significant new capabilities for these products. Third, these scripts created a whole new market with magazine articles, books, third-party software publishers, and training. Fourth, the continuing use of these scripts became an investment by the user in these products. Existing scripts often prevented users from switching to competitive products. And finally, even when a competitive product was introduced with new features, someone would introduce scripts that attempted to add these features into the existing products. Scripts allowed both the publisher and users to advance. ■

Scripting in Macintosh Applications

The most notable use of scripting on the Macintosh is Apple's HyperCard program. This application lets you build a group of cards and hyperlink them together. The cards can contain not only text but multimedia files. The stack of cards that you construct can respond to user input.

The scripting language is such a strong element of HyperCard that many people consider HyperCard itself to be a language. Many Mac owners were initially disappointed with HTML because it lacked many of the capabilities of HyperCard. In many ways, JavaScript brings some of the HyperCard features to the Web.

Perl Started as a UNIX Scripting Language

If you have used the Web, you have used Perl. It is the language used for probably the majority of CGI scripts. These are routines that run on Internet servers and respond to requests from browsers when a user completes a form. There are guestbooks, message boards, voting pages, surveys, and more that use Perl scripts.

Perl is an interpreted language. While you should be able to find a version of Perl for almost any computer platform, it was created for UNIX systems. It is now platform independent. The vast majority of Perl scripts will run without modification on any system. Take a script written on UNIX and it will run perfectly well on DOS.

A CGI script is a type of script that responds to events. In this case, the event is a user submitting data from an HTML form. The attributes of a <FORM> include ACTION, which defines the script to process the data when it is submitted. For example,

```
<FORM ACTION="\cgi-bin\guestbook.pl">
```

will process the data from the form in a script called guestbook.pl. More than likely this routine would store the data in a file and return an HTML page to the browser as feedback. It would probably say something like, "Thanks for your entry into our guestbook."

Perl is freely distributed on the Internet, but please see its license for more detail. You should be able to find a version for your system using any of the Internet search services. Larry Wall is the sole maintainer.

Perl's strength as a language is in manipulating files and text to produce reports. This capability along with its associative arrays make it a natural fit for creating CGI scripts. In a few lines you can process data and return an HTML document in response to an HTML form.

If you are a Perl programmer, you can rather quickly learn JavaScript. Both have a similar control structure and both are interpreted languages. Unlike Perl, JavaScript is object-based but it is not nearly as complex. You might miss the text processing capabilities of Perl, but you will find JavaScript a delightful new language to learn.

There are some cases where JavaScript is not the appropriate solution, but using Perl for a CGI script would fit the requirement. Generally, if you need to store information, you are going to have to do that on the server and Perl would be a good choice.

Extend the Capabilities of the HTML Page

Like other scripting languages that extend the capabilities of the application with which they work, JavaScript extends the standard Web page beyond its normal use. You have already seen in this chapter numerous ways to make your Web site come alive. And given the flexibility of the language, the only limit is your imagination. We must now consider how JavaScript works within HTML pages.

JavaScript Pages Work Differently

With the standard Web site, you get more information by clicking a hypertext link and having the server send you another file. On a more interactive page, you complete a form, submit the results to the server, and wait for a response. In either case you must wait on the server to send a new file. This information is almost always a new page, though it might be a multimedia file like an audio clip or an animation.

With JavaScript-enhanced pages, there is JavaScript code embedded in the HTML code. The JavaScript can instantly provide you information without waiting on the server or your Internet connection (see fig. 1.13). This information can come from user input, code "hidden" with the document, or other documents in frames or other windows.

This JavaScript-enhanced page makes this new information visible by updating the contents of a form or by generating an entirely new document. In a JavaScript calculator (refer to fig. 1.1), the form is updated when numbers are entered. In the Punchline script (refer to fig. 1.5), the user clicks the button and a new document is created from the hidden punchline of the joke.

FIG. 1.13
With standard HTML pages, a Web site serves each page to the browser. With JavaScript-enhanced pages, the source for a page can be the existing page.

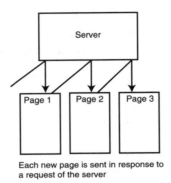

Each new page is sent in response to a request of the server

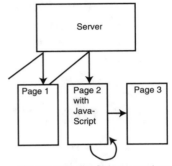

The page with JavaScript can produce a new page without making a request to the server

JavaScript Meets the HTML Page

JavaScript works with browsers by embedding code directly into an HTML page. Netscape added a new generic tag called SCRIPT to recognize scripting languages. To inform the browser that your code is JavaScript, you must add the attribute of LANGUAGE="JavaScript" to the SCRIPT tag. Much of your JavaScript coding is enclosed within these tags, as you can see in the following example:

```
<SCRIPT LANGUAGE="JavaScript">
a = "Hello!"
//...set a variable called 'a' to a value of "Hello!"
</SCRIPT>
```

N O T E   Like most any other computer language, JavaScript allows you to place comments within your code. Single-line and multiple-line comments are possible. A multiple line starts with the two characters /*. It ends with the two characters */.

Consider the following example:

```
/* This is the start of multiple lines of comments.
This is the end */
```

To make a comment at the end of a line or on a single line, just use the characters // and everything after that mark until the end of the line will be considered a comment. ■

Between SCRIPT tags you can write two types of code: *direct statements* and *functions*. Direct statements are executed by the browser as they are loaded. For example, objects are initialized in direct statements. Functions are blocks of code that are executed only by other code or events.

▶ **See** chapter 3, "Events and JavaScript," for more information about code and events, **p. 75**.

For example, mouse-click events usually trigger functions. Most of your programs will use both direct statements and functions.

Many existing HTML tags now have additional attributes to support JavaScript. For example, all elements of a form can now be identified with the NAME element. You should be familiar with the NAME attribute because it has long been used in creating anchors. Using NAME to identify objects in your documents will generally simplify your coding and debugging.

The final addition to HTML is recognizing events like mouse clicks, changes in text boxes, and the loading or unloading of pages. This is how the document recognizes the user interaction. These events are used to trigger JavaScript actions. The code can be quite straightforward, as in the following:

```
<FORM>
<P>Click inside the box and then out to see change.
<INPUT TYPE="text"  NAME="sample" onChange = "sample.value = a">
<!-- ...after any change in this text box, but the value of a in
➥the box -->
</FORM>
```

The JavaScript code that is triggered by an event can be simple or complex. With simple actions, the entire code can be placed in the event element. This is shown in the previous example with sample.value = a. Throughout this book you will see more typical examples of where functions are called by events.

Limited by Objects in the Browser

Like any language, JavaScript manipulates data. Being an object-based language, there are *methods* and *functions* that act on the data in the objects. Other than string, math, and date objects, JavaScript is limited to operating on browser objects and other objects exposed to the browser. These other objects can include plug-ins, Java applets, and ActiveX. This allows you to create new documents, modify your existing forms, and build applications.

JavaScript works with browser objects, which makes the language easier to learn. Most of the code manipulates HTML elements that you already know. For example, it will read properties of a link or write information into a textarea. Use elements you already know about to make pages come alive.

But this is a limitation. There are not any new operations that give you multimedia capability like sound or graphics. To add these types of features, you need to extend the capability of the browser with plug-ins, Java applets, or other external applications. These programs may or may not make their objects available to JavaScript.

CAUTION

Plug-ins are written by software publishers to add capabilities to the Netscape Navigator. These publishers are not required to make these plug-ins work with JavaScript. So you must look at the specifications of a plug-in to see if it supports JavaScript.

This feature is not supported in version 2.0, but is planned for version 2.1 of Netscape Navigator.

JavaScript and Java

JavaScript and Java are alike in more than just name. However, there are significant differences between these two languages. As you learn to understand the differences, you will also understand how they can work together. Each has its place and neither does it all. Table 1.1 provides a quick overview of the differences.

▶ **See** chapter 11, "A Java Tutorial," for more information about Java, **p. 369**.

Table 1.1   Comparing JavaScript and Java

JavaScript	Java
Interpreted by client	Compiled by the author, run on client
Code integrated in HTML documents	Applets distinct from HTML document
Loose typing of data types	Strong typing of data types

JavaScript	Java
Dynamic binding	Static binding
Script limited to browser functions	Stand-alone applications
Works with HTML elements	Goes beyond HTML (for example, multimedia)
Access browser objects and functionality	No access to browser objects or functionality

JavaScript and Java Work in the Same Environment

Both JavaScript and Java are languages for building Internet applications. These applications require browsers. The browsers run these applications by reading code embedded in a HTML page. In other words, they both work in the same environment.

Sun and Netscape have mounted a high profile campaign to ensure the security of these products. Neither product writes to the user's hard drive. Sensitive information about the user is also unavailable to these languages. So both products are limited by security and privacy concerns of their environment.

Because the two products have a similar name and work in the same environment, many people do not realize the distinction between JavaScript and Java.

JavaScript Is NOT Java

It appears that more Internet browsers will support Java than JavaScript, though this is not certain. They display information differently in a browser window. Java applications can stand alone. One is compiled, the other is interpreted. The development tools are different, and they have a surprisingly different audience.

Java Displays Are Limited to a Graphic Area   To display information on a Web page, Java is limited to painting its text and graphics within a defined area. Just like images on a page are drawn within a defined area of the page, so it is with Java programs. Within these areas the Java applets can create animations, paint, and use various fonts. However, an applet cannot affect anything outside its area.

JavaScript gives you access to the entire Web page. You can modify properties of the page or any element of the page. You can create new documents or update parts of a form. Unlike Java, JavaScript lets you change the appearance of any part of your Web documents, not just a limited area.

N O T E The hype on Java is that it is flexible enough to do anything. Currently, it *cannot* affect anything in a Web page outside of the area to which it is assigned. If you want your HTML document to interact with Java, forget it. The only way for Java to control everything on the screen is to write a program from scratch and re-create the entire screen. You basically have to rewrite some browser functions.

To access browser objects, Java is expected to work more closely with JavaScript in future editions. This should enhance the capabilities of both languages.

Directly related to this is Sun's work on a new version of HotJava, its Web browser. Apparently the new version's primary goal is to make available general-purpose browser routines for Java programmers. It is not clear at this time how this will play out, but the development of HotJava is worth watching. ■

Java Applications Can Stand Alone   Java is a general-purpose language that can create stand-alone applications. Unlike the Java applets that run in Web pages, these applications may not even connect to the Internet but perform business functions like accounting. This is an important aspect of Java that has excited many people.

JavaScript, like most other scripting languages, works only with an application. Currently it works with Netscape's Navigator browser and the LiveWire server environment. In the near future it will also work with plug-ins. But JavaScript applications will not function independently.

CAUTION

HotJava (not to be confused with Java or JavaScript) is Sun's own Web browser written in Java. It has shown that Java applications can stand alone. This browser's purpose was to demonstrate the early applets written with the alpha version of Java. With the official release of Java version 1, the original HotJava is no longer a viable browser. It will not run applets written in Java version 1. A new version of HotJava, which will support both Java 1.0 applets and JavaScript, is apparently in the works .

Java Is a Compiled Language   With Java you write your code, compile it, and then run it. The person using your Java applet from a Web page cannot look at the source code. For many programmers, there is a sense of security here that you are not giving away your code.

JavaScript is interpreted. The code you write in JavaScript is the code that the browser executes. There is no intermediate step of creating executable code from the source code. People can look at the source code of the HTML page and read your JavaScript code and your comments.

JavaScript and Java Development Tools   The first generation of development tools for these languages are just being introduced. Since JavaScript and Java are very new languages, this is not surprising. However, looking at the nature of the products, some general distinctions between the development tools can be made.

Java is very much like the C++ language. It is object oriented, uses many of the same statements, uses libraries, and is compiled. Several companies that have strong C++ programming environments are developing similar environments for Java. This will allow the development of large-scale Java applications, but you will have to learn these programming environments.

▶ **See** chapter 18, "Tools for JavaScript Development," for more information, **p. 629**.

JavaScript is tied to the HTML page. The code is embedded in it and it operates on HTML elements. Since the code is interpreted by a browser, it is anticipated that HTML editors will add features for creating JavaScript code.

JavaScript and Java Have Different Audiences   Java requires a multi-tasking, multi-threaded environment. So anyone operating on the UNIX platform, OS/2, Windows NT and 95, or Macintosh will be able to run Java applications and applets. This is a substantial part of the Internet audience.

JavaScript works in any version of Netscape Navigator 2.0 and above, as well as any version of Microsoft Internet Explorer and above. Given the many platforms these browsers support, this is also a substantial part of the Internet audience.

There are some big differences between these audiences. The biggest difference is that millions of people running Windows 3.1 can run Netscape Navigator and thus enjoy JavaScript-enhanced pages. These same people cannot run Java applets or applications.

It appears that more Internet browsers will support Java than JavaScript, though this is not certain. So while you might have a computer that runs JavaScript, your browser might not support it. But those that do not support JavaScript should be a minority with Microsoft and Netscape supporting both languages.

So in the near future it appears that JavaScript has a wider audience due to the Windows 3.1 users. However, as these people upgrade and as new Java-compatible browsers become available, it seems Java will develop a larger audience.

Because JavaScript is an interpreted language, there is a huge audience of potential JavaScript authors. All it takes to write a JavaScript program is a JavaScript-compatible browser like Netscape 2.0 and a text editor. Most HTML editors can also be used to write JavaScript code. So, millions of people now have all the tools they need to create JavaScript applications. In a matter of a few days Netscape was able to distribute probably millions of JavaScript interpreters. It took Microsoft years to distribute nearly as many copies of Microsoft Basic into computers.

Learning JavaScript is almost easy. By typing in just a few lines, you can be running a JavaScript application. As you read through this book you will quickly be incorporating many scripts into your pages. But just as anyone can plant a seed, it does take some patience and skill to create a garden.

Java and JavaScript Working Together

One of the more important aspects of Sun and Netscape's cooperation is the commitment to make the languages work together. They share a similar syntax and control structure that make it easier to write code for either language. But more important, a JavaScript page will be able to communicate with the Java applet referenced by the page.

Another aspect of this sharing takes place not in the browser, but in the server. Netscape's new LiveWire graphic environment will support both Java and JavaScript so the scripting language that works on the browser will also work on the server. Just as interactive scripts currently run as CGI scripts, JavaScript can handle such interaction on these new servers that support LiveWire.

JavaScript and Other Live Content Tools

JavaScript will be incorporated into more Internet tools. While Netscape introduced JavaScript with Navigator 2.0, Sun and Netscape are making it an open, cross-platform scripting language. This means that any publisher can use it as his scripting language. Perhaps this is the primary reason why 28 other companies endorsed JavaScript upon its release.

Several of these companies are expected to either incorporate JavaScript into their products or provide an interface to JavaScript. The most visible products will be the plug-ins to Netscape Navigator, as discussed previously. Also, the Professional version of the LiveWire environment uses JavaScript to access high-end databases. It will be interesting to see how this market develops.

All of this holds great potential for creating an exciting Web experience for your viewers. You will be able to use the same language to enhance your Web page, customize your server, create stunning effects with your plug-ins, and communicate with specialized Java applets. JavaScript can make your Web page come alive; it can make your site an unforgettable experience that your users will want at the top of their bookmarks. ●

JavaScript: The Language

by Mark C. Reynolds

There are many, many different computer programming languages in use today. Each has its own set of special features, which are highly praised by its fans and vigorously panned by its detractors. If you have worked in more than one language then you are aware that there is a continuum of language styles, ranging from highly structured languages such as Ada to more free-wheeling ones such as Lisp. Many are associated with specific settings or applications. Ada, for example, is often found in military projects, while Lisp is often associated with artificial intelligence. Some languages, such as HTML, the language used to describe the layout of World Wide Web pages, have a well-defined organizational structure, but have very little in the way of traditional program structure (there are no data types, for example).

Use operators and expressions

Operators combine individual elements in some specific way; combinations of such elements are called expressions. Look here for a discussion of all JavaScript operators and the ways in which they form expressions.

Manipulate data types and literals

Unlike most programming languages, JavaScript doesn't have explicit data types; however, it does treat elements, such as integers and strings, differently.

Manage the flow of control in several ways

JavaScript provides several ways to execute different sets of code based on prior conditions. Look here for details on flow control structures.

Define JavaScript functions

Find out about JavaScript functions—the means by which Web page events are captured. The syntax for JavaScript functions, and their various uses, are illustrated.

In trying to understand a new language it is not only important to master its syntax, it is also vital to appreciate its style—the way in which that language can be used to accomplish specific goals. We have already reviewed the basic goals of JavaScript in chapter 1, "What Is JavaScript?" as well as contrasted it to the more structured Java language. This chapter describes the JavaScript language from both perspectives. A thorough description of its syntax is given, and some initial concepts on how to structure a JavaScript program are also introduced. Anyone who has programming in almost any modern declarative language, such as C, C++ or Pascal, will feel immediately at home. In addition, HTML authors who have never programmed will be able to rapidly acquire JavaScript proficiency. ■

JavaScript Syntax

JavaScript is based on an action-oriented model of the World Wide Web. Elements of a Web page, such as a button or checkbox, may trigger actions or *events*. When one of these events occurs, a corresponding piece of JavaScript code, usually a JavaScript function, is executed. That function, in turn, is composed of various statements which perform calculations, examine or modify the contents of the Web page, or perform other tasks in order to respond in some way to that event. For example, pressing the SUBMIT button on an online order form might invoke a JavaScript function that validates the contents of that form to ensure that the user entered all the required information.

In this section, we examine the syntax of JavaScript from the bottom up. We begin with the most basic concepts of how to write a JavaScript statement, and what that statement does, and progress upward through more complex and powerful structures in subsequent sections, culminating in a detailed discussion of JavaScript functions and related concepts. Chapter 3, "Events and JavaScript," explores in greater detail how these elements are tied into Web pages through events.

In general, the elements of a JavaScript program can be divided into five categories, as follows:

- Variables and their values
- Expressions, which manipulate those values
- Control structures, which modify how statements are performed

■ Functions, which execute a block of statements

■ Objects and arrays, which are ways of grouping related pieces of data together

This set of categories is very similar to many other languages. As we examine each of these elements in subsequent sections we will discover that JavaScript is somewhat minimalist in its approach. Many familiar elements, such as explicit data types (int, String, REAL), are missing or have been substantially simplified. However, JavaScript also provides a number of powerful object-oriented constructs which greatly simplify program organization. In this way, JavaScript has the expressive power of languages such as C or Java, while also having fewer rules to remember.

Part
I

Ch
2

Variables and Values

One of the main differences between JavaScript and most other languages is that it does not have explicit data types. There is no way to specify that a particular variable represents an integer, a string, or a floating-point (real) number. Any JavaScript variable can be any of these—in fact, the same variable can be interpreted differently in different contexts.

All JavaScript variables are declared using the keyword var. A variable may be initialized, meaning that it is given a value when it is declared, or it may be uninitialized. In addition, multiple variables can be declared on the same line by separating their names with commas. For example, the statements

```
var x = 7
var y,z = "19"
var lk = "lucky"
```

declare a variable named x with initial value 7, an uninitialized variable y and variables named z and lk whose initial values are "19" and "lucky," respectively. It might seem that x is an integer, z and lk are strings, and y is some undefined quantity. In fact, the real story is a little more complicated than this. The value of each variable depends on the context in which it is used. This context is related to the order in which the variables are seen. As you might guess, the expressions

```
5 + x

1k + z
```

evaluate to 12 and "lucky19," seemingly confirming our suspicions about what they really are. However, it is also possible to form the expressions

```
1k + x

x + z
```

which evaluates to "lucky7" and 26, respectively. In the first expression, x has been interpreted as a string, while in the second, z has been interpreted as an integer.

 TIP   JavaScript often attempts to treat all variables within a statement as if they had the same type as the first variable in the statement.

These examples illustrate two *critically* important points about the JavaScript language. First, while JavaScript does not have explicit data types, it does have implicit data types. Second, JavaScript has a set of conversion rules that allow it to decide how to treat a value based on the context in which it is used. The context is established by reading the expression from left to right. In the expression x + z, for example, x is implicitly a numerical value, so that JavaScript also attempts to view z as a number and perform the sum numerically. It succeeds, and the expected 26 results.

What would have happened if we had tried x + 1k? The x variable occurs first on the left, and is really a number at heart. JavaScript thus tries to interpret the variable 1k as a number, too. This is extremely unlucky, in fact, because "lucky" cannot be converted to a number (while z, the string "19," could). JavaScript reports an error if asked to evaluate x + 1k. To understand JavaScript variables and values, therefore, it is necessary to understand its set of implicit types and how they may be converted to one another.

Before we enter into these details, let us consider one final example. In all the preceding cases, the uninitialized variable y was never used. What would be the value of an expression such as

```
x = z + y
```

Of course, as in all other programming languages, the result of using an uninitialized variable is never good. Since y has never been given a value, there is no way this expression can be evaluated. It may result in something seemingly innocent, such as x being assigned the value of z, as if y were zero. It may also result in something much more serious, such as the value of x becoming something strange, or, more likely, a JavaScript error occurring. This leads to the following common sense rule.

 TIP Initialize all JavaScript variables to meaningful default values. If a variable has no meaningful default, initialize it to null.

Implicit Data Types in JavaScript

There are five major implicit data types in JavaScript. A JavaScript value may be as follows:

- A number, such as -5, 0, or 3.3333
- A string, such as "Click Here" or "JavaScript"
- One of the logical values true or false
- A "non-atomic" JavaScript element, such as a function or object
- The special value null

Actually, it would be more correct to say that there are five categories of data type, since it is possible to distinguish two different types of numbers (integers and floating-point numbers), and many different types of JavaScript objects, functions, and other structured types. In fact, part II of this book, "JavaScript Objects," is entirely devoted to explaining the many different JavaScript objects.

Variables and Variable Names It is very important to distinguish between variables and their values. The statement x = 10 contains two components: the variable x and the *literal* value 10. A literal refers to anything that is referred to directly, by its actual value. A variable is just an abstraction that provides a way of giving names to values. Thus the statement x = 10 says, "I am going to refer to the concrete (literal) quantity 10 by the abstract (variable) name x," just as you might say, "I am going to call this lumpy thing I'm sitting on a chair." This also leads to the following important piece of advice.

Part

I

Ch

2

> **CAUTION**
>
> It is bad practice to change the implicit data type of a variable. If a variable is initialized to have a certain type (such as string) it should always have that type.

Thus, since we have started out with x = 10 we should make sure that x always has some numeric value. There is no rule that prohibits us from later saying x = "Fortran", but this will generally lead to confusion or programming errors in most cases. No one will stop you from calling that lumpy thing you are sitting on "bacon and eggs" but many of your guests may become confused if you do so.

One final rule about variable names: a valid JavaScript variable name must begin with a letter or with the underscore character (_). Case is important, so that nor1, NoR1, NORL, and _NORL are all valid JavaScript variable names that refer to different variables.

Numerical Values   There are two numeric types in JavaScript: integers and floating-point numbers. The rules for specifying both types are almost identical to those of C or C++ or Java. Integers may be specified in base 10 (decimal), base 8 (octal), or base 16 (hexadecimal) formats. The three forms are distinguished as follows, based on the first one or two characters:

- 1–9 followed by any set of digits is a decimal integer.
- 0 followed by any set of the digits 0–7 is an octal integer.
- 0x or 0X followed by any of 0–9, a–f, or A–F is a hexadecimal integer.

Any of the three forms can also start with a + or - sign. Thus, -45 is a decimal integer, 017 is an octal integer, and 0x12EF5 is a hexadecimal integer. The minimum and maximum integers that can be used are implementation dependent, but at least 32 bits should be expected.

Floating-point numbers can be specified in either the standard decimal point (.) format or the engineering E-notation. Typical floating-point numbers should contain a decimal point or an exponent, which may begin with either e or E. A floating-point number may also have a + or - sign. 0.0, -1.4e12, and 3.14159 are all valid floating-point numbers. The range of valid floats is again implementation dependent, but you should expect that any valid short floating-point number, as defined by the IEEE standard, is acceptable. (The IEEE is the Institute of Electrical and Electronics Engineers, a professional and standards-making organization.)

Note that the original LiveScript language attempted to treat all the numeric types the same. Since it has become JavaScript there has been a convergence toward the numerical types of the Java language, and the distinction between integer values, such as 5, and floating-point (or real) values, such as 3.3333, has increased.

> **CAUTION**
>
> LiveScript is now completely obsolete. It has been replaced by its descendant, JavaScript. Avoid any code you encounter labeled LiveScript as it will almost certainly not work correctly.

NOTE Watch out for changes in the way JavaScript handles numeric types. In the future, the distinction between integers, single precision floating-point types (floats), and double precision floating-point types (doubles) may become much sharper. ▪

Strings   In JavaScript, strings may be specified using either single quotes ('stuff') or double quotes ("otherstuff"). If you begin a string with one type of quote you must end it with that same form of quote—for example, "badstuff' is not a legal string in JavaScript. Strings may also be nested by alternating the types of quotes used. In fact, you must alternate single and double quotes if you wish to put one string inside another. Here is an example of several nested strings (with apologies to Rudyard Kipling):

"Oh, it's 'Tommy this' and 'Tommy that' and 'throw im out, the brute'"

As in C and Java, JavaScript strings may contain special combinations of characters, known as *escape sequences*, to denote certain special characters. The rules for this are still emerging, but it is probably safe to assume that all the escape sequences defined in C will be supported. Since you will almost always be using formatting directives of HTML (such as <BR> for a line break) you will probably not use these directives very often. At the moment, the following sequences are supported:.

\t	tab
\r	line feed
\n	return
\f	form feed (vertical tab)
\b	backspace

▶ **See** the "Manipulating Text Fields" section of chapter 6, "Interactive HTML Objects," for more information on combining HTML directives with text, **p. 201**.

The special string `""` or `''` represents the zero length string. This is a perfectly valid string whose length is zero. This is the shortest JavaScript string; the length of the longest is, as usual, implementation dependent. It is reasonable to expect that most JavaScript environments will permit very long sonnets (or very short legislative measures) to be represented as single strings.

Logical Values   The logical, or boolean, values `true` and `false` are typically used in expressions that test some condition to determine how to proceed. If that condition is met then one set of statements is executed; if it is not then another set is used instead. The first corresponds to the `true` condition, while the second represents the `false` condition. Not surprisingly, such expressions are known as *conditional expressions*. As you will see in the "Operators" section there are several comparison operators, such as the equality test (`==`), which result in logical values.

It is possible to think of `true` as 1 and `false` as 0. In fact, JavaScript converts these logical values into 1 and 0, respectively. JavaScript also accepts any non-zero integer in place of `true`, for example, so that 5 and -3 can both be used as stand-ins for `true`. Many different programming languages follow this same convention. It should be avoided in JavaScript, as it can lead to type confusion.

The Value *null*   The value `null` has a very special role in the JavaScript language. It is the value of last resort, so to speak, for every variable. For the beginning JavaScript programmer, its primary role will be in initializing variables that do not have any more meaningful initial value. For example, in the set of variable declarations given in the earlier "Variables and Values" section, to initialize `y` to some value, we should have actually written

```
var y = null
```

This prevents JavaScript errors that arise when an uninitialized variable is accidentally used in an expression that requires a value. It is important to realize that the value `null` does not give the variable `y` any implicit data type. `null` also has the property that it may be converted to a benign form of all the other types. When it is converted to a number it becomes `0`, when it is converted to a string it becomes the empty string `""`, and when it is converted to a boolean value it becomes `false`. This is the one case where is it permissible to change the implicit data type of a variable after it is declared.

Therefore, statements such as

```
var lk2 = lk + y
var w = x + y
```

result in `lk2` having the value "lucky" (the same as `lk`) and `w` having the value 10 (the same as `x`). This is why the value `null` is an excellent way of initializing variables—it is guaranteed to be harmless.

Type Conversion

Several of the examples in the previous section use the + operator to combine different types of things. You may recall that when a string is combined with a number in the form

```
stringthing + numberthing
```

the number is converted to a string and the + operator then glues the two strings together (concatenation). However, if they are combined in the opposite order

```
numberthing + stringthing
```

then JavaScript attempts to convert the `stringthing` to a number and add it, numerically, to `numberthing`. If the `stringthing` can be converted to a string, such as "−14," then all goes well; if it cannot then an error results. This illustrates the concept of implicit conversion in JavaScript.

We have already seen that some examples of implicit conversion are completely safe. `false` can be converted to 0, `"5"` can be converted to 5, and `null` can be converted to just about anything. However, some conversions are obviously invalid, and others might be questionable. Questions such as, "May the string '3.0' be legitimately converted to the integer 3?" are actually very difficult to answer with complete generality.

There are two approaches to handling this complex issue: use explicit conversion whenever possible, and use implicit conversion with great care. Both approaches should be used. A detailed study of explicit conversion is in chapter 5, "Built-In JavaScript Objects," beginning with the section "The String Object." For the moment we will use the following rules of thumb.

▶ **See** "The String Object" section of chapter 5, "Built-In JavaScript Objects," which discusses the rules for string-to-number and number-to-string conversion, the source of most conversion errors in JavaScript, **p. 152**.

> **CAUTION**
>
> Use implicit conversion only when converting to a string form. Never use it to convert to numerical form. This is because attempts to convert a non-numerical quantity to a numeric form cause serious JavaScript errors, while conversion to string form generally does not.

You have probably already noticed that conversion to a string is always safe, at least for the data types we have encountered so far. In fact, this type of implicit conversion is a boon to the JavaScript programmer, since it avoids the tedious formatting directives that are necessary in many languages such as C. In JavaScript we can say

```
"This page has been accessed " + cnt + " times today"
```

without having to worry about the data type of the variable cnt. This construction will always give a valid string, and never an error.

The preceding Caution is also based on standard principles of defensive programming. There are many things that cannot be sensibly converted to a numerical form, so the prudent approach is to never try to implicitly convert anything to a number. There are several more robust approaches that can be used in case we have a string that we want to convert to numerical form. These are described in chapter 5. We will also see other exceptions to this rule as our mastery of JavaScript deepens.

Statements and Operators

The basic unit of work in JavaScript is the *statement*, as is the case in most programming languages. A JavaScript statement accomplishes work by causing something to be evaluated. This can be the result of giving a value to a variable, by calling a function, by performing some sort of calculation, or any combination of these. We have already seen variable declaration statements, which not only create (declare) a new variable, but also give it an initial value, such as the following statement:

```
var x = 10
```

JavaScript programs, as mentioned at the beginning of this chapter, are collections of statements, typically organized into functions, which manipulate variables and the HTML environment in which the script itself works, in order to achieve some goal.

The Structure of JavaScript Statements

Before plunging into a detailed description of the various types of statements and the operators they use, let's examine one simple statement in excruciating detail. Consider the statement

```
y = x + 5
```

This statement contains three parts: the result y, the *operator* = and the *expression* x + 5. The result always occurs in the left side, since JavaScript always operates from left to right, and is often called the *lvalue*. The result must always be something that can be modified. It would be erroneous to write null = x + 5, for example, because null is a built-in, unchangeable component of JavaScript itself—it cannot be modified, so it can never appear as a result.

The operator = is the assignment operator, of course. It causes the expression on the right to be evaluated and its value given (assigned) to the result. The expression x + 5 contains another operator, the + operator, which acts to combine x and 5 in some context-specific way. Since x is a number in this case, the + operator performs ordinary addition, and y gets the value 15. As we have already seen, if x had been a string, such as "bleh," then + would have acted as a string concatenation operator and y would be given the value "bleh5" instead. This is an example of *operator overloading*—the + operator can do different things in different situations. Many JavaScript operators are overloaded.

There is one final point to be made about this statement and about the structure of JavaScript programs in general. JavaScript has adopted a line-oriented approach to program flow. This means that it knows that a statement has ended when it reaches the end of a line. It is also possible to explicitly terminate a statement with a semicolon character (;). The statement y = x + 5; is identical in effect to the statement y = x + 5. This also means that you can, in fact, put multiple statements on a single line by separating each of them with a semicolon.

For those just starting out in JavaScript it is often a good idea to terminate each statement with a semicolon, and to also put only a single statement on each line. This might seem both redundant and extraneous, but it is well justified. The end of a line is often a purely visual concept. Anyone who has ever used a word processor has undoubtedly encountered the situation where a very long line looks like two lines. Different platforms (Macintosh, PC, UNIX) also have their own unique ideas as to what the proper end-of-line characters are. It is much safer to put in the extra semicolon character and be explicit about the end of the statement than it is to rely on one's eyesight.

Operators

The set of operators that JavaScript uses is, once again, very similar to that of the C, C++, and Java languages. It provides a number of different ways of combining different values, both literals and variables, into expressions. Some operators require two elements to participate in the operation, and are referred to as *binary* operators. The + operator is a binary operator. Other operators require only a single participant (operand), and are known as *unary* operators. The ++ operator, which adds 1 to its operand, is a unary operator. Operators may also join forces to form aggregate operators, as we shall see next.

JavaScript operators may be classified into the following groups:

- Computational operators
- Logical operators
- Bitwise operators
- Assignment and aggregate operators

This grouping is purely functional, and is based on what the operators actually do. The next four subsections examine each type of operator in more detail. Table 2.1 summarizes the operators in each category and how they are used.

Table 2.1   A Summary of JavaScript Operations

Computational Operators

+	Addition, String Concatenation
−	Subtraction, Unary Negation

*	Multiplication
/	Division
%	Modulus
++	Preincrement, Postincrement
--	Predecrement, Postdecrement

Logical Operators

==, !=	Equality, Inequality
<,<=,=>,>	Arithmetic and String Comparison
!	Logical NOT
&&,||	Logical AND, Logical OR
?	Conditional Selection (trinary)
,	Logical Concatenation

Bitwise Operators

&,|	Bitwise AND, Bitwise OR
^	Bitwise eXclusive OR (XOR)
~	Bitwise NOT
<<,>>,>>>	Shift Left, Shift Right, Unsigned Shift Right

Assignment Operators

=	Assignment
OP=	Aggregate Assignment (+,-,*,/,%,&,|,^,~,<<,>>,>>>)

Computational Operators   The computational operators are addition (+), subtraction and negation (-), division (/), multiplication (*), modulus (%), increment (++), and decrement (--). These operators are often used in performing arithmetic computations, but do not forget that the + operator is overloaded; it also has the extremely important role of string concatenation.

The first five computational operators have their standard mathematical meanings. They add, subtract, divide, or multiply two numeric quantities. By combining two quantities using one of these operators the result is made as precise as possible. If an integer is added to a floating-point number, the result is a floating-point number. The following four statements illustrate the use of these operators:

```
x = 4 + y;
y = 5.5 - z;
z = 10 / w;
w = 1.4e5 * v;
```

Note that division of integer quantities result in an integer result, so that if w had the value 4 in the third statement, z would get the value 2, not 2.5. Note also that the - operator may also be used as a unary operator to compute the negative of a numeric quantity:

```
n = -m;
```

This has exactly the same effect as if we had multiplied m by –1.

The modulus operator (%) is used to compute the remainder from a division. Although it can be used with floating-point numbers, it is typically used with integers, so that 21 % 4 evaluates to 1. The modulus operator always gives a remainder that has the same sign as the corresponding quotient, so that -21 % 4   evaluates to –1, not 3.

The increment and decrement operators are conveniences created to simplify the very common operations of adding or subtracting one from a number. Both these operators are unary and come in two forms: prefix and postfix. The expression ++x is the preincrement form of the ++ operator, while x++ is the postincrement form. This leads to a subtle and often misunderstood point about the increment and decrement operators.

Supposing that x has its usual value 10, consider the two statements

```
y = ++x;
z = x++;
```

These look very similar, but are in fact very different. After both of these statements have been executed, x has the value 11. However, y ends up with the value 11 while z has the value 10. Why? The reason has to do with the complex issue of what order the operators ++ and = are evaluated in these two statements. In the first statement, the ++ is evaluated first, so that x attains the value 11, and then the assignment = is evaluated, so that this value is passed on to y. In the second statement, the assignment operator = is applied first, so that z becomes 10, the current value of x, and then the ++ is applied to x, so that it advances to 11. The same rule applies to the decrement operator (--).

This might seem like it is a violation of the rule of left-to-right evaluation, and it is. Even though the equal sign is to the left of the preincrement operator (++) in the first statement, the ++ operator takes effect first. This is an example of *operator precedence*, the order in which multiple operators are applied. This complex topic is discussed in more detail in the "Order of Evaluation" section later in the chapter.

Part
I

Ch
2

Logical Operators   Logical operators in JavaScript are used either to carry out some form of test, or to combine the results of more than one such test. They are often referred to as conditional operators. The logical operators that perform a test of some sort are the equality/inequality operator (== and !=), the comparison operators (<, <=, >, and =>), and the logical negation operator (!). The operators that combine logical values are logical AND (&&) and logical OR (¦¦). Finally, the conditional operator (?) and the comma operator (,) are also combining operators, although they are only vaguely logical operators.

Equality Operators   The binary equality (==) and inequality (!=) operators are used to test if two quantities are the same or different. These operators are overloaded. On integers, they test for strict equality or inequality. On floating-point numbers, they test to see if the two quantities are equal within the precision of the underlying floating-point type. On strings, they test for exact equality—recall that case is significant in JavaScript strings. These operators all return a boolean value, either true or false.

For example, if x has the value 10, y has the value 3.0, and z has the value "barney," then x == 10 is true, y != -5.0 is also true, and z == "fred" is false. Unfortunately, even operators as simple as these can be a source of error. It is regrettable that the logical operator == looks so much like the assignment operator =. Consider the following incorrect code fragment:

```
if ( x = 3 ) {
    stuff…
```

The purpose of this code is almost certainly to test the value of the variable x against the constant 3, and execute the stuff if that test succeeded. This code fails to realize that purpose in two very dramatic ways, just by inappropriately using = instead of ==.

First of all, x = 3 always gives x the value 3, no matter what its previous value was. Instead of testing x using ==, we have altered it with =. Second, the value of the expression x = 3 is the value of its left side, namely 3. Even though 3 is not a true logical value, it is treated as true by the `if` statement (`if` is described in greater detail in the section, "Control Structure," later in this chapter). This means that `stuff` will always be executed, rather than only being executed when x has the prior value 3.

This type of error occurs in every programming language in which similar operators are used for very different purposes. In this case, we could have adopted another rule of defensive programming and said

```
if ( 3 = x ) {
    stuff…
```

In this case, our typing mistake (= instead of ==) leads to an error, rather than resulting in a subtle programming flaw. Since 3 is a constant, it can never appear on the left side of an assignment, but it is quite capable of appearing on the left side of a logical test. Said another way, since x == 3 and 3 == x are completely equivalent, the form 3 == x is preferable. If it is mistyped as an assignment statement (3 = x) it leads to an immediate error rather than one which might take hours of debugging to uncover. This leads to the following advice.

 TIP   When testing for equality always put constants on the left, especially `null`.

There is another subtle evil about the (in)equality operators when they are used with floating-point numbers. It is very tricky to make floating-point arithmetic completely independent of the underlying machine. This means that z == 3.0 might be `true` on one machine but `false` on another. It can also lead to seemingly absurd results such as 3. != 3.00 being `false` while 3.0 == 2.9999999 is `true`. A remedy for this problem is presented at the end of this section.

Comparison Operators   The comparison operators (<, <=, > and >=) also operate on both numbers and strings. When they act on numbers they perform the usual arithmetic comparisons, yielding boolean values, as with the equality operators. When they act on strings they perform comparisons based on dictionary order, also known as lexicographic order. If a string `str1` occurs earlier in the dictionary than a second string `str2` then the comparison `str1 < str2` (and also `str1 <= str2`) will be `true`. For example, `"barney" < "fred"` is `true`, while `"Franklin" < "Delano"` is `false`.

The Negation Operator   The logical negation operator (`!`) is used to reverse the sense of a logical test. It converts `true` to `false` and `false` to `true`. If `x < 15` is `true` then `!(x < 15)` is `false`, and vice versa. Note that `!` may also be used with integer values, so that `!0` is `true`, while `!5` is `false`. As in other cases, this use of the `!` operator violates type boundaries, and should be avoided.

Boolean Logical Operators   The logical AND (`&&`) and OR (`¦¦`) operators are among the most powerful operators in JavaScript. Both may be used to combine two or more conditions into a composite test. The logical AND of a set of conditions is `true` only if all of its component conditions are `true`. The logical OR of a set of conditions is `true` if any of its component conditions are `true`. Thus

        (x < 17) && buttonPressed && (z == "Meta")

is `true` precisely when `x` is less than 17 *and* the boolean variable `buttonPressed` is `true` *and* `z` is exactly equal to the string "Meta." Similarly,

        (x < 17) ¦¦ buttonPressed ¦¦ (z == "Meta")

is `true` if one or more of the three conditions is `true`.

Lazy Evaluation   JavaScript uses a lazy variant of its usual left-to-right evaluation rule with the `&&` and `¦¦` operators. This lazy evaluation (or short circuit evaluation) rule states that JavaScript stops trying to evaluate the expression as soon as its value is known.

To see how this works, suppose that `x` has the value 20, `buttonPressed` is `true`, and `z` is the string `"Hyper"`. Since `( x < 17 )` is `false` the second and third conditions in the logical AND statement are never evaluated. This is because `false && anything` is always `false`, so the value of the first expression must be `false`. Similarly, the second statement stops as soon as `buttonPressed` is evaluated. Since `true ¦¦ anything` is always `true`, the second expression must be `true`.

Lazy evaluation can be both a boon and a curse. Suppose that `"digofpi(1000000000)"` is a function that computes the billionth digit of *pi*.

The expression

```
( x < 25 ) ¦¦ ( digofpi(1000000000) == 3 )
```

does not actually try to compute the billionth digit of *pi* if x is 20, because the expression is already known to be `true`, and `digofpi()` is never called. As an additional example, consider the following expression:

```
( x < 25 ) && beaupage()
```

Suppose that `beaupage()` is a function that displays a beautiful Web page. If x is 30 this page will never be seen, because the first part of expression (x < 25) is already known to be `false`. As a result the function `beaupage()` is never called. We revisit this phenomenon in the "Functions and Objects" section at the end of this chapter. For the moment, it is wise to be aware of lazy evaluation.

Fuzzy Comparison   The logical AND and OR operators also provide us with one solution to the problem of floating-point comparison. While it may not be possible to ever determine if x is exactly equal to the constant 3.0, you can be certain that it is close using a combined test such as

```
( x - 3.0 ) < epsilon ¦¦ ( 3.0 - x ) < epsilon
```

where `epsilon` is some suitably small value, such as 0.001. This form of test is often referred to as a *fuzzy comparison*.

CAUTION

Floating-point arithmetic is not an exact science. Avoid exact comparison tests such as ==
and !=; use fuzzy comparisons instead.

The Comma and Question Mark Operators   The final two operators in the logical category are the conditional operator (?), often called the question mark operator, and the comma operator (,). These two operators are only vaguely logical, but they don't readily fall into any of the other categories either.

The conditional operator is the only trinary (3 operand) operator in JavaScript. It is used to select one of two possible alternatives based on a conditional test. The syntax for this operator is

```
( conditionthing ? truealt : falsealt )
```

If the `conditionthing` is `true` then the value of this expression is `truealt`; otherwise it is `falsealt`. Note that the colon (:) separating the true alternative from the false alternative is mandatory. This can be used to select an appropriate alternative and simplify code, as in this example:

```
printme = ( errorcode == 0 ? "OK" : "error" );
```

This expression makes the variable `printme` have the string value `"OK"` in case the variable `errorcode` is 0; otherwise, it is set to `"error"`. The question mark operator is often a fast way to select one of two choices when a control structure would be unnecessarily cumbersome.

Finally, the lowly comma operator can be used to force the evaluation of a set of expressions. All intermediate results are discarded, and the value of the very last expression on the right is returned. For example, the expression

```
b = (d = digofpi(1000000000)), beaupage(), (x < 17);
```

always computes the billionth digit of *pi* and assigns it to the variable d, always displays the beautiful page, always compares x against 17, and only returns the result of that comparison since x < 17 is the rightmost expression. The result of that comparison is assigned to the boolean variable b. This might seem like a clever way to outwit JavaScript's lazy evaluation, but it would be clearer to simply write

```
d = digofpi(1000000000);

beaupage();

b = ( x < 17 );
```

In general, the comma operator is only useful when it is inside a `for` loop (see "Control Structures," later in this chapter), and should otherwise be ignored.

Bitwise Operators   In many situations you do not need to know, nor do you wish to know, the precise binary representation of values in your program. There are some situations, however, in which it is absolutely essential to operate at the lowest possible level and deal with the individual bits of a particular value. This often arises in mathematical applications, for example, or when precisely manipulating color values. The bitwise operators are used for this purpose. Table 2.2 shows JavaScript's bitwise operators. Note that all are binary, except for bitwise NOT, which is unary. Each operates on its operands one bit at a time.

Table 2.2 JavaScript's Bitwise Operators

Operator Name	Symbol
Bitwise AND	&
Bitwise OR	¦
Bitwise XOR	^
Bitwise Left Shift	<<
Bitwise Signed Right Shift	>>
Bitwise Unsigned Right Shift	>>>
Bitwise NOT	~

Bitwise AND (&) examines each bit position in each of its operands. If both operands have a 1 bit in a given position, then that bit will also be set to 1 in the result. In all other cases, the output bit position is zero. For example, suppose x = 0x00001234 and y = 0x8000ABCD. Then z = x & y will have the value 0x00000204. You can see this more easily by writing x and y in base 2 (binary) notation, and looking for those positions in which both x and y are 1, as shown in the first part of figure 2.1.

FIG. 2.1

JavaScript's bitwise operators operate on each bit separately.

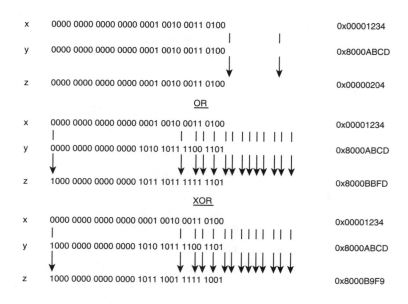

Note that x and y only have the same bits set in highlighted positions, so that those are the only bits set in their logical AND z. In this way, bitwise AND is the bit level analog of the logical AND. Bitwise OR (|) is similar. If either bit is 1 in any bit position, then that bit will be 1 in the result. Thus the value of w = x ¦ y will be 0x8000BBFD, as you see in the middle part of figure 2.1.

Each bit is set in w if either or both of the corresponding bits in x and y is set. The bitwise XOR (exclusive OR) (^) operator is a variation on the bitwise OR operator. It sets a bit in the result if either bit in the operand is set, but not both. The value of v = x ^ y is 0x8000B9F9, as shown at the bottom of figure 2.1.

These three operators may also take more than two operands, so that it is possible to write a very long expression such as

```
n = ( a & b & c & d & e );
```

which operates from left to right, as usual. This expression takes the bitwise AND of a and b, ANDs that result with c, ANDs that result with d, and finally ANDs that result with e. The final result is saved in the variable n.

> **CAUTION**
>
> The bitwise AND (&) and OR (¦) operators bear a shocking similarity to their logical counterparts && and ¦¦. This can lead to painfully undetectable errors. The same care that is exercised with = and == should also be used with these operators.

The unary bitwise NOT operator (~) changes each 0 bit in its operand to a 1 bit, and each 1 bit in its operand to a 0 bit. The bitwise NOT of x will have the value 0xFFFFEDCB:

```
x       0000 0000 0000 0000 0001 0010 0011 0100
~x      1111 1111 1111 1111 1110 1101 1100 1011
```

While &, ¦, ^ and ~ operate on bits in place, the shift operators <<, >>, and >>> are used to move bits around. The left shift operator (<<) shifts a set of bits to the left by a specified number of positions, while both >> and >>> moves that set of bits to the right in two potentially different ways. For example, let us evaluate these three expressions:

```
xleft = x << 5;

ysright = y >> 3;

yusright = y >>> 3;
```

The first of these shifts each bit in x to the left five positions. Zero bits are tacked on at the right, while the bits that are shifted out at the left are lost when they exceed the overall 32-bit length. So the value of xleft must be 0x00024680. The signed right shift operator acts in almost the same way. Each bit of y is shifted to the right three positions. Bits on the right edge of y are lost as they are shifted out. However, rather than shifting in zeros at the left side of y, the most significant bit of y, which happens to be 1 in this case, is shifted in. The resulting value of ysright is 0xF0001579.

This might seem counterintuitive, but it makes good mathematical sense, since it preserves the sign of the operand. If y is negative (most significant bit set, as in our example) then any signed right shifted version of y will also be negative. Similarly, if y had been positive (most significant bit equal to 0) then any right shifted version of y would have been positive. The unsigned right shift operator (>>>) does not preserve the sign of its operand; it always shifts 0 bits in at the left edge. The value of yusright is therefore 0x10001579. The shift processes used to compute xleft, ysright, and yusright are shown in figure 2.2.

FIG. 2.2

JavaScript's shift operators move bits to the right or left, and are equivalent to multiplication or division by a power of two.

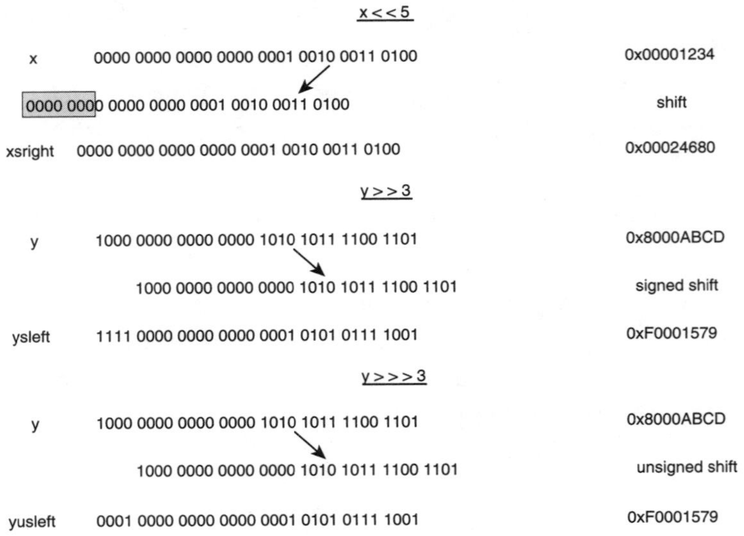

$x << 5$

x	0000 0000 0000 0000 0001 0010 0011 0100	0x00001234
	0000 0000 0000 0000 0001 0010 0011 0100	shift
xsright	0000 0000 0000 0000 0001 0010 0011 0100	0x00024680

$y >> 3$

y	1000 0000 0000 0000 1010 1011 1100 1101	0x8000ABCD
	1000 0000 0000 0000 1010 1011 1100 1101	signed shift
ysleft	1111 0000 0000 0000 0001 0101 0111 1001	0xF0001579

$y >>> 3$

y	1000 0000 0000 0000 1010 1011 1100 1101	0x8000ABCD
	1000 0000 0000 0000 1010 1011 1100 1101	unsigned shift
yusleft	0001 0000 0000 0000 0001 0101 0111 1001	0xF0001579

Since all the bitwise operators act at the bit level, chaos can result if they are applied to a variable that is not an integer. Floating-point numbers are particularly sensitive, since an arbitrary bit pattern need not correspond to a valid floating-point number.

> **CAUTION**
>
> Never perform bitwise operations on floating-point numbers. Your code will be unportable, and floating-point exceptions may result.

Assignment and Aggregate Operators   Our tour of JavaScript operators concludes with the assignment operator and its aggregates. You have already seen many examples of that most fundamental of all operators, the assignment operator (=). You are well aware that it is used to assign the result of an expression or value on the right side of the = sign to the variable or lvalue on the left side of the = sign.

In JavaScript, as in C, C++, and Java, you can also combine the assignment operator with any of the binary computational and logical operators. The expression

```
Left OP= Right ;
```

is just a shorthand for the expression

```
Left = Left OP Right ;
```

where OP is any of the operators +, -, /, *, %, &, ¦, ^, <<, >>, or >>>. So, to add 7 to x, multiply y by 19.5, OR z with 0xAA7700, and perform an unsigned right shift of 10 bits on w you can write

```
x += 7;
y *= 19.5;
z ¦= 0xAA7700;
w >>>= 10;
```

These compact expressions replace the wordier versions x = x + 7; y = y * 19.5, and so forth.

Order of Evaluation   In elementary school math you were probably confronted with questions such as, "What is the value of 3 + 4 * 5? Is it 23 or is it 35?" This was your first exposure to the concept of order of evaluation, or operator precedence.

You probably remember that multiplication has a higher precedence than addition, so that the correct answer is 23. The same issue arises in almost every programming language with the concept of operators—which comes first?

There are two approaches to this issue. The first involves learning, or attempting to learn, the operator precedence table. The more operators there are, the more rules there must be in this table. The second approach is to simply ignore the issue completely and explicitly group your expressions using parentheses. Never write 3 + 4 * 5. Always write 3 + (4 * 5) or even (3 + 4) * 5 if that is what you want.

This recommendation is very much like several others in this chapter. It trades the effort (and perhaps some readability) of using the explicit parenthesized form against the promise that the order of evaluation will always be exactly as you wrote it. Incorrect order of evaluation is almost certainly the second most common source of programming error in JavaScript (confusing = and == is the first). For the daring, figure 2.3 shows the operator precedence table for JavaScript. For everyone else, the following rule of thumb is recommended.

FIG. 2.3

Use the operator precedence table to determine the order of evaluation.

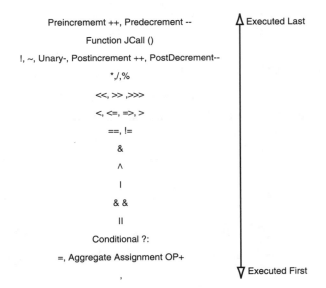

T I P Use parentheses to explicitly specify the order of evaluation in expressions containing more than one operator.

There is one case in which no amount of parentheses will help. When using the increment (++) and decrement (−−) unary operators you must simply know that preincrements and predecrements always happen before anything else.

Part

I

Ch

2

Comments in JavaScript Code

All professional code should have comments that clearly indicate the purpose and logic behind each major section of the code. JavaScript offers two comment styles—the original comment style from C and the single line comment style from C++ and Java.

C style comments are typically used to document major functions or code blocks. Because a C comment may extend over multiple lines it is ideal for detailed discussions of important parts of the code. A C comment begins with `/*` and ends with `*/`. Our aesthetically pleasing function `beaupage()` might begin with a thorough description of just what makes it so beautiful, as follows:

```
/*
   The function beaupage() draws a stunningly beautiful
   Web page by performing the following nineteen steps.
   ... list of the 19 steps
*/
```

By contrast, C++ style comments are most suitable for short, pithy descriptions which will fit on a single line. A C++ style comment begins with `//` and ends at the end of the current line. Critical variables, for example, might merit a Java style comment indicating how they will be used, as follows:

```
var done = false; // set to true when we are all done
```

Both comment styles may be mixed freely in the same JavaScript program. However, such comments should never be nested, as this can lead to confusion. Also, the temptation to use HTML style comments (`<!−` and `−>`) should be strongly resisted, for reasons which will become clear in the next chapter.

▶ **See** the section "The *SCRIPT* Tag" of chapter 3, "Events and JavaScript," for more information on the relationship between HTML comments and JavaScript, **p. 83**.

TROUBLESHOOTING

I have just written my first JavaScript program. Everything looks fine, but the code does nothing. What is wrong? Here is the code:

```
/* My first JavaScript program *?

...many lines of code not shown

/* End of my first JavaScript program */
```

Your comments are well thought out and informative. Unfortunately, your very first comment begins with /* but does not end with */. You have inadvertently typed *? instead of */, so that the comment does not end until very far down in your program. When you use C style comments always make sure that they match.

Control Structures

At this point, you have had just enough of the JavaScript language to declare variables, perform assignments, and do various types of arithmetic, string, and logical calculations. You are not yet able to write any meaningful code because you do not have any higher level constructs. In this section, we will consider various methods of controlling the way in which statements are executed. The next section will expose the highest level of JavaScript—its functions and objects.

There are three types of control structure in JavaScript, as follows:

- `if`
- `while`
- `for`

These three control structures are very similar. Each is introduced by a keyword (`while`, `for`, and `if`, respectively) and each manipulates a *block* of JavaScript statements. A block is introduced by a left brace ({) and terminated with a right brace (}). There can be as many JavaScript statements between { and } as you wish, or as few. A block of code can even be empty, with nothing between the braces. In many ways, a block of statements is like a single gigantic statement. In particular, block structured constructs are often all or nothing—either the entire contents of the block are executed, or none of it is. Since blocks behave like single statements, it is also possible to put blocks inside other blocks, in a nested fashion.

As you will see, each of the three control structures has its own specific format and its own special uses, although it is often possible to achieve the same results using any of the three types, with varying degrees of elegance.

The *if* Statement

The `if` statement is used to conditionally execute a single block of code. It has two forms, the simple `if` statement and the `if…else` statement. The simple `if` statement consists of a conditional expression, known as the `if` test, and a block of code which is executed if that expression evaluates to a boolean `true`. An example of an `if` statement follows:

```
if ( condstmt ) {
     zero or more statements
     }
```

The block of code within the braces is often called the `if` block. The conditional statement `condstmt` can be any expression that yields a logical value. Note that numerical expressions may also be used; 0 is construed as `false` and all other values are taken to be `true`. As stated earlier, an `if` statement should be considered a single statement. Code blocks are not traditionally terminated with a semicolon, although there is no harm in doing so. Listing 2.1 shows an example of a simple `if` statement.

Listing 2.1   The *if* Control Structure

```
if ( ( x < 10 ) && ( -10 < x ) ) {      // if test
     y = ( x * x * x );                   // 1: cube of x
     ystr = "The cube of " + x + " is " + y; // 2: informative string
}
```

In this example, the value of x is tested to see if it is less than 10 and also greater than -10. If the result of this test is `true` then the variable y is set equal to the expression x * x * x , known mathematically as the cube of x, in statement 1 (labeled 1:). The variable ystr is then set to a string that expresses this cubic relationship between x and y, in statement 2. If x fails either of the two tests in the `if` test then neither of the two statements in the `if` block are executed.

It is easy to see even in this simple example that it is often desirable to have a contingency plan in case the if test is false. This leads to the second form of the if statement, the if…else control structure. In this form, one block of code is executed if the if test passes, and a second block is executed if it fails. The format of this type of if statement is as follows:

```
if ( condstmt ) {
        ifblock of statements
} else {
        elseblock of statements
}
```

NOTE   In the current version of JavaScript, the placement of the braces is important. The opening brace ({) should be on the same line as the if keyword. If an else clause is present, the closing brace (}) of the if and the opening brace ({) of the else should both be on the same line as the else keyword. Other placements of the braces are allowed, but may not be understood. ■

In this form of the if statement, the if block is still executed if condstmt is true. However, in this case, the block of code following the else is executed if condstmt is false. Listing 2.2 shows an enhanced version of the code from listing 2.1 using the if...else form.

Listing 2.2   The *if...else* Control Structure

```
if ( ( x < 10 ) && ( -10 < x ) ) {   // if test
    y = ( x * x * x );                // 1: cube of x
    ystr = "The cube of " + x + " is " + y;  // 2: informative string
} else {                             // false case
    y = null;                        // 3: be paranoid; give
                                     //    y a value
    ystr = "Cannot compute the cube of " + x; // 4: explain the failure
}
```

In this example, statements 1 and 2 are still executed if x meets both tests in the if test. If either test fails then statements 3 and 4 in the else block are executed instead. Statement 3 is another example of defensive programming. The variable y is given a value, albeit a meaningless value. This is done so that if y is used later it will be guaranteed to have some value (even if we forgot to initialize) regardless of whether the code flowed through the true part of the if (the if block) or the false part of the if (the else block).

Observe that `ystr` also gets a value no matter which of the two blocks is used. In the `true` case it has the informative string documenting the cube of x; in the `false` case it has a string indicating that the cube of x could not be computed. Since `ystr` will presumably be displayed to the user at some point, it is worthwhile to provide an error message. This is an example of *parallel code design*. Each conditional path modifies the same set of variables. For a simple case, such as listing 2.2, it is easy to ensure that this happens. There are only two variables, y and `ystr`, and we can see exactly where they are set in every case. For more complicated, nested conditional expressions, it can become almost impossible to observe every variable in every case. Parallel code design is a good goal to strive for nonetheless.

The *while* Statement

The `while` statement is used to execute a block of code while a certain condition is `true`. The format of the `while` statement is as follows:

```
while ( condstmt ) {
     zero of more statements
     }
```

The condition clause `condstmt` is evaluated as a logical expression. If it is `true` then the block of statements between the braces is executed. The flow of control then loops back to the top of the `while` statement, and `condstmt` is evaluated again. This process continues until the `condstmt` becomes `false`, or until some statement within the block forces it to terminate. Each pass through the block of code is called an *iteration*. Figure 2.4 illustrates the basic structure of a `while` statement.

FIG. 2.4
JavaScript's `while` control structure executes a block of statements conditionally.

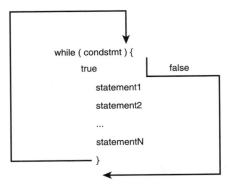

The first fundamental difference between a `while` statement and an `if` statement is that the `while` block may be executed many times, while the `if` or `else` blocks are executed once at most. You might well wonder how a `while` statement ever terminates. The code shown in listing 2.3 illustrates a simple situation in which the `while` block eventually leads to the `condstmt` becoming `false`.

Listing 2.3   A *while* Loop That Adds a Sequence of Numbers

```
var x = 1;
var xsum = 0;

while ( x <= 10 ) {          // loop until x is greater than 10
    xsum += x;               // add x to the running sum xsum
    x++;                     // increment x
}
```

This code accumulates the sum of all the integers between 1 and 10, inclusive, in a variable called `xsum`. `x` starts out as 1, so that `xsum` initially becomes 1 as well. `x` is then incremented to 2 by the `x++` statement. That value is then added to `xsum`, so that it becomes $1 + 2 = 3$. This process continues until `x` finally becomes 11 and the `x <= 10` condition is `false`. `xsum` at this point has the value $1 + 2 + ... + 9 + 10 = 55$. Thus, the loop terminates. Note that it is critically important to initialize `xsum` to 0. If `xsum` is not initialized at all then the statement `xsum += x`, which is just shorthand for `xsum = xsum + x`, gives an error. If `xsum` is initialized to something other than 0, the final result contains that initial value, and is not just the sum of the integers from 1 through 10.

Listing 2.3 shows one way in which a `while` loop can terminate. Statements within the block may cause the conditional statement to become `false`. It could also happen that the conditional statement at the top of the `while` was never `true`, so that the statements within the block are not executed even once. If `x` had started with the value 20 in this example then the `while` test would have been immediately `false`, and the statements `xsum += x` and `x++` would have never been executed. In this event, `xsum` would retain its initial value of 0.

Using the *break* Statement   There is a third way for a `while` loop to terminate. If the special statement `break` is encountered inside the `while` block, the loop is forced to terminate immediately. No further statements are executed and the `condstmt` is not retested. Execution continues with the first statement after the end of the `while` block. Listing 2.4 gives an example of the use of the `break` statement.

Listing 2.4 A *while* Loop with an Internal *break* Statement

```
var x = 1;
var xoddsum = 0;
var xtmp = 0;
var lastx = 0;

while ( true ) {            // 1: loop forever (well, almost)
    xtmp = xoddsum + x;      // 2: compute a trial sum
    if ( xtmp > 100 )        // 3: if it is too large, then...
        break;              // 4: we are done
    xoddsum += x;           // 5: add x to the running sum xoddsum
    x += 2;                 // 6: increment x by 2
}
lastx = x;                  // 7: save the final value of x in the variable
                            //    lastx
```

The test clause of this `while` (statement 1) is `true`, which, you might well suspect, is always `true`. This means that there is no way for this loop to terminate unless it is forced to do so by a `break` statement. In statement 2 a temporary sum is formed in the variable `xtmp`. This sum is tested against the limit 100 in statement 3; if `xtmp` exceeds it then statement 4, the `break` statement, is executed, and the loop terminates. If the test fails (`xtmp` is still less than 100) then the real sum is formed in statement 5. (Note that it would have been equivalent, and slightly more efficient, if we had written statement 5 as `xoddsum = xtmp`.) In statement 6, x is incremented by 2.

What does this `while` loop do? It keeps adding up numbers, odd numbers in fact, until the sum is less than 100. When the next sum would have exceeded 100, the `if` test succeeds, the `break` is executed, and the flow of control of the program reaches the first statement after the entire `while` block, namely statement 7. This statement saves the last value of x in a different variable, `lastx`. So this construction computes the largest sequence of odd numbers that can be added without having the sum exceed 100. You can easily determine for yourself that the value of `lastx` must be 21, since $1 + 3 + \ldots + 21 = 100$ exactly, while $1 + 3 + \ldots + 21 + 23 = 123 > 100$.

The Perils of Infinite Loops Listing 2.4 not only illustrates the use of `break`, it also shows two other elements worth noting. First, listing 2.4 contains a nested conditional: there is an `if` statement inside the `while` block. This sort of construct is extremely common, and many levels of nesting are not at all unusual. Second, this example has another very common but somewhat troublesome feature. Since the while test is always true, there is no way for the while to terminate unless the break statement is executed. In the preceding example, it was terminated quite quickly. Suppose, however, that statement 6 had been incorrectly entered as x -= 2. In this case, xoddsum would be getting constantly smaller and xtmp would never exceed 100. This type of error is known as an *infinite loop*. Listing 2.3 is not immune either, even though it has a conditional test rather than a blanket true. If the final statement of that example had been mistyped as x -, it would never terminate either.

Naturally, infinite loops must be vigorously avoided. They will only terminate when some kind of internal error happens (such as an arithmetic overflow when something becomes too large) or as a result of user intervention. Unfortunately, there is no foolproof way to write a while statement (or a for statement, as we shall see shortly) that is guaranteed to be correct. JavaScript is no different than any other programming language in this respect. However, the following general principles will reduce the opportunity for error:

- Avoid while (true) whenever possible
- Have at least one way of exiting the loop body

If the while (true) construction is used, then the logic that exercises the break statement must be correct. If this logic isn't correct then the loop will never terminate. If you restrict your use of while (true) you will have fewer infinite loops. The second suggestion is based on the observation that the more chances there are to exit the loop, the less likely it is that the loop will last forever. Listing 2.5 shows a modified version of listing 2.4 in which we have moved the test on the sum to the while clause itself, and have also added a very paranoid test on the number of times through the loop (the variable loopcount).

Listing 2.5   An Improved Form of Listing 2.4

```
var x = 1;
var xoddsum = 0;
var lastx = 0;
var loopcount = 0;

while ( ( xoddsum + x ) < 100 ) {        // 1: loop while sum is < 100
    xoddsum += x;                        // 2: add x to the sum xoddsum
    x += 2;                              // 3: increment x by 2
    if ( ++loopcount > 1000 )            // 4: if we're working too
                                         //    late..
```

```
        break;                          // 5: quit
    }
    lastx = x;                          // 6: save the final value of x in
                                        lastx
```

This version satisfies both rules. Of course, the test in statement 4 is completely unnecessary. The code is simple enough that we can reassure ourselves that it is correct and will not go into an infinite loop. Once you are writing slightly more complicated `while` loops, you will find that there are usually multiple possible error conditions that arise. Every time you test for an error you should consider using a `break` statement.

You will often see `while ( true )` written as `while ( 1 )`. These are equivalent, since `true` has the numerical value 1, but the latter form is sloppy. The conditional portion of a `while`, `if`, or `for` statement should always be a true logical expression.

Using the _continue_ Statement   There is another special statement that may be used inside `while` loops: the `continue` statement. The `continue` statement is used to force the flow of control back to the top of the `while` loop. When a `continue` statement is seen, all statements between it and the end of the while block are skipped, and execution continues at the top of the `while`. Listing 2.6 shows a simple use for the `continue` statement.

Listing 2.6   A _continue_ Statement Returns to the Top of a _while_

```
var x = 0;
var xsum = 0;
var loopcount = 0;

while ( loopcount++ < 100 ) {           // 1: loop 100 times
    x++;                    // 2: increment x
    if ( ( x % 5 ) == 0 )           // 3: if x is divisible by 5
        continue;           // 4: skip it
    xsum += x;              // 5: otherwise, add x to xsum
}
```

This example adds up every number between 1 and 100 that is not divisible by 5. The numbers that are divisible by 5 are skipped by virtue of statements 3 and 4. Statement 3 computes the remainder when x is divided by 5. If that remainder is 0 then x must be evenly divisible by 5. In that case, the conditional in statement 3 is true, and statement 4 is executed. The `continue` statement causes execution to continue back to the top of the loop at statement 1. This means that statement 5 is not executed, so the sum always misses those values of x which are divisible by 5, and only those values.

Many programmers would write line 3 as `if ( ! ( x%5 ) )`. While this style is very common, it is also confusing and a potential source of error. One problem with this form is that it confuses JavaScript types by using the numerical value x%5 as if it were a logical value. This form also hides the explicit test for zero of listing 2.6. While this `!` form is more compact, it is also more error prone, and should be avoided.

One striking difference between this listing and previous ones is that x is initialized to 0, not 1, and x is incremented at the top of the loop, not at the bottom. If the x++ were at the bottom, what would happen? The values 1, 2, 3, and 4 would all be gleefully added into xsum. When x reached 5, however, statement 3 would be true, the continue in statement 4 would be executed, and both xsum += x and x++ would be skipped. x would stay equal to 5 forever! Since the x++ statement is critical to the correct functioning of the loop, it must occur before the `continue`. If it occurs after the `continue` it will be skipped.

> **CAUTION**
>
> Any statement that must be executed on every pass through a loop must be placed before any `continue` statements.

The *for* Statement

The `for` statement is the most powerful and complex of the three flow control constructions in JavaScript. The primary purpose of the `for` statement is to iterate over a block of statements for some particular range of values. The `for` statement has the following format:

```
for ( initstmt; condstmt; updstmt ) {
    forblock
}
```

The `for` clause, as shown, has three parts, separated by two mandatory semicolons. The `initstmt` is typically used to initialize a variable, although any valid statement may be used in this position. The `initstmt` is always executed exactly once, when the `for` statement is first encountered. The `condstmt` is a conditional test, and serves exactly the same function as in the `while` statement. It is tested at the top of each loop. The `for` statement terminates when this condition evaluates to `false`. The `updstmt` is executed at the bottom of each loop, as if it were placed immediately after the last statement in the `for` block. It is typically used to update the variable that is initialized by the `initstmt`.

Listing 2.7 shows a simple example of a `for` statement. In fact, the code in this listing accomplishes exactly the same task as the code in listing 2.3. Note that this code does not bother to initialize x when it is declared. This is because the `initstmt` part of the `for` loop sets it equal to 1 immediately.

Listing 2.7   Adding Up a Sequence of Numbers Using *for*

```
var xsum = 0;
var x;

for ( x = 1; x <= 10; x++ ) {        // 1: loop while x is <= 10
    xsum += x;                // 2: add x to xsum
}
```

In many ways, the `for` statement is very much like a fancy version of the `while` statement. Many of the observations that were made for `while` also hold true for the `for` statement. In particular, it is possible to use the `break` and `continue` statements within a `for` loop. One of the advantages of a `for` loop is that its update statement is executed on every pass through the loop, even those passes that are cut short by a `continue`. The `continue` skips every statement in the block, but it does not cause the update statement to be skipped. The `for` statement may also be used unwisely, just like the `while` statement. If the `condstmt` portion of the `for` clause is omitted, it is as if a `true` conditional had been used, so that something within the `for` block must force looping to terminate. You will occasionally see the construction `for(;;)`, which is identical in meaning to `while ( true )`. The two semicolons are mandatory.

The `for` statement also has some unique features that are not shared by `while`. The first is that variables may actually be declared and initialized within the `initstmt` portion. In listing 2.7 we could have dispensed with the external declaration of x, and put `var x = 1;` as the initialization portion of the `for` loop. This is often very convenient, since the loop variable (x in this case) is often used only within the loop itself, often making an external declaration pointless.

NOTE If a variable is only used inside a block of statements it should be declared at the top of that block. This clarifies your code, since it shows which sections of code use which variables (known as variable *scope*). ▪

A second useful feature of the `for` statement is that both the initialization portion and the update portion of the `for` clause may contain multiple statements separated by the comma operator (,). Listing 2.8 shows another version of the code in listing 2.6, rewritten so that both x and lcnt become loop variables.

Listing 2.8   A *for* Loop with Multiple Initialization and Update Statements

```
var xsum = 0;

for ( var x = 1, lcnt = 0; lcnt < 100; x++, lcnt++ ) {
    if ( ( x % 5 ) == 0 )           // if x is divisible by 5
        continue;          // skip it
    xsum += x;                  // otherwise, add x to xsum
}
```

This usage underlines the fact that both x and lcnt are used only within the body of the `for` loop. It is also much more compact than its counterpart in listing 2.6. In this example, we need not worry about the logical effect of the `continue`; we know that both x++ and lcnt++ will always be executed. This is also the most common and useful way to use the comma operator.

Finally, there is another form of the `for` statement that is used exclusively with objects and arrays in JavaScript: the `for…in` statement. We will see how this is used in chapter 4, "JavaScript Objects." Figure 2.5 shows the basic structure of the `for`, `while`, and `if` statements, and the use of the `break` and `continue` statements within them.

▶ **See** the section "Objects, Properties, and Methods in JavaScript" of chapter 4, "JavaScript Objects," for a description of the `for...in` statement, **p. 106**.

FIG. 2.5
Control statements determine the flow of execution in JavaScript.

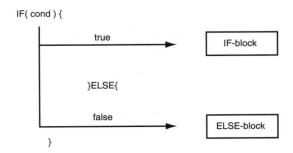

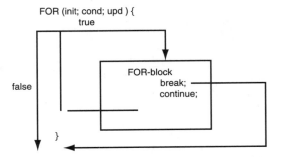

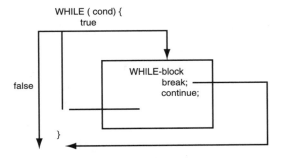

Functions and Objects

The basic statements, expressions, and operators that were discussed at the beginning of this chapter are what computer scientists usually call *primitives*. Primitives are the building blocks from which more complex elements of a program are constructed. The for, while, and if control structures represent the next higher level of organization in JavaScript. Each of these control structures deals with blocks of code whose execution is controlled by the various conditional tests and other clauses. The `for`, `while`, and `if` statements are all block structured.

Functions and objects represent the highest level of organization within the JavaScript language. We will spend many chapters learning how to make effective use of these concepts. The purpose of this section is to introduce them and describe their basic features.

Functions

A *function* is a block of code that has a name. Whenever that name is used the function is called, which means that the code within that function is executed. Functions may also be called with values, known as parameters, which may be used inside the body of the function. Functions serve two purposes. A function is an organizational tool, in the sense that it permits you to perform the same operation without simply copying the same code.

The second purpose of JavaScript functions is to link actions on a Web page with JavaScript code. Mouse clicks, button presses, text selections, and other user actions can call JavaScript functions by including suitable tags in the HTML source for the page.

▶ **See** the "Using JavaScript Event Handlers" section of chapter 3 for further exploration of event handler functions, **p. 92**.

The syntax for a `function` statement in JavaScript is as follows:

```
function Name ( listofparams ) {
     body
}
```

The function's `Name` is given immediately after the `function` keyword. All function names should be unique, and also should not conflict with any of the statement names which JavaScript itself uses (known as the *reserved words*). You cannot have a function named `while`, for example, and you should not have two functions both named `UserHelp`. The `listofparams` is a comma-separated list of the values that are passed into the function. These are referred to as the function's *parameters*, or *arguments*. This list may be empty, indicating that the function does not use any arguments (often called a *void function*). The function's body is the set of statements that make up the function. Listing 2.9 shows a function that adds up all the integers starting at 1 and ending at a value given as the sole argument.

▶ **See** the "Reserved Words" section of appendix C for a complete listing of JavaScript's reserved words, **p. 785**.

Listing 2.9   A Summation function

```
function summation ( endval ) {

    var thesum = 0;                    // this variable will hold the sum

    for ( var iter = 1; iter < endval; iter++ ) {
        thesum += iter;        // add the integer into the sum
    }                          // end of the for loop
    return( thesum );          // return the sum
}
```

This function does the same task that came up in the discussions of the `while` and `for` statements earlier in this chapter. Now that it has been written as a function, this code never needs to be repeated again. Any time you wish to form the sum 1 + 2 + ... + N, you can simply call the function, as `summation(N)`, and it will perform the task. Notice that the `endval` parameter is used as the argument to the function.

When the function is called, as `summation(14)` for example, the actual value 14 is used for `endval` within the function. The function then executes the `for` statement, with `iter < 14` as its termination condition, adding in each successive value into the variable `thesum`. When the `for` loop is done, the function executes the `return` statement. This causes the function to give the value inside the `return` statement back to the caller. This means that if we write

```
var sum14;
sum14 = summation(14);
```

the variable `sum14` is set to the value returned by the summation function when `endval` is given the value 14, namely 105. Functions can return any type of value, and are not restricted to returning integers.

There are several things to notice about this example. First of all, the variables `thesum` and `iter`, which are declared within the body of this function, are local variables. This means that they are only known within the body of this function, and are therefore completely unknown outside it. It is quite possible, even likely, that there are many functions, all of which have a local variable named iter. All these various iters are unrelated. Changing the value of one of these iters would not affect any of the others. This is why the return statement is necessary; it is the only way to communicate the work of the function back to the caller.

This same restriction applies to the parameter endval as well. The arguments to a function may *not* be changed within that function. We could well have written endval = 15 just before the return statement in listing 2.9. This statement would do nothing; it certainly would not change the caller's 14 into a 15. It might seem like every function would always have a return statement. This is not the case, however, since it is possible for a function to have side effects without actually returning a value. This happens by referencing external objects, which are our next topic.

Objects

Functions are used to provide a uniform method for organizing code. Objects serve the same purpose for data. Up to this point, the only data items we have seen are simple variables declared with var. Each of these typeless quantities can only hold a single value of some sort at a time. Objects provide the ability to hold multiple values, so that a group of related data elements can be associated with one another.

What JavaScript calls an object is called a data structure (or class) in many other languages. As with JavaScript functions, there are two aspects to JavaScript objects: creating them and using them. For the moment, we will defer the question of how to create objects and concentrate on how they are used. We will also see that a JavaScript capable browser will provide a number of its own, *built-in objects*.

A JavaScript object is made up of a set of component parts, which are called its *properties*, or *members*. Suppose you have an object named appt which you are using to organize your appointments. The appointment object might have properties that specify the date and time of the appointment, as well as the name of the person with whom the appointment will take place. It might also have a general description field to remind you of the purpose of this meeting. Thus, you can imagine that the appt object will have the following properties:

- day

- month

- time

- who

- why

Each of the properties of the `appt` object are referenced using the dot operator (.). Thus, `appt.month` refers to the `month` property and `appt.why` gives us the reason for the appointment. These references may appear on both the right and left sides of an expression; we may get their values and also set them. Listing 2.10 shows a code fragment that tests the value of `appt` and displays a message about a current appointment.

Listing 2.10   Using the *appt* Object

```
if ( appt.day == Today ) {
    document.write('<BR>You have an appointment today<BR>');
    document.write('See ' + appt.who + ' at ' + appt.time<BR>');
    document.write(appt.why + '<BR>');
}
```

This example assumes that the variable `Today` has somehow been initialized with today's date, so that the equality test with `appt.day` is only `true` for today's appointments. If the test does succeed then the three statements in the `if` block are executed. Each of these references `document.write`. The `document` object is a built-in object of the Netscape Navigator browser. This object has a member known as `write`, which is actually a function. Functional members of JavaScript objects are known as *methods*. This particular method takes a string and displays it on the current Web page.

Each of the three strings that are passed to `document.write` are constructed using + as a string concatenation operator. Each of them references one or more properties of the `appt` object in order to provide meaningful messages to the user. Each also includes `<BR>`, the HTML construction for a line break. This ability to directly issue HTML directives is one of the most powerful aspects of JavaScript, as it allows the programmer to dynamically modify the contents of Web pages using JavaScript functions and objects.

Once you learn more about the Date object, in "The *Date* Object" section of chapter 5, you will be able to construct a much more satisfying version of this example. Even at this stage, however, the advantage of object-based programming should be apparent. Rather than carrying about many variables, you can use objects instead. Each object can contain all the variables of interest to a particular idea. It can also contain method functions that perform related work. Objects can even contain other objects, so that you can organize your data in a hierarchical structure. Subsequent chapters explore these ideas in much greater detail. ●

CHAPTER 3

Events and JavaScript

by Mark C. Reynolds

Although HTML pages can be difficult to develop, they are usually very simple to use. The number of things you can do with an HTML page is quite limited. For the most part you simply look at it— read its text, admire its graphics, and, perhaps, listen to the sounds it can play. For many, the Web experience consists of visiting a series of pages without interacting with them. The only interaction occurs when the user selects a link or clicks an imagemap.

HTML forms have gradually changed that model to increase the level of interaction. A form can have a variety of ways of accepting input, including text fields, buttons, checkboxes, and multiple choice selections. In this way, HTML forms are a lot like paper forms. The user fills in the form, perhaps to purchase some item, and then submits the form. This submission process also mimics real life. It is difficult to tell if the form

- **Use the HTML *SCRIPT* tag**

  This tag is used to incorporate JavaScript code into the <HEAD> of an HTML document

- **Attach event handlers to HTML elements**

  Most user actions on a Web page can be linked to JavaScript functions

- **Intercept button clicks, text entry, and form submission**

  One of the most useful aspects of JavaScript is its ability to monitor and respond to user actions on-the-fly

- **Accept user input, validate it, and provide feedback**

  JavaScript's interactive power allows the browser client to perform many functions that are traditionally done on the server using CGI

has been properly filled in, and the time taken for processing the form is often quite lengthy. In the case of HTML, this processing delay occurs because the contents of the form must be sent across the network to some URL, processed there, and then returned to the user. Even the slightest error causes the form to be rejected, so that the form entry must be repeated.

One of the primary goals of JavaScript is to localize most of this process and perform the form validation within the user's browser. It won't be possible to actually submit an order locally, but it will be possible to make sure that the form is properly filled out locally, and thereby avoid forcing the user to redo the form. JavaScript realizes this goal through event handlers. Event handlers are JavaScript statements (usually functions) that are called whenever something happens. JavaScript functions can be called when a form is submitted, or they can be called whenever the user does anything to the form. If your form requires that a certain field correspond to a number between 2 and 10, for example, you can write a JavaScript function that will validate that field when the user changes it, and complain if the value is out of range.

This chapter describes event handling in JavaScript. We discuss all the events that can be handled, as well as the contexts in which these events may arise. In addition, you learn how JavaScript can be included within Web pages, and how JavaScript functions are connected with different components of that page. ■

Events and Actions

To understand JavaScript's event handling model, you must first think about the things that can actually happen on a Web page. Although there are many different things you can do with the browser, most of these have nothing to do with Web navigation. When you save a page as text, print a page, or edit your hotlist, you are not actually navigating the Web. In these cases, you are using some of the graphical capabilities of the browser, which are independent of the Web.

To understand which browser actions correspond to JavaScript events and which do not, it is important to distinguish those actions that actually cause (or might cause) some change in the Web page being displayed. From the user's standpoint the number of such actions is actually quite limited. In fact, there are really only two types of top level actions: the user can navigate, or the user can interact with an element of an HTML form. Navigation means to change from one Web page to another, or perhaps to open a completely new page in a new window. Interaction with the contents of an HTML form means changing one or more of the elements in such a form that can be changed, such as editable text fields.

Navigation Actions and Events

In the navigation category, you can distinguish the following different actions:

- Selecting a hypertext link
- Moving forward or backward in the history list
- Opening a new URL (possibly in a new window)
- Quitting the browser

Part
I
Ch
3

In most of these cases the current page will be *unloaded*, which means it will no longer be visible in any browser window. In several of these cases a new page will be *loaded*, which means its contents will be displayed in a browser window, perhaps a new one created specifically to display this particular page. Anyone who has used the World Wide Web realizes that selecting a hypertext link may not successfully take you to another. The machine to which that link points may be down, or simply inaccessible. The link may even be dead, meaning that it does not point to a valid destination. Selecting a dead link often unloads the current page, but doesn't load a new page. Most browsers display a blank page or post an error message. You may or may not be left on the current page, depending on the type of error and the browser being used. A sample error alert from Netscape is shown in figure 3.1.

These events, loading and unloading a page, are the two document level events that can be handled by JavaScript. This means that it is possible to write JavaScript code, contained within the HTML definition of a page, that will be executed whenever that page is loaded. You can also have code that is executed whenever that page is unloaded. The dead link example illustrates the important fact that loading and unloading are two separate, unrelated events. When you attempt to activate a dead link, the current page is unloaded, but nothing is loaded in its place. In order to return to the last valid Web page you must use one of your browser's navigation controls. For example, if you select Back in Netscape the last page you visited is reloaded.

FIG. 3.1
Attempting to access a non-existent URL results in an error message on some browsers.

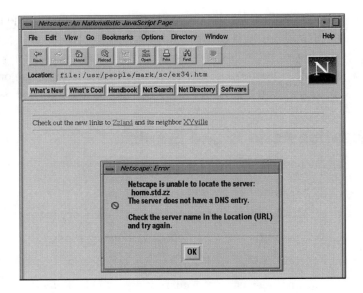

There are two additional events that are vaguely related to navigation. These events are the following:

- mouseover
- statechange

When you move the mouse over a hypertext link, a mouseover event is generated. This event is not associated with clicking the link, it is associated with being *poised* to click it. This event can be used to give the user feedback, such as changing the color of the link or flashing it. The final event is the statechange event. This event has been proposed by Microsoft as part of their planned implementation of an open scripting architecture that will include Visual Basic Script as well as JavaScript. The purpose of this event is to provide staged notifications when a time-consuming operation is taking place. For example, if a movie player plug-in is being loaded, the statechange event might be issued to indicate the plug-in is ready to accept some user interaction, but cannot yet display its movie.

▶ **See** chapter 13, "VB Script and OLE Controls," for more information on the Visual Basic Script language, and its plug-in technology, OLE Controls, **p. 457.**

Forms Input and Events

We have discussed the events that arise if you are using the browser to navigate the Web. Of course, you can also interact with your browser through the elements of an HTML form. Every form element that permits input is associated with one or more JavaScript events. We can broadly characterize the possible components of an HTML form as follows:

- Buttons
- Text fields
- Selection lists

Button Elements in Forms   Buttons come in five varieties, as follows:

- Simple buttons
- Yes/No checkboxes
- Radio buttons
- Submit buttons
- Reset buttons

On the CD

Simple buttons are defined using the HTML `<INPUT TYPE="button">`. Checkboxes define options, which are either off (not checked) or on (checked). These are created using an `<INPUT TYPE="checkbox">` directive. Radio buttons use the `<INPUT TYPE="radio">` directive, and permit the user to select exactly one of a set of choices. Submit buttons and reset buttons are very special. Submit buttons, created by `<INPUT TYPE="submit">`, are used to end input operations on a form. When the submit button is pressed the contents of the form are packaged and sent to the URL target specified in the ACTION attribute of the `<FORM>` definition. Reset buttons bring the form back to its initial state, wiping out any input the user has performed; they are specified as `<INPUT TYPE="reset">`. Figure 3.2 shows a simple HTML form with all five button types; it was generated by the HTML file allbut.htm.

TIP   Hidden fields on HTML forms do not generate JavaScript events.

FIG. 3.2
All five types of HTML
buttons have corresponding
JavaScript events.

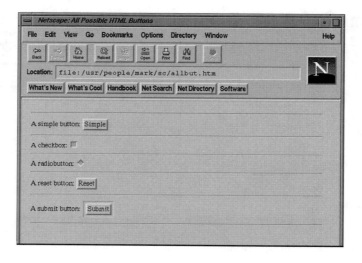

The one thing the five types of buttons have in common is that you click the button to achieve its effect. Because this is an extremely common action, the JavaScript event model defines `click` as one of its HTML form events. This event is generated by each of the five button types. In addition, when a form is actually submitted, a `submit` event is generated. The `submit` event is really owned by the form being submitted, and not the submit button that causes it.

Text Elements in Forms   There are three types of text items possible within an HTML form, as follows:

- Text fields
- Textareas
- Password fields

Single line text fields are created with an `<INPUT TYPE="text">` directive. Any text you type in a text field is displayed as you type it. This behavior is known as *echoing* the input. Single line text fields that are created using `<INPUT TYPE="password">` do not echo their input. Multi-line text fields are created with the `TEXTAREA` tag, and are usually called textareas. An HTML form showing all three types of text elements is shown in figure 3.3, created from the file alltxt.htm on the CD-ROM. Interacting with text is more complex than interacting with a button. There are more things you can do with text. You can click in the text field, enter text, edit text, select text, and decide you are finished with the text and move on.

FIG. 3.3

HTML text elements generate several different JavaScript events.

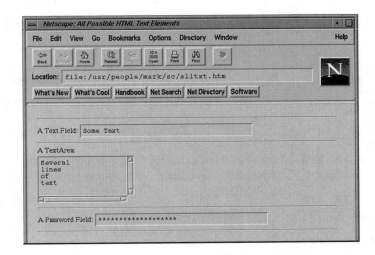

What are the events JavaScript generates in response to these various actions? JavaScript uses a text manipulation model which will be familiar to anyone who has ever used a windowing system. It defines four events that are associated with text fields and textareas, but not passwords fields—change, select, focus, and blur. The first two should be self-explanatory. The change event is generated whenever any text is changed, and the select event is generated whenever text is selected. Selecting text is more than simply clicking in the editable text field or textarea. It means actually highlighting a portion of the text with the mouse.

N O T E Password fields do not generate JavaScript events. This was a conscious design decision to prevent malicious script code from diverting password text. ▪

focus and blur are a little more involved. A text field or textarea is said to have *focus* when it is currently accepting input typed at the keyboard. Clicking anywhere inside a text item is certain to give it focus, and simply moving the mouse over the text field may do so as well. blur is the opposite of focus. *Blur* occurs when the text item no longer has focus. This may happen because some other item now has the focus, or because the focus has simply been lost. You will notice that if you position the mouse over a graphic (other than an imagemap), you can type until your fingers are sore, but nothing happens. This is a case where nothing has focus.

Part

I

Ch

3

Selection Elements in Forms   Selection lists are defined by the SELECT tag; their options are enumerated using the OPTION tag. They operate almost the same as text items; they are capable of generating focus, blur, and change events. Paradoxically, selection lists do not generate select events. You might well wonder why four event types are needed for text and three for lists. This is clarified later in this chapter. Figure 3.4 summarizes the events understood by JavaScript and the HTML elements that generate them.

▶ **See** the section "Manipulating Text Fields," in chapter 6, "Interactive HTML Objects," for more on the topic of text events, **p. 201**

▶ **See** "The Review of HTML Forms" section of chapter 6 for a more detailed review of these form elements, **p. 186**

FIG. 3.4
JavaScript events model different types of user interaction with a Web page.

HTML Elements \ Events	Blur	Click	Change	Focus	Load	Mouseover	Select	Submit	Unload
Button		X							
Checkbox		X		X					X
Document							X		
Form						X			
Link		X							
Radio		X							
Reset		X							
Selection	X		X	X					
Submit		X							
Text	X		X	X			X		
Textarea	X		X	X			X		

Actions That Are Not Events

Anything not mentioned in the previous two sections should be considered an action, not a JavaScript event. Scrolling a window, reading newsgroups, or answering mail are certainly actions, but they are not events. Using the Back, Forward, or Home buttons on Netscape's toolbar are not really JavaScript events, but they ultimately result in JavaScript events being delivered to the current page, since they unload the current document. Creating a bookmark or hotlist entry is not even remotely related to JavaScript events, since that does not affect the current page at all. How does one distinguish actions that might possibly be events from those which are not? The rule is that if an action affects or changes the current page, it is associated with one or more JavaScript events.

It might be argued that scrolling or resizing a window affects the current page, and should therefore result in some kind of event. Those of you who have programmed any kind of windowing system know these are *visibility*, or window damage, events. JavaScript takes a more literal definition of a page. No matter how much or how little of a Web page is visible, it is still the same page. Even if you only read the cartoons in *The New Yorker*, the articles are still there, unchanged.

JavaScript Code in HTML

So far we have talked about JavaScript as a language, and we have talked a bit about HTML, but we have not talked about how JavaScript is used in HTML. Event handlers are the glue that link HTML elements with JavaScript code, but how is it done? This section addresses this question. The answer has two parts: how JavaScript is included or referenced in a Web page, and how event handlers are attached to HTML items.

The *SCRIPT* Tag

In the most general sense, every Web page is constructed from HTML statements that divide the page into two parts: the <HEAD> and the <BODY>. The HTML directives within the context of the <HEAD> give information about the page, while those in the <BODY> make up the page itself. In most simple HTML documents the <HEAD> usually contains only the <TITLE>. It can also contain a BASE tag which specifies a pathname that should be used to resolve relative HREFs within the document, and one or more LINK tags, which indicate the relationship of this document to one or more other documents, such as the browser's home page.

The HEAD section of an HTML document also contains the JavaScript code for your event handlers. While it is not absolutely necessary for all JavaScript code to go with the <HEAD>...</HEAD> delimiters, it is an excellent idea because it ensures that all JavaScript code has been defined before any of the <BODY> of the document is seen. In particular, if the document has a handler for the load event, and that event was triggered before that code had been read, an error would result because the event handler function would be undefined.

Syntax of the *SCRIPT* Tag   JavaScript code is introduced with the SCRIPT tag. Everything between this tag and the closing /SCRIPT tag is assumed to be some kind of client-side script code, such as JavaScript. The syntax for the SCRIPT tag is

```
<SCRIPT LANGUAGE="LangName" [SRC="URL"]>
```

The element LangName gives the language that is used in the subsequent script code; this should be JavaScript. Strictly speaking, the LANGUAGE attribute is not required; at present, Netscape Navigator is the only browser that is widely available and understands any scripting language. Of course, the language it understands is JavaScript. This will certainly change very quickly, so it is a good idea to always include the LANGUAGE attribute.

If the SRC attribute is specified then it should reference a URL containing code in the script language. For JavaScript, this should be a valid URL for a file containing the JavaScript code. The filename should have the suffix .js. If the SRC attribute is given then the <SCRIPT> can be immediately terminated by a </SCRIPT> directive. A <SCRIPT> block that loads JavaScript code from a filename click.js in a directory jscode relative to the document base would look like this:

```
<SCRIPT LANGUAGE="JavaScript" SRC="jscode/click.js">
</SCRIPT>
```

N O T E   Netscape Navigator 2.0 does not yet support the SRC attribute. This feature has been promised for version 2.1. ■

If the SRC attribute is not given then it is expected that all the code between <SCRIPT> and </SCRIPT> is the script source itself. In the glorious future, when the overwhelming majority of browsers understand the SCRIPT tag, or at least benignly ignore it, the JavaScript source may be given literally. Until then it is recommended that source included between <SCRIPT> and </SCRIPT> be enclosed within the

HTML comment delimiters `<!--` and `-->`. A simple example showing a single JavaScript function is shown in listing 3.1.

> **CAUTION**
>
> Use the C-style comments `//` and `/* */` inside JavaScript code. Never use HTML comments *inside* JavaScript.

Listing 3.1   A JavaScript *<SCRIPT>* with a Single Function

```
<SCRIPT LANGUAGE="JavaScript">
<!--
function dontclickme()       {          // an ominous button click handler
     alert("I told you not to click me");
     return( false );
}
<!-- end script -->
</SCRIPT>
```

Use of HTML Comments   The function in listing 3.1 does not do much; it merely uses the `alert()` function to pop up a warning dialog box with its argument as the message. Presumably this function is the `click` event handler for a button you don't want the user to press. The important thing to notice about this simple example is the paradoxical, but important, use of HTML comments. The entire script body is enclosed with a comment, and the comment close `-->` is also paired with a second, seemingly redundant, comment start `<!--` on the last line. At present, you should structure your script according to the following rules:

- Place the comment start (`<!--`) on a line of its own
- Follow it with your JavaScript code
- Terminate the code with `<!--` and `-->` on its own line

You should use this magic incantation not because it makes sense, but because it works. Note that JavaScript code referenced through a SRC URL should also follow these rules, as if it had literally been included in the `<SCRIPT>` block. Note also that you may have both a JavaScript SRC URL, and literal JavaScript between `<SCRIPT>` and `</SCRIPT>`. In this case, the URL referenced by the SRC attribute is read and processed before the literal JavaScript.

CAUTION

HTML comments are one of the least conforming areas of HTML. Most browsers deviate a little from the HTML standards, and some deviate a lot. The preceding comment rules may change in the future, and may be implemented differently on different browsers.

Processing <SCRIPT> Code   There are two important aspects to JavaScript code defined by or within a SCRIPT block. The first important principle is that this JavaScript code is not executed—it is merely read and checked for syntax errors. When the browser sees the code shown in listing 3.1, it does not execute the dontclickme() function, it merely recognizes that this function is a JavaScript function, and saves the definition of that function for later use. This is precisely the opposite behavior of normal HTML. When you say <HR> in an HTML document, you get a horizontal rule. You don't get it immediately, but you do get it when the browser has finished laying out the page (assuming that there are no HTML errors, of course).

This is the way that most interpreted languages work, however. If you create a Sub in BASIC, a defun in lisp, or a proc in Tcl, it is not executed when it is read. Instead, the interpreter *parses* it, which means that it scans through the function looking for obvious syntax errors, such as unbalanced parentheses, and records the function's definition for later use. The function is only used when it is called. In JavaScript, functions can only be called by events.

Binding in JavaScript   Another critically important aspect of JavaScript is that it carries out *dynamic binding*. Binding refers to the way in which names of things, such as variable names, function names, and object names, are associated with the things themselves. If you call the function dontclickme from listing 3.1 by saying dontclickme(), you are not actually referring to the function itself, you are referring to the name of the function. "The Song of the Volga Boatmen" is really the name of that song, it is not the song itself. If you want the sheet music, you go to you favorite music store and ask for it by name; most people do not go in and begin singing "Eh-eh uxhnyot...."

There are two general approaches to binding: static binding and dynamic binding. Many languages, particularly compiled languages like C, C++, and Java, often insist on *static* binding. This means they require that they be able to find all named references when a program is compiled. (Of course, with the advent of dynamically loaded libraries this rule is relaxed a bit.) JavaScript uses the more liberal form, dynamic binding. JavaScript only attempts to resolve names when they are used.

Dynamic binding has several consequences. In the first place, if the function `dontclickme()` is never called, then it can contain all but the most hideous syntax errors and they will never be found. If `dontclickme` is the event handler for a button, and no one ever presses the button, its problems are never exposed. Even if `dontclickme()` is absolutely perfect, but the event handler is erroneously declared to be a function named `noclickme()`, this mismatch will not be detected until someone finally chooses to press the button. JavaScript will only then try to find a function named `noclickme()`. It will fail, and an error will result. Dynamic binding is often called *runtime binding* or *late binding* because the binding process only takes place when the JavaScript interpreter attempts to run the code.

TIP Always check meticulously to ensure that the function, object, and variable names used in HTML match those in the JavaScript code.

Dynamic binding has its advantages and disadvantages. Dynamic binding is used by many interpreters because it simplifies the language, and makes it very easy to add in new functions. Since there is no brooding and melancholy compiler to satisfy, it is possible to build up a complex JavaScript application incrementally. Even if you really need an event handler for every possible event, you can start out with one or two handlers, make them work, and then gradually add more complexity.

The disadvantage of dynamic binding should be clear from the previous discussion. There is very little error checking. When the JavaScript interpreter is reading all the code in the SRC URL, or processing the code between <SCRIPT> and </SCRIPT>, it is performing some checking but it is by no means performing an exhaustive analysis of the code. Errors, particularly mismatched names, are not found until the erroneous code is executed. To see a more complete example of this, look at the HTML page defined in listing 3.2.

Part
I

Ch
3

On the CD

Listing 3.2   ex32.htm   An Illustration of Dynamic Binding

```
<HTML>
<HEAD>
<TITLE>A Potentially Dangerous JavaScript Page</TITLE>
<SCRIPT LANGUAGE="JavaScript">
<!--
function dontclickme() {            // button click handler
    alert("I told you not to click me");
}
<!-- end script -->
</SCRIPT>
</HEAD>
<BODY>
<FORM METHOD="POST" ACTION="mailto:me@myhost.com">
<INPUT TYPE="button" NAME="mycheck" VALUE="HA!" onClick="dontclickme()">
</FORM>
</BODY>
</HTML>
```

If you copy this code, found in ex32.htm in the js directory on the CD-ROM, into a local file, change the e-mail address in the form's ACTION to your own e-mail address, and then read that file into your browser, everything will be fine. Notice that the click event handler for the button is declared using the HTML attribute onClick="dontclickme()", which tells JavaScript that when this button is pressed the function dontclickme should be called. (The exact syntax for declaring event handlers is discussed in the next section.) If you now click that button you should see something like figure 3.5.

FIG. 3.5
Clicking an HTML button invokes a JavaScript event handler that displays an alert.

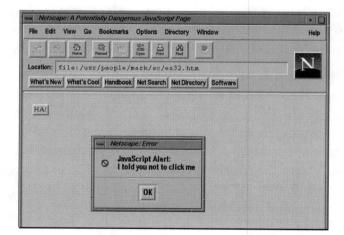

So far so good. The name of the event handler in the HTML statement that created the button matched the name of a JavaScript function in the SCRIPT block. Now try the following experiment. Change the handler declaration from

```
onClick="dontclickme()"
```

to

```
onClick="noclickme()"
```

and then read that file into your browser. You will notice that the initial appearance of the HTML page is exactly as before. No errors have been reported. If you attempt to click the button labeled HA!, your browser reports an error, and the alert dialog box shown in figure 3.5 does not appear. This is dynamic binding at work. JavaScript did not know that the function named noclickme did not correspond to any currently defined function until the user action forced it to try to find one. Technically, the function name noclickme is said to be *unbound*.

It might seem like dynamic binding is a great potential source of error, without providing many benefits as compensation. As you will see when we discuss objects in chapter 4, "JavaScript Objects," objects may be defined and even modified on-the-fly. Dynamic binding allows you to refer to things that do not yet exist, but that will exist when the event handler which uses them is actually called. Dynamic binding, like the loose typing provided by JavaScript's var, is a two-edged sword. It must be used with care, but is very powerful.

▶ **See** the "Defining Your Own Objects: The *new* Statement" section of chapter 4 for more information on creating and modifying JavaScript objects, **p. 107**.

Let's summarize these two critical points about JavaScript parsing and execution, since they will dominate our thinking for several chapters to come:

- JavaScript code is parsed when it is seen in a SCRIPT block; it is only executed when an event occurs.
- JavaScript names are resolved when they are executed, not when they are parsed.

Declaring JavaScript Event Handlers

The previous section demonstrated that JavaScript functions are only executed in response to events. We also know that events themselves only occur when some interaction with or change to the current HTML page occurs. There must be a way in which we can link events to JavaScript functions in HTML. In fact, we have already seen one such example of this in listing 3.2. The mechanism is known as the event handler declaration.

Event handler declarations look exactly like ordinary HTML attributes. Each attribute name begins with the word on and is followed by the event name, so that onClick is the attribute that would be used to declare an event handler for the click event. The full declaration of an event handler looks like

```
onEvent="javascriptcode"
```

Attribute names are not case-sensitive, following the usual HTML convention. It is good practice, however, to use the coding style shown in the preceding line of code, with on in lowercase and the event name with an initial capital. This helps to distinguish it from other attributes, which are often fully capitalized.

The value of the attribute is a set of JavaScript code. The code may be included literally (known as inline JavaScript), or it may reference a JavaScript function. We can completely remove the dontclickme() function of listing 3.2 and write the button statement as

```
<INPUT TYPE="button" NAME="mycheck" VALUE="HA!"
  onClick="alert('I told you not to click me');">
```

This has two disadvantages. First, it tends to lead to very long HTML statements. There is very little you can accomplish in only a few characters. If you have hundreds of characters between the opening (<) and the closing (>) of an HTML statement it will almost certainly be very hard to read, and, if it is too long, may cause your browser to choke. It is also not modular. As you add event handlers for different HTML elements, you may well find that there is a lot of common code. Each of the button handlers might use a variation on the same code. Such common code should always be encapsulated in a JavaScript function, rather than being repeated in several places.

 TIP   Declare all event handlers as JavaScript functions. Avoid inline JavaScript code.

One thing to notice about this example is the fact that the value of the onClick attribute is a quoted string. This follows standard HTML convention. Therefore, to

include a string within the value of the attribute we must alternate single quotes (')
with double quotes ("). This follows the JavaScript standard for strings, as we
learned in the "Implicit Data Types in JavaScript" section of chapter 2. If you
modify the dontclickme function to accept a string argument then you must carefully use quotes when passing in literal strings. Listing 3.3 shows a modified version of dontclickme, called donteventme, and the HTML event handler declarations
which reference it. It can be found in the file ex33.htm on the CD-ROM.

On the CD

**Listing 3.3   ex33.htm   A JavaScript Function Can Be Shared by
Several Event Handlers**

```html
<HTML>
<HEAD>
<TITLE>An Uncooperative JavaScript Page</TITLE>
<SCRIPT LANGUAGE="JavaScript">
<!--
function donteventme( str ) {            // generic diffident handler
     alert("I told you not to " + str + " me");
}
<!-- end script -->
</SCRIPT>
</HEAD>
<BODY>
<FORM METHOD="post" ACTION="mailto:me@myhost.com">
<BR>No<INPUT TYPE="checkbox" NAME="mycheck" VALUE="HA!"
➥onClick="donteventme('click')">
<SELECT NAME="mysel" onChange="donteventme('change')">
<OPTION SELECTED>Nope</OPTION>
<OPTION>Not Me</OPTION>
<OPTION>No Way</OPTION>
</SELECT>
</FORM>
</BODY>
</HTML>
```

Part

I

Ch

3

In this example, the function donteventme is called whenever the checkbox is
checked or any selection is made on the selection list. The alert function within
the donteventme constructs an uncooperative message based on the function's
string argument str. Although this example accomplishes no useful work, it is a
perfect template for a JavaScript page. In general, a JavaScript page has the following three components:

- JavaScript functions inside a SCRIPT block within the <HEAD> of the document
- Non-interactive HTML within the document's <BODY>
- Interactive HTML with event handler attributes whose values are JavaScript functions

You now know how to declare event handlers in general. The next section shows exactly which handlers can be associated with specific HTML tags, and gives various examples of how these event handlers are used.

> **CAUTION**
>
> Netscape Navigator 2.0 has a bug that can prevent JavaScript event handler code from being triggered. This occurs most often if an IMG directive is given without corresponding WIDTH and HEIGHT attributes. Make certain that you include these attributes if you are using images together with JavaScript.

Using JavaScript Event Handlers

JavaScript events occur at three levels—at the level of the entire Web document, at the level of an individual <FORM> within the document, and at the level of an element of a <FORM> within that document. At the same time, any particular element at any of these three levels may result in more than one event. For example, you have already seen that text items can generate up to four different events depending on how they are manipulated. In this section, we examine each level and see which handlers are appropriate for the HTML elements within that level. As you might suspect, most of the action is at the lowest level, within HTML forms.

Document Level Event Handlers

The HTML BODY tag is the container that holds the descriptive content of an HTML page. Just as the material in the HEAD section is about the page, the material between <BODY> and </BODY> is the page. The BODY tag can contain two event handler declarations using the onLoad and onUnload attributes. A JavaScript page might have a BODY declaration that looks like

```
<BODY onLoad="loadfunc()" onUnload="unloadfunc()">
```

The onLoad="loadfunc()" attribute declares a JavaScript handler that will handle the load event. The load event is generated after the entire contents of the page, namely the HTML between <BODY> and </BODY>, has been read, but before it has been displayed. The onLoad event handler is an excellent place to perform any one time initialization. It can also be used to display a splash screen containing company, product, or copyright information. It can even launch a security dialog box which permits only authorized users, with an appropriate password or key, from completely loading the page.

The onUnload="unloadfunc()" attribute declares an event handler that is invoked whenever the page is unloaded. This happens when the user executes any action that brings up a new page in the same browser window. An unload event does not occur if a new page is opened in a new window. Even if a new page is not successfully loaded, the current page is still unloaded, and the unloadfunc is called in that case. An onUnload event handler can be used to ensure that there are no loose ends, and to perform any cleanup necessary. For example, if the user has filled out a form, but has failed to press the Submit button, the onUnload handler should inform the user of that fact. It could even submit the form itself based on the user's response. Note that both the onLoad and onUnload handlers are optional.

There is one final document level event handler, although it is not associated with the BODY tag. Any HTML link can declare an event handler for the mouseOver event, which occurs when the user places the mouse over the HREF of that link. This can be used to achieve a visual effect, or to perform some special processing before the user actually tries to access the link. Listing 3.4 shows a slightly fanciful example. This code can be found in the file ex34.htm on the CD-ROM.

Part

I

Ch

3

CAUTION

In the current implementation of JavaScript, links have event handlers, but anchors do not. This means that you must catch navigation events by attaching event handlers to links. If any of your links point to anchors in the same document, the event must be handled at the link, not at the anchor.

Listing 3.4   ex34.htm   Using the *mouseOver* Event to Mediate Access

```
<HTML>
<HEAD>
<TITLE>A Nationalist JavaScript Page</TITLE>
<SCRIPT LANGUAGE="JavaScript">
<!—
function warnthem( lnk ) {                   // mouseOver event handler
     var theirhost = lnk.hostname;           // 2; get hostname of link
     var domain = "", lastdot = 0, len = 0;
     len = theirhost.length;                 // 4; string length of hostname
     lastdot = theirhost.lastIndexOf(".");   // 5; find last dot
     domain = theirhost.substring(lastdot+1, len); // 6; last part of
                                               ➥hostname
     if ( domain == "zz" ) {                 // 7; warn about country "zz"
         alert("Country zz only has 1200 baud modems");
     }
}
<!— end script —>
</SCRIPT>
</HEAD>
<BODY>
<HR>
Check out the new links to <A HREF="http://home.std.zz"
➥onMouseOver="warnthem(this)">Zzland</A>
➥and its neighbor <A HREF="http://home.xyzzy.xy"
➥onMouseOver="warnthem(this)">XYville</A>
<HR>
</BODY>
</HTML>
```

This HTML creates a page with two elements—links to the fictitious home pages of the countries Zzland and XYville, and sets up a mouseOver event handler for those links. Note that the event handler function warnthem is called with an argument this. The special keyword this is used to refer to the current object. When the warnthem function is called, its parameter lnk is filled in with the object that represents the link over which the mouse just moved.

▶ **See** the chapter 4 section "Defining Your Own Objects: The *new* Statement" for a discussion of the this keyword and other object-oriented concepts, **p. 107**.

Statement 2 extracts the hostname part of that object, which in this example could be either home.std.zz or home.xyzzy.xy, depending on where the mouse is located. The next three statements use some of the string object functions (see "String Content Methods," in chapter 4) to tear off the last part of this fully qualified hostname, namely zz or xy, and save it in the variable domain. This variable is then tested against zz in statement 7. If the test passes then an alert is put up to warn the user that the connection to the zz home page will take longer due to slow modems. Links can also have click event handlers, so this code can be modified not only to warn the user, but also to abort the connection, if necessary. The result of placing the mouse over the Zzland link is shown in figure 3.6.

FIG. 3.6
JavaScript event handlers can be used with any hypertext links.

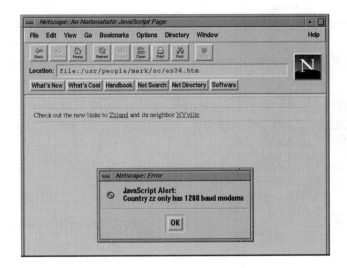

Part
I

Ch
3

Submit Event Handlers in the *FORM* Tag

The FORM tag is used to begin the definition of an HTML form. It includes attributes from the METHOD to be used in submitting the form, the ACTION to be taken, and may also include a single type of event handler attribute, the onSubmit attribute. The syntax for a FORM tag is the following:

```
<FORM NAME="formname" ... onSubmit="submithandler()">
```

 Put event handler attributes last on the attribute list of an HTML tag. This makes them easy to find and modify during debugging.

The onSubmit handler is invoked when the form's contents are about to be submitted. This is a top level action that applies to the entire form. It is also possible to specify an onClick action on the Submit button in a form, as you shall see later in the section, "Button Click Events." The natural use of an onSubmit handler is to validate the contents of a form. The submission proceeds if the contents are valid, and is canceled if they are not.

> **CAUTION**
>
> If you return `false` in an `onSubmit` event handler using UNIX version 2.0 of Netscape Navigator, it does not cancel the submit.

Listing 3.5 (file ex35.htm on the CD-ROM) shows a very simple form with a single element, an editable text field. The value of the field is supposed to be a number between 1 and 9. The submit handler function `checkit` is called when the form is submitted. It validates the user-entered quantity and acts accordingly.

On the CD

Listing 3.5   ex34.htm   Form Content Can Be Validated Using an *onSubmit* Handler

```
<HTML>
<HEAD>
<TITLE>A Simple Form Validation Example</TITLE>
<SCRIPT LANGUAGE="JavaScript">
<!--
function checkit() {                              // submit validation function
    var strval = document.myform.mytext.value;   // 2; input text  value
    var intval = parseInt(strval);               // 3; convert to integer
    if ( 0 < intval && intval < 10 ) {           // 4; input ok
        return( true );                          // 5; allow submit
    } else {                                     // 6; input bad - tell user
        alert("Input value " + strval + " is out of range");
        return( false );                         // 8; forbid submit
    }
}
<!-- end script -->
</SCRIPT>
</HEAD>
<BODY>
<HR>
<FORM NAME="myform" METHOD="post" ACTION="mailto:me@myhost.com"
    onSubmit="checkit()">
<P>Enter a number between 1 and 9:
    <INPUT TYPE="text" NAME="mytext" VALUE="1" SIZE="10"></P>
<BR><INPUT TYPE="submit">
</FORM>
<HR>
</BODY>
</HTML>
```

It is worthwhile to examine this example in some detail, as it exposes a number of points that are more thoroughly discussed later in this chapter. Let us consider the HTML in the <BODY> first. The FORM statement creates a form named myform with a fictitious mailto: destination. It also contains an onSubmit attribute that specifies checkit() as the JavaScript function to call when the form is about to be submitted. Like all of our previous event handlers, this one takes no arguments. You will see very shortly that it is not only possible to pass in arguments, but it can also be very beneficial. For a document this simple, however, it is not necessary.

The first INPUT tag establishes an editable text field named mytext which can hold up to 10 characters, and which will be initialized to the string "1". The second INPUT tag puts a Submit button just below the input text field. Neither of these INPUT statements have any handler attributes, although they could. What happens next?

If the user types in any text, or does anything except press the Submit button, then nothing special happens. This example does not process any events other than the submit event, so changes in the text field or navigation actions do not result in any JavaScript code being executed. If the user does press the Submit button, then the myform form tries to submit itself. This triggers the submit action, which results in its event handler, checkit(), being called.

The checkit function does two somewhat obscure things. In statement 2, it sets the local variable strval equal to the value of document.myform.mytext.value. We know from the "Functions and Objects" section of chapter 2 that the right side of this expression must be an object reference—in fact, a reference to an object within an object within an object. It is reasonable and correct to assume that the myform subobject corresponds to the HTML form named myform within the current document, and that the mytext subobject corresponds to the HTML editable text field named mytext inside myform. This windy construct transfers the value of that text field into the local variable strval. In statement 3, an attempt is made to convert this string to an integer using the built-in function parseInt. The putative integer is stored in intval.

▶ **See** chapter 4, "Built-In Functions," for more information on how to manipulate HTML fields, **p. 140**.

In statement 4, our validation test is performed. If the string in the text field did represent an integer between 1 and 9 inclusive then this if test passes and the checkit function returns true, in statement 5. This is a message from JavaScript to the browser that the submission may complete.

If the text field was out of range then the `else` pathway in statement 6 is taken. Note that `parseInt` returns 0 if its argument cannot be parsed as an integer. This means that if the user entered "five" in the text field rather than "5" the value of `intval` will be 0, and the `else` clause will be taken. Statement 7 puts up an alert dialog box telling the user that the value was out of range. It contains the string representation of the value. This is useful since the alert dialog box may be inadvertently positioned over the text input field. Finally, statement 8 returns `false`, indicating that the submit operation should not complete. The outcome of entering a value that is out of bounds is shown in figure 3.7.

FIG. 3.7
JavaScript submit handlers are often used to validate form input.

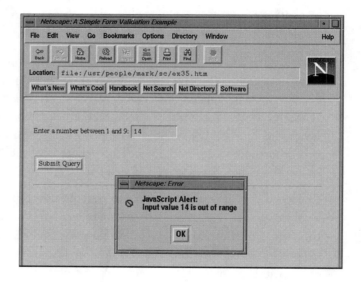

In this particular case it is important to give the `mytext` text field an initial value of 1. This ensures that if the user clicks the Submit button without altering that text field it will have an acceptable value, and the form will be submitted. In many cases, just the opposite is true. The whole point of a catalog order form is to persuade the user to enter critical information, such as his name and e-mail address. In this case, it's a good idea to initialize the text field with a deliberately invalid value, so that if the user hits Submit without typing anything the form is not submitted. Chapters 6, "Interactive HTML Objects," and 16, "Creative User Interaction," provide several more sophisticated examples of customized user interaction using JavaScript.

N O T E Always give the user meaningful feedback on inappropriate input or other error conditions. Indicate why and where the error occurred, not just that an error occurred. Be brief, but specific. ■

Event Handlers in *FORM* Elements

Almost all form elements may have one or more event handlers. The type of event handlers permitted on a given element depends on the type of element itself. You have already seen the linkage between events and HTML entities in figure 3.4. Broadly speaking, buttons can generate `click` events, and text and select items can generate `focus`, `blur`, `select`, and `change` events. The one potentially confusing aspect of this organization of events is that selection lists cannot generate the `select` event. This is because they have no editable text. We will not consider all possible events in this chapter, only a pithy subset.

There are two important exceptions to the rule that all form elements can have handlers. The first exception applies to hidden items, those with `<INPUT TYPE="hidden">`. Since they cannot be seen, they cannot be changed by the user, and therefore cannot generate events. The second exception applies to individual `OPTION` elements within a `SELECT` selection list. The `SELECT` tag itself may have attributes declaring `focus`, `blur`, and `change` handlers, but the `OPTIONS` may not generate their own events. Any acquisition or loss of focus, and any change in the item(s) that have been selected applies to the whole list, not to an individual element.

Button Click Events All button types within an HTML form can have `click` event handlers by adding an `onClick` attribute to their `<INPUT>` declaration. Simple buttons with a `TYPE` attribute of `"button"`, `"reset"`, or `"submit"` merely signal that they have been pressed. (Recall that the act of submitting a form may also be caught using an `onSubmit` handler attached to the `<FORM>` declaration.) Checkboxes and radio buttons also have values. Checkboxes and individual radio buttons can be asked if they are on or off. A group of radio buttons can also be asked for the unique index of the button currently checked.

One very common problem in HTML forms design is the issue of conflicting options. Users are often presented with a variety of different choices, which may even be spread out over more than one HTML form. Some combinations of choices may be invalid or dubious. Unfortunately, in standard HTML there is no way to perform input validation of this kind without actually submitting the form and asking the ACTION URL if that particular combination is acceptable.

JavaScript event handlers are ideal for this kind of validation. As you learn in chapter 4, every HTML form element is also a JavaScript object. You have already seen some examples of this in listings 3.4 and 3.5. Listing 3.6 shows two radio buttons working together with a checkbox using a JavaScript onClick event handler. The code for this listing can be found in file ex36.htm on the CD-ROM. The initial appearance of this form is shown in figure 3.8.

On the CD

Listing 3.6   ex36.htm   Values of Different Form Elements Can Be Accessed in JavaScript

```
<HTML>
<HEAD>
<TITLE>Two Choices Work as One</TITLE>
<SCRIPT LANGUAGE="JavaScript">
<!--
function insok() {  // make sure payment & ins choices are compatible
    var isgold = document.myform.payment[1].checked; // 2; gold checked
    var isins = document.myform.insurance.checked; // 3; insurance elected?
    var ok = null;
                    // 5; if paying in gold without insurance then..
    if ( isgold == true && isins != true ) {
        ok = confirm("Do you want insurance?");    // 6; ask for insurance
        if ( ok == true ) {                        // 7; yes, get insurance
            document.myform.insurance.checked = true;  // 8; check it
        }
}
<!-- end script -->
</SCRIPT>
</HEAD>
<BODY>
<HR>
<FORM NAME="myform" METHOD="POST" ACTION="mailto:me@myhost.com">
<STRONG>Payment Options</STRONG><BR>
<HR>
<INPUT TYPE="radio" NAME="payment" VALUE="1" CHECKED
    onClick="insok()"> Personal Check
<INPUT TYPE="radio" NAME="payment" VALUE="2"
    onClick="insok()"> Gold Bullion
<HR>
<INPUT TYPE="checkbox" NAME="insurance" VALUE="Ins"> Insurance?
</FORM>
<HR>
</BODY>
</HTML>
```

FIG. 3.8
JavaScript onClick
handlers can be used to
exclude invalid user input.

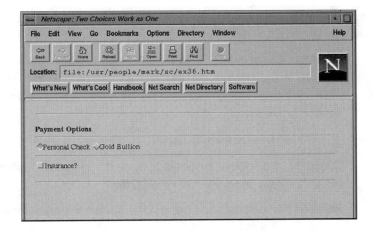

The <BODY> of this page sets up a two-choice radio button named payment, and a checkbox named insurance. The first button is selected, and the checkbox starts off unchecked. The radio button group has the function insok as its click event handler. Whenever either of the buttons is clicked the insok function is called.

In statements 2 and 3 insok fetches the current value of the second radio button named payment. Note that payment actually denotes the entire group of buttons, not any single radio button, so that you must use the array reference payment[1] in order to refer to the second button (0 based indexing is used). That value is stored in the boolean variable isgold. The variable insok gets the state of the insurance checkbox, which is also true if it is checked and false if it is not. A compatibility test is now performed in statement 5. If the radio button group indicates payment in gold bullion, but the insurance button is not checked, then a confirmation dialog box is put up using the confirm() function in statement 6.

The confirmation dialog box has OK and Cancel buttons. If the user presses OK, the function returns true; otherwise it returns false. The return value is tested in statement 7. If it was true, then the user does want insurance, and the method function value of the checked property of the myform.insurance object is set to true. Without worrying too much about what methods and properties really mean just yet, it is easy to infer that this assignment statement has the same effect as a click of the insurance button. That checkbox is now checked.

TROUBLESHOOTING

I modified the code shown in listing 3.6. I added another group of radio buttons to collect information about the user's income level, with its own event handler `doinc()`. I would like to force the `insok()` function to be called from the new event handler. Inside `doinc()` I have a statement

```
myform.insurance.click();
```

This `click()` function is supposed to cause the insurance checkbox to be checked, but the `doins()` handler is never called. Why?

JavaScript has many functions like `click()` that emulate user actions. These emulated actions do not generate events, however, so the corresponding event handler functions are never called. There is nothing mystical about the event handler function `insok()`—it is an ordinary JavaScript function that happens to be linked to an HTML event. If you want to call `insok()` in your `doinc()` event handler, just do the following:

```
insok();
```

Text Edit and Selection Events   HTML text <INPUT> fields with a TYPE attribute of "text" may declare event handlers for any combination of the four text events: focus, blur, change, and select. Multi-line text input items created with a TEXTAREA tag may also have these handlers. Selection lists created with <SELECT> can generate all these events except select.

The focus event is generated when the text item of a list element gets the input focus, usually as a result of a mouse click. Tabbing through form fields also moves the input focus. The blur event is generated when an item which had focus looses it. The change event is generated whenever something changes. In a text item this results when any new text is entered or existing text is deleted. In a selection list it happens whenever a new selection is made, even in a list that permits MULTIPLE selections. The select event is generated when the user selects some text, usually by click-and-drag or double-click operations with the mouse. The select event is almost always accompanied by a visual cue, usually by the selected text becoming highlighted or changing color.

These events can be used to obtain very fine control over the content of text or selection list items. The most common application is to use the change or blur events to ensure that a text field has an appropriate value. If you ask the user to enter her birthdate, for example, and provide separate fields for the month, day, and year, you will almost certainly want to make sure that the value of the day field is a number between 1 and 31. You might even go to greater lengths, and limit the day field's value based on the value of the month field. In any case, you want to avoid erroneous input such as "bleen." Text events can also be used to coordinate the values coming from multiple form elements, as we saw in listing 3.6.

Listing 3.7 (file ex37.htm on the CD-ROM) shows a linguistic application of the blur event for a TEXTAREA. The user is inspired to enter a sentence without a single instance of the letter e. If the user tries and fails he is chided for his lack of creativity. Note that the blur event handler is only called if the user makes an attempt, since blur is only generated when focus is lost. If the user never clicks or types in the TEXTAREA no blur event occurs. Parts II and IV of this book provide many more detailed examples of all the JavaScript events.

On the CD

Listing 3.7   ex37.htm   An Example of JavaScript's Text Events

```
<HTML>
<HEAD>
<TITLE>A Literary Exercise</TITLE>
<SCRIPT LANGUAGE="JavaScript">
<!—
function hasE() {                          // complain if there is an e
    var thestr = document.myform.mytarea.value; // 2; get textarea value
    var uthestr = thestr.toLowerCase();    // 3; convert to lowercase
    if ( uthestr == "" ) {                 // 4; no entry
        return;                            // 5; just return
    }
    if ( uthestr.indexOf("e") >= 0 ) {     // 7; found an 'e'
        alert("Alors! You've got an E in there!");    // 8; failed
    } else {
        if ( uthestr.length <= 20 ) {
            alert("Nice try, but too brief");    // 11; too short
        } else {
            alert("Congratulations!");     // 13; succeeded
        }
    }
}
<!— end script —>
</SCRIPT>
</HEAD>
```

continues

Listing 3.7 Continued

```
<BODY>
<P>The novel <I>A Void</I> does not contain a single &quote&quot.<BR>
Can you create a sentence without one?</P>
<HR>
<FORM NAME="myform" METHOD="POST" ACTION="mailto:me@myhost.com">
<TEXTAREA NAME="mytarea" ROWS="5" COLUMNS="80" onBlur="hasE()">
</TEXTAREA>
</FORM>
<HR>
</BODY>
</HTML>
```

The modulus operandi of this example should be becoming familiar to you now. If the user types or clicks in the textarea nothing happens. When he leaves the textarea and clicks elsewhere a blur event is generated and the handler function hasE invoked. This function gets the contents of the textarea into a local variable named thestr (in statement 2) and then uses one of the string functions to convert it to lowercase (statement 3). This saves a little time, as the function won't have to test for the presence of both e and E. The new lowercase string uthestr is tested against the empty string in statement 4. If there is no text the function returns without complaint.

If there is some text, but it has an e the user is reprimanded in statement 8. If there is no e but the text has less than 20 characters the user is encouraged to try a more ambitious work in statement 11. If the text is long enough and has no e then the user is praised in statement 13. Of course, there is nothing preventing the user from entering gibberish such as zzzzzzzzzzzzzzzzzzzzzzzzz and being congratulated anyway. Much more sophisticated checking would be necessary to ensure that the input was actually a sentence. ●

CHAPTER 4

JavaScript Objects

by Mark C. Reynolds

The idea of object-oriented programming is not a new one. It actually dates back over 30 years, and has gone through several phases of popularity in that time. Currently, object-oriented programming is considered by many to be an established concept that should be part of all modern programming languages. There are several different conflicting definitions of object-oriented programming. Fortunately, there are some key concepts that are shared by (almost) all versions of objected-oriented programming.

At its most basic level, object-oriented programming is a style of programming in which related concepts are grouped together. If you have five data elements and three functions that manipulate those elements, then you group those elements and functions together into a generic container known as an *object*. This is the common ground shared by (almost) all object-oriented programming languages. Differences arise in the details of how such containers are organized, and in how their contents can be accessed and modified.

Use the `Date`, `String`, and `Math` objects

These objects are built in to JavaScript, and provide many functions for date and string manipulation, as well as a large collection of mathematical operations.

Create new objects with specific properties and methods

User-defined objects are a good way of grouping related data items and functions together, and work well with JavaScript's object model.

Build and use arrays

JavaScript arrays can be accessed by using a numerical index or an element name; this simplifies many programming tasks.

Understand the hierarchy of objects on a Web page

Almost every HTML element is associated with a JavaScript object. These objects are arranged in a logical hierarchy, much like a directory tree.

Associate HTML tags with HTML objects

To access HTML objects from JavaScript, it is necessary to explore JavaScript's rules for HTML elements and their attributes.

An analogy can be made between home ownership and object-oriented programming. Everyone's house has a kitchen, some bedrooms and bathrooms, stairs, flooring, and so forth. Some homes have spiral staircases, Art Deco ironwork, and a gazebo in the back yard. Others have a completely utilitarian layout based on a linear architecture with not a rounded corner in sight. When talking about your home, you describe both the basic aspects ("yes, of course we have a basement") and also the embellishments ("the basement has a painfully hard cement floor"). When talking about what an object means in JavaScript, it's necessary to also talk of two levels. The basic aspects of the way JavaScript handles objects is known as its *object model*. The embellishments constitute the extensive set of features of the predefined objects in JavaScript, as well as those aspects of the language that can be used to create and use new, user-defined objects. ■

Objects, Properties, and Methods in JavaScript

Before we can delve into object-oriented programming in JavaScript, it is first necessary to review some of the basic concepts of object-oriented programming itself. You have already had a brief introduction in the "Functions and Objects" section of chapter 2, "JavaScript: The Language." This section takes you further, and explains several critical and often misunderstood ideas.

Object-Oriented Programming Concepts

We already know that an object is basically a container for related items. Rather than carry around money and credit cards in many different pockets and folders, many people choose a more unified method: they keep their money in a wallet. Perhaps they even keep their change in a change purse. The wallet is a container for related items. This is not to say that all such items must be in that wallet; this is often a near-impossible goal for even the most organized individuals. As a flexible principle, however, it is of enormous utility.

Objects operate the same way. Objects collect related data items in a single place and make it simpler, or at least more logical, to access those items. As we have already seen, JavaScript refers to the items collected within an object as its *properties*. You may also recall that JavaScript objects not only store data, they also store functions. It is useful to keep functions that manipulate data items in a specific way with those data items themselves. These functions are known as the *methods* of an object.

The JavaScript Date object is a perfect example of the benefits of this kind of organization. As the name implies, a JavaScript Date object is used to store a date, and also a time. The Date object also has a very particular set of methods that are useful in converting string representations of dates in Date objects. While these functions are vitally important when manipulating strings such as "Nov 23, 1990," they do not really have sweeping application elsewhere. In a word, they are date-specific. It makes good sense to keep these methods with Date objects, rather than making them generally available functions.

In addition to the concepts of object, property, and method there is a fourth, somewhat more subtle, concept that is also of great importance: the *instance*. The relationship between an object and an instance of an object is the same as the relationship between a data type and a variable of that data type. In the typeless language such as JavaScript, this distinction is blurred but is still present. Another way to think of this distinction is to think of an object as a set of shelves, some of which may be occupied while others are not. You convert that object into an instance when you completely fill in all the empty shelves.

While the object Date is an abstract thing that does refer to any specific date, an instance of the Date object must refer to some specific date. Its empty slots, which specify the actual day, month, year, and so forth, have all been assigned specific values.

Defining Your Own Objects: The *new* Statement

Now that we have presented the basic object foundation upon which JavaScript rests, it is time to consider how these concepts are implemented. How does one create objects and instances in JavaScript? In fact, you already know part of the answer to this question, as objects are created by defining a very special sort of function.

Part

I

Ch

4

Let's pursue the home ownership analogy even further and define a house object. The fundamental properties of our house object will be as follows:

- Number of rooms
- Architectural style
- Year built
- Has a garage?

To define an object to hold this information, we write the function shown in listing 4.1. Note that this function makes use of the extremely important keyword `this`, which always refers to the current object. In this case it refers to the current object we are creating.

Listing 4.1   Defining a Function to Create a *house* Object

```
function house( rms, stl, yr, garp ) {        // define a house object
     this.rooms = rms;              // number of rooms (integer)
     this.style = stl;         // style, e.g. Colonial, Tudor, Ranch (string)
     this.yearbuilt = yr;           // year built, integer
     this.hasgarage = garp;            // has a garage? (boolean)
     }
```

There are several things to notice about this object definition. First of all, the name of the function is the name of the object: `house`. Second, this function does not return anything. When functions were first introduced in chapter 2, it might have seemed mysterious how a function could actually do useful work without a `return` statement, since everything inside a function is local. Using a function to create an object works by modifying `this`, so that it need not return anything. You can also have the function `return(this)`. Using this explicit `return` statement has the same effect as the code shown in listing 4.1.

This example shows how a `house` *object* is defined. It does not create a specific `house` *instance*. The `house` object has four slots to hold the four properties `rooms`, `style`, `yearbuilt`, and `hasgarage`. A specific `house` instance will fill those slots with actual values. Instances are created using the `new` statement combined with a function call. The keyword `new` is required, since it tells JavaScript that we are creating an instance rather than just calling a function. We could create an instance of `house`, named `myhouse`, as follows:

```
var myhouse = new house( 10, "Colonial", 1989, true );
```

Note that the instance `myhouse` is treated just like any other variable. It must be declared using `var`. Now that `myhouse` has been created we can refer to its properties using the dot operator (.). `myhouse.rooms` has the value 10, `myhouse.style` is the string "Colonial," `myhouse.yearbuilt` is 1989, and `myhouse.hasgarage` is the boolean value `true`. The fact that `rooms` and `yearbuilt` are integers, `style` is a string, and `hasgarage` is a boolean is only implicit, of course. There is nothing stopping us from creating a `house` instance in which the `hasgarage` property has the string value "yes" rather than a boolean value. Care must be taken to avoid this kind of type confusion.

NOTE   Object properties are typeless, just like all other variables in JavaScript. The `new` operator does not protect you against inadvertently assigning an inappropriate value to a property. ▪

Objects as Arrays

Many programming languages support array data types. An *array* is an indexed collection of items all of which have the same underlying type. In C or Java, for example, we can say `int iarr[10];` which defines a collection of 10 integers. These integers are referred to as `iarr[0]` through `iarr[9]`. These two languages use *zero-based indexing*, which means that the first element of the array is at location 0 and the last element of the array is at one less than the length of the array—9 in this case. Other languages have *one-based indexing*, in which the elements range from 1 up to the length of the array. This might seem more intuitive, but zero-based indexing is actually the more common form.

JavaScript also has arrays that use zero-based indexing. In JavaScript, however, arrays and objects are really two views on the same concept. Every object is an array of its property values, and every array is also an object. Our `myhouse` instance, for example, is an array with the following four elements:

```
myhouse[0] = 10;            // rooms
myhouse[1] = "Colonial";    // style
myhouse[2] = 1989;          // yearbuilt
myhouse[3] = true;          // hasgarage
```

There might not seem to be a lot of advantage to referring to objects in this more numeric and less informative manner. You have to remember which index corresponds to which property. However, this alternate form of access makes it possible to access the properties sequentially, rather than by name, which is sometimes very useful. If we know that house objects always have four members then we can write the function shown in listing 4.2 to display the property values.

Listing 4.2   A Function That Displays the Properties of a *house*

```
function showhouse( somehouse ) {             // display properties of
                                              ➥a house instance
    for( var iter = 0; iter < 4; iter++) {    // four properties exactly
        document.write("<BR>Property " + iter + " is " + somehouse[iter]);
    }
    document.write("<BR>");
}
```

If we call this function as showhouse(myhouse) the four properties of the myhouse instance are displayed. This function must be called with an instance, not an object. It would be an error to try showhouse(house). Since there are several alternative ways of writing it, we will revisit this function when we have learned more about methods and the for…in statement.

One deficiency of the showhouse function should strike you immediately. It relies on the implicit knowledge that every house instance has exactly four properties. If we were to augment the definition of a house object by adding a property known as taxrate (a floating-point number describing the current real estate taxation rate on the house), then the showhouse function would need to be modified to increase the loop count in the for statement from 4 to 5. If we neglect to do so then the showhouse function would only print the first four properties, and would never print the taxrate.

An even more disastrous error would occur if we defined the house object to have only three properties, but forgot to drop the loop count to 3; then the reference to somehouse[3] would refer to a nonexistent array member. This type of error is known as an *out of bounds error*, since it refers to an array element that was not within the boundaries of the array. There is a very simple way to avoid this problem and write the showhouse function in a more general manner.

TIP

Define all objects with a length property, which gives the number of properties in the object. Make the length property the first property.

Using the preceding tip, we can rewrite the definition of the house object to include a length property as the first property, and then generalize the showhouse function to be completely independent of any prior knowledge of the house object. This code for the new house object and showhouse function is shown in listing 4.3. This code can be found in the file house1.js on the CD-ROM.

On the CD

Listing 4.3   house1.js   A Better *house* Object That Knows Its Own Length

```
/*
  This function creates a house instance whose first property,
  at array index 0, contains the number of properties in the house
  instance.
*/

function house ( rms, stl, yr, garp ) {
    this.length = 5;            // four informative properties, and
                                ➥length
    this.rooms = rms;           // rooms
    this.style = stl;           // architecture style
    this.yearbuilt = yr;          // year constructed
    this.hasgarge = garp;          // does it have a garage?
}


/*
  This function displays a house instance using its length property
  to determine how many other properties to display
*/

function showhouse( somehouse ) {                    // display properties of
                                                     ➥a house instance
    var nprops = somehouse.length;        // number of properties
    for( var iter = 1; iter < nprops; iter++) {    // iterate over all
                                                   ➥properties
                                                   ➥except length

        document.write("<BR>Property " + iter + " is " +
        ➥somehouse[iter]);
    }
    document.write("<BR>");
}
```

This house object function takes four parameters, as before. It sets its length property to this number plus 1, since there are four meaningful properties (rooms, style, yearbuilt, and hasgarage) and the length property itself. Each of the meaningful properties have moved up 1, so that if we say myhouse = new house(10, "Colonial", 1989, true) the array representation of myhouse becomes

```
myhouse[0] = 5;              // total # of properties
myhouse[1] = 10;             // rooms
myhouse[2] = "Colonial";     // style
myhouse[3] = 1989;           // yearbuilt
myhouse[4] = true;           // hasgarage
```

The showhouse function starts by looking at the length property and uses that to set the termination condition for the for loop. The constant 4 of listing 4.2 has been replaced by the variable nprops which holds the length of the myhouse array. This version of showhouse only prints the properties of interest; it does not print the length property. This is why the for loop begins at 1 rather than at 0. The property myhouse[0] is the length property.

This use of the length property is a typical example of the true nature of object-oriented programming. One of the fundamental ideas in object-oriented programming is the idea of *encapsulation*, which is a long-winded way of saying keeping related things in the same place. In the previous definitions of house and showhouse (see listings 4.1 and 4.2), the length of the house object was present in two places. It was implicitly present in the definition of house itself, and it was also present explicitly, as the upper limit in the for loop. The doctrine of encapsulation says that this is bad. The length of an object should only be stored in one place—in the object itself. By the same token it might be argued that the showhouse function should really be part of the house object, too. The "Method Functions and *this*" section later in this chapter describes how to do this.

Despite the power of this technique, it might still seem less than obvious to refer to properties by index rather than by property name. JavaScript provides a third technique, which is a hybrid of the dot style (.) and the array style ([ ]). Object properties may be referred to not only as indexed array elements but also as named array elements. This type of array is known as an *associative array*. The set of properties of the myhouse instance could also be listed as

```
myhouse["length"] = 5;
myhouse["rooms"] = 10;
```

```
myhouse["style"] = "Colonial";
myhouse["yearbuilt"] = 1989;
myhouse["hasgarage"] = true;
```

> **CAUTION**
>
> JavaScript arrays can be accessed by integer index or by property names. Property names are case-sensitive. Integer indices are limited by the length of the array. If you refer to non-existent array elements, by name or by index, it either generates a JavaScript error or gives you an invalid value.

Using Variable Length Arrays and Extended Instances

There is one final point to be made about the difference between house object and its various instances. Suppose we create another instance of house, named yourhouse, using the following call to new:

```
yourhouse = new house( 26, "Tudor", 1922, true );
```

myhouse and yourhouse are both instances of the house object. Both result from filling in the four slots in the house template with four specific pieces of information that define myhouse and yourhouse (as well as the fifth, hidden piece of information, the length). It is possible to *dynamically extend* an instance by simply tacking on a new property. If you feel the need to also record the fact that your house has two tool sheds and a gazebo you can write

```
yourhouse.sheds = 2;
yourhouse.hasgazebo = true;
```

These two statements add two new properties to the end of the yourhouse array. The sheds (integer) property is yourhouse[5] and the hasgazebo (boolean) property is yourhouse[6]. Dynamic extensions only apply to specific instances. The myhouse instance is not affected, nor is the house object changed in any way. If we execute showhouse(myhouse) it prints out exactly the same as it did before. If we create a third house named pizza

```
pizza = new house( 3, "Restaurant", 1993, false );
```

it will not have either a sheds property or a hasgazebo property. Figure 4.1 illustrates the relationship between the house object and its various instances.

Part

I

Ch

4

FIG. 4.1

Instances inherit their structure from the underlying object, but can also be extended.

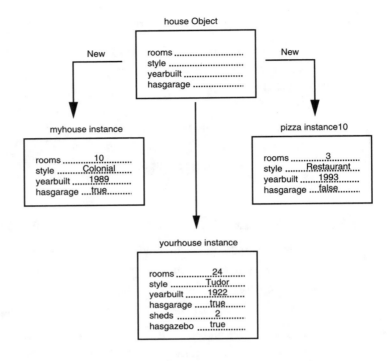

NOTE   Dynamic extensions are completely local to a particular instance. The underlying object and all other instances—past, present, and future—are not affected. ▨

There are some situations in which dynamic extensions are absolutely essential, and dramatically simplify programming. For the most part, however, dynamic extensions should be used with great care, as they can be the source of numerous errors. In fact, we have already made one such error, which shows itself if we attempt to execute the function showhouse(yourhouse). Since the length element of the yourhouse instance has not been modified, it still has the value 5, so that only array elements 1 through 4 (properties "name" through "hasgarage") are displayed. The two new properties will not be displayed. When we added sheds and hasgazebo, we should have also said

```
yourhouse.length += 2;
```

to account for the two new properties in this instance. This is precisely the type of error that is easy to make. In general, it would be much better for the house object to always have `sheds` and `hasgazebo` properties, which are seldom used, than to randomly glue them on. The most efficient way to do this is discussed later in the "Functions with a Variable Number of Arguments" section of this chapter.

The one common case where dynamic extension is extremely useful is in variable length arrays. Since object properties are just array elements, and since these elements can be referred to using a numerical index, it is easy to write an object creation function that creates an array of arbitrary size and content. The function in listing 4.4 can be used to define an object that is an array of strings. The number of strings in the array is the first argument, and the initial value for each element is the second argument.

Listing 4.4   A Variable Length Array-Of-Strings Object

```
function stringarr( howmany, initstr) {    // "howmany" strings
    this.length = howmany;
    for( var i = 1; i <= howmany; i++ ) {
        this[i] = initstr;                 // initial value "initstr"
    }
}
```

If we call this function as

```
mystringarr = new stringarr( 100, "spoon" );
```

it creates an instance with 101 properties. The first, at index 0, is the all-important `length` property. The next 100, at indices 1 through 100 inclusive, are initialized to the string "spoon." Presumably at some point in the future these 100 strings will be set to some other, less uniform values. It is important to initialize all the properties values to something (the empty string "" would do in this case).

If we later find that we need more than 100 strings we do not need to create a new, even longer, `stringarr` instance. Instead we can dynamically extend the array to include these new strings. It is essential that the `length` property be updated in this case, as there is no other way of determining how many elements are in the array, short of counting them with a `for...in` loop (see the following section). The following statements add three new strings and update the length:

```
mystringarr[101] = "I'm";
mystringarr[102] = "doing";
mystringarr[103] = "laundry";
mystringarr.length += 3;
```

The *for...in* Statement

Chapter 2 introduced the extremely useful `for` statement. The standard form of the `for` statement begins with a clause that defines the initial state of the `for` loop, the condition under which it will terminate, and the way in which it is updated at the end of each iteration. There is also a variant of the `for` statement which may be used to iterate over the properties of an object. This statement, the `for...in` statement, has the following form:

```
for ( varname in objname ) {
     forbody
     }
```

In the `for...in` statement `varname` is the name of a variable that takes on the successive property names of the object `objname`. This form of the `for` statement also permits the `varname` to contain a `var` declaration. Using the `for...in` statement we can write yet another form of the `showhouse` function, which does not rely on the presence of a `length` property. This function is shown in listing 4.5. This version actually works on any instance or object, not just on instances of `house`, so it has been renamed `showany`. This function can be found in the file showany.js on the CD-ROM.

Listing 4.5   showany.js   A Function That Displays the Properties of Any Object

```
function showany(anyobj) {        // display properties of an instance
                                  ➡or object
    for( var iter in anyobj ){    // iterate over all properties
        document.write("<BR>Property " + iter + " is " +
        ➡anyobj[iter]);
    }
    document.write("<BR>");
}
```

Method Functions and *this*

One of the most powerful aspects of object-oriented programming in JavaScript is the ability to create objects with functional properties. You may recall that these functional properties are known as methods. Aside from being a convenient organizational principle, there are other distinct advantages to associating functions with objects. We have already seen the special keyword `this` which is used in object creation. It's also used in method functions to refer to the *current object*. To see how this works, consider one more variation on the `house` object and the `showhouse` function shown in listing 4.6 (the file house2.js on the CD-ROM).

Listing 4.6   house2.js   The *showhouse* Function as a Method of *house*

```
/*
  This function creates a house instance with a "show" method
*/

function house( rms, stl, yr, garp ) {
    this.length = 5;               // four info props and length itself
    this.rooms = rm;               // rooms; prop [1]
    this.style = stl;              // style; prop [2]
    this.yearbuilt = yr;           // year built; prop [3]
    this.hasgarage = garp;         // garage?; prop [4]
    this.show = mshowhouse;        // the showhouse method; prop [5]
}

/*
  This function is the show method of the house object
*/

function mshowhouse() {          // note: no arguments!
    var nprops = this.length;  // len of property array not including show
    for ( var iter = 1; iter < nprops; iter++) { //iterate
        document.write("<BR>Property " + iter + " is " + this[iter]);
    }
    document.write("<BR>");
}
```

This version of the instance creation function `house` not only has the usual four pieces of house information (`rooms`, `style`, `yearbuilt`, and `hasgarage`) and the `length` property, which gives the number of properties, it also has a final property named `show`, which is set equal to the function `mshowhouse` (it has been given a new name to emphasize that it is now a method function). Note that we did not count this method in the length of the property array (although we could have).

The method version of the `showhouse` function is shown next. It does not have any arguments. Instead, it refers to its enclosing object as `this`. The usual `for` loop works as before. Since we have deliberately shortened the `length` property by one, only the properties with indices 1 through 4 are displayed. We have used both a dot style (.) reference and an array style ([ ]) reference with `this`, which acts just like any normal instance. If we execute the `show` method on the `myhouse` object, a display something like figure 4.2 appears.

FIG. 4.2

Method functions can be used to display the properties of their instances.

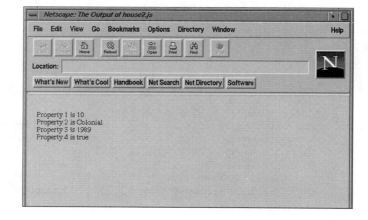

Since this function takes no arguments, you might wonder how it is used. The answer is that since the `show` method is a property just like any other property it may be accessed in the same way. The statements

```
myhouse.show();
yourhouse.show();
pizza.show();
```

all work exactly the same as their nonmethod counterparts

```
showhouse( myhouse );
showhouse( yourhouse );
showhouse( pizza );
```

This particular method function took no arguments, and was also void; it does not return any value. Method functions can take as many arguments as you wish, and can also return values. Listing 4.7 shows a very simple method function that takes the current year and an argument, and returns the age of the house as its value. It checks the argument for validity and returns –1 if the current year is actually earlier than the `yearbuilt` property.

Listing 4.7   A Method Function for Displaying the Age of a House

```
function howold ( curyear ) {            // current year passed as arg
    if ( curyear < this.yearbuilt )      // invalid year: too early
        return(-1);                      // no time travel (yet)
    return( curyear - this.yearbuilt );  // return difference
}
```

This method must be added to the object defining function `house` in order for it to work, of course. This function would be called by a standard property reference such as

```
myhouseage = myhouse.howold( 1996 );
```

This type of function call is no different than a standard function call such as `showhouse( myhouse )`. The only difference between method functions and other functions is that method functions may use `this` as an indirect way of naming the object that contains them.

 T I P   If you have special purpose functions that *only* operate on instances of an object, then those functions should be methods of that object.

Nested Objects

Object properties are typeless quantities. They may be ordinary variables of any implicit type. Our `house` object contains properties that are implicitly integers, strings, and booleans. It also contains functional members (methods). In a very real sense, every new object is a new data type, and every instance of that object is a new variable with its object as the underlying, implicit type of that instance. Since JavaScript is typeless, does this mean that objects can contain other objects? In a word, yes.

Suppose we create a new object called `desc` that holds some common pieces of information about various items. In particular, the `desc` object has properties for length, width, height, and color, and a method for computing the volume. The definition of this object and its volume method are shown in listing 4.8. This code can be found in the file descob.js on the CD-ROM.

Listing 4.8 descob.js A Description Object and Its Volume Method

```
/*
  The object creation function. The len, width and height
  properties will be specified in meters. The color will be
  a string.
*/
function desc( ln, wd, ht, col) {      // describe something
    this.length = 5;              // four properties and length of the
                                    ➥array
    this.len = ln;               // length of the thing; prop [1]
    this.width = wd;             // width of the thing; prop [2]
    this.height = ht;            // height of the thing; prop [3]
    this.color = col;            // color; prop [4]
    this.findvolume = findvolume;    // volume computation method
    }

/*
  The volume computation method. If the ismetric argument is
  true then the metric volume will be returned; otherwise
  the volume in cubic feet will be returned
*/

function findvolume ( ismetric ) {
    var mylen, mywid, myht;
    var conv = ( 39.37 / 12.0 );    // conversion from metric to
                                    ➥English

    if ( ismetric == true ) {
        mylen = this.len;           // metric by default
        mywid = this.width;          // ditto
        myht = this.height;          // ditto
    } else {
        mylen = this.len * conv;     // convert
        mywid = this.width * conv;
        myht = this.height * conv;
    }
    return( mylen * mywid * myht );   // return volume
  }
```

We can now add a desc object as a property of the house object. We could simply add length, width, height, and color properties directly to the definition of house, but this would go against another fundamental principle of object-oriented programming: *object reuse*. The desc object is very general. It can be used to describe a house, a car, a boat, or a tea cozy. It makes good sense to encapsulate these common properties in the desc object and then reuse that object's definition over and over by including it with the house, car, boat, and tea cozy objects. It would be serviceable, but wasteful, to repeat the same information in all these object definitions. Listing 4.9 (part of the CD-ROM file house3.js) shows the latest version of house object creation function.

On the CD

Listing 4.9   house3.js   The *house* Object with a *desc* Sub-Object

```
/*
   This function creates a house instance with a "show" method
   and a "desc" subobject
*/

function house( rms, stl, yr, garp, desci ) {
      this.length = 5;               // four info props and length itself
      this.rooms = rm;               // rooms; prop [1]
      this.style = stl;              // style; prop [2]
      this.yearbuilt = yr;           // year built; prop [3]
      this.hasgarage = garp;         // garage?; prop [4]
      this.descr = desci;            // description instance; prop [5]
      this.show = mshowhouse;        // the showhouse method; prop [6]
      this.howold = howold;          // the howold method; prop [7]
}
```

Part

I

Ch

4

In order to properly create a house instance we must first create a desc instance, and pass it as the fifth argument to house. It would be an error to pass in a desc object. A house instance, even one with a sub-object, must have all its slots filled in; this is what makes it an instance. This means that all the slots in the desc property of house must be filled in, as well, so that it, too, must be an instance. Once this has been done, it is possible to use all the properties and methods of the desc of the house. Listing 4.10 shows code that creates a desc instance, creates a house instance with that description, and then displays the color, age, and volume of the house using the properties and methods of the desc (and myhouse itself). This type of structure, in which objects and instances can be contained within one another, is referred to as an *object hierarchy*. Listing 4.10 is also found in the CD-ROM file house3.js. When this code is executed we obtain a page that looks like figure 4.3.

On the CD

Listing 4.10   house3.js   Creating and Using Sub-Objects

```
/*
  Create a desc instance and use it to create a house instance
*/

var mydesc;
var myhouse;
var mycol, myvol;

mydesc = new desc( 20, 18, 15, "beige" );        // fairly big; ugly color
myhouse = new house( 10, "Colonial", 1989, true, mydesc );  // mine, though

/*
  Display the colorvolume and age of the house using a reference
  to the desc properties of myhouse.
*/

mycol = myhouse.descr.color;                    // property of property
myvol = myhouse.descr.findvolume(true);         // submethod
document.write("<BR>My house is " + mycol);
document.write("<BR>Its " + myhouse.howold( 1996 ) + " years old");
document.write("<BR>My house occupies " + myvol + " cubic meters");
document.write("<BR>");
```

FIG. 4.3
Objects can contain one
another in an object
hierarchy.

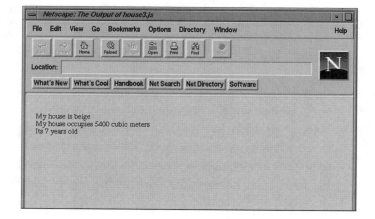

The *with* Statement

Once you have become hooked on object-oriented programming, it often becomes
a pervasive aspect of your coding style. Objects begin to show up everywhere.
JavaScript has a convenient statement, borrowed from the Pascal language, that

performs a set of object manipulations on the same object. Listing 4.10 may have impressed you with the power of its object manipulations. It may have also intimidated you a bit with the amount of typing that is required to get the color of the myhouse instance.

The purpose of the with statement is to permit a number of object references to be made to the same object (or instance) without having to repeat the name of that object. The format of the statement is

```
with ( objname ) {
    statements
    }
```

objname is the name of an object or instance. Inside the with block any reference to properties of objname occurs as if they had been prefixed with objname and the dot operator (.). Listing 4.11 shows an expanded version of the second part of listing 4.10, in which various aspects of myhouse are displayed. The mshowhouse method should now be extended to not only display the properties of its instance, but to also call a similar show method within the desc object (which will also need to be created).

Listing 4.11   Using the *with* Statement as an Implicit Object Reference

```
/*
  Display the color and volume of the house using a reference
  to the desc properties of myhouse.
*/

var mycol, myvol, myage;

with ( myhouse ) {
    mycol = descr.color;        // 1: ref to myhouse.descr.color
    myvol = descr.findvolume(true); // 2: ref to
                                ➥myhouse.descr.findvolume
    myage = yearbuilt;          // 3: reference to myhouse.yearbuilt
    document.write("<BR>My house is " + mycol);              // 4
    document.write("<BR>My house occupies " + myvol + " cubic meters"); // 5
// 6: explicit reference to another instance
    if ( myage > yourhouse.yearbuilt ) {
        document.write("<BR>Its newer than yours!");         // 7
        }
    document.write("<BR>");
    }
```

Each of the statements labeled 1, 2, and 3 makes an implicit reference to the myhouse object, which was established as the default object to use in the with statement. Note that not every statement within the with block needs to refer to myhouse. Statements 4, 5, and 7 make absolutely no reference to any house object. Also, statement 6 makes an explicit reference to a different house instance, namely yourhouse.

Statement 6 exposes one of the weaknesses of the with statement. When JavaScript careens through this with block, it must decide many times when the implicit myhouse is to be used, and when it is to be skipped. It must examine every reference, in fact. So, for mycol it must decide if you meant the local variable mycol or if there is some property of myhouse named myhouse.mycol. Fortunately, there is an unambiguous choice in every case. There is no mycol property of the house object.

Statement 6 uses an explicit reference to yourhouse. If statement 6 had been written as

```
if ( myage > yearbuilt ) {
```

JavaScript would have misinterpreted your intentions as to the meaning of yearbuilt, and would have implicitly translated this statement to

```
if ( myage > myhouse.yearbuilt ) {
```

since there is a yearbuilt property of myhouse. This type of error is both common and pernicious. Since JavaScript is an interpreted language, there is no way to see that this inappropriate translation has taken place. There is no compiled output that can be examined. Such errors are very hard to debug. Even though with is very useful, its use should be strictly circumscribed.

CAUTION

with blocks should be as short as possible. Check all statements within the with block to ensure that there are no ambiguous references to local variables or to properties of other objects.

Functions with a Variable Number of Arguments

Our discussion of the object foundations of JavaScript is almost complete. We have learned that functions are used to define objects and create instances using the new operator. We have also learned that objects, indexed arrays, and associative arrays are really all the same. In fact, the unity between all these concepts goes even deeper. JavaScript functions themselves have properties that can be used to fine-tune their behavior.

This aspect of JavaScript is still evolving at the time of this writing. However, we can say for certain that all JavaScript functions will have at least the following two properties:

- caller
- arguments

The caller property is the name of whoever called the function. The arguments property is an array of all the arguments that are not on the argument list of the function. The caller property permits a function to identify and respond to the environment in which it is called. The arguments property allows us to write functions that take a variable number of arguments. The arguments in the function's argument list are mandatory, while those in the arguments property are optional. Listing 4.12 shows a function that takes one mandatory argument and a potentially unlimited number of option arguments. It returns a string describing its invocation. This function is contained in the CD-ROM file optarg.js.

Listing 4.12   optarg.js   A Function with Mandatory and Optional Arguments

```
/*
 . Demonstrate mandatory and optional
   arguments to a function. Add all optional argument, and return the sum
   as a string.
*/

function addem( str1 ) {                    // one mandatory argument
    var nopt = addem.arguments.length;      // # of arguments
    var sum = 0;                            // sum of optional arguments
    var strres;                             // string result

    for(  var i = 1; i < nopt; i++ ) {      // iterate over all
                                            ➥optionals
```

continues

Listing 4.12   Continued

```
        sum += addem.arguments[i];       // add them
    }
    strres = "Hello " + str1 +   ", sum is " + sum;
    return(strres);
}
```

To see how this works, suppose that this function is called from within another function named test1, with the following invocation:

```
    var str = addem( "there", 1, 3, 5, 7 );
```

What happens? The mandatory argument "there" is assigned to the parameter str1 of the function addem. The complete argument list is also assigned to the variable length array addem.arguments. This has a length property (as do all well be-haved arrays), which has the value 5 since there are five arguments all together—one mandatory argument and four optional arguments. This means that the local variable nopt is 5. Unlike the examples we have used, the length property is not at index 0 of the arguments array. The arguments begin at addem.arguments[0] and continue up to addem.arguments[4] (five elements total). This means that the optional arguments begin at addem.arguments[1]. The for loop in addem adds the optional arguments together, and arrives at $1 + 3 + 5 + 7 = 16$, which is assigned to the local variable sum. Finally, strres is constructed by concatenating various strings, among them the mandatory parameter str1, which is "there", and the value of the sum. The concatenated string is returned, and assigned to str; its value is the string "Hello there, sum is 16."

Notice that both the mandatory argument str1 and the optional arguments are part of the argument list addem.arguments. Notice also that there need not be any optional arguments. The function call

```
    var str = addem( "on a stick" );
```

returns the value "Hello on a stick, sum is 0."

Built-In Objects

Now that we have covered the foundations of object-oriented programming in JavaScript we can begin to look at the actual objects that JavaScript itself provides. These objects can be put into the following three categories:

- Built-in objects
- HTML objects
- Browser objects

Built-in objects include string objects, the Date object, and the Math object. They are referred to as built-in because they really do not have anything to do with Web pages, HTML, URLs, the current browser environment, or anything visual. HTML objects, in turn, are directly associated with elements of Web pages. Every link and anchor is a JavaScript object. Every form, and every element within a form, is an HTML object. The hierarchical organization of display elements on a Web page is reflected almost exactly in a hierarchical set of nested HTML objects. You've already gotten a taste of this hierarchy in the event processing examples of chapter 3.

▶ **See** chapter 3, "Event Handlers in *FORM* Elements" for more information on the relationship between HTML elements and JavaScript functions, **p. 99.**

Browser objects are at the top of JavaScript's object hierarchy. These objects represent large scale elements of the browser's current environment, and include objects such as window (the current window), history (the list of previously visited pages), and location (the URL of the current page).

The rest of this section briefly describes the built-in objects of JavaScript. The next two sections give overviews of the HTML and browser objects. Each of these three categories is quite rich, and chapters 5, "Built-In JavaScript Objects," through 7, "Advanced HTML Objects and Navigation," provide more in-depth information on each of the three categories.

String Objects

String objects are the most built-in of all the built-in JavaScript objects. You do not even use new when creating a string object. Any variable whose value is a string is actually a string object. Literal strings such as "HelloWorld" are also string objects.

String objects have one property, length, and many methods. The length property gives the length of the string. The methods fall into three categories: methods that manipulate the contents of the string, methods that manipulate the appearance of the string, and methods that convert the string into an HTML element.

String Content Methods

The following methods can be used on string objects to access, control, or modify their content:

- `charAt( idx )`
- `indexOf( chr )`
- `lastIndexOf( chr )`
- `substring( fromidx, toidx )`
- `toLowerCase()`
- `toUpperCase()`

The `toLowerCase` and `toUpperCase` methods convert the contents of the string entirely to lower- and uppercase, respectively. So if we define the string variable

```
var mystr = "Look At This"
```

then its `length` property, `mystr.length`, will have the value 12, since there are 12 characters in the string. In addition, we can apply the two case conversion methods and get

```
mystr.toLowerCase() = "look at this"
mystr.toUpperCase() = "LOOK AT THIS"
```

These two functions do nothing to characters that have no case, so the two spaces in this string are unchanged. We could have also applied the methods directly to the literal form of this string object, so `"Look At This".toLowerCase` is also equal to `"look at this"`.

The methods `charAt` and `substring` are used to extract either a single character from a string, at position `idx`, or to extract a range of characters, from position `fromidx` up to but not including position `toidx`. Character positions are zero-based, as are all JavaScript arrays, so that all indices must fall between 0 and one less than the length of the array. For example, using `mystr`, we have

```
mystr.charAt(5) = "A"
mystr.substring(5,7) = "At"
```

Like the method functions `toUpperCase()` and `toLowerCase()` these methods both return strings. Care should be take to give these methods valid indices that are actually within the string. The substring method will forgive you if you accidentally specify a toidx which is <= the corresponding fromidx—it will return the empty string "".

Finally, both the indexOf and lastIndexOf methods are used to search for chr with a string. indexOf searches from the beginning (left side) of the string and lastIndexOf searches from the end (right side). Both return an integer index if they find the character, and -1 if they do not. Using mystr again, we can search for the character o from both sides:

```
mystr.indexOf("o") = 1
mystr.lastIndexOf("o") = 2
```

The first search finds the first o of the word "Look" at position 1 (second character), and the second search finds the second o of "Look" since that is the first o when searching from right to left. Both of these methods also take an optional second argument that specifies an initial index at which to start the search.

String Appearance Methods   The string appearance methods are used to control how a string appears when displayed on a Web page. If you are creating a page with standard HTML tags you would achieve the same effects by using various tags. For example, to make the string "help" appear in italics you would write <I>help</I>. The string appearance methods allow you to obtain the same effects in JavaScript without using the corresponding HTML elements. The string appearance methods are as follows:

- big()
- blink()
- bold()
- fixed()
- fontcolor(colr)
- fontsize(sz)
- italics()
- small()
- strike()
- sub()
- sup()

Part
I

Ch

4

Most of these methods should be self-explanatory. The `italics` method, for example, performs exactly the same function as the `I` tag in HTML. The only two that take arguments are the `fontcolor` and `fontsize` methods. The `fontcolor` method changes the font color of the string, as if the `<FONT COLOR=colr>` attribute had been size. Similarly, the `fontsize` method changes the size of the font used for displaying a string as if the `<FONT SIZE=sz>` attribute had been given. `colr` should be a string; `sz` may be a number or a string. If it's a number then this specifies an absolute font size; if it's a string such as `"+2"` it specifies an increment relative to the current font size. Listing 4.13 shows several examples using the string appearance methods. The output of this code is shown in figure 4.4.

N O T E   Not all HTML style tags have corresponding string appearance methods. You can always directly embed an HTML tag in the string itself if there is no method with the same functionality. ■

Listing 4.13   String Methods Can Be Used to Change How Strings Are Displayed

```
var bstr = "big";
var sstr = "small";

/*
  This displays strings with both big and small text.
*/
document.write("<BR>This is " + bstr.big() + " text");
document.write("<BR>This is " + sstr.small() + "text");
/*
  The following two strings contain directly embedded HTML tags.
  They have exactly the same result as the two method calls above
*/
document.write("<BR>This is <BIG>big</BIG> text");
document.write("<BR>This is <SMALL>small</SMALL> text");
/*
  If your favorite tag does not have a method, just embed it
*/
document.write("<BR>This is <STRONG>strong</STRONG> text");
document.write("<BR>");
```

FIG. 4.4
Many HTML style tags have equivalent JavaScript methods.

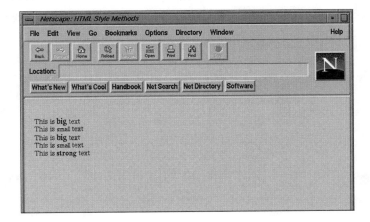

HTML String Methods

JavaScript provides two string methods for converting strings into hypertext entities. These methods should be clearly distinguished from the HTML objects, such as forms, which are discussed in the section "Browser and HTML Objects" later in this chapter. These methods are used to create HTML, while the HTML objects already are HTML. The two methods in this category are as follows:

- anchor(namestr)
- link(hrefstr)

Both these methods are used to create some form of the anchor (<A>) HTML attribute. The difference between them is that the anchor method is used to create an anchor with namestr as the value of the NAME attribute, while link is used to create an anchor with the HREF attribute set to hrefstr. Said another way, anchor creates an anchor that is a target, while link creates an anchor that is a link. Both methods convert the string on which they operate into the text portion of that anchor. namestr may be any valid string which may be a NAME, so it should not have any embedded white space. hrefstr should be a valid URL, since the user is being invited to click it. Listing 4.14 uses these methods and shows a simple example that sets up an anchor target and then links to it.

N O T E   The anchor() string method uses the older but more common HTML NAME attribute rather than the newer ID tag. ■

Listing 4.14   String Methods Can Be Used to Create HTML Anchors and Links

```
var sum4str = "Summary of Chapter 4";
var sum4tar = "Summary4";

/*
  Create a summary target and a link to it. The following two
  statements are completely equivalent to this HTML:

  <A NAME="Summary4">Summary of Chapter 4</A><HR>
  Click here for a <A HREF="#Summary4">Summary of Chapter 4</A>
*/
document.write(sum4str.anchor(sum4tar));
document.write("<HR>");
document.write("Click here for a " + sum4str.link(location + "#" +
➥sum4tar));
document.write("<BR>");
```

The *Math* Object

The Math object is used for various forms of mathematical calculations. It contains several properties that are standard constants, such as *pi* = 3.14159…, as well as a large set of methods that represent common trigonometric and algebraic functions. All Math methods deal with floating-point numbers. Angles are expected to be given in radians, not degrees.

The Math object is our first example of a *static object*. A static object is one that does not change. All of the slots in the Math object already have values. This makes perfect sense, since you cannot change the value of *pi* or invent a new meaning for the cos() function (not without creating chaos). The practical consequence of Math being static is that you never use new with Math; you always refer to the Math object directly. Math is the opposite of the String object. The String object has instances but no explicit object; the Math object has only itself, and no instances.

The Math object has the following properties:

- E
- LN10
- LN2
- PI
- SQRT1_2
- SQRT2

The Math object has the following methods:

- abs(num)
- acos(num)
- asin(num)
- atan(num)
- ceil(num)
- cos(ang)
- exp(num)
- floor(num)
- log(num)
- max(num1, num2)
- max(num1, num2)
- pow(num1, num2)
- random()
- round(num)
- sin(ang)
- sqrt(num)
- tan(ang)

Part
I

Ch
4

These are all the functions and constants you find on any decent calculator. Remember that JavaScript is case-sensitive, so you must write Math.PI exactly to get the value of *pi*. The constants stand for the base of the natural logarithm (Napier's constant, or about 2.71828), the natural log of 10 (about 2.30259), the natural log of

2 (about 0.69315), everyone's favorite *pi* (about 3.141592653589793), the square root of 1/2 (about 0.7071), and the square root of 2 (about 1.4142).

The methods of the Math object include the common trigonometric functions, including the sine (sin), cosine (cos), tangent (tan), and their inverses, the arcsin (asin), arccos (acos), and arctan (atan). Each of the trig functions takes an angle in radians and produces a floating-point number. The values should be between –1 and 1 for the sin and cos methods. Each of the inverse trig functions takes a number, which should be between –1 and 1 for the asin and acos methods, and returns an angle in radians.

The ceil, floor, and round methods all take floating-point numbers as inputs, and return integers as outputs. The ceil method gives the smallest integer that is greater than or equal to its argument, while floor returns the largest integer that is less than or equal to its argument. The round method gives the nearest integer.

The exp, log, pow, and sqrt methods all deal with exponentiation or its inverse. The exp method raises Math.E to the power given by its argument, and is the inverse of the log method, which returns the natural logarithm of its argument, which should be positive. The pow method raises num1, its first argument, to the power num2, its second argument. The sqrt returns the square root of its argument. If you inadvertently give sqrt a negative number it forgives you and returns 0.

Finally, the abs, min, max, and random methods perform various useful operations. The abs method returns the absolute value of its argument. min and max give the minimum and maximum value of their two arguments, respectively. The random method takes no arguments. It returns a random, floating-point number between 0 and 1. For some obscure reason the random method is only available in the UNIX releases of Netscape Navigator 2.0. Listing 4.15 presents some simple uses of the Math object. This example can be found in the CD-ROM file mathex.js.

▶ **See** more detailed examples using the Math object in "The *Math* Object" section of chapter 5, **p. 159**.

On the CD

Listing 4.15   mathex.js   Three Useful Functions Using the *Math* Object

```
/*
   Compute the area of a circle given its diameter
*/
```

```
function areaofcir(diam) {
    var radius = diam / 2;
    return( Math.PI * radius * radius );        // pi times r squared
}

/*
  Given the coordinates of a point on a circle,
  determine how far around the circle we must rotate in order
  to reach that point. Return the angle in radians.
*/

function angoncircum( x, y ) {
    var epsilon = 0.00001;      // a very small number
    if ( Math.abs(x) < epsilon ) {          // if x is very close to zero
        if ( y > 0 ) {                      // positive x axis
            return(0.0);                    // 0 degrees = 0 radians
        } else {                    // negative x axis
            return( Math.PI );              // 180 degrees = pi radians
        }                           // end of inner if-else
    }                               // end of outer if
// division by zero avoided by the "if" test above
    return( Math.atan( y / x ) );
}

/*
  Given the diagonal size of a television, compute its width
  assuming that the screen is square
*/

function tvsize( diag ) {
    return( diag / Math.SQRT2 );
}
```

The *Date* Object

Dealing with dates is one of the most tedious tasks in any language. This is because many people like to represent dates and times in decidedly nondecimal systems. Months come in units of 12, hours in units of 24, and minutes and seconds in units of 60. All these variations are quite illogical from the computer's standpoint. It likes to deal with nice, round numbers, preferably powers of 2, or at least multiples of 10.

The Date object simplifies and automates a lot of the conversion woes associated with going back and forth between a human readable representation, such as

November 23, 1990, and the internal representation. JavaScript's Date object follows the UNIX standard of storing date and time information internally as the number of milliseconds since January 1, 1970. This date is often called "The Epoch," since it is shortly after UNIX was first unleashed on an unsuspecting world.

> **CAUTION**
>
> The current version of JavaScript does not permit you to manipulate dates earlier than The Epoch. Attempting to do so gives unexpected and incorrect results.

The Date object has no properties, but many methods. In order to use the Date object you must first understand how to construct instances of it. There are three basic methods of creating a Date instance, as follows:

- `new Date()`
- `new Date( datestring )`
- `new Date( yr, mon, day )`

The first form constructs a Date instance that represents the current date and time. This should be accurate to within a second, and also include information about your time zone and any corrections to it currently in effect (such as Daylight Savings Time). The second form takes a string of the form "Month Day, Year" such as "November 23, 1990" and converts it to a Date instance. This string may optionally have a time of the form HH:MM:SS at the end, which is used to set the time to HH hours, MM minutes, and SS seconds. Hours should be specified using a 24-hour clock, also known as military time, so that 10:15 PM is represented as 22:15:00. The third form takes three integers representing the year, month, and day. Note that the month is always indexed from zero, so that November is month 10. The year can also be offset by 1900, so that you can use either of these two forms

```
var ndat = new Date(90, 10, 23);
var ndat = new Date(1990, 10, 23);
```

to create a Date instance named ndat for November 23, 1990. Note that for the year 2000 and beyond you must use the second form. This form may optionally take an additional three integer arguments for the time, so that 1:05 PM on November 23, 1990 is

```
var ndat2 = new Date(90, 10, 23, 13, 5, 0);
```

The Date object has a large set of methods for getting and setting the components of a date. These methods are as follows:

- getDate()
- getDay()
- getHours()
- getMinutes()
- getMonth()
- getSeconds()
- getTime()
- getTimeZoneOffset()
- getYear()
- setDate()
- setHours()
- setMinutes()
- setMonth()
- setSeconds()
- setTime()
- setYear()

Most of these methods perform the obvious operation on their Date instance. nvar.getMonth() returns 10, representing November. It is 10, rather than 11, because months are zero-indexed, so that the value of getMonth() is always between 0 and 11, inclusive. The confusingly named getDate, getDay, and getTime are worth a slightly closer look. The getDate method returns the day of the month (1–31), the getDay method returns the day of the week (0–6), and the getTime method returns JavaScript's internal representation of the date, namely the number of milliseconds since The Epoch. This last method might seem to be of dubious utility, but it is useful for comparing two dates to see which is later. The set methods are, of course, used to set the various components of a Date instance. Listing 4.16 shows two simple date manipulation functions. This code can be found in the CD-ROM file datex.js.

Listing 4.16   datex.js   Two Useful Functions Using the *Date* Object

```
/*
   Given a date as a string, return the day of the week
 as an integer between 1 and 7. Note Sunday = 1.
*/

function dayofweek( datestr ) {
    var dati;
    dati = new Date( datestr );          // make datestr into a Date
                                             ➥instance
        return( 1 + dati.getDay() );     // get the day of the week
                                             ➥and add 1
}              // since getDay() returns a number between 0 and 6

/*
   Compute the number of days to your birthday. Your birthday is speci-
   fied as the day and month.
*/

function tobday( dayi, moni ) {
    var today, todayy, todayms;
    var you, youms;
    var tdiff;
    today = new Date();                   // today's date
    todayy = today.getYear();             // current year
    you = new Date(todayy, moni-1, dayi);     // your birthday this year
// need to subtract 1 because months are zero-indexed
        todayms = today.getTime();        // convert today to ms since
                                              ➥The Epoch

    youms = you.getTime();                // convert your birthday to ms
                                              ➥since The Epoch

    if ( youms < todayms ) {              // if your birthday has already
                                              ➥passed..

        you.setYear(1 + todayy);          // look forward to next year
        youms = you.getTime();            // recompute ms since The
                                              ➥Epoch

    }
    tdiff = youms - todayms;              // number of milliseconds until
                                              ➥your next birthday
    tdiff /= 1000;                        // convert to seconds
    tdiff /= 60;                          // minutes
    tdiff /= 60;                          // hours
    tdiff /= 24;                          // convert to days
return( Math.round( tdiff ) );        // round to nearest integer
}
```

In addition to the `get` and `set` methods, the `Date` object also has methods for converting a `Date` instance to a string, and two static methods for parsing dates. These methods are as follows:

- `toGMTString()`
- `toLocaleString()`
- `toString()`
- `parse( datestr )`
- `UTC( datestr )`

The first three of these methods convert a `date` instance into a string representing the date and time relative to Greenwich Mean Time (GMT, also called UTC for Universal Coordinated Time), relative to the current date formatting conventions (which vary between Europe and the U.S., for example), and as just a plain, ordinary string, respectively. The last two methods are used for converting date strings in local time (`parse` method) or in UTC time (`UTC` method) into the number of milliseconds since The Epoch. These methods must be referenced as `Date.parse()` and `Date.UTC()` since they are static; they may not be used with `Date` instances. Since they return the internal representation of dates, these values are often simply passed to `setTime`.

▶ **See** the "Using *Date* Methods" section of chapter 5, "Built-In JavaScript Objects," for a thorough discussion of the methods of the `Date` object, **p. 166**.

Part

I

Ch

4

TROUBLESHOOTING

I have modified your function `tobday` in listing 4.16. My version accepts an arbitrary string as the input birthday. It works perfectly for my birthday, but it fails horribly for my father's birthday. What is wrong? The code looks like:

```
function tobday2( bdaystr ) {
var bdayint = new Date( bdaystr );
... many lines of code not shown
```

Since your father was undoubtedly born before January 1, 1970, the very first line attempts to create a `Date` instance corresponding to a date before The Epoch. This is not currently permitted. Since it seems that you were born after The Epoch, the code will work fine for your birthday. Until this restriction is lifted you must convert the year to one after 1970 before you construct a `Date` instance.

Built-In Functions

You have now had your first exposure to the built-in String, Math, and Date objects. Some of these objects are more built-in than others. While Date acts like an actual object, with the exception of its two static methods, the String object is almost invisible. All normal JavaScript programs manipulate strings as if they are a separate data type. The essence of a string is part of the JavaScript language.

There is also a small set of functions built in to JavaScript itself. They are not methods, and are never applied to an instance using the dot operator (.). They are on the same plane as functions that you create using the function keyword. At present, there are five such built-in functions; they are as follows:

- escape(str)
- eval(str)
- parseFloat(str)
- parseInt(str, radix)
- unEscape(str)

The escape and unEscape functions are used to convert to and from the escape code convention used by HTML. In HTML a number of special characters, such as the HTML delimiters < and >, must be represented in a special way to include them in ordinary text. For example, if you have written any HTML at all then you know that you sometimes need to write %20 to represent a space character. The escape built-in function takes a string representing one of these special characters and returns its escape code in the form %xx, where xx is a two-digit number. Thus, escape(" ") returns %20, the code for a space character. The unEscape function is the inverse of the escape function. It takes an escape code and returns the character which that code represents. Thus unEscape("%20") returns the string " " (a single space character).

The parseFloat built-in function attempts to parse its string argument as a floating-point number. It only continues parsing the str until it encounters a character that could not possibly be part of a valid floating-point number, such as g. The parseInt built-in function performs a similar operation. It attempts to parse its str argument as an integer in base radix. Thus we would obtain the following values:

```
parseFloat("+3.14williamtell5") = 3.14
parseInt(10111, 2) = 23
```

Note that everything after the first w is ignored, since w cannot possibly be part of a floating-point number. The second value is obtained because 23 in binary (base 2) notation is 10111.

Finally, the eval function attempts to evaluate its string argument as a JavaScript expression and return its value. All the normal rules for evaluating expressions, including variable substitution, are performed by the eval function. This function is extremely powerful simply because it evaluates any JavaScript expression, no matter what that expression does. You will see a lot more of this function in several subsequent chapters. For the moment, we briefly look at a simple example in which we ask eval to do some arithmetic for us. If x is a var with the value of 10 then the following two expressions assign 146 to both y and z:

```
y = ( x * 14 ) - ( x / 2 ) + 11;
z = eval("( x * 14 ) - ( x / 2 ) + 11");
```

Browser and HTML Objects

The JavaScript object model and its very interesting set of built-in objects, methods, and functions provide what we would expect from any modern programming language. They provide control structures, encapsulation, functions, mathematical operations, and so forth. Since JavaScript is designed to work with and on the World Wide Web there must also be a linkage between it and the contents of HTML pages.

This linkage is provided by JavaScript's extremely rich set of browser and HTML objects. The browser objects are a reflection of the browser environment, and include objects that can be used to reference the current page, the history list, and the current URL. There are also methods for opening new windows, putting up dialog boxes, and writing HTML directly. We have already been leaning heavily on one such method, the write method of the document object.

The browser (or navigator) objects are at the top of JavaScript's object hierarchy, since they represent overall information and actions that are not necessarily associated with a particular Web page. Within a given Web page, however, each HTML element has a corresponding object, an HTML object, within the object hierarchy. In particular, every HTML form, and every HTML element within every form, has a corresponding object. Figure 4.5 gives an overview of the JavaScript object hierarchy.

FIG. 4.5

JavaScript browser and HTML objects refer to all elements of a Web page.

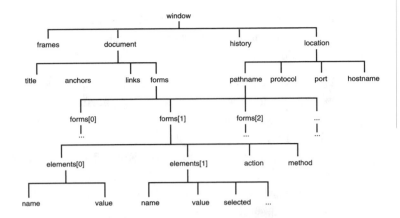

In this section we briefly describe the key JavaScript browser and HTML objects, and show how they relate to one another. Most of the subsequent chapters in this book are devoted to in-depth discussions of how you can make these objects work for you. Each chapter in part II, "JavaScript Objects," in fact, is devoted to a particular category of JavaScript object (built-in, browser, or HTML). The purpose of this section, then, is to acquaint you with the structure of these objects without going into too much detail on how they are used.

Browser Objects

The primary browser objects, in rough order of significance, are as follows:

- `window`
- `document`
- `location`
- `history`

The *window* Object

The `window` object, as figure 4.5 shows, is the top object in the JavaScript object hierarchy. Every browser window that is currently open will have a corresponding `window` object. All the other objects are children of one of the `window` objects. In particular, every window is associated with a particular Web page, and the HTML structure of this page is reflected in the window's `document` object. Every window corresponds to some URL; that URL is reflected in the `location` object. Every window has a history of the previous pages that have been displayed in that window, which are represented by the various properties of the `history` object.

JavaScript maintains an idea of the current window, so that almost all references to sub-objects of the current window do not need to refer to it explicitly. This is why all of our output has been done using `document.write()` rather than `window.document.write()`. `window` objects have the following interesting methods (among others):

- `alert( msgstr )`
- `close()`
- `confirm( msgstr )`
- `open( urlstr, wname )`
- `prompt( msgstr )`

All these methods are used to manipulate the window state of the browser itself. The `alert` and `confirm` methods are used to display their `msgstr` argument in a dialog box. The `alert` method is used to alert the user to something about which the user can do nothing. An alert dialog box contains a single OK button. The `confirm` dialog box is more flexible, and displays its message with both an OK and a Cancel button. If the user selects OK then the `confirm` method returns `true`, otherwise it returns `false`. The `prompt` method is used to solicit user input, in the form of a string. It displays a dialog box with the `msgstr` and an editable text field. This method also accepts a second optional argument that can be used to set a default value in the input field. This method returns whatever the user typed as a string.

You use the `open` method of the `window` object when you wish to open a new browser window. The `urlstr` argument is a string representing the URL that will be loaded into that window. The `wname` argument is a string that gives the new window its name. This method returns an instance of the `window` object representing the new window created. This method also accepts a third argument that can be used to specify a wide variety of display options for the new window (such as whether or not it should display its toolbar). When the `close` method is invoked from a `window` instance the underlying window is closed and the URL in it is unloaded.

▶ **See** several excellent examples of the `open` and `close` methods in the "Dynamic Documents" section of chapter 8, "Dynamic HTML and Browser Objects," **p. 284**.

The *document* Object

Every window is associated with a document object. The document object contains properties for every anchor, link, and form on that page, as well as all of the sub-elements of those elements. It also contains properties for its title (the content of the <TITLE> field of the page), its foreground color (the fgColor property), its background color (the bgColor property), its various link colors, and other attributes of the page itself. The document object has the following methods:

- clear( )
- close( )
- open( )
- write(str)
- writeln(str)

The clear method is used to completely erase a document window. The entire contents are wiped out, regardless of how they got there. The clear method is particularly useful if you are constructing a Web page entirely within JavaScript, and want to make sure it is empty before you start. The open and close methods are used to start and stop buffered output. If you call the open method, perform a series of writes and/or writelns, and then call the close method, the results of your write operations are layed out and appear on the page.

CAUTION

Do not confuse the open and close methods of the document object with the window methods of the same names. They perform very different functions, and are not interchangeable. Use an explicit reference—document.open( ) or window.open( )—to obtain the appropriate one.

Of course we are intimately familiar with the write method by now. The write method is used to write any string expression, including one containing embedded HTML, to the current document. Note that the write method actually takes a variable number of arguments, rather than just one. If more than one argument is given, each of the arguments is interpreted as a string and written in turn. The writeln method is identical to the write method, except that it outputs a carriage return after it has completed writing its argument(s). Note that this carriage return will be ignored by HTML, which really does not like embedded white space, unless the `writeln` is inside preformatted text (within PRE>...</PRE tags).

The *history* and *location* Objects

The `history` object is used to refer to the history list of previously visited URLs. The `history` object has a property known as `length`, which indicates how many URLs are stored on the history list at present. It also has the following three methods:

- `back()`
- `forward()`
- `go( where )`

The `go` method is used to navigate the history list. The `where` argument can be a number or a string. If the `where` argument is a number then it indicates how far we wish to move in the history list. A positive number means that we wish to move that many documents forward in this history list, while a negative number is used to move backward. Thus, `go(5)` has the same effect as using the Forward button five times, while `go(-1)` would be the same as clicking the Back button once. If `where` is a string representing a URL then that URL is loaded, and becomes the current document.

The `location` object describes the URL of a document. It has properties representing the various components of the URL, including its protocol part, its hostname part, its pathname part, and its port number part, among other properties. Unfortunately, these properties are often `null`, at least in the UNIX version of Netscape Navigator 2.0. It also has a `toString` method which can be used to convert it to a string. We can use the following code to display a formatted message giving the current URL:

```
var loc = document.location;
document.write("<BR>URL is " + loc.toString());
document.write("<BR>");
```

HTML Objects

To understand how HTML objects work in JavaScript, let us consider a simple piece of HTML that creates an anchor, a small form, and a link to that anchor. This is not intended to be the HTML for a meaningful Web page, but it will nevertheless illustrate the correspondence between HTML elements and JavaScript HTML objects. Our elementary HTML code is given in listing 4.17. This code can be found in simple.htm on the CD-ROM.

On the CD

Listing 4.17   simple.htm   HTML Code for a Page with a Form, Anchor, and Link

```
<HTML>
<HEAD>
<TITLE>A very simple HTML page</TITLE>
</HEAD>
<BODY>
<A NAME="top">This is the top of the page</A>
<HR>
<FORM METHOD="post" ACTION="mailto:nobody@dev.null">
<P>Enter your name: <INPUT TYPE="text" NAME="me" SIZE="70">
</P>
<INPUT TYPE="reset" VALUE="Oops">
<INPUT TYPE="submit" VALUE="OK">
</FORM>
<HR>
Click here to go to the <A HREF="#top">top</A> of the page
</BODY>
</HTML>
```

This code creates an HTML page with an anchor at the top of the page and a link to that anchor at the bottom. In between is a simple form that allows the user to enter his name. There is a submit button if he gets it right, and a reset button if he doesn't. If the user is successful the form's contents are submitted via a post action to the fictitious e-mail address nobody@dev.null.

The important aspect of this example is not its primitive HTML, but the fact that the HTML elements in it are reflected in the JavaScript object hierarchy. We have already seen that we can access the title of this document through the title property of the document object. We can also access the other HTML elements of this document using the following properties:

- anchors
- forms
- links

These properties of the document object are arrays representing every HTML element that is an anchor, form, or link on the page. In our particular example there is only one of each, so we would refer to the anchor at the top of the page as `document.anchors[0]`, the link at the bottom of the page as `document.links[0]`, and the form in the middle of the page as `document.forms[0]`. These are the top-level HTML objects represented by this document. Each of these elements, in turn, has properties and methods that can be used to describe and manipulate it.

In particular, the `form` object corresponding to `forms[0]` has sub-objects for each of the three form elements (the reset button, the submit button, and the text input field), as well as properties for the `submit` method and the `submit` target. `forms[0].elements[0]` corresponds to the text input field. `forms[0].elements[0].name` is the name of that field, as specified by the NAME field, which is "me" in this case. Figure 4.6 recapitulates this HTML code and shows how each element in the page is associated with an HTML object. We will have many more examples of this in subsequent chapters.

FIG. 4.6
Anchors, links, forms, and form elements are represented as objects in JavaScript.

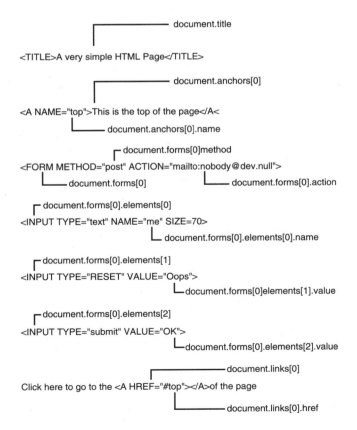

```
                                    ┌───────── document.title
<TITLE>A very simple HTML Page</TITLE>

                                    ┌───────── document.anchors[0]
<A NAME="top">This is the top of the page</A<
              └──── document.anchors[0].name

                      ┌ document.forms[0]method
<FORM METHOD="post" ACTION="mailto:nobody@dev.null">
      └── document.forms[0]            └── document.forms[0].action

  ┌ document.forms[0].elements[0]
<INPUT TYPE="text" NAME="me" SIZE=70>
                   └ document.forms[0].elements[0].name

  ┌document.forms[0].elements[1]
<INPUT TYPE="RESET" VALUE="Oops">
                 └document.forms[0]elements[1].value

  ┌document.forms[0].elements[2]
<INPUT TYPE="submit" VALUE="OK">
                  └document.forms[0].elements[2].value

                          ┌────── document.links[0]
Click here to go to the <A HREF="#top"></A>of the page
                        └────── document.links[0].href
```

JavaScript Objects

CHAPTER 5

Built-In JavaScript Objects

by Andrew Wooldridge

JavaScript is designed to be easy to learn and convenient to use by almost anyone who seeks to create dynamic Web pages and client-side checking of input forms (as well as many other uses discussed in this book). Because the authors of JavaScript have had this in mind, they have provided you, the programmer, with many built-in objects that you will probably use quite often. These built-in objects are available through both the client-side JavaScript (inside the Netscape Navigator on your desktop) and through LiveWire (Netscape's server-side application). In addition, JavaScript has three functions that you can use throughout your scripts without having to declare them.

The three built-in objects are: the String object, the Math object, and the Date object. Each of these provides great functionality, and together they give JavaScript its power as a scripting

How to manipulate text with the String object

Find out how to change the HTML formatting of strings, concatanate them with other strings, and find sub-elements inside strings.

How to use the date and time in JavaScript scripts

Find out how to use the client's machine time to customize your Web pages based on the time of day.

How to create pseudorandom effects

Find out how to use the date and time of day to generate effects, like presenting a different image on the page each time someone visits the site in the span of an hour.

How to use JavaScript for math calculations

Find out how you can do internal calculations within the script and avoid using CGIs for math-intensive applications.

language. These built-in objects are discussed in depth in this chapter and you will find many examples for use in your own projects.

Be sure to review chapter 4, "JavaScript Objects," which introduced you to JavaScript's built-in objects. ■

The String Object

As you saw in chapter 4, you can create a string object by assigning a string literal to a variable.

You call a string's methods by the same dot notation you would in other objects. For example, if `demostring` is `"Some text here!"` then `demostring.bold()` returns **"Some text here!"**.

You can also use string methods on literals, as follows:

```
"This is some text".italics()
```

This line of code returns *"This is some text"*, as displayed by your Web browser.

Table 5.1 shows the various methods that you can call with the string object to alter its HTML formatting.

Table 5.1   String Object Methods for HTML Formatting

Method Name	Example	Returned Value
anchor	`"foo".anchor("anchortext")`	`<A NAME="anchortext">foo</A>`
big	`"foo".big()`	`<BIG>foo</BIG>`
blink	`"foo".blink()`	`<BLINK>foo</BLINK>`
bold	`"foo".bold()`	`<B>foo</B>`
fixed	`"foo".fixed()`	`<TT>foo</TT>`
fontcolor	`"foo".fontcolor("green")`	`<FONT COLOR="green">foo</FONT>`
fontsize	`"foo".fontsize(-1)`	`<FONT SIZE="-1">foo</FONT>`
italics	`"foo".italics()`	`<I>foo</I>`

Method Name	Example	Returned Value
link	"foo".link("linktext")	<A HREF="linktext">foo</A>
small	"foo".small()	<SMALL>foo</SMALL>
strike	"foo".strike()	<STRIKE>foo</STRIKE>
sub	"foo".sub()	_{foo}
sup	"foo".sup()	^{foo}
toLowerCase	"UPPERcase".toLowerCase()	uppercase
toUpperCase	"UPPERcase".toUpperCase()	UPPERCASE

Figure 5.1 shows how the string "foo" would be rendered in your browser if you used each of the methods listed in table 5.1.

Text without any modifications (denoted as Normal Text) is placed between some lines to help you see how each method changes the appearance of the text. Figure 5.2 shows you the source script that was used to create figure 5.1. Note that all of the strings were called as literals—that is, not as variables as you might normally see them.

FIG. 5.1
String methods as rendered by Netscape Navigator.

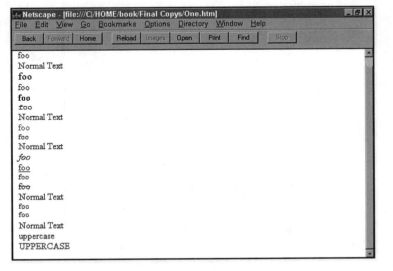

FIG. 5.2
Source code for figure 5.1.

```
Netscape - [Source of: file:///C|/HOME/book/Final Copys/One.htm]

<html>
<script language="javascript">

document.write("foo".anchor("anchortext"))
document.write("<br> Normal Text<br>")
document.write("foo".big())
document.write("<br> ")
document.write("foo".blink())
document.write("<br>")
document.write( "foo".bold())
document.write("<br> ")
document.write( "foo".fixed())
document.write("<br> Normal Text<br>")
document.write( "foo".fontcolor("green"))
document.write("<br> ")
document.write( "foo".fontsize(-1))
document.write("<br> Normal Text<br>")
document.write( "foo".italics())
document.write("<br> ")
document.write( "foo".link("linktext"))
document.write("<br>")
document.write( "foo".small()    )
document.write("<br> ")
document.write( "foo".strike())
document.write("<br> Normal Text<br>")
document.write( "foo".sub())
document.write("<br> ")
document.write("foo".sup())
document.write("<br> Normal Text<br>")
document.write( "UPPERcase".toLowerCase())
document.write("<br> ")
document.write( "UPPERcase".toUpperCase())

</script>
```

Chaining Methods

Not only can you change the formatting of the text in one way at a time, you can "chain" the various methods together to mimic the behavior of nesting HTML tags around a piece of text. This can be particularly useful if you generate HTML automatically via a script. For example, the following displays a blinking "FOO" on the page:

```
document.write("foo".blink().toUpperCase().bold())
```

Remember to include the parentheses after each of the methods even though they do not take any arguments. The preceding code appears to the browser as the following:

```
<B><BLINK>FOO</BLINK></B>
```

You can see that the BLINK tag is nested inside the B tag, since the blink method was called first. (JavaScript reads code from left to right and from top to bottom.) If you wish to have a desired effect with nesting tags, remember that the order of nesting is the leftmost string method nested inside the next method called to the right. The reason you can nest these methods is that they all accept and return a string object so it appears to the next method as a simple string—as if you had typed it in.

Nesting Methods Versus Chaining Methods

There are usually two ways you will see methods called in scripts you encounter. You might see something like this:

```
foo().bar().baz()   "Chaining"
```

or you might see this:

```
foo(bar(baz()))   "Nesting"
```

The difference here can be subtle. With `foo().bar().baz()`, JavaScript will determine the result value of `foo()`, then treat that value as if it were the object called with `.bar()`. You must make sure that the value returned by the leftmost method is valid in order to have the second method "appended" to it, to continue calculations. It is valid here if `foo()` and `bar()` return strings, since string literals (what each of these methods return) can subsequently have other string methods. `foo(bar(baz()))` is different in that evaluation is conducted in right-to-left order. `baz()` is evaluated first and then is passed as a parameter to `bar()`. `bar()` must be able to accept a parameter of this type in order for this to work. For some methods, this difference in evaluation has no effect, but for others, you might get incorrect values.

Anchor and Link

Anchors and links are often confused because they appear to create similar output. An anchor in HTML is a location for a link to point to, and is given a name for subsequent links to identify that anchor. A link is a clickable area of text or an image that jumps the browser to the anchor. See chapter 4 for more discussion of this difference.

Part
II

Ch
5

If you want to create an anchor in JavaScript such as the following:

```
<A NAME="section2">Starting Up</A>
```

you could use:

```
Avariable = "Starting Up"

Avariable.anchor("section2")
```

or you can just use the following:

```
"Starting Up".anchor("section2")
```

It helps to read the string like this:

```
"Starting Up using an anchor of name section2."
```

Links are used in a similar fashion. Only in this case, instead of giving an anchor a name, you are giving a link a URL. For example, to display a link to Yahoo, you would write the code in listing 5.1.

Listing 5.1   list5-1.txt   An Example Using *link*

```
var  linktext = "Yahoo"
var URL = "http://www.yahoo.com"

document.open()
document.write("This is a link to" + linktext.link(URL))
document.close()
```

This is equivalent to writing the following:

```
This is a link to <A HREF="http://www.yahoo.com">Yahoo</A>
```

In this case, you could read the string as:

```
"Yahoo's link is http://www.yahoo.com"
```

TIP

You can quickly create long strings from short ones by using the plus concatenator (+). The expression `"Cat Fish" + " Sandwich"` yields `"Cat Fish Sandwich"`. Also, you can use the += operator (called the "plus-equal" concatenator) to tack a string on the end of another. If `string1 = "hello"`, then `string1+=" there"` would become `"hello there"`.

In addition to changing the formatting of a string object in HTML, you can also return parts of the string without having to know the actual contents of that string. This is extremely useful for parsing out different keywords or commands within some given input string by the user of your script.

Table 5.2 lists the methods of the string object that pertain to displaying subsets of the strings contents.

Table 5.2   String Object Methods for Displaying Subsets of Strings

Method Name	Example(s)	Returned Value
charAt	`"netscape navigator".charAt(0)`	n
	`"netscape navigator" .charAt(10)`	a
indexOf	`"netscape navigator" .indexOf("scape")`	3
	`"netscape navigator" .indexOf("n",2)`	9
lastIndexOf	`"netscape navigator" .lastIndexOf("a")`	14
	`"netscape navigator" .lastIndexOf("a", 12)`	10
substring	`"netscape navigator" .substring(0,7)`	netscap
	`"netscape navigator" .substring(7,0)`	netscap
	`"netscape navigator" .substring(0,50)`	netscape navigator
length	`"netscape navigator" .length`	18
	`"netscape navigator" .substring(0,7).length`	7

Note that `length` is a property of a string and receives its value indirectly based on the number of characters in a string. You cannot directly assign a value to the `length` property.

charAt

The method `charAt` returns the character at the index specified. Characters are numbered from 0 to the length of the string minus 1.

Its syntax is:

```
stringName.charAt(index)
```

For example, the following returns "n":

```
thisstring = "Internet World"

thisstring.charAt(5)
```

indexOf

This method can be used to search down a string (from left to right) until it finds a string fragment matching the specified value. It returns the index of the first character of the matching string. You can use this information with the method substring (mentioned later in this section) to find keywords in a given string. This is useful when you allow the user to input some information and you wish to place parts of that information into different variables. For example, the following returns 9:

```
thisstring = "Internet World"

thisstring.indexOf("World")
```

If the keyword is not in the string, then indexOf returns a -1.

lastIndexOf

This method is identical to indexOf except that the method searches from right to left down the string to find the given keyword. It also returns the index value of the first character of the found keyword. For example, the following returns 5:

```
"Internet World".lastIndexOf("n")
```

substring

substring completes the suite of subset text methods. This method returns a substring given beginning and ending index values. Note that the values do not have to be in numerical order. The string returned from substring(1,9) is identical to the one returned from substring(9,1). Also, if you leave off the second index integer, substring assumes you want it to return everything from the first index to the end of the string. And leaving off both indices returns the entire string. For example, listing 5.2, which can be found on the CD-ROM as list 5-2.txt, returns "World":

On the CD

Listing 5.2	list5-2.txt	An Example Using *substring*

```
thisstring = "Internet World"

thewordnum = thisstring.indexOf("World")

theword = thisstring.substring(thewordnum)

document.open()
document.write(theword)
document.close()
```

Length

The `length` property appears in many types of objects across JavaScript, and pertains to a different value based on the context in which it is used. In strings, this value is an integer based on the number of characters in a string (counting whitespace, etc). For a null string, this value is `zero`. You cannot directly alter this value except by adding or removing characters from a string. Since the value returned by `"foo".length` is a number, you can perform mathematical operations on it like any other number.

For instance, the following returns 7:

```
"Hi There".length - 1
```

The *Math* Object

As you saw in chapter 4, the `Math` object provides built-in constants and methods for performing calculations within the script.

The `Math` object's syntax is the following:

```
Math.propertyname
```

or

```
Math.methodname(parameters)
```

Table 5.3 summarizes the various methods and properties.

Table 5.3 *Math* **Object Methods and Properties**

Method Name	Example	Returned Value
abs	Math.abs(-79)	79
acos	Math.acos(.5)	1.047197551196597631
asin	Math.asin(1)	1.570796326794896558
atan	Math.atan(.5)	0.4636476090008060935
ceil	Math.ceil(7.6)	8
cos	Math.cos(.4)	0.9210609940028851028
exp	Math.exp(8)	2980.957987041728302
floor	Math.floor(8.9)	8
log	Math.log(5)	1.609437912434100282
max	Math.max(1 , 700)	700
min	Math .min(1 , 700)	1
pow	Math.pow(6,2)	36
random (not fully implemented)	Math.random()	.7877896
round	Math.round(.567)	1
sin	Math.sin(Math.PI)	0
sqrt	Math.sqrt(9801)	99
tan	Math.tan(1.5*Math.PI)	INF (infinity)

Math Methods

Although most of the methods used by Math are self-evident—such as using Math.sin to calculate the sine function of a number—they are summarized in the following sections, with examples for your reference.

abs   abs returns the absolute value of its numeric argument.

For example, the following returns 1:

```
Math.abs(-1)
```

acos, asin, atan, cos, sin, tan   These return the appropriate trig function in radians. The a is short for arc, as in atan = arctangent.

For example, the following returns 3.141592653589793116:

```
Math.acos(-1)
```

ceil   Returns the smallest integer greater than or equal to the argument passed to it. This is equivalent to always rounding up to the nearest integer.

For example, the following returns 15:

```
with (Math) {
    foo = ceil(14.49999999);
  }
```

See also floor.

exp   Returns *e* to the power of its argument. Where if x is the argument, exp returns e^x. (e is Euler's constant—the base of natural logarithms.)

For example, the following returns 148.4131591025765999:

```
Math.exp(5)
```

floor   Returns the greatest integer less than or equal to the value passed to it. This is equivalent to always rounding down to the nearest integer.

For example, the following returns 1:

```
numberone = Math.floor(1.9999999);
document.write(numberone);
```

See also ceil.

log   Returns the natural log of the argument passed to it. The base is *e*.

For example, the following returns the log to the base e of *pi*, which is 1.144729885849400164:

```
pie = Math.PI;

pielog = Math.log(pie);

document.write("The log to the base e of PI is: " + pielog + ".");
```

max, min Given two numbers, `max` returns the greater of the two, and `min` returns the lesser of the two.

For example,

```
with (Math) {
    document.write("Between Euler's constant and
 PI, "+ max(E,PI) + " is ──────────── greater.")
}
```

Between Euler's constant and *pi*, 3.141592653589793116 is greater.

pow Given a base and an exponent number, this returns the base to the exponent power.

For example, the following returns 10000:

```
Math.pow(10,4)
```

random Available only to UNIX platforms (Solaris, specifically) as of this writing, this returns a pseudorandom number between 0 and 1.

For example, the following returns 0.09983341664682815475:

```
Math.random()
```

round This method returns the argument rounded to the nearest integer. It rounds up if the number contains an integer of .5 or greater, and down otherwise.

For example, the following returns 1:

```
with(Math) {

java = round(1.4999999999);
document.write(java);
}
```

sqrt Returns the square root of its argument. Note: the argument must be non-negative, otherwise the `sqrt` returns 0.

For example, the following returns 12:

```
Math.sqrt(144);
```

An Example Sine Plotter In figure 5.3, we see a Web site that has implemented a script that quickly generates a sine curve.

FIG. 5.3
A Web site using math methods.

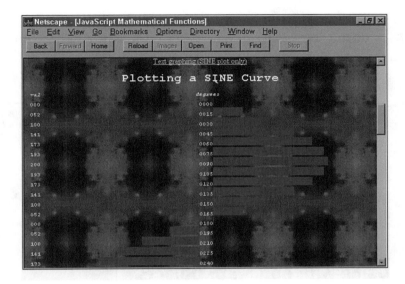

Math Properties

The Math object provides you with a few constants that you can use for various scientific and algebraic functions. Note that these properties are constants and cannot be changed by JavaScript. The following is a list of each property and its approximate values:

Part
II
Ch
5

- E—Euler's constant, the base of natural algorithms. Approximately 2.718.
- LN2—The natural log of 2. Approximately 0.693.
- LN10—The natural log of 10. Approximately 2.302.
- PI—The ratio of the circumference of a circle to its diameter. Approximately 3.1415.
- SQRT1_2—The square root of .5 (one half) or one over the square root of 2. Approximately 0.707.
- SQRT2—The square root of 2. Approximately 1.414.

Table 5.4 sumarizes the Math object properties and gives examples.

Table 5.4 *Math* **Object Properties Summary**

Property Name	Example	Returned Value
E (2.718281828459045091)	Math.E*5	13.59140914229522501
LN10 (2.302585092994045901)	Math.LN10/6	0.3837641821656743168
LN2 (0.69314718055994529)	Math.LN2-Math.E	-2.025134647899099694
PI	Math.sin(2*Math.PI/4)	3.141592653589793116
SQRT2	1/Math.SQRT2	0.7071067811865474617

Using *with* and *Math* Objects

Using the Math object is essentially identical to using other objects in JavaScript with a few exceptions. If you use several Math constants and methods together in a block of code, you can use the with statement to avoid having to retype Math. over and over again.

For example, the following:

```
beta = Math.E * 62;
gamma = Math.PI / 4;
delta = x * Math.sin(theta);
```

becomes

```
with (Math) {
    beta  = E * 62;

    gamma = PI / 4;

    delta = x * sin(theta);
}
```

The *Date* Object

As you saw in chapter 4, the Date object provides information about the current date and time on the client's machine. The Date object is useful for designing sites that are sensitive to the time of day, or use time-based information to present to the user new information without having to use a CGI to access the server's clock.

> **N O T E** You cannot work with dates prior to 1/1/70. This is due to the cross-platform nature of this language—for example, UNIX machines consider 00:00:00 GMT January 1, 1970 to be "zero" on their clocks. Other operating systems have older zero settings (like Macintosh's January 1, 1904) so the most recent of them is considered the baseline for time.

The Date object is similar to the String object in that you create new instances of the object when you assign it to a variable. It differs from the String object in that you use a statement called new to create it. Using the new statement, you create a Date object that contains information down to the millisecond at that instant. Note: This data is created based on the time and date on the client's machine, not the time on your server. So if your page is located on the east coast, and a user visits your site from the west coast, the time reflects his location, not yours. It is important to note this because you have no control over the time on his machine. His clock may be wrong, or not even running (although unlikely). If your script depends heavily on having an accurate time in which to base its calculations, you might get strange effects when your script encounters these special cases. For instance, you might change the foreground text and background colors to reflect the time of day, but if the machine's clock is off, your page will seem "off."

Part
II

Ch
5

The Syntax for Creating a New *Date* Object

To create a new Date object, you use the new operator. The Date object is predefined in JavaScript, and will build this instance filling in the current date and time from the client's system clock. Here is the syntax:

```
variableName = new Date(parameters)
```

For example,

```
today = new Date();
```

You have several optional parameters that you may send to the Date object, as follows:

- `variableName = new Date()`
- `variableName = new Date("month day, year hours:minutes:seconds")`
- `variableName = new Date(year, month, day)`
- `variableName = new Date(year, month, day, hours, minutes, seconds)`

 TIP Each of these forms has a few conventions you should be aware of. The first form, in which you omit all parameters, automatically sets the current date and time in the standard format of:

Day   Month   Date   Hours:Minutes:Seconds   Year

For example,

Sat   Feb   24   14:43:13   1996

If you use the second or fourth form and omit the hours, minutes, or seconds, JavaScript automatically sets them to 0.

Using *Date* Methods

Once you have created a Date object, you can then use the many Date methods to get or set the month, day, year, hours, minutes, or seconds of this instance. Note: You cannot set the Day attribute independently—it depends on the month, year, and date attributes. As with most object methods, you simply call a Date method as follows:

```
varibleName.methodname(parameters)
```

For example,

```
today.setHours(7);
```

There are two exceptions to this rule with the Date object: The UTC and parse methods are "static" methods and are always called with just the generic Date object name.

For example,

```
Date.UTC(parameters)
Date.parse(parameters)
```

Table 5.5 summarizes the different Date methods.

Table 5.5 *Date* **Object Methods**

Method	Example	Returns
getDate	today.getDate()	5
getDay	yesterday.getDay()	2
getHours	today.getHours()	5
getMinutes	today.getMinutes()	30
getMonth	year.getMonth()	6
getSeconds	time.getSeconds()	13
getTime	now.getTime()	*****
getTimeZoneoffset	today.getTimeZoneoffset	******
getYear	now.getYear	96 (the years since 1900)
parse	Date.parse(July 1, 1996)	*****
setDate	now.setDate(6)	-
setHours	now.setHours(14)	-
setMinutes	now.setMinutes(50)	-
setMonth	today.setMonth(7)	-
setSeconds	today.setSeconds(7)	-
setTime	today.setTime (yesterday.getTime())	-
setYear	today.setYear(88)	-
toGMTString	yesterday.toGMTString()	Sat, Feb 24 1996 14:28:15 GMT
toLocaleString	today.toLocaleString()	2/25/96 14:28:15
UTC	Date.UTC(96,11,3,0,0,0)	-

Part

II

Ch

5

Using all these methods' strings and numbers may look like a daunting task, but if you approach the Date object with a few concepts in mind, it makes working with this object much easier.

First, all of the methods can be grouped into four categories: get, set, to, and parse. get methods simply return an integer corresponding to the attribute you requested. set methods allow you to change an existing attribute in a Date object—again by passing an integer—only this time you are sending a number instead of receiving it. to methods take the date and convert it into a string—which then allows you to use any of the string methods to further convert the string into a useful form. parse methods (parse and UTC) simply parse—or interpret—date strings.

Secondly, Date attributes like month, day, or hours are all zero-based numbers. That is, the first month is 0, the second 1, and so on. The same goes for days, where Sunday is 0, Monday is 1, and so on. The reason why numbering starts at 0 instead of 1 is that JavaScript closely mirrors Java in many respects—like always starting an array of "things" with 0. This is a convention followed by many languages and is considered a good programming practice. Table 5.6 lists the numeric conventions.

Table 5.6 *Date* **Object Number Conventions**

Date **Attribute**	**Numeric Range**
seconds, minutes	0 - 59
hours	0 - 23
day (0 = Sunday, 1 = Monday, and so on)	0 - 6
date	1 - 31
month (0 = January, 1 = February, and so on)	0 - 11
year	0 + number of years since 1900

Thirdly, when a Date object is created, it takes the information from the Netscape Navigator's environment—usually right as the Web page is being loaded or sometime shortly after. (The Navigator gets information about its environment from the operating system. Other examples of environment variables are the number of other programs running, the current RAM used, and so on, although these may not be accessible by JavaScript.)

In the following sections, each Date method is described with a brief example.

get Methods

These methods allow you to retrieve information from the current Date object. This information can be the seconds, minutes, hours, day of the month, day of the week, months, or years. Notice that there is a getDay method that will give you the day of the week, but you cannot set this value, since the day of the week is dependent on the month, day, and year. See figure 5.4 for examples of the get methods.

FIG. 5.4

get method examples.

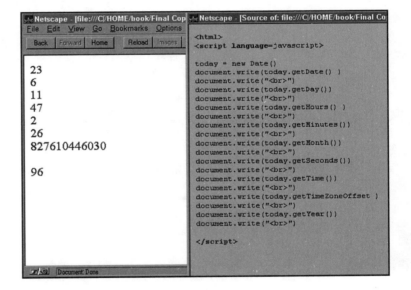

getDate   Given a date object, this returns the date as an integer between 1 and 31.

For example, the following returns 24:

```
today = new Date("February 24, 1996")
document.write(today.getdate())
```

getDay   This returns the day of the week.

For example, the following returns "Today is Saturday":

```
today = new Date("February 24, 1996")

if (today.getDay == 0) {document.write("Today is Sunday")}
if (today.getDay == 1) {document.write("Today is Monday")}
if (today.getDay == 2) {document.write("Today is Tuesday")}
if (today.getDay == 3) {document.write("Today is Wednesday")}
if (today.getDay == 4) {document.write("Today is Thursday")}
if (today.getDay == 5) {document.write("Today is Friday")}
if (today.getDay == 6) {document.write("Today is Saturday")}
```

getHours   This gives you the number of hours since 12:00 A.M.

For example, the following returns, "It's been 16 hours since our party last night!":

```
today = new Date();
document.write("It's been "+ today.getHours +
        " since our party last night!");
```

getMonth   Returns the month attribute of a given Date object.

For example, the following returns 1 (if this month is February):

```
now = newDate()
nowmonth = now.getMonth();
document.write(nowmonth);
```

getSeconds   Returns the seconds of the given Date object.

For example, the following displays a different image about 50 percent of the time the user loads this page:

```
now = newDate();
if (now.getSeconds >30) {document.write("<img src =
➥'randimage1.gif'>")}
if (now.getSeconds <=30) {document.write("<img src =
➥'randimage3.gif'>")}
```

getTime   Returns the number of milliseconds since January 1, 1970. This is useful in setting the time of another Date object.

For example,

```
thisDay = new Date("September 25, 1969");
myBirthday = new Date();
myBirthday.setTime(thisDay.getTime());
```

See also setTime.

getTimeZoneoffset Gives you the difference between the local time and GMT (Greenwich Mean Time).

For example,

```
now = new Date()
timeDifference = now.getTimeZoneoffset;
```

getYear Returns an integer representing the year of the 20th century. Add 1900 to this number to get the current year.

For example,

```
today = new Date("January 1, 1997");
thisYear = new Date();
var output = "Hi!";
if (today.getYear == thisYear.getYear) { output +=" and Happy
➥New Year!"};
document.write(output);
```

If the year is 1996, this returns "Hi!" If it is 1997, it returns "Hi! and Happy New Year!"

set Methods

These methods allow you to add or change attributes of the Date object. You can change the date, month, year, hours, minutes, and seconds of the Date object (see fig. 5.5). All of these methods require integers. Although you will probably use the get methods more often, these methods are handy when you want to quickly create a date and time—perhaps for displaying on a page with a modification date.

setDate Sets the numeric date of a Date object.

For example, the following returns 4:

```
today = new Date("July 1, 1996")
today.setDate(4);
document.write (today.getDate())
```

setHours This sets the hours of the given time.

For example, the following sets the hours attribute ahead 3 hours:

```
today = new Date()
today.setHours=(today.getHours() + 3);
```

FIG. 5.5
set method examples.

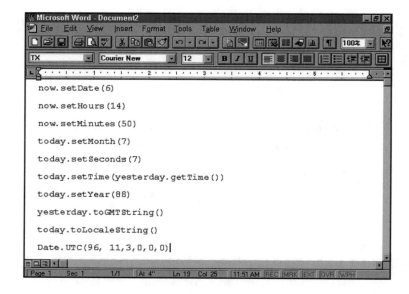

setMinutes This sets the minutes of the given time object (a number between 0 and 59).

For example, the following returns the current Date object (now) with the minutes set for 45:

```
now = new Date()
now.setMinutes(45)
```

setMonth This sets the month integer in the given Date object.

For example, the following returns today (with the month now May):

```
today = newDate()
today.setMonth(4)
```

setSeconds This sets the seconds of the given Date object.

For example, the following returns now (with the seconds set ahead 5 seconds):

```
now = new Date()
now.setSeconds(now.getSeconds()+5)
```

setTime Sets the time value using an integer representing the number of seconds since January 1, 1970.

For example,

```
aDate = new Date();
aDate.setTime(4000*1000*1000*100);
document.write(aDate);
```

returns:

```
Sat Sep 04 08:06:40 1982
```

TIP Instead of using a large integer as a parameter, you could pass a getTime() from another date, such as:

```
thisDay.setime(thatDay.getTime())
```

See also getTime.

setYear   This sets the year of the current date.

For example, the following returns now (with the year now 1997):

```
nowYear = new Date()
nowYear.setYear(97)
```

to Methods

These methods convert date information into another format. You can convert a date into a string (based on some set of conventions—as explained later). Once you have converted the date into a string, it can be treated just like any other string for HTML formatting, etc. (see fig. 5.6). Note that the original date object is not affected. These methods simply parse the date object and return a string based on the information it found.

toGMTString   This method converts the date to a string using the GMT convention.

For example,

```
today = new Date()
document.write((today.toGMTString).bold)
```

This returns `<B>Sat, 24 Feb 1996 17:55:33 GMT</B>`. This is also rendered to the Netscape Navigator in bold text. Note that the bold method appended the `<B>` and the `</B>` to the string, and is not a default action of toGMTString method. This illustrates how you can compact your code based on the assumption that a method returns a known type that you can then use with other methods.

FIG. 5.6
Using to methods.

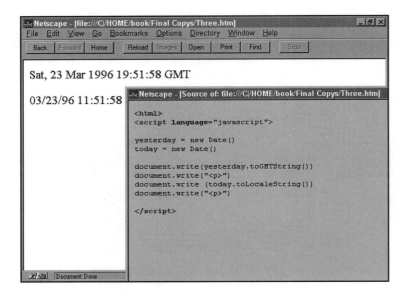

toLocaleString This method converts a date to a string using the locale conventions. Locale conventions are specific to each area that will view this site—meaning that toLocaleString might return a different string in Europe than in the U.S., since in Europe the day is presented before the month. So 09/03/96 might mean September 3rd to the U.S., whereas in Europe, it would mean March 9th.

For example, the following:

```
thisdate.toLocaleString()
```

would return the following in the U.S., if the date was October 4th, 1996:

```
09/04/96 08:06:40
```

In Europe, it might return:

```
04/09/96 08:06:40
```

parse Methods

parse methods take strings and convert them to a resulting date object. These methods complement the to methods, in that they perform the converse of taking a date and coverting it into a string. parse methods are handy in rapidly creating a Date object or simplifying the process of passing a new value to a setTime() method (see fig. 5.7).

FIG. 5.7
Examples of parse
methods.

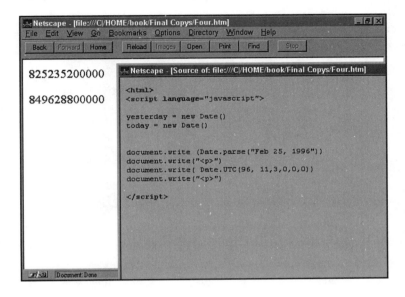

parse   This method returns the number of milliseconds since January 1, 1970 00:00:00. It takes a string such as `Feb 25, 1996` and is useful for setting date objects that already exist. It is acceptable to use the IETF standard date syntax, such as `Sat, 24 Feb 1996 18:15:11 GMT`. It understands U.S. time zone abbreviations, but Netscape recommends you use a time zone offset (thus, the use for the `getTimeZoneoffset` method). Note: The parse function is a static method of `Date`, so it is always called using `Date.parse()`, not with the name of the specific date object instance.

For example,

```
netTime = new Date()
timeString="Jul 10, 1908"
netTime.setTime(Date.parse(timeString));
```

This returns the current `Date` object `netTime` with the changed month, day, and year.

UTC   `UTC` stands for Universal Time Coordinated and is equivalent to GMT. This method is static for `Date`, and is always called via `Date.UTC`. It is called using the following syntax:

```
Date.UTC(year, month, day)
```

or

```
Date.UTC(year, month, day, hours, minutes, seconds)
```

Remember that JavaScript is case-sensitive, so always use uppercase UTC. Also, remember that you use the same integer conventions listed in table 5.6.

For example,

```
theDate = new Date(Date.UTC(96 , 1 , 24 , 12 , 45 , 22));
```

JavaScript Examples Using the *Date* Object

Now that you have survived learning all of the various methods, examples, and numbers listings, it's time to begin doing some interesting things with your knowledge. The following sections show two examples of JavaScript scripts that use the Date object in very different ways. One gives you a straightforward clock to add to your Web pages, and the other gets around the limitation in the current version of JavaScript (in Netscape 2.0) of not having a working random() function. By taking the current hours, minutes, and seconds of a user's visit to your Web page, you can generate a "pseudorandom" number.

A Simple Clock in JavaScript This script samples the time every second, converts that information into a readable string, and displays that string in a small textbox on the screen.

Listing 5.2 A Simple Clock

```
<HTML>
<HEAD>
<TITLE>JavaScript Clock</TITLE>
<script Language="JavaScript">
<!— Hide me from other browsers
// Netscapes Clock - Start
// this code was taken from Netscapes JavaScript documentation at
// www.netscape.com on Jan.25.96

var timerID = null;
var timerRunning = false;
function stopclock (){
        if(timerRunning)
                clearTimeout(timerID);
        timerRunning = false;
```

```
        }

function startclock () {
        // Make sure the clock is stopped
        stopclock();
        showtime();
}

function showtime () {
        var now = new Date();
        var hours = now.getHours();
        var minutes = now.getMinutes();
        var seconds = now.getSeconds()
        var timeValue = "" + ((hours >12) ? hours -12 :hours)
        timeValue += ((minutes < 10) ? ":0" : ":") + minutes
        timeValue += ((seconds < 10) ? ":0" : ":") + seconds
        timeValue += (hours >= 12) ? " P.M." : " A.M."
        document.clock.face.value = timeValue;
        // you could replace the above with this
        // and have a clock on the status bar:
        // window.status = timeValue;
        timerID = setTimeout("showtime()",1000);
        timerRunning = true;
}
// Netscapes Clock - Stop   —>
</script>
</HEAD>
<BODY bgcolor="#ffffff" text="#000000" link="#0000ff"
alink="#008000" vlink="800080" onLoad="startclock()">
<form name="clock" onSubmit="0">
<div align=right>
<input type="text" name="face" size=12 value="">
</div>
</form>
<H1>Now you can add a clock to your pages!</H1>
</BODY>
</HTML>
```

Part

II

Ch

5

Figure 5.8 shows how this would appear on your page.

The heart of this script is the function showtime(). This function creates a Date object called now and pulls out (via getHours, getMinutes, and getSeconds) the hour, minutes, and seconds values. It then creates a variable called timeValue and assigns the hour to it as a string. timeValue is interpreted by JavaScript as a string even though hours is a number because the first value assigned to timeValue was the empty quotes (""). Notice that if the hours value is greater than 12 it is reduced by 12 to account for conventional 12-hour time notation. Notice also that if the number of seconds or minutes is less than 10, the function appends a "0" before that number to keep the number of digits the same space, and to avoid confusion between 03 and 30. This script runs the function `showtime()` every 1000 milliseconds (once a second) to display the current time in a format that is easy for the user to interpret.

FIG. 5.8

A simple clock example.

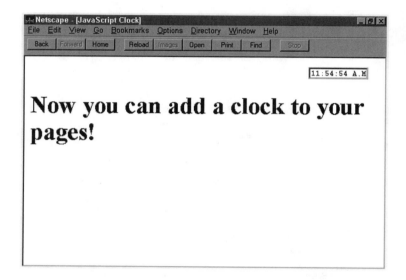

▶ **See** chapter 2 for information about the `setTimeout` and `clearTimeout` methods, **p. 33**.

One of the most useful aspects of JavaScript is that it uses an object-oriented approach to programming. What this means is that you (the scripter) can easily take functions that you worked so hard to perfect in one script and adapt them quickly to another script—often with little or no modifications. You can see in the comments of listing 5.2 that if you want, you can direct the output of the function `showtime()` to the status bar on the bottom of your browser, instead of displaying it in the textbox field on the page. You would do this by commenting out or deleting the following line:

```
document.clock.face.value = timeValue;
```

You would also need to remove the comments (the `//`) from the following line:

```
// window.status = timeValue;
```

It would then look like this:

```
window.status = timeValue;
```

Using the status line has the advantage in that the text is less likely to flicker when it updates, as many rapidly updated form fields tend to do. Also, you can easily modify this code—instead of displaying the current time on the screen—to send it to another function. This function might then use that changing information to reload a clockface image (or almost anything your imagination comes up with).

Pseudorandom Generator   Listing 5.3 shows how you can simulate a seemingly random event. This is currently one of the few ways to work around the fact that the `math.random()` function is not enabled in all versions of Netscape Navigator (across platforms). The background behind this script is this: I wanted to find a way to generate a short three-word sentence based on a list of verbs, adjectives, and objects. These words came together to create a "Magic Talent," which simulates what happens to a number of fictional characters in various fantasy novel series. As someone enters the page, the date is sampled and used as a "seed" number to select one word from each list. These words are then concatenated together on-the-fly and displayed on the page. Essentially, it takes advantage of the fact that someone is unlikely to visit the page at exactly the same hour, minute, and second each day, so it appears to the page visitor that the selection is truly "random." The illusion disappears, though, if he repeatedly reloads this page—since the sentence will change only slightly.

Listing 5.3   The Random Talent Generator

```
<HTML>
<HEAD>
<TITLE>Random Talents Generator</TITLE>
</BODY>
</HEAD>
<BODY bgcolor=#ffffff>
<script language="JavaScript">
<!— Random Talent Generator
var currentdate=0
var spacer= " "
var talent= " "
var theverb= " "
var theadj = " "
var theobjec = " "
var core = 0
var description = "Here is your randomly generated
Random talent. <br> Reload after a while for a new one. <br>"
```

Part
II

Ch

5

continues

Listing 5.3   Continued

```javascript
function StringArray (n) {
        this.length = n;
        for (var i = 1; i <= n; i++) {
                this[i] = ''
        }
        return this
}

verb = new StringArray(10)
verb[0] = 'grow'
verb[1] = 'banish'
verb[2] = 'transform'
verb[3] = 'lift'
verb[4] = 'control'
verb[5] = 'shrink'
verb[6] = 'enlarge'
verb[7] = 'age'
verb[8] = 'youthen'
verb[9] = 'speak to'


adj = new StringArray(10)
adj[0] = 'large'
adj[1] = 'small'
adj[2] = 'green'
adj[3] = 'invisible'
adj[4] = 'mirage'
adj[5] = 'glowing'
adj[6] = 'wooden'
adj[7] = 'armored'
adj[7] = 'imaginary'
adj[8] = 'glass'
adj[9] = 'ghostly'

objec = new StringArray(10)
objec[0] = 'dragons'
objec[1] = 'animals'
objec[2] = 'plants'
objec[3] = 'fruit'
objec[4] = 'humans'
objec[5] = 'centaurs'
objec[6] = 'swords'
objec[7] = 'castles'
objec[8] = 'trees'
objec[9] = 'pies'

function getVerb (){
        currentdate = new Date()
        core = currentdate.getSeconds()
        adcore = Math.floor(core/6)
        core=adcore
```

```
        theverb = verb[core]
        return (theverb)
}

function getAdj (){
        currentdate = new Date()
        core = currentdate.getMinutes()
        adcore = Math.floor(core/6)
        core=adcore
        theadj = adj[core]
        return (theadj)
}

function getObjec (){
        currentdate = new Date()
        core1 = currentdate.getSeconds()
        core2 = currentdate.getMinutes()
        core3 = core1 + core2
        adcore = Math.floor(core3/12)
        core = adcore

        theobjec = objec[core]
        return (theobjec)
}
// main program
document.write("Random Talent Generator".fontsize(6) + "<p>")
document.write(description + spacer + "<p>" +
getVerb() + spacer + getAdj()+ spacer + getObjec())
document.write("<p>")

// -->

</script>

<p>
If you dont see anything above this line, you dont have Netscape
2.0.<br>

</BODY>
</HTML>
```

Figure 5.9 illustrates how this page would appear.

When the user loads this page, the script creates three string arrays and fills them in with the strings I provided. It then uses the getVerb(), getAdj(), and getObjec() to get one of the strings in the array based on the number of seconds, minutes, or the average of the two. This is done by taking the number of seconds in the currentdate.getSeconds, dividing it by 6, and then using the Math.floor method to return an integer between 0 and 9.

FIG. 5.9

The Random Talent
Generator.

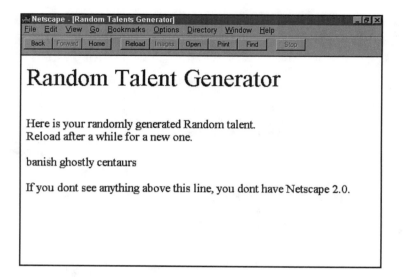

Since there is no real way to know when someone will visit this page, and the seconds change rapidly, there is a good chance that it will be difficult for someone visiting only once or twice a day to discern that the "Talents" aren't actually random.

You also see an example of using the string method `fontsize()`. The method `fontsize()` allows you to replace the `"<FONT SIZE=''>...</FONT>` tags with just a number passed to the `fontsize()` method. Usually this will be a negative or postive 1.

Note that it works fine with the string literal `"Magic Talent Generator"`. We could just as easily have assigned that string to a variable, say `titleString`, and then used `titleString.fontsize(6)`.

 You may find yourself using many of the same functions over and over in many different scripts. It's good practice to keep a personal library of useful functions so you can find them (and use them!) over and over again.

Interactive HTML Objects

by Andrew Wooldridge

If you have been reading this book through to this point, you have proven that you have more than just a casual interest in JavaScript (unless, of course, you've happened to open the book to this page while you are in the book store!). This chapter continues with the "object" theme of this part of the book and introduces you to interactive HTML objects. They are interactive in that they allow you to respond in some way to input from someone who visits your site.

When you finish this chapter, you should be well on your way to building your first set of JavaScript scripts for your site. Most of the sites that you find today were built using many of the concepts in this chapter. The ability to use forms to lay out input and output areas; buttons to accept questions, replies, or other input; and "back end" JavaScript to interpret that input, you have the beginnings of a full-fledged application. The

Review the basics of HTML forms

You will familiarize yourself with the standard HTML tags that make up a user input form and see how you can adapt them to other uses.

Get to know JavaScript buttons, checkboxes, and radio buttons

You will learn how to build thesea.spects of a form through JavaScript and learn to trigger events through buttons.

Manipulate text fields

See how to use JavaScript to read and display information through text fields.

Validate and submit a form

Use JavaScript to check the information a visitor submits without using a CGI.

ability to use the Web browser's GUI (Graphical User Interface) to create small programs very quickly is quite compelling.

What you should take from this chapter is the knowledge of building forms, as well as having a new view of forms. Before JavaScript, the form was basically just for typing in responses to questions, or making a selection among some choices. Now, the form can be a template that instantly responds to some action on your Web site vistor's part. ■

Customizing User Interaction Using JavaScript

JavaScript is one of the first scripting languages that applies an object-oriented approach (via its roots in Java) to writing and modifying Web pages. JavaScript takes expressions in HTML, such as

```
<A HREF="http://www.yahoo.com">Yahoo!</A>
```

and creates an object with methods and properties similar to the ones you read about in chapter 5, "Built-In JavaScript Objects."

This chapter and the next take you through the objects in JavaScript that are created and used when you write HTML code—specifically those related to working with HTML forms. Forms provide a key way for you to build a user interface with which you can create miniature "applettes." An example of this is to use HTML forms buttons and text boxes to allow a user to click buttons on a calculator and see the results immediately (see fig. 6.1). (I use the term *applettes* as an alternative to Java's applet—which is a small program that runs on your browser. JavaScript scripts are smaller, yet might perform many of the same tasks you see in Java. Thus, you can think of them as mini-applets.)

Another example might be for you to create an order form that checks that all of the order fields are filled in correctly and even calculates a running total of the cost of the items ordered (see fig. 6.2).

FIG. 6.1
A Web site using a calculator in JavaScript.

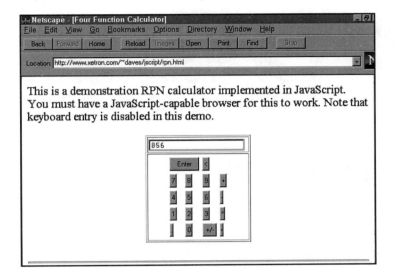

FIG. 6.2
Another Web site, with an order form that automatically calculates your total order.

Before JavaScript, the process of creating and validating information that a user entered via a form depended heavily on sending and receiving information from a server-side CGI script. A CGI was possibly used for creating the actual form (generating HTML), validating the information (such as checking that all of the fields were filled in correctly), and sending a response back to the user confirming that the information had been sent successfully.

Using JavaScript, you can place much of the work on the client-side, which can reduce dramatically the connection times between the client (the Navigator) and the server (your Web server). In terms of validating form information, you do this by allowing the script to inspect the contents of each field that the user has entered and present an alert to the user if the information does not meet some specific requirements—like too many characters or if the field is empty.

Review of HTML Forms

Before we delve into the secrets of JavaScript and forms, let's review the various HTML tags that allow you to create a form. Although you may already be familiar with these tags, it is good to review them in case you discover features you may not be taking advantage of currently. Table 6.1 summarizes these tags.

Table 6.1 Quick Review HTML Form Tags

Tag	Meaning
`<FORM ACTION="URL" METHOD="GET"></FORM>`	Defines a form
`<FORM ENCTYPE="multipart/form-data"></FORM>`	Uploads a file via a form
`<INPUT TYPE="TEXT">`	Input field
`<INPUT NAME="somename">`	Field name
`<INPUT VALUE="somevalue">`	Field value
`<INPUT CHECKED>`	Checked
`<INPUT SIZE=6>`	Field size (in characters)
`<INPUT MAXLENGTH="100">`	Maximum length of field
`<SELECT></SELECT>`	Selection list
`<SELECT NAME="somename">`	Selection list name
`<SELECT SIZE="6">`	Number of options in list

Tag	Meaning
`<SELECT MULTIPLE>`	Multiple selections (more than one)
`<OPTION>sometext`	Option
`<OPTION SELECTED>`	Default Option
`<TEXTAREA ROWS="5" COLS="5">...</TEXTAREA>`	Text area input box size
`<TEXTAREA NAME="somename">...</TEXTAREA>`	Text area name
`<TEXTAREA WRAP=OFF>`	Wraps the text

<FORM>...</FORM>

These tags must begin and end your form.

The following are attributes of the FORM and /FORM tags:

- ACTION is the location where you want this form to go.
- METHOD is the way in which you send this information. The METHOD is usually POST, but sometimes you can use GET.
- ENCTYPE is the MIME type of the information you upload to a server. (At this time, ENCTYPE and file uploads are only available with Netscape.)

<INPUT>

This tag creates various input fields. For example, the following:

```
<INPUT NAME="Address">
```

allows you to establish an input field for addresses within the form.

Pairing this tag with the following attributes allows you to manipulate specific field designations:

- NAME is the name of this field.
- VALUE is the string or numeric value that is sent with this field.

- CHECKED applies to checkboxes and radio boxes and defines if they are checked on page load.
- TYPE determines which type of input this field is. The types are as follows (you can also see some of these types in figure 6.3 and the corresponding HTML code in figure 6.4):
  - TEXT—A plain text box.
  - PASSWORD—A text box that echos bullets when you type into it. The bullets hide the typed text.
  - CHECKBOX—Renders a small box that indicates whether it is selected. Usually for Yes or No questions. They are commonly referred to as checkboxes.
  - RADIO—Renders a small circle that allows you to choose one among many options. They are commonly referred to as radio buttons.
  - IMAGE—Returns the coordinates of the image selected here (with x=num, y=num as the parameters returned). This is very similar to imagemaps, but is useful if you want to just return the xy value that someone clicks. The following is an example:

    ```
    <INPUT NAME="thisimage" TYPE="IMAGE" SRC="foo.gif" ALIGN="TOP">
    ```

    (This use of IMAGE doesn't require you to have a resulting map file on your server, and could be directly sent to a script for interpretation.)
  - HIDDEN—Is not displayed by the browser. Useful for storing special information for the CGI.
  - SUBMIT—When this is clicked, it submits the form.
  - RESET—Clears all input fields and resets to the defaults.
  - SIZE—The size of the input field (in number of characters) for text or password types.
- MAXLENGTH sets the maximum number of characters to be allowed within a field of a text or password type.

FIG. 6.3

Different input fields—
examples of text, password,
checkbox, radio button,
submit, and reset (and
hidden, too).

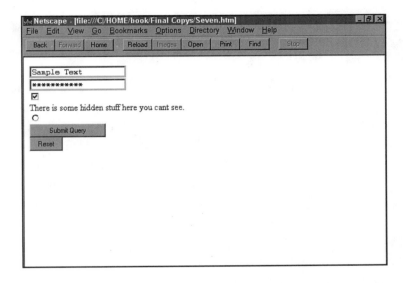

FIG. 6.4

HTML source code of the
input fields in figure 6.3.

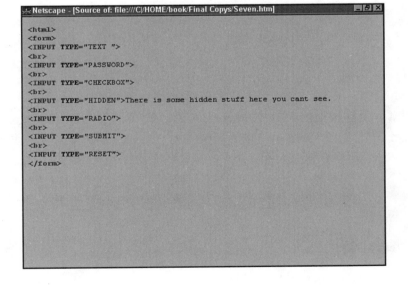

Part

II

Ch

6

<SELECT>...</SELECT>

These tags present either a scrolling list of choices or a pop-up menu. <SELECT> is generated in different ways, based on your choice of options. You can generate a single window that "pops open" to reveal all of the options—from which you can then select one—or you can see a scrolling list of options with up and down arrows much like a regular window—which allows you to see many choices at once. Pull-down windows are best for times when you want someone to choose one option, and it saves screen space. It's best when the number of options are fewer than five or so. If you have more than five, you should set the SIZE attribute to show the first five (or less) and allow the user to scroll through the rest.

The following lists the attributes you use with <SELECT>. Try out many variations on a test Web page to see how changing the attributes changes the way the list is shown:

- NAME is the name of the data (required).
- SIZE determines how many choices to show. If set to 1 or omitted, it renders a pop-up menu. If set to 2 or more it is a scrolling list.
- MULTIPLE allows you to select multiple options and always renders a scrolling list.

 An often underutilized way to use this form element is to place a caption to an image just under the image with <SELECT SIZE=1> and the caption text inside—one line to an <OPTION>.

The result is a nice "pop-open" caption that allows you to use that saved space in other ways. Note though that the bar will be as wide as your longest line in the <OPTION> list.

<OPTION>

Contained within the SELECT and /SELECT tags, this tag designates a selectable item. The following list describes the attributes an <OPTION> might have:

- VALUE is the value returned when the form is submitted if this option was selected.
- SELECTED means when the page is loaded, this option is selected by default.

<TEXTAREA>...</TEXTAREA>

These tags provide an area for a user to enter multiple lines of text. This defaults to four rows in length, with each row 40 characters wide. The following list describes each attribute you might use in a TEXTAREA tag:

- NAME defines the name for the information (required).

- ROWS is the number of rows in this field.

- COLS is the number of characters wide this field is.

- WRAP determines how text flows inside a text area. You have three options for this attribute (you can see examples of WRAP in figure 6.5 and the corresponding HTML code in figure 6.6):

  - OFF—No text wrap.

  - VIRTUAL—Text flows to right border then wraps to next line. It will be submitted as one line, without new lines. So although the text appears to wrap, it will be one line when sent to the server (or script).

  - PHYSICAL—Text flows beyond right border beyond the text area window. When it is submitted, the text will be wrapped based on any new lines.

FIG. 6.5

Two examples of select fields of different sizes.

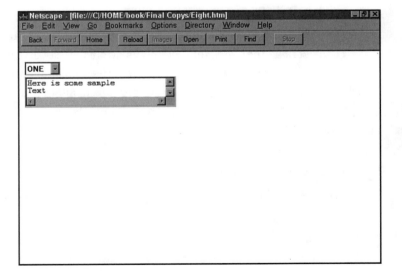

Part

II

Ch

6

FIG. 6.6
HTML source code for
figure 6.5.

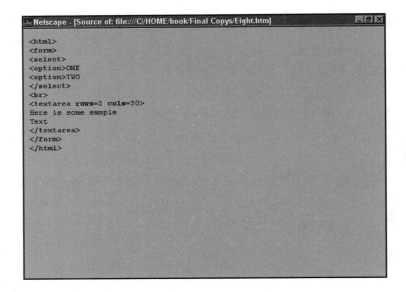

HTML Objects in JavaScript

This section introduces you to JavaScript's HTML objects that relate to forms. With each of these objects, you will see further how to build a form that will be able to respond instantly to user input.

You will learn about buttons, checkboxes, and radio buttons. These form elements consist of all the "clickable" elements. Mouse clicks on these elements can be used to trigger JavaScript functions, or to submit a form to either your home server or another script running elsewhere (perhaps in another frame or window). You will get quite a bit of mileage out of these elements, and JavaScript has enhanced them with its ability to monitor their status (such as if a radio button is on or off).

Buttons, Checkboxes, and Radio Buttons

Now that you've had a brief refresher of the different HTML tags that build a form, you are ready to begin using JavaScript to bring new life to your forms. We will examine how JavaScript builds special objects as it reads your HTML code and explore how to use these objects to create an interactive form.

The *form* Object   Whenever you declare a `<FORM>...</FORM>` in your Web page, JavaScript takes the information contained within that form and builds a `form` object. To create a `form` object, use the syntax in listing 6.1.

Listing 6.1   *form* Attributes

```
<FORM
     NAME = "formname"
     TARGET = "windowname"
     ACTION = "serverURL"
     METHOD = GET ¦ POST
     ENCTYPE = "encodingType"
     [ onSubmit = "handlerText" ] >
</FORM>
```

The new attributes you might notice are `TARGET` and `onSubmit`. `TARGET` specifies the window that the responses go to. The event handler `onSubmit` is optional. The text listed in the `handlerText` is evaluated when you submit this form via the `SUBMIT` button or use the `submit` method in another part of your script.

Once you have created this object, you can address its properties and methods in the following way:

- `formName.propertyName`
- `formName.methodName(parameters)`
- `forms[index].propertyName`
- `forms[index].methodName(parameters)`

JavaScript places each form it finds in a page in an array called `forms`. You can access each form by either its index in this array (with the first form at 0, the next at 1, and so on) or by its name. For example,

```
<form name="thisform">
<input type=text name="input1" value="hi there!">
</form>
```

By doing this you create an object called `thisform` which also exists as `document.forms[0]`.

Figure 6.7 illustrates a review of the object hierarchy to display where a `form` object lies in relation to the other objects generated by JavaScript.

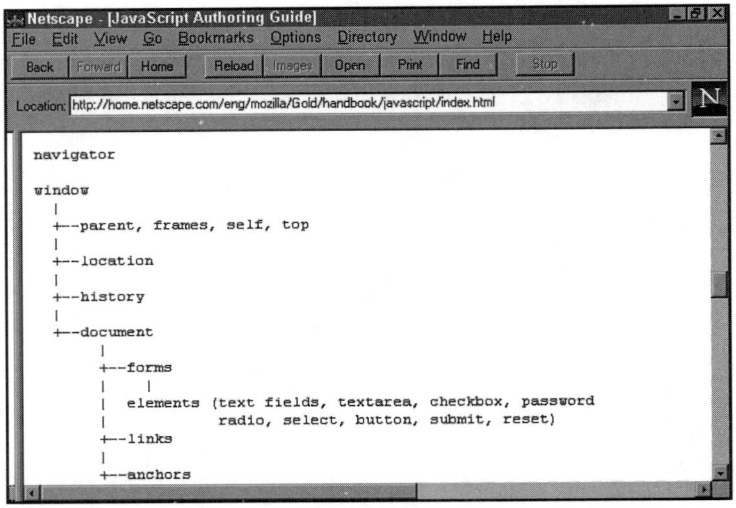

FIG. 6.7
The JavaScript object
hierarchy, showing the
relationship between each
object and its "container"
(higher level objects).

You can access individual fields in this form—where you can either read that field directly or send a new value to that field—which might (depending on the type of input field) dynamically change on the screen. To access information about this form, use the following naming conventions:

- formName.action—From the ACTION argument
- formName.elements—To get to the input (etc.) fields
- formName.encoding—From the ENCTYPE argument
- formName.method—From the METHOD argument
- formName.target—From the TARGET argument

For an example, take a look at listing 6.2.

Listing 6.2 Example of Accessing a *form* Element in JavaScript

```
<script language="javascript">
<form name="thisForm"
    action="foo.html"
    ENCTYPE="text/ascii"
    method="GET">
</form>
<!-- hide this code
document.forms[0].method = "POST'

document.write(document.thisForm.method)
-->
</script>
```

The return of listing 6.2 is the following:

```
POST
```

The *button* Object   The button object is a new type of INPUT tag that allows you to create general purpose buttons in a form. You can use these buttons to activate any function, or to open a new URL, or perform any other action that JavaScript can initiate. To define a button object use the following syntax:

```
<INPUT
    TYPE = "button"
    NAME =" nameInside"
    VALUE = "nameOnButton"
    [onClick = "handlerText"]>
```

This is an extremely useful object, and you will probably find yourself using this often to create buttons to run scripts, open new windows, or even cause the browser to leave your Web site altogether! You must use this inside a set of FORM.../FORM tags. You access a button's properties and methods in the following way:

- buttonName.propertyName

- buttonName.methodName(parameters)

- formName.elements[index].propertyName

- formName.elements[index].methodName(parameters)

For example, listing 6.3 creates a page that looks like figure 6.8. Upon clicking the button, you will see an Alert dialog box that looks like figure 6.9.

Listing 6.3   Using a Button *form* Element in JavaScript

```
<script language="JavaScript">
<!-- hide me from other browsers
function hey() {
    document.alert("Hey there! You pushed the button!")
}
// end hiding from other browsers -->
</script>

<form>

<h1>Click below for an alert!</h1>

<input type="button" name="alertbutton" value="Click Me!"
➥onClick="hey()">

</form>
```

Part

II

Ch

6

FIG. 6.8
Web page with `alert` button example.

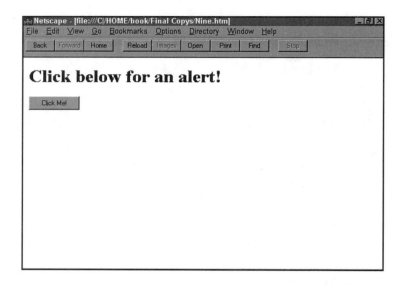

FIG. 6.9
Here's the alert!

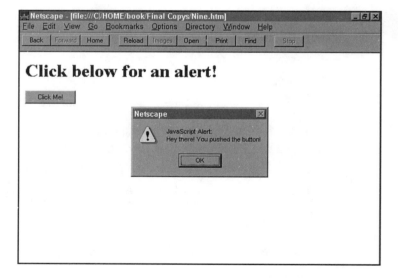

You can access the properties of the button object in listing 6.3 by using one of the following:

```
document.forms[0].elements[0].name
```

or

```
alertbutton.name
```

If you want to retrieve the name of the button as a string object, you could use either of the examples below, which would return "Click Me!":

```
document.forms[0].elements[0].value
```

or

```
alertbutton.value
```

> **NOTE** Once you have created a button object you can change its value, but the text on the button does not change to reflect this. This is because the button was written to the screen when the page was loaded and cannot be changed unless the page is reloaded. And reloading the page alone does not implement the change, since the button reverts to its default value in the HTML code when it is reloaded. The only way to change this value is to set the value equal to some variable that can persist across page reloading. For more information on how to do this, see chapter 12, "More About Java." ■

The *checkbox* Object   The checkbox object is created inside a form and appears as a small box with or without a mark (usually an x) inside it. Think of a checkbox as an On/Off switch.

A user can flip this switch on or off by clicking his mouse inside this box. Clicking here can also trigger an onClick event in your script. You create a checkbox via the syntax in listing 6.4.

Listing 6.4   *checkbox* Object

```
<INPUT
    TYPE = "checkbox"
    NAME = "checkboxName"
    VALUE = "checkboxValue"
    [CHECKED]
    [onClick = "handlerText"]>
    textToDisplay
```

Accessing the properties of this object is very similar to accessing the properties of the button object. The properties are as follows:

- CHECKED indicates true or false to specify if the checkbox is checked.

- DEFAULTCHECKED indicates whether or not the checkbox was marked checked upon page load.

Part
II

Ch
6

- NAME indicates the name of the checkbox.

- VALUE indicates the value that is returned by the form if the checkbox is checked. (This defaults to On.)

Listing 6.5 is an example of using the checkbox object in a script (see fig. 6.10).

Listing 6.5   Using the *checkbox* Object

```html
<html>
<script language="javascript">
function mystatus(){
      (document.theForm.theCheckbox.checked) ?
            alert("The box is checked") :
                  alert("The box is not checked! Oh no!")
}

</script>

<form name="theForm">
<input type="checkbox" name="theCheckbox" value="myValue"
onClick="mystatus()">
</form>
</html>
```

FIG. 6.10
Web page with checkbox.

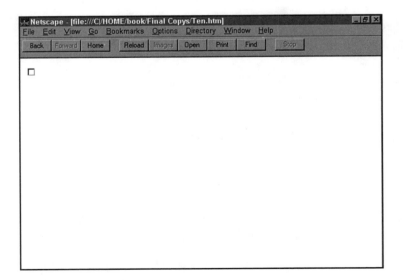

When you click the checkbox so that it is checked, you will see something like what is shown in figure 6.11. If you then "uncheck" it, you will see an alert box like that shown in figure 6.12.

FIG. 6.11
Once the checkbox is checked, you see this alert.

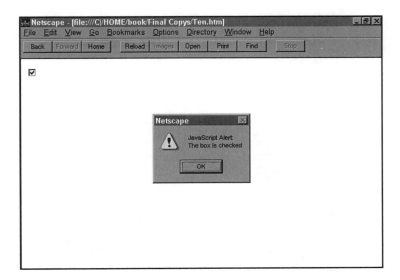

FIG. 6.12
Clicking the checkbox off will give you this alert.

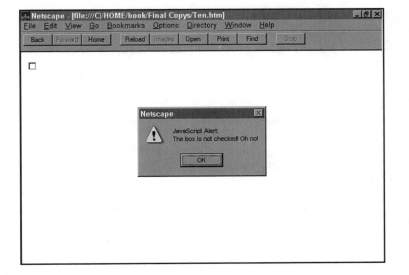

The _radio_ Object This object allows a user to make a choice of a single selection from many. Usually this is a list of related items from which you wish the user to pick only one choice.

The radio object is very similar to the checkbox object, except that a series of radio objects with the same NAME attribute toggle all of the radio buttons off except for the one that was picked. In other words, when you click one radio button in a group of related buttons, all of them will be off except for the one you clicked. You create a radio object using the syntax in listing 6.6.

Listing 6.6 *radio* **Object Syntax**

```
<INPUT
    TYPE="radio"
    NAME = "radioName"
    [CHECKED]
    [onClick = "handlerText"]>
    textToDisplay
```

Accessing information from the radio object is slightly different than from the checkbox object. Since all of the radio buttons of a given group have the same NAME attribute, you access individual radio buttons by adding an index value to the NAME. The format for doing this is as follows:

- radioName[index1].propertyName

- radioName[index1].methodName

- formname.elements[index2].propertyName

- formname.elements[index2].methodName

You can click a specific radio button in JavaScript by using the following:

```
radioName[index1].click
```

Listing 6.7 is an example of using radio buttons with JavaScript. The result is shown in figure 6.13.

Listing 6.7   Radio Button Example

```
<form name = "game">
<input type = "text" name="output" size=15>
<input type = "radio" name="choice" value = "rock"
    onClick ="game.output.value='The Rock'">The rock
<input type = "radio" name="choice" value= "scissors"
    onClick ="game.output.value='The Scissors'">The scissors
<input type = "radio" name="choice" value = "paper"
    onClick = "game.output.value='The Paper'">The paper
</form>
```

FIG. 6.13
Web page example of using
radio buttons to constrain
user input.

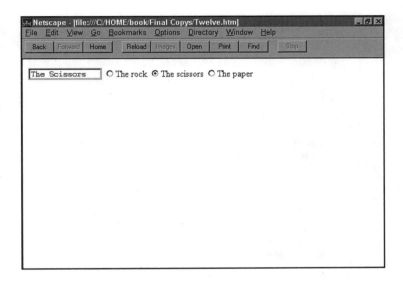

This piece of code allows a user to pick one of the three choices—rock, paper, or scissors—which then shows up in the text field box. If the user wants to choose a fourth alternative, say bomb, then she just has to type it in to the box. This is a quick way for you to offer both a series of preset choices, as well as allow a user to place her own customized choice.

Manipulating Text Fields

This section gives you experience working with the text-based input fields in an HTML form, and shows how you can use JavaScript to enhance these input fields' usefulness to you as a script writer.

The *hidden* Object   Often when you create an interactive form, you want to keep some information hidden, yet still pass this information on to the server when the form is submitted. This is often information about the user—perhaps when he last accessed your page, or some preference that he had set in the previous form that generated this one. You can keep track of this information with hidden fields. This field is often used in place of Netscape's "cookies" for compatability to browsers that do not support the cookie specification. Hidden fields contain text information and are not displayed on the screen with the rest of the form.

Part
II

Ch

6

Netscape cookies are small strings of text stored in your `cookies.txt` file. They are often used to store information about you or your computer that is used by various sites to "remember" some bit of information about you between visits to that Web site. The server writes this code to your machine and will reread it when you visit again. Although this feature is very useful, there are still debates as to its security and validity of use.

To create a `hidden` object, use the following syntax:

```
<INPUT
    TYPE="hidden"
    NAME="hiddenName"
    [VALUE = "textValue"]>
```

You can access the properties of this object by using the following:

- `hiddenName.propertyName`
- `formName.elements[index].propertyName`

For example, the following returns "hi there!":

```
<form>
<input type=hidden name=hideme value="hi there!">
</form>

document.write(hideme.value);
```

When you use hidden fields, it adds a sense of "state" to the Web. What this means is that usually a Web site has no real way of knowing if a visitor to that Web site had just been there moments ago, or if he is visiting for the first time. Using the hidden field, you can place a hidden reminder to yourself (you as the Web site) on the page he receives—such as a timestamp—and retrieve that reminder whenever he submits that form to you for more information. This is very similar to the process one might go through to enter a parking lot, pick up a tag, then return that tag when you leave. Your server can read that hidden field into a CGI script and respond to the user of the page with something like "Welcome Back! Here's what's changed since you were here last!" Another use might be that of a hidden field in a Web-based game which stores the current score, location, and state of a player. This information is sent back to the game engine every time the player moves to a new location.

The *password* Object The password input field in a form is very useful for those times when you need to create a logon screen and keep the password of that logon hidden from view or from being printed by some malicious user who sees the login screen. Any time you want the information hidden from sight as a user types that information on the screen, use the password input field. To create this as an object in JavaScript, use the following syntax:

```
<INPUT
    TYPE="password"
    NAME = "passwordName"
    SIZE=integer
    [VALUE = "textValue"]>
```

Accessing the properties and methods of this object once it is created is identical to previous examples and is as follows:

- `passwordName.propertyName`
- `passwordName.methodName(parameters)`
- `formname.elements[index].propertyname`
- `formname.elements[index].methodname(parameters)`

The password object uses the `focus`, `blur`, and `select` event handlers as methods. Let's say you want to check the validity of a password before a user actually sends it back to the server for a login. You can create a function that checks the password and notifies the user if he entered an invalid password. See listing 6.8 for an example.

Listing 6.8 Form Validation Example

```
<script language="JavaScript">
function checkPass(mypass) {
    if(notpass) {
    alert ("You have entered an invalid password.  Try again.")
    mypass.focus()
    mypass.select()
}

function not

<form onSubmit="checkPass(this)">
<input type="password" name="mypass">
</form>
```

N O T E Don't confuse the `password` object with the `hidden` object. The `password`
object conceals what a user types in to a text entry field, while a `hidden`
object simply hides the whole field. Both input types in some way hide information. ■

The *text* Object   The text input field in an HTML document is your workhorse for
inputting many types of information. Most other types of input in forms are
derivations of this kind of input.

The text input field is simply a small box of a set size that contains a cursor when
you click it. It allows a user using the form to type in information such as a name,
a date, or any other kind of information. If the text a user types is too long for the
box, it scrolls to the left to accomodate the additional text. In JavaScript, this field
serves a new and exciting purpose. Not only can a user using the form enter information into this field, but the script itself can enter information as well. In chapter
5 you saw a script that used this field to display a constantly changing digital clock.

You create a JavaScript `text` object using the syntax in listing 6.9.

Listing 6.9   *text* Object Syntax

```
<INPUT
    TYPE="text"
    NAME="textName"
    VALUE = "textValue"
    SIZE = integer
    [onBlur = "handlerText"]
    [onChange = "handlerText"]
    [onFocus = "handlerText"]
    [onSelect = "handlerText"]>
```

A real-world example of this would be the following:

```
<FORM>
<INPUT TYPE="text" NAME="todaysdate" VALUE="" SIZE="5" onBlur="
➥getDate()" onChange="setDate()"
onFocus="alert('Set the date')"  onSelect="alert('Really change?')">
</FORM>
```

The `text` object properties reflect the information you provide in the tag when you
create the object. Table 6.2 is a listing of those properties with an example of how
you would access them.

Table 6.2 *text* **Object Properties**

Property	Example	Description
defaultValue	myText.defaultValue	The value of the input tag at page load time
name	myText.name	The NAME argument
value	formName.elements[0].value	The VALUE argument

You can act on this object in a number of ways, either indirectly by another function, or directly by using the event handlers contained in the object. Tables 6.3 and 6.4 list the methods and event handlers associated with the text object.

Table 6.3 *text* **Object Methods**

Method	Example	Description
focus	myText.focus()	Equivalent to clicking this field
blur	myText.blur()	Equivalent to clicking another field after using this one
select	myText.select()	Equivalent to dragging the mouse across all the text in this field—selecting it

Table 6.4 *text* **Object Event Handlers**

Event Handler	Example	Description
onBlur	`<input type=text onBlur="alert('blur!')">`	Runs "alert()" when focus leaves this field
onChange	`<input type=text onChange="alert('changed')">`	Runs "alert()" if the text has changed when focus leaves this field
onFocus	`<input type=text onFocus="alert('start typing!')">`	Runs "alert()"when user clicks in (or otherwise gives focus to) this field.

continues

Table 6.4   Continued

Event Handler	Example	Description

onSelect	`<input type=text`
	`onSelect =`
	`"alert('text selected!')">`
		Runs `"alert()"` once some text in this field is selected

The script in listing 6.10 places information about a link in a text field below a series of links when a user passes the mouse over each link. This illustrates how you can use other event handlers to pass information to a text field (see fig. 6.14).

Listing 6.10   Event Handlers and Text Fields

```
<script language = "javascript">
<!-- hide from other browsers
var num =0

function showLink(num){
     if (num==1) {document.forms[0].elements[0].value= "one";
               }
     if (num==2) {document.forms[0].elements[0].value = "two";
               }
     if (num==3) {document.forms[0].elements[0].value = "three";
               }
}


// stop hiding -->
</script>
<form>
<input type=text size=60 >
</form>
<a href="#" onMouseOver="showLink(1)">one</a><br>
<a href="#" onMouseOver="showLink(2)">two</a><br>
<a href="#" onMouseOver="showLink(3)">three</a><br>
```

As you pass your mouse over each link—one, two, or three—you see that the text in the text field changes as well. You can easily modify this code to display helpful information about links on your own page beyond the URL that displays at the bottom left of the Netscape Navigator (which is called the status area).

FIG. 6.14
Using *onMouseOver*, you can display different text in a text field.

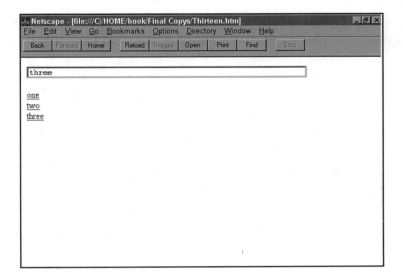

The *textarea* Object   When you need a user to input more than just one line of text in a form you use the textarea input type. This is the case if you are providing to the user an e-mail feedback form and want to allow space for the user to type in a lengthy note. To create a textarea object in JavaScript, use the syntax shown in listing 6.11.

Listing 6.11   *textarea* Object Syntax

```
<TEXTAREA
     NAME ="textareaName"
     ROWS = integer
     COLS = integer
     WRAP = on¦off¦physical¦virtual
     [onBlur = "handlerText"]
     [onChange = "handerText"]
     [onFocus = "handlerText"]
     [onSelect = "handlerText"]>
     textToDisplay
</TEXTAREA>
```

Part

II

Ch

6

A textarea object uses essentially the same attributes, methods, and properties as does the text object (see tables 6.2, 6.3, and 6.4). You can provide default text to display in this field by adding text between the TEXTAREA... /TEXTAREA tags.

Long Example: Foobar the Bazbarian   I use the `textarea` input field in a game I wrote called Foobar the Bazbarian. In this game, the user can click buttons to go north, south, east, and west, and pick up various objects along the way to eventually win the game. The game itself is very simple in its concept, and is long in implementation only because of the many pieces of text input that can be displayed in the textarea window. In a way, this completely turns around the concept of a textarea from one in which you require a user to input long lines of text to displaying something like a miniature computer terminal. Listing 6.12 shows this program's code and figure 6.15 provides a sample display of how it might look on a Web page.

Listing 6.12   Foobar the Bazbarian

```
<HTML>
<HEAD>
<TITLE>FOOBAR! The Bazbarian</TITLE>
</HEAD>
<BODY >
<script language="JavaScript">
<!-- The Engine
//variable declarations
var location="0"
var locDesc= new StringArray(16)
var zero=0
var bonus="10"

locDesc[0]='You are standing at the edge of a small island.
➥Palm trees sprout everywhere and obscure your view to the East and
➥South. The beach is bordered on the North and West'
locDesc[1]='The beach is to the West. You see the remains of your
➥wrecked ship here. The forest is to the East and the beach goes North
➥and South.'
locDesc[2]='The beach is West of you. At the edge of the forest stands a
➥silver cage with a beautiful princess who becons for you to unlock the
➥cage.'
locDesc[3]='The beach lapps at you from the West and South. The palm
➥trees to the North and East sway in the wind. You hear screaming to the
➥North.'
locDesc[4]='The ocean borders the North. On the beach you see empty coke
➥cans and various other washed up trash. '
locDesc[5]='You are surrounded by palm trees.  A monkey waves a you. You
➥hear screaming to the South.'
locDesc[6]='In a clearing, you see a golden cage with a georgeous
➥princess waving at you. She begs you to find the key and let her free.'
```

```
locDesc[7]='The beach borders to the South. There are graves here with
➥names of other warriors like yourself who failed...'
locDesc[8]='The beach borders the North end of the island.
➥The wind blows fiercer here.'
locDesc[9]='You are in the midst of palms.
➥Footprints dot the sand in all directions.'
locDesc[10]='A woman screams to the West.
➥Sharp rocks hurt your bare feet as you wander...'
locDesc[11]='The beach borders the Southern end of the island.
➥You hear a strange sound to the East, like a storm in the distance.'
locDesc[12]='You see a chest full of gold, jewels
➥and many other things. Your search reveals....'
locDesc[13]='The beach stops you short to East.
➥There are the remains of a campfire here.'
locDesc[14]='Bones litter the beach to the East.
➥They look human. You hear a sound like rushing wind to the South.
➥Palms trees obscure your view.'
locDesc[15]='A large green Dragon turns to look at you
➥as you enter the clearing. Its growl is like a Mac Truck stuck in
➥high gear.'

// functions

function StringArray (n) {
    this.length = n;
    for (var i = 1; i <= n; i++) {
        this[i] = ''
        }
    return this
}
function initgame(){
    var intro = "Welcome to Foobar the Bazbarian! \r\nClick on
buttons to navigate\r\nClick RESET to start over\r"
    document.forms[0].dialogbox.value=intro+locDesc[0]
    document.forms[5].score.value=zero
    document.forms[5].itemhere.value="None"
    document.forms[5].your1.value="Empty"
    document.forms[5].your2.value="Empty"
    document.forms[5].your3.value="Empty"
    document.forms[5].your4.value="Empty"
    location=0
}
function upscore(addscore){
    oldscore=document.forms[5].score.value;
    num1=parseFloat(addscore);
    num2=parseFloat(oldscore);
    newscore=num1 + num2;
    document.forms[5].score.value=newscore
    }
```

Part

II

Ch

6

continues

Listing 6.12 Continued

```
function changeLocation(index){
    force=parseFloat(location) + parseFloat(index);
    location=force;
    if (location==0){
        document.forms[0].dialogbox.value=locDesc[0];
        document.forms[5].itemhere.value="None";
        }
    if (location==1){
        document.forms[0].dialogbox.value=locDesc[1];
        document.forms[5].itemhere.value="None";
        }
    if (location==2){
        document.forms[0].dialogbox.value=locDesc[2];
        document.forms[5].itemhere.value="None";
        }
    if (location==3){
        document.forms[0].dialogbox.value=locDesc[3];
        document.forms[5].itemhere.value="None";
        }
    if (location==10){
        document.forms[0].dialogbox.value=locDesc[4];
        document.forms[5].itemhere.value="None";
        }
    if (location==11){
        document.forms[0].dialogbox.value=locDesc[5];
        document.forms[5].itemhere.value="None";
        }
    if (location==12){
        document.forms[0].dialogbox.value=locDesc[6];
        document.forms[5].itemhere.value="None";
        }
    if (location==13){
        document.forms[0].dialogbox.value=locDesc[7];
        document.forms[5].itemhere.value="None";
        }
    if (location==20){
        document.forms[0].dialogbox.value=locDesc[8];
        document.forms[5].itemhere.value="None";
        }
    if (location==21){
        document.forms[0].dialogbox.value=locDesc[9];
        document.forms[5].itemhere.value="None";
        }
    if (location==22){
        document.forms[0].dialogbox.value=locDesc[10];
        document.forms[5].itemhere.value="None";
        }
    if (location==23){
        document.forms[0].dialogbox.value=locDesc[11];
```

```
                document.forms[5].itemhere.value="None";
                }

        if (location==30){
            document.forms[0].dialogbox.value=locDesc[12];
            document.forms[5].itemhere.value="Key";
            }

        if (location==31){
            document.forms[0].dialogbox.value=locDesc[13];
            document.forms[5].itemhere.value="None";
            }

        if (location==32){
            document.forms[0].dialogbox.value=locDesc[14];
            document.forms[5].itemhere.value="None";
            }

        if (location==33){
            document.forms[0].dialogbox.value=locDesc[15];
            document.forms[5].itemhere.value="None";
            pit();
            }
        if (location != 0 && location != 1 && location != 2 && location !=
            ➥3 &&
            location !=10 && location !=11 && location !=12 && location
            ➥!=13 &&
            location !=20 && location !=21 && location !=22 && location
            ➥!=23 &&
            location !=30 && location !=31 && location !=32 && location
            ➥!=33 )
            {
                alert ("You cant go there! The water blocks your way.");
                location=parseFloat(location) - parseFloat(index);
            }


    //alert(force + " and location" + location);
    }

function takeItem(){
    if (document.forms[5].itemhere.value != "None") {
        document.forms[5].your1.value=document.forms[5].itemhere.value;
        upscore(bonus);
        }
    else {
        alert("There's nothing here!")
        }
    }
```

continues

Listing 6.12   Continued

```
function useItem(itemtouse) {

        if (itemtouse == "Key" && location == 2) {
        document.forms[0].dialogbox.value="You Win! The Princess
        ➥gives you a big Kiss, and Hillary reluctantly returns
        ➥you to the land of Bat....\rYAY!"
        upscore(1000);
        }
        else {
            if (itemtouse == "Key" && location == 12) {
                document.forms[0].dialogbox.value="You picked the
                ➥wrong Princess. The Witch cackles as she shoots a
                ➥bolt of flame at your head. You Die!"
                document.forms[5].score.value=zero
            }
            else{
                alert ("I cannot use that here");
                }}
 }

 function pit() {
      document.forms[0].dialogbox.value=
document.forms[0].dialogbox.value + "\rDid I forget to mention the
➥Dragon? Oops. This huge monster thunders up and takes a big bite out of
➥your face. You die."
                document.forms[5].score.value=zero
            }

// end Functions
// end The Engine --></script>
<h1 align=center>Foobar the Bazbarian!</h1>
<table border align=left><tr><td colspan=2><form><!-- form 0 -->
<textarea rows="10" cols="50" name="dialogbox" wrap="virtual">
</textarea></form><tr><td><h4 align="center">Movement</h4>
<table border ><tr><td></td><td><form><!-- form 1 -->
<input type="button" Value="North" Name="GoNorth"
➥onClick="changeLocation(-1)">
</form></td><td></td><tr><td><form><!-- form 2 -->
<input type="button" Value="West" Name="GoWest"
➥onClick="changeLocation(-10)">
</form></td><td align=center><B>GO</B></td><td><form><!-- form 3 -->
<input type="button" Value="East" Name="GoEast"
➥onClick="changeLocation(10)">
</form></td><tr><td><tr><td></td><td><form><!-- form 4 -->
<input type="button" Value="South" Name="GoSouth"
➥onClick="changeLocation(1)">
</form></td><td></td></table>
<td valign=top><form><!-- form 5 -->Your Score: <input type="text"
➥name="score"><br>
```

```
Items Here: <input type="text" name="itemhere"><br>
Your Items:<br>
<input type="text" name="your1"><input type="button" Value="USE"
➥Name="use1" onClick="useItem(document.forms[5].your1.value)"><br>
<input type="text" name="your2"><input type="button" Value="USE"
➥Name="use2" onClick="useItem(document.forms[5].your2.value)"><br>
<input type="text" name="your3"><input type="button" Value="USE"
➥Name="use3" onClick="useItem(document.forms[5].your3.value)"><br>
<input type="text" name="your4"><input type="button" Value="USE"
➥Name="use4" onClick="useItem(document.forms[5].your4.value)"><br>
<input type="button" Value="TAKE ITEM" name="takeme"
➥onClick="takeItem()">
<input type="button" Value="QUIT" name="quitme" onClick="history.go(-
➥1)">
<input type="button" Value="RESET" name="resetme" onClick="initgame()">
</form></table><p><font size="-1">Created and copyright Andrew
Wooldridge</font><p>
<hr align="50%">
You are FOOBAR, the Bazbarian from the land of Bat.
You and the Princess of Zfoeps have been kidnapped by the Wicked
Witch Hillary. As a challenge, Hillary has imprisoned herself
and the Princess in two cages.
You must search this small island to free the Princess!
Search around and find the key to unlock her cage.
If you let out the wrong girl you die! If you
free the Princess you win!
Click RESET to Start. <br clear=left>
Email me if you find a bug.
<a href="mailto:andreww@c2.org">andreww@c2.org</a>
</BODY>
</HTML>
```

FIG. 6.15
Web page view of Foobar
the Bazbarian.

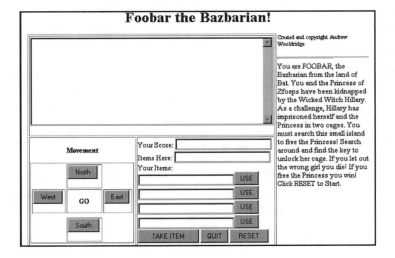

Validating and Submitting a Form

This section covers the final pieces of information you need to complete your exploration of JavaScript and forms. The last two form-based objects, submit and reset, are accompanied with an example of a simple mail-in form that checks the input before it is sent back to you.

The *submit* Object   The submit button was originally intended in HTML to be the final button a user would click to send a form back to the server. It would submit information, send feedback, or present a structured request for new information (you see this in search engines like Yahoo!). With JavaScript, you can now use this button to also send all of the information collected in a form to another window on your browser, or to the same window itself, which causes the contents of the window to change in some way. An example of this is changing the background color of the window based on the user's preference on a form. You create a submit object by using the following syntax:

```
<INPUT
     TYPE="submit"
     NAME="submitName"
     VALUE="buttonText"
     [onClick = "handlerText"]>
```

You access this object's properties and methods by the following syntax:

- submitName.propertyName

- submitName.methodName(parameters)

- formName.elements[index].propertyName

- formName.elements[index].methodName(parameters)

When you click a submit button, it always loads a new page—even if that page is the same page you were already on. This is useful in that you can use a form to change attributes of the current page and see them change when you submit the form. The submit object uses the onClick event handler and can be clicked by using the submitName.click method.

The *reset* Object   The reset button allows a user to completely reset a form's input fields to their defaults. You create a reset object in JavaScript by using the following syntax:

```
<INPUT
     TYPE="reset"
```

```
                NAME="resetName"
                VALUE="buttonText"
                [onClick ="handlerText"]>
```

To access its methods and properties, you use the same familiar syntax, as follows:

- ■ resetName.propertyName

- ■ resetName.methodName(parameters)

- ■ formName.elements[index].propertyName

- ■ formName.elements[index].methodName(parameters)

The reset button uses the same onClick event handler and click method as the submit object.

A Simple Form Validation Example   Listing 6.13 is a simple script that checks all of your input to see that you have placed the correct information inside each field. It then submits the form.

Listing 6.13   Form Input Validation Example

```
<html>
<script language=JavaScript>
<!-- hide me
function testone() {
      if (document.forms[0].elements[0].value==""){
          alert("Please put a name in the first field!")
      }
}

function testtwo (){
     if (document.forms[0].elements[2].value.length <5){
          alert("Please input at least 5 characters")
     }
}

function testthree(){
     if (document.forms[0].elements[4].value=="No"){
          alert("Please change field three!")
     }
}


// end hiding -->


<form>
<h1>Below is a series of fields that you must set before you can send
this form</h1>
```

continues

Part

II

Ch

6

Listing 6.13   Continued

```
<input type=text name=one value=""> Input your name (any text)
<input type=button name=check value=checkme onClick="testone()"><p>
<input type =text name=two >Input at least 5 characters
<input type = button name=checktwo value=checkme onClick="testtwo()"><p>
<input type = text name=three value="No">Change this to something else
<input type=button name=three value=checkme onClick="testthree()"><p>
</form>

</html>
```

From the example in listing 6.13, you can see how an input of type button was used in place of an input of type submit. In a real-world script, you could either use a button input type with an onClick event handler which would then run a check on that specific field, or you could keep the submit button and use an onSubmit event handler to run checks on all of the input fields at once. The difference here is that when you use onClick and the button, you can be more specific as to which area you are checking; whereas, using the more general onSubmit, you can check all the fields at once without asking the visitor to check them. ●

CHAPTER 7

Advanced HTML Objects and Navigation

by Ray Daly

Your users will demand quicker response time as you add more interactivity to your pages. Before JavaScript, most interactive features required your Web page to invoke a CGI script on the server. The more interactivity, the more the users have to wait on the server to deliver new documents. The response time improves dramatically as JavaScript handles interactivity on the browser side instead of waiting on CGI scripts.

To meet this increasing demand for better response time, you will increase the size of your Web documents with JavaScript. This is because your pages are more like applications and less like plain reading material. As your document gets larger, you will incorporate more navigational aids. You will create dynamic elements with JavaScript to let users quickly see the

JavaScript is a new URL type

Use the new `javascript:` URL to execute a function without jumping. This is very useful for replacing grey, rectangular buttons with colorful icons.

Change the hyperlinks

Though you can't change the displayed text of a hyperlink, you can dynamically change where a link will take your user.

Learn the importance of the NAME attribute

JavaScript puts document elements into arrays. You can reference by the array index, if you know it, but you will find names easier to use.

Select input verification

Multiple choice often leads to more accurate responses from users. JavaScript allows verification with the `select` element.

Build a browser within a browser

With frames and dynamic hyperlinks you can build a new type of browser. Take a look at an example with Internet cameras and an FTP auto dialer.

material they want and skip irrelevant information. And you will do this without waiting on the server.

Controlling the flow of user interaction is critical to good design. You can confuse your users with the multiple windows and frames possible in the new browsers. The dynamic capability of JavaScript allows you to create new documents in response to your users' preferences. For example, if the viewer selects a favorite sport, the hyperlink named "Last Year's Champion" could vary based on the viewer's selection.

With JavaScript features, you can transform the browser from static displays to interactive applications. There are a variety of examples in this chapter which let you try out the new dynamics of hyperlinks, anchors, and selection lists. The chapter concludes with a much larger application that shows you the possibilities of the new browser. ■

Link In with JavaScript

Click and follow the designer's lead. That's how people navigate the Web: they follow the links chosen by the designer. Click the same link a hundred times and it takes you to the same page every time. Every user is different and has different expectations. For example, a link that's appropriate for an adult might be too complex for a young child.

This limitation of HTML drives many people to build a better Web page. You probably looked at a few poorly designed Web pages and were frustrated by the hyperlinks designed into those pages. As a designer, you might have chosen other sites to link to. So people build other Web pages and try to make them perfect for their audiences. They still end up with pages in which the viewer follows the designer.

Your links are now dynamic with JavaScript. Based on options a user can select, clicking the link takes the user to different places without waiting on a CGI script to feed a page from the server. Also, by using the frames and windows, your existing page is not necessarily replaced by the new page. Your browser can be a kaleidoscope on the Web simultaneously viewing multiple sites around the world. Or you can pull in different publications based on the day of the week.

Additions to the *LINK* Syntax

You are probably familiar with using the `link` tag in an HTML document. A very simple example is the following:

```
<A HREF="http://www.yoursite.com">Click here</A>
```

Your browser would display "Click here" as a hyperlink.

The reference of a `LINK` is a URL or a location. You know the World Wide Web protocol, which is `http://` as you see in the preceding example. You could also have used the `MailTo` protocol (for example, **mailto:info@mailcall.com**). There are formats for FTP, Gopher, and File. JavaScript makes two additional protocols available: `javascript:` and `about`.

***javascript:* protocol** A new URL type is now defined in JavaScript for the `LINK` tag. The protocol is simply `javascript:`. For example, you could specify `javascript: history.go(-1)` as the URL. When used as the URL for a LINK, the browser executes the statement following the colon. In the following example it executes: `history.go(-1)`. As a useful example, try adding the following line to any page:

```
<A HREF="javascript: history.go(-1)">Go back to previous page</A>
```

This is particularly useful on documents displayed in browser windows where you have disabled the toolbar.

When you click this hyperlink, the browser takes you back to the previous page in your history list. If you want to test this, open your browser and load your default home page. Then load the page in listing 7.1 called history.htm on the CD-ROM. Clicking the hyperlink returns you to your default home page.

On the CD

Listing 7.1   history.htm   Demo of *javascript* URL

```
<HTML><HEAD><TITLE>history.htm by Ray Daly</TITLE>
</HEAD><BODY>
<P>Juno said, "<A HREF="javascript:history.go(-1)">
History will repeat itself.</A>"<P>
</BODY></HTML>
```

Part

II

Ch

7

Hyperlinks can also behave like buttons in forms. Instead of placing a function in an `onClick` event, place the function behind the `javascript:` protocol. Clicking the hyperlink will have the same effect as clicking a button. In other words, replace the following code for a button in a form:

```
<INPUT TYPE="botton" VALUE="click here" onClick="myfunction()">
```

with this code for using a hyperlink:

```
<A HREF="javascript: myfunction()">click here</A>
```

Now let's take this a step further and replace the grey, rectangular JavaScript button with your own colorful icons. Again, use the javascript: protocol, but this time use it with the IMG tag. Here's some sample code:

```
<A HREF="javascript: myfunction()"><IMG SRC="youricon.gif"></A>
```

This gives you the ability to make your own shape, size, and color buttons! Imagine how bright and colorful a simple calculator can now appear.

The code for creating a button, a text link, and an icon is in listing 7.2. Pressing any one of these items produces the same result.

On the CD

Listing 7.2   Substituting Text and Icons for Buttons

```
<HTML><HEAD><TITLE>jsbutton.htm by Ray Daly </TITLE>
<SCRIPT LANGUAGE="JavaScript">
function netalert() {
     alert('Any function could go here')
}
</SCRIPT>
</HEAD><BODY>
<P><B>You can substitute icons for buttons or links for buttons</B><BR>
<FORM><INPUT TYPE="button"  VALUE="same as link or icon"
    onClick="netalert()"></FORM>
<A HREF="javascript: netalert()">same as icon or button</A><BR>
<P>This icon will function the same as a button or link<BR>
<A HREF="javascript: netalert()"> <IMG SRC="helpmark.gif"></A>
</P></BODY></HTML>
```

You can take this concept one step further by using imagemaps. Imagemaps are graphics with active areas. Click one area and you link to one site, click another part of the image and you link to another. Geographical maps and directories are common uses of imagemaps.

When coding an imagemap you use URLs to instruct the browser. By substituting in the javascript: protocol, you can now create imagemaps that execute various JavaScript functions instead of jumping to another location.

Prior to Netscape Navigator 2.0, all imagemaps were executed on the server. Now you can create client-side imagemaps where the browser does not need to wait on results from the server. Click an image and the browser immediately executes the instruction.

Coding an imagemap requires that URLs be specified for various regions of the image. With client-side imagemaps, you can substitute the javascript: protocol. Clicking the imagemap can now execute JavaScript functions as well as jump to locations specified in URLs.

NOTE To enable client-side imagemaps, Netscape introduced a new attribute to the IMG element called USEMAP (see **http://home.netscape.com/assist/ net_sites/html_extensions_3.html**). It is added to the IMG tag to tell the browser to invoke client-side imagemapping by reading information from a MAP element. The syntax is:

```
<IMG SRC="yourimage.gif" USEMAP="yourfile.html#mapname">
```

where mapname is the name of a MAP element in the document called yourfile.html.

The MAP element must have a name in order to be referenced by the USEMAP attribute. Contained within the MAP element are AREA tags. A MAP element usually contains more than one AREA tag, one for each different region of the imagemap. The syntax is:

```
<AREA [SHAPE="shape"] COORDS="x,y,..." [HREF="reference"] [NOHREF]>
```

where shape can be RECT (retangles), POLY (polygons), CIRCLE (circle), and DEFAULT (default). COORDS specifies the points that define the shape. You then have the option to specify an action using the HREF attribute. Or you can specify no action using NOHREF. ■

In JavaScript, you can specify the reference to use the javascript: protocol. For example, this code defines a rectangular area where the browser loads the previous page from the history list:

```
<AREA SHAPE="rect" COORDS="0,0,100,50" HREF="javascript:history.go(-1)">
```

You can have the browser take you to new locations, execute a JavaScript statement, or a JavaScript function. Your Web pages are more alive than ever now. Listing 7.3 shows a script for creating a client-side imagemap with the javascript: protocol.

Listing 7.3   Client-Side Imagemap with *javascript:* Protocol

```
<HTML><HEAD><TITLE>imagesid.htm by Ray Daly</TITLE>
<SCRIPT LANGUAGE="JavaScript">
function sayhi () {
    alert ('Alert poped up from an Image Map')
}
</SCRIPT></HEAD><BODY>
<P><B>Demo of Client Side Image Mapping and the <I>javascript</I>
➥protocol.</B><P>
<IMG SRC="imagesid.gif" USEMAP="#mapdemo">
<MAP NAME="mapdemo">
<AREA SHAPE="rect" COORDS="0,0,100,100" HREF="javascript:history.go(-
➥1)">
<AREA SHAPE="rect" COORDS="100,0,200,100" HREF="javascript:sayhi()">
<AREA SHAPE="rect" COORDS="200,0,300,100" HREF="http://www.yahoo.com">
</MAP>
</BODY></HTML>
```

CAUTION

A `javascript:xxx()` call replaces a URL. The browser tries to interpret any return from a function call as if it were a URL. If the browser does not understand the return value, it reloads the current page. When that occurs, any window globals that you set during the `xxx()` function call will be lost.

The other new protocol is the `about:` protocol. When used as a location for a link, it provides Navigator information (see listing 7.4, which can also be found in the about.htm file on the CD-ROM). In its basic format without any arguments, it is the same as selecting About Netscape from the Help menu. When used with the plug-ins argument, the page displayed is the same as About Plugs from the Help window. The last usage is with the argument cache which is supposed to display the disk cache statistics.

N O T E   On Windows NT, this features does not work.

On the CD

Listing 7.4   about.htm   Demo of *about:* Protocol

```
<HTML><HEAD><TITLE>about.htm by Ray Daly</TITLE>
</HEAD><BODY>
<P>Demo of the <I>about:</I> protocol:
<UL><LI><A HREF="about:">about:</A></LI>
```

```
<LI><A HREF="about:cache">about:cache</A></LI>
<LI><A HREF="about:plug-ins">about:plug-ins</A></LI>
</UL><P>
</BODY></HTML>
```

Properties of the *LINK* Object

Each object has properties. The properties of the LINK object tell you about the URL. There is also a property to tell you the target for the document. I have created a small page that shows all of the LINK properties in action (see fig. 7.1 and listing 7.5). The code for this page can also be found in the linkprop.htm file on the CD-ROM.

FIG. 7.1
All of the properties, except TARGET, extract substrings from the HREF property.

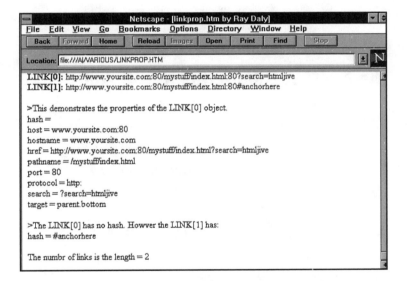

Listing 7.5   linkprop.htm   Demo of *LINK* Object Properties

```
<HTML><HEAD><TITLE>linkprop.htm by Ray Daly</TITLE></HEAD><BODY><P>
<B>LINK[0]:   </B>
<A HREF="http://www.yoursite.com:80/mystuff/index.html?search=htmljive"
TARGET="parent.bottom">
http://www.yoursite.com:80/mystuff/index.html:80?search=htmljive</A>
<BR><B>LINK[1]:   </B>
<A HREF="http://www.yoursite.com:80/mystuff/index.html#anchorhere"
TARGET="parent.bottom">
http://www.yoursite.com:80/mystuff/index.html:80#anchorhere</A>
```

continues

Part

II

Ch

7

Listing 7.5 Continued

```
<BR><BR>>This demonstrates the properties of the LINK[0] object.
<SCRIPT LANGUAGE="JavaScript">
document.write( "<BR>hash = " + document.links[0].hash)
document.write( "<BR>host = " + document.links[0].host)
document.write( "<BR>hostname = " + document.links[0].hostname)
document.write( "<BR>href = " + document.links[0].href)
document.write( "<BR>pathname = " + document.links[0].pathname)
document.write( "<BR>port = " + document.links[0].port)
document.write( "<BR>protocol = " + document.links[0].protocol)
document.write( "<BR>search = " + document.links[0].search)
document.write( "<BR>target = " + document.links[0].target)
document.write( "<P>>The LINK[0] has no hash.  ")
document.write("Howver the LINK[1] has:<BR>")
document.write( "hash = " + document.links[1].hash)
document.write("<BR><BR>The numbr of links is the length = ")
document.write( document.links.length)
</SCRIPT></BODY></HTML>
```

The *NAME* Attribute Has New Significance

Prior to putting JavaScript into HTML pages, there was not much point in using the NAME attribute, so my tags remained nameless. NAME was only used for anchors and when sending form information to a CGI script.

As you use JavaScript to make your links dynamic, you need to distinguish between the various links on your page. The properties of the link object are accessible using the following format:

```
document.links[index].propertyname
```

In using this format, you need to know the index number. The index number is assigned to each LINK object in sequence as it is loaded by the browser. The first link loaded has the index of 0, the second is 1, and so on. So you need to keep track of the order in which the LINK objects are loaded. This is the default method of accessing properties.

Often, a simpler means is to name the elements that are referenced by your JavaScript code. Therefore, using our first example, add the NAME attribute:

```
<A NAME="myname" HREF="http://www.yoursite.com">Click here</A>
```

Now your JavaScript code can access the properties of this object without having to know the index number. Simply use the following format:

```
document.name.propertyName
```

Using the NAME attribute is probably familiar to you if you have used anchors in your HTML documents. It is the identical format and is still how you create anchors. So whenever you use the NAME attribute for your JavaScript code, you are also adding a new anchor.

LINK Events: *onMouseOver* and *onClick*

JavaScript code executes when the browser recognizes certain events. The link object recognizes two events: onClick and onMouseOver. You will probably use onClick in most of your code and onMouseOver only occasionally. The following will remind you of the format of these events used with the LINK tag.

▶ **See** "Event Handlers in *<FORM>* Elements," in chapter 3, **p. 99**.

 TIP When debugging code involving the status bar, make sure you include the statement `return true`.

The format is the same as for other events. Use our example, as follows:

```
<A NAME="myname" HREF="http://www.yoursite.com"
onMouseOver="window.status='Please visit my site.'; return true">
Click here</A>
```

This places the message `Please visit my site.` in the status bar when the viewer places the mouse pointer over the hyperlink. This overrides most browsers that would display the URL in the status bar in this event.

You can use this feature to change the look and feel of your pages. Instead of showing the URL, which is geek talk to many, change your links to verbally tell people where the links take them. So instead of displaying something like

```
http://www.cris.com/~raydaly/sponsors.html
```

you can display an easier to understand message in the status bar, such as

```
Hyperlink to "Sponsor of the Day"
```

The `onClick` event uses the same format. Also, the example application for this chapter makes frequent use of the `onClick` event. The following is a short example:

```
<A NAME="mymessage" HREF="http://www.newsite.com"
onClick="alert('Thanks for visiting.  Enjoy the new site.')">
Visit Newsite</A>
```

This code displays an alert dialog box prior to jumping to the new site (see fig. 7.2). Only after the user clicks OK in the dialog box does the browser hyperlink to www.newsite.com.

CAUTION

The `onMouseOver` event is trapped at each boundary of a link. This results in an event occuring twice as the point enters and leaves the link.

If you use the `onMouseOver` event to write to the status bar, you find that if you move your mouse too quickly you miss the status write. This is because it is rapidly replaced by the browser's own response to the event. When you exit, the status written stays there until you encounter another link. If you want to use the content of your link in a function called from an `onMouseOver` handler, you can pass the function the keyword `this`. Links are treated like any other JavaScript object.

FIG. 7.2

You can display a dialog box prior to hyperlinking to a new site.

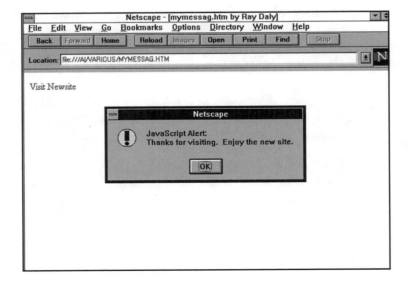

CAUTION

You might confuse your users by changing the HREF using onClick. Users often look to the status bar to see the URL that the hyperlink will take them to. When you assign the HREF attribute of the LINK, it is displayed in the status bar. When using the onClick event you can set the HREF to a different URL. By reading the status bar the user may assume he is going to the first URL, but instead your JavaScript code takes him to the URL specified by the onClick statement.

In the following example, the status bar makes it appear that the link is to Yahoo's site, but the code takes you to Infoseek. It goes to show that you cannot even trust links anymore.

```
<A NAME="searchme" HREF="http://www.yahoo.com"
onClick="this.href='http://www.infoseek.com'">
Search Internet for a Topic</A>
```

To avoid such a deception in the status bar, just add onMouseOver to change the contents of status bar. For the preceding example, just insert the following as the second line:

```
onMouseOver="window.status='Will take you to a search engine.';
➥return true"
```

Change Link URLs, Not the Displayed Text

Unlike text boxes, JavaScript cannot change the hyperlink text displayed by the browser. In listing 7.6, the hyperlink text is Yahoo!. Regardless of the changes you make to this object, this stays on the screen.

As you design your dynamic links, consider the words and images that reflect the new nature of your hyperlinks. For example, you could write a simple random URL function. When you click the link, it takes you to a random search site. You might use the words, "Spin the wheel to a random search site," or add a graphic image of a roulette wheel.

Listing 7.6 is an example showing how to make a dynamic link to Yahoo! The browser simply displays the hyperlink text Yahoo! When you click this link before 6:00 p.m., you link to the text-only version of Yahoo! But after 6:00 p.m., you link to the regular graphic version of Yahoo! So the HREF changes, but the displayed text stays the same. The following code can also be found in the file atlyahoo.htm on the CD-ROM.

On the CD

Listing 7.6   atlyahoo.htm   Page with Alternative Yahoo! Links

```
<HTML>
<HEAD><SCRIPT Language="JavaScript">
function timeText () {
    today=new Date()
    hour = today.getHours()   //...get hour of the dat
    if (hour>18 ) {
        //...after 6:00 p.m use graphics
        yahooURL= "http://www.yahoo.com/"
    } else {
        //...all other times use test mode
        yahooURL = "http://www.yahoo.com/text/"
    }
    return yahooURL    //...result of function is a URL
}
</SCRIPT></HEAD>
<BODY>
<A NAME="yahooLink" HREF=""
onClick="this.href=timeText()"   //...get the right URL
onMouseOver="window.status='Hyperlink to Yahoo!'; return true">
Yahoo!</A>
</BODY></HTML>
```

The URLs are not just for the Web. For example, suppose you have a fairly lengthy form to be completed by a customer, and one of the first entries asks about the customer's location. Based on that entry, you might dynamically change the mailto address. Then any e-mail the customer might send is directed to the proper salesperson. Listing 7.5 asks the user where he is located. (This code is included on the CD-ROM as atlmail2.htm.) Based on his selection, e-mail goes to a different address. Figure 7.3 shows the result of listing 7.7.

On the CD

Listing 7.7   atlmail2.htm   Page that Switches *Mailto:* Addresses

```
<HTML><HEAD></HEAD>
<BODY>
<FORM>
<B>Where are you located?</B><BR>
<INPUT TYPE="radio" NAME="country" onClick="salespersonMailto=
    'mailto:worldsales@company.com'"> Outside North America<BR>
<INPUT TYPE="radio" NAME="country" onClick="salespersonMailto=
    'mailto:nasales@company.com'"> North America<BR>
</FORM>
<A NAME="salesperson" HREF="mailto:info@yoursite.com"
➥onClick="this.href=salespersonMailto">
Email your salesperson.</A>
</BODY></HTML>
```

FIG. 7.3
Depending on the selection, e-mail goes to a different address. Remember to include a default address or use a dialog box to ask the user to make a choice before trying to send e-mail.

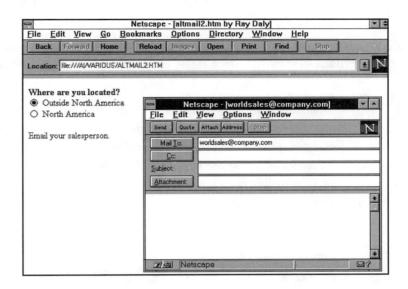

Display Documents in Frames and Windows

The LINK tag now enables the designer to specify the TARGET for the URL. This is an optional attribute. If it is not used, the new page simply replaces the previous page as before. But JavaScript allows you to display these new pages in frames or new windows.

One target for your link can be a new browser window. The windows will generally look and function as if you opened a second browser. Therefore, the original page is still displayed in your first window, and the new page is displayed in the second. You can reduce the functionality of these windows by changing their features when the windows are open.

A frame is the other possible target for your link. Frames divide your browser window into two or more areas. Inside these frames you can display standard Web pages or create your own documents. The applications constructed in this chapter use frames.

▶ **See** the section "Frames and JavaScript" in chapter 19, "Using Frames and Cookies in Advanced Applications," for more information on using frames, **p. 661**.

The following code displays the Yahoo! page in the frame labeled "three."

```
<A HREF=" "onClick="this.href=http://www.yahoo.com" "
➥TARGET="three">Show picture Tri</A>
```

Part

II

Ch

7

Windows and frames are often a vital part of a design with dynamic links. Using JavaScript code behind a link, you can build new types of browsers. You can also build new tools. For example, you might bring a page into a frame, analyze it, and display the results in another frame.

One area of a frame is often like a control panel that can control the display in another. For example, researchers constantly use different search engines on the Web, and these sites are bookmarked. But it would be handier if these sites were always available like the Directory buttons in Netscape Navigator. Listings 7.8, 7.9, and 7.10, (called searchdr.htm, display.htm, and search.htm on the CD-ROM), show how the top frame contains one line with hyperlinks to eight different search engines. This frame is like a control panel with the documents targeted at the lower frame. Figure 7.4 shows the result.

Listing 7.8   searchdr.htm   Top Page for SearchDr

```
<HTML><HEAD><TITLE> searchdr.htm </TITLE></HEAD>
<FRAMESET ROWS="60,*">
   <FRAME SRC="search.htm" NAME="buttons">
   <FRAME SRC="display.htm" NAME="display">
</FRAMESET>
</HTML>
```

Listing 7.9   display.htm   Initial Screen in Display Frame

```
<HTML><HEAD><TITLE>Part of searchdr.htm: display.htm</TITLE></HEAD>
<BODY><H1>Display Area</H1>
<P>Click on any hyperlink above to display a search engine here.
</BODY></HTML>
```

Listing 7.10   search.htm   Frame for SearchDr with Hyperlinks

```
<HTML><HEAD><TITLE>Part of searchdr.htm:  search.htm</TITLE></HEAD>
<BODY>
<A HREF="http://www.altavista.digital.com/" TARGET="display"> Alta
➥Vista</A>   --
<A HREF="http://www.excite.com" TARGET="display">Excite</A>   --
<A HREF="http://www.lycos.com/" TARGET="display">Lycos</A>   --
<A HREF="http://www.mckinley.com/" TARGET="display">Magellan</A>   --
<A HREF="http://www.nlightn.com/" TARGET="display">NlightN</A>   --
<A HREF="http://www.opentext.com:8080/" TARGET="display">Open Text</A>   --
```

```
<A HREF="http://www.webcrawler.com" TARGET="display">WebCrawler</A> --
<A HREF="http://www.yahoo.com" TARGET="display">Yahoo!</A>
</BODY>
</HTML>
```

For a more substantial example, we will construct an application in this chapter called Internet Tri-Eye. It will truly give you a different view of the world. In listing 7.11 and its corresponding figure 7.5, you see the frames used in creating Internet Tri-Eye. This code can be found in the file trieye.htm on the CD-ROM.

Although this will be displayed using your browser, it is not the same old browser anymore. Frames and dynamic hyperlinks let you reshape the browser.

FIG. 7.4
SearchDr puts any of the listed search engines in the frame marked Display. When you create frames, let the default frames provide instructions to the new users.

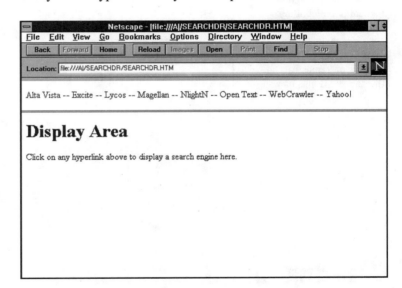

Listing 7.11   trieye.htm   Frame Document for Internet Tri-Eye

On the CD

```
<HTML><HEAD><TITLE>Internet Tri-Eye</TITLE></HEAD>
<FRAMESET ROWS="*,200">
    <FRAMESET COLS="33%,34%, 33%">
        <FRAME SRC="one.htm" NAME="one">
        <FRAME SRC="two.htm" NAME="two">
        <FRAME SRC="three.htm" NAME="three">
    </FRAMESET>
    <FRAME SRC="guide.htm" NAME="guide">
```

continues

Part
II

Ch

7

Listing 7.11 Continued

```
<NOFRAMES>
<H1>Internet Tri-Eye</H1>
<P><B>Internet Tri-Eye</B> is a demonstration of several features of
Javascript.  To view and use this program you need a Javascript
compatible browser like Netscape 2.0.
</NOFRAMES>

</FRAMESET></HTML>
```

FIG. 7.5

The frames used to create Internet Tri-Eye will contain the control panel at the bottom and display Internet camera pictures from around the world. The contents of frames can be .GIF and .JPEG files as well as HTML documents.

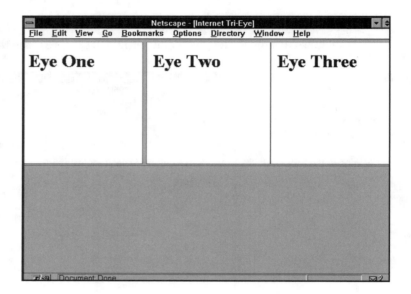

Creating and Using Anchors

Anchors are not commonly used on Web pages. If you have an alphabetical listing, an anchor might take you to a particular section. However, most sites have tended to use rather short pages. These pages might be one or two screens in length and do not often need anchors.

As you develop JavaScript applications, your documents will get longer. Also, with frames and multiple windows, less of your document is displayed on-screen. Your users will want you to take them right to the information instead of being required to scroll through your page. Anchors help you deliver your information more directly.

Your HTML Elements

The pages you design with JavaScript are fundamentally different from most other HTML pages. Because they are so interactive, your viewers will spend more time on your pages than the average HTML page. They may also save the page because it is not just a page of text anymore, but an application.

These differences should make you consider making your pages bigger than before. The user may be willing to wait a little longer for a page to load if that means it will be richer.

Since your pages are now applications, users will expect quick responses to their inputs; you cannot deliver that promise if you have to keep requesting documents from the server. Instead, take what you might have normally put on several different pages and build it into one big page. This can also benefit users because when they save the page, they can have the complete application.

For example, with your Great JavaScript Application you might have a page of help and documentation. Given the sophistication of your application, this could be fairly lengthy, and normally you might consider separating it from the application page. However, if you follow that course, when users save the application, they will not have the help when loading it from their hard drives. Instead, consider making a bigger page that includes all of the help information and documentation. Then set up anchors to the help topics so people can easily refer to them (see fig. 7.6).

FIG. 7.6
By combining multiple pages into one, your JavaScript application becomes more responsive. The fewer the requests to the server, the more responsive your application is.

Regular HTML Page

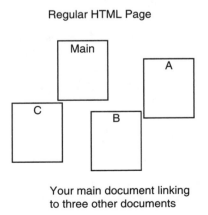

Your main document linking to three other documents

Longer JavaScript Page

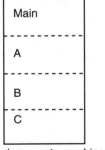

All documents combined into one document with hyperlinks now going to anchors

When you have longer documents, anchors become crucial for navigating around the document. Instead of scrolling through screen after screen, click the keyword and you have found your place. Use this technique for documentation, help, or other reference material.

Anchor Any Text or Element

Use anchors in the standard way and in new ways with JavaScript. Anchors enable you to specify a destination for a hyperlink within a document. For example, assume you want to be able to jump to the words, "Part Two." Then you would put this code in your document:

```
<A NAME="jumphere">Part Two</A>
```

Note that the name does not have to be the same as the text. In this example the name is jumphere, and the text displayed by the browser is "Part Two." To create the hyperlink to this section, use the following code:

```
<A HREF="#jumphere"> Go To Part Two</A>
```

This is useful not only within the current document, but also when pulling up information within frames or in other windows. For example, take the case of a form in which you are verifying the input. You would probably use a dialog box to notify the viewer that the input is out of range; then use an anchor at the description of the text box, and link the browser to it with hypertext. Now the text box is right at the top of the screen awaiting a new input.

N O T E   You can use the anchor to scroll the page to the place you want. The FOCUS and the SELECT methods can do the same with form elements. However, if your form elements have labels, these methods will move the element to the top of the screen cutting off your label. If you want your users to be able to read the labels, anchor the labels and jump to them.

For comparison, both techniques are used in the code formname.htm on the CD-ROM (see listing 7.12 and fig. 7.7). ■

Anchors can also provide you with a new way to control the flow in completing a form, as shown in listing 7.12 and figure 7.7. Many times in completing paper forms, you see such instruction as "If you answered NO to question 6, skip to question 9." With JavaScript and anchors, you can look at the response to a question, then—depending on the answer—automatically jump to the anchor for the next appropriate question.

On the CD

Listing 7.12   veriname.htm   Anchors in Form Verification

```html
<HTML><HEAD><TITLE>verfname.htm by Ray Daly</TITLE>
<SCRIPT LANGUAGE="JavaScript">
function skip2 (form) {
    if (form.q1.value>11) {
        alert ('You get FREE Overnite Shipping.  Skip to question 12.')
         form.q2.value="FREE Overnight"
         window.location="#a12"
         //...jump to anchor a12
    }
    if (form.q1.value<0) {
        alert ('You can not return these items')
        form.q1.value=""
        form.q1.focus()
        form.q1.select()
        //...instead of jumping to an anchor, this uses focus and select method
    }
  }
</SCRIPT></HEAD><BODY><FORM>
<P>Try filling in quanties of 16, 8 and -3.  </P>
<B>1.)  How many do you want?</B><BR>
FREE Overnite shipping when ordering 12 or more.<BR>
<INPUT NAME="q1" TYPE="Text" onBlur="skip2(this.form)"><BR>
<a NAME="a2">
<B>2.)  How do you want it shipped?</B><BR>
<INPUT NAME="q2" TYPE="Text" ><BR>
<BR><BR><BR><BR><BR><BR>
<I>(more questions are listed here)
<BR><BR><BR><BR><BR><BR>
<BR><BR><BR><BR><BR><BR>
<B>12.)  What color do you want?</B><BR>
<A NAME="a12"><INPUT NAME="q12" TYPE="Text" ><BR>
<BR><BR><BR><BR><BR><BR>
<I>(more questions are listed here)
<BR><BR><BR><BR><BR><BR>
<BR><BR><BR><BR><BR><BR>
</FORM>
</BODY></HTML>
```

FIG. 7.7
You will see a visual difference in comparing the use of anchors to control the flow or the use of the FOCUS and SELECT methods.

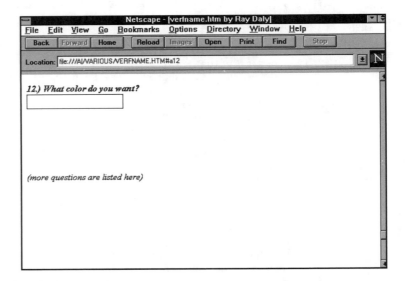

 TIP When debugging your JavaScript, check your quotes. Although double quotes and single quotes work the same, you cannot start with a double quote and end with a single quote, or vice versa. Your quotes must match or you will end up with errors several lines later.

Selection or Scrolling—Your Option

What kind of test did you prefer in school: multiple choice or essay? You probably found multiple choice easier. Certainly, your teacher found multiple choice easier to grade.

When you design interactive forms, your viewers probably also find your requests easier to understand in a multiple choice format. Understanding this aspect of form design, you have probably used radio buttons and checkboxes. These are excellent devices for presenting a limited number of choices.

When you present the viewer with a large number of choices, use the SELECT element. This enables you to present a large list without cluttering up your page. A good use would be geographical lists, such as states or countries in address forms.

Syntax in Review

Although using the SELECT element makes it easier for your viewer, you have to do more work. Remember, SELECT is an element within a form, so it must be between the <FORM>...</FORM> tags. The syntax of SELECT is one of the most complicated of all the HTML elements. You should be familiar with most of this specification. To support JavaScript you can optionally include event handlers of onBlur, onChange, and onFocus (see listing 7.13).

Listing 7.13   Using *onBlur, onChange,* and *onFocus* with the *SELECT* Element

```
<SELECT
   NAME="selectName"
   [SIZE="integer"]
   [MULTIPLE]
   [onBlur="handlerText"]
   [onChange="handlerText"]
   [onFocus="handlerText"]>
   <OPTION VALUE="optionValue" [SELECTED]> textToDisplay
      [ ... <OPTION> textToDisplay]
</SELECT>
```

The SELECT tag has one required attribute: NAME. This name and a value associated with the selected OPTION element are sent to the server when a form is submitted. The NAME attribute can also be used as an anchor. An optional attribute is SIZE, which tells the browser how many options to display.

MULTIPLE is an optional attribute of SELECT, which changes the list so that one or multiple items can be selected by the user. This type of list is called a *scrolling list*.

The SELECT tag always contains two or more OPTION elements. This is where you list the items for the user to select. Each OPTION has a text property that is displayed in the select box. There is also an associated VALUE property that is sent to the server when the form is submitted along with the name of the SELECT tag. The last attribute of OPTION is itself optional. The SELECTED attribute is a means to have

Part
II

Ch
7

one of the items in your selection list be the default when the page is displayed. The only additions to this specification for JavaScript are the events discussed in the next section.

onChange, onBlur, and onFocus Events for SELECT

Like other objects in JavaScript, the SELECT object responds to events. Here you will learn specific uses of onFocus, onChange, and onBlur with the SELECT objects.

▶ **See** the section "Event Handlers in *<FORM>* Elements" in chapter 3 for more on focus, blur, and change events, **p. 99**.

onChange   onChange is the most common event that you monitor in SELECT. It looks for change from one selection to another. When the event is triggered, your code executes. An example of using onChange, by selecting a country, is shown in listing 7.14 and figure 7.8. Say you change a country selection from the United States to Mexico. Then onChange triggers a JavaScript function that changes the currency type from U.S. dollars to pesos. However, if you did not change the selection, the event would not trigger.

 TIP   When using SELECT, you have a built-in associate array. Each OPTION value relates to a selection.

Listing 7.14   money.htm   Currency by Country Using *onChange*

```
<HTML><HEAD><TITLE>money.htm by Ray Daly</TITLE>
<SCRIPT LANGUAGE="JavaScript">
function changeCurrency(form) {
   form.currency.value=form.country.options[form.country.selectedIndex].value
}
</SCRIPT></HEAD>
<BODY><FORM>
<P>Demonstrates <I>onChange</I> event.  After you make a country selection,
the currency does not change until you click somewhere else.</P>
<B>Select your country</B><BR>
<SELECT NAME="country" onChange="changeCurrency(this.form)">
<OPTION VALUE="US Dollars">USA
<OPTION VALUE="Canadian Dollars">Canada
<OPTION VALUE="Peso">Mexico
</SELECT>
<P><B>Prices are displayed in:</B><BR>
<INPUT TYPE="text" NAME="currency">
</FORM></BODY>
</HTML>
```

FIG. 7.8
You will probably find that onChange does not work as you expect with SELECT. You have to click somewhere outside the SELECT box for the change to take effect.

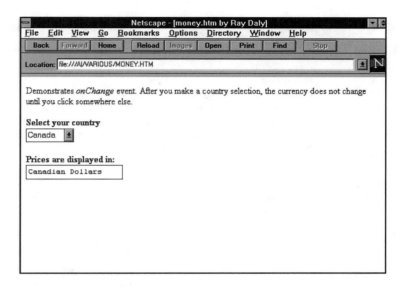

onBlur onBlur is a good way to verify proper selections. This event looks for when the focus is no longer on the SELECT object. In other words, it looks for when you click somewhere other than the current element. When the event is triggered, you could execute a verification function. Although you can use the onChange event to verify selections, using onBlur might ensure the viewer's choice. This is because the onBlur event triggers JavaScript code even if a change has not occurred.

Verification is not always simply an *either/or* choice. For example, you might have a selection with some uncommon, but acceptable answers. This might be an unusual color for a piece of merchandise. For this circumstance, you might verify that this is indeed the correct selection, even if the user made no change in his selection. In listing 7.15, the user is simply notified with an alert dialog box if he wants to buy less than a dozen eggs (see fig. 7.9).

Listing 7.15 eggs.htm Eggs Come by the Dozen Using *onBlur*

```
<HTML><HEAD><TITLE>eggs.htm by Ray Daly</TITLE>
<SCRIPT LANGUAGE="JavaScript">
function checkEggs(form) {
  form.eggs.value=form.quantity.options[form.quantity.selectedIndex].value
    if (form.quantity.selectedIndex==0) {
        alert ('People usually order eggs by the dozen.')
    }
```

Part

II

Ch

7

continues

Listing 7.15   Continued

```
}
</SCRIPT></HEAD>
<BODY><FORM>
<P>Demonstrates <I>onBlur</I> event.  After you select a quanity,
the number on-hold is not updated until you click somewhere else.</P>
<B>How many eggs do you want:</B><BR>
<SELECT NAME="quantity" onBlur="checkEggs(this.form)">
    <OPTION VALUE="6">Half dozen
    <OPTION VALUE="12">Dozen
    <OPTION VALUE="24">Two dozen
</SELECT>
<P><B>We are holding this many eggs for you:</B><BR>
<INPUT TYPE="text" NAME="eggs">
</FORM></BODY>
</HTML>
```

FIG. 7.9

The event onBlur works almost exactly like onChange, except the JavaScript code is executed even if the selection does not change.

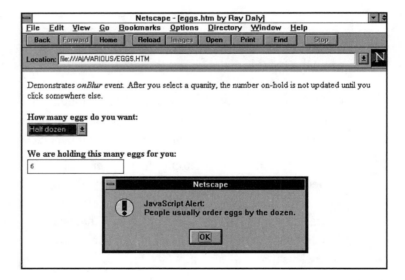

onFocus   onFocus is an excellent way to assist the viewer in completing your form. It looks for the viewer moving the cursor to the SELECT element and then triggers code prior to any entry by the viewer.

For example, each question in your form can include particular instructions that assist the viewer in making a proper selection. When onFocus is triggered, your code could display in a separate window or frame the instructions related to that question. Or if you require a numeric answer to be calculated, why not pop up a calculator in a new window? That's what happens in the math word problem presented in listing 7.16 (see fig. 7.10).

T I P It is possible to create an endless loop using the onBlur event. To avoid this trap, create a flag variable. Initially set it to zero. Every time you call the routine, check the value of the flag. If the flag is zero, then execute the rest of the routine and set the flag to one. If the flag is not zero, then the routine has already been executed once so you don't need to execute it again.

On the CD

Listing 7.16 wordprob.htm Tricky Math Word Problem Using *onFocus*

```
<HTML><HEAD><TITLE>wordprob.htm by Dr. Ray Daly III </TITLE>
<SCRIPT LANGUAGE="JavaScript">
function giveAnswer(form) {
    if (form.answer.selectedIndex==2) {
        alert ('People usually forget trains run on two tracks.')
    }
}
already=0
function callCalculator(form) {
if (already==0) {
    already = 1  //...only need to open this window once
newWindow=window.open("http://www.netscape.com/comprod/products/
➥navigator/version_2.0/script/calc.html")
}
}
</SCRIPT></HEAD>
<BODY><FORM>
<P>Demonstrates <I>onFocus</I> event.  As soon as you put click on the
SELECT element, then a calculator pops up.</P>
<P><B>Railroad track is ordered for three sections of track.  The first
is 15 miles long.  The second is 23 miles long and the third is 6 miles
long.  How many miles of track needs to be ordered to complete construc-
tion?
</B></P>
<P><B>What is your answer:</B><BR>
<SELECT NAME="answer" onFocus="callCalculator(this.form)"
    onBlur="giveAnswer(this.form)">
    <OPTION VALUE="21">21
    <OPTION VALUE="29">29
    <OPTION VALUE="88">88
</SELECT>
</FORM></BODY>
</HTML>
```

Part

II

Ch

7

FIG. 7.10
When you design your JavaScript applications, remember that you can call up other people's applications like calculators.

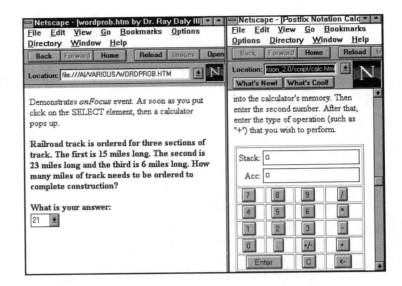

Dynamically Change the Selection, Not the Text

Unlike its textbox cousins, TEXT and TEXTAREA, your code cannot change the text displayed in the SELECT list. Although your viewer may have chosen Canada as the country, your code cannot substitute the name of the provinces for the names of the states as the text displayed by the options.

However, your code can dynamically change the selection made. The selected property reflects the selection status of an option. You can set selected which immediately changes the selection displayed on the browser display. You can see how this works by using radio buttons to change a SELECT list dynamically (see listing 7.17 and fig. 7.11).

On the CD

Listing 7.17   dinner.htm   Pizza for Dinner Using SELECTED Property

```
<HTML><HEAD><TITLE>dinner.htm by Red Daly</TITLE></HEAD>
<BODY><FORM>
<P>Demonstrates <I>selected</I> property.  See what you can afford for
dinner.  Click on the radio button for a dollar amount and show your
dinner in the select box..</P>
<P><B>How much money do you have for dinner?</B><BR>
```

```
<INPUT TYPE="radio" NAME="a"
onClick="this.form.meal.options[0].selected=1">$10<BR>
<INPUT TYPE="radio"
NAME="a"onClick="this.form.meal.options[1].selected=1">$15<BR>
<INPUT TYPE="radio"
NAME="a"onClick="this.form.meal.options[2].selected=1">$20<BR></P>
<B>Your dinner tonite is:</B><BR>
<SELECT NAME="meal" >
<OPTION VALUE="$10">Pizza
<OPTION VALUE="$15">Extra Cheese Pizza
<OPTION VALUE="$20">Extra Veggies Pizza
</SELECT>
</FORM></BODY>
</HTML>
```

FIG. 7.11

You can really confuse your users by having one form element change another. Be sure to think through your design.

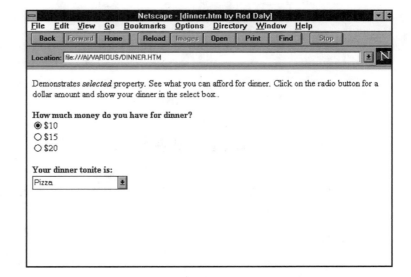

CAUTION

With text boxes, the information displayed in the box is the `value` property. With `select`, the value property is not displayed. This is like radio buttons and checkboxes. So don't change the `value` property of `select` and expect the display to change.

Part
II

Ch
7

Example: An Application Using Advanced Navigation

This example is designed to explain the concepts discussed in this chapter. There are several suggestions on how you can make them more robust, but the key is the explanation. You will see how links, as well as anchors, can be dynamic. The select is also used.

Internet Tri-Eye is truly a kaleidoscope on the Web. With a few clicks, you can see New York, Hollywood, and Pike's Peak; Hong Kong, the Antarctic, and the Netherlands; or fish, a cat, and some ants. It is a great way to demonstrate not only JavaScript, but also the Web.

The purpose of Internet Tri-Eye is to simultaneously display pictures from multiple cameras connected to the Internet. You select a set, say the U.S., International, or Animals. Then you click Show Picture to display one view of the world. Further information about each camera is also available.

Expand the View with Frames

Listing 7.18 shows the basic layout for the browser window. This layout is defined by the HTML page. The file is named trieye.htm and can be found on the CD-ROM. The window is divided into two frames with the top frame divided into three additional frames (see fig. 7.12).

N O T E   Internet Tri-Eye is a JavaScript application that uses frames. As a result, the entire application consists of five files: trieye.htm, one.htm, two.htm, three.htm, and guide.htm. The code for the first four files is in listings 7.18, 7.19, 7.20, and 7.21. The last file, guide.htm, is developed as you work through this section. The completed application is available on the CD-ROM. You start the application by loading the file trieye.htm. ■

On the CD

Listing 7.18   trieye.htm   Frameset for Internet Tri-Eye Application

```
<HTML><HEAD><TITLE>Internet Tri-Eye</TITLE></HEAD>

<FRAMESET ROWS="*,200">
    <FRAMESET COLS="33%,34%, 33%">
```

```
            <FRAME SRC="one.htm" NAME="one">
            <FRAME SRC="two.htm" NAME="two">
            <FRAME SRC="three.htm" NAME="three">
        </FRAMESET>
        <FRAME SRC="guide.htm" NAME="guide">

    <NOFRAMES>
    <H1>Internet Tri-Eye</H1>
    <P><B>Internet Tri-Eye</B> is a demonstration of several features of
    JavaScript.  To view and use this program you need a Javascript
    compatible browser like Netscape 2.0.
    </NOFRAMES>

    </FRAMESET>
    </HTML>
```

FIG. 7.12
The basic frames for
Internet Tri-Eye are resizable
so the user can change their
shape to match their screen
size.

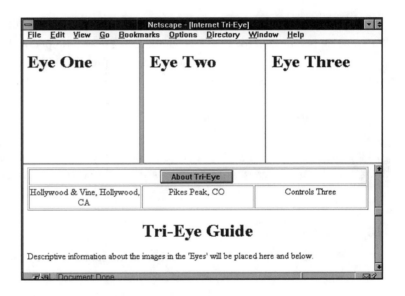

The content of the top three frames, the eyes, are files one.htm, two.htm, and three.htm (see listings 7.19, 7.20, and 7.21). These are extremely small files that are only used when the application is first loaded.

On the CD

Listing 7.19 one.htm Initial Contents of Frame One for Tri-Eye

```
<HTML><HEAD></HEAD><BODY>
<H1>Eye One</H2>
</BODY></HTML>
```

Part
II

Ch
7

Listing 7.20   two.htm   Initial Contents of Frame Two for Tri-Eye

```
<HTML><HEAD></HEAD><BODY>
<H1>Eye Two</H2>
</BODY></HTML>
```

Listing 7.21   three.htm   Initial Contents of Frame Three for Tri-Eye

```
<HTML><HEAD></HEAD><BODY>
<H1>Eye Tri</H2>
</BODY></HTML>
```

Files two.htm and three.htm are identical to the file one.htm except that the headline is changed to "Eye Two" and "Eye Three," respectively. The guts of Tri-Eye and all of the JavaScript code is found in the file guide.htm. This file contains the contents of the lower frame. As we progress in building the application, all of the changes are made to this file. So far, the four files, trieye.htm, one.htm, two.htm and three.htm, are complete.

 Most people find it easier to write JavaScript after doing the layout. Do your frames, your tables, your controls, and even some windows; then write the code to pull it all together.

Objects for Tri-Eye

Now that we have the framework, the next step is to set up objects for each "eye" or camera. We start by defining an object called cam. The object has three properties: the description of the camera, the name for the anchor (more later), and the URL for the image. The code in guide.htm starts with the standard header, the SCRIPT tag, and then defines the cam object (see listing 7.22).

Listing 7.22   guide.htm   Start of the Coding for Tri-Eye

```
<HTML><HEAD><TITLE>Internet Tri-Eye by Ray Daly</TITLE></HEAD>
<SCRIPT LANGUAGE="JavaScript">
<!--
function cam (name, anchor, url) {
    this.name = name
```

```
        this. anchor = anchor
        this.url = url
}
```

Next, for each camera a new object is established. In this example, there are nine different cameras, so create nine different objects labeled cam1 to cam9 (see listing 7.23). You can add more if you like.

Listing 7.23 guide.htm Setting Properties for *Cam* Objects for Tri-Eye

```
cam1 = new cam ("Hollywood, CA", "#Hollywood", "http://
➥hollywood.bhi.hollywood.ca.us:8000/pictures/image01.gif")
cam2 = new cam ("Pikes Pike, CO",  "#Pikes",
➥"http://www.softronics.com/peak_cam/cam.jpg")
cam3 = new cam ("New York City, NY", "#New York City",
➥"http://www.metaverse.com/gate/images/empire.jpg")
cam4 = new cam ("Zandvoort, NE", "#Zandvoort",
➥"http://www.dataplace.nl//images/zandv-gr.jpg")
cam5 = new cam ("Hong Kong",  "#Hong Kong",
➥"http://www.hkstar.com/images/capture1.jpg")
cam6 = new cam (" Australian Antarctic",  "#Antartic",
➥"http://www.antdiv.gov.au/aad/exop/sfo/mawson/video.gif")
cam7 = new cam ("Fishcam", "#Fishcam",
➥"http://www.netscape.com/fishcam/fishcam.gif")
cam8 = new cam ("Mojo - Cat",  "#Mojo",
➥"http://www.lowcomdom.com/mojo.gif")
cam9 = new cam ("Steve's Ant Farm", "#Ant Farm",
➥"http://sec.dgsys.com/images/zANTPIX/Untitled.jpeg")
```

We now have nine different objects. In order to make it easier to reference these objects, create another object called camset (see listing 7.24). From this object, an object called camindex is created. The first property in camindex is cam1, the second is cam2, etc. Thus, to get the contents of cam5, you reference the fifth element in camindex.

Listing 7.24 guide.htm Putting Nine Objects into One for Tri-Eye

```
function camset (eye1, eye2, eye3, eye4, eye5, eye6, eye7, eye8, eye9 )
{
    this.eye1 = eye1
    this.eye2 = eye2
    this.eye3 = eye3
```

Part

II

Ch

7

continues

Listing 7.24 Continued

```
    this.eye4 = eye4
    this.eye5 = eye5
    this.eye6 = eye6
    this.eye7 = eye7
    this.eye8 = eye8
    this.eye9 = eye9
}
camindex = new camset (cam1, cam2, cam3, cam4, cam5, cam6, cam7, cam8, cam9)
```

We do not need to create so many different objects, but this method seems more straightforward than the other options. If you are good with objects, have fun minimizing.

The final two lines of the JavaScript for this section initialize two variables to one, as follows:

```
        var setnumber=1
        var camnumber=1
    //-->
    </SCRIPT>
    </HEAD>
```

Controls To make anything happen with Internet Tri-Eye, controls need to be added. So far, all we have in guide.htm is the JavaScript defining the objects. Now the HTML code is added for the controls (see listing 7.25).

To hold the controls, there is a table of three rows and three columns. Across the entire first row is a button and a select element. The button is very simple and labeled About. When you click it, an alert dialog box tells you about Internet Tri-Eye.

The next element in the top row is a SELECT box. Here you select which set of cameras you want to look at. The first three cameras are locations in the United States, the next three are international, and the last three are pets. When you make a selection, it sets the variable setnumber to 1 or 2 or 3.

Listing 7.25 guide.htm Laying Out the Control Table for Tri-Eye

```
<BODY><FORM>
<TABLE BORDER="1" WIDTH="100%">
<TR>
   <TD ALIGN=CENTER COLSPAN=3>
```

```
      <A NAME="top">
      <INPUT TYPE="button" NAME="aboutTE"  VALUE="About Tri-Eye"
onClick="alert('Tri-Eye is a demo from the book:  JavaScript Special
➥Edition')">
      <SELECT
         NAME="setselect"
          onBlur="setnumber=setselect.selectedIndex+1">
         <OPTION VALUE="US" SELECTED> U.S.
         <OPTION VALUE="World">World
         <OPTION VALUE="Pets">Pets
      </SELECT>
   </TD>
</TR><TR>
   <TD ALIGN=CENTER VALIGN=TOP WIDTH="33%">
<A HREF=" "onClick="this.href=findHREF(1)" " TARGET="one">Show picture
➥One </A>
      </TD>
         <TD ALIGN=CENTER VALIGN=TOP WIDTH="34%">
<A HREF=" "onClick="this.href=findHREF(2)" " TARGET="two">Show picture
➥Two</A>
   </TD>
   <TD ALIGN=CENTER VALIGN=TOP WIDTH="33%">
<A HREF=" "onClick="this.href=findHREF(3)" " TARGET="three">Show picture
Tri</A>
   </TD>
</TR><TR>
    <TD ALIGN=CENTER>
     <A HREF=" "onClick="this.href=findHASH(1)" " NAME="Info1">-- Info --</A>
     </TD>
     <TD ALIGN=CENTER>
     <A HREF=" "onClick="this.href=findHASH(2)" " NAME="Info1">-- Info --</A>
     </TD>
     <TD ALIGN=CENTER>
     <A HREF=" "onClick="this.href=findHASH(2)" " NAME="Info1">-- Info --</A>
     </TD></TR>
</TABLE>
```

The final two rows of controls are for demonstrating dynamic links and anchors.

Dynamic Links

The middle row of controls is for the dynamic links. When you press on these
links, one picture from one camera is displayed. There is one control for each of
the "eyes." The code we need pulls in the proper URL, given "eye" 1, 2, or 3, and is
based on the set chosen with the SELECT box (see listing 7.26). These variables are
camnumber and setnumber.

Part

II

Ch

7

Listing 7.26   guide.htm   *findHREF* Function for Tri-Eye

```
function findHREF (eye) {
        // ...eye is 1, 2 or 3  -- the target frame
        indexnumber = (eye-1) +( 3 * (setnumber -1)
        //the value of indexnumber is between 0 and 8
        return camindex[indexnumber].url
}       //returns the url of the camera
```

This code is added between the SCRIPT tags in the header section. In most cases you will want to place functions in the header so they are loaded prior to the page be displayed. Once you have the URL, the code is fairly simple. When the hyperlink is clicked, the findHREF function is called. It returns the URL, and the href property is changed. The target for the URL is the appropriate "eye" frame. Change the href property to the URL. For "eye" 3, the code is:

```
<A HREF=" "onClick="this.href=findHREF(3)" " TARGET="three">Show
➥picture Tri</A>
```

For simplicity, the hyperlink text is "Show picture one" or "two" or "tri." To polish up the application, an icon could be used here.

Anchors to Complete the Story

So far, Internet Tri-Eye is already spectacular. It is a true kaleidoscope on the world. However, it does not tell us anything about these pictures. Anchors are used in two different ways to complete the story.

Anchors to the Reference Information   The final row of the controls is for information links. Press the text "—Info—" and the frame scrolls down to a description of the site. For this example, there is a short, three-line description with a link to the host site if you would like more information.

When the objects were created for this page, anchors were included. So the same technique that was used earlier for links is now used for anchors. The function has only a minor difference: it returns the anchor property.

```
function findHASH (eye) {
        // ...eye is 1, 2 or 3 -- the target frame
        indexnumber = (eye-1) + ( 3 * (setnumber -1))
        return camindex[indexnumber].anchor
}
```

The control itself is also similar:

```
<A HREF=" "onClick="this.href=findHASH(3)" " NAME="Info1">-- Info -- </A>
```

Anchors to Take You Back   Once you read the information on the picture, you probably want to go back to the controls. Notice that the title of each description is followed by a hyperlink labeled (top). What you may not have noticed is that there is no anchor with the name (top). Instead, (top) is the name of the About button. So press on (top), and the About button is at the top of the page.

```
<A HREF="#top">(top)</A>
```

N O T E   This code completes the guide.htm file (see listing 7.27). All five files that make up this application are found on the CD-ROM. You start the application by loading trieye.htm. ■

On the CD

Listing 7.27   guide.htm   Anchor Section for Tri-Eye

```
<CENTER><H1>Tri-Eye Guide</H1></CENTER>
<DL><DT><A NAME="Hollywood">Hollywood, CA</A>
➥<I><A HREF="#top">(top)</A></I></DT>
<DD>Not your typical American street corner, this is
<A HREF="http://www.geocities.com/cgi-bin/main/BHI/look.html">Hollywood
and Vine from GeoCities</A>.  Just remember that &quot;nobody walks in
L.A.&quot;</DD>
<DT><A NAME="Pikes">Pikes Pike, CO</A>   <I><A HREF="#top">(top)</A>
➥</I></DT>
<DD>One of America's most famous mountains.
<A HREF="http://www.softronics.com/peak_cam.html">Pikes Peak Cam from
Softronics</A> gives you the view from Colorado Springs.</DD>
<DT><A NAME="NYC">New York City, NY</A>   <I><A HREF="#top">(top)</A>
➥</I></DT>
<DD>New York City's most famous building.
<A HREF="http://www.metaverse.com/empire.html">Empire Cam from
Metaverse</A>
has a view across part of the skyline.  Check the weather.</DD>
<DT><A NAME="Zandvoort">Zandvoort, the Netherlands</A>
➥<I><A HREF="#top">(top)</A></I></DT>
<DD>No close ups of the people on the beach.  This
<A HREF="http://www.dataplace.nl/dp/pages/foto.htm">Livecam from
Dataplace</A>
points northwest across a traffic circle and up the beach.</DD>
<DT><A NAME="Hong">Hong Kong</A>   <I><A HREF="#top">(top)</A></I></DT>
```

continues

Part

II

Ch

7

Listing 7.27   Continued

```
<DD>Street scene that is colorful almost anytime.  The
<A HREF="http://www.hkstar.com/starcam.html">STARcam from HK Star
➥Internet Ltd.</A>
shows more cars than people.</DD>
<DT><A NAME="Antartic">Australian Antarctic</A>   ¦
➥<I><A HREF="#top">(top)</A></I></DT>
<DD>While often black, some previous pictures are available.  The
<A HREF="http://www.antdiv.gov.au/aad/exop/sfo/mawson/video.html">camera
at Mawson Station</A> captures the pictures and though a variety of
technology gets it to your desk.</DD>
<DT><A NAME="Fishcam">Fishcam</A>    <I><A HREF="#top">(top)</A></I></DT>
<DD>Perhaps the most famous fish in the world.
<A HREF="http://www.netscape.com/fishcam/fishcam.html">Fishcam from
➥Netscape</A>
now has multiple cameras and formats.  Who ever imagined an aquarium as
a revenue source?</DD>
<DT><A NAME="Mojo">Mojo</A>    <I><A HREF="#top">(top)</A></I></DT>
<DD>You won't believe the technology used to bring you these images.
<A HREF="http://www.lowcomdom.com/mojo_cam.html">Mojo-Cam</A> isn't from
a fixed view so it worth following.</DD>
<DT><A NAME="Ant">Ant Farm</A>    <I><A HREF="#top">(top)</A></I></DT>
<DD>Some people won't even think that this is a safe distance away.
<A HREF="http://sec.dgsys.com/AntFarm.html">Steve's Ant Farm</A> also
has a movie available.</DD></DL></FORM></BODY></HTML>
```

Now Internet Tri-Eye is complete.

Other Possible Improvements to and Uses of Internet Tri-Eye

Internet Tri-Eye was written to keep the code simple to explain, not dazzle you with graphics. The following are several suggestions for improving Tri-Eye or expanding its use:

- When you press —Info—, the control scrolls off the frame. Add one frame just for the table of controls. Show the information in another frame.

- Don't use any frames, but put everything in its own window. Press the control to show a picture, and it pops up as a new window. Then every "eye" can be free floating.

- Replace the text links with icons. Although —Info— is easy to explain in a book, the page will look better with graphics.

■ Add more cameras. People are hooking up cameras all of the time: some silly, some beautiful, and some scenic. Grab your favorite, and create some more objects.

■ Instead of doing cameras, do eZines or other publications. Take a collection of eZines and put them in as objects. This would obviously work much better with windows instead of frames.

Example: Tri-Eye FTP Auto Dialer

Trying to FTP a popular new piece of Internet software can be frustrating. You press on a link, and it seems like minutes before you're asked to try again later because the site is busy.

N O T E Tri-Eye FTP Auto Dialer (see fig. 7.13) uses the same files as Internet Tri-Eye. The only change is to the guide.htm file. To start the application, load trieye.htm. ■

FIG. 7.13
Tri-Eye FTP Auto Dialer looks rather bland when you start it up. The action comes from the user interacting.

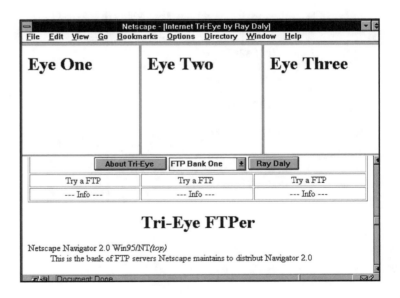

You can create the Tri-Eye FTP Auto Dialer with a simple modification to one file of the Internet Tri-Eye application (see fig. 7.14). Simply change the values of the properties for each cam object in the guide.htm file. These properties are the URLs for the information displayed in each of the upper frames. For example, for Netscape's FTP site, use the Windows NT/95 version of Navigator 2.0:

```
ftp://ftp2.netscape.com/2.0/windows/n32e20.exe
```

Do the same for each FTP location by just changing the host from ftp2 to ftp3, and so on; the last one is ftp10. The function looks nearly the same; only the contents of the properties have changed (see listing 7.28).

On the CD

Listing 7.28   guide.htm   Redefined *cam* Object for Tri-Eye FTP Auto Dialer

```
function cam (name, anchor, url) {
   this.name = name
   this.anchor = anchor
   this.url = url
}
cam1 = new cam ("FTP2", "#Netscape FTP", "ftp://ftp2.netscape.com/2.0/
➥windows/n32e20.exe")
cam2 = new cam ("FTP3", "#Netscape FTP", "ftp://ftp3.netscape.com/2.0/
➥windows/n32e20.exe")
cam3 = new cam ("FTP4", "#Netscape FTP", "ftp://ftp4.netscape.com/2.0/
➥windows/n32e20.exe")
cam4 = new cam ("FTP5", "#Netscape FTP", "ftp://ftp5.netscape.com/2.0/
➥windows/n32e20.exe")
cam5 = new cam ("FTP6", "#Netscape FTP", "ftp://ftp6.netscape.com/2.0/
➥windows/n32e20.exe")
cam6 = new cam ("FTP7", "#Netscape FTP", "ftp://ftp7.netscape.com/2.0/
➥windows/n32e20.exe")
cam7 = new cam ("FTP8", "#Netscape FTP", "ftp://ftp8.netscape.com/2.0/
➥windows/n32e20.exe")
cam8 = new cam ("FTP9", "#Netscape FTP", "ftp://ftp9.netscape.com/2.0/
➥windows/n32e20.exe")
cam9 = new cam ("FTP10", "#Netscape FTP", "ftp://ftp10.netscape.com/2.0/
➥windows/n32e20.exe")
```

FIG. 7.14
Tri-Eye FTP Auto Dialer will make multiple attempts to make an FTP connection. This should increase your chances of success.

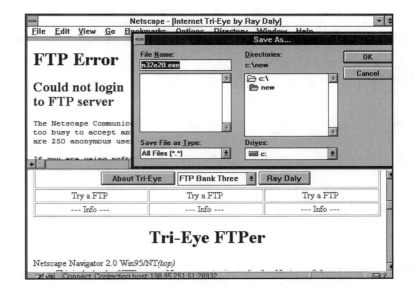

CHAPTER 8

Dynamic HTML and Browser Objects

by Mark C. Reynolds

This chapter describes the creation of dynamic documents and windows as well as the interaction between windows and their components. This chapter presumes that you now have a working knowledge of JavaScript syntax; the material covered is somewhat more complex than in earlier chapters (see chapter 4, "JavaScript Objects").

The first theme of the chapter is the creation of pop-up windows. The entire content of those windows is defined by a creation function, rather than a URL. We will examine various examples, including pop-ups with text, pop-ups with buttons, and editable pop-ups.

We will next examine the history, status, and location objects. You will see how to hurl the user to a specific URL on the history list, how to examine the various parts of the location object, and how to store and retrieve information using

Write JavaScript statements that can access objects in windows and documents

Almost every HTML element, as well as a large number of browser components, may be accessed from JavaScript.

Create and format new Netscape windows

The open( ) method is a very powerful statement which JavaScript programmers may use to open new browser windows.

Add new elements by rewriting documents dynamically

The HTML code for existing documents may be modified to change the appearance of a Web page.

Create entirely new documents for JavaScript

It is also possible to construct the entire HTML for a new page in JavaScript.

Manipulate the history list and the location object

This browser component describes the page currently being visited.

the search property of the `location` object. Finally, you will learn how to create dynamic documents. In fact, you will create a page entirely from JavaScript. You will also learn how to rewrite pages on-the-fly. ■

▶ **See** the "Browser and HTML Objects" section of chapter 4, for a discussion of how JavaScript code accesses HTML and browser components, **p. 141**.

JavaScript Object Hierarchy

You have already learned a lot about objects in JavaScript. In fact, the previous four chapters have been devoted to exploring the various JavaScript objects and their uses. You have already been exposed to the various built-in objects and HTML objects that JavaScript provides. To go further and explore dynamic HTML creation, we must first take a closer look at the hierarchy of objects in JavaScript.

If you are familiar with any object-oriented languages, you expect an object hierarchy to begin with a generic object from which all other objects are descendants or children. Unfortunately, the JavaScript object hierarchy does not really follow this model. It might be best described as a system of ownership, and, even then, the analogy is not really exact. For example, a window that creates another window could be thought of as the parent of the new window. However, if you try to refer to the original window from the child by saying `parent.someobject`, it will not work.

On the other hand, frames within a frameset have a parent-child relationship with the original window, and asking for `parent.someobject` will likely yield the object. Other ownership relationships are not characterized by a parent-child relationship at all. For example, form elements belong to a form, but to obtain the form, you use `this.form`—not `this.parent`. With these disconcerting thoughts in mind, let's attempt to sort out the dependencies among Netscape Navigator objects.

The Navigator is, in a way, the parent of all other JavaScript objects. It is the executable that runs the browser. The Navigator is responsible for the creation of all browser windows. It is also responsible for responding to general window events. The Navigator is *not* a visual object. You cannot see it. You only interact with it through its visual construct: its windows.

Browser Windows

Most Navigator window components can only be manipulated in a yes/no fashion at the time of window creation. These include the menu, button bar, location display, status display, history list display, and scroll bars. At the time of window creation, you can determine whether the window can be resized as well as find its dimensions.

This might seem like a significant restriction. By rewriting the document, however, you can change the contents of a window. This technique enables you to change the values of form elements, the content of the status bar, the position of the pointer in the history list, and the location (the URL that the window contains) at any time. Table 8.1 lists these various elements, when they can be modified, and how they can be modified. Note that the last two items in this table are not really window elements; they control what is displayed, but are not explicitly displayed themselves.

Table 8.1   Modification Rules for JavaScript Controls

Object	When	How	Rewrite?
Button bar	Window creation	Yes/No	NA
Menu	Window creation	Yes/No	NA
Location display	Window creation	Yes/No	NA
Status bar	Window creation	Yes/No	NA
History	Window creation	Yes/No	NA
Document	During rewrite	Complete	NA
Many form element properties	Any time	Complete	No
Status bar content	Any time	Complete	No
Location	Any time	Complete	Yes
History list	Any time	Complete	Yes

Dynamic Window Creation

One of the more advanced projects later in this book is the creation of a *sticky notes* application (in the "Dynamic Documents" section). To do that, you need to have a small note window in which to present the note. Let's create a primordial note window now. To do that, you must already have a window open with an element that enables you to call a JavaScript function (such as a button with an onClick handler). This base window is the parent of the child note window. The child can always find its parent with self.parent but the parent can only refer to the child by its name. There is no self.child[] reference nor is there a windows array available to JavaScript because of security concerns.

> **CAUTION**
>
> Netscape Navigator is a mimic. If you create a window under JavaScript control, the next window that is created by Navigator will have the same dimensions as the last window created by JavaScript.

The element that we will use is an image that behaves as a button, which is triggered by a HREF=javascript:myfunc included in the LINK tag. This works very well if you need to call only one function and you need no return value. When you try to use this mechanism in a window constructed on-the-fly, however, the image refuses to display. In fact, any image that uses relative addressing refuses to display in a dynamic window.

The solution is to either use a completely static reference for the image or to set the base directory of your page with <BASE>path</BASE> in the header. This latter approach helps JavaScript find the image. If you need an object that will be accessed later, you might want to use a form input element, rather than one of these button images. JavaScript will have less trouble finding it.

The following three steps are necessary to use an image as a button for executing a JavaScript function:

1. Write an appropriate HTML declaration for the desired image.
2. Enclose this HTML declaration within reference tags.
3. Resolve the HREF to a JavaScript function declaration.

These three steps are shown in listing 8.1.

Listing 8.1   Creating a Button Image

```
<IMG WIDTH=23 HEIGHT= 22 VSPACE=2 HSPACE= 2 ALIGN=LEFT
      SRC="Images/gobtn.gif" BORDER=0>
<A HREF='xxxxxx'><IMG WIDTH=23 HEIGHT= 22 VSPACE=2 HSPACE= 2 ALIGN=LEFT
      SRC="Images /gobtn.gif" BORDER=0><A>
<A HREF='javascript: openNote'><IMG WIDTH=23 HEIGHT= 22
VSPACE=2 HSPACE= 2 ALIGN=LEFT SRC="Images/gobtn.gif"
  BORDER=0><A>
```

The function used in this example is the openNote() function, the source for which is given in listing 8.2. Before we plunge into this code, it is worthwhile to notice that the border has explicitly been set to zero. This is the only way you can keep Navigator from drawing a border around your image if it is within a reference statement. Listing 8.2 contains the HTML for the base window with the Image button. It includes the openNotes() function in a header script. Once you open a note window, make sure you close it before it gets lost. Navigator will not open a second window by the same name: it just updates the first one. When this code is executed by pressing the Make Note button you will see something like figure 8.1.

Listing 8.2   Creating a New Window in JavaScript

```
<HTML>
<HEAD>
<TITLE>Opening a Window with JavaScript</TITLE>
<SCRIPT>

//window globals
     var aNoteWin

function openNote(topic)
{
     aPopUp= window.open('','Note','toolbar=no,location=no, ¬
         directories=no,status=no,scrollbars=yes,resizable=yes, ¬
         copyhistory=no,width=300,height=200')
     ndoc= aPopUp.document
     astr ='<HTML><HEAD><BR><TITLE>' + topic + '</TITLE>'
     astr +='</HEAD>'
     astr +='<BODY>'
     astr +=topic +  '<BR>'
     astr +='</BODY></HTML>'
```

continues

Listing 8.2   Continued

```
        ndoc.write(astr)
        ndoc.close()
        self.aNoteWin = aPopUp
}

function closeNote(which)
{
        self.aNoteWin.close()
}

</SCRIPT>
</HEAD>
<BODY>
<H3><BR><HR><BR></H3>
<CENTER>
<FONT SIZE=5 COLOR='darkred'><B>Example 1</B></FONT>:  <FONT SIZE=5 ¬
     COLOR='darkblue'><B>Opening a New Window</B></FONT>
<FORM NAME='noteForm'>
<INPUT TYPE='button' NAME='makeBtn' VALUE='Make Note' ¬
     onclick='openNote("JoAnn Murphy at 7:00; bring salad")'>
<INPUT TYPE='button' NAME='closeBtn' VALUE='Close note'  ¬
     onclick='closeNote()'>
</FORM>
</CENTER>
<H3><BR><HR><BR></H3>
</BODY>
</HTML>
```

CAUTION

In a windows.open statement, there are three things to bear in mind, as follows:

1. You only need the first two parameters (the URL, which can be empty, and the window name) to open a window. If you do not include the third parameter, the window attributes list, then the window will have all of its window attributes set to yes (present).

2. If you specify any of the windows attributes, then you must include the whole list of attributes. Otherwise, the results will be unpredictable.

3. Enclose the attributes list in quotation marks, separate the items with commas, and do not leave spaces.

FIG. 8.1
A dynamically created window may be tied to button events in JavaScript.

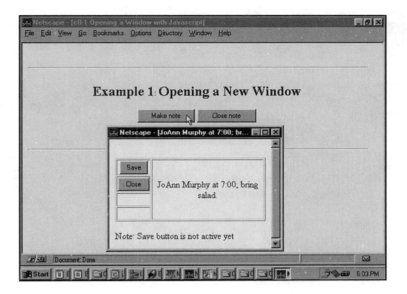

This small script illustrates several points. First, you can set a window global by defining it outside of any function and preceding it with var. Here we set the window global aNoteWin with var aNoteWin. This variable is global so that you could use it to refer to aNoteWin in other functions. Although we did not do so here, you might want to save a number of notes in an array. Second, when you create a window *de novo* via a script and no URL is specified, the window document is still open and you can write to it. Here we wrote the note topic and then closed the document.

A window that you create can be as simple as the note window. However, you can also make this window quite complex. In order to do so, you must write everything to the document, including form elements, images, and JavaScript functions, before you close it. Listing 8.3 shows a second version of the openNote() function. This more elaborate version furnishes the note window with two buttons, including onClick handlers, the topic text, a warning message, and two JavaScript functions. It may be found in the file c8-1.htm on the CD-ROM. Note that the save function is stubbed. The topic of data storage is discussed in chapter 19. All the display elements are neatly wrapped in a table.

▶ **See** the "Parameter Specification and Data Storage" section of chapter 19 for information on how data may be stored transiently in the `location.search` property and persistently in `cookies`, **p. 650**.

On the CD

Listing 8.3   c8-1.htm   A More Sophisticated Notes Window

```
function openNote(topic)
{
    aPopUp= window.open('','Note','toolbar=no,location=no,¬
    directories=no,status=no,scrollbars=yes,resizable=yes, ¬
copyhistory=no,width=300,height=200')
    ndoc= aPopUp.document
    ndoc.close()
    ndoc.open()
    astr ='<HTML><HEAD><BR><TITLE>' + topic + '</TITLE>'
    astr +='</HEAD>'
    astr +='<SCRIPT>'
    astr +='function closeNote(aName){'
    astr +='self.close()'
    astr +='}'
    astr +='function saveNote(aName){'
    astr +='}'
    astr +='<\/SCRIPT>'
    astr +='<BODY>'
    astr +='<FORM>'
    astr +='<TABLE ALIGN=LEFT BORDER><TR ALIGN=CENTER><TD>'
    astr +='<INPUT TYPE=button NAME=saveBtn VALUE="Save"  ¬
        ONCLICK="saveNote()" \>'
    astr +='</TD>'
    astr +='<TD ROWSPAN=4>' + topic
    astr +='</TD>'
    astr +='</TR><TR ALIGN=CENTER><TD>'
    astr +='<INPUT TYPE=button NAME=closeBtn VALUE="Close"  ¬
        ONCLICK="closeNote()" \>'
    astr +='</TD></TR>'
    astr +='<TR><TD><BR></TD></TR>'
    astr +='<TR><TD><BR></TD></TR>'
    astr +='</TABLE>'
    astr +='</FORM>'
    astr +='<BR CLEAR=ALL><H3><BR></H3>'
    astr +='Note:  Save button is not active yet'
    astr +='</BODY></HTML>'
    ndoc.write(astr)
    ndoc.close()
    self.aNoteWin = aPopUp
}
```

Window Status

Netscape Navigator keeps you appraised of which link or button your mouse pointer is over via its status bar. Occasionally, it sends you other messages via that method, too. Perhaps you have seen it busily scrolling text to catch your attention. The *status* (not the status bar itself) is a property of a window and is accessible to you as `self.status = Some message`. When you change the status, Navigator immediately displays it in the status bar. You can also set a property called `defaultStatus`, which is the default message displayed in the status bar. Listing 8.4 illustrates the use of the `status` property in Netscape Navigator. This code can be found in the file c8-2.htm on the CD-ROM.

On the CD

Listing 8.4   c8-2.htm   Manipulating the Status Bar

```
<HTML>
<HEAD>
<TITLE>Manipulating the Status Bar</TITLE>
<SCRIPT>
// set up a window global so that the new window can be accessed
// from all functions.
var aStatWin = null

function openStatus(defmsg,msg)
{
    aStatWin=window.open('','statWin','toolbar=no,location=no, ¬
        directories=no,status=yes,scrollbars=no,resizable=yes, ¬
        copyhistory=no,width=550,height=2')
    if (aStatWin != null)
        {
            aStatWin.document.write('<FORM NAME="dform"> ¬
                <INPUT TYPE=TEXT NAME="dummy"></FORM>')
            aStatWin.document.close
            aStatWin.defaultStatus = defmsg
            aStatWin.status = msg
            setFocus()
        }
}

function setStatus()
{
    if(self.aStatWin == null )
        alert('Status window is closed!')
```

continues

Listing 8.4   Continued

```
        else
            {
                    self.aStatWin.status = document.statForm.statMsg.value
                    setFocus()
            }
}

function setFocus()
{
    self.aStatWin.document.dform.dummy.focus()
}

function close()
{
    self.aStatWin.close()
    aStatWin = null
}

//This function is a work-around to make sure that the table
//      overlay is drawn correctly.
function fixup()
{
    blankWin=window.open('','blankWin','toolbar=no,location=no, ¬
        directories=no,status=yes,scrollbars=no,resizable=no, ¬
        copyhistory=no,width=600,height=450')
    blankWin.close()
}

</SCRIPT>
</HEAD>
<!-- fixup forces redraw of window after everything, including images,
  has loaded.  The redraw is necessary to enforce correct drawing
  of table overlays.  -->
<BODY onLoad='fixup()'>
<H3><BR><HR><BR></H3>
<CENTER>
<FONT SIZE=5 COLOR='darkred'><B>Example : </B></FONT> ¬
    <FONT SIZE=5 COLOR='darkblue'><B>Setting the Contents of the ¬
     Status Bar</B></FONT>
<H3><BR><HR><BR></H3>
<H3><BR></H3>
</CENTER>
<CENTER>
<FORM NAME='statForm'>
<TABLE WIDTH=520 ALIGN=CENTER BORDER><TR ALIGN=CENTER><TD>
<TABLE WIDTH=500 ALIGN=CENTER >
<TR ALIGN=CENTER>
<TD WIDTH=35 ALIGN=CENTER>
```

```
<IMG WIDTH=485 HEIGHT=50 VSPACE=2 HSPACE= 2 ¬
    ALIGN=CENTER SRC="Images/gotray.gif">
</TD>
<TD>
<!-- <INPUT TYPE=button VALUE='Make Status Window' ¬
    onClick='openStatus("Status is GO!", ¬
    document.statForm.statMsg.value)'> -->
<A HREF='javascript: openStatus("Status is GO!", ¬
    document.statForm.statMsg.value)'>
<IMG WIDTH=23 HEIGHT=22 VSPACE=2 HSPACE=2  ALIGN=absMiddle ¬
    SRC="Images/gobtn1.gif" BORDER=0>
Open Status Window</A>
</TD>
<TD ALIGN=LEFT >
<A HREF='javascript: setStatus()'>
<IMG WIDTH=23 HEIGHT=22 VSPACE=2 HSPACE=2  ALIGN=absMiddle ¬
    SRC="Images/gobtn2.gif" BORDER=0>
Set Status</A>
</TD>
<TD ALIGN=CENTER >
<A HREF= 'javascript: close()'>
<IMG WIDTH=31 HEIGHT=30 VSPACE=2 HSPACE= 2 ALIGN=absMiddle BORDER=0 ¬
    SRC="Imagesokbtn.gif">
Close Status
</A>
</TD>
</TR>

<TR ALIGN=CENTER>
<TD ALIGN=CENTER COLSPAN=4>
Msg <INPUT TYPE=text NAME='statMsg' VALUE='Howdy!' ¬
    SIZE= 50 MAXLENGTH=80>
</TD>
</TR>
</TABLE>
</TD></TR></TABLE>
</FORM>
</CENTER>
<H3><BR></H3>
</BODY>
</HTML>
```

This example builds a window with a status bar included. Just to make things interesting, we will set the content of the status bar from the parent window. In addition, this script provides an example of the advanced HTML concept of *table overlays*, and an onLoad() handler, which provides a work-around for Netscape's unpredictable order of drawing images. We will say a little more about table overlays later, when we discuss the fixup() function.

The status window is created with a `javascript: openStatus(defMsg,msg)` link attached to an image. This function, `openStatus(defMsg, msg)`, performs the following tasks:

- It creates a new window with everything turned off but the status bar. It also sizes the window so that only the status bar is showing.

- It checks that the window was actually created by examining `aStatWin` for a `null` value. It is important to perform this, since attempts to access objects in a nonexistent window will result in errors. The usual reason why a window will fail to be created is lack of memory. This routine aborts with a message if the window was not created.

- It places a dummy button in `aStatWin`. This button is just used as an object to set the focus, so that we can bring the window to the front. Otherwise, small windows can get lost.

- It sets the initial and default status. Netscape immediately makes its presence known by writing to your status bar.

We will set the status of the status window with a call to `setStatus()`. This call is made from a `javascript: setStatus(document.statForm.statMsg.value)` link attached to an image.

The `setStatus()` function also checks to see if `aStatWin` exists before it tries to address one of its objects. If `aStatWin` does exist, `setStatus` changes the content of its status bar. `setStatus()` then sets the focus on the dummy button in `aStatWin` to bring the window to the front. This is done by a call to the `setFocus()` method. The resulting window is shown in figure 8.2. When you are done with the window you can close it using an image button linked with a call to `close()`. The `close()` function simply closes `aStatWin` and makes sure that its value is reset to `null`.

The function `fixup()` is worth looking at in more detail. The order in which Netscape Navigator draws images depends upon where the images are coming from, whether they are in the cache, and whether their height and width are given explicitly. It can also depend on the size of the images. Extremely attractive presentations can be made by overlaying text and graphics on other graphics via the overlay feature of Netscape tables.

FIG. 8.2

A status bar window may be created dynamically by the parent window.

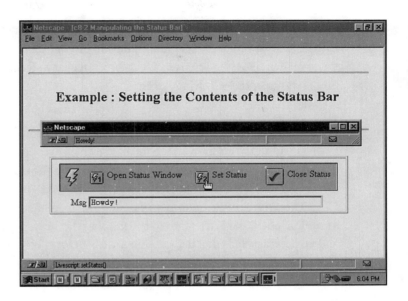

However, Netscape will invariably draw your bottom image last when the page first loads. Scrolling the screen causes the correct redraw, but you cannot expect or require your users to do that. One way to force the redraw is to open and quickly close another window over your page. You need to do this *after* all of the page elements have been loaded. When this occurs, Navigator sends an onLoad event, which you can capture in the BODY tag. The fixup() function ensures that all of the image buttons are visible. Although this is far from an ideal solution, it is effective.

 Always check that a newly created window exists before you try to address its properties or methods. Do this by checking to see if the window is null. If it is null, use an alert to inform the user.

The *Location* Object

The location object essentially holds information about the URL to which the browser points. The browser reads this marked up text from the server's disk and interprets it just like Microsoft Word reads and interprets a file on your disk. In addition to the URL, the `location` object also contains any post parameters of an HTML form submitted via a Submit button or your call to `submit()`. Because of this, you can use the `location` object for temporary storage. In Netscape, the location consists of the following parts:

```
protocol//hostname: (port) pathname search hash
```

`Protocol` is the type of protocol used for this file. Examples are `http`, `ftp`, `gopher`, `telnet`, and `file` (for files on the local disk). `Hostname` and `port` are only valid when the document is on a remote server. They contain the domain name/IP address of the server and the server port, respectively. They are not usually a visible part of a URL. The Web `port` is a number denoting the type of service, and is usually `80` for `http`. The `pathname` is the path to the file that the browser displays. `Search` includes any post parameters that are compiled when a form is submitted. `Hash` is usually a link to a local anchor.

The `location` object also has a `host` property, which consists of the combination of `hostname` and `port`. The `location` object also has an extremely important property, known as `href`, which contains the entire URL.

Finding Out Where You Are   This next example is a page that has no body. It is written entirely by the header script. As the page is written, it dissects the `location` object and lists all of its properties in a table. To see a non-empty `location.search`, you have to submit the little form included after the table. To see a non-empty `location.search`, click the dummy link and then Netscape's Reload button. The `host`, `port`, and `hostname` properties will be non-empty only if you have loaded some page from a server. Listing 8.5 shows the code for the Location Display script. This code is in the file c8-3.htm on the CD-ROM.

On the CD

Listing 8.5   c8-3.htm   Displaying the Properties of the *Location* Object

```
<HTML>
<HEAD>
<!-- Created 08 Feb 1996 a2:41 PM 02:41 PM -->
<TITLE>Parts of the Location Object</TITLE>
<SCRIPT>
```

```
var aline = '<H3><BR></H3><HR><H3><BR></H3>'
var skip='<H3><BR></H3>'

document.write('<CENTER>')
document.write('<FONT SIZE=5 COLOR="darkred"><B>Example : </B></FONT> ¬
    <FONT SIZE=5 COLOR="darkblue"> ¬
    <B>What\'s in the Location       Object?</B></FONT>') ¬
document.write('<BR>')
document.write('<BLOCKQUOTE><BLOCKQUOTE>If you are viewing this ¬
    document from your hard disk, host, hostname, and port will ¬
    be empty.</BLOCKQUOTE></BLOCKQUOTE>')
document.write('<BR>')

document.write('<CENTER><TABLE ALIGN= CENTER BORDER CELLPADDING=3>')
document.write('<TR><TD><B>Property</B></TD><TD ALIGN=CENTER> ¬
    <B>Value</B></TD></TR>')
document.write('<TR><TD>href</TD><TD>' + location.href + '</TD></TR>')
document.write('<TR><TD>protocol</TD><TD>' + location.protocol ¬
    + '</TD></TR>')
document.write('<TR><TD>hostname</TD><TD>' + location.hostname ¬
    + '</TD></TR>')
document.write('<TR><TD>host</TD><TD>' + location.host + '</TD></TR>')
document.write('<TR><TD>port</TD><TD>' + location.port + '</TD></TR>')
document.write('<TR><TD>pathname</TD><TD>' + location.pathname ¬
    + '</TD></TR>')
document.write('<TR><TD>search</TD><TD>' + location.search ¬
    + '</TD></TR>')
document.write('<TR><TD>hash</TD><TD>' + location.hash + '</TD></TR>')
document.write('</TABLE></CENTER>')
document.write(aline)
document.write('<CENTER>')
document.write('<FORM NAME="nameForm" >')
document.write('Your name\: <INPUT TYPE=text NAME="yourName" ¬
    VALUE="John Smith" WIDTH=30 MAXLENGTH=30>')
document.write('<INPUT TYPE=submit VALUE="Click Me to Add a ¬
    Search Parameter!" >')
document.write('</FORM>')
document.write('<A HREF=' + location.href + '#myAnchor >Click on me ¬
    and then RELOAD to enter a hash parameter!</A>')
document.write(aline)
</SCRIPT>
</HEAD>

</HTML>
```

Sending the User Elsewhere   Not only can you obtain useful information by examining the location object, you can also modify it and send the user elsewhere. This is useful if you should want to dynamically generate a URL or a reference to an anchor. The example shown in listing 8.6 builds a URL dynamically and sends the current browser to that URL. This code implements a "Message Center," which retrieves messages from URLs created via button clicks. Five users have been created to demonstrate this aspect of the location object. The CD-ROM file c8-4.htm contains this message center code.

On the CD

> **Listing 8.6   c8-4.htm   Modifying the Current URL Dynamically**

```
<HEAD>
<!-- Created 08 Feb 1996 a4:08 PM 04:08 PM -->
<TITLE>Message Center</TITLE>
<SCRIPT>
function getMessage(who)
{
     loc = self.location
     document.forms[0].translate.value = loc
     loc = document.forms[0].translate.value
     k = loc.lastIndexOf('/')
     loc = loc.substring(0,k+1)
     nloc = loc.substring(0,k+1)+ who.value + '.htm'
     self.location=nloc
}
</SCRIPT>
</HEAD>
<BODY>
<CENTER><HR>
<FONT SIZE=5 COLOR='darkred'><B>Example 4</B></FONT>:  <FONT SIZE=5 ¬
     COLOR='darkblue'><B>Moving Around Dynamically</B></FONT><BR>
<HR><FONT SIZE=6 COLOR='darkslateblue'><B>Message Center</B></FONT><BR>
</CENTER>

<CENTER>
<FORM>
<TABLE BORDER ALIGN=CENTER><TR><TD>
<INPUT TYPE=radio NAME='getMsgR' VALUE='John' ¬
     onClick='getMessage(this)'>John
<INPUT TYPE=radio NAME='getMsgR' VALUE='George' ¬
     onClick='getMessage(this)'>George
<INPUT TYPE=radio NAME='getMsgR' VALUE='Barbara' ¬
     onClick='getMessage(this)'>Barbara
<INPUT TYPE=radio NAME='getMsgR' VALUE='Ken' ¬
     onClick='getMessage(this)'>Ken
<INPUT TYPE=radio NAME='getMsgR' VALUE='Julie' ¬
     onClick='getMessage(this)'>Julie
<INPUT TYPE=hidden NAME='translate' VALUE='' >
</TD></TR></TABLE>
</FORM>
</CENTER>
```

```
<H3><BR><HR><BR></H3>
<H3><BR><HR SIZE=5 WIDTH=80%><BR></H3>
</BODY>
</HTML>
```

The script works by first obtaining the current location. It then strips off the filename and replaces it with the value of the radio button clicked. It also makes sure to tack on the suffix, `.htm`. This presumes that the message HTML files are in the same directory as the current page. However, it would be easy enough to build in a subdirectory name just for the messages or even have a separate subdirectory for each person. The `location` object is then set to the newly constructed URL. Setting the `location` object retrieves the file at that location. In our example, this file represents the set of messages for the particular user whose button was pressed.

 T I P   You can force a page to be reloaded by setting the `location` object to the URL corresponding to that page.

Using the *Search* Property   When you submit a form, all the values of the various form elements are retrieved, parsed, and concatenated with the `location` object; they are placed after the path and preceded by question marks (?). The value of `location.search` is precisely that string, including the question mark (?).

This string is not just a simple list of element contents, however. Each element value is placed in the string in the form `elementName=elementValue` and followed by an ampersand (&). Any non-alphanumeric characters are coded or escaped. The ASCII value of any such character is changed into a two-digit hex number preceded by a percent sign (%). If text field or textarea elements have multiple words, these words are separated by a plus sign (+). Consequently, when you get the `location.search` string, you have to decode it to get the various form elements that it contains.

▶ **See** the section on "Global and Local Variables" in chapter 9, which discusses character encoding in more detail, **p. 300.**

You can place your own form element values, or anything else, in the location's `search` property. As long as you precede it with a question mark (?), `location.search` will retrieve it. However, not all non-alphanumeric characters can be placed in the string or retrieved intact. If you are going to concoct a home-grown search string, you may either need to encode the parameters yourself or not allow non-alphanumeric characters. Listing 8.7 is a simple page that shows you how to manipulate location.search.

Listing 8.7   Using the *Search* Property of the *Location* Object

```
<HTML>
<HEAD>
<!-- Created 08 Feb 1996 a6:10 PM 06:10 PM -->
<TITLE>Forcing a Reload with Location</TITLE>
<SCRIPT>
function reloadMe()
{
    astr = document.nameForm.myName.value
    astr= self.location.pathname  + '?' + astr
    self.location = astr
}

function clearUp()
{
  self.location = self.location.pathname
}

if (self.location.search != null && self.location.search !='')
    {
        document.write('<CENTER><FONT SIZE=4 COLOR="darkslategray"><B> ¬
            Form Entry Data: </B></FONT></CENTER>')
          document.write('<CENTER><FONT SIZE=4 COLOR="red"><B>' + ¬
            self.location.search + '</B></FONT></CENTER>')
    }
</SCRIPT>
</HEAD>
<H3><HR></H3>
<CENTER><FONT SIZE=6 COLOR="blue"><B>Forcing a Reload with ¬
    Location</B></FONT></CENTER>
<H3><BR><HR><BR></H3>

<CENTER>

<FORM NAME=nameForm>
<INPUT TYPE=text NAME=myName VALUE='abracadabra&#^$()'>
<INPUT TYPE=button NAME=reloadBtn VALUE='Reload Page' ¬
    onClick='reloadMe()'>
<INPUT TYPE=button NAME=submitBtn VALUE= 'Submit Form' ¬
    onClick='this.form.submit()'>
```

```
<INPUT TYPE=button NAME=clearBtn VALUE= 'Clear' onClick='clearUp()'>
<INPUT TYPE=hidden NAME=hideFld >
</FORM>
</CENTER>
<H3><BR><HR><BR></H3>
<H3><BR><HR SIZE=5 WIDTH=80%><BR></H3>
</BODY>
</HTML>
```

A script in the <HEAD> part of an HTML document can pick up the command-line parameters with location.search and write something to the document being loaded based on what it finds. This example just reads the parameter string and writes it for you at the head of the page. Note that this write is guarded by a test to see if location.search is null or empty. If location.search is not a valid string and you attempt to parse it into variables that are used later, you will encounter error after error. Always test for a null string or an empty string.

The code in listing 8.7 has two useful functions. ClearUp() simply strips the search string from the location by setting the location object to location.path. The reloadMe() function takes the value from the text box and adds it to location.path. It then sets the location to that result.

The *History* Object

The history object is a list that contains the locations of all the URLs that you have visited. You can move backward and forward through the history list with history.back and history.forward. You can also move around in the list in a relative fashion with history.go(). This function takes a positive or negative integer argument and moves you that many URLs forward or backward in the history list. The only property of a history list you can access is its length, which is the number of items in the list. You can neither set nor retrieve history list items.

To show how to manipulate the history list, we will build another pop-up window that boasts only a Close button and four directional buttons. The buttons enable you to manipulate the history list of the parent window. You can move backward and forward by one step or five. This code is shown in listing 8.8, and can be found in the file c8-6.htm on the CD-ROM.

Listing 8.8   c8-6.htm   Using the *History* Object in a Pop-up Window

```
<HTML>
<HEAD>
<!-- Created 08 Feb 1996 a9:21 PM 09:21 PM -->
<TITLE>Running through the History List</TITLE>
<SCRIPT>
var aNoteWin
var myDummyVar = 'Apples, peaches, pumpkin pie...'

function openNote(topic)
{
    aPopUp= window.open('','Note','toolbar=no,location=no, ¬
        directories=no,status=no,scrollbars=yes,resizable=yes, ¬
        copyhistory=no,width=110,height=150')
    ndoc= aPopUp.document
    ndoc.close()
    ndoc.open()
    astr ='<HTML><HEAD><BR><TITLE>' + topic + '</TITLE>'
    astr +='<SCRIPT>'
    astr +='function closeNote(aName){'
    astr +='self.close()'
    astr +='}\n'
    astr +='function saveNote(aName){'
    astr +='}\n'

    astr +='function goNext(){'
    astr +='creator.history.forward()\n'
    astr +='}\n'
    astr +='function goBack(){'
    astr +='creator.history.back()\n'
    astr +='}\n'
    astr +='function goStart(){'
    astr += 'creator.history.go(-5)\n'
    astr +='}\n'
    astr +='function goEnd(){'
    astr +='creator.history.go(5)\n'
    astr +='}\n'
    astr +='<\/SCRIPT>'
    astr +='</HEAD>'
    ndoc.write(astr)
    astr ='<BODY>'
    astr +='<FORM NAME="popForm">'
    astr +='<TABLE ALIGN=LEFT BORDER>'
    astr +='</TR><TR ALIGN=CENTER><TD>'
    astr +='\<INPUT TYPE=button NAME=closeBtn VALUE="Close" ¬
        ONCLICK="closeNote()" \>'
    astr +='</TD>'
    astr +='</TR>'
    astr +='<TR><TD>'
    astr +='<INPUT TYPE="button" NAME="startBtn" VALUE=&lt;&lt; ¬
        onclick="goStart()">'
```

```
        astr +='<INPUT TYPE="button" NAME="backBtn" VALUE=&lt; ¬
            onclick="goBack()">'
        astr +='<INPUT TYPE="button" NAME="nextBtn" VALUE=&gt; ¬
            onclick="goNext()">'
        astr +='<INPUT TYPE="button" NAME="endBtn" VALUE=&gt;&gt; ¬
            onclick="goEnd()">'
        astr +='</TD></TR>'
        astr +='<TR><TD>'
        astr +='<INPUT TYPE="hidden" NAME="IAm" VALUE="0">'
        astr +='</TD></TR>'
        astr +='</TABLE>'
        astr +='</FORM>'
        astr +='<BR CLEAR=ALL><H3><BR></H3>'
        astr +='</BODY></HTML>'
        ndoc.write(astr)
        ndoc.close()
        self.aNoteWin = aPopUp
        self.aNoteWin.creator = self
        aNoteWin.document.popForm.startBtn.focus()
}

function closeNote(which)
{
        self.aNoteWin.close()
}

</SCRIPT>
</HEAD>
<BODY >
<CENTER>
<FONT SIZE=5 COLOR='darkred'><B>Example 6</B></FONT>: ¬
    <FONT SIZE=5 COLOR='darkblue'><B>Running through the History List ¬
    </B></FONT>
</CENTER>
<H3><BR><HR><BR></H3>


<BODY>
<H3><BR><HR><BR></H3>

<CENTER>
<FORM NAME='noteForm'>
<INPUT TYPE='button' NAME='makeBtn' VALUE='Make Popup' ¬
    onclick='openNote("JoAnn Murphy at 7:00; bring salad.")'>
<INPUT TYPE='button' NAME='closeBtn' VALUE='Close Popup' ¬
    onclick='closeNote()'>
</FORM>
</CENTER>
<H3><BR><HR><BR></H3>
```

continues

Listing 8.8 Continued

```
<H3><BR><HR><BR></H3>
<H3><BR><HR SIZE=5 WIDTH=80%><BR></H3>
</BODY>
</HTML>
```

This pop-up is a variation on our old friend, aNoteWin. It can access its parent's variables through an artificial property of aNoteWin, the creator property. At the end of the openNote() function, which creates and draws the window, aNoteWin.creator is set to self. This automatically creates a new property of the aNoteWin. This enables you to have ready access to the parent window's variables, functions, and objects.

Security Aspects of JavaScript Objects

Although it would be useful to retrieve history list items, this functionality has been removed from JavaScript. Unfortunately, each history list entry contains the entire location, including the search string. If this information could be retrieved, the possibility exists that credit card or other personal information might be gleaned by malicious individuals.

You may have wondered why there is no windows array. This also does not exist in JavaScript for security reasons. If it did, a script from one window might reach into another unrelated window and scavenge information from its form elements or its location object. Again, what might be perceived as a limitation in JavaScript has been imposed to protect you.

The *Document* Object

The document object encapsulates all JavaScript objects that correspond to the HTML elements. It is the parent of forms, links, and anchors. These objects occur as arrays and are accessed as document.Forms[*xx*], document.Links[*xx*], and document.anchors[*xx*], where *xx* is an array index. The document object also has several other useful properties. It has a property, for example, for all of the standard object colors, such as the background color, text color, and link colors. You cannot change the property of a static closed document, however, so these properties are useful only when building a document.

Four properties that are useful in keeping your documents up to date are the `location`, `title`, `lastModified`, and `referrer` properties. These are used to dynamically write a header or a footer for your documents. Listing 8.9 shows a typical example of how you could use the `document` object in this way. Note that the properties of the `document` object are read-only. The attempt to set `document.title` in this listing will fail.

Listing 8.9   Writing the Document Header

```
<HTML>
<HEAD>
<!-- Created 08 Feb 1996 a11:32 PM 11:32 PM -->
<TITLE>Writing a Document Header</TITLE>
<SCRIPT>
document.bgcolor = 'linen'
document.text = 'darkslateblue'
document.link = 'coral'
document.vlink='peach'
document.alink='red'
document.title='Dynamic Headers'
document.write('<TABLE ALIGN=RIGHT WIDTH=300 BORDER=1>')
document.write('<TR><TD>')
document.write('<FONT SIZE=7 COLOR= "navy">')
document.write('<CENTER>' +document.title + '</CENTER>')
document.write('</TD></TR></TABLE>')
document.write('<CENTER><B>')
document.write('<HR>')
document.write('This document was last modified on<BR> ¬
    <FONT COLOR="red">' + document.lastmodified + '</FONT><BR>')
document.write('Save this URL: <BR><FONT COLOR="red">' ¬
    + document.location + '</FONT><BR>')
document.write('You arrived here from <BR><FONT COLOR="red">' ¬
    + document.referrer + '</FONT><BR>')
document.write('<BR><HR><BR>')
document.write('</B></CENTER>')
document.write('')
</SCRIPT>
</HEAD>
<H3><BR><HR><BR></H3>
<H3><BR><HR SIZE=5 WIDTH=80%><BR></H3>
</BODY>
</HTML>
```

Forms   You can get input from your users via HTML form elements (sometimes known as widgets). You can have many forms on a page. If they are named (by an HTML NAME directive) you can refer to them by name. You can also refer to a form by its index into the zero based `forms` array. Each form can have any one of the standard HTML form elements. These include single-line `text`, `radio`, `checkbox`, `hidden`, `password`, `reset`, and `submit`. There is also a `select` widget, which can be either a drop-down list or a plain list, and a `textarea` widget, which can be used to collect large amounts of text spanning multiple lines.

▶ **See** the section on "Using JavaScript Event Handlers" in chapter 3 for a discussion on the correspondence between HTML form elements, the events that they generate, and their JavaScript counterparts, **p. 92**.

The CD-ROM file c8-10.htm, is a page with several forms on it. This page demonstrates the interaction of form elements. It also has a script that iterates through all of the forms in the document and prints out their element names and values.

TIP A script can only access elements that have already been created. They cannot be accessed in a document <HEAD> because the forms and their elements do not yet exist.

Links   Links are the bread and butter of any hypertext system, especially HTML. In JavaScript, the `links` array can be canvassed in order to provide a list of links in a document. Links have only one property, the `target`. The `target` is *not* the URL pointed to by the link; rather, it is the window into which that URL will be loaded. Any link is also a `location` object, so that you can dissect the link in the same way you dissect a `location` object.

Links can have an `onClick` handler just as buttons do. However, when the `onClick` handler finishes, the URL specified by the link will be loaded. If you do not want the link to go anywhere, just specify the current URL as its destination. If you want to use a link to execute a function, use HREF= `'javascript: myfunc()'`. Myfunc() can call a function or contain JavaScript code. For example, HREF=`'javascript: self.close()'`, immediately closes the current window.

CAUTION

A `javascript:xxx()` call replaces a URL. The browser will try to interpret any return from a function call as if it were a URL. If the browser does not understand the return value, it reloads the current page. When that occurs, any window globals that you set during the *xxx()* function call will be lost.

Both text and images can be links. You can include both in the same link if you want so that clicking either the text or the image will activate the link's events. Because images can be links, you can use them as buttons to call functions if you use `javascript:xxx()` as the HREF instead of a URL. Unfortunately, because you cannot replace images dynamically, you cannot modify the appearance of the image to simulate a button down effect.

Links can also trap the `onMouseOver` event. However, it traps this event at the boundaries of the link. What that means is that if you run your mouse pointer over a link, the event will be fired twice: once when you enter the bounding box of the link and once when you leave it.

If you use the `onMouseOver` event to write to the status bar, you find that if you move your mouse too quickly you miss the status write. This is because it is rapidly replaced by the browser's own response to the event. When you exit, the status written will stay there until you encounter another link. If you want to use the content of your link in a function called from an `onMouseOver` handler, you can pass the function the keyword `this`. Links are treated like any other JavaScript object. Figure 8.3 shows a `onMouseOver` event being triggered just as the mouse moves over the link.

FIG. 8.3
MouseOver is only fired when the mouse pointer enters or leaves the linked object.

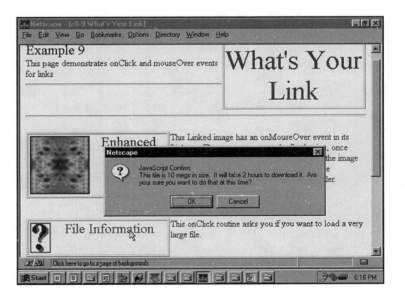

Figure 8.3 was generated by the code in listing 8.10, which includes examples of trapping onClick and onMouseOver events from links. It also includes a script that uses the document.links array to write a list of all of the links on the page. Examples of using a javascript:xxx replacement for a URL in a link can also be found in listing 8.2, which uses linked images as buttons.

Listing 8.10   Event Processing for the *Link* Object

```
<HTML>
<HEAD>
<!-- Created 09 Feb 1996 a2:45 AM 02:45 AM -->
<TITLE>What's Your Link</TITLE>
<SCRIPT>
function checkOut()
{
    a = (confirm("This file is 10 megs in size.  It will take 2 hours ¬
    to download it.  Are your sure you want to do that at ¬
        this time?"))
    if (a == true)
        {
            alert ('loading file...')
        }
    else
        {
            alert('NOT loading file!')
            self.location = self.location
        }
}

function enhance(what)
{
    astr = what.href
    self.status = 'Click here to go to a page of backgrounds.'
}


</SCRIPT>
</HEAD>
<BODY>
<TABLE ALIGN=RIGHT WIDTH=250 BORDER=1>
<TR><TD>
<FONT SIZE=7 COLOR= "darkcorel">
<CENTER>What's Your Link</CENTER>
</TD></TR></TABLE>
<FONT SIZE=5 >Example 9</FONT><BR>
This page demonstrates onClick and mouseOver events for links
```

```
<HR>
<H3><BR><HR><BR></H3>
<TABLE ALIGN=LEFT BORDER WIDTH=250>
<TR><TD>
<A HREF='C8-8.HTM' onMouseOver='enhance(this)'>
<IMG WIDTH=100 HEIGHT=100  VSPACE=2 HSPACE= 2 ALIGN=Left ¬
      SRC="Images/grkaleid.jpg">
<CENTER><FONT SIZE=5>Enhanced Status</FONT></CENTER></A>
</TD></TR></TABLE>
This Linked image has an onMouseOver event in its Link tag.
This event appears to be fired twice, once when the mouse passes
into the boundary of the image and once when it passes out.
Move the mouse SLOWLY to see the effect of the event handler.<BR CLEAR ALL>
<H3><BR></H3>

<TABLE ALIGN=LEFT BORDER WIDTH=250>
<TR><TD>
<A HREF='C8-9.HTM' onClick='checkOut()'>
<IMG WIDTH=32 HEIGHT= 50 VSPACE=2 HSPACE= 2 BORDER=2 ALIGN=Left ¬
      SRC="Images/answer_u.gif">
<CENTER><FONT SIZE=5>File Information</FONT></CENTER></A>
</TD></TR></TABLE>
This onClick routine asks you if you want to load a very large file. ¬
      <FONT SIZE=4 COLOR='red'> </FONT>
<BR CLEAR ALL>
<H3><BR><HR><BR></H3>
<H3><BR><HR SIZE=5 WIDTH=80%><BR></H3>
</BODY>
<SCRIPT>
k = document.links.length
document.write('This page has ' + k + ' links.  They are: <BR>')
for (i = 0 ; i < k ; i++)
    {
          document.write(i + '   ' + document.links[i] + '<BR>')
    }
</SCRIPT>
</HTML>
```

Anchors   Anchors consist of text or images in your document that are marked, usually named, and can be referenced by a link within the same document (known as a *local* link). The document object has an anchors array, but at this time its use is quite limited. You can find out how many anchors are on the page using the length property. The property arrays anchors[i].value or anchors[i].name can be accessed without error, but will also be empty.

Dynamic Documents

Dynamic documents created using JavaScript provide all the functionality of static documents written in HTML. If you can write it in HTML, you can write it on-the-fly in a document script. In fact, you can write your whole document in a script. You have already seen an example of this in listing 8.8, which converts document properties into a formatted area that can be placed at the beginning of any document you write. You can also have a script after the BODY tag that writes a document footer in a similar fashion.

Restrictions on *document.write*

Unfortunately, you cannot change anything on your current page once the document is finished. If you want to write to the current document, you have to open it and write to it via scripts placed at the beginning and end of the document. You can also choose to rewrite the entire document.

Using the document.write method is like printing on a dot matrix printer: it is top down only. This makes it particularly hard to do graphing or other innovative work that requires accurate positioning of objects on the page because you cannot know in advance where they will end up.

You must also be careful when enclosing an HTML statement within a document.write clause. This innocent statement will give you at least one error:

```
Document.write('<FONT SIZE=5 COLOR='red'>Mozilla is GREAT!</FONT>')
```

Many HTML parameters need to be quoted, and it is much easier to use single quotes than double quotes. Unfortunately, the write statement above will terminate with the leading quote of 'red'. The closing parenthesis of the write statement will not be found, and an error will occur. The problem is easily fixed in this case: just use double quotes around the word "red".

But what do you do if there is a need for a third level of nested quotes? Take this HTML statement for example:

```
<INPUT TYPE='radio' NAME='mycolor' VALUE='red' onClick='Alert("You chose red!")'>
```

This statement already has nested quotes. If you want to enclose this within a `document.write()` clause, you have two choices:

- Use a backslash to escape one set of quotes, usually the ones most deeply nested:

```
document.write(<INPUT TYPE="radio" NAME="mycolor" VALUE="red"
onClick="Alert(\"You chose red!\")">
```

- Put the contents of the deepest quotes into a variable:

```
astr = "You chose red!"
document.write(<INPUT TYPE="radio" NAME="mycolor" VALUE="red"
onClick="Alert(astr)">
```

If you have more than three levels of quotes, then you *must* use the second option.

▶ **See** the "Variables and Values" section of chapter 2, which gives the basic rules for string quoting, **p. 35**.

Using Nascent Documents

To provide a canvas for yourself to write on, use the `document.open()` command. It is a good idea to precede this with a `document.close()` command as a safety precaution, in case there is already a document open. You can open or reopen a document in the current window or any window for which you have a reference. Opening a document in that window clears anything that is already there. Once the document is open, you can write to it.

> **CAUTION**
>
> If you issue a `document.open()` command from within a script in the current page and it is not preceded by a window reference, the current page will be opened. Whatever is on the page is *gone!* This can be quite a surprise. Don't worry. You can recover the page with a reload, but your users might not know that. Check all `document.open()` references carefully.

A document is open until you specifically close it or until the browser runs out of things to write on it. When you first open a window, the document associated with that window is also opened. You can then write to it with a header script. Then the browser writes all of the body, if there is one, and anything it finds in the footer script, if there is one. When it reaches the end of the HTML text, it automatically closes the document. Note that if you open a new window with `myNewWin = self.open('', 'NewWin')`, you do not have to issue a `document.open()`. Just start writing on the blank page.

We have already noted some items to be careful of in using document write statements. If you try to write to a document that is not open, nothing will happen. No error will occur—the command will simply fail. You can write anything to a nascent document, including scripts. If you are creating a window from scratch, then you *have* to write everything. Listings 8.1 and 8.2 at the beginning of this chapter illustrate this approach.

TROUBLESHOOTING

I opened a fresh document using `document.open()`, wrote to it for quite a long time using `document.write()`, and nothing happened. Where did I go wrong?

`Document.write()` places all of its output into an ASCII stream. Think of it as one big string that exists somewhere in memory. The browser does not get to interpret the stream until you specifically say, "That's all, folks!" with a `document.close()`. Once you close the document, everything that you have written (hopefully) is rendered in the browser window. This also means than any script errors will not be noticed until the document is actually closed.

A Page Generated Entirely by JavaScript

If you examine listing 8.9, you see that this document is written totally within the header. Let's revisit this document and add a little to it. Suppose that you have a number of images that have the same prefix and differ only in a final numerical suffix. Let us also suppose that these numbers are sequential. With very little JavaScript, you can dynamically generate the image citations and write them to the page.

Listing 8.11 takes this approach. The `for` loop is particularly worthy of close examination. It keeps adding citation information to a continuously growing string. When it is finished, it uses one `document.write()` statement to put the string on the document stream. There are several reasons to use this type of an iterative construct:

- It is easier to debug. You could use a separate string for each individual citation and pop it up in an alert so that you can check its syntax.
- It gets rid of some of the nested quote problems.
- You can save the resulting output string. This is particularly useful if you want to actually write the HTML for the citations as text, rather than have the browser interpret what you write. To do that, you need to replace each < with < and each > with >.

Listing 8.12   Generating an Entire Document in JavaScript

```
<HTML>
<HEAD>
<!-- Created 08 Feb 1996 a11:32 PM 11:32 PM -->
<TITLE>Writing a Document with JavaScript</TITLE>
<SCRIPT>
document.bgcolor = 'linen'
document.text = 'darkslateblue'
document.link = 'coral'
document.vlink='peach'
document.alink='red'
document.write('<TABLE ALIGN=RIGHT WIDTH=350 BORDER=1>')
document.write('<TR><TD>')
document.write('<FONT SIZE=7 COLOR= "indianred">')
document.write('<CENTER>' +document.title + '</CENTER>')
document.write('</TD></TR></TABLE>')
document.write('<BR>')
document.write('<LEFT>')
document.write('This page is an example of a document written ¬
      completely within a script. The reference for each image is  ¬
      generated dynamically')
document.write('</LEFT>')
document.write('<BR CLEAR ALL>')
document.write('<HR>')
bstr = 'BLACE'
kstr = ''
for (i = 1 ; i <= 10 ; i++)
{
      var xstr = bstr + i + '.jpg'
      kstr += '<IMG SRC=\"NewImages\/' + xstr + '" '
      kstr += 'HEIGHT=100 WIDTH=100 VSPACE=5 HSPACE=5 BORDER=2
ALIGN=LEFT>'
      kstr += '<H3><BR><H3>'
      kstr += '<CENTER><FONT SIZE=4 COLOR="coral">' + xstr ¬
            + '</FONT></CENTER>'
      kstr += '<HR><BR CLEAR ALL>'
}
```

continues

Listing 8.12   Continued

```
document.write(kstr)
document.write('<BR><HR><BR>')
document.write('This document was last modified on<BR> ¬
    <FONT COLOR="red"><B>' + document.lastModified + '</FONT><BR>')
document.write('<BR><HR><BR>')
document.write('</B></CENTER>')
document.write('')
</SCRIPT>
</HEAD>
<H3><BR><HR SIZE=5 WIDTH=80%><BR></H3>
</BODY>
</HTML>
```

Dynamically Rewriting Your Page

There are many reasons why you might want to rewrite your page dynamically. You might want to try out various background images and colors, for example. There are two steps to this process: obtaining (or generating) the current information that you will modify, and also saving that information somewhere. Obtaining the information is easy. Storing and retrieving it is not because JavaScript does not enable you to read or write files (another security restriction).

One approach is to use a form and submit that form with no action listed. This places the form's parameters in the `search` property of the `location` object. This requires quite a bit of parsing, though. We have already seen in listing 8.7 that you can write your own `location.search` string. This approach is often simpler than using `submit`—with its awkward results—provided that you have no escaped characters and are able to process the parameters in order. Listing 8.12 shows an example of this. It can be easily extended to include a number of different items. In fact, you can build a simple page with it. This code can be found in the CD-ROM file c8-11.htm.

On the CD

Listing 8.12   c8-11.htm   Using JavaScript to Dynamically Rewrite a Document

```
<HTML>
<HEAD>
<!-- Created 08 Feb 1996 a6:10 PM 06:10 PM -->
<TITLE>Dynamic Modification of Documents</TITLE>
```

```
<SCRIPT>

function reloadMe()
{
    self.location = self.location
    astr= self.location.pathname  + '?'
    astr += document.forms[0].aname.value + '*'
    astr += document.forms[0].mytext.value + '*'
    astr += document.forms[0].mylink.value + '*'
    astr += document.forms[0].myvlink.value + '*'
    astr += document.forms[0].myimage.value + '*@'
    self.location = astr
}

function clearUp()
{
  self.location = self.location.pathname
}


function doTC(what)
{
    what.form.mytext.value = what.value
}

function doLC(what)
{
    what.form.mylink.value = what.value
}

function doVC(what)
{
    what.form.myvlink.value = what.value
}

function doImage(what)
{
    document.forms[0].myimage.value = 'DBLACE' + what + '.jpg'
}

function doname(what)
{
    what.form.aname.value = what.value
}

function createArray(n)
{
    this.length = n
    return this
}
```

continues

Listing 8.13 Continued

```
function arrayParms(astr)
{
    var k = astr.length
    astr = astr.substring(1,k)
    var n = 0
    var a = 1
    var i = 1
    var counter=0
    while(a > 0)
    {
        a = astr.indexOf('*',n)
        var bstr = astr.substring(n,a)
        if (bstr != '@' && counter <10 )
            {
                    parms[i] = bstr
                    n=a+1
                    i++
            }
        else a = 0
        counter++
    }
}
var parms = new createArray(5)
var astr = location.search
arrayParms(astr)

astr = '<BODY BACKGROUND = "Images/' + parms[5] + '" '
astr += 'TEXT="'+ parms[2] + '" '
astr += 'LINK="'+ parms[3] + '" '
astr += 'VLINK="'+ parms[4] + '" '
astr += 'ALINK="red" '
astr += '>\n'
document.write(astr)
document.write('<TABLE ALIGN=RIGHT WIDTH=350 BORDER=1>')
document.write('<TR><TD>')
document.write('<FONT SIZE=7 COLOR= "indianred">')
document.write('<CENTER>' +document.title + '</CENTER>')
document.write('</TD></TR></TABLE>')
document.write('<LEFT><B>')
document.write('This page is an example of dynamically revised by ¬
        a header script which acts on information stored in the command ¬
        line.  That information is based on user\' choices.')
document.write('</B></LEFT>')
document.write('<BR CLEAR ALL>')
document.write('<HR>')
astr ='<CENTER><FONT SIZE=7 COLOR="' + parms[3] + '"><B> '
astr += parms[1] + '</B></FONT></CENTER>'
document.write(astr)
document.write('<HR><BR>')
```

```
</SCRIPT>
</HEAD>

<CENTER>

<FORM NAME=nameForm>
Enter your first name here:<BR>
<INPUT TYPE=text NAME=myname  SIZE= 20 ¬
     onChange='doname(this)'><H3><BR></H3>
<CENTER>
<TABLE ALIGN=LEFT WIDTH=100 BORDER CELLPADDING=5>
<TR ALIGN=LEFT><TD>
<CENTER><B>Text</B></CENTER>
<INPUT TYPE="RADIO" NAME="tc" VALUE='white' ONCLICK='doTC(this)'>white
<INPUT TYPE="RADIO" NAME="tc" VALUE='yellow' ONCLICK='doTC(this)'>yellow
<INPUT TYPE="RADIO" NAME="tc" VALUE='navy' ONCLICK='doTC(this)'>navy
<INPUT TYPE="RADIO" NAME="tc" VALUE='blue' ONCLICK='doTC(this)'>blue
<INPUT TYPE="RADIO" NAME="tc" VALUE='orange' ONCLICK='doTC(this)'>orange
<INPUT TYPE="RADIO" NAME="tc" VALUE='red' ONCLICK='doTC(this)'>red
<INPUT TYPE="RADIO" NAME="tc" VALUE='black' ONCLICK='doTC(this)'>black
</TD></TR></TABLE>

<TABLE ALIGN=LEFT WIDTH=100 BORDER CELLPADDING=5>
<TR ALIGN=LEFT><TD>
<CENTER><B>Link</B></CENTER>
<INPUT TYPE="RADIO" NAME="lc" VALUE='white' ONCLICK='doLC(this)'>white
<INPUT TYPE="RADIO" NAME="lc" VALUE='yellow' ONCLICK='doLC(this)'>yellow
<INPUT TYPE="RADIO" NAME="lc" VALUE='navy' ONCLICK='doLC(this)'>navy
<INPUT TYPE="RADIO" NAME="lc" VALUE='blue' ONCLICK='doLC(this)'>blue
<INPUT TYPE="RADIO" NAME="lc" VALUE='orange' ONCLICK='doLC(this)'>orange
<INPUT TYPE="RADIO" NAME="lc" VALUE='red' ONCLICK='doLC(this)'>red
<INPUT TYPE="RADIO" NAME="lc" VALUE='black' ONCLICK='doLC(this)'>black
</TD></TR></TABLE>

<TABLE ALIGN=LEFT WIDTH=100 BORDER CELLPADDING=5>
<TR ALIGN=LEFT><TD>
<CENTER><B>VLink</B></CENTER>
<INPUT TYPE="RADIO" NAME="vc" VALUE='white' ONCLICK='doVC(this)'>white
<INPUT TYPE="RADIO" NAME="vc" VALUE='yellow' ONCLICK='doVC(this)'>yellow
<INPUT TYPE="RADIO" NAME="vc" VALUE='navy' ONCLICK='doVC(this)'>navy
<INPUT TYPE="RADIO" NAME="vc" VALUE='blue' ONCLICK='doVC(this)'>blue
<INPUT TYPE="RADIO" NAME="vc" VALUE='orange' ONCLICK='doVC(this)'>orange
<INPUT TYPE="RADIO" NAME="vc" VALUE='red' ONCLICK='doVC(this)'>red
<INPUT TYPE="RADIO" NAME="vc" VALUE='black' ONCLICK='doVC(this)'>black
</TD></TR></TABLE>
</CENTER>

<BR CLEAR ALL>
<HR>
<CENTER><FONT SIZE=4>Click on the image that you want for a ¬
     background.</FONT></CENTER>
```

continues

Listing 8.13 Continued

```
<H3><BR></H3>
<A HREF='javascript:doImage(1)'>
<IMG WIDTH=100 HEIGHT= 100 VSPACE=5 HSPACE= 5 BORDER=2 ALIGN=Left
SRC="Images/DBLACE1.jpg"></A>

<A HREF='javascript:doImage(2)'>
<IMG WIDTH=100 HEIGHT= 100 VSPACE=5 HSPACE= 5 BORDER=2 ALIGN=Left
SRC="Images/DBLACE2.jpg"></A>

<A HREF='javascript:doImage(3)'>
<IMG WIDTH=100 HEIGHT= 100 VSPACE=5 HSPACE= 5 BORDER=2 ALIGN=Left
SRC="Images/DBLACE3.jpg"></A>

<A HREF='javascript:doImage(4)'>
<IMG WIDTH=100 HEIGHT= 100 VSPACE=5 HSPACE= 5 BORDER=2 ALIGN=Left
SRC="Images/DBLACE4.jpg"></A>

<A HREF='javascript:doImage(5)'>
<IMG WIDTH=100 HEIGHT= 100 VSPACE=5 HSPACE= 5 BORDER=2 ALIGN=Left
SRC="Images/DBLACE5.jpg"></A>
<BR CLEAR ALL>
<HR>
</CENTER>
<TABLE ALIGN= RIGHT WIDTH=300><TR ALIGN=RIGHT><TD>
Name: <INPUT TYPE=text NAME=aname ><BR>
My Image: <INPUT TYPE=text NAME=myimage ><BR>
My Text: <INPUT TYPE=text NAME=mytext ><BR>
My Link: <INPUT TYPE=text NAME=mylink ><BR>
My VLink: <INPUT TYPE=text NAME=myvlink ><BR>
</TD></TR></TABLE>

<INPUT TYPE=button NAME=reloadBtn VALUE='Rewrite Page' ¬
     onClick='reloadMe()'>
<INPUT TYPE=button NAME=clearBtn VALUE= 'Clear' onClick='clearUp()'>
<INPUT TYPE=hidden NAME=hideFld >
</FORM>
<HR>
Click on Netscape's reload button before you click on the Rewrite ¬
     Page button.
<H3><BR><HR><BR></H3>
<H3><BR><HR SIZE=5 WIDTH=80%><BR></H3>
</BODY>
</HTML>
```

This page illustrates the following points that we have touched upon before:

■ It uses a script in the document <HEAD> to write to the document as it is being created.

- It dynamically changes the location.search string to store parameter information.

- It uses that information during the next rewrite operation to pick up where it had left off.

Figure 8.4 shows the result of loading this page (only the top part of the page is shown). The page starts out in the default Netscape colors. It gives the user the opportunity to select text and link colors, and a background tile. The user is in the process of selecting a tile.

FIG. 8.4
A dynamically rewritten page stores information for use in the next rewrite operation.

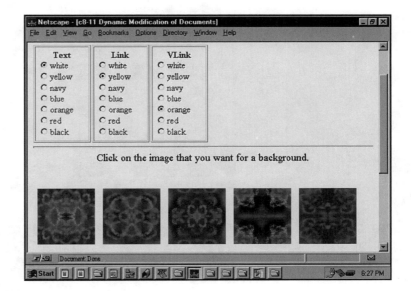

This script does several things that are worth noting, as follows:

- It creates a global array named parms. It does not bother to initialize the array because the program knows which parts of the array it is going to use later.

- It has a simple routine named reloadMe() to gather all of the form elements and write them to the location object.

- It has a simple parsing routine, named arrayParms(), to dissect location.search and place the pieces in an array.

- Its header script acts on the information provided by the user to dynamically reconstruct the page.

Figure 8.5 shows all the choices being placed in the summary form as the user clicks and enters text. Figure 8.6 shows the browser window after it has been rewritten dynamically to use the colors and tiles chosen by the user. Note that the summary form's contents have been added to the command line.

FIG. 8.5
Dynamic documents may modify their own appearance under user control.

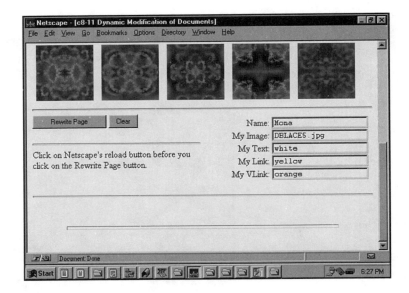

FIG. 8.6
Dynamic documents can rewrite their own background.

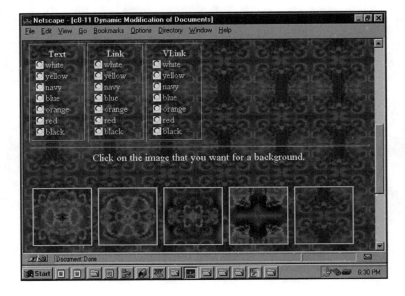

You can write to any page that appears in your window hierarchy. You cannot write to a page that is not a part of that hierarchy. Consequently, a parent can write to a child window and a child can write to its parent. If you want a parent window to write to a newly created child window, then you need to keep a handle to that window. The window.open() method returns such a handle; you should store this value as a global variable. It can then be used subsequently to access the child. If you do not use a global variable, then you will not be able to access the child window from any function other than the one that created it.

The *openNote()* Script Revisited

Let's examine the very first complete example in this chapter (listing 8.2) again now that you have more knowledge and experience. The parent window has two buttons, one to open the window and one to close it. These buttons call the parent window's functions, openNote() and closeNote(), respectively. The parent stores the handle to the openNote window in the global variable, aNoteWin. The responsibilities of the open routine are as follows:

- It defines the appearance of the window using the open(...) parameters.
- It writes the script of the window, including any event handle functions that are called by window objects and any initialization for the window.
- It writes the HTML for all of the objects in the window. In this case, the objects are a table with two buttons and the note text. The Close button includes the onClick handler that calls the closeNote() function of the child window.

The open routine also exemplifies a common and useful time-saving practice, known as *aliasing*. The full hierarchical representation of aNoteWin's document (self.aNoteWin.document) is collected in the short and easy to write variable, known as ndoc.

Finally, it is worth pointing out the utility of having the child window's Close button in the parent window, especially if the child window is small. The open() method will not create a second window of the same name, although it can do some updating if you make a second open() call with different parameters. If you click the Make Note button and nothing happens, it is possible that you did not get rid of the last window you made.

Murphy's Law dictates that the forgotten child will be at the very bottom of the eight other large windows on your screen. Being able to close the window from the parent is a great time saver and an excellent debugging tool.

Writing a Text Graph

In this section, we will write a simple text graph using an approach similar to that described in the section, "A Page Generated Entirely by JavaScript." We will provide entry fields on a form in which the user can enter some numbers. We will then use those numbers to dynamically generate the text graph using *X*s. Because we need to keep the size of the graph such that it will fit on the display, we will check all of the input in the form. This code is found on the CD-ROM in the file TextGraph.htm. Figure 8.7 shows the initial appearance of the form.

FIG. 8.7
The text graph page enables the user to enter data that will be graphed.

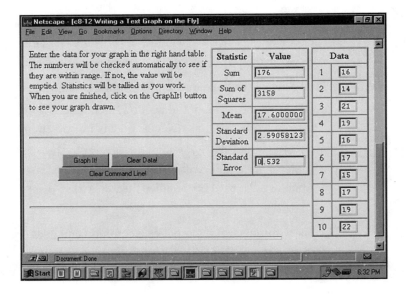

Data is entered into the form on the right. Up to 10 numbers can be added. As the data is entered, the program automatically does summary statistics. This is really useful if you want to see whether data *outliers* can be gracefully thrown away. (Data outliers are elements which are very far away from all other elements, such as 1000 in the sequence 1,3,1000,19,-4.) Once the data is entered, the user has the option of drawing the graph.

There are several points to examine in this example. The first thing to notice is that data is parsed and saved in exactly the same way as the previous example. Second, the code that draws the graph is conditional on location.search being non-empty. If no parameters have been added, then no graph is displayed; instructions are given instead.

As the user enters data, it is checked to see whether it falls within an acceptable range. As this is done, cumulative statistics are also kept. These are presented in a table adjacent to the data itself. Finally, if the location is reset, then all the fields in the form are cleared. This approach is much more polite than using Netscape's Reload button. Note that a footer script is used to reload the data fields. Figure 8.8 shows the result after user input has been entered and a graph drawn.

FIG. 8.8
Numerical data may be converted to a text graph using dynamic documents.

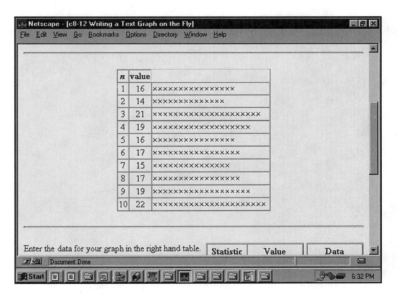

CHAPTER 9

Creating Your Own JavaScript Objects

by Mona Everett with Mark C. Reynolds

In chapter 4, "JavaScript Objects," we learned about JavaScript arrays and their close relationship with JavaScript objects. That same chapter also taught us how to create functions to do meaningful work. In this chapter, we build upon that foundation and learn how to create complex arrays, functions, and objects. In the process of this exploration, we reveal some of the hidden power of JavaScript.

Many of the examples in this chapter are too large to be listed in their entirety within the chapter. All the source code can be found on the CD-ROM. ■

How to build a reusable function library

JavaScript's object-oriented model makes it easy to write modular and reusable functions.

Learn about parameter checking and validation

A function may be called from different contexts, so it is important that functions validate their arguments before using them.

Use eval to execute functions written as strings

Building functions dynamically in the form of strings is a very powerful technique in JavaScript.

Look here for info on array initialization and storage

Arrays must be properly initialized to be used without error.

Create extended arrays and multi-dimensional arrays

JavaScript arrays are very flexible. Array elements may be added at will (so long as one is careful) and arrays may even contain other arrays.

Global and Local Variables

We have already explored the distinction between global variables, which are visible in every function, and local variables, which are only visible in the function in which they are declared. If you want to declare variables global to the whole window, define them outside of any function. Whether you precede the declaration with var or not it is still global. However, any declarations that you make inside of functions should be preceded with var if you want them to remain local. As you know, it is not strictly necessary to declare variables within functions. JavaScript treats any unknown variable it sees as a new variable, as if you had declared it. If you do not explicitly declare such a variable, or do not precede it with var, it becomes a window global variable. Check your functions very carefully for variable declarations. If you accidentally make a variable a global variable by not using var it can cause no end to trouble.

 TIP Particular care should be taken with variables having common names, such as i, j, or iter. Always check the declaration of these variables carefully.

It is unfortunate that the rules for the use of var are confusing. Remember that placing var in front of a variable declaration restricts it to the *scope* in which it is declared. The scope of a variable is the context in which that variable can be used. In the case of a local variable declared in a function, the scope of that variable is the function itself. In the case of a window script, it is the window. If you do not use var in a function or a window script, the variable's scope is global—it can be used anywhere in the window.

Although Javascript does not force you to declare or initialize variables before you begin function statements, it is often very useful to do so. First, it allows you to document the purpose of each variable. This is not only good programming practice, it is also genuinely useful. When you return to a function six months after you wrote it you may not remember what the variable countme does, unless you explicitly document it as // array index variable. Second, if you explicitly declare each variable, then you have the opportunity to initialize them to some meaningful default value.

▶ **See** the "Objects, Properties, and Methods in JavaScript" section of chapter 4 for a description of the basic rules for JavaScript functions and their parameters and variables, **p. 106**.

> **CAUTION**
>
> If you declare global variables *within* a function, you must execute the function first for the variables to be defined.

Figure 9.1 illustrates this idea. When the first button is pressed, an alert dialog box results, which tells you that there is an undefined variable. Since the variable was declared with `var` inside a function, it is local and "out of scope" to anything outside the function. The other three buttons all access global variables which have been defined outside of a function or within a function without the use of `var`. Pressing these buttons gives you the value of the variable. The source code for this example can be found in c9-2.htm on the CD-ROM.

Part II Ch 9

FIG. 9.1
JavaScript alerts you when you have used an undefined variable.

Parameter Checking

Functions, particularly ones that carry out critical tasks like opening windows, should always check to see if their parameters are valid. This usually involves making sure that they are the correct type and/or are within some expected range. First and foremost, then, we need routines to determine if the parameters are valid. Strings are relatively safe as parameters, but numbers and booleans are not. This is because JavaScript often converts a non-string, such as 5, to the corresponding string "5," but it only converts to numerical or boolean values if it can. If a string parameter is specified as the number 5, no error occurs, because the numerical value 5 and the string "5" may be freely converted to one another. If a numerical parameter is specified as the string "five," an error very definitely occurs, because JavaScript does not know how to convert that string to a number.

If you discover a bad parameter, you have two choices. You can simply abandon all processing, or you can change the bad parameter to some safe default. It is often preferable to do the latter, and place an error message in a variable that calling routines can check. The library functions which we will develop later in this chapter use two of these; they are `aWinErr` and `aStringErr`. Of course, there is nothing you can do to keep the user from entering something totally unanticipated in a text field. The best you can do is try to limit the destruction that ensues.

Now let's examine a few functions from our repertoire to see how they work. Three checking functions are presented: one for numbers or restricted characters, one for booleans, and one for character encoding/decoding.

Numbers or Restricted Character Sets   The function isIn, shown in listing 9.1, is multipurpose. It can check to see if all of the characters in a parameter string are also found within a comparison string. If the comparison string is empty, it uses a string of digits (0-9) as the comparison string. This function returns a boolean value to indicate if the comparison succeeded or failed. It can also strip unwanted characters from the parameter value and return a string that contains only acceptable characters. The test code is found in the file c9-testr.htm on the CD-ROM.

On the CD

Listing 9.1   c9-testr.htm   A Multipurpose Parameter Checking Function

```
function isIn(astr,nstr,strip)
// astr :  item in question
// nstr :  allowable character string; defaults to numbers
// strip:  determines whether return is true/false
// or only allowable characters.  Defaults to false.
{
    //declare and initialize variables to make sure they stay local
    var cc=''
    var dd=''
    var bstr = ''
    var isit
    var i = 0
    // make error string empty
    aStringErr = ''
    //force number to a string
    astr = '' + astr
    //default to checking for a number
    if (nstr== null || nstr == '') nstr = '1234567890'
    //make sure that 'strip' is a boolean
    strip = (isBoolean(strip))
    //force to string; remember, this can return a boolean
    strip += ''
    //NOT a boolean--complain
    if (strip == 'false')
        {
                strip = false
                aStringErr = '"Value" must be (T/t)rue or (F/f)alse.'
```

```
            aStringErr += 'It is neither. Defaulting to false.'
        }

    //now that everything is set up, let's get down to business

    isit=false

    // begin loop which cycles through all of the characters in astr
    for (i = 0 ; i < astr.length ; i++)
        {
            cc=astr.substring(i, i+1)

            // begin loop which cycles through
            // all of the characters in nstr
            for (j =0 ; j< nstr.length ; j++)
                {
                    dd = nstr.substring(j, j + 1)
                    isit = false
                    if (cc == dd)        // so far so good
                        {
                            isit = true
                            bstr += cc      // accumulate good
                                            ➥characters
                            break           // no need to go
                                            ➥further
                        }
                } // end of j loop
            //you found a mismatch; disqualify the item
                ➥immediately unless you are going to strip the
                ➥string.
            if (isit == false && strip == 'F')
                    break;
            else continue
        } // end of i loop

    if (strip=='T') return bstr  // return stripped string
    else return isit             // or return true/false (boolean)
}
```

The isIn() function takes three parameters. The parameter astr is the item to be checked. The parameter nstr contains the set of characters which are permissible in astr. By default, nstr will be "1234567890" which will have the effect of checking to see if astr is a numerical quantity. The boolean parameter strip indicates if unacceptable characters (characters not in nstr) should be stripped out of astr.

The first portion of the isIn() function makes sure that astr and nstr are both strings, and initializes nstr to its default value if it was given as the empty string. It also ensures that `strip` is boolean (the function `isBoolean()` is described in the later section "Boolean Validation"). The `for` loop then examines every character in `astr`. The `substring` function extracts each character into the local variable `cc` and checks to see if that character may be found in `nstr` using a second `for` loop. If any unacceptable characters are found the `isit` variable is set to `true`. This `for` loop is also responsible for building a new string, in the local variable `bstr`, which contains only acceptable characters.

If the `strip` parameter is `true` then the function will return the stripped string `bstr` at the end of its processing. An example of this is shown in figure 9.2. The characters l and v are out of range, and are removed. If `strip` was `false` then the function returns a boolean value which indicates whether the `astr` parameter contained any unacceptable characters. This case is illustrated in figure 9.3, using the same set of string values.

FIG. 9.2
JavaScript functions may convert unacceptable parameters to an acceptable form.

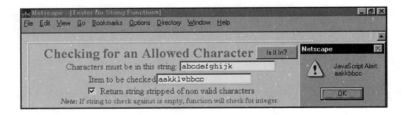

FIG. 9.3
JavaScript functions may choose to reject parameters which are out of range.

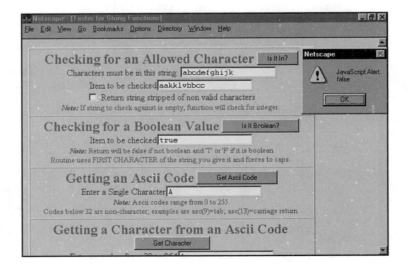

Boolean Validation   When we write code it is easy to forget exactly how we are supposed to pass a variable. One of the nice things about JavaScript the language is that it is relatively untyped when compared with strongly typed languages like Ada or Pascal. In JavaScript the same function can return a boolean or a string or a number with impunity. The calling routine may have some trouble though; it complains if you try to hand it a string when it thinks it should get a number. One way out of this dilemma is to forcibly convert the variable to the form you want. You can force an arbitrary value to be a string by concatenating it with an empty string. You can force an arbitrary value to be an integer with `parseInt()`.

▶ **See** "The String Object" section of chapter 5 for a discussion of string conversion rules and methods, **p. 152**.

This kind of type confusion occurs frequently with boolean values. Should a function return `true` or "true" or "t" or "T" to indicate success? Listing 9.2 shows the `isBoolean()` routine. It takes the first character of a putative boolean, changes it to uppercase, and checks to see if it is "T" or "F." If the resulting value is either "T" or "F" then the function returns `true` or `false`, respectively. If the resulting value is neither "T" nor "F" then `isBoolean` returns false. Note that only the first letter of the `astr` parameter is examined, so that fear, FORTRAN, and felicity will all be interpreted as `false`, while tundra and TECO will be seen as `true`.

Listing 9.2   c9-testr.htm   A Boolean Validation Function

```
function isBoolean(astr)
//astr is the object to check
{
     var isit=''
     astr +=''
     if (astr == null ¦¦ astr == '') isit= false
     else
          {
                    astr = astr.substring(0,1)      // just get first
                                                      ➥letter
                    astr = astr.toUpperCase()      // make it caps
                    if (astr != "T" && astr != "F")
                         {
                               // unacceptable value entered
                               isit = false
                         }
                    else
                         //returns value which caller can test for true/
                          ➥false
```

continues

Listing 9.2   Continued

```
                          //without having to do substrings, etc.
                          isit= astr
        }
   //return is mixed:  can be either a boolean or a string.
   return isit
}
```

Character Validation and Conversion   Most languages have a means of defining a character as a numeric code and, conversely, converting the code back to the character. The ASCII standard is often used for this conversion these days, just as EBCDIC was used 20 years ago. All these character encoding systems, such as ASCII, represent each character as a unique numeric value. In ASCII, for example, the space character has the decimal character code 32 (or 0x20 in hexadecimal), the letter b has the decimal code 98 (0x62), and the punctuation mark ampersand has the decimal code 38 (0x26). There are many such character encoding systems, some of which also include characters from languages other than English.

▶ **See** chapter 11, which discusses the Unicode international character encoding standard in the section entitled "The Java Language," **p. 370**.

In fact, if we had functions to convert between the character respresentation and the numerical representation then many forms of parameter validation would become much easier. For example, an `isNumber` function, which attempts to determine if a parameter is a number, becomes extremely easy to write. One just examines each variable's numerical ASCII code to see if it is in the range represented by the numerical codes for the characters 0 through 9.

These two conversion functions are relatively easy to write. We first need to construct a string that contains all of the printable ASCII characters. We will construct such a string (called the `charset` string) with a utility function called `makeCharsetString()`. To convert from the character representation to the numerical representation we search for the character within the `charset` string. The numerical representation of that character is its index in the `charset` string, plus 32. The additional 32 is needed since that is the numerical code of the first printable ASCII character, the space character.

To convert from the numerical representation we reverse the process. We subtract 32 from the numerical value and then extract the character in the `charset` string at that location. Listing 9.3 shows the asc function, which converts from character to numeric code, while listing 9.4 shows the chr function, which converts from numeric code to character. The asc() and chr() functions, along with the makeCharsetString() function (which is not listed in the following) will all be found in the c9-testr.htm file on the CD-ROM.

> **N O T E** Case always matters in character encoding. The numerical code for an uppercase letter will always be different from that of the corresponding lowercase letter. For example, b is 98 (0x62) in ASCII, while B is 66 (0x42). ■

On the CD

Listing 9.3 c9-testr.htm A Function to Return the ASCII Code of a Character

```
?
function asc(achar)
//achar character whose ascii code you want
{
    var n = 0
    var csstr = makeCharsetString()  //get ascii char string
    //alert(csstr)
    n = csstr.lastIndexOf(achar)
    //printable characters begin at 32 with [space]
    return n + 32
}
```

On the CD

Listing 9.4 c9-testr.htm A Function to Return a Character Given an ASCII Code

```
function chr(x)
{
    var ar = ''
    var astr = makeCharsetString()      //get ascii string
    //alert(astr)
    result = ''
    if (x >= 32 )              // printable
        {
            x = x - 32
             ar = astr.charAt(x)
            result = ar
        }
    else                       // non printable, return text
                               ➥representation
```

continues

Listing 9.4   Continued

```
        {
                if ( x == 9 ) result = 'tab'
                if ( x == 13 ) result = 'return'
                if ( x == 10 ) result = 'linefeed'

        }
        return result
}
```

Note that there are some strategically placed `alert()` calls in these functions that are commented out. These alerts are for debugging purposes, to ensure that the functions are actually delivering what you want. Note also that the `chr()` function does not handle most of the *control characters*, whose numeric codes are below 32. The only control characters which it tells you about are the tab, a return, and linefeed characters. This can be used in an ugly but useful way to insert a carriage return/linefeed combination into a string using the expression + `chr(13)` + `chr(10)`.

There is one additional function we will present. This is the extremely useful `word()` function, which extracts an indexed phrase from a delimited string. A delimited string is one containing one or more entries separated by a special character referred to as the delimiter or separator. For example, the string "My:name:is:Hanover:Fiste" contains five components—My, name, is, Hanover, and Fiste—separated by the delimiter colon (:).

N O T E   Delimited strings are used frequently in JavaScript and other loosely typed languages. Delimited strings are convenient because they allow multiple elements to be represented as a single string. Many spreadsheet and database programs, for example, can export their data as delimited strings. The comma (,) and colon (:) characters are frequently used as delimiters. ▪

The `word()` function is shown in listing 9.5. It takes three parameters: the delimited string `inwhat`, the delimiter `sep`, and the index `which` of the component required. It returns the component requested. Thus, if you ask `word()` for the third component of the string "My:name:is:Hanover:Fiste," it returns "is." Figure 9.4 shows some sample output from the `word()` function. In this case we have used the @ character as the delimiter and asked for the second item in the string. Note that the `word()` function uses 1-based indexing.

Listing 9.5   c9-testr.htm   The Delimited String Processing Function
word()

```
function word(sep,which,inwhat)
// separator character
// which word/phrase
// text in which to look
{
    //alert(inwhat)
    var n = 0               // start of a phrase
    var wstr = 0            // holds substring
    var i = 0              // loop counter
    var s = 0              // start of winning phrase
    var f = 0              // end of winning phrase
    for (i = 1 ; i < which ; i++)
        {
            n = inwhat.indexOf(sep,n)       // look for separator
            if (n < 0 )                     // if you do not find it
                {
                    return ''                // return is empty string
                    break                    // jump out of loop
                }
            n++                              // otherwise, loop again
        }

    // now we should be at the right place
    if ( n >= 0)                             // ... but do this only if
    {                                        // we found the separator
        //alert(n + '==' + wstr)
        var s = n                            // phrase starts with n,
                                             ➥now s
        var f = inwhat.indexOf(sep,n)        // get next instance of sep
        if (f < 0 ) f = inwhat.length        // but if there is none ...
        wstr = inwhat.substring(n,f)         // must be last phrase in
                                             ➥string
    }
    //alert(f + '--' + wstr)
    return wstr                              // return string; it will
                                             // be empty if sep was not
                                             ➥found.

}
```

The word() function does its job by using a simple algorithm. The first for loop in this function uses the string method indexOf() to find each occurrence of the delimiter character sep in the input string inwhat. The local variable n is used to hold the current position of the delimiter, while the iteration variable i counts the number of such delimiters found so far. If fewer than the required number of which are found then the word() function returns the empty string.

FIG. 9.4

The word() function extracts an indexed phrase from within a character delimited string.

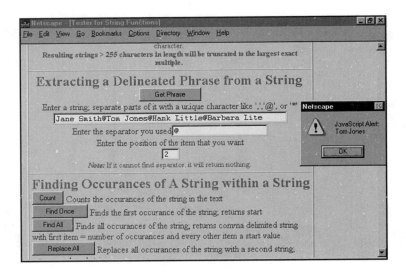

If the required number are present then the `if` test just after the `for` loop will succeed. At this point `n` is positioned at the beginning of the element which we want; it is now necessary to locate the end of that element. This will either be the next occurrence of the delimiter, or the end of the `inwhat` string itself. The local variable `f` is used to hold the location of the end of the element. Once `n` and `f` have been computed the `word()` function uses the `substring()` method to store the desired element in the local variable `wstr`, which is then returned as the value of the `word()` function.

More on JavaScript Functions

You may recall from chapter 4 that functions are developed by declaring them within a script. This section briefly reviews some of things to remember when writing functions, and then delves a little deeper into some of the fine points of functions in JavaScript. This material is developed further in the next section on associative arrays.

Make sure that you declare your most elementary functions earliest in the header script. This ensures that later functions are able to use them. The same rule applies to objects. Make sure that you do not reference any objects that have not yet been created in any of your functions. Functions in a header script cannot see objects created by the HTML on your page, nor can they see objects created by code executing later in the script. If there is something that *must* be done with an HTML generated object, place it in a footer script.

Proper error checking is also very important. If a function fails, provide a mechanism for the calling routine to detect the failure. If you can, try to keep the damage to a minimum. It is a sign of very poor design when the Netscape Navigator JavaScript Error dialog box comes up immediately after your page is loaded. One major problem with using functions has to do with passing the parameters in incorrect order. If some function expects three parameters that represent two numerical values and a string, but you give it a numerical value, a string, and then the second numerical value, an error very likely occurs. A similar problem arises when a calling function misinterprets what should be passed in a parameter. If a function relies on unchecked input from a user, check that the parameter is at least of the right type. If you detect that it is incorrect, flag it, and, if you can, fix it.

CAUTION

Make sure that all local variables within a function are preceded by `var`. If a function inadvertently declares a global variable which has the same name as a local variable in another function, inexplicable behavior will often result. In particular, function parameters may become garbled. This type of error is particularly difficult to diagnose, so particular care should always be taken with variable declarations.

Storing Your Functions

JavaScript cannot read (or write) local data files, but it can load and use HTML files. Therefore, even though you cannot create a JavaScript function library in an ordinary file, you can write a function library in an HTML header and load that library inconspicuously when you want to use it. Function libraries may also be used with frames, by designating one particular frame as the "owner" of the library. All of the other frame documents have a global variable called `funcs`, which refers to that special frame from the perspective of the calling frame. Consequently, you can call a function named `myfunction` in the function library by using the reference `funcs.myfunction` from anywhere in any of the nested frames. You can also make a function library in a frameset itself. Finally, some future version of the Netscape browser will have the ability to load JavaScript files using the SRC attribute of the SCRIPT tag, much as images are loaded.

▶ **See** the section "A Bug Database in JavaScript," in chapter 19 for a comprehensive example of using a function library with frames, **p. 673**.

Note that the functions given here are meant to be introductory only. Since JavaScript, at the moment, lacks many of the functions that have become standard in most programming languages, we have provided you with a library of some commonly used functions. They can be found in the file function.htm on the CD-ROM. Function.htm is also the document in the upper-left frame of c9-1.htm, the frameset document used for the demos in chapter 20.

If you are in that document, clicking the tile image in that frame pops up a window with all of the function declarations and variable definitions. You can try out all of the string functions from the file c9-funcs.htm, which is also on the CD-ROM. This HTML file is a little test page that allows you to enter parameters and call a given function with them. It is also useful if you want to quickly look up an ASCII code or convert some HTML text to a form in which it can be displayed by the browser without being interpreted as HTML by the browser.

Functions on the Fly

We have used the construct javascript: xxx as a replacement for a URL reference in linked text or images. We can also use this idea to create a one line scratchpad to execute code any time we want. First of all, you can attach just javascript: to a link. When this link is exercised a window pops up with two frames—a text widget on the bottom and a blank window on top. If you type some script into the text box, and then hit Return, the text is executed. You can even rewrite the document in the top frame.

N O T E   The javascript: construction does not work uniformly on all platforms. In addition, there are behavioral differences between Netscape version 2.0 and version 2.0.1. Use this technique with caution. ■

▶ **See** chapter 8, which describes the use of the javascript: construct in several places. See the "Links" and "Anchors" sections in particular, **p. 280, 283**.

Rather than writing script code, there is an even easier way to get the same behavior. Just type **javascript:** in the location display and hit Return. Up pops the scratchpad! In fact, you can even type your code directly into the location text box and have it be executed. Figure 9.5 illustrates this simple JavaScript scratchpad.

FIG. 9.5
The JavaScript one line scratchpad is created with the javascript: URL.

The *eval* Function

In HyperCard, one can write Hypertalk in a text field and then "do" the field, which executes the contents of that field. Because of this your HyperCard scripts can write and execute code on the fly. You can do something similar in JavaScript using `eval()`. Although `eval()` sounds like it should be used only to evaluate mathematical equations, this function can actually do much more. It can evaluate any string that is a JavaScript statement. Try this experiment. Create an HTML button and attach the following statement as its `onClick` event handler:

```
eval('alert("I did it!")')
```

On the CD

When you click the button the alert box pops up. In the same way, you can pass the contents of an HTML text field or textarea to a JavaScript event handler. This is illustrated by the function `evaluate()`, which is found in the file c9-3.htm on the CD-ROM. This function consists of a single line of code, `eval(what)`. A single HTML button arranges to pass the contents of a textarea to this function, which promptly tries to execute the contents of that textarea as JavaScript code. The `eval` statement can be placed directly in the button handler, of course. By placing it in the separate (but trivial) `evaluate` function we make it easier to extend in the future. Figure 9.6 shows this simple textarea evaluator at work.

FIG. 9.6

The contents of a `textarea` can be evaluated as JavaScript code using `eval`.

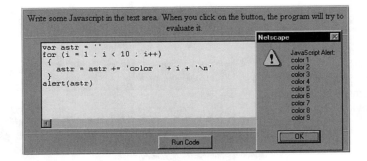

JavaScript's Associative Arrays

Associative arrays were introduced in chapter 4 and have been used in several previous chapters in this book. You are already aware that an associative array is a one dimensional array of pairs. You access the left member of the pair with a numeric index. You access the right member of the pair with a string index equal to the value of the left member of the pair. For example, (left) `myArray[1] = "red"` but (right) `myArray["red"]= "FF0000"`. Arrays must be explicitly created by a function that takes a generic `this` object and gives it a size. You can also create other properties for the array in this function. To actually create the array, you use the `new` operator together with our array creation function. For example, the statement

```
myNewArray = new createArray(6,'')
```

creates an array called `myNewArray` with 6 elements and initializes all of the left members to `''`. Note that this is not being done for you by JavaScript in some magical way. You have to write the creation function and then invoke it with the appropriate parameters.

An array is a primordial JavaScript object. Its properties, which represent the array members, can be anything. You must set the special property known as `size`, however, in your creation function. This property gives the length of the array (and is occasionally referred to as `length` for that reason). The `size` property is usually put in the zeroth element of the array during initialization. This means that your arrays will actually have $n+1$ elements in total: n elements for data, and one extra element at index zero to hold the array size. You need to be sure that your array access functions do not overwrite the zero element. Listing 9.6 shows a general purpose `createArray()` function.

> **Listing 9.6   A General Purpose *createArray* Function**
>
> ```
> function createArray(n, init)
> {
>     this.size = n  //This initialization is absolutely necessary
>     for (i = 1 ; i <= n ; i++)
>         {
>                 this[i] = init      //Initialize all of the left hand
>                                 ↳elements
>         }
>     return this        //Return the  array object to the caller
> }
> ```

Notice that there is no initialization of the right members of the array. You can also arrange to do this in the createArray function, but only with some effort. This is because the left element must be unique, and we have initialized all the array elements to the same value, namely the value init. If you have two array members containing the same value, you are only able to get to the first one.

In addition to creating arrays, it is often desirable to be able to reset or clear an array so that it may be reused. A special procedure, known as a *double replacement scheme*, must be used to clear or reset an existing array. (You can always create a completely new array, of course.) This special approach is needed because you have no way of knowing what values are already stored in the array. In particular, you have no way of knowing that they are unique. The double replacement method uses the following loop to safely reset the array myArray:

```
myArray[i] = '@@@@@'
myArray['@@@@@'] = ''
myArray[i] = ''
```

This method uses a special dummy replacement value to manipulate both the left and right sides of the pair. In the preceding example, the string '@@@@@' is used. To avoid the problem of non-unique indices, this dummy value must be highly unusual so that it is extremely unlikely to actually appear in the array.

> **CAUTION**
>
> Do *not* try to initialize the right side of an array in the same loop in which you initialize the left side. Javascript mixes left and right values for you. If you need to initialize the right side then do it in a separate loop.

Using Associative Pairs

Associative arrays occur far more often than you might think. They even occur in everyday life, although most people do not think of them that way. The picture on the top of a TV dinner box is related to what is in the box. You choose your dinner by looking at the picture because the picture conjures up thoughts of what is in the box. You would not open every box in the freezer and examine its actual contents in order to decide which one to put in the microwave. Programmers tend to think of an association in somewhat less colorful terms such as $a = b$, $x = 3y^2$, and so on. A Windows.ini file is an excellent example of the use of associative pairs. Every entry has a left element, such as *.doc, and a right element, such as c:\winword.winword.exe. In this case, the association is a relationship between a file suffix and the application that created it. Hypertext links are also associations; they are just ordered backward. The following HTML:

```
<A HREF='http://www.myfavoritelink.com'>My favorite link</A>
```

is actually an associative pair. If we were to place this into an array, most of us would place My favorite link on the left side, and 'http:// www.myfavoritelink.com' on the right. We often reference complicated, large, and sometimes obtuse objects with less complicated words or nicknames.

An Enhanced Array Object   A simple associative pair array may not be sufficient for your needs. Since an array is just an unstructured object, we can conveniently make it into a more complex object. For example, we can add a description property to an array. This is useful because the array may have a short name that is easy to use elsewhere in our code, but that name may not be very illustrative of the array's purpose.

Another property we might want to add is a property that reflects the "element of interest right this minute" or the "current" element. An example of this might be the strings in a listbox. The current property could refer to the currently selected item. This might be called the currentIndex property, or, more tersely, the nDx property. (Remember that JavaScript is case-sensitive.) Finally, if we are using the list as some kind of a stack, or if we are keeping track of items that are constantly being added or deleted from the list, we might need to know where the next open slot is located. We will call this property the nextIndex property.

But where do we put these properties? Well, properties are just array elements, so the question is where in the element list they should be placed. If we put them at the beginning, the array elements proper do not start at `index=1`. If we put them at the end, the array elements are in the right place, but it is now more difficult to increase the size of the array. This is because there are referencing problems if you access the properties by their array index, rather than by their names. We will examine the advantages and drawbacks of both approaches.

Array Initialization and Storage   While Netscape's description of arrays and their capabilities is glowing, there are some pitfalls in using arrays. Most of them stem from a lack of initialization or from incorrect initialization. The file c9-4.htm on the CD-ROM contains several array initialization and array manipulation functions. Various array functions are given that present different approaches to the location of the enhanced array object properties, such as `currentIndex` and `nextIndex`, and how (or if), the array is initialized.

The page generated by this file has buttons to allow you to initialize various arrays, reset them, clear them to `null`, enter a single value, and fill the arrays. Each array is treated in the same fashion. After you have exercised one or more of these functions you can then look at the contents of each array to see the effect. The array creation functions are organized into two catgories: those that place the enhanced properties at the end, and those that place the enhanced properties at the beginning. The first four array creation methods place the enhanced properties at the end of the array and initialize all empty slots to `"@"`. They differ in how they handle the enhanced properties.

The final three creation methods place the enhanced properties at the beginning of the array. This set of methods can be used to examine the consequences of not initializing the array, or initializing all of the elements (including those of the special properties) to the same thing, and of initializing only the empty elements. These functions are obviously not the only possible ways in which such array functions can be written. Listings 9.7 and 9.8 show two of these functions. Notice that it is not possible to create an uninitialized array and still place the extended properties at the bottom.

Listing 9.7   c9-4.htm   A Function to Create an Array with Special Properties Added at the End

```
function createArray1_d(n,init)
{
    var i = 0
    this.length = n + 3
        for (i = 1 ; i <= n ; i++)
        {
            this[i] = init
        }
    this.description = 'desc'
    this.nDx = 'nx'
    this.nextIndex = 'ni'
    return this
}
```

Listing 9.8   c9-4.htm   An Array Creation Routine with Extended Properties at the Beginning

```
function createArray3(n,init)
{
    var i = 0
    this.length = n + 3
    this.description = 'dc'
    this.nDx = 'nx'
    this.nextIndex = 'ni'
        for (i = 4 ; i <= n + 4 ; i++)
        {
            this[i] = init
        }
    return this
}
```

When you first load the c9-4.htm page, all of its arrays have been created; those arrays which initialize themselves have done so. Initialization has been done only for the left elements. No initialization has been done for the right elements. The viewing routine has been set to look at the first unused element. This will be the element at index n + 1, which is not yet processed or initialized in any way.

For purposes of this discussion, we call those array elements that are not directly related to a property the *empty* elements. Those that are associated with properties are called the *special* elements. Each array element consists of a left and right element. The left element of the zeroth element of the array has the array size in it. Note that the array size does not include the zeroth element itself, so that if the array size is 100, the array actually has 101 elements (the 101st being the size element). Said another way, the size includes elements 1...array.size. You should structure your for loops so that you iterate from element 1 up to and including element array.size.

> **CAUTION**
>
> Platform dependencies have been reported in the current release of Netscape Navigator. You may find array functionality to be different depending on the platform on which you are running the Navigator. Try the code in c9-4.htm and c9-4x.htm as test cases.

First, let's look at the those arrays that have the special elements at the end of the array. Click the 1a button. This creation routine initializes all of the empty elements to "@" and the special elements to " ". Did you expect to see the property names in the special elements? They do not appear here. They are properties associated with the array object, not values within the array object. You might expect the right element of anArray[0] to be undefined. It appears to be merely empty instead.

Before you breathe a sigh of relief, let's look at the next array creation method (associated with button 1b). Because we could not tell which element was which, we decided to initialize the left side of each special element with the name of the property associated with it. We did not do anything to the right side of the properties...well, we didn't, but JavaScript did! Notice that the right element has also been filled in with the name of the property, as shown in figure 9.7. This should provide your first clue that JavaScript arrays seem to have a mind of their own. Further, the right side of anArray[0] has the last special property assignment in it.

Button 1c manipulates an array in which all of the special elements have been initialized to the same value as the empty elements. There are no surprises here, except for the "@" put into the anArray[0] right side element. The final creation method of the first series initializes the special elements to two unique characters for each related property. This creation routine is also the most well-behaved of all, as shown in figure 9.8. The presence of the last special element assignment on the right side of anArray[0] is no longer a surprise.

FIG. 9.7
JavaScript often fills associative array values autonomously.

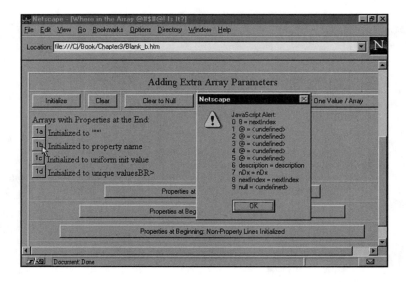

FIG. 9.8
Initializing a JavaScript array to unique values works best.

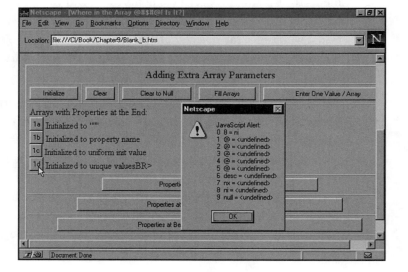

The three creation methods in the second series put the special elements at the beginning of the array. Using the first of these three methods it is possible to produce a completely uninitialized array. Still, nothing unusual happens; the empty elements are just `null`, as shown in figure 9.9. The second of these creation methods initializes the special elements, except that the initialization spans the whole array instead of just the empty elements. The very last creation method is designed and behaves properly, although, once again, `anArray[0]` is mysteriously filled in by JavaScript.

FIG. 9.9
Accessing a completely uninitialized array yields null values.

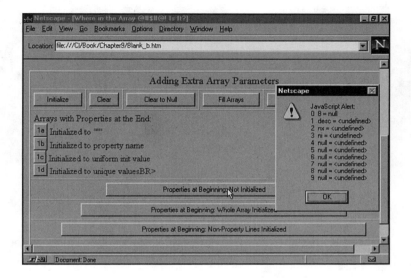

Instead of clearing or reinitializing the arrays at this point, click the rightmost button named `Enter One Value/Array`. This button does exactly that. It enters a `"red","FF0000"` pair into `anArray[2]` for those arrays with special properties at the end and into `anArray[6]` for those arrays with special properties at the beginning.

The array created by method 1a offers up no more surprises in this case. The value pair has been entered in the correct place. Notice that the array uses one-based indexing in terms of reference as well. The arrays created by the other methods with the special elements at the end (methods 2 through 4) are also well behaved. However, when we get to the first of the methods that puts the special elements at the beginning, trouble appears. The data pair is placed in `anArray[6]` but the `"FF0000"` is also placed in the left element of `anArray[7]`, as shown in figure 9.10.

It is worthwhile to note that this array is the one that was not initialized. To see this effect, reload the page. If you initialize the array in any way, even to `null`, it becomes well behaved. This should be a strong indication that initialization is always a good idea. The next two methods behave well within the array proper; notice, however, that an "`FF0000`" has been placed in the left element of the first unused element.

FIG. 9.10

Using an uninitialized array can overwrite array elements; once it is initialized all is well.

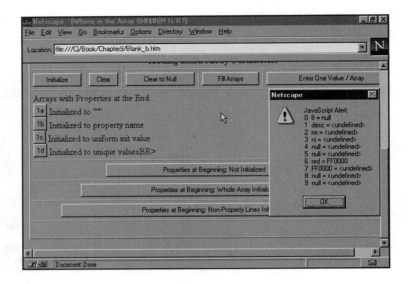

To continue our array experimentation, let's reinitialize the arrays, preferably by reloading the file. Then click the `Fill Arrays` button. This fills the empty elements of the array with pairs in the form of name=month. Repeat your inspection process. Array 1a is filled properly but now an `"FF0000"` has appeared in the first unused element. The same is true for the other three arrays which have their special properties last. As might be expected, the uninitialized array with special properties first fails to perform as desired, as shown in figure 9.11. The other two arrays with properties first behave well, except for the standard quirks: the left element of the last array element ends up in the right element of anArray[0] and the left side of the first unused element is set to the right side of the now discarded color pair. Clearing the array solves all the problems associated with not being initialized, as shown at the bottom of figure 9.12.

You can perform a variation on this experiment by reinitializing the arrays and then clearing them, using either method. Use the Initialize and Clear (or Clear to Null) buttons, and then add a single value to all of the arrays, or simply fill the arrays. The 0 element and first unused elements remain quirky, but the array elements themselves behave properly.

FIG. 9.11
Entering data into an uninitialized array scrambles the values.

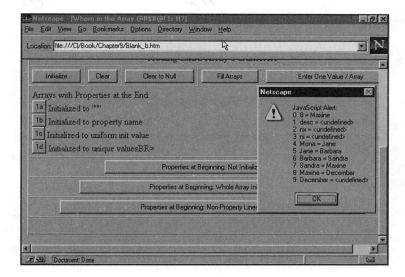

FIG. 9.12
After an uninitialized array has been cleared, all reference problems are resolved.

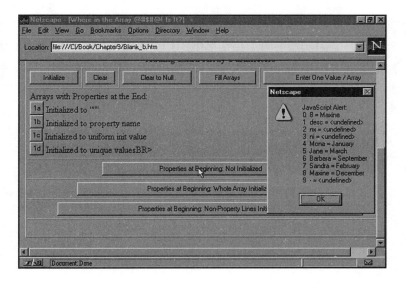

The companion page in the file c9-4x.htm provides a variation on the same theme. It is the same as the code in c9-4.htm, except that all its arrays have an extra uninitialized element, just after the original eight array elements. As before, a first unused element is displayed. If you go through the same procedures, you see that this extra element causes even more confusion.

CAUTION

Initialize your arrays before you use them! Uninitialized arrays cannot be trusted to provide correct results when referenced. They cannot even be trusted to provide consistently incorrect results, and can be a nightmare to debug.

Filling Arrays from Paired Lists   Listing 9.9 is worth special attention. It provides a function named `fillArrayFromLists()` which will fill the associative pairs of an array from two parallel lists of delimited elements. It is a lot faster to write such lists than it is to specifically set each right and left element in an array. This function uses the library function `word()` which is described earlier in this chapter. You may recall that this function uses a character delimiter to separate the elements in the list. The separator can be any character; the most common one is a comma (,). HyperCard enthusiasts will recognize this as an item list. The `fillArrayFromLists` function will be found in the file c9-4.htm on the CD-ROM.

On the CD

Listing 9.9   c9-4.htm   A Function to Load an Associative Array from Two Delimited Lists

```
function fillArrayFromLists(anArray,aaList,bbList,sep,s,f)
{
    var lstr = ''                   // left hand array element
    var rstr = ''                   // right hand array element
    var i = 0                       // iteration variable
    var counter = 1
     for (i = s ; i <=f ; i++)
        {
            anArray[i] = word(sep,counter,aaList)
            anArray[anArray[i]] = word(sep,counter,bbList)
            counter++
        }
}
```

This function takes six parameters: the array `anArray` whose values are to be set, two delimited strings `aaList` and `bbList` which hold the right and left elements, the string delimiter `sep`, and the first `s` and last `f` indices in `anArray` which are to be set. The function executes a simple `for` loop over all the array indices from `s` to `f` inclusive. In each iteration it calls the `word()` function twice, to the right and left elements from `aaList` and `bbList`.

As a demonstration of the power of this function, let us invoke it using two short lists. In our case, we use the asterisk character (*) as the delimiter. The following code shows each person on the list aList being associated with a particular month, as given in the list bList:

```
var aList = 'Mona*Jane*Barbara*Sandra*Maxine'
var bList = 'January*March*September*February*December'
fillArrayFromLists(array1,aList,bList,'*',1,5)
```

Using the Enhanced Array Object   Now that we have created our enhanced array object and dissected it at great length, how can we use it and which version should we adopt? Although most of the creation methods we have tested work if the array is properly initialized, we will use the final version of the methods which place their special properties first in our subsequent code. This is the one that did *not* overwrite our special properties. Most of the time only the left elements of the associative pair are used, but these lists can also hold an associated object (right element).

T I P   The enhanced array object may be used to implement a string list, object list, or a stack.

One array which arises frequently in JavaScript applications is an array of newly created child windows, since JavaScript does not provide such an array by default. Listing 9.10 shows the function winArrayAdd( ), which can be used to add a window to such a window array. Note that this function uses global variables to keep track of the next available array slot (in nextWin) as well as the current window (in curWin).

Listing 9.10   A Function to Add a Window to a Window Tracking Array

```
function winArrayAdd(aWinHdl)
{
    // set next open slot in winArray to hold this window handle
    // and that windows creator
    aWinArray[nextWin] = aNewWin
    aWinArray[aWinArray[nextWin]] = aNewWin.creator
    curWin = nextWin    // make this the current window
    nextWin++                // increment next available slot pointer
}
```

Instead of using global variables we can, of course, use an array with special properties as well. The code in listing 9.11 illustrates this form of the window addition function. While listing 9.11 does not look much different from 9.10, the latter version is the preferred one. This is because it keeps essential window tracking information together. Other functions may therefore access all the relevant data by simply examining appropriate elements of the array, rather than having to look at the array and also consult some global variables.

Listing 9.11   A Better Version of the Window Add Function Using Special Properties

```
function winArrayAdd(aWinHdl)
{
    // set next open slot in winArray to hold this window handle
    // and that windows creator
    aWinArray[aWinArray.nextIndex] = aNewWin
    aWinArray[aWinArray[nextWin]] = aNewWin.creator
    aWinArray.ndx = aWinArray.nextIndex     // make this the current
                                            ➥window

    nextWin++          // increment next available slot pointer
}
```

Arrays of Arrays

One of the biggest criticisms of associative arrays is that they are one dimensional. The argument can be made that the left and right sides constitute a second dimension, of size two, but this is not really a true multi-dimensional array. In fact, two-dimensional arrays are really just arrays of arrays. Because of the nature of associative arrays, one can develop such complex structures with relative ease.

Simulating Multi-Dimensional Arrays   Imagine, if you will, an array of colors. In a simple implementation of such an array, the left element contains the name of the color, such as "red," and the right member contains the hexadecimal value for the color. For red this value is 0xFF0000. There are many shades of red, however, and Netscape has even named a few specific ones. Of course, we could add all of these variant names to the array. It would be much nicer to be able to go to an array, find "red," and then access into a list of colors which were various shades of red. Let's now construct an example in which we can do that. As usual, the left element is initialized to "red." The right element, however, holds a handle to another array called moreReds. The array moreReds contains the typical colorname=hexvalue pair. Listing 9.12 shows a very simple-minded way of creating such a multi-dimensional array.

Listing 9.12   A First Approach to Creating a Multi-Dimensional Array

```
colors = new createArray(9,'')

moreRed = new createArray(20,'')
moreYellow = new createArray(20,'')
moreOrange = new createArray(20,'')
moreBrown = new createArray(20,'')
moreGreen = new createArray(20,'')
moreBlue = new createArray(20,'')
morePurple = new createArray(20,'')
moreGray = new createArray(20,'')
moreWhite = new createArray(20,'')

...
```

Part
II
Ch
9

Not only is this tedious, but it's not even a complete solution. We have to put each of these secondary arrays into the right elements of the first array. There must be an easier way to do this. We need to develop an approach to getting the various values into the multi-dimensional array and getting them out again.

Listing 9.13 contains three functions. The createArray() function is very similar to the array constructor we have already seen. The fillcolorArray() function fills both the left and right elements of an associative array, which is passed in as a parameter. This means that if you execute the statement

```
anArray = fillColorArray(anArray,'green','gr')
```

the left elements are filled with green1, green2,..., and the right elements are filled with gr1, gr2,.... The third function, lotsOfColors(), is used to orchestrate the creation and initialization of this array. This function also uses our old friend the word() function.

One might think of using eval() to metamorphose a constructed string into an array handle, as in the following statement:

```
dstr = eval(dstr = new createArray(20,''))
```

In fact, this is not necessary. Here we see another tribute to the flexibility of JavaScript variables because the following statement works just fine:

```
dstr = new createArray(20,'')
```

Try this in C or Pascal! The resulting value of dstr is then passed to fillColorArray() to be stuffed with values. When this function returns, dstr is plugged into the right value of the current array pair.

Listing 9.13   Three Functions Used to Create an Associative Array of Associative Arrays

```
function createArray(n,init)
//n          size of array
//init    what you want all values initialized to
{
        var i = 0
        this.length = n              // set the size of the array
        for (i = 1 ; i < n ; i++)
            {
                    this[i] = init    // fill the array with "init"
            }
        return this                  // return the newly created array
}

function fillColorArray(anArray,init,init2)
//   anArray is the array to be filled
//   init holds the values for the left side
//   init2 holds the values for the right side
{
        var i = 0
        var astr = ''
        var bstr = ''
        var n = anArray.length    // get array length
        for (i = 1 ; i <= n ; i++) // iterate over each element
            {
                    astr = init + i       // get left value
                    bstr = init2 + i      // get right value
                    anArray[i] = astr     // set left
                    anArray[astr] = bstr  // set right
            }
        return anArray                    // return modified array
}


function lotsOfColors()
{
    var cstr
// colors will be an array of 9 colors
```

```
// colorstring will be the names of those colors, delimited by commas
    var colors = new createArray(9,'')
    var colorstring =
 ➥'red,yellow,orange,brown,green,blue,purple,gray,white'
    for (i = 1 ; i <= 9 ; i++ )    // iterate over array
        {
            cstr = word(',', i , colorstring)  // extract the i-th
            ➥element
            colors[i] = cstr          // set left value
            dstr = 'more' + cstr
// create and initialize right value in next two statements
            dstr = eval(dstr = new createArray(20,''))
            dstr = fillColorArray(dstr,cstr,cstr.substring(0,2))
            colors[colors[i]] = dstr  // set right value
// next three statements are for debugging
// they display the values set in an alert
            astr = colors[cstr][3]
            bstr = colors[cstr][astr]
            alert( astr + '\n' + bstr)
        }
}
```

The function `lotsOfColors()` warrants close attention. It starts off by creating the associative array, `colors`, as well as a comma delimited string that lists the colors it uses. It then cycles through a loop for each color to be processed. It first extracts the color we want from `colorstring` (as a string) and then sets the left element of the current associative pair to that string. Thus `colors[1]` yields "red." That's the easy part. How do we name the array handles that we place into the right member? We can construct an element named `"moreRed"` but the `"moreRed"` is a string. Fortunately, JavaScript permits a string to be enough of a chameleon that it can be turned into an array handle.

> **CAUTION**
>
> Arrays should be initialized and filled in different routines. If you attempt to perform these operations in the same routine, strange substitutions, which are symptomatic of an uninitialized array, will result.

Using a Multi-Dimensional Array   So far, we have not tried to access the secondary members of this construction. Surprisingly enough, that is not much harder than accessing the usual one-dimensional associative array. In fact, the debugging code at the end of `lotsOfColors()` already shows how this is done.

```
astr = colors[cstr][3]
bstr = colors[cstr][astr]
alert( astr + '\n' + bstr)
```

The variable `astr` holds the left element, and `bstr` the right element. If you attempt to do this in one step it appears confusing. If you substitute the value of `astr` in the second expression, you get the following massive expression:

```
bstr = colors[cstr][colors[cstr][3]]
```

Note that we placed some convenient, but arbitrary, values into our subsidiary arrays. We could have had the `fillColorArray()` function generate successive, properly spaced hex values that were within the appropriate color range. In general, it is more likely that you will want to use these kinds of arrays to keep arbitrary data.

Some JavaScript HTML Objects

This section reviews some of the fundamental concepts of HTML objects in JavaScript, and then proceeds to the more complex `Image` and `Text` objects described at the beginning of this chapter. By this point you are well acquainted with the various HTML objects in JavaScript. The focus of this section is to explore some of their innovative uses. Many of the "tricks" of JavaScript revolve around its *polymorphism*, namely its capability to view a single thing in different ways.

JavaScript strings provide an excellent example of this polymorphism. Strings in JavaScript can be thought of as HTML objects, in addition to their usual meaning. This is because JavaScript provides methods for giving strings many of the formatted characteristics of HTML text, such as bold (`<B>`), italics (`<I>`), big (`<BIG>`), link (`<A>`), and so on. When you use a construction such as

```
mystring = 'This is some text.'
mystring = mystring.bold,
```

`mystring` becomes '`<B>This is some text.</B>`'. We will use methods such as these in the `Text` object we create.

▶ **See** "The String Object" section of chapter 5, where HTML string methods are discussed in great detail, **p. 152**.

Objects Revisited

By now you are intimately aware that objects are just arrays of properties. However, properties are accessed somewhat differently than array elements, and they usually only use the left side of the array. New properties can be added to an object at any time. This is possible because *only* the left element of the array is used. Trying to add new array elements on-the-fly when you are using both sides of the array element is fraught with disaster, as we have seen previously.

Objects can have properties and/or methods. Methods are simply functions that have been declared as properties. For example, you might have a color object. Colors are cited in terms of their red, green, and blue components (at least in browsers; there are other color mixing schemes). Many of Netscape's colors also have common names. To declare a color object, we must make a constructor/creator, as shown in listing 9.14. This is no different than the type of construction methods we have seen for arrays.

Listing 9.14   Creating a Simple Color Object

```
function createColor(name,red,green,blue)
{
    this.name       =       name
    this.red        =       red
    this.green      =       green
    this.blue       =       blue
    this.length   =     4
    return this
}

myGreenColorObject = new createColor('green','22','DD','22')
```

Property Taxes   Object constructors really just reserve space for the property array elements. We can access the property values by their array indices, as well as by using the dot operator (.). This is sometimes extremely useful for storing objects. To convert the color object into a string delimiter with the @ character, the code in listing 9.15 might be used. This type of string is often useful for storing objects persistently, as we shall see in chapter 20.

▶ **See** the "Storing Parameters and Other Data" section of chapter 19, which describes the cookies approach in great detail. *Cookies* may be used to store objects represented as delimited strings, **p. 650**.

Listing 9.15 Storing an Object's Properties as a Delimited String

```
function storeColor(aColorObject)
{
    var k = aColorObject.length    // number of elements in object
    var astr = ''                  // initialize to empty string
    var i = 0
    for(i = 1 ; i <= k ; i++)      // iterate over elements
        {
            astr += aColorObject[i] + '@'       // append to astr.
        }
    return astr                    // return delimited string
}
```

You can easily reverse this process, as listing 9.16 shows. The function getColor() undoes the work done by the function storeColor of listing 9.15. It tears apart the delimited string passed as its second argument astr, and sets the properties of aColorObject accordingly.

Listing 9.16 Retrieving an Object's Properties from a Delimited String

```
function getColor(aColorObject,astr)
{
    var lastloc = astr.lastIndexOf('@')    // final delimiter
    var n =0                  // number of delimiters found
    var f = 0                 // location of current delimited
    var i = 1        // current array index
    while ( n >= 0 )
        {
// find next delimiter, store in local variable f
            f = astr.indexOf(astr,n)
// set the i-th array element to the string between the last delimiter
// ( at location n ) and the current delimiter ( at location f )
            aColorObject[i] = astr.substring(n,f)
// if we are at the very last delimiter ( at location lastloc )
            if (f == lastloc)
                {
// then take the substring from the current position up to the end
// of the string and break out of the while loop
                    aColorObject[i+1] =
                    ↪astr.substring(f+1,astr.length)
                    break
                }
// if we are not at the very last delimiter then repeat the process
            else n = f  + 1
```

```
// update array index
            i++
        }
}
```

These examples are not the only ways to perform either of these operations. The storage function `storeColor()` of listing 9.15 could also have been implemented as shown in listing 9.17, for example. We could also use the `word()` function to retrieve the properties of an object from a string in the `getColor()` function. This would be slower than the approach shown in listing 9.16, however.

Part
II

Ch
9

Listing 9.17   An Alternative Color Storage Function using the *for...in* Statement

```
function storeColor(aColorObject)
    {
        var astr = ""
        for (var i in aColorObject)
                astr += aColorObject[i] + '@'
        return astr
    }
```

Creating Your Own Methods   It would be nice if the `color` object knew how to do its own conversion to and from the delimited string representation. Since we have already written the essential conversion functions, it's easy to make them methods of the `color` object: we just assign them as properties of the object itself. If we use this approach our `color` object constructor is as shown in listing 9.18.

Listing 9.18   Creating a *color* Object with Methods and Properties

```
function createBetterColor(name,red,green,blue)
{
    this.name               =        name
    this.red                =        red
    this.green              =        green
    this.blue               =        blue
    this.toString           =        storeColor
    this.fromString         =      getColor
    this.length             =        6
    return this
}

myGreenColorObject = new createBetterColor('green','22','DD','22')
```

N O T E Always set the `length` property of an object in your constructor. Some implementations of JavaScript will automatically create a `length` property in the element at `index=0`, and keep that `length` property updated as new elements are added, but this behavior is not guaranteed. ▪

If you are going to convert a function into a method, you can (and should) alter it somewhat to exploit the fact that it is now a method function. If a function is not a method function of an object, then it may only access that object if the object is passed as a parameter to the function, or if the object has been declared globally. Once you make the function a method of the object, the function can reference the object that contains it via the keyword `this`. Consequently, we can rewrite the `storeColor` method to look like listing 9.19.

Listing 9.19 Storing an Object's Properties Using a Method Function

```
function storeColor()
{
     var k = this.length
     var astr = ''
     var i = 0
     for(i = 1 ; i <= k ; i++)
         {
              astr += this[i] + '@'
         }
     return astr
}
```

N O T E In order to change a function into a method function of an object, follow these three steps:

1. Make the method a property of the object, as in `aColor.toString = storeColor`.

2. Do not pass the object as a parameter to the function.

3. Change all explicit references to the object to the keyword `this`; for example, `l = aColorObject.length` becomes `l = this.length`. ▪

Images as Objects

Drawing images is a complex affair. One of the most important things to remember about image manipulation in terms of JavaScript is that all images *must* be characterized by HEIGHT and WIDTH modifiers in their HTML tags. If you leave these modifiers out, JavaScript misbehaves or doesn't function at all. We will create an Image object that encapsulates all the important Image properties, including the height and width. The Image object will also know how to display itself in several contexts. The constructor for the Image object is shown in listing 9.20. All of the code for the Image object can be found on the file c9-5.htm on the CD-ROM.

On the CD

Listing 9.20   c9-5.htm   A Comprehensive Constructor for an *Image* Object

```
?
function createImage(title, filename, height, width, vspace, hspace,
                     border, bordercolor, frame, framecolor, href, notes)
{
    this.title              = title
    this.filename           = filename
    this.height           = height
    this.width          = width
    this.vspace             = vspace
    this.hspace             = hspace
    this.border             = border
    this.bordercolor        = bordercolor
    this.frame              = frame
    this.framecolor        = framecolor
    this.href               = href
    this.notes              = notes
    this.draw               = drawImage
    this.frame              = frameImage
     this.reference         = referenceImage
     this.popup             = popImage
    return this
}
```

Properties and Methods of the *Image* Object   If you examine the constructor for the Image object shown in listing 9.20, you see that it not only encapsulates the normal HTML qualifiers for an image, but it also has properties for a file spec, a title, an associated URL, and notes. It can present itself as a plain image, a framed image, or a linked image. It can also pop itself up in a window of its own. The image "draws" itself by presenting you with a string that you can send to a nascent document using `document.write()`. The code in listings 9.21, 9.22, and 9.23 shows the methods used to draw a plain image, a linked image, and a framed image.

▶ **See** the "Using Nascent Documents" section of chapter 8, "Dynamic HTML and Browser Objects," for a thorough discussion of documents created on-the-fly, **p. 285**.

Listing 9.21 c9-5.htm   The *Image* Object's Plain *draw* Method

```
function drawImage(how,border)
{
      var astr = ''
// if the image does not use this modifier
// the parameter can be empty or '^'
            astr = '<IMG SRC="' + this.filename + '"'
            if (how != '') astr += ' ALIGN=' + how
            if (this.height != '') astr += ' HEIGHT=' + this.height
            if (this.width != '' && this.width != '^')
                astr += ' WIDTH=' + this.width
            if (this.vspace != '' && this.vspace != '^')
                astr += ' VSPACE=' + this.vspace
            if (this.hspace != '' && this.hspace != '^')
                astr += ' HSPACE=' + this.hspace
            if (this.border != '' && this.border != '^')
                astr += ' BORDER=' + this.border
            astr +='>'
            if (this.border != '' && this.border != '^')
                astr = '<FONT COLOR=' +
                    this.bordercolor + '>' + astr + '</FONT>'
            return astr

}
```

Listing 9.22 c9-5.htm   The *Image* Object's Linked *draw* (Reference) Method

```
function referenceImage(how,border,ref,atext)
{
      if (ref == '') ref=this.href
      if (ref == '') ref = location.href
          if (atext == '') atext = 'Your text here!'
      var astr = '<A HREF=' + ref + '>'
```

```
astr += '<IMG SRC="' + this.filename + '"'
if (how != '') astr += ' ALIGN=' + how
if (this.height != '') astr += ' HEIGHT=' + this.height
if (this.width != '' && this.width != '^')
    astr += ' WIDTH=' + this.width
if (this.vspace != '' && this.width != '^')
    astr += ' VSPACE=' + this.vspace
if (this.hspace != '' && this.width != '^')
    astr += ' WIDTH=' + this.hspace
if ('' + border != '') astr += ' BORDER=' + this.border
astr +='>'
astr += atext
astr += '</A>'
return astr

}
```

Listing 9.23 c9-5.htm The *Image* Object's Framed *draw* Method

```
function frameImage(how,border,leading)
{
    var astr = '<TABLE '
    if (how != '') astr += ' ALIGN=' + how
    if ('' + border != '') astr += ' BORDER=' + border
    if ('' + leading != '') astr += ' CELLSPACING=' + leading
    astr += '><TR><TD ALIGN=CENTER>'
    var bstr = '</TD></TR></TABLE>'
    astr += this.draw('',2)
    astr += bstr
    return astr
}
```

Notice that the frameImage method essentially draws the table structure, which is the "frame," and then calls the drawImage method to draw the image. In all cases, the image can have a border. In both the drawImage and frameImage methods, the border color is determined by the current font color. Since the Image object encapsulates the border color, it is as easy to include it as it is to include any other modifier. Referenced image borders, though, do not have such a choice; they will be the link color or vlink color specified for the page.

Using the *Image* Object You can use the Image object to make a database of your images. A filename, notes (which can include a caption for the image), and a URL are included as part of the object, as we have seen. The example program on the CD-ROM (file c9-5.htm) arbitrarily sets up a trivial database of six Image objects held in an array. It can present these images as plain, framed, or referenced. It can also pop up any image in its own window. Listing 9.24 shows the method function that creates the pop-up.

Listing 9.24   c9-5.htm   The Pop-Up Method of the *Image* Object

```
function popImage(title)
{
    var w = 50 + parseInt(this.width)        // image width as displayed
    var h = parseInt(this.height) + 50       // image height as displayed
    scrl = 'no'                              // do scrolling?
    if (w>640){w=640;scrl='yes'}    // if width too big then scroll
    if (h>480){h=480;scrl='yes'}    // if height too big then scroll
// create HTML attributes for the image
    var whstr ='WIDTH=' + w + ',HEIGHT=' + h +
                'RESIZABLE=yes,SCROLLBARS=' + scrl
// open a new window
    aNewWin = self.open('',title,whstr)
// if the new window could not be created…
    if (!aNewWin)
        {
// notify the user that it failed, and try to indicate
// possible causes
            var alertstr = "Could not open a new window."
            alertstr += " A window of named " + title
            alertstr += " may already be open."
            alertstr += " You may also be out of memory"
            alert(alertstr)
}
// if new window was created successfully…
    else
        {
// create the HTML to display the image
            var astr = '<HTML><HEAD>'
            astr += '<BASE HREF="' + location.href + '">'
            astr += '<TITLE>' + this.title + '</TITLE>'
            astr += '</HEAD><BODY>'
// write out that HTML
            aNewWin.document.write(astr)
            var bstr = '<CENTER>' + this.draw('CENTER') + '</CENTER>'
            aNewWin.document.write(bstr)
            aNewWin.document.write('</BODY></HTML>')
// close the document
            aNewWin.document.close()
        }
}
```

The resulting image display is shown in figure 9.13. The page generated by the CD-ROM file c9-5.htm is covered with pop-up windows containing its tiny database of six images. The images were placed in the pages arbitrarily; the page has no input interface. Any single image can be popped up by placing its number in the text box next to the Image button and clicking the button. Figures 9.14 and 9.15 show the plain and framed versions of the image displayed in a catalog format. The image catalog is nothing more than a scrolling display of all the images in the database.

FIG. 9.13
The Image object can be activated to pop up an image database.

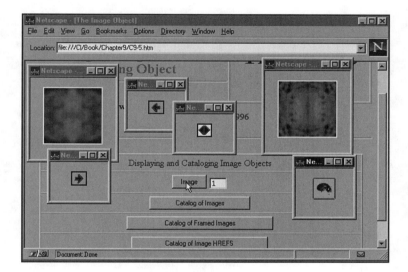

Most of the draw methods presented here accept a string terminator as a parameter, and also return a string. The terminator is usually the carriage return character, \n. This results in a string with linebreaks suitable for an alert. You can also use <BR> as the string terminator; this yields a string that can be nicely presented in a window. The utility function showInWindow in listing 9.25 pops up a window and tries to put anything you hand it into that window. We will use this function quite often in chapter 20.

FIG. 9.14
The image database may
be displayed as a scrolling
catalog of plain images.

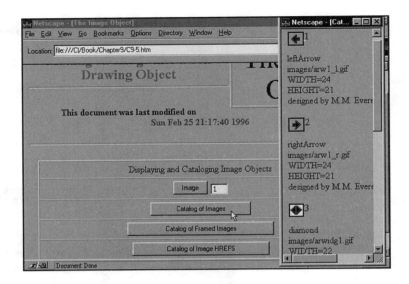

FIG. 9.15
The image database may be
displayed as a scrolling
catalog of framed images.

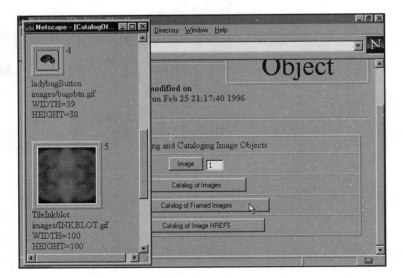

Listing 9.25 c9-5.htm A Function That Shows an Object in a Pop-up Window

```
function showInWindow(tstr,title)
{
    var w = 300
    var h = 300
```

```
        scrl = 'yes'
        if (w>640){w=640;scrl='yes'}
        if (h>480){h=480;scrl='yes'}
        var whstr ='SCROLLBARS=' + scrl + ',RESIZABLE=yes,WIDTH=' + w +
                ',HEIGHT=' + h
          aNewWin = self.open('',title,whstr)
        var astr = '<HTML><HEAD>'
        astr += '<BASE HREF="' + location.href + '">'
        astr += '<TITLE>' + title + '</TITLE>'
        astr += '</HEAD><BODY>'
        aNewWin.document.write(astr)
        aNewWin.document.write(tstr)
        aNewWin.document.write('</BODY></HTML>')
        aNewWin.document.close()
    }
```

The *Text* Object

The approach we employed for the Image object can be used for text manipulation as well. We will create a Text object that holds various important properties related to how the text is displayed. This Text object will be very similar to the Image object in terms of the type of draw methods it supports. The constructor function for the Text object is shown in listing 9.26. All the code for the Text object can be found on the CD-ROM file c9-6.htm.

On the CD

Listing 9.26   c9-6.htm   The Constructor Function for the *Text* Object

```
function createText(type,title,text,size,color,bold,italic,
                  supersub,frame,href,notes)
{
    this.type =type
    this.title= title
    this.text = text
    this.size = size
    this.color = color
    this.bold = bold
    this.italic  =  italic
    this.supersub = supersub
    this.frame =        frame
    this.href  =        href
    this.notes  =  notes
    this.draw = drawText
    this.frame = frameText
```

continues

Listing 9.26   Continued

```
        this.reference = referenceText
        this.popup = popText
      this.lines = stringToList
      this.word = word
      return this
  }
```

Notice that this function is very similar to the constructor for the `Image` object. It encapsulates some of Netscape's own string properties. This object, too, knows how to present itself as plain, framed, or referenced text. It can also pop itself up in a window. Note that it has a `type` property; that is, the text can be a list, a paragraph, and so on. Its `draw` method accepts a parameter that allows you to draw the text according to a predefined `type` method or to draw the text using the properties you have set.

The `Text` object has some methods that can access the text as lines or words. Again, this is a crude emulation of HyperCard. These methods allow you to define the separator which separates one phrase from another. The `stringToList` method accepts a prefix and a suffix as well as the list separator. It separates the string into phrases and then adds the prefix and suffix given. Use the `\n` character as the separator to get logical lines. Our old friend, the `word()` function, is used to return the word at the position you specify. The implementation of the `stringToList` method is shown in listing 9.27.

Listing 9.27   c9-6.htm   A Function to Separate Delimited Strings into Phrases

```
function stringToList(sep, pref,suf)
// sep = separator (delimiter)
// pref = prefix to prepend
// suf = suffix to append
{
        var n = 0          // location of current separator
        var f = 0          // location of next separator
        var astr = ''      // string being built
        var nstr = ''      // work string
        var finished = false
        while (f >= 0 )
            {
// get position of next separator
                    f = this.indexOf(sep,n)
```

```
// if this the last one?
                if (f == this.lastIndexOf(sep))
                        {
// if so then get the end of the string
                           f = this.length
// and set the finished flag
                           finished = true
                        }
// get the string, prepend the prefix and append the suffix
                 nstr = pref + this.substring(n,f) + suf
// add the current working string onto the final string
                 astr += nstr
// if all done then break out of the loop
                 if (finished ) break
// advance to the next separator
                 n = f + 1
         }
    return astr        // return the completed string
}
```

Note that this function uses an interesting trick to decide when it has come to the
end of the string. It uses lastIndexOf() to get the character position of the last
occurrence of the separator. As it walks the string, it checks to see if the character
found equals the last instance of that character. If it does, it sets the phrase end to
the end of the string, performs its usual string separation, and then quits.

Another useful routine, which can easily be modified for your own purpose, is the
makeTitle method. MakeTitle goes through a string and eliminates spaces, but
capitalizes the letter after the space. This is useful for catching two word window
names, such as "Hi there," which a user has entered. If you hand the open() command more than one word, it simply does not open the window, nor does it tell you
why. The makeTitle method converts such strings into more acceptable titles, such
as "HiThere" in this case. The makeTitle function is shown in listing 9.28. Figure
9.16 shows the result of exercising the pop-up capabilities of the Text object. This
page was created using the file c9-2.htm on the CD-ROM.

On the CD

Listing 9.28   c9-2.htm   A Function to Create Window Title Strings

```
function makeTitle(what)
{
    var n = what.length      // length of string "what"
    var i = 0                // iteration variable
    var cc = ''              // current character
```

continues

Listing 9.28 Continued

```
      var accstr=''            // output string being built
      for (i = 0 ; i < n ; i++)       // iterate over the whole string
         {
// get character at position "i"
            cc = what.substring(i,i+ 1)
// if that character is not a space, then add it to the output string
               if ( cc != ' ' )
                  {
                       accstr += cc
                       continue
                  }
            else
               {
// if that character is a space then skip it
                    I++
// grab the first character after the space
                           cc=what.substring(i,i + 1)
// convert it to uppercase
                      cc = cc.toUpperCase()
// add that uppercase letter onto the output string
                      accstr += cc
               }
         }
      return accstr        // return the output string
      }
```

FIG. 9.16
The database of text objects can display itself in pop-up windows.

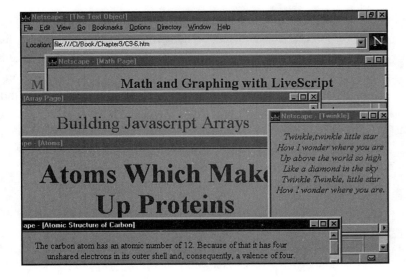

JavaScript and Live Objects

CHAPTER 10

Netscape Plug-Ins and JavaScript

by Andrew Wooldridge

Netscape Navigator allows you to extend its functionality almost indefinitely using a new construct called a *plug-in*. Other programs, such as Adobe's Photoshop, have used the concept of plug-ins for some time. In Photoshop, plug-ins act as enhanced filters that allow the image designer greater flexibility in either manipulating an image or converting that image into another format. Basically, plug-ins enhance the abilities of their host application. Before plug-ins, the only way you could handle new data types (say, a JPEG image) in a Web browser environment was through linking subsidiary programs, called helper apps, to your browser. *Helper apps* are small, usually specialized programs (or applications—thus the name apps) that receive a file of a specific type from your Web browser and display, or otherwise load, and interpret that file.

What Netscape plug-ins are

We will discuss the basic concepts of plug-ins, and how they function within your browser.

How to use Netscape plug-ins

You will see how to install a plug-in, and learn how it can help you enhance your Web pages.

How to embed a plug-in in your Web pages

Learn how to use <EMBED> to place new content-types on your page.

Where to find plug-ins

Find where to download and view samples of new plug-ins.

How to use JavaScript with plug-ins

Learn how Netscape plans to use JavaScript with plug-ins.

For example, in the early days of the Web, the popular browser of the time—Mosaic—would not allow you to view JPEG images inside the page. You had to click the JPEG link, and watch as the browser downloaded the file, then launched some viewer (Jpegview, for example, on Macintosh). Dealing with helper apps was at best a confusing process where the user had to manually configure the browser to find the helper app (assuming that you had already downloaded it and configured it correctly). You had to deal with directory paths, temporary files, missing helper apps, and so on.

When you viewed a Web page with a new file type, you usually had to temporarily launch a new application and leave the Web browser (perhaps hidden behind the new window of the helper app). This would be equivalent to working on a file in Microsoft Word, and having to launch NotePad every time you wanted to read a plain text file.

Netscape has improved upon this relatively clumsy system with its plug-in architecture. Instead of using a helper app and manually configuring the browser to launch it, you, as a Web user, simply download the correct plug-in, drop it into the correct folder (or point the installer to the correct directory), and launch Netscape. Instead of viewing the new data in a separate window/application it is now *inlined* in the browser. Inlined refers to the fact that you see the information in a box within the browser window. An example is to see an MPEG file that you can play inside the browser window beside some text and links that might explain the MPEG movie. ■

Plug-Ins versus Helper Apps

Before we talk further about plug-ins, you might be curious as to the differences between Netscape plug-ins and helper apps. Both of these act as a way to augment the browser's viewing capability, and expand the number of file types that the browser can handle. The advantage of the plug-in is that it is more closely integrated with the browser's environment. The API for creating a plug-in is freely available from Netscape's Web site, and this allows third-party developers to create new "mini-apps" that can be more closely managed by the browser. Plug-ins can be loaded and unloaded from memory on the fly—using your RAM more efficiently than helper apps, which commonly will remain active even after you've left the site you were viewing, or even after you've exited your browser all together. Figure 10.1 shows how a Quicktime Movie file would look using a helper app (Movie Player) and figure 10.2 shows how an MPEG might look within a browser page.

FIG. 10.1

A Quicktime movie as seen in a helper application (Movie Player).

FIG. 10.2

An MPEG movie as seen in a browser using an MPEG viewer plug-in.

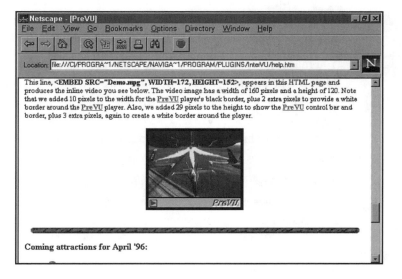

Plug-ins allow you to seamlessly integrate new content within your pages. Since Netscape can determine which plug-ins your client browser currently has—you will be able (in future versions of JavaScript) to check the client browser to see if it has the correct plug-in and displays the file accordingly. If it does not, your JavaScript can display another default format. To view the current list of plug-ins your browser has, select File, Open Location, and type **about:plugins**. This will display a list of the plug-ins your browser uses. If you currently don't have any plug-ins, you will still see a "*", which represents a default plug-in. In Netscape 3.0, there will be two new sub-objects of the `navigator` object that can also get this information: `navigator.plugins` and `navigator.mimeTypes`.

Plug-Ins and MIME Types

Netscape plug-ins depend on a system of file type identification called MIME. MIME stands for Multi-purpose Internet Mail Extensions. Originally devised as a way to allow e-mail applications to view new multimedia file types, MIME has become the standard way in which Internet applications learn about the type of file that is being retrieved from the Internet. MIME can handle just about any kind of format that has been created to this date. This includes text formats, images, sounds, movies, compressed files (like ZIP and TAR files), PostScript, and many others. All Web browsers and most Internet software depend on MIME types to tell the software how to handle each new file downloaded.

You may have noticed when using helper apps that every app has an associated MIME type and file extension—such as .AVI. Most data formats you encounter via the Web have an associated MIME type. For example, a Windows AVI file would have a MIME type of `video/x-msvideo`. The first part of that type is the Content-type, which defines the major scope of this file—for example `video`, `multipart`, `audio`, `application`, or `text`.

The second part, after the slash, refers to the subtype, which is usually the specific type the browser needs to interpret the file—such as `postscript`. If you view the Helpers window of your general preferences (in Netscape 2.0 select Options,

General Preferences, Helpers), you will find many examples of MIME types (see table 10.1). When you encounter something like application/x-gzip the x usually indicates that the subtype is a proposed standard and is often used for newly developed file types, or ones that have yet to gain wide acceptance. If you read through your Helpers window in Netscape you will begin to become familiar with the kinds of MIME types that your browser can handle.

When the Navigator starts up, it scans its Plug-ins folder and "registers" a given MIME type to the corresponding plug-in that can read files of that type. Then, when that type is encountered in a Web page, an instance of that plug-in is loaded into memory and the information is used in one of three ways. It may be displayed inline (as in the MPEG file example in figure 10.3) which is also called embedded; full page (for example an Adobe Acrobat file in figure 10.4) where the entire window under the nav-buttons is occupied by the plug-in; or hidden (as in the case of a MIDI sound player which may not have any information displayed in the window, but plays in the background).

FIG. 10.3
An MPEG file viewed inside Netscape.

MPEG file —

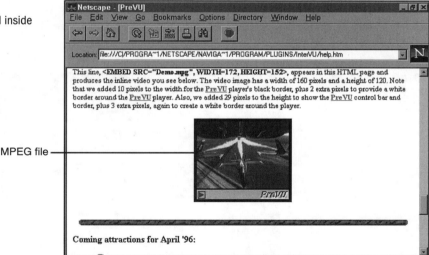

FIG. 10.4
An Adobe Acrobat file
viewed in Netscape.

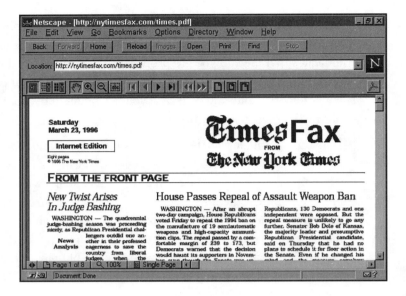

Each plug-in may be capable of handling more than one MIME type—for example, a sound player that reads both AU and MIDI sound types (see fig. 10.5). Another example would be an image viewer that reads progressive JPEG and regular JPEG.

FIG. 10.5
MIDI file player within a
browser window.

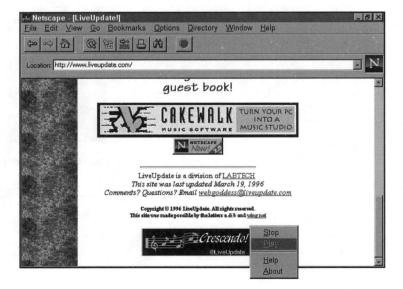

Although each plug-in may read more than one file type, two plug-ins cannot both read the same file type. During the registration process, only the first plug-in encountered is used. Table 10.1 lists briefly the most common MIME types.

Table 10.1   Common MIME Types

Content-Type	Subtype
text	text
	richtext
	enriched
	tab-separated-values
	sgml
multipart	mixed
	alternative
	digest
	parallel
	form-data
message	rfc822
	partial
	external-body
	news
application	octet-stream
	postscript
	oda
	mac-binhex40
	wordperfect5.1
	pdf
	zip
	cybercash
image	jpeg
	gif
	tiff

continues

Table 10.1 Continued	
Content-Type	**Subtype**
audio	basic
	32kadpcm
video	mpeg
	quicktime

If you decide to use a new file type in your site, you need to make sure that the Web server is configured to send the appropriate MIME type to the browser. This is so the Web browser interprets the file correctly and loads the right plug-in.

Using Plug-Ins with HTML

Once you decide on a new format you wish to support on your Web site, you need to add the correct tags to display that file. You usually can just create a link to the file with a URL such as

```
<a href="http://foo.bar.com/whoopie.AVI">Whoopie!</a>
```

However, you need a new tag to display that format from within the page itself. You do this with <EMBED>. This tag must include the attributes that determine the size and kind of plug-in to be called, as well as special information specific to that plug-in. Its syntax is as follows:

```
<embed src="filename" width="num" height="num"
palette="foreground¦background">
```

There are also additional attributes specific to the plug-in. For example,

```
<EMBED
    SRC="theavi.avi"
    WIDTH="300"
    HEIGHT="200"
    AUTOSTART=true
    LOOP=true>
```

Although this format is in wide use today—and will continue to be supported—the fact that you can add unlimited attributes to this tag, such as FOO=""HI"", MY=""WIFE"", and so on, does not conform with the rest of the HTML specification and will be replaced with a new tag called the INSERT tag. This tag is being developed by the w3.org as a replacement for many of the existing tags that insert multimedia objects in Web pages.

The World Wide Web Consortium

The World Wide Web Consortium (at www.w3.org) is an organization that develops standards for the Web. It is based at the Masachusetts Institute of Technology, run by the Laboratory for Computer Science. It acts as a single point of information about the Web, develops reference programming code to implement standards, and develops standards through Internet Drafts (documents which specify developing standards). This is the organization that developed the HTML 1.0 and 2.0 standards, and is working toward new standards based on a proposed 3.0 version.

The following is an example of the proposed <INSERT>:

```
<insert data=TheEarth.avi
    type="application/avi">
    <param name=loop value=infinite>
    <img src=TheEarth.gif alt="The Earth">
    </insert>
```

There are a large number of attributes associated with the INSERT tag; these are summarized in table 10.2.

Table 10.2   *INSERT* Tag Attributes

Attribute	Description
ID	Used to define a document-wide identifier.
CLASS	A space separated list of SGML NAME tokens.
LANG	An attribute that identifies the natural language used by the content of the associated element.
DIR	Specifies the direction in which the tokens should be read. For international adaptability.

continues

Table 10.2 Continued

Attribute	Description
STYLE	An attribute that allows you to include rendering information.
CLASSID	Used to specify a class identifier for an object.
CODE	Specifies a URL referencing where to find the code that implements the object's behavior.
DATA	Specifies a URL referencing the object's data.
TYPE	The MIME type of the object.
ALIGN	Determines where to place the object; it can be TEXTTOP, MIDDLE, TEXTMIDDLE, BASELINE, or TEXTBOTTOM.
WIDTH	Width of the box enclosing this area.
HEIGHT	Height of the box enclosing the object.
BORDER	An attribute that applies to the border shown when the object forms part of a hypertext link, as specified by an enclosing anchor element.
HSPACE	The amount of space beyond the left and right of the box containing the object.
VSPACE	The minimum space above and below the box containing the object.
USEMAP	If used as an imagemap, this specifies the location of the client-side imagemap.
ISMAP	If used as an imagemap, this specifies the URL of the map file on the server.

To further expand this tag to accommodate plug-ins and applets like Java applets, there are two other elements—the PARAM tag and the ALIAS tag. With Java, you would use the PARAM tag in the same way you do with the existing APPLET tag (see listing 10.1):

> **Listing 10.1 Java Applet using *INSERT* tag**
>
> ```
> <insert
>       classid="java:NervousText.class"
>       code="http://java.acme.com/applets/NervousText.class"
>       width=400
>       height=75
>       align=baseline
>   >
>   <param name=text value="This is the Applet Viewer">
>   </insert>
> ```

The PARAM tag can take these attributes, as follows:

- NAME—The name of the property
- VALUE—The value of that property
- VALUEREF—Refers to the object's ALIAS
- TYPE—The parameter's MIME type if the data: URL is used

The ALIAS tag allows you to define an object without actually inserting it into the page. It is used along with the VALUEREF of the PARAM tag. It can take the following attributes:

- ID—Defines the name of the alias
- DATA—The object's data
- CODE—The object's code
- CLASSID—The object's UUID
- TYPE—The object's MIME type

Until this specification is implemented by the major browsers, you should continue to use the EMBED tag.

Plug-In Considerations

"Why use a plug-in? Is it really worth my time to set up my server and learn all of this new HTML?" Yes. Many Web sites now display mostly text, with a scattering of pictures which are mainly GIF and JPEG files. Although this is adequate for most standard Web sites, it is very static and really rather boring after someone visits there more than once. The growth of the Web has pushed developers to find new ways to attract people to come to their sites. A dynamic new format—such as Shockwave files—adds an entirely new level of interactivity to the Web and allows Web sites to explore new ways to express their creativity. Also, there are many file formats such as Microsoft Word DOC files that most Web browsers cannot read, even though that format is commonly used outside the Web.

Plug-ins of this type allow sites to leverage their existing files, and take the advantages of that format to the Web. Netscape's site and Browserwatch (**http://www.netscape.com** and **http://www.browserwatch.com/plug-in.html**) provide the Net community with a large list of available plug-ins, and are very likely to have a more up-to-date list of plug-ins than the list that follows, but the list is provided so you can begin to see what kinds of plug-ins are being developed.

Sound Players

- Crescendo by Liveupdate

  http://www.liveupdate.com/
- Realaudio by Progressive Networks

  http://www.realaudio.com/
- Talker Plug-In by MVP Solutions

  http://www.mvpsolutions.com/
- Toolvox by Voxware

  http://www.voxware.com/

Text Readers

These plug-ins allow you to read text-based formats that Netscape cannot read on its own. Many of these take over the browser window entirely in order to view the new file format, although Netscape's navigational buttons still appear at the top. Note that already popular word processing formats like Microsoft Word are viewable by Netscape because of plug-ins.

- Acrobat Amber Reader by Adobe

  http://www.adobe.com
- Envoy Plug-In by Tumbleweed Software

  http://www.twcorp.com
- Word Viewer Plug-In by Inso Corporation

  http://www.inso.com

VRML and 3-D Viewers

These plug-ins allow you to view three dimensional models—either inlined (in a specified box size) or in an entirely new browser window. Live3d from Netscape uses a new format for VRML 2.0 that allows for motion, sound, and behaviors using Java.

- Chemscape Chime by Mdl Information Systems

  http://www.mdli.com/
- DWG/DXF Plug-In by Softsource

  http://www.softsource.com/softsource/
- Live3d by Netscape

  http://home.netscape.com/comprod/products/
  navigator/live3d/download_live3d.html
- SVF Plug-In by Softsource

  http://www.softsource.com/softsource/
- VR Scout VRML Plug-In by Chaco Communications

  http://www.chaco.com
- Vrealm by Integrated Data Systems

  http://www.ids-net.com
- WIRL Virtual Reality Browser by Vream

  http://www.vream.com

Part
III

Ch
10

Graphic Formats Viewers

- Corel Vector Graphics

  http://www.corel.com/corelcmx/

- Figleaf Inline by Carberry Technology/EBT

  http://www.ct.ebt.com/

- Lightning Strike by Infinet Op

  http://www.infinop.com

- Vdolive by Vdonet

  http://www.vdolive.com/

- Wavelet Image Viewer by Summus

  http://www.summus.com/

Multimedia Players

These are the fastest-growing and most interesting of the plug-ins. These (and many others, by the time you read this) display animation, sound, and interactivity that will dramatically change the way a Web page is used by Web site developers. For instance, Shockwave from Macromedia allows you to play small arcade-style games in a browser window, or display an interactive kiosk-style demo of a college campus.

- ASAP Webshow by Software Publishing Corporation

  http://www.spco.com

- Astound Web Player by Gold Disk

  http://www.golddisk.com

- Shockwave For Director by Macromedia

  http://www.macromedia.com

- Sizzler by Totally Hip

  http://www.totallyhip.com/

There are many more plug-ins available, most of which are available for the Windows 3.1 and Windows 95 operating systems. Macintosh plug-ins had a late start due to Netscape delaying the standardization of its Macintosh plug-in API, but, as of this writing, there are many new plug-ins for Mac. There will be UNIX-based plug-ins in the future as well, but the SDK (software development kit) for that operating system was only released a few months ago as of this writing.

Considerations in Using Plug-In Based Formats

There are many factors a Web designer must take into consideration when he designs online content for the Web. There are a few factors that I tend to use when I start a Web-based project that seeks to use plug-in based formats: Simplicity, Size, Appropriateness, and Ubiquity. The following are questions you might ask yourself that address each of these factors:

Might this information be displayed just as easily in an existing format? (Simplicity)

Just because you *can* use a plug-in specific format doesn't necessarily mean you *should*. If you have image files you want to display and you can convert them to GIF or JPEG, you should consider doing that instead. It dramatically improves the chances of your images being seen. Although both Netscape and Microsoft Internet Explorer use plug-ins, many older browsers cannot, and you will not reach as many people with your images as you would using the tried and true image formats.

Will these files increase the load on my server because of their size? (Size)

Some file formats were not originally intended to be sent down the Internet pipeline, and thus they may be huge in size. If you force someone to download these files, be prepared to see a large load increase on your Web server, and probably a decrease in the number of hits your site receives.

Is this format appropriate for my intended audience? (Appropriateness)

Sometimes a specific file format is inappropriate for a given Web audience. If you are targeting modem users, you might not want to use large files, or if you are simply writing documents, PostScript might be overkill for what you want to display. One good rule of thumb is KISS: Keep It Simple, Silly.

Is this format widely accepted? (Ubiquity)

As the number of plug-ins grows dramatically, you will begin to encounter competing plug-ins for the same MIME types, or differing types that effectively do the same thing for your Web site. For example, Macromedia's Shockwave plug-in has recently seen competition for multimedia viewing with a plug-in called Sizzler. You should do some research into the most prevalent type of plug-in for your media type, or style of display, before you invest a lot of time in developing content for a media type that is too new, too obscure, or too out of style. All of these things decrease the chances that people who come to your site will have the same plug-in that you intend to be used for this type, and most likely they will not take the time to divert themselves from their browsing path just to get your specific plug-in.

Can I use multiple plug-in types on a page?

Using more than one type of plug-in oriented file format on a page is asking for trouble at this stage of the Web. For every plug-in that you introduce to your page, you increase the memory requirements of the browser that uses the plug-in.

Note, however, that once you leave a page with a given plug-in, the browser frees up that memory for use by other plug-ins. So if you want to display many different media types requiring different style plug-ins, you might want to separate them out into different pages. Also, you should test your site on the lowest level computer system that you expect to browse your site and see how the increased memory requirements affect it.

Is this plug-in cross-platform?

A lot is being said and done about Java these days, and with good reason. Sun is hoping Java will become a completely cross-platform way of running distributed applications across the Net. Its main selling point is that it's cross-platform. If the kind of file type you want to display via a plug-in requires a plug-in that is only available for one operating system (since plug-ins are OS specific) you might want to reconsider using that plug-in until it does become cross-platform. If not, you will be effectively cutting off anyone who uses that other OS from seeing or enjoying your nifty movie or slick sound file. If you must use that plug-in type, you should consider offering an alternate route for others to see that information.

Plug-In Examples

Included on the CD-ROM are a number of plug-ins for you install on your machine to enhance Netscape. Before you take all of these plug-ins and fill your Plug-ins folder (or directory, for you DOS folks), remember that some plug-ins overlap in the kinds of media types they read, and others you might never use (such as a CAD reader, when you don't use CAD tools or are interested in CAD).

Figures 10.6 through 10.9 are images that display a few of the many kinds of plug-ins you might encounter on a Web site. These give you an idea of how to incorporate plug-ins in your own pages.

Macromedia Shockwave

Shockwave is a plug-in that allows you to view Macromedia Director files within your browser. Director files originally weren't designed for sending across the Internet, and tend to be large. So Macromedia created a small utility called AfterBurner, which takes a native DCR file and converts it into a "shocked" file. The resulting file is much smaller, and has the added benefit that it can no longer be edited by someone else using Director, which discourages others from decomposing a Director file and stealing its elements. An example of a Shockwave game is shown in figure 10.6.

FIG. 10.6
Macromedia Shockwave's dart game.

Part
III

Ch
10

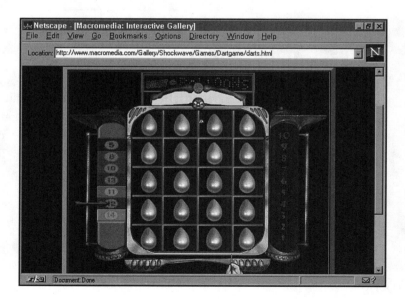

Adobe Acrobat

Adobe Acrobat allows you to have much larger control over the layout and formatting of your documents. You can have layered images, hyperlinks, and embedded images all within a single PDF file. Now that you can view these files using Acrobat Amber, you can publish those files across the Web. Figure 10.7 is an example of an Acrobat file.

FIG. 10.7
Adobe Acrobat plug-in example.

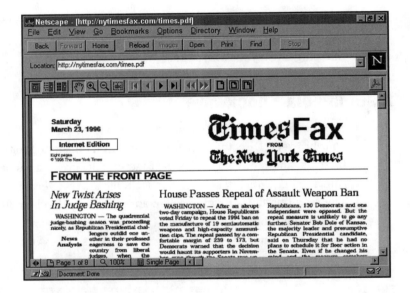

Microsoft Word Viewer

Inso Corporation (**http://www.inso.com/**) has developed a Microsoft Word 6.0 (and 7.0) document viewer. The uses of this plug-in should be quite obvious in that you need not even save the file in a different format to allow others to view your Word files. All files from 6.0 and earlier are now available for publishing via the web. Figure 10.8 shows a small example of a word format file.

FIG. 10.8
Microsoft Word plug-in example.

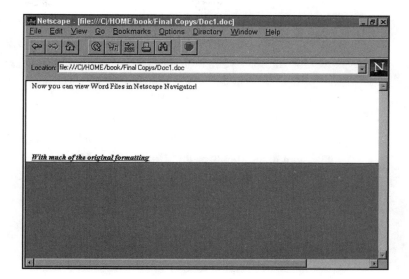

Virtual Reality Modeling Language

Originally called the Virtual Reality Markup Language, which points to its association with HTML, this language specifies how 3-D images can be displayed across operating systems, and also allows for low- and hi-resolution image loading across the Internet, lighting, shading, and much more. Netscape's Live3d adds a new dimension with movement and Java support. Figure 10.9 is an example of a VRML file.

FIG. 10.9
Live3d (a VRML viewer) plug-in example.

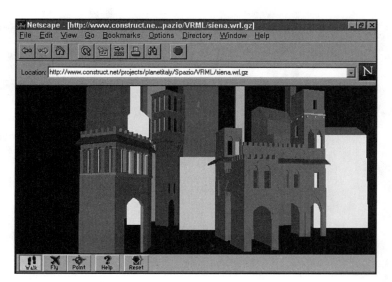

Plug-Ins and JavaScript

Now that you have seen and learned about plug-ins, you are probably wondering how JavaScript is able to communicate freely with these plug-ins and Java applets. As of this writing, the specifications for that communication have not yet been released to the public. You can, though, use JavaScript to control the EMBED tag just as you would control other tags. Suppose you had a plug-in that displayed a clock based on a file it uploaded and the TIME parameter. You can create a JavaScript script that takes the current time and sends that time to the plug-in on loading. The following is a code snippet:

```
var currentTimeObj = new Date()
var theTime = currentTimeObj.getTime


document.write("<embed src="theClock.tim" height=50 width=50 TIME=" +
theTime+ ">")
```

This gets the current time that the client has on his machine and displays the clock in the correct way. The only other way to do this is to use a server script that might build the correct HTML, but the time would be subtly off due to location differences.

You can also use a JavaScript snippet of code to check if a browser has a given plug-in and displays your page accordingly. This is accomplished by very briefly opening a sub-window and attempting to open a file of the given MIME type in that window. If the plug-in exists, then the script returns true. This code only checks to see if your browser has *any* plug-in that reads that MIME type, not a specific plug-in; see listing 10.2 for an example.

Listing 10.2 Checking the MIME Type in JavaScript

```
function probePlugIn(mimeType) {
    var havePlugIn = false
    var tiny = window.open (" ", "teensy", "width=1, height=1")
    if (tiny !=null) {
        if (tiny.document.open(mimeType) !=null)
            havePlugIn = true
        tiny.close()
        }
    return havePlugIn
}
```

To test for a specific plug-in, say Shockwave (or some other Director plug-in), you use the following:

```
var haveShockWavePlugIn = probePlugIn ("application/x-director")
```

If the browser has the Shockwave plug-in, the value of `haveShockWavePlugIn` is `true`.

I also mentioned earlier in this chapter that a future version of Netscape will have two new objects: `navigator.plugins` and `navigator.mimeTypes`. `Navigator.plugins` will be an array of all the plug-ins that the client browser supports, and `navigator.mimeTypes` will be an array of all the MIME types that the browser supports, which will include not only the plug-ins but also the browser's own support, and any helper apps.

Once these objects are available in JavaScript, you should be able to access this information quickly, and perhaps even change the properties of the plug-ins. ●

CHAPTER 11

A Java Tutorial

by Mark C. Reynolds

JavaScript is an extremely powerful tool for developing Web pages. You have already seen a number of significant applications using JavaScript in the preceding chapters. The complexity and power of applications that can be developed in JavaScript is almost unlimited. There are certain situations in which the Java programming language may be a better solution, however.

The difference between JavaScript and Java is very much like the difference between hand tools and power tools. Anything you can do with a lathe you can also do with a rasp, a hand saw, and sandpaper. It is quite possible to produce beautiful woodwork using only the simplest tools. One gains time, and perhaps uniformity, by using a lathe. To do this, however, one must know how to operate a lathe properly, without losing fingers. (In this analogy JavaScript is the lathe.) JavaScript is a simpler language than Java, with fewer built-in functions, yet it is still extremely expressive. Java has a much larger set of capabilities, yet it is also a bit more difficult to use.

Define and use Java methods and classes

Java classes are analogous to JavaScript's objects, while methods fulfill the same role in both languages.

Create Java applets

A Java applet is a small application that is embedded into a Web page. When the Web page is accessed the applet can perform tasks that provide live content to that page.

Use the Java Development Kit to compile applets

The Java Development Kit is a set of tools used to create the binary versions of Java applets, which are used in Web pages.

Embed applets in a Web page

The HTML APPLET tag is used to perform the actual embedding of Java applets. It has a number of attributes that can be used to influence the applet's behavior.

The correct approach, of course, is to use all the tools that are available. Nevertheless, it is very important to realize when to pick up the fine grit sandpaper and when to power up the lathe. This chapter introduces the Java language, and describes its differences with JavaScript. The basic constructs of Java applets are explored, and some simple examples given. ■

The Java Language

If you have ever seen any Java code you have probably noticed that it bears a substantial resemblance to JavaScript. A large part of the Java language is identical to JavaScript. There are several significant differences between Java and JavaScript that are critical in learning how to effectively use both tools. These differences can be grouped into the following three categories:

- The object models
- Interactions with the browser environment
- Language differences

The way in which the two languages handle objects is fundamental to how each is used. Their interactions with the Web browser are also fundamentally different—the concept of an event is completely different in Java. Finally, the Java language is much stricter in its usage than JavaScript. Before we plunge into a detailed description of Java code, it is useful to look at these differences in a little more detail. Java and JavaScript are very different under the hood.

Java and JavaScript Compared

In part II of this book, "JavaScript Objects," we take a very close look at objects in JavaScript. JavaScript objects are used to access the built-in mathematical, string, and date functions. JavaScript objects are also used to access and manipulate HTML elements inside JavaScript code. Java takes this object-oriented approach even further. Everything in Java is based on objects (known as *classes* in Java), and their properties (*instance variables* in Java) and methods. In JavaScript you often create functions that are methods of your own objects. You are also perfectly free to have functions that are not methods. Event handler functions are usually not method functions, for example. In Java, all functions must be methods of some object, and all variables must be properties of some object.

In JavaScript the focus is on responding to events. A user action produces an event that triggers a JavaScript event handler, which does something useful. In Java, user events are handled very differently. When the user loads a Web page containing Java code, in the form of a Java *applet*, the browser tells the applet to start. When the user leaves that page the applet is told to stop. While JavaScript code is ultimately event driven, and intimately tied to its HTML environment, Java applets are much more independent. An applet may respond to a mouse click within its active area, but it won't be listening for the sound of a Submit button being pressed. An applet is a little application that lives in its own world, for the most part. JavaScript code is more like a *Dynamically Loaded Library* (DLL) which is activated in response to something.

Finally, we know that JavaScript takes a very relaxed attitude towards variables and functions. Variables are typeless, and the distinction between functions, objects, and arrays is blurry at best. By contrast, Java is an extremely strict language. All Java variables have an explicit data type. Types may only be converted to one another under very well defined conditions, and only by using explicit type conversion functions. Java also enforces static name binding, instead of JavaScript's dynamic binding. It is impossible (so they say) to reference an undefined function.

▶ **See** the "Dynamic Binding" section of chapter 4 for a discussion of the name binding concept, **p. 219**.

Java is actually a very small language when compared with other object-oriented programming languages such as C++. Nevertheless, it has a large number of capabilities. The extensive set of built-in functions and objects known as the Java *class hierarchy*, for example, implements an extremely rich and powerful set of tools for image manipulation and network access, among other things. This Java tutorial focuses on the core part of Java necessary to create meaningful and interesting Web content.

Data Types in Java

Java variables must be explicitly declared with a particular data type. Java is very similar to the C and C++ programming languages in terms of the types it supports.

Java, however, rigidly specifies the size and representation of its various types so that there can be no confusion. If you have ever tried to port a C program from a DOS or Windows environment with 16-bit integers to a UNIX or Windows-NT environment with 32-bit integers, you know from firsthand experience how frustrating such low-level problems can be.

In addition to its primitive types, such as `int`, `float`, and `boolean`, Java also has object types, just like JavaScript. In Java, however, you must say which object was used to create a particular instance. The declarations that follow say that s is an instance of the `String` object, and that d is an instance of the `Date` object.

```
String s;
Date d;
```

N O T E   For the most part Java statements are similar in form to their JavaScript counterparts. Every Java statement *must* end in a semicolon, however. ■

As you might suspect, these are uninitialized instances. The variables s and d are of type `String` and `Date`, respectively, but have no values yet. They are unbound, just as the JavaScript declaration

```
var myvar;
```

creates an uninitialized (unbound) variable `myvar`. The only difference between the two languages is that in Java we at least know what the underlying type of s and d are, while in JavaScript `myvar` is a complete mystery until it is given some value.

There are several differences between the object models of Java and JavaScript, as well as their terminologies. Note that Java refers to its objects as *classes*, unlike JavaScript. Java object members are referred to as *instance variables*, rather than properties. Instances and methods have the same meaning in both languages. Note particularly that Java has no independent functions, only methods. These differences arise from the fact that Java is both explicitly typed and strongly typed. In Java every piece of data must have a type. Every structured data type, such as `String`, is a class, while the data itself is an instance of that class. This concept of strong typing pervades all of Java, and is even reflected in the differences in terminology with JavaScript.

In Java almost all the built-in data types are numeric. This is a reflection of the fact that everything that is more complex than a number is represented by a Java class. The built-in data types in Java are as follows:

- `boolean`
- `byte`
- `char`
- `short`
- `int`
- `long`
- `float`
- `double`

The `boolean` data is a 1-bit type which may have the familiar values `true` and `false`. Java is more strict than JavaScript in that it does not allow you to use a numeric expression in a context in which a boolean value is expected. You must say `while ( true )` rather than `while ( 1 )`, for example, because the clause of a `while` statement must be a logical (boolean) value.

The `byte`, `short`, `int`, and `long` types are the basic fixed-point numeric types. All are signed quantities. They are represented using 8, 16, 32, and 64 bits, respectively. If you are a C programmer from either the 16- or 32-bit worlds this may seem a little confusing. In the 16-bit world `int` and `short` are mostly the same, while in the 32-bit world `int` and `long` are often the same. Java is actually more explicit. All the basic types are platform independent. Their sizes are fixed as part of the language itself.

You may be wondering what the `char` data type is. Java has taken a very modern approach, and adopted a standard known as the *Unicode* standard for character representation. Unicode is a way of representing almost any character in any language of the world using a fixed Unicode sequence. Unicode sequences look like \u*NNNN*, where *NNNN* is a four-digit hexadecimal number. This is something like an extension to the escape sequences of the C programming language. In C you can write '\007' to represent the character with ASCII code 7 (Ctrl+G, which usually makes the computer go 'ding'). In Unicode, you can write '\u212B' to represent the Angstrom symbol Å and '\u1039' for the Tibetan Rinchanphungshad.

TIP With the exception of Unicode characters, Java has the same syntax for literals as JavaScript.

> **CAUTION**
>
> What you see is not necessarily what you get with Unicode. Many browsers and most display devices are not able to properly handle most Unicode sequences. Avoid Unicode in your Java code unless you are sure your users have the appropriate fonts and software to display it.

The `char` data type is a Unicode character. It is 16 bits wide, and is an unsigned quantity, unlike all the other Java data types. This can also lead to some confusion for programmers who are familiar with 8-bit characters, since a `char` is twice as big as a `byte` in Java. One immediate consequence of the use of Unicode is that strings and arrays of bytes are not the same; some work must be done to convert from one to another. Another consequence is that if you ask a string such as "Hiya" how long it is, it will tell you 4. This means that it is 4 `chars` long, which is actually 8 bytes.

The `float` and `double` data types are standard single and double precision floating-point data types. The Java language mandates that these data types conform to the IEEE (Institute of Electrical and Electronics Engineers) 754 standard, so that a `float` will always be a 32-bit quantity and a `double` a 64-bit quantity, with very precisely defined notions of accuracy, precision, and permitted maximum and minimum values. Imposing a particular standard may be pushy, but at least it ensures that correct implementations will all work the same way.

On the surface Java variables and JavaScript variables seem to behave in the same way. Because Java is a strongly typed language, unlike JavaScript, Java variables can be used only in much more restrictive ways. It is not possible to change the data type of a variable in Java, as it is in JavaScript. In order to convert between different data types you must use explicit conversion routines. We will see several examples of this, particularly in the final section of this chapter, "An Accounting Applet in Java."

Java Classes as Structured Data Types

Java would be very underpowered if it had only the built-in types listed in the previous section. Of course, it not only has these primitive types, it also has complex types which are built up from smaller components. These are classes in Java. They are very similar to JavaScript objects, and also to the classes of C++. In fact, the Java class model is a very simplified version of the one used by C++. Java has a very rich set of predefined classes, known as the Java class hierarchy. Some of the components of this hierarchy are described in the final section of this chapter. Still more are discussed in chapter 12, "More About Java." In this section, we discuss the basic concept of a class, and show how they are defined and used.

The Java concept of a class is quite close to the JavaScript concept of an object. The primary difference is that Java is much stricter about how instances may be used, and has a more detailed set of rules that must be followed. For example, it is not possible to dynamically extend a Java instance, as it is in JavaScript.

▶ **See** the section on "Using Variable Length Arrays and Extended Instances" in chapter 4, which describes how to extend JavaScript instances, **p. 219**.

A Java class is a collection of variables and methods. When a class is created, its variables and methods are defined as part of the class definition. Therefore, the shape of the class is fixed when it is created. Listing 11.1 shows a very simple Java class definition.

Part III

Ch 11

Listing 11.1 A Java Class for Keeping Track of Money

```
class Account {              // name of the class is "Account"
    int ivegot = 0;          // instance variable, initialized to zero

    void deposit ( int n ) {    // method for adding money
        ivegot += n;
    }

    int balance( ) {            // method for determining how much is
                                ➡left
        return(ivegot);
    }

    boolean withdraw( int n ) {    // method for attempting to
                                   ➡withdraw money
        boolean result;      // local variable
        if ( n <= ivegot ) {
```

continues

Listing 11.1 Continued

```
            ivegot -= n;
            result = true;
        } else {
            result = false;
        }
        return(result);
    }
}
```

 TIP Java class names should begin with an uppercase letter. Instance names often begin with a lowercase letter, and contain the class name of which they are an instance.

Listing 11.1 defines a class known as Account. It has a single instance variable, ivegot, which records the total amount of money stored in the Account. It is initialized to 0. It also has three method functions: deposit, balance, and withdraw. These method functions perform the operations specified by their names; they deposit money, get the account balance, and attempt to withdraw money.

There are several things to notice about this class definition. The first and most obvious thing about the class Account is that all its components are declared inside the class definition. In particular, all the class methods are given explicitly as part of the class itself. Methods and variables are not attached as they are in JavaScript—they are a required part of the definition itself.

The second important aspect of these methods is the fact that each of them is declared with its own data type. The balance method is declared to be an int method, which indicates that it returns an int value, the amount of money left in the account given by the int ivegot. The balance method is said to have a return type of int. Similarly, the withdraw method has a return type of boolean; it returns a boolean quantity.

N O T E The return type of a method must match the value returned. It is a serious error to attempt to return something whose type is different than the return type. ■

The *void* Keyword   The deposit method is interesting because it introduces a new keyword: void. The void keyword is used to indicate that nothing is returned. The `deposit` method simply takes its argument, adds it to the instance variable `ivegot`, and then falls off the end of its { } definition block. There is no `return` statement. `void` means what it says—there is nothing being returned.

The same rule applies for the empty argument list of the `balance` method. This indicates that the `balance` function accepts no arguments. This is in contrast to the `deposit` and `withdraw` methods, both of which accept a single argument, which we are told is an `int`. Just as it would be an error to pass a floating-point value to `deposit`, it would also be an error to pass any value to `balance`, or to try to take the value of a method function declared to be `void`.

If we assume `myacct` is an instance of the `Account` class, then both of the following statements would be in error by virtue of misusing the `void` type:

```
int i = myacct.balance(0);  // bad: void args

int j = myacct.deposit(10); // bad: void return
```

Declaring Java Classes   With the example of listing 11.1 in mind, you can see the general pattern for declaring both kinds of class members, namely instance variables and method functions. The general structure of a class declaration looks like the template shown in listing 11.2.

Part
III

Ch
11

Listing 11.2   Declaring a Java Class and Its Members

```
class Classname {          // a class named Classname
    Type1 Var1;            // instance variable Var1 of type Type1
    Type2 Var2;            // instance variable Var2 of type Type2
    ...                    // more instance variables
// Method Method1, return type RetType, arguments Arglist
    RetType Method1( Arglist ) {
        ...
        return( Thing );    // return statement if not void
        }                  // end of Method1
    ...                    // more methods
}                          // end of class definition
```

This class declaration consists of three basic parts, as follows:

- The class declaration line
- The instance variable declarations
- The method declarations

The class declaration line declares the name of the class. It is Java tradition that this name begin with an uppercase letter, as noted earlier. This makes it easy to distinguish class names from variable names (and from the names' built-in types) which traditionally begin with a lowercase letter. In listing 11.1, we declared a class named Account.

The instance variables are then declared immediately following the opening of the class definition, which is indicated by the opening bracket ({). It is possible in Java to declare instance variables anywhere outside a method definition, but it is simpler and easier to understand if they are all placed at the very top of the class definition. Our Account example had a single instance variable ivegot. Note that every instance variable must have a type, and may be initialized. The Account variable ivegot was initialized to 0, for example. As usual, it is good programming practice to initialize all instance variables to reasonable defaults, if possible.

The method function should be placed after the instance variables have been declared. Each method function declaration itself is composed of the following four parts, all of which are mandatory for (almost) every method:

- The return type
- The method name
- The argument list
- The method body

The return type is given immediately before the name of the method itself. With one critical exception (constructor methods, which are described next) all methods must have a return type. If the method executes the return statement, then it must declare what type of quantity it is returning in its return type. If the method does not return anything then it must declare its return type to be void. Java is very strict about mismatches of this form.

The method name is the name by which the method is invoked. This is exactly the same as the function and method names of JavaScript, with one exception. If the name of a method is exactly the same as the name of the class, then the method is known as a *constructor method*, or simply a *constructor*. Later in this section, you will see how these are used.

The argument list declares which arguments, if any, will be given to this method function. The argument list should contain the argument types, as well as the names of the arguments. In listing 11.1, there is a method named deposit with a void return type and a single int argument named n; a balance method with int return type and no (void) arguments; and a boolean withdraw method which also takes a single int argument named n, just like deposit. The argument list must match the arguments used exactly. We cannot call deposit with two arguments or with a string argument, and we cannot call balance with any arguments at all.

Finally, the set of Java code between the opening and closing brackets ({}) constitutes the method *body*. The method body does the work of the method. In general, the method body may make use of its arguments and of the instance variables. The method function deposit is a perfect example of this. Its method body consists of a single statement

```
ivegot += n;
```

which adds the argument n, the amount being deposited, to the instance variable ivegot. Method functions can also call other method functions within the class.

Let's consider an example that makes use of the Account class. In this example, we will open an account, make a deposit of 100, and then make successive withdrawals of 40 and 70. The code to do this is shown in listing 11.3. (Note that these deposits and withdrawals are not associated with any specific currency. The deposit of 100 could be 100 dollars, 100 Francs, or even 100 coconuts.)

Part III

Ch 11

Listing 11.3 Using the *Account* Class

```
Account myacct;                    // 1; declare an instance of the
                                   ➥Account class
boolean gotit;                     // 2; got the money?

myacct = new Account();            // 3; initialize it
myacct.deposit(100);               // 4; deposit 100
gotit = myacct.withdraw(40);       // 5; try to withdraw 40
if ( gotit == true ) {             // 6; got it
    System.out.println("Withdrawal ok");     // 7; print a message
} else {                           // 8; didn't get it
    System.out.println("Insufficient funds");
    System.out.println("Balance: " + myacct.balance()); // 10; print balance
}
```

continues

Listing 11.3 Continued

```
gotit = myacct.withdraw(70);              // 12; try for 70 now
if ( gotit == true ) {                    // 13; got it
    System.out.println("Withdrawal ok");
} else {                                  // 15; didn't get it
    System.out.println("Insufficient funds");        // 16; print
                                                  ➡failure message
    System.out.println("Balance: " + myacct.balance()); // 17; print
                                                  ➡balance
}
```

This code shows a typical sequence of operations in Java. Statement 1 declares an instance of the class Account. It is an uninitialized instance, so it cannot be used until we initialize it. This initialization happens in statement 3 using the familiar new operator:

```
myacct = new Account();              // 3; initialize it
```

Note that the Account class is invoked as if it were a function (with no arguments). The variable myacct is now a fully initialized instance of the class Account, so we are free to use its methods.

CAUTION

Do not confuse instances with instance variables. Instances are structured data items created from classes using the new operator. Instance variables are variables contained within a class definition.

In statement 4 we make a deposit of 100, so that the ivegot now has the value 100. Similarly, statement 5 withdraws 40, so that ivegot is then reduced to 60. Both these statements invoke methods of the myacct instance, as follows:

```
myacct.deposit(100);                 // 4; deposit 100
gotit = myacct.withdraw(40);         // 5; try to withdraw 40
```

This withdrawal succeeds so that the boolean variable gotit, which holds the return value of the method function withdraw, is true. Therefore, the if test in statement 6 succeeds, and statement 7 is executed, as follows:

```
if ( gotit == true ) {               // 6; got it
    System.out.println("Withdrawal ok");    // 7; print a message
}
```

We have enough experience to guess that `System.out.println` calls the `println` method of the sub-object `out` of the system object `System`, and prints a message somehow.

> **N O T E** The dot operator (`.`) works the same way in Java and JavaScript. It is used to reference an element (instance variable, property, or method) of an instance. ▪

We now grow bold and attempt to withdraw 70 from the account represented by the instance `myacct` by calling the method function `withdraw` again in statement 12, as follows:

```
gotit = myacct.withdraw(70);                    // 12; try for 70 now
```

This time it doesn't work, however, since the account holds only 60 at this time. If you examine the body of the method function `withdraw` in listing 11.1 you see that it is quite careful to test and make sure that there are sufficient funds. In this case, therefore, `myacct.withdraw` returns `false`.

The `if` test of statement 13 fails and the `else` pathway of statement 15 takes us to statement 16, which prints out a discouraging but accurate assessment of our financial state. Statement 17 is also invoked to print our balance, as follows:

```
if ( gotit == true ) {                    // 13; got it
    System.out.println("Withdrawal ok");
} else {                                  // 15; didn't get it
    System.out.println("Insufficient funds");        // 16; print
                                                    ➥failure message
    System.out.println("Balance: " + myacct.balance()); // 17; print
                                                    ➥balance
}
```

Statement 17 uses the method function `balance` to get the value, and also makes use of + as a string concatenation operator. This is one of the few cases in which Java relaxes its strict rules on data types. It is usually possible to use + to convert non-strings into strings, but there are certain exceptions. We learn more about this topic in the next chapter. For the moment, just know that converting any of Java's built-in numerical types to strings, as line 17 does, is safe. Figure 11.1 displays a time history of the code in listing 11.3.

FIG. 11.1
Java instance variables
keep their value throughout
the life of an instance.

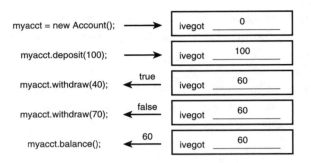

This example probably raises several questions. Based on your experience with JavaScript you are probably wondering why we need any of the methods of the Account class. After all, can't we just refer to the instance variable ivegot as myacct.ivegot, and use the following statements:

```
myacct.ivegot += n;
myacct.ivegot -= n;
int howmuch = myacct.ivegot;
```

to deposit n, withdraw n, and get the account balance into the variable howmuch? This example code in listing 11.3 is also very unrealistic. Banks do not simply let you open an account, they want you to open an account with an initial balance. There should be some way of specifying that initial balance when we call new, just as we do in JavaScript. Finally, this example is insecure. We really do not want anyone to have access to our account balance, nor do we want people to withdraw our money. They should be able to deposit as much as they like.

All three of these observations are valid. To make this example more meaningful we must introduce two more Java constructions—private instance variables and constructor methods.

Private Variables The basic deficiency of the class Account defined in listing 11.1 is that the instance variable ivegot is completely wide open. After the account is opened (new is called to create an instance of Account) we can simply manipulate the balance directly. This makes the three methods of Account fairly useless, and is also very insecure. We would like to hide ivegot from prying eyes, and also restrict the withdraw and balance methods. Listing 11.4 shows a revised definition of the Account class which does this. This file is ex11_4.java on the CD-ROM.

Listing 11.4   ex11_4.java   A Safer Version of the _Account_ Class

```java
class Account {                      // new and improved Account
    private int ivegot = 0;          // 2; amount on deposit
    private int password = 29;  // 3; instance variable for account
                              ➥password
    boolean isopen = false;          // 4; account actually has money

    void deposit(int n) {            // 5; any one can deposit
        if ( n > 0 )                 // 6; cannot deposit negative money
            ivegot += n;             // 7; do the deposit
/*
   Check account and make sure it is open
*/
        isopen = ( ivegot > 0 ? true : false );     // 8; update
                                          ➥isopen
    }                                // end of deposit method

    int balance(int pword) {     // 10; password protected balance
                              ➥method
        if ( pword == password )     // 11; correct password
            return( ivegot );        // 12; return accurate balance
        else                         // 13; incorrect password
            return( -1 );            // 14; return bogus balance
    }                                // 15; end of balance method

    boolean withdraw(int pword, int n) {  // 16; password protection
                              ➥here too
        boolean ok = true;           // 17; ok to withdraw?
        if ( pword != password )     // 18; bad password
            ok = false;              // 19; cannot withdraw
        if ( n > ivegot )            // 20; too much
            ok = false;              // 21; cannot withdraw
        if ( ok == true ) {          // 22; withdrawal allowed
            ivegot -= n;             // 23; update balance
// 24; update isopen variable
            isopen = ( ivegot > 0 ? true : false );
        }
        return(ok);                  // 26; return status
    }                                // end of withdraw method
}                                    // end of Account class
```

This version of the Account class has three instance variables: ivegot, password, and isopen. The first two are declared to be of type int, and also have the special keyword private. A private variable is one that cannot be accessed outside the class. We can no longer refer to myacct.ivegot, nor can we refer to myacct.password, since both are declared `private`. We can, however, refer to the boolean variable `isopen` using `myacct.isopen`. This variable will be used to indicate whether the account has any money, so it is initialized to `false`. We can redundantly declare `isopen` as

```
public boolean isopen = false;
```

using the `public` keyword. `public` is the opposite of `private`, and indicates that `isopen` may be accessed outside the class. By default, instance variables are `public` unless specified otherwise.

The methods `deposit`, `withdraw`, and `balance` are now essential. Because these methods are all within the `Account` class they are permitted to access the class's private variables, as well as its public ones. The `deposit` method illustrates this in a very simple way. In statement 6 it tests its argument to ensure that it is positive, so that no one can make a sneaky withdrawal by depositing a negative amount. If the test passes, then statement 7 is executed. It adds the argument `n` to the private variable `ivegot`. It also updates the public instance variable `isopen` in statement 8. If there is some money on deposit the account is declared to be open (`isopen` is `true`) otherwise it is closed (`isopen` is `false`). The following three statements constitute the body of the deposit method:

```
if ( n > 0 )           // 6; cannot deposit negative money
    ivegot += n;       // 7; do the deposit
isopen = ( ivegot > 0 ? true : false );    // 8; update isopen
```

The new version of the `balance` method now makes use of password protection. To successfully call this method function, a password must be supplied as the argument `pword`. This argument is tested against the private variable `password`. If the passwords match then the actual balance is returned via the statement `return(ivegot)` on line 12. If they do not match then -1 is returned in statement 14. Note that since external access to a private variable is prohibited, it is not possible to steal the password by saying

```
int ha = myacct.password;
```

It is also not possible to gain access to the balance without supplying a password. The statement

```
int left = myacct.balance();
```

will be instantly rejected by Java, since any call to `balance()` must have exactly one `int` argument. The `withdraw` method operates in a similar way. It now takes two arguments, the password argument `pword` and the amount to withdraw `n`. If the passwords do not match (`pword != password` on line 18) or the amount is too great (`n > ivegot` on line 20) then the local variable `ok` is set to `false`. If `ok` remains `true` then both tests must have passed and the withdrawal takes place (statement 23). In this case the status of the account is also updated in statement 24. If there is no money left the account is automatically closed (`isopen` is set to `false`). Finally, the status of the transaction is returned using `return(ok)` on line 26.

N O T E Variables declared inside methods are known as *local variables*. They may only be accessed within the body of the method in which they are declared. ■

This version of the `Account` class satisfies our security concerns. No one can tamper with our `myacct` instance and withdraw money, or even get our balance without the proper password. The password and the account balance are hidden. However, we have allowed anyone to determine whether or not we have an active account using the public instance variable `myacct.isopen`. Anyone can also deposit as much money as he likes.

We still do not have any way of simulating the real life experience of opening an account, since we must still execute two separate statements to open the account, as follows:

```
Account myacct = new Account();
myacct.deposit(100);
```

In addition, there is no way to set the account password. It is stuck at 29 forever. This means that any instance of the `Account` class will have this password. If you know the password on `youracct`, which is 29, then you also know the password on `myacct`, which is also 29. We can, of course, add a `newpassword()` method, which changes the password, but then we would have to execute three statements to open the account: a `new` statement to create the instance, a call to `deposit` to deposit some money, and a call to `newpassword` to change the password. The solution to this inefficient situation is the use of constructor methods.

Part
III

Ch
11

Constructor Methods   Constructor methods, or *constructors* as they are often called, are used to initialize instances. They are called when the new operator is used on a Java class. From your experience with JavaScript, this would seem to be the natural approach. In JavaScript, you call new on a function, and pass it arguments which become the properties and methods of that new instance. You use the special keyword this to denote the current instance.

In Java, constructors are used somewhat differently. For one thing, constructors are methods of the class itself. Constructors have two special aspects, as follows:

- The name of a constructor must be identical to the class name.
- A constructor has no return type.

The second aspect is the only case in which a method function does not have a return type. Other than these two special rules a constructor is the same as any other method. Typically, you use a constructor to perform initialization, such as depositing money and setting the password to our Account class. Listing 11.5 shows the code for a constructor for Account which performs these two operations.

Listing 11.5   A Constructor for the *Account* Class

```
Account(int initdep, int newpword) {          // Constructor
                                              ➥declaration

    ivegot = initdep;              // initialize amount on
                                   ➥deposit
    password = newpword;               // set new password
    isopen = true;                   // declare account open
}                                  // end of constructor
```

This code must be inside the definition of the Account class, of course. This constructor meets both our requirements. It initializes the private variables ivegot and password with the two arguments to the constructor, and also sets the public instance variable isopen to true to declare to the world that the account is now open. We must now use the new operator with two integer arguments to create a new account:

```
Account myacct = new Account(100, 12345);
```

This statement creates an instance `myacct` of the Java class `Account`, with an initial deposit of 100 and a new password of 12345. There is still a problem with this class definition, since there is nothing stopping us from making the erroneous statement

```
Account badacct = new Account(-100, 12345);
```

This creates a perfectly valid instance, named `badacct`, with an initial balance of 100! The result here is simply nonsensical, but in other cases spurious initialization can lead to disastrous results. There is, in fact, a way of providing error checking by using the `isopen` instance variable. Listing 11.6 shows a modified version of the `Account` constructor, which checks the initial deposit and makes sure that it is at least 100.

Listing 11.6 A Constructor for the *Account* Class with Error Checking

```
Account(int initdep, int newpword) {         // Constructor
    if ( initdep >= 100 ) {          // 2; minimum deposit requirement
                                      ➥met
        ivegot = initdep;
        password = newpword;
        isopen = true;
    }
    else                             // 7; minimum deposit requirement not
                                      ➥met
        isopen = false;              // 8; declare failure
}
```

This constructor tests the argument `initdep`, in statement 2, to make sure that it passes the minimum deposit test. If it does pass then the same three initialization statements of listing 11.5 are executed. The constructor then sets the `isopen` variable to `true` to indicate that the instance was successfully constructed (line 6). If the initial deposit test failed then the code branches to line 8 instead. This statement ensures that `isopen` is set to `false` to indicate that the instance construction failed.

Method Signatures in Java   At this point, our `Account` class has many of the features of a real bank account. We have password protection, all the methods that represent everyday transactions, and a reasonably accurate constructor. A little fine tuning will give it even more verisimilitude, as well as illustrate one of the most important aspects of Java methods.

In real life, many bank accounts are rarely this simple. Accounts often have several different pools of money (savings, checking, checking/NOW, CD) with different rules on how these pools must be handled. You might want to open a checking account and a savings account at the same time. We could accommodate this by rewriting the Account constructor to accept three arguments, representing the initial savings deposit, the initial checking deposit, and the new password. If either of the two initial deposit amounts is zero then we would interpret this as meaning that no account of that type was to be opened.

There is a simpler way, however. In Java, we can have more than one method with the same name, so long as all the argument lists are different. Suppose we assume that the default is to open only a checking account, and use the constructor shown in listing 11.6 to perform that operation. We now need another constructor that will open both a checking and a savings account. Listing 11.7 shows this new constructor. Note that it references a new private instance variable named ivegotsav, which holds the savings account balance.

Listing 11.7   An Alternate Constructor for the *Account* Class

```
Account(int initdep, int initsdep, int newpword) { // 3 argument
                                                  ➥constructor
     if ( initdep >= 100 && initsdep >= 1 ) {     // minimum balance
                                                  ➥tests
          ivegot = initdep;                // initialize checking
          ivegotsav = initsdep;               // initialize savings
          password = pword;                // reset password
          isopen = true;                    // accounts are open
          }
     else
          isopen = false;                  // below minima; don't open
account
     }
```

The constructor of listings 11.6 and 11.7 can both be used. Java tells them apart by virtue of the fact that their argument lists are different. The constructor of listing 11.6 takes two int arguments, while that of listing 11.7 takes three. This is often referred to as the *method signature* or the *method shape*, and is written as (int, int) or (int, int, int), respectively. The following statements open two new accounts (create two new instances of the Account class):

```
Account myacct = new Account(100, 12345);

Account wifesacct = new Account(500, 100, 54321);
```

The instance `myacct` represents a checking account with an initial deposit of 100, and a password of 12345. The instance `wifesacct` has both a checking account and a savings account, with initial deposits of 500 and 100, respectively, and a password of 54321.

> **N O T E** Multiple class methods can have the same name so long as they have different method signatures. This technique is known as *overloading*. While overloading is most useful for constructors, because the name of the constructor is fixed by the name of the class, it can be used for any class methods. ∎

The *static* and *final* Keywords   Now that we have introduced the concept of two pools of money within an `Account`, we must obviously modify the `deposit`, `balance`, and `withdraw` methods to make them aware of this fact. Let us suppose that we can withdraw money only from the checking account, but we can deposit money to either account, and query either account's balance. It would be nice to give the `deposit` and `balance` methods a tag indicating which pool of money to use.

If we were writing this code in C or C++ (or several other languages), we could make the tag be the member of an enumerated type. We could also use the `#define` construct to define symbolic constants to stand for the two types of accounts. Finally, we could create `const`s in C++ and use those for the two account types. How does one create a constant in Java? This question is answered as we dissect the code in listing 11.8 which shows our final version of the `Account` class. This file is ex11_8.java on the CD-ROM.

Listing 11.8   ex11_8.java   A Fully Functional Version of the *Account* Class

```
class Account {               // Account Class
    private int ivegot = 0;       // 2; amount on deposit in checking
                              ➥account
    private int ivegotsav = 0;       // 3; amount on deposit in savings
                              ➥account
    private int password = 29;    // 4; account password
    public boolean isopen = false;       // 5; account actually has
                              ➥money
// these constants refer to the checking and saving accounts
```

continues

Listing 11.8   Continued

```
    public static final int CHECKING = 1;         // 6;
    public static final int SAVINGS = 2;          // 7;
// all accts at this bank have this id
    public static int Bankid = 2167;              // 8;
// Constructor: open checking acct only
    Account(int initdep, int newpword) {          // 9;
        if ( initdep >= 100 ) {         // 10; minimum deposit
                                        ➥requirement met
            ivegot = initdep;           // 11; initialize checking
                                        ➥acct
            password = newpword;        // 12; set acct password
            isopen = true;              // 13; the acct is open for
                                        ➥business

        }
        else                    // 15; minimum deposit requirement not met
            isopen = false;             // 16; insure failure
    }                                   // 17; end of first constructor
// 3 argument constructor
    Account(int initdep, int initsdep, int newpword) {      // 18;
        if ( initdep >= 100 && initsdep >= 1 ) {    // 19; min
                                        ➥balance?

            ivegot = initdep;           // 20; initialize checking
            ivegotsav = initsdep;       // 21; initialize savings
            password = pword;           // 22; set password
            isopen = true;              // 23; accounts are open
        }
        else
            isopen = false;        // 26; below minima; don't open
                                   ➥account
    }                              // 27; end of 3 arg constructor
// deposit method: any one can deposit anywhere ( no password )
    void deposit(int n, int which) {          // 28;
        if ( n <= 0 ) return;           // 29; negative deposit
                                        ➥forbidden
        if ( which == Account.CHECKING )    // 30; checking account
                                        ➥deposit
            ivegot += n;                // 31; deposit to checking
        else if  ( which == Account.SAVINGS )    // 32; saving acct
                                        ➥deposit
            ivegotsav += n;             // 33; deposit to savings
    }                               // 34; end of deposit method
// password protected balance method
    int balance(int pword, int which) {          // 35;
        if ( pword != password )        // 36; incorrect password
            return( -1 );               // 37; return bogus balance
// checking account balance wanted
        if ( which == Account.CHECKING )    // 38;
            return(ivegot);             // 39; return it
// savings account balance wanted
```

```
                else if ( which == Account.SAVINGS )    // 40;
                    return(ivegotsav);                // 41; return it
                else                                  // 42; some strange value for
                                                      ➥where
                    return( -2 );                     // 43; return error code
        }                                             // 44; end of balance method
// password protected checking acct withdrawal
        boolean withdraw(int pword, int n) {          // 45;
            if ( pword != password )                  // 46; bad password
                return(false);                        // 47; cannot withdraw
            if ( n > ivegot )                         // 48; too much
                return(false);                        // 49; cannot withdraw
            ivegot -= n;                              // 50; update checking acct
                                                      ➥balance
            isopen = ( (ivegot+ivegotsav) > 0 ? true : false ); // 51;
                                                      ➥open?
            return(true);                             // 52; return status
        }                                             // 53; end of withdraw method
    }                                                 // 54; end of Account class
```

For the most part, this version of the Account class is an amalgamation of the two constructor methods we introduced in the previous sections together with updated versions of the deposit, withdraw, and balance methods from listing 11.4. This version does introduce two new keywords, static and final, and one new concept, that of a *class variable*. We will examine in detail how this class now works.

There are seven variables declared, in lines 2 through 8. The first four have already been introduced: ivegot and ivegotsav hold the checking and savings account balances, password holds the account password, and isopen is the overall account status. The only change we have made is to explicitly declare isopen to be public. These four variables are instance variables; the first three are also private. The next three statements (lines 6 through 8) use the new keywords, as follows:

```
public static final int CHECKING = 1;         // 6
public static final int SAVINGS = 2;          // 7
public static int Bankid = 2167;              // 8
```

The final keyword simply states that this value may never be altered. A final variable must be initialized. final in Java serves the same purpose as const does in C++. The static keyword has a different purpose. It indicates that all instances refer to exactly the same shared variable. The static keyword makes a variable a *class variable* rather than an instance variable.

TIP   Declare class constants to be both final and static.

To understand the difference between a class (static) variable and an instance variable, consider the difference between the instance variable ivegot and the class variable Bankid, which we have just invented to hold an identifier associated with all accounts at this particular bank. Every instance of the Account class will have its own copy of the instance variable ivegot. The amount of money in my account, represented by the myacct instance, is unrelated to the amount of money in your account, represented by the youracct instance. You can conduct thousands of transactions, and amass millions of dollars in the ivegot instance variable of youracct without it having any effect on the ivegot instance variable of myacct (unfortunately).

This is not the case with the class variable Bankid. There is exactly one such variable, and it is shared among all instances of the Account class. This is what makes it a class variable: it belongs to the class, and not to the individual instances of the class. This also means that we may refer to it as Account.Bankid, as well as myacct.Bankid and youracct.Bankid. Note that the static and final keywords may also be applied to methods. We have already seen examples of static methods in JavaScript, in the Date object.

▶ **See** the section "The *Date* Object" in chapter 5, "Built-In JavaScript Objects," for a complete description of its static methods and how they are used, **p. 219.**

The Account class has two constructors, which we have already seen. The two argument constructor is given in lines 9 through 17. It creates a checking account only. The three argument constructor, which allows us to open both checking and saving accounts simultaneously, is shown in lines 18 through 27. Both constructors check their arguments to ensure that minimum deposit requirements are met, and set isopen to false if they are not.

We have rewritten the deposit method so that is takes a second mandatory argument, called which. This argument is used to indicate which account should receive the deposit of n. Error checking of n happens in statement 29, which refuses to make a deposit if the amount is negative, as follows:

```
    if ( n <= 0 ) return;         // 29; negative deposit forbidden
```

If the test passes then the value of which is examined. It is expected to refer to one of the class constants CHECKING or SAVINGS. Note that we refer to them as Account.CHECKING and Account.SAVINGS, in statements 30 and 32. This is a class reference, which is permitted since they are static. We could just as well have used the instance references this.CHECKING and this.SAVINGS, since these constants are part of each instance, too.

If this is a checking account deposit then the test in statement 30 passes and n is added to the checking account instance variable ivegot, in statement 31. If which is Account.SAVINGS instead then n is added to ivegotsav in statement 33, as follows:

```
    if ( which == Account.CHECKING )     // 30; checking account
    deposit
            ivegot += n;                 // 31; deposit to checking
    else if ( which == Account.SAVINGS ) // 32; saving acct deposit
            ivegotsav += n;              // 33; deposit to savings
```

If which is not equal to either constant then nothing happens. We just fall off the end of the deposit method, which is quite acceptable since it is a void method.

The code for the balance method, on lines 35 to 44, operates in the same way as the deposit method. It performs its usual password test (line 36). If that test passes then it tests the value of which and returns the corresponding balance. If which is neither CHECKING nor SAVINGS the method returns an error code of -2. This value was deliberately chosen to be different from the bad password error return of -1, on line 37. The caller can distinguish the two error cases based on which bogus balance was returned.

The implementation of the withdraw method (lines 45 to 53) is almost unchanged from our previous version. We assume that we are only permitted to withdraw from the checking account, so no which parameter is needed. The test that updates the isopen variable has been updated to keep the account open so long as the total balance in both accounts (ivegot+ivegotsav) is greater than 0. This test is shown on line 51, as follows:

```
    isopen = ( (ivegot+ivegotsav) > 0 ? true : false ); // 51; open?
```

Arrays in Java   There is one final piece of Java object machinery that we need before we can launch forward and actually make something appear on a Web page. We need Java arrays. It should come as absolutely no surprise that arrays are actually objects (classes) in Java. The similarity with JavaScript arrays end there, however. There are no associative arrays in Java, and there are no extensible arrays. Java's usual strictness is carried to fanatic extremes in dealing with arrays.

Java enforces the following five rules for all of its arrays:

- Arrays must be created with the new operator or by explicit initialization.
- Every array has fixed length, given by its length instance variable.
- Every array element must have the same type.
- It is impossible to access memory before the beginning of an array.
- It is impossible to access memory beyond the end of an array.

This very restrictive approach is part of Java's security model. One of the most common ways of accessing memory which is not really yours is to declare an array, say int i[10] , and then look at elements like i[-6]. Veteran FORTRAN and C programmers will recognize this as the famous "stack creep" technique for reaching into system memory. Of course, arrays are also a source of completely innocent but vicious errors, such as referring to i[10], even though only i[0] through i[9] really belong to us.

TIP Java arrays are zero-indexed, as in C, C++, and JavaScript.

Let us briefly consider how to use arrays in Java. If we actually do want an array of 10 ints, we must declare a variable to hold this array, and then allocate it using the new operator. The following statements do the trick:

```
int iarr[]; // declare an int array variable
iarr = new int[10]; // allocate space
```

Before we call the new operator the variable iarr is absolutely uninitialized, just as the statement Account myacct; declares an instance myacct of the Account class, but does not actually create such an instance. It is absolutely prohibited to attempt to make an array declaration such as

```
int badiarr[10];// hopelessly bad, awful, and wrong
```

The format used to allocate iarr is the pattern that should be followed to allocate an array of anything; do not attempt anything like the declaration of badiarr. In particular, we can use these two statements to allocate an array of Account instances:

```
Account acctarr[];

acctarr = new Account[10];
```

The variable `iarr` represent an array of 10 `ints`, and the variable `acctarr` represents an array of 10 `Account` instances. None of these is initialized yet, however, so it is unwise to attempt to refer to `iarr[5]` or `acctarr[3]`. Each of the array slots must be initialized. Array creation is really a two-step process, in which the memory is first allocated using `new`, and the individual values are then set. We could say

```
acctarr[0] = myacct;

acctarr[1] = youracct;

acctarr[2] = new Account(2000, 14141);
```

and so forth, to fill in the various slots in the `acctarr`. We can also use explicit initialization, which creates an array and fills in its values at the same time. The following statement, for example, creates an array of four floating-point values:

```
float fltarr[] = { 3.14159, 2.71828, 1.4141, 0.7071 };
```

In each of these cases we may get the length of the array using the instance variable, so both `iarr.length` and `acctarr.length` are 10, while `fltarr.length` is 4. The valid elements of the array range from index 0 through index (length-1). An out of bounds error results if any other elements are accessed.

Part

III

Ch

11

> **CAUTION**
>
> It is often worthwhile to check an array reference to make sure that it is in bounds. This can be accomplished using an `if` test against the length member, as follows:
>
> ```
> if ( 0 <= idx && idx < arr.length )
> ok to use arr[idx];
> ```

The other grievous mistake in Java is to attempt to set an array element to any type other than its base type. Therefore, any member of `iarr[]` must be an `int`, any member of `acctarr[]` must be an instance of the `Account` class, and every member of `fltarr` must be a float. A statement such as `fltarr[2]` = `"pi"` generates a Java exception.

Java Statements

So far we have said very little about statements in Java. You have no doubt noticed in each of the previous listings that Java statements greatly resemble JavaScript statements. Java has a few extra rules, and also a few new statement types that are not supported in JavaScript. There are also some JavaScript constructions that cannot be done, or can only be done very awkwardly, in Java. The reader is strongly encouraged to review chapter 2, "JavaScript: The Language," particularly the section on "Control Structures" and the discussion of "Operator Precedence."

Since Java follows almost the same set of rules as JavaScript we will not attempt an exhaustive discussion of those rules. Instead, we will focus on a few of the major differences. As mentioned quite early in this chapter, Java statements *must* be terminated with a semicolon. While this is a matter of style in JavaScript, it is mandatory in Java. If you omit the semicolons Java attempts to interpret your program as a single gigantic statement, to your eternal embarrassment.

It is already apparent that Java has the `if` statement; it also has the `while` and `for` statements of JavaScript. Java has three more very interesting control structures which are not present in JavaScript: the `do...while` statement, the `switch` statement, and a variant on the `break` and `continue` statements which take a label. In compensation, Java does not have the `for...in` statement of JavaScript. The reason for this latter omission has to do with the more circumscribed way that Java defines objects, as we have just seen.

The *do...while* Statement   The `while` statement in Java and the `while` statement in JavaScript are identical. Both evaluate their `while` clause and then execute the `while` body only if the conditional in the `while` clause was `true`. This means that the `while` body may be executed an infinite number of times, once, or not at all. If we were foolish enough to write

```
while ( false ) {
find the meaning of life;
}
```

the `while` body would never be executed. The valid but meaningless `while`
(`false`) would never be used in practice, of course, but it is quite possible to
have a `while` clause that does evaluate to `false` immediately. This is unfortunate
in the case that it is desirable to execute the `while` body at least once.

The `do...while` statement solves this problem. A `do...while` statement still contains a `while` body and a `while` test, but the `while` test is at the end, ensuring that
the body of the `do...while` loop is executed at least once. The format of this statement is as follows:

```
do {
while-body;
} while ( conditional ) ;
```

CAUTION

The semicolon at the end of the `while` clause in a `do...while` statement is mandatory. The
usual rule that the closing brace of a { } code body terminates the body does not apply to
the do...while statement, since the `while` clause must occur after the closing brace.

The *switch* Statement   The `switch` statement is used to select one alternative
from a set of possible choices. It is designed to be a more compact form of the
`if...else` construction, particularly in case there are many possibilities. The
format of the `switch` statement is shown in listing 11.9.

Listing 11.9   The Java *switch* Statement

```
switch ( numberthing ) {
    case firstval:
        statements;
        break;
    case secondval:
        statements;
        break;
        ...
    default:
        statements;
    break;
}
```

Unlike the other conditional statements the `numberthing` element inside the `switch` test is not a logical value; it is a numerical value. In particular, it must be a numerical value whose underlying type is `byte`, `short`, `char`, or `int`. The value of the `numberthing` is compared against each of the numerical values in the `case` statements. Note that each `case` statement ends with a colon (:). This is mandatory. If it finds a match then it executes the statements after the `case` statement but before the first `break` statement. If none of the case clauses provides a match then it looks for a clause of the form

```
default:
```

which matches anything that is not otherwise matched. In this situation, all the statements between the `default` and the next `break` statement are executed. As an example, consider the `balance` method in listing 11.8. It does a three-way test on its argument `which`. This three-way test can be easily rewritten as a `switch` statement; the code is shown in listing 11.10.

TIP Default cases in `switch` statements are not required, but are recommended. They often catch otherwise mysterious errors.

Listing 11.10   The *Account.balance* Method Rewritten Using the *switch* Statement

```
int balance(int pword, int which) {        // password protected
                                           ➥balance method
    int retval;                        // 2; local variable for return
    if ( pword != password )             // 3; incorrect password
        return( -1 );                    // 4; return bogus balance
    switch ( which ) {                   // 5; switch on the value of
                                         ➥"which"
        case Account.CHECKING:             // 6; which ==
                                           ➥Account.CHECKING
            retval = ivegot;           // 7; return code is checking
                                       ➥balance
            break;                     // 8; done with checking case
        case Account.SAVINGS:              // 9; which == Account.SAVINGS
            retval = ivegotsav;          // 10; return code is savings
                                         ➥balance
            break;                     // 11; done with savings case
```

```
        default:                // 12; which has any other value
            retval = (-2);          // 13; return code indicates an
                                    ➥error
            break;                  // 14; done with the default case
        }                       // 15; end of switch statement
    return(retval);             // 16; return the return code
}                               // 17; end of the balance method
```

This version of the balance method performs the usual password test and then immediately enters a switch in statement 5. The numerical value being tested is which, which is an int. If the value of which is Account.CHECKING then the case Account.CHECKING: statement at line 6 matches, and statement 7 is executed:

```
case Account.CHECKING:      // 6; which == Account.CHECKING
    retval = ivegot;        // 7; return code is checking balance
    break;                  // 8; done with checking case
```

This assigns the checking account balance ivegot to the local variable retval. The break statement at line 8 is then executed. Like any good break statement it directs the flow of control to the first statement after the switch, namely statement 16 which returns retval.

If which has the other valid value Account.SAVINGS then a similar block of code is executed, which gives retval the value of the savings account balance ivegotsav instead (lines 10 and 11). If which has any value other than Account.CHECKING or Account.SAVINGS then the default case, at line 12, matches and statements 13 and 14 execute, as follows:

```
default:                // 12; which has any other value
    retval = (-2);      // 13; return code indicates an error
    break;              // 14; done with the default case
```

In any case, the code ends up at line 16 with retval having one of the two valid values, ivegot or ivegotsav, or the error value -2. In a situation such as this, where there are only three possible alternatives, the amount of code saved by using a switch statement versus multiple if...else statements is minimal. If there had been a few more alternatives, the savings would have been dramatic, however.

Part
III

Ch
11

TROUBLESHOOTING

I have a very simple `switch` statement that examines an integer variable `i`. Based on the value of `i` it sets a local variable `j`. For some reason, the two cases `i==1` and `i==2` always give the same result, even though they have different code in their case blocks. What is wrong? The code looks like this:

```
switch ( i ) {
    case 1:
        j = 2*i;
    case 2:
        j = 3*i;
        break;
    ...
}
```

You have made the most common error in using a `switch` statement. There is no `break` statement to conclude case 1. When `i` is equal to 2 the statement `j = 3*i` is executed, and `j` gets the value 6, as it should. However, when `i` is equal to 1 the statement `j = 2*i` is executed, and then the statement `j = 3*i` is also executed, so that `j` has the incorrect value 3 rather than the correct value 2.

The `switch` statement is more than happy to execute multiple blocks of code. The only way it knows to stop is when it encounters a `break` statement. The presence of another `case` statement, as you have included, won't even slow it down. This is known as "falling through" a `case` statement. Sometimes this is desirable, but usually it is just an error.

The Labeled *break* and *continue* Statements   With the `if`, `while`, `for`, and the new `switch` statement, Java has a rich collection of techniques for controlling statement execution. Java also has one more trick up its sleeve, which can prove very valuable in cases where there are many nested conditionals. It might seem like overkill to add more and more new control structures, since this often leads to confusion. There is a school of thought that says everything can, and should, be reduced to just a single type control, such as `while`. This may be accurate in a purely theoretical sense, but it often is impractical.

On the other hand, it is also true that multiple control structures, particularly nested ones, can be hard to manage. If you have a `for` inside an `if` inside a `while`, and you say `break`, where do you go? You certainly know by now that the correct answer is that the `break` sends you to the first statement after the `while` block, wherever that is. This may be the correct answer, but it is often not the answer you want. If some kind of error or exceptional condition occurs, or if you have finally completed a calculation, you might just want to exit completely from the `for`, `if`, and `while` blocks. This is a situation in which many long for a `goto` statement.

Java does not have a `goto` statement. It does have a mechanism for going to an arbitrary location when a `break` or `continue` statement is executed. This is known as the *labeled* `break` or *labeled* `continue` statement, since the keyword is followed by a label that indicates the desired destination. Listing 11.11 shows a very peculiar set of Java code which illustrates the labeled `break`.

Listing 11.11   Using the Labeled *break* in Java

```
int i, j, k, w;
outtahere:                                   // 2; label
for(i=0;i<200;i++) {
    if ( i%3 == 0 ) {
        j = 7*i; k = 0;
        while ( k++ < j ) {
            if ( k == 29 )                   // eureka!
                break outtahere;     // 8; this gets us out of here
        }                            // end of while
    }                                // end of if
}                                    // end of for
w = j;              // 12; this is where you will actually end up
```

Note that the label `outtahere` must come before the outermost loop, at statement 2. When the labeled `break` of statement 8 is executed, control actually flows to the first statement after the outermost (`for`) block, at statement 12 (which is `w = j;` in this example). This counterintuitive structure is necessary since the label must occur before any statement which uses it. Note also that the label must end with a colon (:).

Think of the label `outtahere` as a name for the next statement, which is the entire mass of the `for` statement in this case. A labeled `break` goes to the first statement after the labeled statement, while a labeled `continue` goes back to the labeled statement. If statement 8 had said `continue outtahere` then the mathematical madness of listing 11.11 would have started all over again.

Developing Java Applets

We have now learned a considerable amount about the Java language itself. The next topic to consider is how it can be used on a Web page. The answer is surprisingly different from the JavaScript approach. Writing JavaScript is almost like writing HTML. You fire up your favorite text editor, create JavaScript event handlers and utility functions, link them to events on a Web page, and you are done. When you load the page, the JavaScript is executed when events arrive.

Java is fundamentally different. JavaScript is (almost) always interpreted, meaning that the Web browser analyzes the text content of the JavaScript code on-the-fly, as it is needed. Java, on the other hand, is a compiled language. Java source is never included directly on a Web page. Instead, a special APPLET tag is used to reference Java code in a special binary format.

The Java Development Cycle

Java is actually both compiled and interpreted, as contradictory as that seems. To understand how this is possible, we must examine the process used to develop Java code. The first step, of course, is to write Java source code. We have already seen a substantial amount of Java source in the various listings in this chapter. If we were writing JavaScript we would now be almost done, since we could embed the code directly on a Web page. With Java we must first convert the source in a binary format, known as Java *bytecodes*.

One of the fundamental principles of Java is that it is architecture neutral: it can run on any type of machine with a Java-capable Web browser. This goal could not be met if Java were compiled in Intel 486 binaries, or Sparc-5 binaries, or any specific machine's binary format. Instead, Java is compiled into the binary format for an abstract (or virtual) machine. For quite a while this virtual machine did not have a physical counterpart—it was simply an abstract instruction set. In March 1996, however, Sun Microsystems announced that it would begin construction on a set of "Java microprocessors," which will actually run the Java instruction set directly. Every other machine must still translate the Java instructions into its own native instructions, however.

When we write Java we must therefore perform three steps, as follows:

- Create the Java source code
- Convert the Java source code to the abstract binary format
- Reference the Java binary code on a Web page

The second step of this process requires that we use a Java compiler to create Java binary code. There are several compilers available; the most widely used is part of a set of tools from Sun known as the *Java Development Kit (JDK)*. The third step makes use of the APPLET HTML tag. These two steps are discussed in the next two sections. First, the question of why Java is both interpreted and compiled is still open.

The answer is that we, the Java programmers, compile Java into its abstract binary format, but the Web browsers must then interpret that format. When a Web browser accesses a page that contains an APPLET tag specifying Java code, the Web browser fetches the binary version of that code (not the Java source). The Web browser must then interpret those abstract instructions to do real work on a real machine. After all, if you have Netscape running under Windows 95 on a Pentium, and Netscape tries to hand the Java bytecodes to the Pentium chip, the Pentium chip will spurn them.

Java Compilers and the JDK

The Java Development Kit, or JDK, is a set of tools for manipulating Java source and binary files. The JDK was the first such set of tools, but is not the only set. Since the JDK is still the most widely used Java development environment, this section describes it in some detail. Other Java compilation environments are discussed at the end of this section.

It is also important to realize that there are several different versions of the JDK. The Macintosh version of the JDK has no command-line interface, and does not support the same set of capabilities as the Solaris version, for example. It is beyond the scope of this book to provide a comprehensive description of all the tools in the JDK, or to discuss how each has been customized for various platforms. However, we will at least mention all its major components, which are as follows:

- appletviewer
- java
- javac
- javadoc
- javah
- javap
- jdb

The `appletviewer` and `javac` tools are the two you will use the most often, at least at the beginning of your Java career. The `appletviewer` is an application that can be used to view Java applets outside of any Web browser. Usually, you write a Java applet, compile it using the Java compiler `javac`, and then test it using the `appletviewer`. The `appletviewer` frees you from having to debug both your HTML and your Java code at the same time. It is also useful in tracking down browser-dependent bugs, since `appletviewer` is not itself a browser. The `appletviewer` and the Java compiler `javac` are available on all platforms supported by the JDK.

The JDK can be downloaded free from Sun Microsystems' site **http:// www.javasoft.com**. Currently, the JDK is available for Windows 95, Windows NT, Solaris 2.4 and 2.5, Linux and several other versions of UNIX, and the Macintosh. This list will no doubt continue to grow, so you are advised to check javasoft's Web site regularly for the latest information.

Components of the JDK   The unfortunately named `java` application is a Java interpreter. If you give the `java` application a Java binary file it executes the contents of that file. This application is not really of interest to us, since it is primarily used to test and execute stand-alone Java applications rather than applets. Java is a large enough language that it is possible to write full blown applications in Java. `java` is then used to execute them.

The `javadoc` application automatically generates HTML documentation from Java source code. It looks for specially formatted comments with the source and uses those to construct the corresponding documentation. We will see a few simple examples of such comments in the next chapter.

The `javah` application is used when you want to mix Java code with C or C++ code. `javah` generates files that allow Java, C, and C++ to interoperate. At the moment

Java applets are forbidden to use modules written in any language other than Java (known as *native methods*), so javah is not of interest to us. Java enforces this prohibition for security reasons.

javap is the Java profiler. It allows you to instrument Java code to discover which portions of it are taking the most time. jdb is the Java debugger. It permits symbolic debugging of Java binaries. Once you are a bit further along the Java learning curve you will certainly want to explore these tools further.

The Java Compiler   The javac tool is the Java compiler. It is invoked by giving it the name of one or more Java source files. If the files contain valid Java then they will be converted to the binary format of the Java instruction set. Let us take the source code of listing 11.8, contained in the file ex11_8.java on the CD-ROM, and make a very tiny change—modify the class declaration to say "public class Account" instead of "class Account." If we do this and then attempt to compile it using the following statement:

```
javac ex11_8.java
```

the Java compiler complains with a message saying that "the public class Account must be defined in a file called 'Account.java'." Well, if it must then it must. If we oblige and rename the file to Account.java (which can also be found on the CD-ROM), and then try

```
javac Account.java
```

On the CD

it succeeds, and the file Account.class is created. Files with the suffix .class are Java binary files. This seemingly peculiar restriction on the filename of the source code for a public class is something that must simply be tolerated in this revision of the JDK. In addition, we must make the Account class be a public class if we wish to refer to it in other files. Finally, there is no flexibility in the name of the binary output file, either. The compiled version of the public Account class must be contained in a file named Account.class. The underlying reasons for these file name restrictions are complex, and cannot really be explained without a long and painful discussion of Java internals. For our purposes we will simply accept these rules, which are summarized in the Note that follows.

N O T E Public classes in Java should follow these rules:

- Put only one public class definition in a Java source file.

- The name of the source file must match the name of the public class.

- Do not rename the compiled output file. It must be the name of the public class, followed by the suffix `.class`. ▓

Other Java Development Environments   For a long time the JDK was the only game in town. Since Java was developed by Sun it is only natural to expect that its development environment would be the first, and also the most comprehensive. Because of Java's explosive popularity, a number of other environments have been created. Some are free, like the JDK, while others are commercial products.

One effect of Java's overwhelming growth rate is that any list or description of Java tools would be hopelessly out of date before it could be printed. No attempt will be made to present such a list in this book. Instead, the best way to learn about such tools is on the Web itself. There are two resources which can be used to obtain the most up-to-date information.

The Gamelan repository, at **http://www.gamelan.com**, contains a very large collection of information about Java, JavaScript, and many other Web-related topics. Their site boasts several hundred Java entries. Some are simple applet demonstrations, while others are full-blown development tools. Both commercial offerings and public domain code are represented. Their Java page is well worth visiting.

After some initial reluctance Microsoft (**http://www.microsoft.com**) has also entered the Java arena. Their Java development environment is known as Jakarta. It is intended to be fully integrated with the Microsoft philosophy towards software products. This means that it will have a visual development environment similar to Visual Basic and Visual C++. It is also designed to interface smoothly with Microsoft's object system (known as COM).

One of the most interesting features that Microsoft has announced is the ability to compile Java directly to native machine code in addition to producing standard `.class` output files. Of course, the native code will not be platform independent, but significant performance improvements can be expected. If you will be developing Java on any of the Windows platforms you should plan on regular visits to Microsoft's Web page for the latest information.

The *APPLET* Tag

Now that we have a compiled Java file we are at last approaching the point at which we can actually create a fully functional Java applet. Since Java applets are binary files, there is no way we can literally include them in HTML, as we did using the <SCRIPT>...</SCRIPT> block for JavaScript. Instead, we must use a new HTML tag, the APPLET tag, to reference the Java binaries for our applet.

An APPLET block consists of the following four parts:

- The <APPLET> declaration itself
- A set of parameters which may be given to the applet using the PARAM tag
- Alternate text
- The closing </APPLET>

Part
III

Ch
11

An example showing the basic HTML syntax for an APPLET block is shown in listing 11.12.

Listing 11.12   Example of an *APPLET* Block in HTML

```
<APPLET CODE="Something.class" WIDTH=100 HEIGHT=50>
<PARAM NAME="var1" VALUE="5">
<PARAM NAME="othervar" VALUE="somestring">
This alternate text is displayed on Java-impaired browsers
</APPLET>
```

Mandatory Attributes   This example in listing 11.12 attempts to load and execute the Java binary code from a file named Something.class given as the value of the mandatory CODE attribute. By default, a Java-capable browser searches for files referenced by CODE relative to the HTML document's BASE, although this search strategy can be changed by the optional attribute CODEBASE, described in the next section.

The mandatory WIDTH and HEIGHT describe the size of the box that is allocated for this applet. The applet may later attempt to change this size itself. The values of the WIDTH and HEIGHT attributes are in pixels. On a Java-enabled browser the example of listing 11.12 is drawn inside a box of 100×50 pixels. Other browsers instead display the alternate text This alternate text is displayed by Java-impaired browsers. The alignment of the applet's bounding box may be influenced by the optional ALIGN attribute.

 TIP The APPLET tag is not an HTML block attribute. APPLET tags should be enclosed in a heading (<Hn>), paragraph (<P>), division (<DIV>) block, or some other block delimiter.

Optional Attributes   The APPLET tag also accepts the following optional attributes:

- ALIGN
- CODEBASE
- HSPACE
- NAME
- VSPACE

The ALIGN attribute is used to specify the alignment of the applet's bounding box with respect to other adjacent text and graphics. The values of the ALIGN attribute include BOTTOM, MIDDLE, and TOP, much like the IMG tag. They also include an additional set including ABSBOTTOM, ABSMIDDLE, BASELINE, LEFT, RIGHT, and TEXTTOP for more precise control.

The CODEBASE attribute is used to specify an alternate location at which to find the Java binary specified in the CODE attribute. If the value of the CODEBASE attribute is an absolute path then that path is searched for the Java code. If CODEBASE is specified as a relative path, such as java/classes then that path is appended to the document's BASE, and the code is sought in that relative location. This is often useful if you wish to keep your HTML in one place, and your Java binaries in another.

HSPACE and VSPACE are used to define the amount of horizontal and vertical space that should be created as a border for the applet. Both specify a numerical value in pixels. The NAME attribute is used to give the applet a name, which may be completely unrelated to any of the names of the classes it uses. Applet NAMEs are used for applet-to-applet communication, and also reserve a place for the applet in the

JavaScript HTML hierarchy. This point is explored further in chapter 12, "More About Java," in the section on "JavaScript to Java Communication."

> **N O T E** The APPLET tag does not currently accept an ALT attribute to specify alternate text for Java-impaired browsers. Such text must be embedded in the <APPLET>...</APPLET> block itself. ▓

The *PARAM* Tag   The <APPLET>...</APPLET> block may contain any number of PARAM tags. Each PARAM tag takes two attributes: NAME and VALUE. The value of each of these attributes is an uninterpreted string. This is the standard mechanism for passing in initialization parameters from the Web page to a Java applet. Java applets have a special method, called getParameter(), to retrieve such values from their environment. Note that each PARAM tag specifies exactly one parameter.

A Simple Applet

On the CD

We are now ready to construct a simple Java applet. This applet doesn't do much. In fact, all it does is display a string in color. We will arrange to pass in a string to be displayed using a PARAM tag. This applet shows us most of the fundamental components of Java applet design. The HTML code for a page containing the applet is shown in listing 11.13, while the code for the applet itself is shown in listing 11.14. These files are ex11_13.html and PStr.java, respectively, on the CD-ROM.

Part
III

Ch
11

Listing 11.13   ex11_13.html   A Web Page Containing a Simple Applet

```
<HTML>
<HEAD>
<TITLE>Displaying a String in Java</TITLE>
</HEAD>
<BODY>
<P>
<HR>
<APPLET CODE="PStr.class" WIDTH=400 HEIGHT=40 ALIGN="CENTER">
<PARAM NAME="mystring" VALUE="cocoanuts">
You will see this text if your browser does not understand Java.
</APPLET>
<HR>
The <A HREF="PStr.java">source</A>
</P>
</BODY>
</HTML>
```

Listing 11.14   PStr.java   A Java Applet That Displays a String

```
import java.lang.* ;                            // 1; get Java language
                                                ↪package
import java.awt.* ;                             // 2; get Java AWT package

public class PStr extends java.applet.Applet {  // 3; define our applet
                                                ↪type
    String userstring = null;                   // 4; instance variable

    public void init() {        // 5; called when applet is loaded
// get value of PARAM NAME="mystring"
        userstring = getParameter("mystring");      // 6;
    }
// called when applet starts
    public void start() {                       // 8;
        Dimension d = preferredSize();          // 9; get preferred size
        resize(d);                              // 10; make applet that size
        repaint();                              // 11; redraw the screen - calls paint()
    }
// override built-in paint()
    public void paint( Graphics g ) {           // 13;
        String outstr;
// string concatentation
        outstr = "I've got a lovely bunch of " + userstring;     // 15;
        g.setColor(Color.green);                // 16; get output color to
                                                ↪green
// draw the string offset from the corner
        g.drawString(outstr, 10, 10);           // 17;
    }

}
```

The code in listing 11.13 should be self-explanatory. An APPLET is declared to be implemented by the CODE at URL PStr.class, relative to the document's BASE. Its dimensions are 100×40 pixels, and its alignment is CENTER. Some alternate text has been provided after the single PARAM tag, which gives the parameter mystring the value cocoanuts. A pointer is given to the source PStr.java in an HREF at the end of the <BODY>.

To run this applet we must create the file Cstr.class from the file PStr.java, which is shown in listing 11.14. This is done using the javac tools, with the command

```
javac PStr.java
```

This command creates the java binary `PStr.class`. We can now view the results by pointing our favorite Java capable browswer at the file `ex11_13.html`, or by invoking the appletviewer on it using the command "appletviewer ex11_13.html." The results of viewing this HTML in Netscape are shown in figure 11.2.

FIG. 11.2
Java applets allow you to create text and graphics on-the-fly.

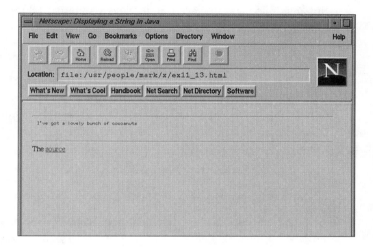

Part
III

Ch
11

Anatomy of an Applet

Just how does the `PStr` applet work? The code in listing 11.14 contains a number of new concepts which we describe next. The `PStr` applet begins with two new statements using the `import` directive, as follows:

```
import java.lang.*;
import java.awt.*;
```

This directive is used to inform the Java compiler that externally defined classes may be needed. Statement 1 says to `import java.lang.*` ;, where the `*` is a wild card indicating all the classes within the *package* `java.lang`. A package is a related collection of classes.

Of course, this applet does not use all the classes in the `java.lang` package, but it does not hurt to overspecify when using an `import` statement. Only those elements that are actually needed are used. Statement 2 makes a similar request for the `java.awt` package. The AWT is Java's Abstract Windowing Toolkit, a collection of graphic utilities.

▶ **See** chapter 12, "More About Java," which describes the class in the AWT and shows how several of them are used to load and manage images, **p. 425.**

Statement 3 declares the applet's class PStr. As indicated previously, this class name should be the same as the name of the file in which it is found. Rather than being a simple class declaration, however, statement 3 introduces one more new keyword, extends, as follows:

```
public class PStr extends java.applet.Applet {
```

Java supports the object-oriented notion of *inheritance*. This means that classes may be built on other classes, and inherit some of their properties and methods. In this case the built-in applet class java.applet.Applet is being used as the *base class* (or *superclass*) and our customization PStr is the *derived class* (or *subclass*). This frees us from having to write a lot of code which would only duplicate the standard behavior of java.applet.Applet. All applets begin with a declaration of the form

```
public class Myclass extents java.applet.Applet {
```

The PStr class contains a single instance variable, userstring, declared in statement 4. This variable is of type String, the Java string class. It also contains three methods, init(), start(), and paint(). The init() and start() methods are two of four standard methods that are called during the life of an applet. The init method is called when an applet is first loaded, and should be used to perform any one time initialization. The start method is called when an applet begins running, generally right after init completes. There are two other complementary methods, stop and destroy, which are called when an applet is stopped (when another page is visited, for example), and when the browser is completely finished with an applet (when it falls off the end of the browser's cache, for example).

This particular applet does not need to do anything when it is stopped or destroyed, so these methods are not provided. In fact, the default java.applet.Applet class provides implementations of all of these methods, so that an applet need not actually provide any of them. The PStr class *overrides* the init and start methods of its parent java.applet.Applet. A method is overridden when a subclass implements a method that is also implemented in its superclass. When this happens the method in the subclass is used. Thus the PStr class uses the superclass implementations of stop and destroy and its own implementations of init and start.

When the PStr.class file is loaded the first thing that happens is the init method is called. The init method executes a single statement (at line 6), as follows:

```
userstring = getParameter("mystring");
```

which uses the Java function getParameter(). This function is used to retrieve the value of a PARAM tag whose name is given as an argument. Therefore, if there is a PARAM whose NAME attribute is "mystring", the getParameter() call in statement 6 returns the VALUE of that PARAM. If not, it returns null. In our HTML code of listing 11.13 there is such a parameter, and its VALUE is the string "cocoanuts."

N O T E   PARAM values are always interpreted as strings in Java. ▪

The initialization is now complete, and the method function start is called next. This function performs three actions, as follows:

```
Dimension d = preferredSize();      // 9
resize(d);                          // 10
repaint();                          // 11
```

In statement 9 it gets the preferred size of the applet's drawing area using the Java function preferredSize(). This returns the WIDTH and HEIGHT as specified in the APPLET tag in the form of an instance d of the class Dimension. This value is immediately passed to the Java function resize() which attempts to ensure that the applet's drawing area is that size. These two statements are not strictly necessary, but are good examples of defensive programming.

The final statement of the start method is statement 11. This statement calls the Java function repaint(), which forces the entire drawing area of the applet to be redrawn. In particular, it forces a call to the paint() method, which this PStr has also overridden. Unlike the init and start methods, which both have void signatures, the paint method accepts a single argument, g, which is an instance of the Graphics class. The methods of the Graphics class are used to actually do graphics. The paint method looks like the following:

```
String outstr;
outstr = "I've got a lovely bunch of " + userstring;  // 15
g.setColor(Color.red);                    // 16
g.drawString(outstr, 10, 10);    // 17
```

Statement 15 constructs the output string outstr, by concatenating a constant string with the value of userstring. Note that if userstring had been null the value of `outstr` would be the string "I've got a lovely bunch of null" since the quantity `null` is converted to the string "null." Statement 16 sets the drawing color to red by using the `red` (static, final) class variable of the `Color` class. Finally, statement 17 draws the string `outstr` in that color. We place the string at relative coordinates (10,10), meaning that the string is offset 10 pixels from the top edge and 10 pixels from the left side of the applet's bounding box.

Even though this applet is extremely simple, it does illustrate all the major aspects of applet design. The more complex applet we describe in the next section has the same basic components, as do the applets of chapter 12.

An Accounting Applet in Java

In this section we examine a slightly more sophisticated Java applet. This applet exercises the `Account` class which we have meticulously built up in the previous sections of this chapter. Our Java applet uses the `PARAM` tag mechanism to process a set of transactions. When it is done it displays an account status in its applet window.

On the CD

The `PARAM` mechanism we use is extremely simple. We specify the number of transactions using a `PARAM` whose `NAME` is "ntrans." The `VALUE` of this parameter is the total number of transaction parameters to follow. Each one of those `PARAM`s has a name of the form `trans#` followed by a number. Thus, the first transaction has `PARAM NAME="trans#1"`, the second `NAME="trans#2"`, and so forth. The `VALUE`s of these transaction parameters encode what we want. If the value is of the form `"deposit:100"` that indicates a deposit of 100, while it is of the form `"withdraw:150"`, that indicates a withdrawal of 150. The Java source for this applet is shown in listing 11.15. The source code for this applet can be found in the CD-ROM file Acex.java.

Listing 11.15   Acex.java   A Java Applet That Processes Account Transactions

```
import java.lang.* ;
import java.awt.* ;

public class Acex extends java.applet.Applet {      // 3; declaration of
                                                     ➡class
```

```
        int ntrans = 0;                         // 4; number of transactions
                                                ➥requested
        int ntransdone = 0;                      // 5; number of transactions
                                                 ➥done
        int ndeposits = 0;                      // 6; number of deposits done
        int nwithdrawals = 0;                    // 7; number of
                                                 ➥withdrawals done
        int noverdrafts = 0;                     // 8; number of overdrafts
        private Account myacct = null;           // 9; Account instance
                                                 ➥itself
        private static final int MyPass = 1492;      // 10; secret password
// private method to do 1 transaction
        private void do1trans(String thetrans) {       // 11;
            String numpart;                      // 12; numerical part of a
                                                 ➥transaction
            int wherecolon;                      // 13; location of colon
                                                 ➥separator
            int valu;                            // 14; transaction' value
            int len;                             // 15; length of string
            boolean ok;                          // 16; withdrew ok?

            wherecolon = thetrans.indexOf(":");      // 17; find the
                                                     ➥separator
            if ( wherecolon <= 0 ) return;       // 18; bad transaction
            len = thetrans.length();             // 19; overall length of
                                                 ➥string
// get numerical part
            numpart = thetrans.substring(wherecolon+1, len);       // 20;
            valu = Integer.parseInt(numpart);      // 21; convert it to an
                                                   ➥int
            if ( valu <= 0 ) return;             // 22; bad transaction
            switch ( thetrans.charAt(0) ) {      // 23; type of
                                                 ➥transaction?
// deposit ( 100 = numerical value of "d" )
                case 100:                // 24;
                    myacct.deposit(valu, Account.CHECKING);       // 25;
                                                                  ➥do it
                    ndeposits++;              // 26; update counters
                    ntransdone++;
                    break;
                case 119:                // 29; withdrawal ( 119 = "w" )
                    ok = myacct.withdraw(MyPass, valu);       // 30;
                                                              ➥try it
                    if ( ok == true ) {      // 31; success; update
                                             ➥counters
                        nwithdrawals++, ntransdone++;       // 32;
            } else {                 // 33; failure
                        noverdrafts++;              // 34; flag an
                                                    ➥overdraft
                    }
                    break;
```

continues

Listing 11.15 Continued

```
        }                                      // 37; end of switch
    }                                          // 38; end of do1trans() method

    public void init() {                       // 39; init method
        String tmp;
        myacct = new Account(1000, 100, MyPass);   // 41; fire up
                                                      ➥account
        tmp = getParameter("ntrans");          // 42; get # of
                                                      ➥transactions
// if not null then convert to integer and set ntrans
        if ( tmp != null )                     // 43;
            ntrans = Integer.parseInt(tmp);    // 44;
    }                                          // 45; end of init()

    public void start() {                      // 46; start method
        String onetrans;                       // 47; will hold one
                                                      ➥transaction

        int i;

        for(i=1;i<=ntrans;i++) {               // 49; for all
                                                      ➥transactions
// try to find the parameter
            onetrans = getParameter("trans#" + i);   // 50;
            if ( onetrans != null )            // 51; if found then..
                do1trans(onetrans);            // 52; do it
        }
        resize(preferredSize());               // 54; request
                                                      ➥preferred size

        repaint();                             // 55; force repaint
    }                                          // 56; end of start()

    public void paint( Graphics g ) {          // 57; paint method
        String msg1, msg2, msg3, msg4;         // 58; temp strings for
                                                      ➥messages
        int thebalance;                        // 59; final balance
        int loc = 15;                          // 60; drawing location

        thebalance = myacct.balance(MyPass, Account.CHECKING);
// msg1 contains a report on number of transactions requested and
➥performed
        msg1 = "Transactions requested: " + ntrans;
        msg1 += "; transactions performed: " + ntransdone;
// msg2 contains a report on number of deposits and withdrawals done
        msg2 = "Deposits: " + ndeposits;
        msg2 += "; withdrawals: " + nwithdrawals;
        g.setColor(Color.black);               // 66; draw it in neutral
                                                      ➥black
        g.drawString(msg1, 10, loc);           // 67; first
```

```
                                                          ➥message
            loc += 15;                        // 68; update y coordinate
            g.drawString(msg2, 10, loc);           // 69; second
                                                          ➥message
            loc += 15;                        // 70; update y again
            if ( noverdrafts > 0 ) {            // 71; oops,
                                                 ➥overdrafts...
                msg3 = "Overdrafts: " + noverdrafts;    // 72; report
                                                    ➥how many
                g.setColor(Color.red);            // 73; draw it in panicky
                                                 ➥red
                g.drawString(10, loc);           // 74; overdraft message
                loc += 15;                        // 75; update y
            }
            msg4 = "Balance: " + thebalance;        // 77; balance
                                                          ➥message
    // If the balance is nonzero then draw it in green, otherwise red
            g.setColor(thebalance > 0 ? Color.green : Color.red);
            g.drawString(msg4, 10, loc);           // 79; balance
                                                          ➥message
        }                                  // 80; end of paint
    }                                      // 81; end of Acex
```

The *init* Method

To understand how this applet works, let us approach it from a functional point of view. We know that the first thing in this applet that is executed is its init() method, which begins on line 39. The following extract shows the body of the init() method:

```
String tmp;
myacct = new Account(1000, 100, MyPass);    // 41; fire up account
tmp = getParameter("ntrans");               // 42; get # of
                                              ➥transactions
// if not null then convert to integer and set ntrans
if ( tmp != null )                          // 43;
    ntrans = Integer.parseInt(tmp);         // 44;
```

The first thing the init method does is initialize our Account instance, myacct, with starting balances of 1000 in checking and 100 in savings. It also sets the account password to the private variable MyPass.

This illustrates one very important point about Java. The Account class is referenced indirectly, through its Account constructor. It is not necessary for us to include the Account class code. When the Acex applet is loaded and the `init` method is called, the Java interpreter within the browser detects that there is a reference to an external class on line 41. It knows that the name of that class must be the same as the name of the constructor. This tells it that it must load the file `Account.class` over the network to actually call the `Account` constructor. This only works, however, now that we have made the `Account` class be `public`.

This is the reason that we may not put the binary Java code for the `Account` class in a file named kickme.class, or in any file other than `Account.class`. If we do, the Java interpreter will not be able to find the class code. Even though the Java language has static binding, it also has dynamic loading. This keeps Java binary files as small as possible, since external classes are only loaded when they are needed. This is very desirable, since those binary files are being accessed across a potentially very slow network.

After the `Account` class code has been implicitly loaded and the constructor called, the `init` method then calls the `getParameter()` function to retrieve the number of transactions from the parameter `ntrans`. If it can find such a parameter it then attempts to convert that `String` value into an integer, on line 44. It uses the `parseInt` method of the `Integer` class, which has exactly the same purpose as JavaScript's built-in function of the same name.

 TIP Many Java methods are the same in JavaScript.

The *start* Method

Once the `init` method completes the `start` method is called. The `start` method executes a `for` loop, beginning on line 49. The body of the `start` method is as follows:

```
String onetrans;                    // 47; will hold one transaction
int i;

for(i=1;i<=ntrans;i++) {            // 49; for all transactions
// try to find the parameter
    onetrans = getParameter("trans#" + i);    // 50;
    if ( onetrans != null )                    // 51; if found then..
        do1trans(onetrans);                    // 52; do it
    }
```

```
resize(preferredSize());        // 54; request preferred size
repaint();                      // 55; force repaint
```

It iterates for the number of transactions requested. If the `init` method did not set the `ntrans` value, it will have its default value of 0 (given in the instance variable section of the class definition, on line 4). For each iteration an attempt is made to find a parameter whose NAME begins with `trans#`. These parameters contain the transaction requests as their VALUEs. If a parameter of this type is found, the `start` method makes a call to the private method `do1trans()` to actually process the transaction. When all transactions are complete the `start` method requests that the applet's drawing area be resized to its preferred size (line 54) and then forces a repaint (line 55).

The *do1trans* Method

The `do1trans` method is the workhorse for transaction processing. It accepts a `String` argument that contains the requested transaction in the form `request:amount`. To process such a request, it must separate the request type (`deposit` or `withdraw`), which occurs before the colon (:), from the request amount, which occurs after the colon. Let's examine exactly how this works on a request such as "deposit:400." The first few lines of the `do1trans()` method handle this type of parsing, as follows:

```
wherecolon = thetrans.indexOf(":");   // 17; find the separator
if ( wherecolon <= 0 ) return;        // 18; bad transaction
len = thetrans.length();              // 19; overall length of string
// get numerical part
numpart = thetrans.substring(wherecolon+1, len);   // 20;
valu = Integer.parseInt(numpart);     // 21; convert it to an int
if ( valu <= 0 ) return;              // 22; bad transaction
```

In line 17 a call is made to the `String` method `indexOf`. This call attempts to find the character index of the colon separator. In our case that separator is the eighth character, so this method call returns 7 (since character indexing is zero-based). Line 20 uses the `String` method `substring` to extract the portion of the transaction string beginning at character index 8 to the end of the string. This is just the string "400" in our case, which, of course, corresponds to the numerical part of the transaction. The result is saved in the local `String` variable `numpart`. Line 21 uses the `parseInt` method again to convert this value from a `String` to an integer. The next block of code in the do1trans() method is used to actually process the transaction, as follows:

```
switch ( thetrans.charAt(0) ) {        // 23; type of transaction?
// deposit ( 100 = numerical value of "d" )
     case 100:                   // 24;
         myacct.deposit(valu, Account.CHECKING);        // 25; do it
             ndeposits++;          // 26; update counters
         ntransdone++;
         break;
     case 119:                         // 29; withdrawal ( 119 = "w" )
         ok = myacct.withdraw(MyPass, valu);            // 30; try
                                                        ➥it
         if ( ok == true ) {     // 31; success; update counters
             nwithdrawals++, ntransdone++;      // 32;
         } else {                 // 33; failure
             noverdrafts++;       // 34; flag an overdraft
         }
         break;
     }                           // 37; end of switch
```

The switch statement on line 23 now examines the first character of the transaction string thetrans using the String method charAt. This method returns numerical values, so that we must use the numerical codes for the characters "d" and "w" in the case statements. If the first character is "d" (line 24) then this must be a deposit transaction. Line 25 carries out the transaction, and lines 26 and 27 update the counting variables ndeposits and ntransdone, which record the number of deposits and successful transactions, respectively.

If the first character is "w" (line 29) then this is a withdrawal. We know that withdrawals may fail, so we record the result of calling the withdraw method of the Account class in the local variable ok on line 31. If the withdrawal succeeds we again update counting variables (line 32). If it fails we update a different counting variable, noverdrafts, which records the number of attempted overdrafts.

Note that the do1trans method ignores any invalid input. If the input string was "deposit:xxx" or "gag:45," both would be silently rejected. The former would fail the test on line 22, since "xxx" cannot be successfully parsed as an integer. The latter would simply fall off the end of the switch statement, since the first letter "g" matches neither "d" nor "w."

Note also that the do1trans() also accepts a string of the form "deltatron:200" as a deposit request (in the amount of 200), since it only examines the first character of the input. Most of the real syntax checking on deposits and withdrawals that you would find in a genuine accounting package has been eliminated from this example. This was done because the goal of this chapter is to introduce you to Java, not teach you about string parsing or bring you up to date on modern accounting practices. A fully robust version of the do1trans() method would have been many times longer, without any significant new Java content.

The *paint* Method

After the start method has finished calling do1trans, it forces the paint method to be called by invoking repaint. The paint method draws a series of strings in various colors summarizing the transactions. The following is the body of the paint method:

```
thebalance = myacct.balance(MyPass, Account.CHECKING);   // 61;
msg1 = "Transactions requested: " + ntrans;
msg1 += "; transactions performed: " + ntransdone;
msg2 = "Deposits: " + ndeposits;
msg2 += "; withdrawals: " + nwithdrawals;
g.setColor(Color.black);                // 66; draw it in neutral black
g.drawString(msg1, 10, loc);            // 67; first message
loc += 15;                              // 68; update y coordinate
g.drawString(msg2, 10, loc);            // 69; second message
loc += 15;                              // 70; update y again
if ( noverdrafts > 0 ) {                // 71; oops, overdrafts...
    msg3 = "Overdrafts: " + noverdrafts;     // 72; report how many
        g.setColor(Color.red);          // 73; draw it in panicky red
        g.drawString(10, loc);          // 74; overdraft message
        loc += 15;                      // 75; update y
        }
msg4 = "Balance: " + thebalance;        // 77; balance message
g.setColor(thebalance > 0 ? Color.green : Color.red);   // 78
g.drawString(msg4, 10, loc);            // 79; balance message
```

It gets the current account balance (line 61), and then constructs two strings recording the number of transactions requested, the number actually processed, and the total number of deposits and withdrawals (lines 62 to 65). It displays these strings in basic black (lines 66 to 70). Note that the x coordinate of the strings is the same—it is always 10, while the y coordinate, stored in the variable loc, is incremented after each call to drawString. This ensures that the strings are not drawn on top of one another.

Having displayed this basic information, it next checks to see if any overdrafts occurred on line 71. If they did it constructs a message indicating how many (line 72), sets the drawing color to red (line 73), and then draws that string (line 74). It also updates the y coordinate for the next draw on line 75. Finally, the current balance is displayed. The color this string uses is determined by comparing the balance to 0. If the balance is greater than 0 then green is used, while if it is 0, red is used (line 78). The final balance string is drawn in line 79.

Executing the Account Example Applet

To execute this Java applet we must do two things: we must compile it and place the code in the appropriate directory, and we must also create some appropriate HTML that invokes it. The applet is compiled using the command

```
javac Acex.java
```

which creates the binary file Acex.class. This must be placed in the same directory with the binary Account.class file, since that file needs to be loaded to resolve the various references to methods in the Account class. Finally, we must have a small piece of HTML that issues some transactions. This is shown in listing 11.16 (the CD-ROM file ex11_16.html). The result of browsing this tiny Web page is shown in figure 11.3.

Listing 11.16   ex11_16.html   Executing the Accounting Applet on a Web Page

```
<HTML>
<HEAD>
<TITLE>Using the Accounting Applet</TITLE>
</HEAD>
<BODY>
<P>
<HR>
<APPLET CODE="Acex.class" WIDTH=400 HEIGHT=400 ALIGN="CENTER">
<PARAM NAME="ntrans" VALUE="5">
<PARAM NAME="trans#1" VALUE="withdraw:400">
<PARAM NAME="trans#2" VALUE="deposit:10">
<PARAM NAME="trans#3" VALUE="withdraw:900">
<PARAM NAME="trans#4" VALUE="withdraw:330">
<PARAM NAME="trans#5" VALUE="deposit:250">
You will see this text if your browser does not understand Java.
</APPLET>
```

```
<HR>
The Example <A HREF="Acex.java">source</A>.
<BR>
The <A HREF="Account.java">Account</A> base class.
</P>
</BODY>
</HTML>
```

FIG. 11.3

The Java Accounting applet processes transactions in vivid color.

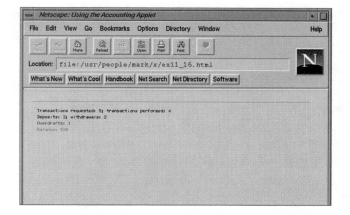

Part

III

Ch

11

CHAPTER 12

More About Java

by Mark C. Reynolds

One of the major advantages of the Java language is its power and flexibility. Java is a full-featured programming language with all the constructs one needs to develop object-oriented applications. However, as you have already seen in chapter 11, "A Java Tutorial," Java is not as directly connected with the environment of its Web page as JavaScript. Java cannot really access HTML elements on a Web page in a direct manner. As compensation for this deficiency, Java provides some extremely powerful tools for manipulating images and URLs. Java also has a set of components, known as the *Advanced Windowing Toolkit* (AWT), which enable Java applets to create pushbuttons, text entry fields, and other HTML-like entities.

The term *Java* encompasses many things. In chapter 11, we focused on gaining some initial understanding of Java as a programming language. In the process, you encountered some

Use Java packages

All the major packages in the Java Class Hierarchy will be described, with special emphasis on the most important methods and classes.

Load and display images in Java

The image package is a key component in Java's graphics system. We will examine several of its elements in detail.

Layout components in the applet window

Layout is often the most challenging aspect in any windowing system. All of Java's built-in layout methods will be described, and two of the most common will be used in detailed examples.

Manipulate URLs

Java imposes certain rules on opening other Web pages. We will see what those rules are, as well as examine how Java cooperates with the browser in handling URLs.

old familiar methods, such as parseInt() and charAt(), and also some new ones, such as paint(). This points to the fact that Java is more than a language. Java is also a set of methods, organized into a collection known as the Java Class Hierarchy, which enables us to do complex tasks. Much of the expressiveness of Java only becomes clear when we learn more about some of the components of the Java Class Hierarchy and what they can do for us.

This chapter explores the Java Class Hierarchy with particular emphasis on image and URL manipulation. It presents the basic concepts necessary to explore Java further, as well as enabling you to write more complex and interesting Java applets. ■

The Java Class Hierarchy

In chapter 11, "A Java Tutorial," you were first exposed to the concept of *inheritance* in Java. In particular, in the applet described in the section "An Accounting Applet in Java," you saw three Java classes working together: the Account class, the Acex class, which drove the applet itself, and, implicitly, the Java class java.applet.Applet. We were introduced to the special keyword extends and we saw that Acex was said to extend the built-in class java.applet.Applet. This idea of having one class extend another, also known as *subclassing*, is critical to understanding the Java Class Hierarchy.

▶ **See** "An Accounting Applet in Java" in chapter 11 for a detailed example of subclassing the Applet class, **p. 414**.

Classes and Subclasses

In chapter 11, we built our Account class from the ground up and gradually refined the methods to perform a set of simple, but useful, operations. We could have continued this process *ad infinitum,* adding more and more functions for more and more specialized situations. This would make the Account class cover a larger number of situations, but it would also lead to dramatic overkill in some cases. It would be nice to have the capability to handle escrow accounts, foreign currency transactions, and the like, but in many situations, you would not use these extra capabilities.

This leads to the notion that perhaps we do not want to extend a class by adding more and more to it, but rather by creating specialized versions of that class. The specialized versions would have all the capabilities of the generalized class, but would also have their own unique features. The specialized classes, such as EscrowAccount and InternationalAccount, have all the methods and instance variables of Account, but also have their own methods, which Account does not have. The specialized classes *inherit* the attributes of their parent. The specialized classes are *subclasses* of their parent class, which is known as the *superclass*.

> **N O T E** There is no *multiple inheritance* in Java. Every Java class has exactly one parent class. ■

Naturally, this simple idea of inheritance acquires some twists and turns when it is actually implemented. The first such variation is the idea of having a subclass *override* a method in the superclass. The Acex applet discussed at the end of chapter 11 overrides the paint method of its java.applet.Applet superclass. It does not override the inherited method repaint—it just uses it as is.

You can imagine that the international version of Acex would keep the withdraw and balance methods the same and would add convert and transfer methods (to convert between different currencies and to transfer money). It might also override the deposit method so that deposits could be made in foreign as well as local currency. A subclass not only extends its superclass, it also tends to modify its behavior for special situations.

Java has a special keyword, super, that is used to refer to the superclass of a class. Superclass instance variables can be accessed as super.varname, and superclass methods can be invoked as super.methodname(). This keyword is particularly useful if you want the subclass to use its own method named NAME and also use its parent's method, also named NAME.

For example, our internationalized version of the deposit method might look something like listing 12.1. This version of deposit simply converts the deposit amount, in any arbitrary currency, into the local equivalent (line 3) and then calls the deposit method in the superclass (Acex) to perform the deposit. This avoids the tedious approach of copying all the deposit code in any subclass that overrides it.

Part III

Ch 12

Listing 12.1   A Class Method Calls Its Superclass Method

```
// Assume that "currency" is a variable specifying the type of currency,
// and that convert is a method that converts between currencies
// this is the subclass deposit method
void deposit(int amount, int which, int currency) {          // 1;
     int localamount;
     localamount = convert(amount, currency);            // 3; convert to
                                                            ➥local
     super.deposit(localamount, which);            // 4; invoke superclass
                                                       ➥method
}
```

What happens to instance variables of a class when a subclass is derived from it?
As one might imagine, public instance variables remain public. Interestingly
enough, private instance variables (and private methods) are completely private—
they are unknown in the subclass just as they are unknown outside the class.
This means that no subclass can reference private instance variables or make use
of private methods of its superclass. Java also has a third category, known as
protected variables and methods, which are known to the class and to all its subclasses, but remain invisible outside the class. Figure 12.1 illustrates the relationship between the various types of class members and their subclass counterparts.

FIG. 12.1

Subclassing can be used in
Java to create specialized
classes.

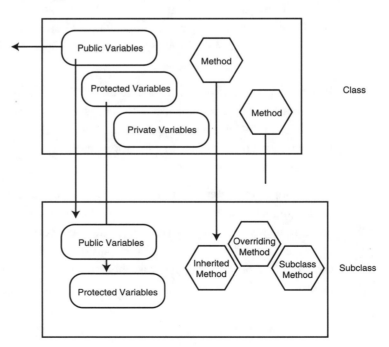

Packages in Java

The Java Class Hierarchy is the collection of all the classes that are provided as a standard part of Java. These classes are organized in a class hierarchy, as previously described, with a series of very general classes—such as the ubiquitous class known as Object—at the top of this hierarchy. This might lead you to guess that the class java.applet.Applet, which is the superclass of all applets, is a subclass of java.applet, which is in turn a subclass of an all encompassing java class. This is an excellent guess, but it is incorrect.

Java actually has two kinds of organization for its classes. It has a strict class hierarchy, which describes all the children of each class. It also has a more horizontal organizational structure, known as the Java *package* system. Packages are used to group together similar, but not necessarily directly related, classes into a set of groups. These groups are the Java packages. Packages can be distinguished notationally from classes because they all begin with a lowercase letter, while classes always start with an uppercase letter. Thus Applet is a class in the java.applet package, which is a part of the java package. As a class, Applet is derived as follows:

```
Object -> Component -> Container -> Panel -> Applet
```

An applet is therefore actually a specialized form of the graphics class Panel, which is derived from two other graphics classes, Container and Component, and ultimately from Object. This is an excellent example of the matrix organization of classes and packages. Applet is a member of the java.applet package; Panel, Container, and Component are members of the java.awt (Advanced Windowing Toolkit) package; and Object is the member of the java.lang package.

The top of the Java package hierarchy is the java package. There are other top level hierarchies, such as the sun hierarchy, which are platform and/or operating system dependent. The java hierarchy, however, is always guaranteed to be present. It contains the following packages:

- lang
- net
- awt
- applet
- util
- io

The *java.lang* Package   The `java.lang` package is one of the most important and fundamental of the Java packages. It defines the basic object types that correspond to elements of the language. It also includes several very interesting pieces of machinery that are used throughout Java programming, including the critical concept of a *thread*, which will be reviewed shortly.

The data type classes contained within `java.lang` include `Boolean`, `Character`, and `String`, as well as the numerical types `Integer`, `Long`, `Float`, and `Double`. These latter four classes are actually subclasses of a generic `Number` class. As one might expect, each of the numerical types defines conversion methods. You have already seen one of these, namely the `parseInt` method of the `Integer` class, which is used to convert strings to integers.

▶ **See** the section "An Accounting Applet in Java" in chapter 11, which illustrates the use of this method, **p. 414**.

The `java.lang` package also contains a class known as `Math`, which is very similar to the JavaScript object of the same name. `Math` provides an expanded set of mathematical operations. The same can be said for the `String` class, which is a full-fledged class (object) in Java—unlike its implicit counterpart in JavaScript. Java also provides a second string class within the `java.lang` package known as `StringBuffer`. This is used for extensible strings. Whenever you concatenate strings using the plus sign (+) operator, you are actually using a `StringBuffer`. More precisely, whenever the Java compiler sees an expression that involves merging two strings, it rewrites that expression to use a `StringBuffer` behind the scenes.

Finally, the `java.lang` package contains two critical classes with enormous utility: `System` and `Thread`. The `System` class provides system-level functionality with a platform-independent interface. The way in which it is actually implemented, of course, depends heavily on the actual platform. You have already seen an example of the `System` class in the print statement, `System.out.println("message")`, which sends the string "message," with a subsequent carriage return, to the *standard output*. Where this output actually goes is, of course, platform dependent. `Threads` are the subject of the next section and are used in the "Image Viewer Applet" section at the end of this chapter.

N O T E   In Netscape Navigator, the output generated by `System.out.println` can be seen by activating the Java Console under the Options menu. ■

Using Java Threads   It is often very useful to do several things at once. Not only does this get more done, it brings everything to completion earlier. Of course, in this aspect, most humans are like most computers. It is not really possible to do more than one meaningful thing at a time, such as reading two books at once, but it is often highly desirable (particularly for one's image) to make it appear that way. This is the advantage of modern multitasking. Each user process gets its own set of tiny slices of a single CPU, and the illusion of simultaneous processing is maintained. Most modern operating systems enable you to seem to perform several tasks, such as editing while printing.

In this hustle and bustle world of ours, there is never enough time to do all the things we want to do without it looking like we are ignoring someone or something. The same can be said for the programs we write. In the days of plain old DOS, for instance, people were used to waiting for the program to finish printing or repaginating before they could do something else. Microsoft brought Windows to the DOS world, and suddenly you could run more than one program at a time, thus enabling you to do more than one thing at a time. You were, however, the computer was not.

A CPU (Central Processing Unit) really only executes one instruction at a time, and each instruction belongs to a particular program. But, and here's where it gets interesting, the CPU does not care where the instruction comes from; it just executes it. Essentially what operating systems for UNIX, Windows, and Macintosh computers do is cleverly pass instructions to the CPU from the loaded programs so that it looks like they are all running at the same time, but in fact each of them is getting its slice of the CPU's time in a sort of round-robin fashion. This enables the programs to print or repaginate while you're off playing Solitaire or something.

There are often cases in which it is highly desirable to be able to perform many tasks within a single program. This is particularly true in graphics programs. In attempting to display multiple images, it is advantageous to be working on image 5, while image 4 is being displayed, for example. Java provides such a capability as part of its `java.lang` package through the medium of the `Thread` class.

A Java thread is very similar to an ordinary thread in a garment. It has a definite starting point, a definite endpoint, and can weave through the garment in tandem with other threads. A complete description of Java threads is well beyond the scope of this chapter. However, we can examine the general structure of a threaded Java applet. This structure is used in the Image Display applet to realize precisely the goal described previously: interleaving graphic operations and other operations. The template for a multithreaded Java applet is shown in listing 12.2.

Listing 12.2   The Structure of a Runnable Java Applet

```
public class MTApplet extends java.applet.Applet implements Runnable {
    Thread mythread = null;       // the thread we will create

    public void init() {          // init method, as before
        ...                       // initialization stuff goes here
    }

    public void start() {         // start method, creates thread
        if ( mythread == null ) {
            mythread = new Thread();
            mythread.start();
        }
    }

    public void stop() {          // stop method, stops thread
        if ( mythread != null ) {
            mythread.stop();
            mythread = null;
        }
    }

    public void paint( Graphics g ) {    // local paint method
        ...                              // custom drawing goes here
    }

    public void run() {           // the work method of the thread
        ...                       // the main body of the thread
    }
}
```

This template has several familiar features as well as some new wrinkles. The first thing to notice is that the class declaration for this MTApplet class not only extends java.applet.Applet, as it must, but it also implements Runnable. Runnable is a new type of Java element: a Java *interface*. An interface, like a superclass, expresses a set of methods. A class, such as MTApplet, which implements this interface, must also implement these methods. In particular, it must implement a run method. The purpose of the run method will become clear in a moment.

The MTApplet class has the very familiar init() method, which is used to do whatever initialization is required. This usually involves parsing user parameters accessed via the getParameter() method. If images are to be manipulated, the init() method is also a good place to begin loading those images. The paint() method is also much as before: it is used to perform our applet-specific drawing operations. These operations are now done in parallel, however, using threads.

The start() and stop() methods shown in listing 12.2 are not templates or placeholders; they are shown in their entirety. The start method examines the instance variable mythread to see if it is null (its initial value). If it is, then the start method creates a new Thread instance by invoking the new operator and sets mythread to be that instance. The effect of creating a new thread is that there is now one extra task that can be run. This new thread is not yet running, however. The final statement in the start method launches this new thread by saying mythread.start(). This calls the start method of the new thread. The new thread now runs as an independent entity within the applet.

The stop method is the mirror image of the start method. It also examines the mythread instance variable. If it is not null, then that thread is halted by calling its stop method. Cleanup is then performed by setting the mythread variable back to null. The interplay between start and stop is such that at most, one new thread will be created. If start finds that mythread is not null, it will do nothing. Also, stop ensures that the new thread will never be stopped twice. None of this yet explains how the new thread accomplishes anything, however.

The answer to this mystery is provided by the new run() method. When a class implements the Runnable interface and a new thread is created and set running by that class, then its run() method will be entered. In fact, every applet is already a thread, known as the main thread. Unless a new thread is created by instantiating the Thread class, the main thread is the only thread, so there is effectively no parallelism.

Once the second thread is activated and the `run` method entered, the new thread can do one set of operations while the `main` thread is doing something else. This is the key idea behind parallelism in Java. If the `run` method performs some graphical operations and ends up triggering `paint()`, the actual drawing is performed in the `main` thread, while the computations leading up to it are performed in the second thread.

CAUTION

The actual implementation of Java threads is platform dependent at this time. This is because threads require some cooperation from the underlying operating system, and different operating systems cooperate in different ways. A thread-based applet that works perfectly under Solaris may fail on Windows NT, and vice versa. Applets using threads should be thoroughly tested on all major platform types (UNIX, Windows, and Macintosh).

The *java.net* Package The `java.net` package contains the basic classes and methods that are used for network communications. This package contains classes representing network connections (sockets), network addresses, and, most significantly, URLs. This might sound like an extremely rich source for interesting Java programming ideas, but the Java security model limits what you can do with this package quite severely. It is worthwhile to review these limitations because they have a significant effect on what is possible and what is not.

Every Java applet is activated within the context of a Web page via that page's APPLET tag. This Web page in turn was obtained from some URL and is therefore associated with a particular Web server. We will refer to the Web page that activated the applet as that applet's document and the server from which that page was obtained as the applet's server.

The first restriction on network access within Java is that it is prohibited from opening a network connection to any host other than the applet's server. This means that it is not even possible to make a network connection to the user's own host! The second restriction is that a Java applet can only access documents within the directory hierarchy rooted at the applet's document BASE. These two restrictions combined might seem quite grim because the set of documents accessible within Java is rendered very small.

Fortunately, there are no restrictions on documents that Java can ask its browser to open. This concept is one of the subtleties of Java. Java does not actually implement graphics, network connections, or anything else that impacts the external environment. It has a series of methods where it can ask its browser to do these things for it. When you create a button or open a URL in Java, it is actually the browser that is doing these things for you.

Having said all this, there is one very important class in the `java.net` package that you can (and will) use quite effectively: the URL class. As the name implies, this class is used to construct an abstract representation of a URL. This class has several different constructions, as follows:

```
URL(String)

URL(URL, String)

URL(String, String, String)

URL(String, String, int, String)
```

The first form takes a `String`, such as the literal `http://home.netscape.com`, and attempts to construct a URL instance from it. The second form is used to concatenate a `String` representing a relative pathname onto an existing URL. This form can be used to descend from the applet's document BASE to an HTML file within its tree.

The third and fourth forms are used to build a URL from its component parts. The third form takes a protocol name, such as `http`, a hostname, such as `home.netscape.com`, and a filename, such as `index.html`, and produces a URL from that combination. The fourth form enables you to also explicitly set the port number for those rare cases in which the protocol is not being accessed on its default port. (`http` is occasionally received on port 1080 or 8080 rather than its default 80, for example.)

When we review our two major Java applets later in this chapter, you will see the first two forms of the URL class constructor, and also how one politely asks one's browser to open a "foreign" URL. The discussion on the `java.applet` package also shows how to obtain the URL that corresponds to the applet's document BASE.

The Advanced Windowing Toolkit We have already observed that Java cannot interact directly with HTML elements, unlike JavaScript. There are no HTML FORM components within the Java Class Hierarchy. This means that Java programmers must construct their own buttons, text entry fields, and the like if they want such items to be part of their applets. The Advanced Windowing Toolkit (AWT) is Java's set of capabilities for doing this. It is contained within the package.

The classes in the AWT can be subdivided into three categories: display items (such as Button), layouts (such as FlowLayout), and overall graphics items (such as Color and Font). The first category, display items, is the largest and includes an extensive set of elements, including the following:

- Button—a standard button
- Checkbox—a button with an on/off indicator
- CheckboxGroup—a set of radio buttons
- Choice—a pop-up menu of choices
- Dialog—a pop-up dialog box
- Frame—an entirely new window
- Image—a GIF or JPEG image
- Label—a static text item
- List—a listbox of items
- Menu—a menu of items
- Panel—an organizational item that can contain other items
- Point—a single pixel
- Polygon—a region bounded by line segments
- Rectangle—a rectangular region
- Scrollbar—a scroll bar, usually associated with a List or TextArea
- TextArea—an editable text item that can have more than one line, and can be scrolled
- TextField—a single line editable text item with fixed size

As you can see from this enumeration, many familiar HTML elements are also present in the AWT. As in HTML, it is quite simple to glue together a set of graphical items in a page, but it is somewhat more difficult to make the presentation attractive and crisp. HTML has a number of markup styles and directives that can be used to control the visual format of various elements, including tables and forms.

The means to control where elements are placed, how they are aligned with one another, and how they are sized and spaced is always an issue in graphics programming. This applies to all windowing systems. Java is no exception. The Java AWT has chosen an approach with several different, quite distinct layout styles. Within each style, the display elements that you create, such as `Buttons` and `TextAreas`, are placed according to a well-defined system. However, it can still take time to get things looking just the way you want, and if all else fails, you can still programmatically position objects at specific coordinates.

 TIP The default Java layout is `FlowLayout` with `CENTER` justification. Use this until you become more comfortable with the AWT.

At present, there are five Java layout styles. Each has its own peculiarities, and you will almost certainly find yourself using a combination of styles once you acquire some skill with the AWT. The Java layout classes are:

- BorderLayout
- CardLayout
- FlowLayout
- GridLayout
- GridBagLayout

The `BorderLayout` approach is based on the idea of placing elements at one of the four cardinal points—North, South, East, or West—or in the Center. It is often ideal for arranging items in case you would like two or three arranged in a vertical (North, Center, South) or horizontal (West, Center, East) stacking order. `BorderLayout` is also used with `Panels` for hierarchical organization of items. If you would like a top row of `Buttons` and perhaps a `Label` below, you would create two `Panels`, place them at the North and South locations in a `BorderLayout`, and then add the `Buttons` to the northern `Panel`, and a `Label` to the southern `Panel`. Listing 12.3 shows a code fragment that does just this.

Part
III

Ch
12

Listing 12.3 An Example of Hierarchical Layout in Java

```
BorderLayout bl;
Button but[];
Panel nopa, sopa;
Label la;

bl = new BorderLayout();              // 5; create a new BorderLayout
                                      ➥instance
setLayout(bl);                        // 6; make it the default layout
nopa = new Panel();                   // 7; create two new panels
sopa = new Panel();
add("North", nopa);                   // 9; put nopa at the North edge
add("South", sopa);                   // 10; add sopa at the South edge
but = new Button[4];              // 11; allocate space for 4 buttons
but[0] = new Button("Back");       // 12; create the buttons with
                                      ➥various labels
but[1] = new Button("Forward");
but[2] = new Button("Home");
but[3] = new Button("Done");
for(int i = 0; i < 4; i++) {       // 16; add the buttons to the North
                                      ➥panel
    nopa.add(but[i]);               // 17; it will default to a
                                      ➥FlowLayout
la = new Label("Southern Label");   // 18; create new label
sopa.add(la);                       // 19; add to south Panel
}
```

This example begins by allocating a new instance of the BorderLayout class (line 5) and then calling the setLayout method to make this the current layout. Remember that a Java applet is actually a subclass of a Panel, so that the bare call to setLayout on line 6 applies to the Panel containing the entire applet. The next two statements create Panel instances. Note that one can create instances of graphical items all day long, but they are not displayed until they are added to the applet.

The North and South Panels are added in lines 9 and 10 using the add method. The add method is overridden in all the layout classes, which means that it has its own distinct syntax for each one. In the case of a BorderLayout, the first argument to add must be one of the five permissible directions. We use North and South to split the applet vertically. The next five lines create four Buttons with some text to name them. Lines 16 and 17 then add those buttons to the North Panel. This is accomplished by explicitly invoking the add method of nopa, the North Panel instance. If we had mistakenly just used add(but[i]) on line 17, this would have attempted to add these buttons to the entire applet's panel. Lines 18 and 19 create and add a `Label` to the `South Panel` in a similar way.

N O T E At the moment, button labels must be text. It is not currently possible to put an image inside a button using the `Button` class. A subclass of the `Button` class would have to be written to do this. ▪

The `FlowLayout` class implements an approach in which elements are added incrementally across one or more rows. Elements can be justified within a given row using `LEFT`, `CENTER` (the default), or `RIGHT` justification. If an element does not fit on a given row, the layout wraps around to the beginning of the next row. `FlowLayout` is often used for rows of buttons or other components of similar size and shape. As mentioned earlier, `FlowLayout` is the default layout for any newly created graphical container (such as a `Frame` or `Panel`).

The other three layout types are more specialized. `CardLayout` is used to create slide-show-like presentations. Elements of a `CardLayout` are presented sequentially rather than displayed simultaneously on the screen. `GridLayout` lives up to its name. It enables you to position elements based on their row and column location. It is used by first specifying the number of rows and columns to be allocated, and then placing individual elements in their desired (row,column) location. `GridBagLayout` is a much more powerful version of `GridLayout`. It is also regrettably complex because it is necessary to first construct a description of the layout, using the subsidiary class `GridBagConstraints`, and then actually build the layout on top of that.

Part
III

Ch
12

The final set of classes in the immense `java.awt` package is the classes that correspond to general graphical constructs rather than things that are actually drawn. We have already seen three examples of these classes in our tiny applets from chapter 11, "A Java Tutorial": the `Color`, `Dimension`, and `Graphics` classes. The `Color` class is usually used by invoking its static instance variables that name the primary colors (such as `Color.Red`), although it can also be used to construct arbitrary color values directly from red, green, and blue levels. The `Dimension` class is used to hold information about the size of a component. The `Graphics` class captures the entire graphical state of an applet. Recall that the method signature for the applet `paint()` method is `public void paint( Graphics g )`.

Within `paint()`, you can call a set of methods too numerous to mention to draw strings, rectangles, and other common primitive graphics operations. Some of the other important classes in this general graphics category are the following:

- `Event`
- `Font`
- `MediaTracker`

The `Event` class is extremely important because it enables us to respond to user events, such as a button being pushed inside our applet. The `Applet` class has another method, known as `action()`, that is called whenever user interaction takes place. Its method signature is `public Boolean action( Event ev, Object arg )`. It is called whenever the Object `arg` (a `Button`, for example) is pushed and generates the Event `ev`. If you override the default `action` method, you can control what happens when events occur, just as in JavaScript.

> **CAUTION**
>
> Java events and JavaScript events are not directly related. At present, Java cannot respond to events outside its applet. It is also not possible to install a JavaScript event handler for `Events` inside a Java applet.

The `Font` class is used to manipulate the text appearance of any item that contains text. It can be used to load a particular font by name (such as `TimesRoman` or `Helvetica`), to set the font style (such as `PLAIN`, `BOLD`, or `ITALICS`), and also to set the font size. The oddly named `MediaTracker` class is Java's answer to the patient projectionist. It is almost always used to track the progress of images being progressively loaded over the network. You will see examples of all three of these AWT classes below.

The *java.applet* Package   The `java.applet` package is quite small and has just one interesting class, `Applet`, with a small number of interesting methods. You have already seen the `getParameter()` method, which accepts a `String` argument giving the NAME of a PARAM, and returns the VALUE of the PARAM (or `null` if there is no matching name). The other three `Applet` methods that you will use most frequently are the following:

```
URL getDocumentBase();

URL getCodeBase();

AppletContext getAppletContext();
```

You can probably guess that the first of these methods returns a URL instance representing the value of the BASE attribute of the applet's document. It is the top of the document directory tree that the applet can access on the server host. The second of these methods is similar: it returns the URL representing the value of the CODEBASE attribute given in the APPLET tag, if any. This is used when all the Java class binaries are kept in a different server directory than the HTML files. That directory would be named in the CODEBASE attribute.

 TIP The URLs returned by getDocumentBase() and getCodeBase() are always valid for use in Java applets as long as they are not null.

▶ **See** "The *APPLET* Tag," section of chapter 11 for a description of the HTML elements used in declaring an applet, **p. 407**.

The getAppletContext method is used to talk directly to the browser. The applet context really refers to the browser environment in which the applet is running. Once you have obtained the applet context, you can then use it to ask the browser to display a URL, for example. This is not a task that you can perform directly in Java because of security restrictions. You will see an example of this in the section entitled "A Pop-Up Document Viewer Applet" later in this chapter.

The *java.util* and *java.io* Packages   These packages are the last two on our tour of the Java Class Hierarchy. The java.util package provides various utility classes, while the java.io package handles input and output to files and streams. The java.util package contains the Date object for manipulating date items, as in JavaScript. It also contains a series of classes that can be used to manipulate structured collections of things, including the Vector, HashTable, Dictionary, and Stack classes.

One of the most useful utility classes is StringTokenizer. This class is used to solve the age-old problem of decomposing a string, such as the following:

"this,is,a,comma,separated,list"

into its individual components, which will be delimited by a separator:

"this" "is" "a" "comma" "separated" "list"

Part

III

Ch

12

The traditional way of solving this problem would be to search for the separator character, which is the comma character (,) in this case, and keep track of the individual substrings that occurred between the separators. We would find the first comma and separate the initial string into "this" and "is,a,comma,separated,list" and then repeat the procedure until each of the individual elements was extracted. The StringTokenizer class completely automates this tedious, but extremely common parsing task.

Anyone who has ever written string manipulation code that attempts to interpret a series of separate items (tokens) will appreciate the StringTokenizer class.

There is not much to be said about the java.io class for applet developers. One of Java's security restrictions prohibits local file access of any kind inside an applet. While we can certainly ask the browser to open a document using the file: protocol, the applet cannot do so itself. This restriction may be weakened in some future version of Java, but at the moment Java cannot touch the local file system.

A Pop-Up Document Viewer Applet

This section analyzes and presents a pop-up document viewer applet in Java. This applet enables the user to specify the communication protocol to be used via a pop-up menu and also permits a full document name to be entered into a text field. Once the user commits to a particular document name by pressing a button, the applet requests that the browser open that document in a new window. This applet is designed as a simple demonstration of some of the capabilities of the java.applet and java.awt packages. It also illustrates Java's variety of event handling. The code is shown in listing 12.4. It can also be found on the CD-ROM in the file SD.java.

On the CD

Listing 12.4   SD.java   Viewing a Document in a New Browser Window Using Java

```
/**
  A Java Applet to launch a document in a new window
  Comments for "javadoc" follow.
  @author Mark C. Reynolds
  @version 1.0
*/
```

```
import java.awt.*;                        // 1; get AWT components
import java.net.*;                        // 2; get URL and friends
import java.applet.*;                      // 3; get Applet class methods

public class SD extends java.applet.Applet {
     String whatproto = "http";             // 5; initial protocol to use
     String prevproto = whatproto;            // 6; previous protocol used
     Choice ch;                       // 7; A pop-up menu choice
     TextField tf;                     // 8; User entered document name
     AppletContext ac;                  // 9; Ask the browser…

     public void init() {                  // 10; Init method
          FlowLayout fl;
          Button bu;
          Font fo;
// create a new left-justified flowlayout with 10 pixels of spacing
//on each side of each item
          fl = new FlowLayout(FlowLayout.LEFT, 10, 10); // 14
          setLayout(fl);                   // 15; make it the current
                                        ➥layout
          fo = new Font("TimesRoman", Font.PLAIN, 18); // 16; a fairly
                                        ➥big font
          setFont(fo);                    // 17; make it the
                                        ➥current font
          ch = new Choice();              // 18; create a Choice instance
          ch.setFont(fo);                 // 19; make this the current font
          ch.addItem(whatproto);            // 20; add "http" as a choice
          ch.addItem("gopher");            // 21; add literal "gopher" as a
                                        ➥choice
          ch.addItem("ftp");
          ch.addItem("file");
          add(ch);                       // 24; add the pop-up menu to our
                                        ➥flowlayout
          bu = new Button("Open");           // 25; create "Open" button
          add(bu);                       // 26; add the button to our flowlayout
// create a textfield of length 70, and put the string "http://" in it
          tf = new TextField(whatproto + "://", 70);      // 27
          tf.setEditable(true);    // 28; enable the user to modify the
                                        ➥field
          add(tf);                       // 29; add the text field to our
                                        ➥flowlayout
          ac = getAppletContext();        // 30; discover our context
     }                                 // 31; end of init method

     public void start() {                  // 32; start method does
                                        ➥nothing
     }

     public void stop() {                  // 34; stop method does nothing
                                        ➥too
     }
```

continues

Part
III

Ch
12

Listing 12.4 Continued

```
// change the text entry when user changes protocol
    private void modifytext() {              // 36;
        int len = prevproto.length();   // 37; string len of prev
                                        ➡protocol
        String cur = tf.getText();          // 38; get the current
                                        ➡text
        String left = cur.substring(len);  // 39; get the document
                                        ➡name part
// new name = new proto + old document name
        tf.setText(whatproto + left);        // 40;
    }                                    // 41; end of modifytext() private
                                        ➡method

    private void launchdoc() {          // 42; ask browser to open a
                                        ➡document
        String doc = tf.getText();          // 43; get document name
        URL u = null;                       // 44; document's URL
// test to ensure that there is a doc name, more than just proto://
        if ( doc.length() <= ( whatproto.length() + 3 ) ) return; // 45
        try {                               // 46; execute something that might
                                        ➡abort
            u = new URL(doc);       // 47; convert doc name to URL
                                        ➡instance
        } catch (MalformedURLException ue) {      // 48;
// if it failed then print a message indicating why
            System.err.println("Invalid URL: " + ue.getMessage()); // 49;
            return;                        // 50; and give up
        }                                  // 51; end of try clause
// ask for the document to be opened in a new window named "New Window"
        ac.showDocument(u, "New Window");        // 52
    }                                    // 53; end of launchdoc

    public boolean action(Event ev, Object arg) {      // 54; event
                                        ➡handler
        if ( ev.target instanceof Choice ) {          // 55; Choice
                                        ➡event
            prevproto = whatproto;           // 56; save prev protocol
                                        ➡name
            whatproto = arg.toString();      // 57; get the choice
                                        ➡selected
            modifytext();                   // 58; change the text
                                        ➡displayed
            return(true);                  // 59; indicate event handled
        }                                  // 60; end of Choice event
        if ( ev.target instanceof Button ) {     // 61; Button event
// if the "Open" button was selected then...
```

```
        if ( arg.toString().equals("Open") ) {      // 62;
            launchdoc();               // 63; try to launch the
                                              ↪document
            return(true);              // 64; event handled
        }                        // 65; end of if statement
    }                         // 66; end of Button event
    return(false);                 // 67; did not handle event
}                           // 68; end of action method
}                            // 69; end of SD class
```

Initializing the SD Applet

The `init()` method for the SD (Show Document) applet begins on line 10. Its job is to construct all the graphical elements that are displayed and, in the process, to initialize various instance variables that are used in the event handling methods `modifytext()` and `launchdoc()`. It starts out by creating a `FlowLayout` instance on line 14. This instance is left justified so that new elements are added starting at the left edge of each row. We also indicate that we would like at least 10 pixels between each element in a row (the second argument to the constructor), and between rows (the third argument). Line 15 makes this layout the current layout. Because an applet is actually a `Panel`, this now applies to the entire applet.

Line 16 accesses a plain Times Roman font with 18 point type. If your system does not have this particular font, you may need to adjust this statement to choose another font name (such as Helvetica or Geneva) and perhaps another font size (such as 24 point). You can also specify the empty string `" "` as the first parameter to the `Font` constructor; this will select a default font. Line 17 makes this font the current font for the applet's panel. Now, three items are put into the flow layout beginning at line 18: a pop-up menu, a button, and a single line text field.

The pop-up menu is created on line 18. Because pop-ups have their own fonts, which may be separate from the `Panel` in which they reside, you must set the font of the pop-up (line 19). This pop-up presents the user with a choice of four communication protocols that will be used. These are added to the pop-up in lines 20 through 23. Note that the default item, which represents the default protocol, is the one added first. That will be the initial value of the instance variable `whatproto`, which is the `String` "http." Line 24 finally adds this pop-up to the layout.

Line 25 creates a `Button` whose label is "Open." This is the button that the user presses to attempt to load a new document. It is added to the layout in line 26. The third item in our layout is an editable text field, which is created in line 27. The initial `String` that will be displayed is "http://", obtained by concatenating the default protocol "http" with the literal delimiter "://."

Line 28 makes this text field read/write, and line 29 adds it to the layout. Because this text field is quite long, it will be added in a new row below the pop-up menu and the Open button. Finally, line 30 initializes the instance variable, `ac`, to the applet's context. This is used in the `launchdoc()` method. Figure 12.2 shows the initial appearance of the SD applet after the `init()` method has been executed.

FIG. 12.2
The Show Document Applet uses AWT elements, which are very similar to HTML forms components.

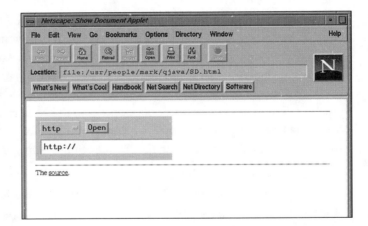

Event Handling in the SD Applet

You will notice immediately that the `start()` and `stop()` methods of the SD applet do absolutely nothing. All of the activity in this applet is triggered in response to user interaction. As a result, all of our code is within the `action` method and none in `start` or `stop`. There is also no `run` method in this applet because we are not implementing any threads (the next applet we consider uses threads).

There are many different ways of performing event handling in Java. For example, Java applets that desire to handle only mouse down events can override a specialized method known as `mouseDown`. If you were only interested in button clicks on the Open button, you could use this approach. Because we are actually interested in handling events on the pop-up menu and button clicks on Open, the SD applet uses the more general approach.

If an applet overrides the action method, this indicates that it wants to handle more than one event type. The code for the action method begins on line 54. Note that this method accepts two arguments: an Event instance indicating the type of event, and an Object instance indicating where the event occurred. The target element of an Event indicates which graphical element was associated with the event.

On line 55, the Java keyword, instanceof, is used to ask if the event was associated with a Choice item (a pop-up menu). If the result is true, then the code in lines 56 through 59 is executed. This code saves the previous choice value (line 56), stores the new choice value by extracting the String version of the Object selected (line 57), and then invokes the modifytext() private method to fix up the document name being displayed. It then returns true in line 59 to indicate that this event was successfully processed.

> **CAUTION**
>
> All applet event handling methods must return true to indicate that the event has been handled and false to say that it has not. Failure to do so may cause the applet (and the browser) to become horribly confused.

To understand what is going on, consider a concrete example. Suppose that the user had typed the document name, "http://ftp.javasoft.com", in the text field and then suddenly realized that this was not going to work because it would require the FTP protocol rather than the http protocol. The user then invokes the pop-up choice menu and selects FTP.

This selection triggers the action method of the SD applet. The test on line 55 will pass; prevproto will become the string "http" and whatproto the string "ftp." The modifytext() method on line 36 is now executed. It gets the length of the prevproto string (which will be 4), and also fetches the current document string on line 38. This will be the string "http://ftp.javasoft.com". It then peels off the substring that contains everything except the protocol name in line 39.

The local variable `left` will be the string "://ftp.javasoft.com." Finally, it glues the new protocol (stored in `whatproto`) onto the front of this substring and pushes that string out to the text field in line 40. The text now reads, "ftp://ftp.javasoft.com." You are encouraged to perform this experiment and verify that the protocol part of the text field changes in lockstep with the value of the choice selected from the pop-up menu.

Opening a New Document with the SD Applet

The `action` method is also equipped to handle `Button` events. If the test on line 61 succeeds, this indicates that some button has been pressed, and the code on line 62 will be executed. Line 62 is a bit of defensive programming in which you test to make sure that it was the Open button that was pressed.

In our example, this test is superfluous because we have only one button. This line compactly converts the `arg` argument to a `String` and then uses its `equals` method to test against the literal "Open." This test must pass in our case, so line 63 will be executed and the `launchdoc()` method invoked. When that method returns, the `action` method returns `true` to indicate that the button press was handled (line 64). If this event was neither a pop-up selection nor a button press, then the `action` method returns `false` on line 67.

The `launchdoc()` method is used to actually ask the browser to open a document URL. It first gets the text of the document name in line 43. It then checks to make sure that that string is long enough on line 45. If the string is just a bare protocol, such as "file://", this test fails and the method returns at that line. The extra 3 in this test accounts for the three characters `://`.

We now have a string representing a URL stored in the local variable `doc`, say "http://home.netscape.com." We would like to convert this to a URL instance because that is what we need for the subsequent request to the browser. This is executed in the `try` block beginning on line 46. A `try` block is required whenever a method invocation might generate a Java *exception*. Without being too specific, we can say that an exception results when you attempt to do something and it fails in a potentially unpleasant way. The `URL` constructor on line 47 is such a statement.

How did we know this? Is it necessary to remember all the functions that can generate exceptions? Fortunately, the answer is *no*. If you had tried to write `u = new`

URL(doc); without enclosing it in a `try` block, the Java compiler would thoughtfully tell you that URL constructors can generate exceptions and that you should try to catch the `MalformedURLException`. We have complied with this request and enclosed the ominous statement in a `try` block, which always takes the following form:

```
try {
    ominous statement(s)
    } catch (SomeException e) {
        do something if an exception occurs
    }
```

In our case, if `doc` does not correspond to a valid URL for any reason, the applet receives the `MalformedURLException` and the code on lines 49 and 50 (within the `catch` clause) is executed. This code prints out a message indicating the reason for the failure on line 49, and then returns. Note that all exceptions have a `getMessage()` method that we have used to tell the user why the URL was malformed. A URL might be malformed because it was entered incorrectly, referred to a nonexistent server, or mentioned a document that the server did not want the user to see, among other reasons.

If the URL was well formed, then the `catch` clause will not be executed and the code will arrive at line 52. This is the critical statement that actually communicates with the browser. We use the `showDocument` method of the `AppletContext` `ac` to ask it to open the URL `u` in a new window whose name is "New Window." This method call can still fail, of course, even if the URL `u` is well constructed. You should experiment with this applet by typing in various valid and invalid URLs, hitting the Open button, and observing the results.

Part
III

Ch
12

TROUBLESHOOTING

The `modifytext()` method is the workhorse that handles the event associated with changing the choice. When you clear the text field, you are wiping out the protocol part ("http" for example) of the document name. The applet does not know this, however, because it is assuming that you will only change the protocol using the Choice item. Said another way, once you have cleared the text field, the protocol part of the document name is `null`, but the value of the instance variable, `whatproto`, is still set to the last protocol used.

continues

continued

If you are going to enable the user to change the protocol directly, then `modifytext()` has to become smarter. Use the following algorithm:

1. Read in the document string using `tf.getText()`.

2. Find the first colon character using the `String` method, `charAt()`.

3. Set the local variable, `len`, to the length of the substring up to that colon.

4. Continue as written in listing 12.4

An Image Viewer Applet

The real power of Java comes through in its capability to rapidly display multiple images, giving the appearance of true animation on a Web page. You now have enough knowledge about Java threads and also about the AWT, that you can present a simple image viewer applet in Java. This applet provides the first concrete example of something that would be extremely difficult to accomplish in JavaScript. This applet can also be used as a template for writing more sophisticated applets that use Java threads. The code for the image viewer is shown in listing 12.5. This code appears in the file Simimg.java on the CD-ROM.

On the CD

Listing 12.5   Simimg.java   Displaying Multiple Images Is Easy Using Java Threads

```
import java.applet.*;
import java.awt.*;
import java.net.*;

public class Simimg extends Applet implements Runnable {
    Image imgs[];                      // 6; the images themselves
    int imgidx = 0;                // 7; image currently being displayed
    int nimg = 0;                  // 8; total number of images
    Thread mythread  = null;         // 9; animation thread

    public void init() {              // 10; get params and images
        MediaTracker mt;          // 11; track image loading using
                                        ➥this class
        String tmp;               // 12; tmp string
        String imgloc;            // 13; location of images
```

```
        URL db;                              // 14; Applet's document BASE

        imgloc = getParameter("imgloc");     // 15; locate image
                                                  ➥directory
        if ( imgloc == null ) return;        // 16; no image directory—
                                                  ➥give up
        tmp = getParameter("nimg");          // 17; get number of
                                                  ➥images
        if ( tmp == null ) return;           // 18; no images—give up
        nimg = Integer.parseInt(tmp);        // 19; convert to
                                                  ➥integer
        if ( nimg <= 0 ) return;             // 20; invalid image count—
                                                  ➥give up
        imgs = new Image[nimg];              // 21; allocate array for
                                                  ➥images
// create a mediatracker for the images
        mt = new MediaTracker(this);         // 22;
        db = getDocumentBase();              // 23; find Applet's doc BASE
// this loop starts loading all the images
        for(int i = 0, j = 1; i < nimg; i++, j++) {        // 24;
            imgs[i] = getImage(db, imgloc + j + ".gif");   // 25;
// tell the MediaTracker instance to track this image as ID 0
            mt.addImage(imgs[i], 0);                       // 26;
        }                           // 27; end of image loading loop
        try { mt.waitForID(0);      // 28; wait for all images
} catch (InterruptedException e) {
        nimg = 0;                            // 30; if it failed set # images
                                                  ➥to 0
        }                                    // 31; end of catch clause of try
                                                  ➥block
    }                                        // 32; end of init method

    public void run() {                      // 33; thread's run method
        Thread me;                           // 34; current thread

        me = Thread.currentThread();         // 35; get current
                                                  ➥thread
        me.setPriority(Thread.NORM_PRIORITY-1);   // 36; decrease
                                                  ➥priority
        while ( imgidx < nimg ) {            // 37; loop over images
            repaint();                       // 38; draw current image
            try {
                Thread.sleep(100);           // 40; wait a little while
                } catch (InterruptedException e) {}
            imgidx++;                        // 42; update index to next image
        }                                    // 43; end of while loop
    }                                        // 44; end of run method

    public void start() {
        if ( mythread == null ) {
            mythread = new Thread(this);
```

continues

Listing 12.5   Continued

```
                mythread.start();
            }
        }

    public void stop() {
        if ( mythread != null ) {
            mythread.stop();
            mythread = null;
        }
    }

    public void paint( Graphics g ) {               // 57; draw the current
                                                    ➥image
        if ( ( imgs != null ) && ( 0 <= imgidx ) && ( imgidx < nimg )
        ➥&&
            imgs[imgidx] != null ) {       // 59; sanity check all
                                                    ➥values
            g.drawImage(imgs[imgidx], 0, 0, this);     // 60; draw
                                                    ➥it!
        }
    }

        for(int i = 0, j = 1; i < nimg; i++, j++) {          // 24;
                                        ➥loop to load all images
            imgs[i] = getImage(db, imgloc + j + ".gif");     // 25;
                                        ➥begin loading
    to
        for(int i = 0; i < nimg; i++) {          // 24; loop to load
                                                    ➥all images
            imgs[i] = getImage(db, imgloc + (i + 1) + ".gif"); // 25;
                                                    ➥begin loading
```

Initializing the Simple Image Viewer

The init method for the Simimg applet performs two functions: it gets user parameters and it loads the images. This applet requires two PARAM tags to be specified, indicating where the images are to be found and how many there are. On line 15, the imgloc parameter is accessed; if it is not present, the init method returns immediately (line 16). Lines 17 through 20 get the nimg parameter, convert it to an integer, and make sure that it is a positive number. If this parameter is not present or is not a valid positive number, the init method returns.

Line 21 allocates an array just large enough to hold the indicated number of images. Line 22 initializes a `MediaTracker` instance. This instance will be used shortly to ensure that all images are loaded before the `init` method completes. Line 23 uses the `getDocumentBase()` method from the `java.applet` package to discover the applet's document BASE, saving that value in the local URL variable, `db`.

Statement 24 sets up a `for` loop to load all the images into the image array `imgs`. Note that two iteration variables, `i` and `j`, are used. This is because the `imgs` array is indexed from zero, but we are assuming that the names of the images will be something like IMG1.gif, IMG2.gif, and so forth. The `i` iteration variable marches through the array, while the `j` variable is used to build the names of the successive images.

The `getImage()` method is used on line 25 to launch the image loading process. It takes two arguments: a `URL` specifying a server directory and a `String` giving the name of the file within that directory that is to be loaded. We are using the applet's document BASE as the first argument, and we are constructing the successive image names using the value of the `imgloc` parameter (with a numeric suffix) as the second argument. This particular version assumes that all the images are GIFs.

N O T E At present, the `getImage()` method only understands the GIF and JPEG image formats. Other formats will be added in the future. ▪

The `getImage()` method is slightly deceptive in that it does not guarantee that the image is actually gotten when the method returns. All it does is begin to load the image. This is the purpose of statement 26. We add the image being loaded to the `MediaTracker` instance `mt`, which indicates that we are going to subsequently watch the loading process, presumably to ensure that it is done.

The `addImage` method takes two arguments: an `Image` instance, and an integer ID. The ID is used to group images into pools. We could, for example, track the first half of the images as ID 0 and the second half as ID 1. In this way we could be displaying the completely loaded ID 0 images while the ID 1 images were still being loaded.

This applet takes a brute force approach. All images are declared to have ID 0. On line 28, we actually wait for all the ID 0 images, which are all the images, to be fully loaded. Because this method can generate an `InterruptedException`, it must be executed within a `try` block, as we have seen in the SD applet. If this exception occurs, then we set the number of images `nimg` to 0, ensuring that none will be displayed.

The Simimg applet, unlike the SD applet, requires `PARAM` tags to properly function. A sample HTML file (Simimg.html on the CD-ROM) that uses this applet is shown in listing 12.6. Note that this particular HTML file indicates that we will load 16 images, that they will be located in the subdirectory "images" of the document's base directory, and that they will have the prefix "T." This means that the applet will attempt to load 16 images named images/T1.gif, images/T2.gif,…images/T16.gif. It is also worth noting that this HTML implicitly assumes that all the images will fit in a drawing area that is 300×150.

On the CD

Listing 12.6   Simimg.html   HTML for the Simimg Applet

```
<HTML>
<HEAD>
<TITLE>A Simple Image Player</TITLE>
</HEAD>
<BODY>
<HR>
<APPLET CODE="Simimg.class" WIDTH=300 HEIGHT=150>
<PARAM NAME="imgloc" VALUE="images/T">
<PARAM NAME="nimg" VALUE="16">
</APPLET>
<HR>
The <A HREF="Simimg.java">source</A>.
</BODY>
</HTML>
```

Running the Simple Image Applet

The formal structure of this applet is exactly the same as we described earlier in our discussion of threads. The start() and stop() methods are each responsible for creating the "animation" thread and for stopping it, respectively. The actual work is done by the run() method and indirectly by the paint() method.

The run method first discovers the identity of its own thread by invoking the static method currentThread() of the Thread class on line 35. It then lowers its own priority to be just slightly less than the default priority for threads (line 36). This makes sense if we think of threads in terms of a standard multitasking operating system. Higher priority tasks get more of the real CPU and generally execute more frequently. The same model applies to Java threads. By declaring itself less important, it is implicitly declaring that the drawing activity is more important.

Line 37 is the main image loop. As long as the instance variable, imgidx, is less than the total number of images, nimg, the loop will continue. Each pass through the loop issues a call to repaint(), which results in the paint() method being executed (line 38). Each pass through the loop also puts the animation thread to sleep for 100 microseconds (line 40). This is another way to give the drawing activity even more time and to also ensure that it is actually executed.

One of the side effects of using the static sleep method of the Thread class is to ensure that other threads that are waiting to run get a chance to do so. This method can also generate an exception, which we dutifully ignore. Finally, at the end of the loop, we update imgidx to process the next image.

The paint method, which begins on line 57, is a model of defensive programming. It checks to make sure that the imgs array is not null, that imgidx is neither too small nor too large, and that the actual image in the imgs array itself is not null. If all these tests pass, then it uses the drawImage method of the Graphics instance, g, to actually draw the image (line 60). Figure 12.3 shows the result after 16 images have been loaded and successfully displayed.

FIG. 12.3
Java simplifies the tasks of image manipulation and animation.

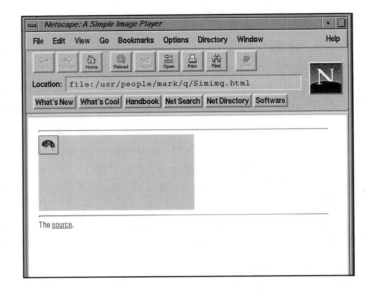

CHAPTER 13

VBScript and OLE Controls

by Andrew Wooldridge

If you have been programming for any length of time, you have probably run across the programming language called Visual Basic. Visual Basic is a compiled language that is relatively simple to learn and comes with a lot of pre-built code to enable programmers to reuse code. Furthermore, Microsoft intends to incorporate a subset of its Visual Basic syntax into its new Web browser, Microsoft Internet Explorer. Visual Basic Script represents the competing scripting language to JavaScript. Microsoft has changed its overall strategy to incorporate the Internet in a big way—which means it is moving to compete directly with Netscape for browser market share.

What Visual Basic Script is

You learn what Visual Basic Script is and how it fits into Microsoft's Internet strategy.

The syntax of Visual Basic Script

This chapter covers the language of Visual Basic Script, its syntax, and more.

How Visual Basic Script compares to JavaScript

See how Visual Basic script differs from JavaScript, as well as some of the comparitive advantages of both.

About OLE controls and Visual Basic Script

A brief explanation of OLE controls and how you can use OLE controls in your Web pages.

Visual Basic Script (or VBScript, as it is often called) enables Web content creators to script, automate, and customize their Web pages in a similar fashion to JavaScript. VBScript takes scripts embedded in HTML pages and sends them to a compiler on the client side, which then compiles and runs the script—much like a regular Visual Basic Program. You can validate form submissions, generate HTML on-the-fly, or even create a client-side game that is compiled on-the-fly. You might even include special information that the user provided just moments before.

Visual Basic Script is a subset of the total Visual Basic language. Many of the potentially hazardous features of Visual Basic have been eliminated from VBScript to disallow such constructs as VB viruses or Trojan horses being loaded along with the interactive content on the Web page. Visual Basic script is at the bottom of a three-tiered level of complexity of packages that use Visual Basic. ■

Language Overview

If you have learned to some extent the syntax of JavaScript, it will go a long way toward helping you learn about Visual Basic Script, and knowing something about Visual Basic will help you even more. Many of the features you find in JavaScript have their mirrors in Visual Basic script, which is primarily due to the fact that there is a basic set of features all scripting languages should have in order to handle conditional execution of code, or handling text input and output, etc. What you will find as you begin to learn about Visual Basic script is that you have a powerful new set of tools that have in the past been applied to programming applications, which are now being applied to the web.

Each of the sections below talks about a different aspect of Visual Basic Script, and to some extent builds on the knowlege gained from the previous section. My best recommendation to you as a scripter is to download the SDK for the Microsoft ActiveX[a] enviroment (which includes the pre-release version of Microsoft Internet Explorer) at http://www.microsoft.com/intdev/sdk/. From there, you should visit Microsoft's Visual Basic web site (at **http://www.microsoft.com/vbscript/ vbsmain.htm**). Once you get familiar with the language from here and the web site, you should be well on your way to creating interactive web sites (literally Internet-based applications) with Visual Basic Script.

Table 13.1 gives you an overview of the syntax of the language.

Table 13.1   Visual Basic Script Syntax

Category of Element	Syntax Used
Arrays	
	Declaration (Dim, Static, etc.)
	LBound, UBound
	ReDim, Erase
Assignment	
	=
	Let
	Set
Comments	
	Using REM and '
Control flow	
	Do...Loop
	For...Next, For Each...Next
	While...Wend
	If...Then...Else
Error trapping	
	On Error Resume Next
	Err object
Literals	
	Empty
	Nothing
	Null

continues

Table 13.1 Continued	
Category of Element	**Syntax Used**
Literals	
	True, False
	User-defined literals:
	123.456; "Foo", etc.
Miscellaneous	
	Line continuation character (_)
	Line separation character (:)
Nonconforming Identifiers	
	o.[My long method name]
Operators	
	Arithmetic:
	+, –, *, /, \, ^, Mod
	Negation (–)
	String concatenation (&)
	Comparison:
	=, < >,, <,, >,, < =, > =, Is
	Logical:
	Not
	And, Or, Xor
	Eqv, Imp
Options	
	Option Explicit

Category of Element	Syntax Used
Procedures	
	Declaring procedures:
	Function
	Sub
	Calling Procedures:
	Call
	Exiting procedures:
	Exit Function
	Exit Sub
	Parameters for procedures:
	ByVal, ByRef
Variables	
	Procedure-level:
	Dim
	Static
	Module-level:
	Private, Dim

Data Types

Visual basic uses only one data type: *variant*. It needs only this one type because VBScript takes the data within some variable and treats it as a number when appropriate and treats it as a text string if that is the logical intended type. VBScript uses the context in which a variable is called to determine how a variable is "typed." VBScript enables you to use *subtypes,* which can further define how the variant type is interpreted. Table 13.2 lists the various subtypes that VBScript understands.

Part

III

Ch

13

Table 13.2 Listing of Subtypes to the Data Type *variant*

Subtype	Explanation
Empty	Variant is not initialized. Value is either zero for numeric variables or a zero-length string ("") for string variables.
Null	Variant intentionally contains no valid data.
Boolean	Contains either True or False.
Byte	Contains integer in the range zero to 255.
Integer	Contains integer in the range –32,768 to 32,767.
Long	Contains integer in the range –2,147,483,648 to 2,147,483,647.
Single	Contains a single-precision, floating-point number in the range –3.402823E38 to –1.401298E–45 for negative values; 1.401298E–45 to 3.402823E38 for positive values.
Double	Contains a double-precision, floating-point number in the range –1.79769313486232E308 to –4.94065645841247E–324 for negative values; 4.94065645841247E–324 to 1.79769313486232E308 for positive values.
Date (Time)	Contains a number that represents a date between January 1, 100 to December 31, 9999.
String	Contains a variable-length string that can be up to about 2 billion characters in length.
Object	Contains an OLE Automation object.
Error	Contains an error number.

Variables

VBScript enables you to create and use many kinds of variables—which are similar to JavaScript variables in that they are locations where values of a given kind are held.

To define a variable in VBScript, you use the DIM command. This is the mirror image of the VAR command in JavaScript and is used similarly:

```
<SCRIPT LANGUAGE="VBS">
          <!--
           Dim MyVariable
          -->
          </SCRIPT>
```

VBScript variables follow the same kinds of conventions as JavaScript variables; for example, they must begin with an alphanumeric character, are limited to 255 characters, and must be unique to the scope in which they are called. Unlike JavaScript, where variables are limited by the scope in which they are called, you can declare `static` variables in VBScript, which enables them to persist after the function calling them has finished. Listing 13.1 is an example.

Listing 13.1   Creating a Static Variable (Accumulator)

```
<SCRIPT LANGUAGE="VBS">
          <!--
           Function ClockTime(anumber)
              Static Accumulator
              Accumulator = Accumulator + anumber
              ClockTime = Accumulator
           End Function
          -->
          </SCRIPT>
```

In this case, you would be able to execute the function ClockTime over and over and be able to rely on the fact that the variable `Accumulator` continued to persist between calls. In this way, `Accumulator` would be able to consistently increase based on the variable `anumber` that you pass to it each time.

N O T E   Note that when you set a variable to be Static it will persist between function calls, yet is still only avaliable to that function because its scope is limited to the function. ▪

Arrays   Arrays in VBScript are created in a way somewhat different from JavaScript. In VBScript, you create an array by using the DIM statement and setting an upper limit for the size of the array, for example, `Dim Foo(30)`. This would create an array of 31 items, starting with `Foo(0)` and ending with `Foo(30)`. If you want to assign a value to any of the items in this array, simply use the equal sign (=), as follows:

Part
III

Ch
13

```
Foo(10) = 100
Foo(11) = 99
```

Contrast this to JavaScript, in which you first create an array constructor, as in listing 13.2.

Listing 13.2   Creating an Array in JavaScript

```
function MakeMyArray(x){
     this.length=x;
     for (var i=1; i<= ; i++) {
          this[i]=0}
     return this
     }
}
```

Then you use `new` to create an instance of that array, as in

```
var thisValue = new MakeMyArray(500);
```

In VBScript, you can create arrays of up to 60 dimensions. For example, if you want to create a 3-dimensional array with 100 elements in the first dimension, 50 in the second, and 10 in the third, you could call the array as shown in listing 13.3.

Listing 13.3   Creating a 3D Array in VBScript

```
<SCRIPT LANGUAGE="VBS">
<!-- A 3D array
     Dim theArray(99, 49, 9)
-->
</SCRIPT>
```

N O T E Note that when you create an array in VBScript, you are sending not the size of the dimension, but the name of the highest value in that dimension, which is one less than the size of the dimension. So an array of size 10 is created with an index of 9. ■

This next feature seems unique to VBScript, although JavaScript may have this functionality as well: you can create an array whose size can change dynamically over time. This is called (appropriately) a Dynamic array and is created the same way you would create a regular array only you do not place a value in the parentheses when you first create it. You must use ReDim with a value to set the correct size for that time. Every time you want to resize that array, you use ReDim again with the correct index values.

N O T E If you ReDim an array to a smaller size you will lose the data in the upper levels of your data.

VBScript Constants

Although JavaScript does have a few constants in its Math() method, VBScript uses many more for various programming functions. Many of the functions in VBScript have their own built-in constants—which cannot assume different values. Table 13.3 lists a few of the more common ones.

Table 13.3 Commonly Used Constants

Constant	Description
vbCr	Carriage return character
vbCrLf	Carriage return and line feed characters
vbFalse	Boolean value represented by 0
vbLf	Line feed character
vbTrue	Boolean value represented by –1

VBScript Operators

VBScript operators work in much the same way as those in JavaScript, and they follow the same order of precedence as most fifth generation languages, such as Java, C++, and Perl. Table 13.4 shows the arithmetic, comparison, and logical operators in order of precedence.

Table 13.4 Visual Basic Script Operators

Arithmetic Operators		Comparison Operators		Logical Operators	
Description	**Symbol**	**Description**	**Symbol**	**Description**	**Symbol**
Exponentiation	^	Equality	=	Logical negation	Not
Unary negation	–	Inequality	<>	Logical conjunction	And
Multiplication	*	Less than	<	Logical disjunction	Or
Division	/	Greater than	>	Logical exclusion	Xor
Integer division	\	Less than or equal to	<=	Logical equivalence	Eqv
Modulo arithmetic	Mod	Greater than or equal to	>=	Logical implication	Imp
Addition	+	Object equivalence	Is		
Subtraction	–				
String concatenation	&				

Control Flow in VBScript

Most languages need some form of control of program flow, such as IF...THEN...ELSE statements, loops, and so on. VBScript provides its own syntax, which is similar in some ways to JavaScript, but does not use parentheses. This is due to VBScript's roots in BASIC, as opposed to JavaScript's roots in C++, which groups items together using parentheses. Listings 13.4 and 13.5 are some examples of using control statements in Visual Basic Script.

Listing 13.4   *IF...THEN...ELSE* Example

```
<SCRIPT LANGUAGE="VBS">
            <!--
            Sub ShowtUser(value)
                If value = 0 Then
                    Musicplay.Jazz = True
                    Videoplay.Batman = Slow
                Else
                    Musicplay.Jazz = False
                    Videoplay.Batman = Fast
                End If
            End Sub
            -->
            </SCRIPT>
```

Listing 13.5   *DO...WHILE* Loop Example

```
<SCRIPT LANGUAGE="VBS">
            <!--
            Sub ChkFirstWhile()
                Dim counter, myNum
                counter = 0
                myNum = 20
                Do While myNum > 10
                    myNum = myNum - 1
                    counter = counter + 1
                Loop
                MsgBox "The loop made " & counter & " repetitions."
            End Sub

            Sub ChkLastWhile()
                Dim counter, myNum
                counter = 0
                myNum = 9
                Do
                    myNum = myNum - 1
                    counter = counter + 1
                Loop While myNum > 10
                MsgBox "The loop made " & counter & " repetitions."
            End Sub
            -->
        </SCRIPT>
```

Part
III

Ch
13

When you use DO...WHILE you can perform some action repeatedly until some condition is met. You can use UNTIL to perform a loop until the condtion is true. If you want to check another condition and exit the loop early, you can use the EXIT DO command with an IF...THEN condition within the loop. If you wish to perform some function on a series of objects, you can use FOR EACH...NEXT, as seen in listing 13.6.

Listing 13.6   Using *For Each...Next* in VBScript

```
<SCRIPT LANGUAGE="VBS">
            <!--
            Sub
            For Each myState in myCountry
                    If myState.Governer = "Democrat" Then
                            myState.Color="green"
                    End If
            Next
            End Sub
        -->
    </SCRIPT>
```

Visual Basic Script Procedures

VBScript uses two different kinds of procedures, as opposed to JavaScript's one function statement. In VBScript, you have the SUB procedure and the FUNCTION procedure. With the SUB procedure, you can send it values and it can perform actions, but it does not return a value. The FUNCTION procedure is identical, except that it returns a value. Listings 13.7 and 13.8 are examples of the SUB and FUNCTION procedures.

Listing 13.7   Using *Sub*

```
<SCRIPT LANGUAGE="VBS">
            <!--
            Sub ConvertTime()
                time = InputBox("Please enter the time in seconds.",1)
                MsgBox "The time is " & Seconds(time) & " O'clock
            End Sub
        -->
            </SCRIPT>
```

Listing 13.8   Using Function

```
<SCRIPT LANGUAGE="VBS">
            <!--
            Sub ConvertTime()
                time = InputBox("Please enter the time in seconds.",1)
                MsgBox "The number of hours is " & Seconds(time) & "
                ➡O'clock
            End Sub


            Function Seconds(theTime)
                Seconds=theTime / 120
            End Function
            -->
            </SCRIPT>
```

Syntax Summary

Although VBScript is easy to learn, there are a large number of keywords to learn for the various functions, methods, operators, etc. Tables 13.5 through 13.9 are tables that supply you with these keywords grouped by type as a reference.

Table 13.5   Functions in VBScript

Functions

Abs	Array	Asc
Atn	C	CBool
CByte	CDate	CDbl
Chr	CInt	CLng
Cos	CreateObject	CSng
CStr	CVErr	D
Date	DateSerial	DateValue
Day	E	Exp
H	Hex	Hour
I	InputBox	InStr

Part
III

Ch
13

continues

Table 13.5 Continued

Functions

Int, Fix s	IsArray	IsDate
IsEmpty	IsError	IsNull
IsNumeric	IsObject	
LBound	LCase	Left
Len	Log	LTrim, RTrim, and Trim
Mid	Minute	Month
MsgBox	Now	Oct
Right	Rnd	Second
Sgn	Sin	Sqr
Str	StrComp	String
Tan	Time	TimeSerial
TimeValue	UBound	UCase
Val	VarType	Weekday
Year		

Table 13.6 VBScript Methods

Methods

Raise	Clear

Table 13.7 VBScript Operators

Operators

+	And	&
/	Eqv	^

Operators

Imp	\	Is
Mod	*	Not
Or	-	Xor

Table 13.8   VBScript Statements

Statements

Call	Dim	Do...Loop
Erase	Exit	For...Next
For Each...Next	Function	If...Then...Else
Let	LSet	Mid
On Error	Private	Public
Randomize	ReDim	Rem
RSet	Select Case	Set
Static	Sub	While...Wend

Table 13.9   VBScript Objects and Properties

Objects	Properties
Err	Description
	HelpContext
	HelpFile
	Number
	Source

Part
III

Ch
13

Visual Basic Script in HTML

As you have seen in many of the previous listings, Visual Basic Script uses the same SCRIPT.../SCRIPT tags that JavaScript does. Listing 13.9 is an example of a simple VBScript.

Listing 13.9 Simple Script

```
<SCRIPT LANGUAGE="VBS">
            <!--
                Function CanDeliver(Dt)
                    CanDeliver = (CDate(Dt) - Now()) > 2
                End Function
            -->
            </SCRIPT>
```

Notice that this follows much of the same rules as JavaScript—especially to the extent that you must use comments to keep older browsers from viewing the code inline. Listing 13.10 is an example of a VBScript that opens a dialog box in the browser when the user clicks a FORM button.

Listing 13.10 "Hello There" in VBScript

```
<HTML>
<HEAD><TITLE>A Simple First Page</TITLE>
<SCRIPT LANGUAGE="VBS">
<!--
Sub Button1_OnClick
        MsgBox "Hello There!"
End Sub
-->
</SCRIPT>
</HEAD>
<BODY>
<H3>A Simple First Page</H3><HR>
<FORM><INPUT NAME="Button1" TYPE="BUTTON" VALUE="Click
➥Here"></FORM>
</BODY>
</HTML>
```

VBScript expands on the <SCRIPT> format and allows you to add additional attributes to this tag. Suppose you had a button in a form such as

```
<form>
<input type="button" name="screamer" Value="yell" >
</form>
```

You could create a script that opens a window with a message "HELLO THERE!" like this:

```
<SCRIPT LANGUAGE="VBS" EVENT="OnClick" FOR="Button1">
<!-- the message
   MsgBox "HELLO THERE!"
-->
</SCRIPT>
```

The EVENT attribute tells VBScript which event handler to monitor for this script, and the FOR attribute indicates which element (in this case a form input button) to monitor the event handler.

Visual Basic Script and OLE Automation

Visual Basic Script also enables programmers to set properties and methods of OLE controls as well as applets created with Java. Listing 13.11 gives an example of an OLE controller using a proposed INSERT tag.

Listing 13.11 An Example OLE Control Using the *INSERT* Tag

```
<Insert>
clsid = {"000effe0000005045454504342"}
OLEcontrol.forecolor = true
OLEcontrol.animate
javaapplet.forecolor = olecontrol.forecolor
<\Insert>
```

Part
III

Ch
13

OLE controls, now known as ActiveX[a] controls, consist of binary software objects that are highly reusable. They contain well-defined properties and I/O interfaces. The advantage of using OLE controls is that you can quickly create sophisticated applications by pulling together simpler objects through a language such as Visual Basic, although you could develop them in other languages such as Perl, or C++. OLE controls could consist of animated graphics, floating toolbars, dynamically built forms, and more. You can get and set properties of OLE controls and invoke its methods just as if this were a form element that you might check or set (see the following section, "VBScript and Forms"). Let's suppose you had a (fictional) OLE control embedded in an HTML document using <OBJECT> that displayed a spinning earth—as in listing 13.12.

Listing 13.12 The World OLE Control

```
<OBJECT
      CLASSID="clsid:{5t5636y3i-6e45w-23r37}"
      id=theWorld
      width=300
      height=200
      align=top
      hspace=2
      vspace=0
>
<PARAM NAME="Name" VALUE="Earth">
<PARAM NAME="Size" VALUE="large">
<PARAM NAME="Color" VALUE="blue-green">
</OBJECT>
```

A form to change the color might be:

```
<FORM NAME="WorldChange">
<INPUT TYPE="TEXT" NAME="newColorValue" SIZE=10>
<INPUT TYPE="BUTTON" NAME="cmdChangeColor" VALUE="Change Color">
</FORM>
```

And the VBScript that might change the object's value might look like that shown in listing 13.13.

Listing 13.13 VBScript for the World Color Control

```
<SCRIPT LANGUAGE="VBS">
<!--
Sub cmdChangeColor_onClick
      theWorld.Color = Document.WorldChange.newColorValue.Value
End Sub
-->
</SCRIPT>
```

This is one area that VBScript has leaped ahead of JavaScript, at least as of this writing. The fact that VBScript can modify attributes and methods of OLE controls would be equivalent to JavaScript being able to do the same with plug-ins and Java. Until this happens, VBScript has a clear advantage for creating Internet-based applications using OLE controls instead of Java applets.

VBScript and Forms

VBScript can perform the same kinds of form input validation as JavaScript. Although it uses syntax specific to VBScript, it has many similarities to JavaScript, such as the `OnClick` event handler. Listing 13.14 is an example of a form with a simple validation function.

Listing 13.14   A Simple Form Validation Example

```
<HTML>
<HEAD><TITLE>Simple Validation</TITLE>
<SCRIPT LANGUAGE="VBS">
<!--
Sub Submit_OnClick
        If IsNumeric(Document.myForm.Foo1.Value) Then
                If Document.myForm.Foo1.Value < 100 Or
                        Document.myForm.Foo1.Value > 1000 Then
                        MsgBox "Please enter a number
                        ➥between 100 and 1000."
                Else
                        MsgBox "Your Number Has Been
                        ➥Accepted"
                End If
        Else
                MsgBox "Please enter a numeric value."
        End If
End Sub
-->
</SCRIPT></HEAD>
<BODY>
<FORM name="myForm">
Enter a value between 10 and 1000:
 <INPUT NAME="Foo1" TYPE="TEXT" SIZE="2">
<INPUT NAME="Submit" TYPE="BUTTON" VALUE="Submit">
</FORM>
</BODY>
</HTML>
```

Part
III

Ch
13

Basically, what the script in listing 13.14 does is it presents a page with a small text entry box with a submit button. When the user clicks on the Submit button it triggers the `Submit_OnClick` event. VBScript knows to execute the `Sub` upon this trigger and it checks to see if the value in `Foo1` is numeric. If it is numeric, it further checks to see if the value is between 100 and 1000, whereupon it gives a dialog box based on that value. If the number is not numeric it presents a dialog box asking the user to type in another value. Notice that the value is not really sent anywhere from the form. If you want the value to actually be sent back to the server you could use `Document.myForm.Submit`.

VBScript is similar to JavaScript in that it is very useful for checking form data for errors or omissions on the client machine (in the Web browser instead of the server). Using OLE controls, you can even pass data into a control via a form and add or change that control's attributes or behavior.

VBScript Is Growing

In figure 13.1, you see the three tiers of Visual Basic, as well as how Visual Basic Scripting Edition (the long name for VBScript) fits in with the rest of the Visual Basic family of products.

At the bottom is VBScript: a free, small, and fast subset of Visual Basic that runs directly from Web pages. Next is Visual Basic for Applications, which is usually packaged with Microsoft Office. It features OLE automation and includes a debugger and script editor. At the top is Visual Basic 4.0, which is targeted at hardcore programmers, students, professionals, and hobbyists. It features client-server data access and distributed computing support, and it enables teams to create code using source control.

VBScript is a very new language specification. As of this writing, there is only one software implementation of it: Microsoft Internet Explorer version 3.0 Alpha. Microsoft has a client architecture called Sweeper, which is an API using Win32 and OLE to allow developers to add Internet capability to their applications. You will see other applications that begin to use Sweeper and as such will be able to read and interpret Visual Basic Script scripts. On the server side, Microsoft's Internet Information Server will also be using OLE and VBScript to automate many tasks as well as dynamic new capabilities.

FIG. 13.1
Visual Basic is offered in
three versions, which are
targeted at different levels
of users.

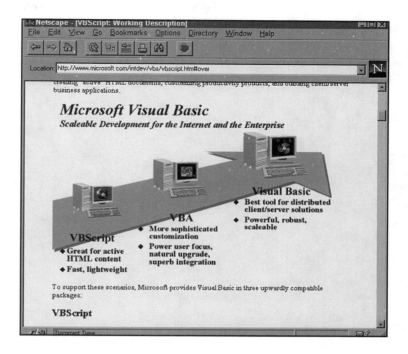

As this language continues to develop, it will probably be targeted toward people who are already Visual Basic programmers and want to leverage their knowledge of VB to the Web. Further, Visual Basic Script is being developed as a language that will enable novice programmers to control a wide range of object types (specifically, Microsoft's OLE objects and Sun's Java applets). VBScript will also appeal as well to Web site developers who seek to expand the interactivity of their site by using OLE controls for everything from small animations to complex full-blown Internet applications (like an inlined IRC client or a mini FTP client).

The specification will probably change considerably before it is ready for a final release—although unlike JavaScript, it is a subset of an already robust language that has been around for quite some time and will take advantage of that stability to seek wider acceptance than JavaScript.

Only time will decide which script language becomes more widely adopted, with VBScript having a huge following of Visual Basic programmers and JavaScript a very quickly growing base of Java programmers. As the spec is released, look for new additions to the Microsoft Visual Basic home page on the Web at **www.microsoft.com/vbscript/**. ●

Part
III

Ch
13

JavaScript Special Effects

CHAPTER 14

Controlling Web Page Appearance

by Ray Daly

As you are already aware, HTML is not desktop publishing. It provides structure and style to your Web page, but no control of the page width, size, or typography. This is what enables the Web to work on so many different platforms. Now with JavaScript and recent extensions to the HTML specification, you have more control over page appearance. In fact, your whole site can almost be considered as one application.

This chapter focuses on the appearance of text on your user's Web browser. The first section covers building JavaScript applications with a control panel. Next, text properties, font colors, and font methods are discussed. The chapter ends with a detailed example of a message editor, which uses all of the font methods of JavaScript. ■

JavaScript applications

Designing an application can involve building multiple, related pages with JavaScript. You can do this using frames and multiple windows.

Storing data

Though you cannot save data to the user's hard drive, there are ways to put information into bookmarks and cookies on the browser.

Color properties

Colors can now be specified by name without using hexadecimal numbers. Now Webmasters must be color coordinators.

Designing a frame application

Learn about child-parent relations when referring to objects between frames.

JavaScript for text editing

We will develop a message editor application. Although text editing methods are minimal, you will still be able to create a practical application.

Page Building with JavaScript

Before applying specific JavaScript properties, methods, and techniques, you must be aware of layout. This includes how the browser processes a page and its related documents as well as some design principles about good layout. You can build multiple pages with JavaScript to design your application.

Even the First Page Can Come Alive

The first time a user requests a page from your site the user has not yet given you any feedback, so you simply serve the page. When the page reaches the browser, however, the following two facts become available and can make the page come alive:

- JavaScript-enhanced browsers can recognize code that other browsers will ignore. You can add a special welcome to your opening document that only JavaScript users can view. The code in listing 14.1 makes a menu of links available only to JavaScript users.

- JavaScript-enhanced browsers know the time of day and the date. Using this information, you can change the appearance. Although this has limited application, it is still worth considering. For example, you can display holiday greetings (see fig. 14.1). Listing 14.1 is code for a greeting based on the hour of the day.

  For an example, look at Katipodesign (**http:/ourworld.compuserve.com/ homepages/tuckey/kmain.htm**) shown in figure 14.2.

On the CD

Listing 14.1   greeting.htm   JavaScript Only Greeting and Menu

```
<HTML><HEAD><TITLE>greeting.htm by Ray Daly</TITLE></HEAD>
<BODY><H1>WTFIN:  Where to Find it Now</H1>
<SCRIPT LANGUAGE="JavaScript">
<!-- hidden from other browsers
today=new Date()      //..get data and time
x=today.getHours()    //..pull out the hours
document.write ('<H2>Welcome JavaScript Surfers</H2>')
```

```
if (x<12) {
   document.write('<H3>Good Morning!</H3>')
} else {
   document.write('<H3>Hello on this beautiful day!</H3>')
}
//...you could substitute graphics instead of text greetings.
document.write('<P>Hidden away for your use only are several
➥applications:</P>')
document.write('<OL><LI><A HREF="messedit.htm">Message Editor</A></LI>')
document.write('<LI>More applications here.</LI></OL>')
//  all done with JavaScript-->
</SCRIPT>
<A HREF="nextpage.htm">Continue to <I>Find it Now</I>.</A>
</BODY></HTML>
```

FIG. 14.1

Greetings based on the time or date are possible with JavaScript. You can also offer links just for JavaScript users.

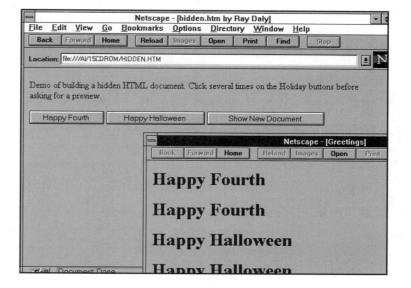

One of the first things you learn about JavaScript is that you cannot really change much about a page that is already displayed. Change a property and most likely it doesn't change the display. The text and layout of form elements are fixed.

You can, however, change the background color. For most pages, this may seem trivial and it probably is. But you can be creative with this feature. This is covered in more detail later in the section, "Practical Uses of Text Properties."

Part
IV
Ch
14

FIG. 14.2
Katipodesign shows how
graphic design can be
enhanced with JavaScript.
But you have to visit it at
different times of the day to
see it all.

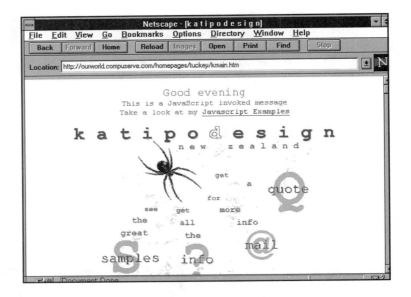

First Page as a Control Panel

Although the user can't control the currently displayed page, data from this page can change the appearance and content of related documents. In many ways, you can consider the first page to be a *control panel* that enables the user to make a choice that affects all related documents.

As an example, you can create a frameset in which one frame is the "control panel." In this frame, the user can click a choice of font and background colors. The rest of the documents in the other frames are then displayed using this selection.

TIP With frames, you have the frame document and related documents. You may not want the user to be able to load the related documents without the frameset. In these related documents, you can use the onLoad event handler to verify that the document was loaded with the frameset.

The first page can also control content. For example, a sports site might start by asking which sports interest you. The rest of the site can omit links and information on teams and games that don't match your interest.

JavaScript Enhanced Pages as an Application

These "control panels" could be more sophisticated. You might develop a whole series of questions, like on a registration page, and all subsequent documents could be modified by the registration data from the control panel. These control panels are coming up more and more on sites (see fig. 14.3).

FIG. 14.3
Dave's Tekno Dive (**http://www.dream.com**) gets better with each visit. If you register, he saves your background preference for 30 days. The control panel changes the way you browse his site.

It is possible to build very advanced JavaScript applications. I envision that URLs of frame contents and new windows will force the loading of the "control panel." The dependence on data from the first page is like a parent-child relationship. (This is very different from today's Web sites in which most pages can stand on their own.) Although the server can send what appears to be static pages, the JavaScript in these pages makes them come alive in the browser.

N O T E As you will see in this chapter, you can create documents that are only a part of an application. Often, these pages make little or no sense on their own. Yet, all pages look the same to a search engine.

To discourage people from directly accessing these secondary documents, consider hiding these pages from the search engines. You should consult your Webmaster about how your system can hide files.

Part
IV
Ch
14

continues

continued

Or, you may want to read up on the `robots.txt` file. When a search engine indexes a site, it uses a program called a robot or a spider. When the engine visits a site, the first file it reads is `robots.txt`. Using the information in this file, the search engine's robot omits specified areas from its search on the site. Take a moment to read "A Standard for Robot Exclusion," which is available at **http://info.webcrawler.com/mak/projects/ robots/norobots.html**. ■

▶ **See** "Frames and JavaScript," in chapter 19, "Using Frames and Cookies in Advanced Applications," for more detail on frames, **p. 661**.

Storing Control Panel Information

As you develop JavaScript applications, you will have multiple related documents. Sharing information between these documents is part of the process of building these applications. But now that you have collected all of this information, you may want to start storing it.

Cookies Store Information in the Browser   One means of storing information between pages is to use *cookies* (client-side persistent information). The browser, not the server, maintains this information. When using cookies, each time the browser makes a certain request to a server, the request includes this stored information. The server may or may not use this information.

Let's look at a simple example. Say you want to store a customer's name—Smith. The information is stored by the browser, and when the browser requests another related page, this information is sent to the server by the browser.

Cookie data uses the format of NAME=VALUE. For this example it would be `customer=Smith`. If you have multiple pairs of data, just separate them with semi-colons—for example, `customer=Smith ; phone=8005551212`.

To store information in a cookie with JavaScript, you can use the `cookie` property of the document. To store a value use a statement like this

```
document.cookie = "customer=Smith"
```

In the default mode, the cookie information is maintained until a session ends. Also, the information is only sent when requesting pages from the same server. More details are available in Netscape's Preliminary Specification (**http:// home.netscape.com/newsref/std/cookie_spec.html**).

You retrieve information from the cookie also using the `cookie` property. Then, using string methods, you could extract the information. For our customer Smith example,

```
var pair=document.cookie
lastname = pair.substring(pair.indexOf("=")+1,pair.length)
///...lastname should now equal Smith
```

You can store cookie information two ways. First, as you gather important information, you might want to immediately store it in the cookie. The other method is to create an exit function. This function is called by an `unLoad` event and saves the information into the cookie.

While the cookie specification is considered preliminary, the standard is supported by a wide number of browsers. So while you should use it with some degree of caution, cookies will certainly become more common.

Bookmarks and URLs for Storage   Though it's infrequently used, you can store information in the URL for your page. Using the search property of a location, you can add text to the end of your URL. While extremely long URLs can cause server problems, storing small amounts of data should work flawlessly. Search data is the information after a question mark (?) in a URL. In the following example, `?info=htmljive` is the search portion of the URL:

```
http://www.yoursite.com?info=htmljive
```

After a user enters registration information, you can take him to a post-registration page. Have your code add registration information to the URL using the search property (see listing 14.2). Recommend to the user that he make that page a bookmark. This saves the user's registration information as part of the bookmark.

When the customer returns to your site using the bookmark, you can read the search property of the URL. Now you have the registration information and your user can be immediately directed into your site.

On the CD

Listing 14.2   search.htm   Store Information in a URL

```
<HTML><HEAD><TITLE>search.htm by Ray Daly </TITLE></HEAD><BODY>
<P>Save this page as a bookmark to avoid the registration page on your
next visit..</P>
<script language="JavaScript">
```

Part
IV

Ch
14

continues

Listing 14.2   Continued

```
if (location.search==""){
    //...need this if control to avoid an endless loop
    window.location.search="?infohere"
    //..add information to URL
    document.write("window.location.href")
}
</script></BODY></HTML>
```

Most often you will see search information stored in a format of associative pairs. In this format you have *field=value*. Multiple pairs are separated by the ampersand (&), and spaces are not permitted. Go to almost any search engine and do a simple search. The page that is returned to you will have search text in its URL. For example,

```
http://www.altavista.digital.com/cgi-bin/
query?pg=q&what=web&q=htmljive
```

Though the format of associative pairs is common, there appears to be no requirement to use them. I've found that you can put almost any text or numeric data you want into this portion of the URL.

Parent Knows All   While cookies and bookmarks with search information allow user information to be stored between visits, you can also maintain information during the current visit using the control panel concept.

JavaScript works with both frames and multiple windows. As long as a window from your application stays open, the browser can store data. For example, a user can work within your application and then hyperlink to another site. You can design all of your external links to open up new browser windows. This way your original window is not unloaded and your data is retained.

Good Design

Whether a Web page looks good is a matter of taste: what you like, I might avoid. This factor should be part of your design. Enable users to change the appearance even to a style that you would not normally choose. For example, many of the people I work with set their word processor colors to vibrant green and rich purple. This is a style I might only use on Easter.

Although everyone has individual tastes, the following are different principles that can produce good-looking pages (see fig. 14.4):

- Keep it simple: focus the document on a topic.

- Leave white space: don't fill your page with text or images (especially large ones).

- Employ only the styles you need: don't use every option.

- Shorter lines of text are easier to read.

FIG. 14.4
Almost everyone agrees that Yahoo!'s design is elegant and to the point. The graphic is all that is necessary and functional. The text is easy to read in multiple columns with spacing between the lines.

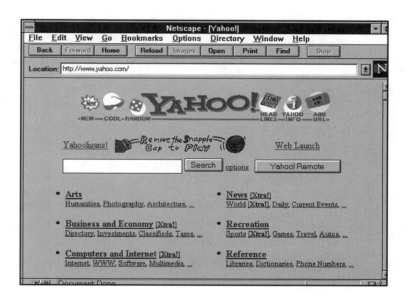

Text Properties and Color Values

Background color and tiles have forever changed the Web. A site without a background is considered old fashioned and behind the times. This puts a burden on the designer to be a color coordinator.

If you change the background color, you also need to be able to modify the colors used to display text. Having the background color match the text color makes the text invisible. Although you might want to use this as an effect, most of the time you will want a pleasant contrast between these two colors.

Part
IV

Ch
14

Text Properties

There are five text properties available from the browser. These all reflect the values of the TEXT attribute of the BODY tag. The first two are the color for the background and for the text of the document. Their properties are called bgColor and fgColor.

The three other text properties reflect the three different colors applied to hyperlink text. Usually you want your hyperlinks to stand out from the rest of the text. Although early browsers displayed these links by underlining the text, now most browsers distinguish these links by color. They also provide feedback to the user by changing this color momentarily when the user clicks the link. After a link is visited, the color is also changed. Respectively, these properties are called linkColor, alinkColor, and vlinkColor.

The syntax for these properties is as follows:

```
document.fgColor [= [<RGB Triplet> ¦ <Color Name>]]
document.bgColor [= [<RGB Triplet> ¦ <Color Name>]]
document.alinkColor [= [<RGB Triplet> ¦ <Color Name>]]
document.linkColor [= [<RGB Triplet> ¦ <Color Name>]]
document.vlinkColor [= [<RGB Triplet> ¦ <Color Name>]]
```

Where <RGB Triplet> is a string of hexadecimal values representing a combination of the colors red, green, and blue; <Color Name> is a string representing a specific color's name as defined in the Color Table. See appendix D for both the hexadecimal and the literal names for predefined colors.

Color Values

You specify the color for TEXT properties just as you would any other color element. The general syntax is:

```
document.textproperty = "colorvalue"
```

where colorvalue is either a hexadecimal or a literal name representing a color.

Hexadecimal Values for Color   Prior to JavaScript, all color values were specified using the RGB hexadecimal values. This is a six-digit number. It is often called a triplet because it is divided into three sets of two digits each: the first two digits specify the amount of red, the second two the amount of green, and the last two the amount of blue.

Because the numbers are hexadecimal, the values range from 00 to FF. (255 is the decimal equivalent of FF hexadecimal.) For example, black is FFFFFF and white is 000000. Aqua, which is an equal mix of green and blue, is represented by 00FFFF:

```
document.fgColor = "00FFFF"
```

Using Color Names   JavaScript provides another option, besides hexadecimal numbers, for specifying color values: you can use names. Instead of coding

```
document.fgColor = "0000FF"
```

you can use the word *blue* like this:

```
document.fgColor = "blue"
```

You have a choice of over 150 predefined colors. Of course you have standard colors such as blue, violet, cyan, and maroon. But now, such colors as dodger blue, tomato, Navajo white, firebrick, peach puff, and Alice blue are hard coded into JavaScript.

▶ **See** "Color Values" in appendix C for a list of all the color names, **p. 787.**

> **N O T E**   You probably remember the primary colors: red, yellow, and blue. Why are the colors red, green, and blue used for computers? Why green instead of yellow?
>
> Red, yellow, and blue paints are commonly used on paper to learn about primary colors. In that case, white light reflects off the mixture of paints to produce the desired color. No paint produces white, and equal amounts of each color absorbs all of the reflected light, producing black. The important point is the reflected light. The color you see is a result of reflected light.
>
> Red, green, and blue (RGB) are the primary colors when the light itself provides the color. It doesn't matter whether you mix red, green, and blue lights on a darkened theatrical stage or from inside a monitor or television. No light produces black; an equal amount of all lights produces white. ■

Color Tools   As you work with color you will find having a few tools will make things easier. For example, what is the hexadecimal number for light purple? What color text looks good on a coral background?

A chart that shows the hexadecimal representation of a desired color is a great tool. There are numerous charts available. I use the *RGB Hex Triplet Color Chart* at **www.phoenix.net/~jacobson/rgb.html**. I have saved this page on my hard drive. Whenever I need it I just load the page and really see what the color looks

Part
IV

Ch
14

like on a monitor. (You can print it out, but the colors don't look the same as onscreen.)

A program that actually lets you experiment with color properties and background tiles is hIdaho Design's Color Center™ (**http://www.hidaho.com/colorcenter/**) by Bill Dortch (see fig. 14.5). You select colors and actually see the results on your screen. Not only is it a great way to find pleasant color schemes, but it is also a brilliant JavaScript application.

FIG. 14.5
hIdaho Design's Color Center™ is even more brilliant on your monitor. You can work in hex, decimal, or percentage. The logo is an animated GIF file.

Practical Uses of Text Properties

Knowing the text properties of the current document, you can use these values to set the text properties for any new documents. Make the new documents the same as the current one, or create a new color by manipulating the current property values.

Another use is to provide feedback that the user's action was recognized. You can either replace the existing background or possibly flash the background. You can also use it with a countdown sequence like ticks of a clock.

For example, upon a user's action (say, clicking a hyperlink) you can make the background color change to the standard text color. This makes the text "disappear" and notifies the user that his action was accepted. The code for this example is in listing 14.3 and can also be found on the CD-ROM as color16.htm.

On the CD

Listing 14.3   color16.htm   Changing Background Color

```
<HTML><HEAD><TITLE>color16.htm by Ray Daly</TITLE></HEAD>
<BODY bgColor="red" fgColor="black" >
<P>Simple example of changing background color.</P>
<P><FONT COLOR="green">Why did the chicken cross the road?</P>
<P><FONT COLOR="document.bgColor">To get to the other side.</P>
<!--...make color same as background to make invisible -->
<FORM><INPUT TYPE="button" VALUE="Red"  onclick='document.bgColor="red"'>
<INPUT TYPE="button" VALUE="Green" onclick='document.bgColor="green"
➥'><BR>
</FORM>
<P><A HREF="http://www.yahooligans.com/"
onClick='document.bgColor="black" '>Yahooligans</A>
</BODY></HTML>
```

Overriding *fgColor*

Normally, the color specified with fgColor is the color of all the text on the page, except hyperlinks. You can override this color by using the fontcolor element. For example, you can place one paragraph of text in between <FONT COLOR="chocolate"> and </FONT>. The text of this paragraph would then be displayed in the color chocolate instead of the color specified by fgColor.

JavaScript provides for a method for placing FONTCOLOR tags around a string. This is the topic for the next section.

Fonts and Font Methods

You certainly have used physical styles for your HTML pages, such as bold, fixed, and italics. JavaScript has methods for these three styles as well as blink, strikeout, subscript, and superscript. It also has methods for big, small, fontsize, and fontcolor. This chapter groups these methods under the name of *font methods*.

Description of Font Methods

The result of a font method places the appropriate tags at the front and end of the string. For example, for the physical style of bold, if testString="example", then the result of testString.bold() is <B>example</B>. In other words, the result of a font method is a new string with HTML code embedded in it.

Below you will see three figures that demonstrate all the JavaScript font methods. Listing 14.4 shows the use of each font method on the same string. Listing 14.5 shows the equivalent HTML code. Figure 14.3 is a screen shot showing the display of each style.

Using Font Methods

The font methods are useful in four primary ways, as follows:

- Your page can directly create a new document in a new window or a frame.
- Your page can collect a sequence of inputs and only build the new document when the user signals completion.
- Your user can create an HTML document that is submitted to the server. The server can then save this page and make it available to other users. Your user may never see the new document.
- JavaScript is also used on servers using the LiveWire environment. Font methods are very advantageous in creating pages there.

Using Font Methods Directly   You create new documents using the document.write or document.writeln methods. As part of the string used in a document.write method, you can use the font methods instead of hard coding in the style tags.

▶ **See** the section "Browser Objects" in chapter 4, "JavaScript Objects," for details on the document.write. method, **p. 105**.

It can be easier to debug using document.write (promptstring.bold()) than document.write ("<B>" + promptstring + "</B>"). It also allows for the browser to handle implementation of HTML tags, for which specifications may change in the future. In the following example, you see the JavaScript code using `document.write` (see listing 14.4), the equivalent HTML code (see listing 14.5), and the display of that HTML code (see fig. 14.6). This shows the use of each of the different font methods. Figure 14.6 shows how either one of these documents will display on a browser.

Because the HTML code does not actually specify a font, the results will vary depending on your browser. The appearance also will depend on your browser preferences.

On the CD

Listing 14.4   fontmeth.htm   All Font Methods in Use

```
<HTML><HEAD><TITLE>fontactu.htm by Ray Daly</TITLE></HEAD><BODY>
<SCRIPT LANUAGUAG="JavaScript">
var testString = "JavaScript Font Methods "
document.write ('<P>')
document.write (testString.bold()+"<BR>")
document.write (testString.fixed()+"<BR>")
document.write (testString.italics()+"<BR>")
document.write (testString.blink()+"<BR>")
document.write (testString.strike()+"<BR>")
document.write (testString.sub()+"<BR>")
document.write (testString.sup()+"<BR>")
document.write (testString.big()+"<BR>")
document.write (testString.small()+"<BR>")
document.write (testString.fontsize(1)+"<BR>")
document.write (testString.fontsize(2)+"<BR>")
document.write (testString.fontsize(3)+"<BR>")
document.write (testString.fontsize(4)+"<BR>")
document.write (testString.fontsize(5)+"<BR>")
document.write (testString.fontsize(6)+"<BR>")
document.write (testString.fontsize(7)+"<BR>")
document.write (testString.fontcolor("FA8072")+"<BR>")
document.write (testString.fontcolor("salmon")+"<BR>")
document.write ('</P>')
</SCRIPT></BODY></HTML>
```

TIP   You can combine font methods to act on one string. For example, to produce a bold, size 4 font in the color of salmon, use the following code:

```
testString.bold.fontsize(4).fontcolor("salmon")
```

Listing 14.5   fontactu.htm   Equivalent HTML Code to Font Methods

```
<HTML><HEAD><TITLE>fontactu.htm by Ray Daly</TITLE></HEAD><BODY>
<B>JavaScript Font Methods </B><BR>
<TT>JavaScript Font Methods </TT><BR>
<I>JavaScript Font Methods </I><BR>
<BLINK>JavaScript Font Methods </BLINK><BR>
<STRIKE>JavaScript Font Methods </STRIKE><BR>
<SUB>JavaScript Font Methods </SUB><BR>
<SUP>JavaScript Font Methods </SUP><BR>
<BIG>JavaScript Font Methods </BIG><BR>
<SMALL>JavaScript Font Methods </SMALL><BR>
<FONT SIZE="1">JavaScript Font Methods </FONT><BR>
<FONT SIZE="2">JavaScript Font Methods </FONT><BR>
<FONT SIZE="3">JavaScript Font Methods </FONT><BR>
<FONT SIZE="4">JavaScript Font Methods </FONT><BR>
<FONT SIZE="5">JavaScript Font Methods </FONT><BR>
<FONT SIZE="6">JavaScript Font Methods </FONT><BR>
<FONT SIZE="7">JavaScript Font Methods </FONT><BR>
<FONT COLOR="FA8072">JavaScript Font Methods </FONT><BR>
<FONT COLOR="salmon">JavaScript Font Methods </FONT><BR>
</P></BODY></HTML>
```

FIG. 14.6

How the browser displays the HTML code for font methods (see listings 14.4 and 14.5). The code is different; the result is the same.

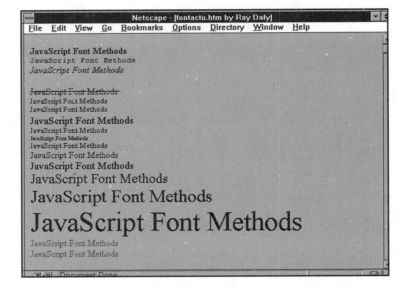

Using Font Methods Indirectly   There are many cases in which you want to build a document as user inputs are gathered, instead of immediately. This enables users to select components to be used for their documents. By putting the components together in different sequences, users create different HTML pages. Using an indirect technique, they can preview the page prior to finalizing it.

A very practical example is an HTML editor (see fig 14.7). The user builds the page using various form inputs, such as buttons. These activate functions that insert HTML tags using the font methods. As the user builds the page by making various choices, the raw HTML code is displayed in a text area of a form. The text area functions like a text editor in which the user can make changes prior to finalizing the document.

FIG. 14.7

HTMLJive is an HTML editor written in JavaScript. You build a document in the textarea with the option to preview it.

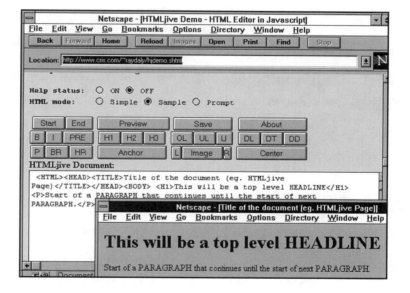

In other cases, you may not want the user to be capable of directly editing the HTML code. Instead of building the HTML page in a test area, you can use a hidden form element. Just use the value of that hidden element to store the code until it is ready to be directed to a new document (see fig. 14.8). The code for this example is in listing 14.6.

Part
IV

Ch
14

FIG. 14.8

In this example, code is stored in the hidden form element but you don't see it until you click the Show New Document button.

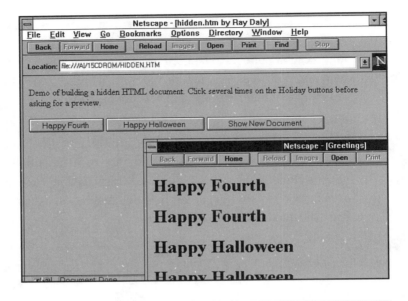

Listing 14.6   hidden.htm   Storing New Document in Hidden Value

```
<HTML><HEAD><TITLE>hidden.htm by Ray Daly</TITLE>
<SCRIPT LANGUAGE="JavaScript">
<!-- hide code from other browsers
function preview (form) {
     msg=open ("", "DisplayWindow","toolbar=yes,scrollbars=yes")
        msg.document.write(form.storage.value)
}
// end hiding -->
</SCRIPT>
</HEAD><BODY>
<P>Demo of building a hidden HTML document.  Click several times
on the Holiday buttons before asking for a preview.</B>
<FORM>
<INPUT TYPE="hidden" NAME="storage"
VALUE="<HTML><HEAD><TITLE>Greetings</TITLE></HEAD><BODY>">
<!--...this hidden element is where the HTML document is created -->
<INPUT TYPE="button" VALUE="Happy Fourth"
onClick='this.form.storage.value += "<H1>Happy Fourth</H1>" '>
<INPUT TYPE="button" VALUE="Happy Halloween"
onClick='this.form.storage.value += "<H1>Happy Halloween</H1>" '>
<INPUT TYPE="button" VALUE="Show New Document"
onClick="preview(this.form)">
</BODY></HTML>
```

HTML Strings as a Submission   There is also the case in which the new HTML code is never directly displayed by the browser. Instead, using the various user inputs, the HTML code is stored in either a text box or in a hidden value. When complete, the resulting code is submitted to the server, which processes it.

A practical example is a Web-based message board. Users can compose messages using a JavaScript-enhanced message editor. Because the messages become part of a Web page, they contain various physical styles, such as bold and italics. Buttons can be part of the form, so users do not necessarily need to know the HTML code to add italics or bold to their messages. When a message is complete, it can be sent to the server and appended to an existing page.

Another example is a salesperson's weekly report. A salesperson can complete a Web form about her activity. This might include invoice numbers, dollar amounts, and comments. When the report is complete, the JavaScript code adds HTML code to the various inputs. The final document is submitted to the server where it is simply appended to the sales manager's page for his review on Monday morning.

Font Methods on the Server   The primary purpose of the Web server is to respond to requests with HTML pages. LiveWire creates live pages by responding to user input. Because the server is building a live HTML page, the font methods are used extensively in LiveWire applications.

▶ **See** "External Process Communications: JavaScript and CGIs" in chapter 17, "JavaScript on the Server," which discusses building HTML pages on the server with LiveWire, **p. 616**.

Design of JavaScript Message Editor

For a detailed and practical example, we are building a message editor. This JavaScript-enhanced page provides controls for the user to easily add HTML style tags to messages. This final text is then submitted to a server where the message is added to a guest book, a message board, or any other site that accepts HTML-enhanced messages.

Designing JavaScript applications often works best if you lay out the interface first. This is a way to decide not only the layout, but the events for which you need to write code. Once you have the layout, then write the code that works behind each event. This is a common technique for event-driven programs, and it is the approach taken for our message editor.

> **CAUTION**
>
> The initial release of JavaScript has limited methods available for text editing. First, the string methods are limited. For example, there is no search and replace method.
>
> The other limitation relates to the fact that text editing takes place in a textarea. The textarea object has no properties related to the cursor position. Therefore, text functions can only append new text to the end of the text and not at the cursor.
>
> Despite these considerable limitations, interesting applications can be created.

How the Message Editor Works

This application basically works like any other page with a text box in a form. The users complete their information, and they can edit it. When it is finalized, the text is submitted to a server where it is processed.

JavaScript enhances this process. We will design a control panel in which the user can select a text style. The program will then prompt the user for the text to highlight with a style. After the user has finished typing, the text and the HTML code is appended to the message in the text area.

The other main feature of the message editor is the preview window. Users will be able to preview their HTML documents prior to submitting them to the server. This will be activated by a button on the control panel. Because all of this activity takes place in the browser (on the client side), the load on the server is reduced. It also provides a much quicker response time than waiting for the server to return a previewed document.

Layout Decision

You must decide whether to create this application in one document or multiple documents. There are trade-offs with either choice.

You can make one long document with all of the HTML and JavaScript code. The user may then need to scroll around the page to use it. This choice can also be easier to code. The real benefit is that the user can save and recall the application in a single file on his hard drive.

The other option is to create a frame for the control panel and another for the text window. Users will not be able to easily save the application on their hard drives because it is now in several files. The real benefit is ease of use because the user will not have to scroll around as much.

For our example, we will use a page with frames. There will also be a dialog box and two other windows.

Framing the Message Editor

For the message editor, there are two main frames. The top frame displays the control panel. It is as wide as the browser allows and it has a fixed height large enough to contain all of the controls.

The top panel is subdivided into a left and right section. The left simply displays the last font color used. This is a fixed width. The right contains all of the controls and extends to the edge of the screen.

The second frame will contain the text box. This is where the message is edited. Like the other frame, the width is the same as the screen. Its height is variable, taking up the remainder of the vertical space.

Listing 14.7 is the code for creating the frames. To test the frames, three test documents are created (see listings 14.8, 14.9, and 14.10). These documents will be modified as we develop the application. Our test result is shown in figure 14.9.

N O T E The message editor is an application written using frames. As such, the complete application consists of five files: messedit.htm, messarea.htm, messcolr.htm, and messcont.htm. The application starts by loading messedit.html. There is also a file for help information in messhelp.htm. These pages are developed as we go through to the end of this chapter. The CD-ROM contains the complete application and none of the development listings. ▩

Part

IV

Ch

14

Listing 14.7 messedit.htm Frameset Document for Message Editor

```
<HTML><HEAD><TITLE>Message Editor by Ray Daly</TITLE>
<FRAMESET ROWS = " 110, * ">
     <FRAMESET COLS="20,*">
     <!-- this is the upper frame, divided into two more frames -->
          <FRAME NAME="messcolr" SCROLLING="no" NORESIZE
          ➥SRC="messcolr.htm">
     <FRAME NAME="messcont" SCROLLING ="no" NORESIZE SRC =
     ➥"messcont.htm">
     </FRAMESET>
     <FRAME NAME="messarea"  NORESIZE SRC="messarea.htm">
     <!-- this is the lower frame -->
</FRAMESET>
</HTML>
```

Using frames with Netscape requires multiple documents. The primary document is a new type of HTML document because it has no <BODY>. Instead, the document uses the FRAMESET element. The contents of the FRAMESET tag are FRAME tags. The primary attribute of the FRAME is the source document, which is displayed in the frame. So for a page with two frames, you would have two FRAME elements, each specifying a source document.

One other optional element of a FRAMESET is another FRAMESET. You would use this in the case where you want to subdivide a frame into different frames. This is how we create the message editor example.

Listing 14.8 messcont.htm Test Document for Upper Frame

```
<HTML><HEAD><TITLE>Message Editor by Ray Daly</TITLE>
<BODY bgcolor ="white">
<H1>messcont.htm</H1>
</BODY></HTML>
```

Listing 14.9 messarea.htm Test Document for Lower Frame

```
<HTML><HEAD><TITLE>Message Editor by Ray Daly</TITLE>
<BODY bgcolor ="white">
<H1>messarea.htm</H1>
</BODY></HTML>
```

On the CD

Listing 14.10 messcolr.htm Test Document for Color Frame

```
<HTML><HEAD><TITLE>Message Editor by Ray Daly</TITLE>
<BODY bgcolor ="black">
</BODY></HTML>
```

FIG. 14.9

It's always a good idea to test your frames to see if they are the size you expect.

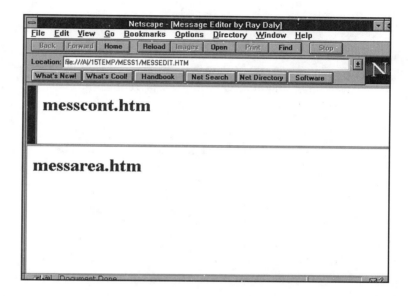

Framesets Nest, Frames Objects Don't

The message editor contains a case of nested framesets. The primary, or top, frameset contains another frameset. This is done to subdivide a frame into two other frames. You might think of these frames and framesets as a tree structure. Using the filenames from our example, a tree might break down to resemble the following:

Part
IV

Ch
14

Frameset: `messedit.htm`   Parent

   Frame: `messtext.htm`   Child

   Frameset: Child

      Frame: `messcont.htm`   Grandchildren?

      Frame: `messcolr.htm`

Because the top file is considered the parent by JavaScript, you would consider messtext and the Frameset to be children. So the other two frames would be considered grandchildren, right? Surprisingly, the answer is no!

When JavaScript creates the objects from the framesets, all of the frames get "flattened." In other words, each frame, regardless of how deeply it is nested, is considered a child and is placed into the same frame array. All frames are placed into the array in the same sequence that they appear in the HTML file. All nesting is ignored, for example,

```
frames[0].document.name is messcolr
frames[1].document.name is messcont
frames[2].document.name is messarea
```

This makes it easier to properly refer to a property in another frame. You don't need to know the relative relationship between frames since they are each a child to the parent.

Later in the chapter we will add to a value of a textarea (called `messtext`) in a form (called `heavy`) in a frame (named `messarea`) from a function in the other frame (called `messcont`). This value is referenced from the other frame using the following code:

```
parent.messarea.document.heavy.messtext.value
```

Please note the word `document` in this code. Since a frame has several properties, you must specify that you are referring to the `document` property.

HTML Code for a Layout

In deciding on a layout, we will provide just enough code to see what the application will look like. For the text area, no further coding is needed other than layout. For the control pane, we will display the various buttons and other controls with practically no JavaScript coding.

HTML Code for the Text Area   This frame will consist primarily of a form. You can also select a background color for the form elements to sit on. There will also be one line of instruction at the top of the text area. As defined by the frame coding above, this document is called messarea.html.

Let's start with the standard tags and define the background color as aqua:

```
<HTML><HEAD><TITLE>Message Editor by Ray Daly</TITLE></HEAD>
<BODY bgcolor="aqua">
```

Next is the start of the form and the single line of instruction:

```
<FORM NAME="heavy"><P><B>Type your message in this box:</B><BR>
```

This form will contain only three elements. The first element of the form is the text area: this one is defined with a column width of 70 and a height of 16 lines. You can make these whatever dimensions you choose.

TIP   You can choose a text area that is longer that the frame. Then the user will have to scroll the frame to get to the Submit and Reset buttons. In this case, you might consider putting one set of buttons at the top of the text area and another at the bottom. This is a design choice.

The coding of the text area follows the standard format. There is also an attribute of wrap=virtual.

```
<TEXTAREA NAME="messtext" ROWS="10" COLS="70" WRAP="virtual">
</TEXTAREA>
```

N O T E   A form enhancement was one of the less publicized additions to HTML that Netscape proposed and has implemented within Navigator 2.0 (**www.netscape.com/assist/net_sites/new_html3_prop.html**).

An attribute was added to the TEXTAREA tag called WRAP. There are three different options, as follows:

off—This is the default setting. There is no wrapping; lines are sent exactly as typed.

virtual—With this option, the display is word-wrapped, but the actual text is not. In other words, you see a long line wrapped, but the browser sends it as one long line to the server.

Part
IV

Ch
14

continues

continued

> `physical`—With this option, the display is word-wrapped and the text is sent with all wrap points.

The syntax is:

```
<TEXTAREA WRAP="wrapvalue"> ▓
```

The final two elements are the buttons for submitting the document and an optional Reset button. The default wording is not used. Because this program is like a word processor or text editor, those types of terms are used.

```
<INPUT TYPE="submit" VALUE="Submit Message">
<INPUT TYPE="reset" VALUE="Reset:  Erase all text">
```

To finish this document, we only need to close the tags for both the FORM and HTML:

```
</FORM> </HTML>
```

The code for this entire document is shown in listing 14.11. Figure 14.10 shows how this document looks inside our frame.

On the CD

Listing 14.11   messcont.htm   Text Area in Lower Frame

```
<HTML><HEAD><TITLE>Message Editor by Ray Daly</TITLE></HEAD>
<BODY bgcolor ="aqua">
<FORM NAME="heavy"><P><B>Type your message in this box:</B><BR>
<TEXTAREA NAME="messarea" ROWS="10" COLS="70" WRAP="virtual">
</TEXTAREA>
<INPUT TYPE="submit" VALUE = "Submit Message" >
<INPUT TYPE="reset" VALUE = "Reset:  Erase all text">
</BODY></HTML>
```

You can add another button to this frame, as users might appreciate having a Preview button right next to the Submit button. This button allows users to preview their messages prior to submitting them. The Preview button is detailed in the section "The Preview" later in this chapter.

At this point, three of the four documents that make up the message editor are complete. The main code is in the control panel, which we will now develop.

FIG. 14.10
Notice the large message area waiting for a user to type something. The wrap attribute is set to virtual to force word-wrapping.

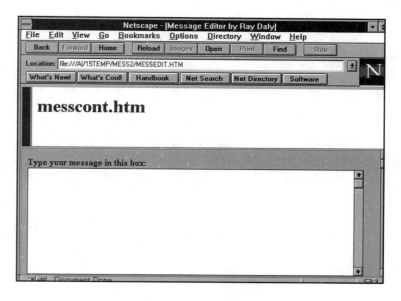

The Controls in the Control Panel The control panel will have three rows of controls. These controls prompt the user for text to be appended to the text in the text area with the appropriate HTML codes.

The first row will contain eight buttons all of approximately the same size. These buttons are for the physical styles: bold, italics, fixed, strike, blink, sup, and sub. (The buttons will display these words.) There will be an eighth button on this row called About.

The second row will contain nine controls. The first two buttons are of the same size as those in the first row. These are for the styles big and small. Then there will be much smaller buttons for font sizes 1 to 7. The last button on this row will be for Help.

The third row is a set of seven hyperlinks. The text for these are eight standard colors, except white. Each text will be displayed in its corresponding font color. The last control on the row will be a button for the preview feature.

Putting the Controls into a Table The controls should appear properly spaced to make it easier for the user to find the button he wants. Aligning the buttons also

Part

IV

Ch

14

makes it easier on the eyes. Figure 14.11 shows what we are trying to achieve. Figure 14.12 shows what it would look like without the table providing spacing and alignment.

FIG. 14.11

This is how we want the control panel to appear. The alignment and spacing is more pleasing and the slightly different size of the buttons is less noticeable.

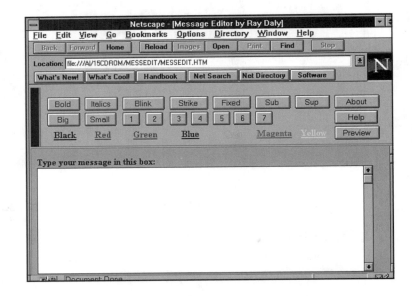

FIG. 14.12

Without a table all of the controls are squished together, which makes it hard for the user to find the proper button.

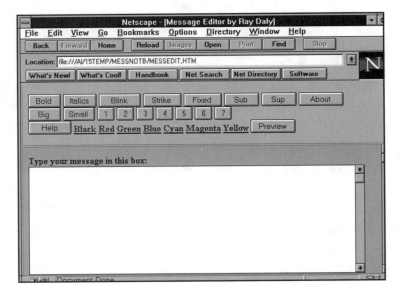

To accomplish the desired layout of these controls, each will be centered within a cell of a table. The <TABLE> is being used only for layout purposes and has no borders. It will be effectively invisible to the user.

Given three rows of controls, the table will also have three rows. With both the top and bottom rows having eight controls, we know the minimum number of columns is also eight. Because the middle row has several smaller buttons and a total count of ten, we are going to double the number of columns to sixteen.

 Centering buttons within cells of a table hides the fact that the buttons are different sizes.

The standard size buttons—those from the top and bottom rows—will be placed in cells that span two columns. The seven smaller buttons for font sizes in the second row will each be placed within single cells. The coding for this table is in listing 14.12.

There are comments inserted into the cells where coding will go for each control. Also, the entire table is between FORM tags because each button is a form element. The standard elements that define an HTML document are also there, including a background color of light gray. This code is shown in listing 14.12.

Listing 14.12   messcont.htm   Tabled Layout of Controls

```
<HTML><HEAD><TITLE>Message Editor by Ray Daly</TITLE>
</HEAD><BODY bgcolor ="white">
<TABLE WIDTH="100%" HEIGHT="100%" BORDER="0">
   <TR><TD COLSPAN=2><!—bold here—>bold</TD>
       <TD COLSPAN=2><!—italics here—>italics</TD>
       <TD COLSPAN=2><!—blink here—>blink</TD>
       <TD COLSPAN=2><!—strike here—>strike</TD>
       <TD COLSPAN=2><!—fixed here—>fixed</TD>
       <TD COLSPAN=2><!—sub here—>sub</TD>
       <TD COLSPAN=2><!—sup here—>sup</TD>
       <TD COLSPAN=2><!—about here—>about</TD>
   </TR><TR><TD COLSPAN=2><!—big here—>big</TD>
       <TD COLSPAN=2><!—small here—>small</TD>
       <TD><!—fontsize 1 here—>1</TD>
       <TD><!—fontsize 2 here—>2</TD>
       <TD><!—fontsize 3 here—>3</TD>
       <TD><!—fontsize 4 here—>4</TD>
```

Part

IV

Ch

14

continues

Listing 14.12 Continued

```
       <TD><!—fontsize 5 here—>5</TD>
       <TD><!—fontsize 6 here—>6</TD>
       <TD><!—fontsize 7 here—>7</TD>
       <TD><BR></TD><TD COLSPAN=2><BR></TD>
       <TD COLSPAN=2><!—help here—>help</TD>
    </TR><TR><TD COLSPAN=2><!—black fontcolor—>black</TD>
       <TD COLSPAN=2><!—red fontcolor—>red</TD>
       <TD COLSPAN=2><!—green fontcolor—>green</TD>
       <TD COLSPAN=2><!—blue fontcolor—>blue</TD>
       <TD COLSPAN=2><!—cyan fontcolor—>cyan</TD>
       <TD COLSPAN=2><!—magenta fontcolor—>magenta</TD>
       <TD COLSPAN=2><!—yellow fontcolor—>yellow</TD>
       <TD COLSPAN=2><!—preview button—>Preview</TD>
    </TR></TABLE>
 </BODY></HTML>
```

Putting Buttons into the Table   The coding for each of the buttons follows the same format. The HTML code creates a button displaying the name of the style (e.g., bold). Each contains an onClick event, which will call a function specifically to implement that feature. However, this coding will not be written until the next phase of developing this program. The following is the code for the Bold button:

```
<INPUT name="bold" type="button" value="  Bold  "
onClick="stylemethod('bold')">
```

This same coding is created for Italics, Fixed, Blink, Strike, Sub, Sup, Big, Small, 1, 2, 3, 4, 5, 6, and 7. Insert this coding into the correct cells of the table. The coding for all of these is shown in listing 14.13.

On the CD

Listing 14.13 messcont.htm Button Inputs Defined

```
<INPUT name="bold" type="button" value="  Bold  "
onClick="stylemethod('bold')">
<INPUT NAME="italics" TYPE="button" VALUE="Italics"
onClick="stylemethod('italics')">
<INPUT NAME="blink" TYPE="button" VALUE="  Blink  "
onClick="stylemethod('blink')">
<INPUT NAME="strike" TYPE="button" VALUE=" Strike "
onClick="stylemethod('strike')">
<INPUT NAME="fixed" TYPE="button" VALUE=" Fixed "
onClick="stylemethod('fixed')">
<INPUT NAME="sub" TYPE="button" VALUE="  Sub  "
```

```
onClick="stylemethod('sub')">
<INPUT NAME="sup" TYPE="button" VALUE="  Sup  "
onClick="stylemethod('sup')">
<INPUT NAME="big" TYPE="button" VALUE="  Big  "
onClick="stylemethod('big')">
<INPUT NAME="small" TYPE="button" VALUE="Small"
onClick="stylemethod('small')">
<INPUT NAME="1" TYPE="button" VALUE="  1 " onClick="stylemethod('Size 1')">
<INPUT NAME="2" TYPE="button" VALUE="  2 " onClick="stylemethod('Size 2')">
<INPUT NAME="3" TYPE="button" VALUE="  3 " onClick="stylemethod('Size 3')">
<INPUT NAME="4" TYPE="button" VALUE="  4 " onClick="stylemethod('Size 4')">
<INPUT NAME="5" TYPE="button" VALUE="  5 " onClick="stylemethod('Size 5')">
<INPUT NAME="6" TYPE="button" VALUE="  6 " onClick="stylemethod('Size 6')">
<INPUT NAME="7" TYPE="button" VALUE="  7 " onClick="stylemethod('Size 7')">
```

About, Help, and Preview will have their own specialized functions so they do not call the same `stylemethod`. The code for these buttons is:

```
<INPUT NAME="about" TYPE="button" VALUE="  About  "
onClick="aboutalert()"><
<INPUT NAME="help" TYPE="button" VALUE="   Help   "
onClick="helppage()">
<INPUT NAME="preview" TYPE="button" VALUE="Preview"
onClick="apreview(this.form)">
```

TIP When you create a button, JavaScript makes the button just large enough to hold the text stored in the VALUE property. You can widen a button by adding extra spaces to the text of the VALUE property.

With a little experimenting, you can make most buttons appear to be the same width. However, browsers on other platforms and with other preferences may display different widths.

Hyperlinks as Controls The third row of the control panel has seven hyperlinks that are used as controls. These are used instead of buttons to enable the user to actually see the different colors. This is essentially a simple color selector.

N O T E   A color selector can be done in a variety of ways. You can have a SELECT list showing the string literals for all 150 colors. You can create a text box for users to input hexadecimal values, or you can create a SELECT drop-down list that has the names of the colors.

An exciting way would be to create a client-side image map of a color bar. The user can select a color and execute the appropriate JavaScript code by clicking anywhere on the color bar. ■

Originally I wrote the coding for these hyperlinks using the OnClick event. The problem was that I had to specify an HREF for either an anchor or a URL. All I wanted was to implement a JavaScript function without jumping to an anchor or loading a URL. So I set the HREF to a nonexistent anchor. This worked, however a future version of JavaScript might produce an error message. The following is an example of the code I originally used:

```
<A HREF=#bold  onClick="stylecolor('red')"> <FONT color="red">Red </
➥FONT></A>
```

It turns out that this is a perfect case for using the new javascript: protocol. Instead of specifying an anchor, a URL, or even a mailto:, you can specify JavaScript code. In our case, we want to specify executing a function for the color represented by the hyperlink. So now the code looks like this:

```
<A HREF="javascript: stylecolor('red')"> <FONT color="red">Red </
➥FONT></A>
```

T I P   *Easter Egg* is a term in video games for an undocumented, hidden feature. By using fontcolor methods, you can make a hyperlink invisible. Just make the fontcolor the same as the normal text color. The only clue would be in the status bar.

T I P   The javascript: protocol allows you to make hyperlinks behave like buttons. So if you don't like being limited to the predefined buttons, use a hyperlink, the javascript: protocol, and your own image as an icon.

```
<A HREF=#bold  onClick="stylemethod('red')">
<FONT color="red">Red </FONT></A>
```

Create this same coding for black, green, blue, yellow, cyan, and magenta. Obviously, if you don't like these colors, just pick another set. Insert this code into the correct cells of the table. The complete code for the tables with all of the hyperlinks and buttons is shown in listing 14.14.

Listing 14.14 messcont.htm Tabled Layout of Buttons

```
<HTML><HEAD><TITLE>Message Editor by Ray Daly</TITLE>
</HEAD><BODY bgcolor ="lightgrey">
<TABLE WIDTH="100%" HEIGHT="100%" BORDER="0">
 <FORM><TR><TD COLSPAN=2>
   <INPUT NAME="bold" TYPE="button" VALUE=" Bold "
onClick="stylemethod('bold')"></TD>
   <TD COLSPAN=2>
   <INPUT NAME="italics" TYPE="button" VALUE="Italics"
onClick="stylemethod('italics')"></TD>
   <TD COLSPAN=2>
   <INPUT NAME="blink" TYPE="button" VALUE="  Blink  "
onClick="stylemethod('blink')"></TD>
   <TD COLSPAN=2>
   <INPUT NAME="strike" TYPE="button" VALUE=" Strike "
onClick="stylemethod('strike')"></TD>
   <TD COLSPAN=2>
   <INPUT NAME="fixed" TYPE="button" VALUE=" Fixed "
onClick="stylemethod('fixed')"></TD>
   <TD COLSPAN=2>
   <INPUT NAME="sub" TYPE="button" VALUE="  Sub  "
onClick="stylemethod('sub')"></TD>
   <TD COLSPAN=2>
   <INPUT NAME="sup" TYPE="button" VALUE="  Sup  "
onClick="stylemethod('sup')"></TD>
   <TD COLSPAN=2>
   <INPUT NAME="about" TYPE="button" VALUE="  About  "
onClick="aboutalert()"></TD>
  </TR><TR><TD COLSPAN=2>
   <INPUT NAME="big" TYPE="button" VALUE="  Big  "
onClick="stylemethod('big')"></TD>
   <TD COLSPAN=2>
   <INPUT NAME="small" TYPE="button" VALUE="Small"
onClick="stylemethod('small')"></TD>
   <TD><INPUT NAME="1" TYPE="button" VALUE="  1  "
onClick="stylemethod('Size1')"></TD>
   <TD><INPUT NAME="2" TYPE="button" VALUE="  2  "
onClick="stylemethod('Size 2')"></TD>
   <TD><INPUT NAME="3" TYPE="button" VALUE="  3  "
onClick="stylemethod('Size 3')"></TD>
   <TD><INPUT NAME="4" TYPE="button" VALUE="  4  "
onClick="stylemethod('Size 4')"></TD>
   <TD><INPUT NAME="5" TYPE="button" VALUE="  5  "
onClick="stylemethod('Size 5')"></TD>
   <TD><INPUT NAME="6" TYPE="button" VALUE="  6  "
```

Part
IV

Ch
14

continues

Listing 14.14 Continued

```
onClick="stylemethod('Size 6')"></TD>
   <TD><INPUT NAME="7" TYPE="button" VALUE="  7 "
onClick="stylemethod('Size 7')"></TD>
   <TD><BR></TD>
   <TD COLSPAN=2><BR></TD>
   <TD COLSPAN=2>
   <INPUT NAME="help" TYPE="button" VALUE="   Help   "
onClick="helppage()"></TD>
</TR><TR><TD COLSPAN=2 ALIGN="center">
<A HREF="javascript: stylecolor('black')">
          <FONT COLOR="black"><B>Black</B></FONT></A></TD>
      <TD COLSPAN=2 ALIGN="center">
      <A HREF="javascript: stylecolor('red')">
          <FONT COLOR="red"><B>Red</FONT></B></A></TD>
      <TD COLSPAN=2 ALIGN="center">
      <A HREF="javascript: stylecolor('green')">
          <FONT COLOR="green"><B>Green</B></FONT></A></TD>
      <TD COLSPAN=2 ALIGN="center">
      <A HREF="javascript: stylecolor('blue')">
          <FONT COLOR="blue"><B>Blue</B></FONT></A></TD>
      <TD COLSPAN=2 ALIGN="center">
      <A HREF="javascript: stylecolor('cyan')">
          <FONT COLOR="cyan">Cyan</FONT></B></A></TD>
      <TD COLSPAN=2 ALIGN="center">
      <A HREF="javascript: stylecolor('magenta')">
          <FONT COLOR="magenta"><B>Magenta</B></FONT></A></TD>
      <TD COLSPAN=2 ALIGN="center">
      <A HREF="javascript: stylecolor('yellow')">
          <FONT COLOR="yellow"><B>Yellow</B></FONT></A></TD>
      <TD COLSPAN=2>
      <INPUT NAME="preview" TYPE="button" VALUE="Preview"
        onClick="apreview(this.form)">></TD>
   </TR></FORM></TABLE>
</BODY></HTML>
```

Double Check the Layout You now have enough code to check your layout. Start your browser and load the code you have so far. You should see a layout just like that shown in figure 14.13.

Normally at this point in your program development, you would spend some time polishing the layout. You might rearrange the controls, change a description, or decide on a different color background. You may or may not want to do this now, depending on how you like the choices made so far. If you like what you see, let's proceed and make this thing do some work.

FIG. 14.13
The layout of the message editor is only a facade at this point, but it is better to get the layout done and then put code behind it.

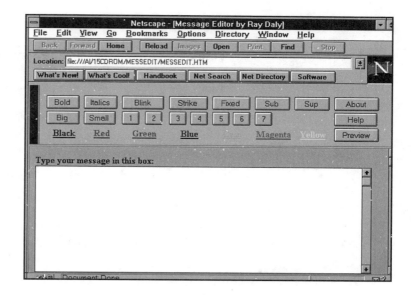

Program Structure or Coding the Events

Although the message editor has 26 different controls on the control panel, most perform nearly identical functions. Most controls prompt for a text string, apply a font method to the string, and then append it to the text in the text area. The Help and About buttons simply display text. And finally, we have the best feature of all: the Preview button.

Font Methods

For all of the font style buttons, there is one function. Each button calls this function and passes a single value: the name of the style. The function uses this value in the prompt box text and to decide which method to apply to the text. Although it creates a rather long function, it does keep down the number of functions.

The Function *stylemethod( )* The first thing `stylemethod()` does is display a dialog box in which the user can enter the text. This is the text that will be highlighted in the given style. You will note that the prompt message reminds the user of the style selected. This goes after `</TITLE>` and before `</HEAD>`, and is shown in listing 14.15.

Part
IV

Ch
14

On the CD

Listing 14.15   messcont.htm   Start Adding Functions

```
<SCRIPT LANGUAGE = "JavaScript">
<!-- hide code from other browsers
function stylemethod (style) {
    x = prompt ("Enter your text for the style:" + style, "")
    if ((x!=null) && (x!="")) {
        <!-- many if statements will go here -->
    }
}
// no more hiding -->
</SCRIPT>
```

The next several lines of code are a series of if statements. To the text string returned from the prompt dialog box, we must now apply the proper font method. This is the section of code for the condition in which the style was bold.

```
if (style=="bold") {
    x = x.bold()
}
```

Additional if statements must be created for each of the additional 15 font methods using buttons. This code is shown in listing 14.16.

Each of the above if statements produces a string with the appropriate HTML tags surrounding the string to be highlighted. This string is now simply appended to the existing text in the text area.

On the CD

Listing 14.16   messcont.htm   If Statements of Style Function

```
        if (style == "bold") {
            x = x.bold()
        }
        if (style == "italics") {
            x = x.italics()
        }
        if (style == "blink") {
            x = x.blink()
        }
        if (style == "strike") {
            x = x.strike()
        }
        if (style == "fixed") {
            x = x.fixed()
        }
```

```
    if (style == "sub") {
        x = x.sub()
    }
    if (style == "sup") {
        x = x.sup()
    }
    if (style == "big") {
        x = x.big()
    }
    if (style == "small") {
        x = x.small()
    }
    if (style == "Size 1") {
        x = x.fontsize(1)
    }
    if (style == "Size 2") {
        x = x.fontsize(2)
    }
    if (style == "Size 3") {
        x = x.fontsize(3)
    }
    if (style == "Size 4") {
        x = x.fontsize(4)
    }
    if (style == "Size 5") {
        x = x.fontsize(5)
    }
    if (style == "Size 6") {
        x = x.fontsize(6)
    }
     if (style == "Size 7") {
        x = x.fontsize(7)
    }
}
```

The Function *stylecolor( )*   Though the method of applying color to strings is
the same as other font methods, we are going to add a feature when using the
fontcolor method. So we need a function just for colors, which we will call
stylecolor( ). When you select a color control, you will change the color in the
small frame in the upper-left corner. This provides the user with feedback and
visually reminds the user which color he has selected. The code for this function is
shown in listing 14.17.

Part

IV

Ch

14

Listing 14.17 messcont.htm Function *stylecolor( )*

```
function stylecolor(style) {
  parent.messcolr.document.bgColor = style
  x = prompt ("Enter your text for the style: "+ style, "")
    if ((x!=null)&&(x!="")) {
          x = x.fontcolor(style)
parent.messarea.document.heavy.messtext.value =
                    parent.messarea.document.heavy.messtext.value + x
  + ' '
      }
```

Adding the String to the Textarea   We now have the text string with the proper method applied to it. The goal is to append this string to the text already in the textarea in the lower frame.

In a case without frames and with a single form, this task is simple. We would just add the string to the existing value of the textarea. For a string of x with a form named `heavy` and a textarea named `messtext`, the code would simply be as follows:

```
heavy.messtext.value=heavy.messtext.value + x + " "
```

A space is added at the end of each insertion for separation.

In our message editor example we have an application using frames. We are trying to add text from code in one frame (the control panel) to the textarea in another frame. We need to reach across the frames. To do this we will use the name of the frame, the form, and the textarea. In our case these names are `messarea`, `heavy`, and `messtext`. We also know that both frames are part of the same frameset. So our final line of the function looks like the following:

```
parent.messarea.document.heavy.messtext.value =
            parent.messarea.document.heavy.messtext.value + x + "
```

From the control panel we are adding the text to `messtext`, which is in form `heavy`, which is part of the document in the frame named `messarea`. This frame is part of the same frameset as the control panel so they both have the same parent.

The About and Help Features

So far we have treated the About and Help buttons as part of the style function. This was great for testing the application, but we now want to make these buttons work.

The About button simply tells the user such information as where the program originated, the name of the author, and the version number. The coding is straightforward:

```
function aboutalert () {
     alert ("Message Editor by Ray Daly from JavaScript Special
     ➥Edition")
}
```

The Help function opens a new window with a help message, as seen in figure 14.14. This comes from another file, messhelp.htm (see listing 14.18). The code to open this window is as follows:

```
function helppage () {
     helpwin=open ("messhelp.htm",
"HelpWindow","toolbar=no,scrollbars=yes")
}
```

FIG. 14.14
The Help screen for Message Editor is static. A more elaborate Help screen could contain the same controls as the control panel and provide help for each control.

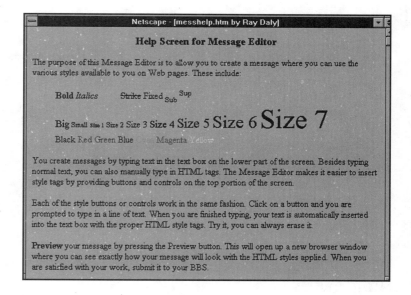

Listing 14.18 messhelp.htm Help Screen for Message Editor

```
<HTML><HEAD><TITLE>messhelp.htm by Ray Daly </TITLE></HEAD><BODY>
<CENTER><H3>Help Screen for Message Editor</H3></CENTER>
<P>The purpose of this Message Editor is to allow you to create a mes-
sage where you
can use the various styles available to you on Web pages.   These in-
clude:</P>
```

continues

Listing 14.18   Continued

```
<DL><DD>
<B>Bold</B> <I>Italics</I> <BLINK>Blink</BLINK> <STRIKE>Strike</STRIKE>
Fixed
<SUB>Sub</SUB> <SUP>Sup</SUP> <BR>
<BIG>Big</BIG> <SMALL>Small</SMALL> <FONT SIZE="1">Size 1</FONT>
<FONT SIZE="2">Size 2</FONT> <FONT SIZE="3">Size 3</FONT> <FONT
SIZE="4">Size 4</FONT>
<FONT SIZE="5">Size 5</FONT> <FONT SIZE="6">Size 6</FONT> <FONT
SIZE="7">Size 7</FONT> <BR>
<FONT COLOR="black">Black</FONT> <FONT COLOR="red">Red</FONT>
<FONT COLOR="green">Green</FONT> <FONT COLOR="blue">Blue</FONT>
<FONT COLOR="cyan">Cyan</FONT> <FONT COLOR="magenta">Magenta</FONT>
<FONT COLOR="yellow">Yellow</FONT>
</DD></DL>
<P>You create messages by typing text in the text box on the lower part
of the screen.
Besides typing normal text, you can also manually type in HTML tags.
The Message Editor
makes it easier to insert style tags by providing buttons and controls
on the top
portion of the screen.</P>
<P>Each of the style buttons or controls work in the same fashion.
Click on a button
and you are prompted to type in a line of text.  When you are finished
typing, your text
is automatically inserted into the text box with the proper HTML style
tags.  Try it,
you can always erase it.</B>
<P><B>Preview</B> your message by pressing the Preview button.  This
will open up a new
browser window where you can see exactly how your message will look with
the HTML styles
applied.  When you are satisfied with your work, submit it to your
BBS.</P>
</BODY></HTML>
```

The Preview

You have waited to the very end of this chapter for the best feature of this program. You may be disappointed at how short this code is. The purpose of this code is to take the HTML document created in the text area and display it on its own page. The code is shown in listing 14.19.

On the CD

Listing 14.19 messcont.htm Preview Function

```
function apreview (form) {
        msg = open ("","DisplayWindow","toolbar=yes")
        starttags ="<HTML><HEAD><TITLE>Preview</TITLE></
        ➥HEAD><BODY><P><PRE>"
        endtags = "</PRE></P></BODY></HTML>"
        y = starttags + parent.messarea.document.heavy.messtext.value +
        ➥endtags
        msg.document.write (y)
}
```

CAUTION

The function for preview is called `apreview`, not preview. This is because the button itself is already using the name preview (see fig. 14.15). Unlike some other languages, function and object names can conflict.

FIG. 14.15
The message in the text box can be typed in or entered by pressing the control buttons. You can see how your message displays in a browser in figure 14.16.

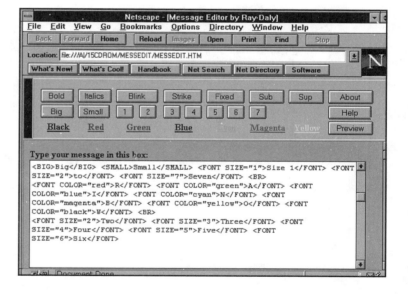

Part
IV

Ch
14

FIG. 14.16

This is the preview window, which shows how your message will appear in a browser. Once you approve, then you submit your message.

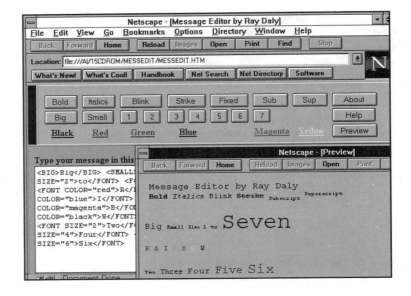

CAUTION

The limitation built into this design is that only one style can be applied at a time. For example, using the controls, it does not allow bold italics or green big. Of course, you can manually enter the codes in the text area to create these physical styles. This limitation does force your users to keep their affects simple. Such simplicity can produce better design.

 As the message editor was designed, it only allows a single paragraph message. To make it more useful, include a control to add the paragraph tags.

CHAPTER 15

Visual Effects

by Bill Dortch

The flat, static Web page may not yet be a thing of the past. But as the number of pages on the Web spirals into the tens of millions, new creative approaches are required both to catch viewers' attention and to hold their interest. Web page designers may now choose from a growing array of tools to lend visual impact to their creations.

In this chapter, you'll see how JavaScript can be used to create several useful visual effects, including alternating color schemes, fades, scrolling marquees, and dynamic graphics. Unlike effects created using other tools, JavaScript effects load quickly as part of your document, and can start even before a page is completely loaded. ■

Create a color alternator

The Alternator object alternates between two color schemes, producing a flashing effect.

Build an event scheduler

The Event and EventQueue objects are used to manage timer-based events. They provide the basis for many of the effects described in this chapter.

Write a color fader

The Fader object produces a smooth fade from one color scheme to another.

Make a scrolling marquee

The Marquee object is used to create a scrolling marquee. Marquees can include multiple fonts, font sizes, and colors, and can scroll left or right.

Generate XBM images

The xbmImage object is used to generate graphic images in real time. A drawing application based on xbmImage is included on the accompanying CD.

Creating Dynamic Framesets

Before we get started, let's take a look at the frameset environment we'll use to create visual effects.

Because Netscape 2.0 does not provide a way to update a document directly once it has been written to the screen, all of the effects we create here require that we write a new document to the screen for each step in an animation, marquee, or other effect. Rather than load each successive document from the server (which would be much too slow), we'll generate our documents on-the-fly and then slap them into frames. Listing 15.1 shows the skeleton frameset that we'll develop in the examples that follow.

Listing 15.1   Skeleton Frameset

```
<html>
<head>
<title>Visual Effects</title>
<script language="JavaScript">
<!— begin script
var emptyFrame = '<html></html>';
function headFrame () {
  return '<html><body bgcolor="#FFFFFF" text="#000000">' +
    '<h1 align="center">Visual Effects</h1>' +
    '</body></html>';
}
function initialize () {
  self.head.location = "javascript:parent.headFrame()";
}
// end script —>
</script>
<frameset rows="52,*" onLoad="initialize()">
 <frame name="head" src="javascript:parent.emptyFrame"
     marginwidth=1 marginheight=1 scrolling="no" noresize>
  <frame name="body" src="javascript:parent.emptyFrame">
</frameset>
<noframes>
<h2 align="center">Netscape 2.0 or other
JavaScript-enabled browser required</h2>
</noframes>
</html>
```

Some of the syntax and techniques used here are a bit different from what you've seen so far. But it's all perfectly legal. Let's take a minute to dissect this skeleton script.

The *javascript:* Protocol

You've often seen `http:` or `ftp:` at the beginning of a URL. This is the *protocol:* it tells the browser which protocol handler to use to retrieve the object referred to after the colon. The `javascript:` protocol is really no different; it simply instructs the browser to let JavaScript retrieve the object. But rather than initiate communication with another server, the JavaScript handler returns the value of the variable or function cited after the colon. The value returned should be HTML or some other MIME type the browser knows how to display.

When using a `javascript:` URL, keep in mind that the reference after the colon is specified from the perspective of the receiving frame. In our example, from the point of view of the head frame, the `headFrame()` function is in the parent frame.

Empty Frames

Sometimes it's desirable to initially leave a frame blank and load the contents later. For instance, the value of the frame may depend on user input or the result of a lengthy calculation or process. You could load an empty document from the server, but that wastes a server access. It's faster and easier to use the `javascript:` protocol to load the empty document internally.

The `<HTML></HTML>` pair used in our `emptyFrame` variable isn't strictly necessary under Netscape—an empty string works just as well. But other JavaScript-enabled browsers, when they're available, may not be as forgiving.

You may be wondering why we need to use an empty frame at all in this example, at least for the head frame, when we could load it directly. In fact, it should not be necessary to do this, but a bug in Netscape 2.0 causes frames loaded using the `javascript:` protocol to align incorrectly if they are loaded directly from a FRAME tag. So instead, we must load an empty document in the FRAME tag and then load the intended document from the `onLoad` handler for the frameset.

You might also be tempted to simply leave off the SRC= attribute. However, due to another odd Netscape behavior, frames that do not have an initial location specified cannot be updated with a new location.

> **N O T E** You may have seen frameset documents that use about:blank to specify an empty frame. This is a Netscape-specific construction and should be avoided. Also, frames initialized with about:blank have been known to display spurious messages on some platforms. ■

Content Variables versus Functions

In our skeleton frameset, emptyFrame is a variable containing HTML, while headFrame() is a function that returns HTML. Either method can be used. In general, use variables if the content will not change. Use functions to return dynamic content.

A Simple Color Alternator

One of the easiest visual effects to create is a color alternator, which switches between two color schemes in a frame. This effect is best used in small frames containing large, bold headlines. It should not generally be used with smaller, detail text, as it will make such text difficult to read while the effect is in progress. It would also be wise to use this effect in moderation—a brief burst of alternating colors can be very effective when your page first loads, when making a transition to a new topic, or to underscore a point. However, continuous flashing quickly becomes annoying to the viewer. (Remember the fate of the BLINK tag!)

Let's start with a simple, direct example. Building on our skeleton frameset, in listing 15.2, we modify the headFrame() function to return one of two BODY tags, depending on the state of a variable called headColor.

Listing 15.2   The Modified *headFrame()* Function

```
var headColor = "white";
function headFrame () {
  return '<html>' +
    ((headColor == "white") ?
```

```
          '<body bgcolor="#FFFFFF" text="#000000">' :
           '<body bgcolor="#000000" text="#FFFFFF">') +
        '<h1 align="center">Visual Effects</h1>' +
        '</body></html>';
}
```

In listing 15.3, we create a function called setHead() that uses JavaScript's setTimeout() function to create a timer loop. We'll update the head frame six times, alternating colors each time.

Listing 15.3   The *setHead()* Function Alternates Colors

```
var headLoops = 6;
function setHead () {
  if (headColor == "white")
    headColor = "black";
  else
    headColor = "white";
  if (—headLoops > 0)
    setTimeout ('setHead()', 100);
  self.head.location = "javascript:parent.headFrame()";
}
```

Finally, we'll call setHead() in our initialize() function:

```
function initialize() {
  setHead();
}
```

When our example page is loaded, the head frame will alternate rapidly between white-on-black and black-on-white. The entire effect lasts less than one second. The output is shown in figures 15.1 and 15.2.

N O T E Due to an implementation problem in Netscape 2.0, timer events are called a maximum of three times per second on Windows platforms. This limitation is expected to be removed in a future release. ■

FIG. 15.1

The heading frame alternates between black-on-white (shown here) and and white-on-black (shown in fig. 15.2).

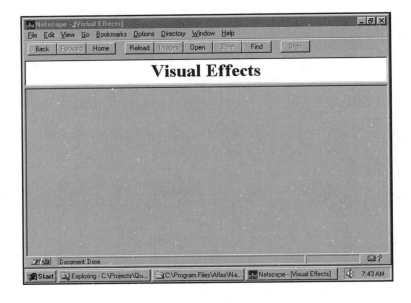

FIG. 15.2

Here is an example of white-on-black.

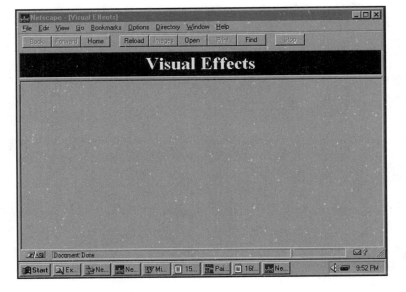

Listing 15.4 shows the complete code for this example.

Listing 15.4 The Simple Color Alternator

```html
<html>
<head>
<title>Visual Effects</title>
<script language="JavaScript">
<!-- begin script
var emptyFrame = '<html></html>';
var headColor = "white";
function headFrame () {
  return '<html>' +
    ((headColor == "white") ?
      '<body bgcolor="#FFFFFF" text="#000000">' :
      '<body bgcolor="#000000" text="#FFFFFF">') +
    '<h1 align="center">Visual Effects</h1>' +
    '</body></html>';
}
var headLoops = 6;
function setHead () {
  if (headColor == "white")
    headColor = "black";
  else
    headColor = "white";
  if (—headLoops > 0)
    setTimeout ('setHead()', 125);
  self.head.location = "javascript:parent.headFrame()";
}
function initialize () {
  setHead();
}
// end script -->
</script>
<frameset rows="52,*" onLoad="initialize()">
  <frame name="head" src="javascript:parent.emptyFrame"
    marginwidth=1 marginheight=1 scrolling="no" noresize>
  <frame name="body" src="javascript:parent.emptyFrame">
</frameset>
<noframes>
<h2 align="center">Netscape 2.0 or other
JavaScript-enabled browser required</h2>
</noframes>
</html>
```

A Better Color Alternator

Our first color alternator works fine if you plan to only use the effect once with one set of colors in a single frame. But if you plan to use this effect more extensively, you'll end up duplicating a lot of code. In this section, we'll develop a generalized version of the color alternator that offers greater flexibility and can easily be reused.

We'll take an object-oriented, component-based approach in this example. This might initially appear to be overkill, but as you will see, the components we create here provide the foundation for more complex effects.

Color Objects

Let's start by defining a `Color` object and some related functions. As you know, colors in HTML (and JavaScript) are represented by hexadecimal triplets of the form RRGGBB, in which each two-digit hexadecimal code represents the red, green, or blue component of a color. Values range between 00 and FF hex, corresponding to zero to 255 decimal. Our `Color` object constructor, shown in listing 15.5, accepts a hexadecimal string, but stores the individual components as numbers, which are easier to manipulate.

Listing 15.5 The *Color* Object Constructor

```
var hexchars = '0123456789ABCDEF';
function fromHex (str) {
  var high = str.charAt(0); // Note: Netscape 2.0 bug workaround
  var low = str.charAt(1);
  return (16 * hexchars.indexOf(high)) +
    hexchars.indexOf(low);
}
function toHex (num) {
  return hexchars.charAt(num >> 4) + hexchars.charAt(num & 0xF);
}
function Color (str) {
  this.red = fromHex(str.substring(0,2));
  this.green = fromHex(str.substring(2,4));
  this.blue = fromHex(str.substring(4,6));
  this.toString = ColorString;
  return this;
}
function ColorString () {
  return toHex(this.red) + toHex(this.green) + toHex(this.blue);
}
```

As you might expect, the fromHex() and toHex() functions convert between numeric and hexadecimal values. Note that these functions will only work with values in the range 00 to FF hex (zero to 255 decimal). By the way, it should be possible to write the fromHex() function more compactly, as

```
function fromHex (str) {
return (16 * hexchars.indexOf(str.charAt(0))) +
    hexchars.indexOf(str.charAt(1));
}
```

However, a bug in the JavaScript implementation in Netscape 2.0 prevents this from working correctly.

The ColorString() function is defined as the Color object's toString() method. This function converts the color back to an RGB triplet, and is automatically invoked any time a Color object is used in a context that requires a string.

 TIP Any JavaScript object can be given a toString() method, which is automatically called whenever an object needs to be converted to a string value.

Let's use the Color constructor to define a few colors:

```
var black = new Color ("000000");
var white = new Color ("FFFFFF");
var blue = new Color ("0000FF");
var magenta = new Color ("FF00FF");
var yellow = new Color ("FFFF00");
```

Now that we've got our colors in a convenient form, let's define an object to contain all the colors in use by a document at a given moment. We'll call this the BodyColor object. Its constructor is shown in listing 15.6.

Listing 15.6 The *BodyColor* Object Constructor

```
function BodyColor (bgColor,fgColor,linkColor,vlinkColor,alinkColor) {
  this.bgColor = bgColor;
  this.fgColor = fgColor;
  this.linkColor = linkColor;
  this.vlinkColor = vlinkColor;
  this.alinkColor = alinkColor;
  this.toString = BodyColorString;
  return this;
}
function BodyColorString () {
  return '<body' +
```

continues

Listing 15.6 Continued

```
  ((this.bgColor == null) ? '' : ' bgcolor="#' + this.bgColor + '"') +
  ((this.fgColor == null) ? '' : ' text="#' + this.fgColor + '"') +
  ((this.linkColor == null) ? '' : ' link="#' + this.linkColor + '"')
➡+
  ((this.vlinkColor == null) ? '' : ' vlink="#' + this.vlinkColor +
➡'"') +
  ((this.alinkColor == null) ? '' : ' alink="#' + this.alinkColor +
➡'"') +
  '>';
}
```

The `BodyColor()` constructor accepts up to five `Color` objects as parameters, one for each HTML body color attribute. The colors are specified in the order of generally accepted importance; trailing colors can be omitted if they will not be used. So, for instance, if a document does not contain any links, the last three parameters can safely be left off.

Like the `Color` constructor, the `BodyColor` constructor includes a `toString()` method: the `BodyColorString()` function. In this case, a complete `BODY` tag is returned, including any color attributes specified.

Note that the individual `Color` objects are used directly in the construction of the `BODY` tag string. Because they are used in a context requiring a string, the `Color` object's `toString()` method will automatically be called to translate these into hexadecimal triplet strings!

Let's define a few `BodyColor` objects. Because we won't be using any links in this example, we'll omit the three link parameters:

```
var blackOnWhite = new BodyColor (white, black);
var whiteOnBlack = new BodyColor (black, white);
var blueOnWhite = new BodyColor (white, blue);
var magentaOnYellow = new BodyColor (yellow, magenta);
var yellowOnBlue = new BodyColor (blue, yellow);
```

In this case, we've used colors we defined previously. Because we're likely to reuse these colors, it was worthwhile to assign them to named variables. But suppose we wanted to use a color only once in a specific `BodyColor` object. It seems—and is—inefficient to define a variable just to hold an object we're going to use immediately:

```
var weirdOne = new Color ("123ABC");
var oddBody = new BodyColor (weirdOne, yellow);
```

Instead, we can invoke the `Color` constructor directly from the `BodyColor` constructor parameter list without ever assigning a name to the color:

```
var oddBody = new BodyColor (new Color ("123ABC"), yellow);
```

 TIP When creating an object that is referred to by name only once, you can invoke its constructor in the parameter list of the function or method that will use it instead of assigning it to a named variable.

The *Alternator* Object

Our next step is to create an object that generates HTML that alternates between two `BodyColor` specifications. We'll call this the `Alternator` object. Its constructor is shown in listing 15.7.

Listing 15.7 The *Alternator* Object Constructor

```
function Alternator (bodyA, bodyB, text) {
  this.bodyA = bodyA;
  this.bodyB = bodyB;
  this.currentBody = "A";
  this.text = text;
  this.toString = AlternatorString;
  return this;
}
function AlternatorString () {
  var str = "<html>";
  with (this) {
    if (currentBody == "A") {
      str += bodyA;
      currentBody = "B";
    }
    else {
      str += bodyB;
      currentBody = "A";
    }
    str += text + '</body></html>';
  }
  return str;
}
```

The `Alternator()` constructor accepts two `BodyColor` objects plus a string containing whatever is to appear between <BODY> and </BODY>. In theory, the text string can be arbitrarily long, but 4K seems to be the maximum usable length on some Netscape platforms. In our examples, this string will be much shorter.

The `currentBody` variable indicates which `BodyColor` object is used to generate the `BODY` tag. This is switched by the `toString()` method, `AlternatorString()`, each time it is invoked.

Let's create an `Alternator` object now. We'll use the same text that appeared in the head frame of our simple alternator example:

```
var flashyText = new Alternator (blackOnWhite, whiteOnBlack,
  '<h1 align="center">Visual Effects</h1>' );
```

Each time `flashyText` is referenced, it will alternate between black-on-white and white-on-black output. For example, suppose we loaded `flashyText` into three frames consecutively:

```
self.frameA.location = "javascript:parent.flashyText";
self.frameB.location = "javascript:parent.flashyText";
self.frameC.location = "javascript:parent.flashyText";
```

The output is shown in figure 15.3.

FIG. 15.3
The *Alternator* object alternates between color schemes each time it is used.

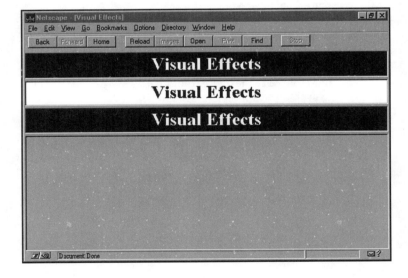

Events and the Event Queue

All that's left is to write our `flashyText` object to the screen at regular intervals. To do this, we'll create an object called an `Event`, which—in this context—is an action that is scheduled to take place at a particular time. We can define our `Event` object so that a separate event was required for each write to the screen, but this would require a lot of extra coding. Instead, we'll build a looping mechanism into our `Event` object because most of the effects we create in this chapter involve multiple writes to the screen. Listing 15.8 shows the `Event` constructor.

Listing 15.8   The *Event* Object Constructor

```
function Event (start, loops, delay, action) {
  this.start = start * 1000;
  this.next = this.start;
  this.loops = loops;
  this.loopsRemaining = loops;
  this.delay = delay * 1000;
  this.action = action;
  return this;
}
```

The `Event` constructor takes the start time for the event (relative to the time the program is launched or the time the `EventQueue` is started), the number of times (loops) to execute the event, the delay between each execution, and the action to be performed for the event.

The start time and delay are specified in seconds, but are converted to milliseconds for internal use. The action can be any valid JavaScript statement enclosed in quotes. (This is similar to the way you specify an action for JavaScript's `setTimeout()` function.) The following is the `Event` constructor for our `flashyText` object:

```
var flashEvent = new Event (0, 10, 0.1,
  'self.head.location="javascript:parent.flashyText"');
```

We will start the event at time zero, that is, as soon as the `EventQueue` is started. We'll loop ten times with each loop one-tenth of a second apart. The action for the event is to load the `flashyText` object into the head frame.

We've defined an Event, but it's still just sitting there. This is where the EventQueue object comes in. The EventQueue contains a list of Event objects to be acted upon. It handles the scheduling and looping of events and executes the associated actions. Listing 15.9 shows the EventQueue constructor and related functions. This is a fairly complex bit of code; I won't go through it line-by-line, but, following the listing, I'll cover the key parameters and methods.

Listing 15.9   The *EventQueue* Object Constructor

```
function EventQueue (name, delay, loopAfter, loops, stopAfter) {
  this.active = true;
  this.name = name;
  this.delay = delay * 1000;
  this.loopAfter = loopAfter * 1000;
  this.loops = loops;
  this.loopsRemaining = loops;
  this.stopAfter = stopAfter * 1000;
  this.event = new Object;
  this.start = new Date ();
  this.loopStart = new Date();
  this.eventID = 0;
  this.addEvent = AddEvent;
  this.processEvents = ProcessEvents;
  this.startQueue = StartQueue;
  this.stopQueue = StopQueue;
  return this;
}
function AddEvent (event) {
  this.event[this.eventID++] = event;
}
function StartQueue () {
  with (this) {
    active = true;
    start = new Date();
    loopStart = new Date();
    loopsRemaining = loops;
    setTimeout (name + ".processEvents()", this.delay);
  }
}
function StopQueue () {
  this.active = false;
}
function ProcessEvents () {
  with (this) {
    if (!active) return;
    var now = new Date();
    if (now.getTime() - start.getTime() >= stopAfter) {
      active = false;
      return;
```

```
    }
    var elapsed = now.getTime() - loopStart.getTime();
    if (elapsed >= loopAfter) {
      if (—loopsRemaining <= 0) {
        active = false;
        return;
      }
      loopStart = new Date();
      elapsed = now.getTime() - loopStart.getTime();
      for (var i in event)
        if (event[i] != null) {
          event[i].next = event[i].start;
          event[i].loopsRemaining = event[i].loops;
        }
    }
    for (var i in event)
      if (event[i] != null) // Note: Netscape 2.0 bug workaround
        if (event[i].next <= elapsed)
          if (event[i].loopsRemaining— > 0) {
            event[i].next = elapsed + event[i].delay;
            eval (event[i].action);
          }
    setTimeout (this.name + ".processEvents()", this.delay);
  }
}
```

The first parameter to the EventQueue constructor is the queue name. This *must* be the same as the variable name to which the EventQueue object is assigned. (This is a bit of a kluge, but is required for the event processor to make setTimeout() calls to itself.)

Next, the delay parameter specifies how often the events in the queue are checked. This is important because it determines the maximum rate of actions for all events in the queue. If you specify a queue delay of 0.10 seconds, but an event delay of 0.05 seconds, the event will only be executed every 0.10 seconds. Therefore, the delay should be set to the smallest value required by your events. Values smaller than 0.05 seconds are not recommended.

CAUTION

Due to a bug in Netscape 2.0, memory allocated to the action string in a setTimeout() call is not released until the page is exited. Therefore, because each processing loop of the EventQueue object calls setTimeout(), set the delay to the highest usable value to minimize calls to setTimeout(). This bug is expected to be fixed in a future release.

The loopAfter parameter specifies the number of seconds after which the entire EventQueue will start over. This enables entire complex sequences of events to be repeated.

The loops parameter specifies the number of times the entire EventQueue repeats. Set this to zero if you do not want the queue to repeat.

The stopAfter parameter indicates the number of seconds after which the queue stops processing events, regardless of the number of loops remaining. Set this to an arbitrarily chosen high number, such as 99999, if you do not want the queue to stop after any particular length of time.

Once the EventQueue has been defined, you can then use the addEvent() method to add events to the queue. Let's create an event queue and add our flashEvent object to it.

```
var evq = new EventQueue ("evq", 0.1, 30, 10, 99999);
evq.addEvent (flashEvent);
```

Our event queue will check for events every 0.1 seconds. It will start over every 30 seconds, repeating 10 times. If for some reason it is still active after 99999 seconds, it will stop processing.

The final step is to start the queue. We'll do this in our initialize() function, which is the onLoad handler for our frameset.

```
function initialize () {
  evq.startQueue();
}
```

That's it! We're in business! After creating numerous functions and scores of lines of code, we now have exactly what we started with in our first, "simple" example. But wait—there's more.

Scheduling Multiple Events

As noted at the beginning of this section, this somewhat complex approach to generating the Alternator effect isn't really necessary if you are only going to use a single effect once in your program. But the advantages quickly multiply when you create complex effects or sequences of events. Each new event requires just a few lines of code, as listing 15.10 demonstrates.

Listing 15.10   Adding New Alternator Events

```
var dance1 = new Alternator (yellowOnBlue, magentaOnYellow,
  '<h1 align="center">Dancing...</h1>');
var inthe1 = new Alternator (magentaOnYellow, yellowOnBlue,
  '<h1 align="center">...in the...</h1>');
var streets1 = new Alternator (whiteOnBlack, yellowOnBlue,
  '<h1 align="center">...streets!</h1>');
var d1e = new Event (0, 10, .1,
  'self.f1.location="javascript:parent.dance1"');
var i1e = new Event (3, 10, .1,
  'self.f1.location="javascript:parent.inthe1"');
var s1e = new Event (6, 10, .1,
  'self.f1.location="javascript:parent.streets1"');
evq.addEvent(d1e);
evq.addEvent(i1e);
evq.addEvent(s1e);
```

Listing 15.11 shows the complete code for the improved alternator with an expanded example. (This script can also be found in the file 15exm01.htm on the CD-ROM.) The output is shown in figure 15.4. In the sections that follow, you'll see how you can easily build on our event model to create even more interesting effects.

On the CD

Listing 15.11   15exm01.htm   Complete Code for the Improved Alternator

```
<html>
<head>
<title>Visual Effects</title>
<script language="JavaScript">
<!— begin script
var emptyFrame = '<html></html>';
var hexchars = '0123456789ABCDEF';
function fromHex (str) {
  var high = str.charAt(0); // Note: Netscape 2.0 bug workaround
  var low = str.charAt(1);
  return (16 * hexchars.indexOf(high)) +
    hexchars.indexOf(low);
}
function toHex (num) {
  return hexchars.charAt(num >> 4) + hexchars.charAt(num & 0xF);
}
function Color (str) {
  this.red = fromHex(str.substring(0,2));
  this.green = fromHex(str.substring(2,4));
  this.blue = fromHex(str.substring(4,6));
```

continues

Listing 15.11 Continued

```
  this.toString = ColorString;
  return this;
}
function ColorString () {
  return toHex(this.red) + toHex(this.green) + toHex(this.blue);
}
function BodyColor (bgColor,fgColor,linkColor,vlinkColor,alinkColor) {
  this.bgColor = bgColor;
  this.fgColor = fgColor;
  this.linkColor = linkColor;
  this.vlinkColor = vlinkColor;
  this.alinkColor = alinkColor;
  this.toString = BodyColorString;
  return this;
}
function BodyColorString () {
  return '<body' +
    ((this.bgColor == null) ? '' : ' bgcolor="#' + this.bgColor + '"') +
    ((this.fgColor == null) ? '' : ' text="#' + this.fgColor + '"') +
    ((this.linkColor == null) ? '' : ' link="#' + this.linkColor + '"')
    ➥+
    ((this.vlinkColor == null) ? '' : ' vlink="#' + this.vlinkColor +
    ➥'"') +
    ((this.alinkColor == null) ? '' : ' alink="#' + this.alinkColor +
    ➥'"') +
    '>';
}
function Alternator (bodyA, bodyB, text) {
  this.bodyA = bodyA;
  this.bodyB = bodyB;
  this.currentBody = "A";
  this.text = text;
  this.toString = AlternatorString;
  return this;
}
function AlternatorString () {
  var str = "<html>";
  with (this) {
    if (currentBody == "A") {
      str += bodyA;
      currentBody = "B";
    }
    else {
      str += bodyB;
      currentBody = "A";
    }
    str += text + '</body></html>';
  }
```

```
    return str;
  }
  function Event (start, loops, delay, action) {
    this.start = start * 1000;
    this.next = this.start;
    this.loops = loops;
    this.loopsRemaining = loops;
    this.delay = delay * 1000;
    this.action = action;
    return this;
  }
  function EventQueue (name, delay, loopAfter, loops, stopAfter) {
    this.active = true;
    this.name = name;
    this.delay = delay * 1000;
    this.loopAfter = loopAfter * 1000;
    this.loops = loops;
    this.loopsRemaining = loops;
    this.stopAfter = stopAfter * 1000;
    this.event = new Object;
    this.start = new Date ();
    this.loopStart = new Date();
    this.eventID = 0;
    this.addEvent = AddEvent;
    this.processEvents = ProcessEvents;
    this.startQueue = StartQueue;
    this.stopQueue = StopQueue;
    return this;
  }
  function AddEvent (event) {
    this.event[this.eventID++] = event;
  }
  function StartQueue () {
    with (this) {
      active = true;
      start = new Date();
      loopStart = new Date();
      loopsRemaining = loops;
      setTimeout (name + ".processEvents()", this.delay);
    }
  }
  function StopQueue () {
    this.active = false;
  }
  function ProcessEvents () {
    with (this) {
      if (!active) return;
      var now = new Date();
      if (now.getTime() - start.getTime() >= stopAfter) {
        active = false;
        return;
```

continues

Listing 15.11 Continued

```
      }
    var elapsed = now.getTime() - loopStart.getTime();
    if (elapsed >= loopAfter) {
      if ( —loopsRemaining <= 0) {
        active = false;
        return;
      }
      loopStart = new Date();
      elapsed = now.getTime() - loopStart.getTime();
      for (var i in event)
        if (event[i] != null) {
          event[i].next = event[i].start;
          event[i].loopsRemaining = event[i].loops;
        }
    }
    for (var i in event)
      if (event[i] != null)
        if (event[i].next <= elapsed)
          if (event[i].loopsRemaining— > 0) {
            event[i].next = elapsed + event[i].delay;
            eval (event[i].action);
          }
    setTimeout (this.name + ".processEvents()", this.delay);
  }
}
var black = new Color ("000000");
var white = new Color ("FFFFFF");
var blue = new Color ("0000FF");
var magenta = new Color ("FF00FF");
var yellow = new Color ("FFFF00");

var blackOnWhite = new BodyColor (white, black);
var whiteOnBlack = new BodyColor (black, white);
var blueOnWhite = new BodyColor (white, blue);
var yellowOnBlue = new BodyColor (blue, yellow);
var magentaOnYellow = new BodyColor (yellow, magenta);

var flashyText = new Alternator (blackOnWhite, whiteOnBlack,
  '<h1 align="center">Visual Effects</h1>');
var dance1 = new Alternator (yellowOnBlue, magentaOnYellow,
  '<h1 align="center">Dancing...</h1>');
var dance2 = new Alternator (whiteOnBlack, yellowOnBlue,
  '<h1 align="center">Dancing...</h1>');
var dance3 = new Alternator (new BodyColor(black,yellow),
magentaOnYellow,
  '<h1 align="center">Dancing...</h1>');
var inthe1 = new Alternator (magentaOnYellow, yellowOnBlue,
  '<h1 align="center">...in the...</h1>');
var inthe2 = new Alternator (blackOnWhite, whiteOnBlack,
```

```
  '<h1 align="center">...in the...</h1>');
var inthe3 = new Alternator (yellowOnBlue, blueOnWhite,
  '<h1 align="center">...in the...</h1>');
var streets1 = new Alternator (whiteOnBlack, yellowOnBlue,
  '<h1 align="center">...streets!</h1>');
var streets2 = new Alternator (blueOnWhite, magentaOnYellow,
  '<h1 align="center">...streets!</h1>');
var streets3 = new Alternator (yellowOnBlue, blackOnWhite,
  '<h1 align="center">...streets!</h1>');

var flashEvent = new Event (0, 10, 0.1,
  'self.head.location="javascript:parent.flashyText"');
var d1e = new Event (0, 10, .1,
  'self.f1.location="javascript:parent.dance1"');
var d2e = new Event (5, 10, .1,
  'self.f2.location="javascript:parent.dance2"');
var d3e = new Event (10, 10, .1,
  'self.f3.location="javascript:parent.dance3"');
var i1e = new Event (3, 10, .1,
  'self.f1.location="javascript:parent.inthe1"');
var i2e = new Event (8, 10, .1,
  'self.f2.location="javascript:parent.inthe2"');
var i3e = new Event (13, 10, .1,
  'self.f3.location="javascript:parent.inthe3"');
var s1e = new Event (6, 10, .1,
  'self.f1.location="javascript:parent.streets1"');
var s2e = new Event (11, 10, .1,
  'self.f2.location="javascript:parent.streets2"');
var s3e = new Event (16, 10, .1,
  'self.f3.location="javascript:parent.streets3"');

var evq = new EventQueue ("evq", 0.1, 20, 10, 60);
evq.addEvent (flashEvent);
evq.addEvent(d1e);
evq.addEvent(i1e);
evq.addEvent(s1e);
evq.addEvent(d2e);
evq.addEvent(i2e);
evq.addEvent(s2e);
evq.addEvent(d3e);
evq.addEvent(i3e);
evq.addEvent(s3e);

function initialize () {
  evq.startQueue();
}
// end script —>
</script>
<frameset rows="52,52,52,52,*" onLoad="initialize()">
  <frame name="head" src="javascript:parent.emptyFrame"
    marginwidth=1 marginheight=1 scrolling="no" noresize>
```

continues

Listing 15.11 Continued

```
<frame name="f1" src="javascript:parent.emptyFrame"
    marginwidth=1 marginheight=1 scrolling="no" noresize>
<frame name="f2" src="javascript:parent.emptyFrame"
    marginwidth=1 marginheight=1 scrolling="no" noresize>
<frame name="f3" src="javascript:parent.emptyFrame"
    marginwidth=1 marginheight=1 scrolling="no" noresize>
<frame name="body" src="javascript:parent.emptyFrame">
</frameset>
<noframes>
<h2 align="center">Netscape 2.0 or other JavaScript-enabled browser
➥required</h2>
</noframes>
</html>
```

FIG. 15.4
Alternating text events are scheduled in four frames.

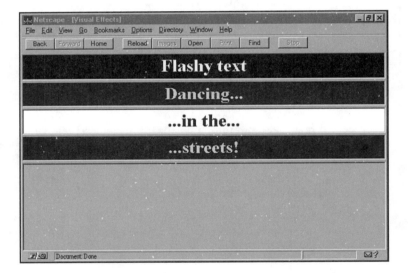

A Color Fader

Like the Alternator effect, the Fader effect involves the transition from one color scheme to another. But instead of jumping abruptly between colors, the Fader displays a series of intermediate shades, creating the illusion of a smooth transition. Although the Alternator effect is noisy and jarring, the Fader effect is calm, serene, even solemn. In particular, a slow fade up from (or down to) black can lend a somber, serious tone to the message being conveyed. Or the Fader can be used to create wild, psychedelic effects—whichever best suits your purpose.

By now, it should come as no surprise that we'll start by creating a new object type. But before we create the Fader object itself, we need to create a special object that calculates an intermediate color value between two Color objects. I'll call this the IntColor object. Its constructor is show in listing 15.12.

Listing 15.12   The *IntColor* Object Constructor

```
function IntColor (start, end, step, steps) {
  this.red =
    Math.round(start.red+(((end.red-start.red)/(steps-1))*step));
  this.green =
    Math.round(start.green+(((end.green-start.green)/(steps-1))*step));
  this.blue =
    Math.round(start.blue+(((end.blue-start.blue)/(steps-1))*step));
  this.toString = ColorString;
  return this;
}
```

The IntColor() constructor takes two Color objects—start and end—plus the number of steps between the start and end colors and the current step. The resultant object is identical to a Color object and can be used as such. It may be convenient to think of IntColor() as just another constructor for a Color object.

Now that we have a way to calculate intermediate colors, we can create our Fader object. Listing 15.13 shows its constructor.

Listing 15.13   The *Fader* Object Constructor

```
function Fader (bodyA, bodyB, steps, text) {
  this.bodyA = bodyA;
  this.bodyB = bodyB;
  this.step = 0;
  this.steps = steps;
  this.text = text;
  this.toString = FaderString;
  return this;
}
function FaderString () {
  var intBody = new BodyColor();
  with (this) {
```

continues

Listing 15.13 Continued

```
    if (bodyA.bgColor != null && bodyB.bgColor != null)
      intBody.bgColor =
        new IntColor (bodyA.bgColor, bodyB.bgColor, step, steps);
    if (bodyA.fgColor != null && bodyB.fgColor != null)
      intBody.fgColor =
        new IntColor (bodyA.fgColor, bodyB.fgColor, step, steps);
    if (bodyA.linkColor != null && bodyB.linkColor != null)
      intBody.linkColor =
        new IntColor (bodyA.linkColor, bodyB.linkColor, step, steps);
    if (bodyA.vlinkColor != null && bodyB.vlinkColor != null)
      intBody.vlinkColor =
        new IntColor (bodyA.vlinkColor, bodyB.vlinkColor, step, steps);
    if (bodyA.alinkColor != null && bodyB.alinkColor != null)
      intBody.alinkColor =
        new IntColor (bodyA.alinkColor, bodyB.alinkColor, step, steps);
    step++;
    if (step >= steps)
      step = 0;
  }
  return '<html>' + intBody + this.text + '</body></html>';
}
```

The Fader object itself is similar in construction to the Alternator object. The Fader() constructor takes a beginning BodyColor object (bodyA), an ending BodyColor object (bodyB), and a text string containing the HTML and text to be displayed. In addition, the Fader() constructor takes the number of steps to be used in the transition from the beginning colors to the ending colors.

The toString() method, FaderString(), is a bit more complex than its Alternator counterpart. It creates a temporary BodyColor object, and populates it with IntColor objects for each color attribute that is present in both the beginning and ending BodyColor objects. It then increments the current step. When all steps have been completed, it resets the current step to zero, so the object can be reused. It returns the specified text, along with an embedded BODY tag generated from the temporary BodyColor object.

It may have occurred to you that a Fader object with steps set to 2 performs exactly the same function as an Alternator object. However, the code is a little longer and involves more processing.

> **TIP** If you are using both `Alternator` and `Fader` objects, you can use a `Fader` object with two steps in place of an `Alternator` object and omit the alternator code to save space.

A `Fader` object is defined in much the same way as an `Alternator` object, as shown in listing 15.14.

Listing 15.14   Using the *Fader* Object

```
var fadingText = new Fader (yellowOnBlue, magentaOnYellow, 10,
  '<h1 align="center">Visual Effects</h1>');
var evq = new EventQueue ("evq", 0.1, 20, 10, 60);
evq.addEvent (new Event (0, 10, 0.1,
  'self.head.location="javascript:parent.fadingText"'));
```

Notice that instead of creating a named variable for our `Fader` event, we defined it in the parameter list for the `addEvent()` method. If you have a lot of events, making up names for them can be a chore—not to mention a source of confusion.

When creating events for `Fader` objects, it's important to remember that the number of loops specified for the event should normally be the same as the number of steps in the fade. If you specify a smaller number of loops, you'll get an incomplete fade; specify a larger number, and the fade will start over with the initial color.

A Scrolling Marquee

By now, you've probably seen dozens of pages with a scrolling text ticker down at the bottom in the status area. Besides being hard to read, these tend to block out the usual status messages associated with cursor actions. The Java applet marquees and tickers are much better, but they take awhile to load and won't run on all platforms. However, you can enjoy the best of both worlds by creating a JavaScript marquee that's both readable and quick to load.

Ideally, our marquee should be able to display text in a variety of fonts, sizes, and colors, in any combination. So before we define the `Marquee` object itself, let's create some text-handling objects that will help us do just that. The `Text` and `Block` object constructors are shown in listing 15.15.

Listing 15.15   The *Text* and *Block* Object Constructors

```
function Text (text, size, format, color) {
  this.text = text;
  this.length = text.length;
  this.size = size;
  this.format = format;
  this.color = color;
  this.toString = TextString;
  this.substring = TextString;
  return this;
}
function TextString (start, end) {
  with (this) {
    if (TextString.arguments.length < 2 || start >= length) start = 0;
    if (TextString.arguments.length < 2 || end > length) end = length;
    var str = text.substring(start,end);
    if (format != null) {
      if (format.indexOf("b") >= 0) str = str.bold();
      if (format.indexOf("i") >= 0) str = str.italics();
      if (format.indexOf("f") >= 0) str = str.fixed();
    }
    if (size != null) str = str.fontsize(size);
    if (color != null) {
      var colorstr = color.toString(); // Note: Netscape 2.0 bug
      ➥workaround
      str = str.fontcolor(colorstr);
    }
  }
  return str;
}
function Block () {
  var argv = Block.arguments;
  var argc = argv.length;
  var length = 0;
  for (var i = 0; i < argc; i++) {
    length += argv[i].length;
    this[i] = argv[i];
  }
  this.length = length;
  this.entries = argc;
  this.toString = BlockString;
  this.substring = BlockString;
  return this;
}
function BlockString (start, end) {
  with (this) {
    if (BlockString.arguments.length < 2 || start >= length) start = 0;
    if (BlockString.arguments.length < 2 || end > length) end = length;
  }
  var str = "";
```

```
  var segstart = 0;
  var segend = 0;
  for (var i = 0; i < this.entries; i++) {
    segend = segstart + this[i].length;
    if (segend > start)
      str += this[i].substring(Math.max(start,segstart)-segstart,
        Math.min(end,segend)-segstart);
    segstart += this[i].length;
    if (segstart >= end)
      break;
  }
  return str;
}
```

The Text object is used to contain a string, along with font, size, and color information. If you look closely, you'll see that the Text object has some interesting properties, both figuratively and literally.

The Text object is designed to mimic JavaScript strings, but with some important differences. The Text object has a length property, for instance, and a substring() method. But while the length property returns the length of the text itself, the substring() method returns the requested substring *plus* the HTML tags required to render the substring in the desired font, size, and color.

Why is this important? Because the Marquee object must display segments of text to produce its scrolling effect; so to maintain proper formatting, it needs to be able to retrieve substrings as small as a single character with all their HTML attributes intact.

The Text() constructor takes a text string, and, optionally, a font size, a Color object, and a format string. The format string can contain the lowercase letters *b, i,* or *f,* or any combination of the three, which stand for bold, italic, and fixed, respectively. The Color object specifies the foreground color to be used when displaying the text.

NOTE Due to a JavaScript bug in Netscape 2.0, font size must be passed as a string (e.g., "7"), rather than a number, when specified as a parameter to the Text() constructor.

The `Block` object is used to combine two or more `Text` objects, JavaScript strings, or even other `Block` objects in any combination. Like the `Text` object, the `Block` object mimics JavaScript string behavior. A call to its `substring()` method might return portions of several of its constituent objects, with all their HTML formatting intact.

The `Block()` constructor accepts any number of `Text`, string, or `Block` objects. These can be considered to be logically concatenated in the order specified in the argument list.

Listing 15.16 shows an example of using `Text` and `Block` objects.

Listing 15.16   Using *Text* and *Block* Objects

```
var t1 = new Text ("When shall ", "5", "", blue);
var t2 = new Text ("we three ", "6", "fb", red);
var t3 = new Text ("meet again, ", "5", "bfi", yellow);
var t4 = new Text ("or in rain? ", "6", "ib", red);
var b1 = new Block (t3, "In thunder, lightning, ", t4);
var b2 = new Block (t1, t2, b1);
```

A call to `b2.substring(5,25)` would then return the following:

```
<FONT COLOR="#0000FF"><FONT SIZE="5">shall </FONT></FONT>
<FONT COLOR="#FF0000"><FONT SIZE="6"><TT><B>we three </B></TT></
FONT></FONT>
<FONT COLOR="#FFFF00"><FONT SIZE="5"><I><B>meet </B></I></FONT></
FONT>
Your
```

Using `Text` and `Block` objects, you can create marquees in a wide variety of styles. Now let's take a look at the `Marquee` object itself. Listing 15.17 shows its constructor.

Listing 15.17   The *Marquee* Object Constructor

```
function Marquee (body, text, maxlength, step) {
  this.body = body;
  this.text = text;
  this.length = text.length;
  this.maxlength = maxlength;
  this.step = step;
  this.offset = 0;
  this.toString = MarqueeString;
```

```
      return this;
    }
  function MarqueeString () {
    with (this) {
      var endstr = offset + maxlength;
      var remstr = 0;
      if (endstr > text.length) {
        remstr = endstr - text.length;
        endstr = text.length;
      }
      var str = nbsp(text.substring(offset,endstr) +
        ((remstr == 0) ? "" : text.substring(0,remstr)));
      offset += step;
      if (offset >= text.length)
        offset = 0;
      else if (offset < 0)
        offset = text.length - 1;
    }
    return '<html>' + this.body + '<table border=0 width=100%
    ➥height=100%><tr>' +
      '<td align="center" valign="center">' + str + '</td></tr></table></
      ➥body></html>';
  }
function nbsp (strin) {
  var strout = "";
  var intag = false;
  var len = strin.length;
  for(var i=0, j=0; i < len; i++) {
    var ch = strin.charAt(i);
    if (ch == "<")
      intag = true;
    else if (ch == ">")
      intag = false;
    else if (ch == " " && !intag) {
      strout += strin.substring(j,i) + " ";
      j = i + 1;
    }
  }
  return strout + strin.substring(j,len);
}
```

The body parameter to the Marquee() constructor accepts a BodyColor object. This object determines the overall color scheme for the marquee.

The text parameter can be a Block object, a Text object, or a JavaScript string object. The text produced by this object will be scrolled across the screen to create the marquee effect. Any colors embedded in this object will override the foreground color specified in the body parameter for the corresponding section of text.

The `maxlength` parameter is the maximum length of the text returned by the `Marquee` object, not counting HTML formatting tags. You will need to experiment with this a bit to get the right width. A good starting point is to use the width of the marquee frame divided by ten. So for a 400-pixel-wide window, start with 40 and then adjust as necessary. It's okay to specify a length slightly larger than the frame width, but if you specify a much longer length, it will slow down processing and increase memory usage.

The `step` parameter specifies the number of characters the marquee will scroll each time it is invoked. You will generally want to set this to 1 or 2, or, to scroll backwards, –1 or –2. Combined with the delay time defined for the `Marquee` event, the `step` parameter determines how fast the `Marquee` scrolls across the screen.

The `toString()` method, `MarqueeString()`, uses a table to center the text vertically and horizontally within the frame. (Depending on how you use the `Alternator` and `Fader` objects, you may want to modify their `toString()` methods to do this as well.) Note that if you use a combination of large and small fonts in your marquee, the text may "wobble" vertically during the transition from one size to another.

The `nbsp()` function is used to replace all space characters with nonbreaking spaces (` `). This enables you to include consecutive spaces (normally ignored by HTML) in your text. It also prevents the scrolling text from breaking into two or more lines when the font is small enough or the marquee window large enough that this would otherwise occur.

In listing 15.18, we create a marquee, using the opening lines from Shakespeare's Macbeth for our text.

Listing 15.18 Using the *Marquee* Object

```
var mbScene = new Block (
  new Text ("When shall we three meet again, ", "5", "b", red),
  new Text ("In thunder, lightning, or in rain? ", "6", "bf", blue),
  new Text ("When the hurlyburly\'s done, ", "5", "ib", yellow),
  new Text ("When the battle\'s lost and won. ", "6", "bfi", magenta),
  new Text ("That will be ere the set of sun. ", "6", "fb", red),
  "..............."
  );

var mbMarquee = new Marquee (whiteOnBlack, mbScene, 50, 2);
var evq = new EventQueue ("evq", 0.1, 120, 5, 600);
evq.addEvent (new Event (0, mbMarquee.length * 3, 0.125,
  'self.f1.location = "javascript:parent.mbMarquee"'));
```

There are several points to note in this example. First, rather than define a separate named variable for each Text object, I created them in the parameter list for the Block constructor. Again, this is usually preferable to cluttering your program with a lot of variables that are only referenced once.

Next, notice that I *escaped* the apostrophes in the text using the \ character. It's sometimes easy to forget to do this when you're working with real-world text in JavaScript applications.

The line of dots at the end of the Block acts as a separator between the end of the text and the beginning when the marquee wraps around. In this particular case, it would have been better to use a Text object with a larger font size because the rest of the text in the block uses larger fonts. But the point to keep in mind is that you *can* use plain strings in Block objects if you want to.

Finally, when creating the Event for the marquee, the number of loops is specified as a multiple of the length of the Marquee object. This is much easier than counting all the characters in the Block object manually!

On the CD

The complete code for this example is included on the accompanying CD (see 15exm02.htm). Its output is shown in figure 15.5.

FIG. 15.5
A scrolling marquee can include multiple font styles, colors, and sizes.

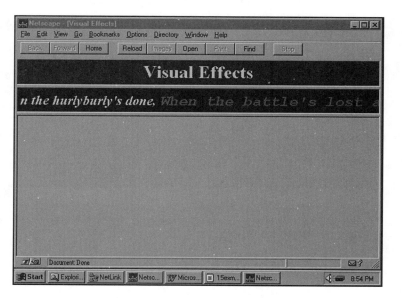

The *Static* Object

In some cases, you may just want to put some text in a frame at a particular time. This isn't really an effect, per se, but it would be convenient to have an object similar to the rest of our objects for this purpose. The `Static` object fills this need. Its constructor is shown in listing 15.19.

Listing 15.19 The *Static* Object Constructor

```
function Static (body, text) {
  this.body = body;
  this.text = text;
  this.toString = StaticString;
  return this;
}
function StaticString () {
  return '<html>' + this.body + this.text + '</body></html>';
}
```

The `Static()` constructor takes a `BodyColor` object and a text string, which may contain HTML. You could also use a `Text` object or a `Block` object for the text parameter. The following is an example of using the `Static` object:

```
var beHere = new Static (blackOnWhite, '<h1 align="center">Be Here
Now</h1>');
var evq = new EventQueue ("evq", 0.1, 120, 5, 600);
evq.addEvent (new Event (12, 1, 10,
  'self.f4.location = "javascript:parent.beHere"'));
```

Animating Images

The best way to animate images using JavaScript is not to. Netscape 2.0 supports GIF89a multipart images, which contain built-in timing and looping instructions. These load faster and run more smoothly than animation created using JavaScript and can be placed anywhere on the page (whereas JavaScript animation currently require their own frame). A number of inexpensive shareware utilities are available for creating GIF animation, the best-known of which is probably *GIF Construction Set* by Alchemy Mindworks. While GIF89a images are currently supported only by Netscape, it's pretty safe to assume that when other browsers support JavaScript, they'll also support GIF animation.

All that said, there may be cases when you want or need to create an animation using JavaScript. In particular, you may want to do so when you're creating images on-the-fly, a subject that will be treated in depth in the next section.

Before we create our Animator object, we'll need an object to hold information about individual images. Listing 15.20 shows the constructor for the Image object.

Listing 15.20   The *Image* Object Constructor

```
function Image (url, width, height) {
  this.url = url;
  this.width = width;
  this.height = height;
  return this;
}
```

The url parameter to the Image() constructor must be a fully specified URL; relative URLs won't work within the framework we've developed because the default protocol is always assumed to be javascript:. The width and height parameters are required, but don't necessarily have to be accurate: Netscape automatically scales images to the width and height specified.

Now let's take a look at our Animator object. Its constructor is shown in listing 15.21.

Listing 15.21   The *Animator* Object Constructor

```
function Animator (name, body) {
  var argv = Animator.arguments;
  var argc = argv.length;
  for (var i = 2; i < argc; i++)
    this[i-2] = argv[i];
  this.name = name;
  this.body = body;
  this.images = argc - 2;
  this.image = 0;
  this.ready = "y";
  this.toString = AnimatorString;
  return this;
}
function AnimatorString () {
  var bodystr = this.body.toString();
  var bodystr = bodystr.substring(0, bodystr.length - 1) +
```

continues

Listing 15.21   Continued

```
     ' onLoad="parent.' + this.name + '.ready=\'y\'">';
  var str = '<html>' + bodystr +
    '<table border=0 width=100% height=100%><tr><td align="center"
    ➥valign="center">' +
    '<img src="' + this[this.image].url + '" width=' +
    ➥this[this.image].width +
    ' height=' + this[this.image].height + '></td></table></body></
    ➥html>';
  this.image++;
  if (this.image >= this.images)
    this.image = 0;
  this.ready = "n";
  return str;
}
```

The `Animator()` constructor takes a name parameter, which *must* be the same as the variable name assigned to the `Animator` object. This is followed by a `BodyColor` object, and any number of `Image` objects. You will generally want to create your `Image` objects in the parameter list for the `Animator()` constructor.

Unlike the `Color`, `Text`, and other objects we've used in our effects so far, images are not immediately available when we want to put them on the screen—they are usually loaded from a server. And there's no reliable way of guessing how long that will take. If you try to display them on a fixed timetable, most likely none of them would get a chance to load completely: the next image you try to display would clobber the one currently loading, and Netscape would start loading it again from scratch the next time it was called for.

The only way to get around this is to let each image load completely before displaying the next image. The `Animator` object does this by including an `onLoad` handler in the `BODY` tag for each image it writes to the screen. When the `Animator` object's `toString()` method, `AnimatorString()`, generates a new frame, it sets the `ready` flag in the object to *n*, meaning that the Animator is not ready to display a new frame. Once the image has loaded completely, the `onLoad` handler is called and sets the `ready` flag back to *y*. (This is the reason you need to specify the name of the `Animator` object: so the `onLoad` handler knows which object to update.)

The last part of this trick falls to the `Event` object we create for the `Animator`. You may recall that an `Event`'s action can be any valid JavaScript statement, so simply

Part
IV

Ch
15

include an if statement in the action to test whether the Animator is ready before updating the frame. Listing 15.22 shows an example of using the Animator. Figure 15.6 shows the output.

Listing 15.22   Using the *Animator* Object

```
var anim = new Animator ("anim", blackOnWhite,
  new Image ("http://www.hidaho.com/colorcenter/img/logo1.gif", 32, 32),
  new Image ("http://www.hidaho.com/colorcenter/img/logo2.gif", 32, 32),
  new Image ("http://www.hidaho.com/colorcenter/img/logo3.gif", 32, 32),
  new Image ("http://www.hidaho.com/colorcenter/img/logo4.gif", 32, 32),
  new Image ("http://www.hidaho.com/colorcenter/img/logo5.gif", 32, 32),
  new Image ("http://www.hidaho.com/colorcenter/img/logo6.gif", 32, 32),
  new Image ("http://www.hidaho.com/colorcenter/img/logo7.gif", 32, 32),
  new Image ("http://www.hidaho.com/colorcenter/img/logo8.gif", 32, 32)
  );
var evq = new EventQueue ("evq", 0.1, 120, 5, 600);
evq.addEvent (new Event (0, 60, 0.1,
  'if (anim.ready=="y") self.f1.location="javascript:parent.anim"'));
```

N O T E   Due to a JavaScript bug in Netscape 2.0, in some cases it is not possible to read or set boolean or numeric values across frames. This is why the Animator object uses a string for the ready flag.

FIG. 15.6
A logo can be animated using the Animator object.

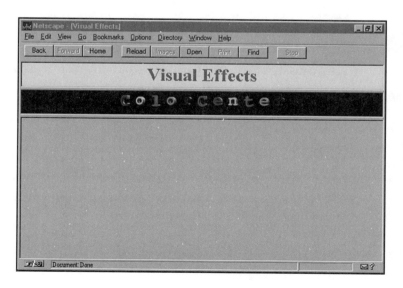

Generating Images

Loading images from a server has its limitations. Apart from the amount of time this can take—especially over a slow connection—you generally have a fixed set of images to work with (unless you generate images on the server using a CGI program). There are times when it is useful to create images on-the-fly, perhaps in response to user input or to create a dynamic animation.

JavaScript offers two solutions. The first is to use single-pixel GIF files to construct images. Because Netscape automatically scales images to the specified width and height, you can create rectangles of various dimensions from a 1×1 GIF image of a particular color. This technique is especially useful for creating dynamic bar charts; but beyond that, its applications are very limited. I won't cover this technique here, but I encourage you to experiment with it on your own.

The second solution is to generate XBM-format images. You may not have heard of these before, but you've probably seen them. They're often used as icons in server directory listings. You are most likely to see one when downloading a file via FTP.

The greatest drawback to XBM images is that they're monochromatic—in other words, black-and-white, though Netscape renders them as black-and-gray. But this is also something of an advantage to us because they can be represented internally as a string of bits, one per pixel, on or off. This also makes manipulating them fairly straightforward and not too costly in terms of processor cycles—an important consideration when working with an interpreted language, such as JavaScript. Also important to us, the XBM file's native format is ASCII text, which can be represented using JavaScript strings.

The XBM Format

An XBM image consists of a header specifying its width and height in pixels and a string of hexadecimal byte codes. As shown in listing 15.23, it looks a lot like something you'd find in a C-language source file.

Listing 15.23   An XBM Image File Header

```
#define xbm_width 32
#define xbm_height 32
```

```
static char xbm_bits[] = {
  0xFF,0x02,0x88,0x25,0x3C,0xB4,0x11,0xDB,
  ...
};
```

The names `xbm_width`, `xbm_height`, and `xbm_bits` are not part of the specification. We chose these because they are descriptive, but the names could be any valid C-style identifiers—it's the format that's important.

Each byte code is a bitmap corresponding to eight pixels in a row of pixels. The first byte code represents the upper-leftmost eight pixels in an image. Bits are processed from left to right until the specified width is reached. The next set of bits then defines the next row of pixels, and so on, until the entire image is drawn.

Representing an XBM Image

We'll represent the XBM bits internally as JavaScript numbers. Because JavaScript uses 32-bit integers, it makes sense to store 32 XBM bits in each JavaScript number. However, it turns out that the high-order sign bit can't be set on some platforms, so we'll use 16-bit numbers instead. This wastes some space, but the math is much easier if we stick with powers of 2.

Our XBM images will be made up of two types of objects: the `xbmRow` object, which contains an array of 16-bit numbers, and the `xbmImage` object, which contains an array of `xbmRow` objects. These objects both contain additional information used in manipulating the image and in translating it to ASCII text for display. Listing 15.24 shows their constructors.

Listing 15.24   The *xbmRow* and *xbmImage* Object Constructors

```
function xbmRow (parent, columns, initialValue) {
  this.redraw = true;
  this.text = null;
  this.parent = parent;
  this.col = new Object();
  for (var i = 0; i < columns; i++)
    this.col[i] = initialValue;
  this.toString = xbmRowString;
  return this;
}
function xbmImage (width, height, initialValue) {
```

continues

Listing 15.24   Continued

```
  this.width = (width+15)>>4;
  this.pixelWidth = this.width<<4;
  this.height = height;
  this.head = "#define xbm_width " + (this.pixelWidth) +
    "\n#define xbm_height " + this.height +
    "\nstatic char xbm_bits[] = {\n";
  this.initialValue = ((initialValue == null) ? 0 : initialValue);
  this.negative = false;
  this.row = new Object();
  for (var i = 0; i < height; i++)
    this.row[i] = new xbmRow(this, this.width, this.initialValue);
  this.drawPoint = xbmDrawPoint;
  this.drawLine = xbmDrawLine;
  this.drawRect = xbmDrawRect;
  this.drawFilledRect = xbmDrawFilledRect;
  this.drawCircle = xbmDrawCircle;
  this.drawFilledCircle = xbmDrawFilledCircle;
  this.reverse = xbmReverse;
  this.clear = xbmClear;
  this.partition = xbmPartitionString;
  this.toString = xbmString;
  return this;
}
```

The xbmImage() constructor takes the width and height of the image, in pixels, as parameters. An optional initial value can also be specified—if supplied; this will create a pattern of vertical lines in the image. Otherwise, a zero is assumed, which results in a blank image.

The xbmImage() constructor calls the xbmRow() constructor to create each row in the image. xbmRow() should be considered an internal function. You don't need to call it directly.

Both xbmImage and xbmRow have toString() methods: xbmImageString() and xbmRowString(), respectively. These create the ASCII representation of the XBM image when it's time to display it. A third method, xbmPartitionString(), optimizes the string-building process, which would otherwise consume an excessive amount of memory. These are shown in listing 15.25.

Listing15.25 The *xbmImage toString()* Methods

```
function xbmRowString () {
  if (this.redraw) {
    this.redraw = false;
    this.text = "";
    for (var i = 0; i < this.parent.width; i++) {
      var pixels = this.col[i];
      if (this.parent.negative)
        pixels ^= 0xFFFF;
      var buf = "0x" + hexchars.charAt((pixels>>4)&0xF) +
        hexchars.charAt(pixels&0xF) + ",0x" +
        hexchars.charAt((pixels>>12)&0xF) +
        hexchars.charAt((pixels>>8)&0xF) + ",";
      this.text += buf;
    }
  }
  return this.text;
}
function xbmPartitionString (left,right) {
  if (left == right) {
    var str = this.row[left].toString();
    if (left == 0)
      str = this.head + str;
    else if (left == this.height - 1)
      str += "};\n";
    return str;
  }
  var mid = (left+right)>>1;
  return this.partition(left,mid) + this.partition(mid+1,right);
}
function xbmString () {
  return this.partition(0,this.height - 1);
}
```

XBM Drawing Methods

The foundation of our XBM drawing capability is the drawPoint() method, xbmDrawPoint(), shown in listing 15.26. As all of our XBM drawing methods, the drawPoint() method doesn't actually draw anything on the screen. Instead, it updates the internal state of the xbmImage object to indicate that the specified point needs to be drawn.

Listing 15.26   The *xbmDrawPoint()* Function

```
function xbmDrawPoint (x,y) {
  if (x < 0 || x >= this.pixelWidth ||
      y < 0 || y >= this.height)
    return;
  this.row[y].col[x>>4] |= 1<<(x&0xF);
  this.row[y].redraw = true;
}
```

The `drawPoint()` method takes the *x* and *y* coordinates of the point to be drawn. These are specified relative to the upper-left corner of the image, which is point (0,0).

The *y* coordinate is used as an index into the array of `xbmRow` objects. The high-order bits of the *x* coordinate are used to compute an index into the array of JavaScript numbers representing the row. The low-order bits are then used to calculate the bit offset for the desired pixel coordinate, which is turned on.

Let's create an `xbmImage` object and draw a point:

```
var picture = new xbmImage (64,64);
picture.drawPoint(10,15);
```

Drawing points can be useful for creating fine detail within an image, but it would take a lot of `drawPoint()` calls to create a useful image. Fortunately, we have some more powerful drawing methods at our disposal.

Listing 15.27   The *xbmDrawLine()* Function

```
function xbmDrawLine (x1,y1,x2,y2) {
  var x,y,e,temp;
  var dx = Math.abs(x1-x2);
  var dy = Math.abs(y1-y2);
  if ((dx >= dy && x1 > x2) || (dy > dx && y1 > y2)) {
    temp = x2;
    x2 = x1;
    x1 = temp;
    temp = y2;
    y2 = y1;
    y1 = temp;
  }
  if (dx >= dy) {
    e = (y2-y1)/((dx == 0) ? 1 : dx);
    for (x = x1, y = y1; x <= x2; x++, y += e)
      this.drawPoint(x,Math.round(y));
```

```
    }
    else {
      e = (x2-x1)/dy;
      for (y = y1, x = x1; y <= y2; y++, x += e)
        this.drawPoint(Math.round(x),y);
    }
  }
```

The drawLine() method, xbmDrawLine(), shown in listing 15.27, draws a line between two points by making a series of calls to drawPoint(). It takes two pairs of coordinates, (x1,y1) and (x2,y2), as parameters. The algorithm is reasonably efficient, at least in the context of an interpreted language. The drawLine() method forms the basis of our rectangle-drawing algorithms, shown in listing 15.28.

Listing 15.28   Rectangle Drawing Functions

```
function xbmDrawRect (x1,y1,x2,y2) {
  this.drawLine (x1,y1,x2,y1);
  this.drawLine (x1,y1,x1,y2);
  this.drawLine (x1,y2,x2,y2);
  this.drawLine (x2,y1,x2,y2);
}
function xbmDrawFilledRect (x1,y1,x2,y2) {
  var x,temp;
  if (x1 > x2) {
    temp = x2;
    x2 = x1;
    x1 = temp;
    temp = y2;
    y2 = y1;
    y1 = temp;
  }
  for (x = x1; x <= x2; x++)
    this.drawLine(x,y1,x,y2);
}
```

The drawRect() method, xbmDrawRect(), draws a hollow rectangle, given two opposing corner coordinate pairs, (x1,y1) and (xy,y2). The drawFilledRect() method, xbmDrawFilledRect(), draws a filled rectangle, as you probably guessed.

Let's draw some lines and rectangles. Figure 15.7 shows the results.

```
var picture = new xbmImage (64,64);
picture.drawLine (0,0,63,63);
picture.drawRect (32,0,63,32);
picture.drawFilledRect (0,32,32,63);
```

FIG. 15.7
Lines and rectangles drawn
using the xbmImage
object.

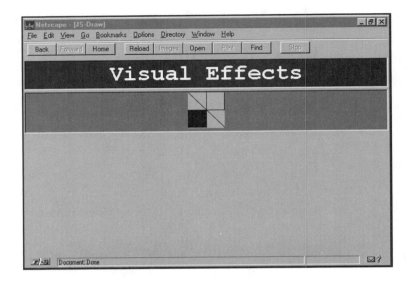

Our last two drawing methods, shown in listing 15.29, draw hollow and filled
circles.

Listing 15.29   Circle Drawing Functions

```
function xbmDrawCircle (x,y,radius) {
  for (var a=0, b=1; a < b; a++) {
    b = Math.round(Math.sqrt(Math.pow(radius,2)-Math.pow(a,2)));
    this.drawPoint(x+a,y+b);
    this.drawPoint(x+a,y-b);
    this.drawPoint(x-a,y+b);
    this.drawPoint(x-a,y-b);
    this.drawPoint(x+b,y+a);
    this.drawPoint(x+b,y-a);
    this.drawPoint(x-b,y+a);
    this.drawPoint(x-b,y-a);
  }
}
function xbmDrawFilledCircle (x,y,radius) {
  for (var a=0, b=1; a < b; a++) {
    b = Math.round(Math.sqrt(Math.pow(radius,2)-Math.pow(a,2)));
    this.drawLine(x+a,y+b,x+a,y-b);
    this.drawLine(x-a,y+b,x-a,y-b);
    this.drawLine(x+b,y+a,x+b,y-a);
    this.drawLine(x-b,y+a,x-b,y-a);
  }
}
```

The drawCircle() method, xbmDrawCircle(), and the drawFilledCircle() method, xbmDrawFilledCircle(), take the coordinates of the center point of the circle plus the radius. These methods take advantage of the fact that it's necessary only to compute the points for a single octant (one-eighth) of a circle. They compute these points relative to an origin of (0,0), and then translate them to the eight octants relative to the *x* and *y* coordinates.

Because the drawPoint() method automatically "clips" any points that don't lie within the image area, we can draw circles that only partially intersect our image (as shown in figure 15.8):

```
var picture = new xbmImage (64,64);
picture.drawCircle (32,32,20); // completely within image
picture.drawCircle (0,0,30); // only 90 degrees of arc appear
```

FIG. 15.8
Circle and arc drawn using the xbmImage object.

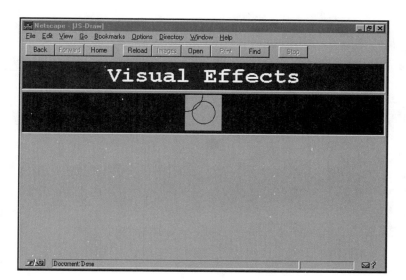

Displaying Generated Images

A generated xbmImage object can be displayed in much the same way that an ordinary image would be displayed, except that it has a javascript: URL. Listing 15.30 shows an example of using the Static object to supply the surrounding HTML.

Listing 15.30   Displaying an *xbmImage* Object

```
picture = new xbmImage (64,64);
picture.drawLine (0,0,63,63);
picture.drawLine (0,63,63,0);
var pictureFrame = new Static (whiteOnBlack,
  '<img src="javascript:parent.picture" width=64 height=64>');
self.frameA.location = "javascript:parent.pictureFrame";
```

Note, however, that once an xbmImage has been displayed, any subsequent changes to it will not be displayed when you redraw the frame. Netscape assumes that images of a given name don't change, so it uses its cached copy after the first draw. The workaround is to assign the xbmImage object to an object with a different name and then redraw it. The JS-Draw application, shown in the next section, uses an array for this purpose.

You can animate a series of xbmImages using the Animator object we created earlier. Just specify the javascript: URL of the image in the Image object.

A Drawing Application: JS-Draw

JS-Draw is a drawing application based on the xbmImage object and its methods. A couple of methods have been added to clear the image and to display it in negative (white on black).

On the CD

The complete code is included on the accompanying CD (see 15exm03.htm). An example of its output is shown in figure 15.9.

FIG. 15.9
The JS-Draw application was built using `xbmImage()` objects.

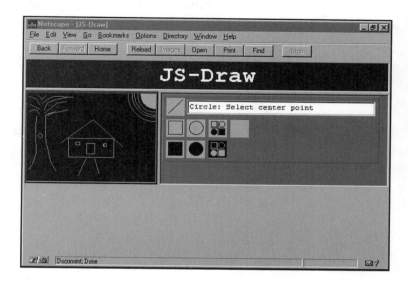

The Show

The final example, included on the accompanying CD (see 15exm04.htm), uses every trick in the book—or at least, every trick in this chapter.

While it is a little too busy to make a good Web page, you might think of it as a laboratory, a starting point for your ongoing experiments with visual effects. ●

CHAPTER 16

Creative User Interaction

by Bill Dortch

JavaScript offers tremendous flexibility in interacting with the user. You can create entire documents on-the-fly. You can dynamically customize both the content of a document and its appearance according to user criteria and other factors. User input also benefits from this flexibility: prompts can be dynamically generated, and even free-form input can be processed. In this chapter, you develop techniques for performing all these tasks.

This chapter builds on several of the objects you created in chapter 15, "Visual Effects," and some of the techniques you developed there, so you might want to review that chapter before you begin, or refer to it as you go along. ■

Create dynamic output

Page content and layout are generated on-the-fly based on user input and other factors.

Generate random numbers

The RandomNumberGenerator object is used to create random phrases and display them using random fonts and color schemes.

Sort an array

A Quicksort array-sorting function is used to sort words for the phrase generator, and rank scores in a database-lookup application.

Parse free-form user input

Keywords are extracted from a query string and used for database lookup.

Create an indexed database

A multiple-key indexing and retrieval mechanism is used to build a bookstore catalog with author, title, and subject indexes.

Creating Dynamic Output

JavaScript provides two methods of updating the screen with dynamic content: you can use the document.write() function, or you can write the entire contents of a frame to the screen using the javascript: protocol. As in chapter 15, you use the latter approach here because it is better suited to the examples in this chapter.

The skeleton frameset shown in listing 16.1 is essentially the same as that used in chapter 15.

Listing 16.1   The Skeleton Frameset

```
<html>
<head>
<title>Creative User Interaction</title>
<script language="JavaScript">
<!— begin script
var emptyFrame = '<html></html>';
function headFrame () {
   return '<html><body bgcolor="#FFFFFF" text="#000000">' +
      '<h1 align="center">Creative User Interaction</h1>' +
      '</body></html>';
}
function initialize () {
   self.head.location = "javascript:parent.headFrame()";
}
// end script —>
</script>
<frameset rows="52,*" onLoad="initialize()">
   <frame name="head" src="javascript:parent.emptyFrame"
      marginwidth=1 marginheight=1 scrolling="no" noresize>
   <frame name="body" src="javascript:parent.emptyFrame">
</frameset>
<noframes>
<h2 align="center">Netscape 2.0 or other
➥JavaScript-enabled browser required</h2>
</noframes>
</html>
```

In this listing, you start by initializing the frames to point to the emptyFrame variable in the FRAME SRC= tag and then set the true location from the initialize() function, which is the onLoad handler for the frameset. As noted in the preceding chapter, this gets around an alignment bug in Netscape 2.0 that appears when loading a frame directly using the javascript: protocol.

You can specify either a variable or a function name on the right side of the colon in a `javascript:` URL. Normally, you use a variable to return an unchanging (or static) value, whereas you use a function to return dynamic content. If a variable name refers to an object, however, and that object has a `toString()` method defined, the function associated with the `toString()` method is called when the object is referenced in a `javascript:` URL, in which case dynamic content may be returned. You see an example of this behavior in the later section entitled "A Random Phrase Generator."

You have defined `headFrame()` as a function, although it currently returns a static value. You can jazz it up with a little bit of dynamism, as shown in listing 16.2.

Listing 16.2   Returning Dynamic Content

```
function headFrame () {
  var now = new Date();
  var body;
  if (now.getHours() >= 6 && now.getHours() < 18)
    body = '<body bgcolor="#FFFFFF" text="#000000">';
  else
    body = '<body bgcolor="#000000" text="#FFFFFF">';
  return '<html>' + body +
    '<h1 align="center">Creative User Interaction</h1>' +
    '</body></html>';
}
```

Now, when `headFrame()` is loaded between 6:00 a.m. and 6:00 p.m., it comes up in "daylight" mode, with a white background. From 6:00 p.m. until 6:00 a.m., the function displays its nocturnal mode.

But why stop here? You can give the user an appropriate greeting as well, as shown in listing 16.3.

Listing 16.3   Returning a Timely Greeting

```
function headFrame () {
  var now = new Date();
  var hour = now.getHours();
  var body;
  var greeting;
  if (hour >= 6 && hour < 18)
    body = '<body bgcolor="#FFFFFF" text="#000000">';
```

continues

Listing 16.3   Continued

```
  else
    body = '<body bgcolor="#000000" text="#FFFFFF">';
  if (hour < 6)
    greeting = "Up late, or up early?";
  else if (hour < 12)
    greeting = "Good morning!";
  else if (hour < 18)
    greeting = "Good afternoon!";
  else
    greeting = "Good evening!";
  return '<html>' + body +
    '<h1 align="center">Creative User Interaction</h1>' +
    '<h3 align="center">' + greeting + '</h3>' +
    '</body></html>';
}
```

One result of this listing is shown in figure 16.1.

FIG. 16.1
The current time is used to generate an appropriate greeting.

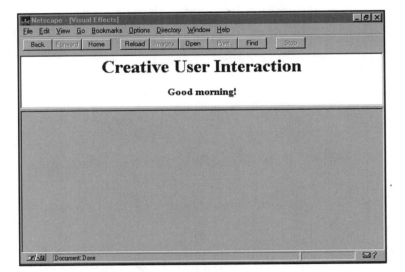

Generating Random Numbers

In the preceding example, you used the time of day to determine which colors and messages to use in generating a dynamic header frame. You can take this example even further; for instance, you might define a different message for every hour of the day, or even for every minute of the hour. You can use this technique to give your pages many different looks.

For many applications in which a degree of apparent randomness is desirable, using the Date object alone yields acceptable results. When you need a series of "random" numbers one after another, however, the Date object isn't of much help. Chances are, whatever calculations you're performing or effects you're creating will be finished before the Date object advances to a new value. A *Random Number Generator* (RNG) comes into play here.

In truth, no such thing as a software-generated "random" number really exists. Software is hopelessly logical—given a particular set of input values, a function performs a predefined set of steps in a predictable order, yielding predictable results. (Even a buggy function yields predictable, if undesirable, results.)

Even the best algorithms, such as the one presented in the next paragraph, don't generate truly random numbers. Instead, they generate very long sequences of numbers that simulate random behavior. However, eventually the sequences repeat. The numbers generated are therefore properly known as *pseudorandom* numbers.

The RNG shown in listing 16.4 is an implementation of the Park-Miller algorithm. (See "Random Number Generators: Good Ones Are Hard to Find," by Stephen K. Park and Keith W. Miller, Communications of the ACM, 31(10):1192—1201, 1988.) The JavaScript version was written by David N. Smith of IBM's T.J. Watson Research Center. Mr. Smith notes that his version has not been subjected to the rigorous testing required of a mission-critical RNG.

Listing 16.4   The *RandomNumberGenerator* Object

```
function NextRandomNumber()  {
  var hi   = this.seed / this.Q;
  var lo   = this.seed % this.Q;
  var test = this.A * lo - this.R * hi;
  if (test > 0)
    this.seed = test;
  else
    this.seed = test + this.M;
  return (this.seed * this.oneOverM);
}
```

continues

Listing 16.4 Continued

```
function RandomNumberGenerator() {
  var d = new Date();
  this.seed = 2345678901 +
    (d.getSeconds() * 0xFFFFFF) +
    (d.getMinutes() * 0xFFFF);
  this.A = 48271;
  this.M = 2147483647;
  this.Q = this.M / this.A;
  this.R = this.M % this.A;
  this.oneOverM = 1.0 / this.M;
  this.next = NextRandomNumber;
  return this;
}
```

In the preceding listing, the RandomNumberGenerator() constructor uses the system time, in minutes and seconds, to "seed" itself; that is, to create the initial values from which it will generate a sequence of numbers. If you are familiar with random number generators, you might have reason to use some other value for the seed. Otherwise, you should probably not change it.

This RNG is implemented as an object. To use it, you create an instance of the object and then invoke its next() method to return a number. Each call to the next() method returns a new random number, as in the following:

```
var rand = new RandomNumberGenerator();

// Display five random numbers
for (var i = 0; i < 5; i++)
  document.write ("The number is: " + rand.next() + "<br>");
```

Like many random number generators, this RNG returns a fraction between 0 and 1—for example, .2755983265971, or something similar. To convert this number to an integer between 0 and *n,* you must multiply *n* times the random number and then round the result. Here's an example that returns a random number between 0 and 255:

```
function random255 () {
  return Math.round(255 * rand.next());
}
```

This example works fine if you need only random integers between 0 and 255. But you can rewrite it to return a number between 0 and any integer, as follows:

```
function random (n) {
  return Math.round(n * rand.next());
}
```

By now, you might be starting to wonder, why all the fuss about random numbers? What use are they, anyway? Well, they have many serious and important uses; in simulations, in software testing and verification, and so on. They also happen to be great for creating games and other fun things, as you see in the next section.

N O T E You might have noticed that Netscape's `Math` object includes a built-in `random()` method. Unfortunately, it was implemented only on UNIX platforms in Netscape 2.0. Furthermore, the implementation varies from one UNIX platform to another. The version presented here should work as well as, if not better than, most UNIX implementations, and will work on all Netscape platforms, including Macintosh and Windows. ▧

A Random Phrase Generator

According to one popular theory, if you put enough monkeys in a room full of typewriters, eventually, by hit and miss, they will bang out the complete works of Shakespeare. Although we suspect it would take several generations of monkeys just to tap out a decent sonnet, try a similar, but less ambitious experiment here, using the random number generator in place of monkeys.

The goal here is to generate some simple phrases by randomly combining words from lists of verbs, articles, adjectives, and nouns. In this exercise, you can cheat a little bit by imposing a structure on the phrases. Your formula is as follows:

verb + article (or possessive pronoun) + adjective + noun.

For example,

Have a nice day.

Random Words

Start creating the random phrase generator by defining an object to contain a list of words, as shown in listing 16.5.

Listing 16.5   The *Word* Object Constructor

```
function Word () {
  var argv = Word.arguments;
  var argc = argv.length;
  this.list = new Object();
  for (var i = 0; i < argc; i++)
    this.list[i] = argv[i];
  this.count = argc;
  this.toString = WordString;
  return this;
}
function WordString () {
  var i = Math.round((this.count - 1) * rand.next());
  return this.list[i];
}
```

The Word() constructor is designed to accept a variable number of parameters, or arguments. Every JavaScript function has a built-in property called arguments. The arguments property is an array containing all the arguments passed to the function, indexed beginning with 0. The arguments property also has a length property, which is the number of arguments passed to the function. I assigned them to variables argv and argc primarily because variables by those names play a similar role in C programs.

The Word() constructor takes the words passed in the argument list and puts them in an internal array called list. To keep the numbering scheme simple, you can make list a separate object rather than make each word a property of the Word object itself.

The toString() method WordString() does the monkey's job of returning random words. As you learned in chapter 15, JavaScript automatically calls an object's toString() method any time the object is used in a context requiring a string. WordString() uses the random number object rand to generate an integer between 0 and the number of words in the list, minus one. (If you have a list containing five words, the generated integer is 0–4.) This integer is then used as the index into the list array.

To start, use the Word() constructor to create a list of nouns:

```
var noun = new Word ("dog", "cat", "shoe", "doorknob", "umbrella");
```

Now, each time you refer to the `noun` object in a context requiring a string (thus invisibly calling its `toString()` method), you get a random selection from the list. For instance, consider this code snippet:

```
for (var i = 0; i < 5; i++)
   document.write ("Have a " + noun + "<br>");
```

It returns a list of offerings that might look something like the following:

```
Have a shoe
Have a umbrella
Have a umbrella
Have a dog
Have a doorknob
```

As you can see, just because you reference the `noun` object five times does not mean that each of the five words will be listed. Randomness means that you might get just one of the words repeated five times. Or you might get all five perfectly alphabetized. Over time, these instances will roughly average out, but you have no way of knowing what you'll get in any given sample.

Now go ahead and define the rest of the word types, and take a crack at some random phrases, as follows:

```
var verb = new Word ("have", "get", "eat", "pet", "feed");
var article = new Word ("a", "the", "my", "your");
var adjective = new Word ("nice", "pretty", "smelly", "hairy",
➥"yellow");

for (var i = 0; i < 5; i++)
   document.write (verb + " " + article + " " +
   ➥adjective + " " + noun + "<br>");
```

To add variety to the phrases, you can include a couple of possessive pronouns in the `article` object, as shown in the preceding code. Here's one possible set of generated phrases:

```
get your nice shoe
pet a smelly umbrella
pet your hairy shoe
feed my yellow dog
eat the hairy doorknob
```

How many different phrases can you generate? Right now, you can calculate the number of phrases as the number of verbs (5) times the number of articles (4) times the number of adjectives (5) times the number of nouns (5), or a total of 500 phrases. But you're about to increase that number more than tenfold.

The Phrasemaker

Having a function that returns a complete phrase would be convenient. While you're at it, you can add the ability to vary the structure of the phrases and include some special handling for plural nouns, as well as adjectives or nouns that begin with vowels. Listing 16.6 gets you started.

Listing 16.6   The *phrase()* Function

```
function isVowel (ch) {
  if (ch == 'a' || ch == 'e' || ch == 'i' ||
      ch == 'o' || ch == 'u')
    return true;
  return false;
}
function phrase (adjs) {
  var plural = (rand.next() >= .5); // Sets plural to true or false
  var vb = verb.toString();
  var first = vb.charAt(0);
  var vb = first.toUpperCase() + vb.substring(1,vb.length);
  var art = article.toString();
  var adj = new Object();
  for (var i = 0; i < adjs; i++)
    adj[i] = adjective.toString();
  var nn = (plural) ? pluralNoun.toString() : singularNoun.toString();
  if (plural && art == "a")
    art = "some";
  if (art == "a") {
    if (adjs > 0)
      first = adj[0].charAt(0);
    else
      first = nn.charAt(0);
    if (isVowel(first))
      art = "an";
  }
  var ph = vb + " " + art + " ";
  for (i = 0; i < adjs; i++)
    ph += adj[i] + " ";
  ph += nn;
  return ph;
}
var singularNoun = new Word ("dog", "cat", "shoe", "doorknob",
➥"umbrella");
var pluralNoun = new Word ("dogs", "cats", "shoes", "doorknobs",
➥"umbrellas");
```

In this listing, the `phrase()` function takes as a parameter the number of adjectives to be included in the phrase, and it returns a complete phrase with the first letter capitalized. The function uses the random number generator to decide whether the noun will be singular or plural. The article "a" is also given special handling: if the noun is plural, "a" is changed to "some"; if it precedes a word beginning with a vowel, it is changed to "an."

Notice that you call the `toString()` methods for the Word objects directly here. Because of the special handling you're doing, you aren't using them in a string context, so `toString()` isn't called automatically by JavaScript.

In this listing, you also define new Word objects for singular and plural nouns. Although plural nouns could be created from the singular nouns used here by appending "s" to the end of each, many irregular nouns cannot be transformed easily. Note that the `singularNoun` and `pluralNoun` objects could contain completely different words, and even different numbers of words.

Here's an example of using the `phrase()` function:

```
document.write (phrase(0) + "<br>");
document.write (phrase(1) + "<br>");
document.write (phrase(2) + "<br>");
```

The phrases generated might look something like this:

```
Buy an umbrella
Eat your smelly cats
Have the nice yellow doorknob
```

Colors, Fonts, and All

Up to this point, you've been testing the phrase generator using simple `document.write()` calls. Put it in a frameset now, with all the trimmings. Because you're experimenting with random numbers, you can use them in the display process as well, to generate random color schemes and fonts for the phrases.

Briefly review a few of the objects you created in chapter 15 for putting text on the screen. These objects simplify the process of creating random colors and fonts for the phrase generator. Listing 16.7 shows the `Color` object.

Listing 16.7   The *Color* Object Constructor

```
var hexchars = '0123456789ABCDEF';
function fromHex (str) {
  var high = str.charAt(0); // Note: Netscape 2.0 bug workaround
  var low = str.charAt(1);
  return (16 * hexchars.indexOf(high)) +
    hexchars.indexOf(low);
}
function toHex (num) {
  return hexchars.charAt(num >> 4) + hexchars.charAt(num & 0xF);
}
function Color (str) {
  this.red = fromHex(str.substring(0,2));
  this.green = fromHex(str.substring(2,4));
  this.blue = fromHex(str.substring(4,6));
  this.toString = ColorString;
  return this;
}
function ColorString () {
  return toHex(this.red) + toHex(this.green) + toHex(this.blue);
}
```

The `Color` object holds a color. It stores the red, green, and blue components as numbers (0–255). The `Color()` constructor accepts a hexadecimal triplet of the form RRGGBB, whereas the `toString()` method, `ColorString()`, converts the internal values back to this format.

Listing 16.8 shows the `BodyColor` object.

Listing 16.8   The *BodyColor* Object Constructor

```
function BodyColor (bgColor,fgColor,linkColor,vlinkColor,alinkColor) {
  this.bgColor = bgColor;
  this.fgColor = fgColor;
  this.linkColor = linkColor;
  this.vlinkColor = vlinkColor;
  this.alinkColor = alinkColor;
  this.toString = BodyColorString;
  return this;
}
function BodyColorString () {
  return '<body' +
    ((this.bgColor == null) ? '' : ' bgcolor="#' + this.bgColor + '"') +
    ((this.fgColor == null) ? '' : ' text="#' + this.fgColor + '"') +
    ((this.linkColor == null) ? '' : ' link="#' + this.linkColor + '"') +
```

```
      ((this.vlinkColor == null) ? '' : ' vlink="#' + this.vlinkColor +
      ➥'"') +
      ((this.alinkColor == null) ? '' : ' alink="#' + this.alinkColor +
      ➥'"') +
      '>';
}
```

The `BodyColor` object contains one or more `Color` objects corresponding to the HTML color attributes that can be specified in a `body` tag. Its `toString()` method returns a formatted `body` tag, including any specified colors.

Listing 16.9 shows the `Text` constructor.

Listing 16.9   The *Text* Object Constructor

```
function Text (text, size, format, color) {
  this.text = text;
  this.length = text.length;
  this.size = size;
  this.format = format;
  this.color = color;
  this.toString = TextString;
  this.substring = TextString;
  return this;
}
function TextString (start, end) {
  with (this) {
    if (TextString.arguments.length < 2 || start >= length) start = 0;
    if (TextString.arguments.length < 2 || end > length) end = length;
    var str = text.substring(start,end);
    if (format != null) {
      if (format.indexOf("b") >= 0) str = str.bold();
      if (format.indexOf("i") >= 0) str = str.italics();
      if (format.indexOf("f") >= 0) str = str.fixed();
    }
    if (size != null) str = str.fontsize(size);
    if (color != null) {
      var colorstr = color.toString(); // Note: Netscape 2.0 bug
      ➥workaround
      str = str.fontcolor(colorstr);
    }
  }
  return str;
}
```

The Text object contains a text string, along with optional font size, font color, and format information. The format string can contain any combination of the letters "b," "i," or "f," corresponding to bold, italic, or fixed (<tt>) formatting. Text objects mimic some JavaScript string behaviors—they have a length property and a substring() method.

Listing 16.10 shows the Static object.

Listing 16.10 The *Static* Object Constructor

```
function Static (body, text) {
  this.body = body;
  this.text = text;
  this.toString = StaticString;
  return this;
}
function StaticString () {
  return '<html>' + this.body + this.text + '</body></html>';
}
```

The Static object holds a BodyColor object and any text, including HTML, that is to appear between the body and /body tags. Its toString() method returns a complete HTML page ready for display.

Now you can also create a new helper function, center(), to center the text on the page, as follows:

```
function center (text) {
  return '<table width=100% height=100% border=0 ' +
    'cellpadding=0 cellspacing=0>' +
    '<tr><td align="center" valign="center">' +
    text + '</td></tr></table>';
}
```

The center() function accepts a text parameter, which can be either a JavaScript string or any object that has a toString() method. The function returns the text embedded in a one-cell table with width and height set to 100 percent, and horizontal and vertical centering specified. This way, the text is centered within the frame.

To generate random colors for the display, create two new objects, called DarkColor and LightColor, as shown in listing 16.11.

Listing 16.11   The *DarkColor* and *LightColor* Object Constructors

```
function DarkColor () {
  this.red = Math.round (127 * rand.next());
  this.green = Math.round (127 * rand.next());
  this.blue = Math.round (127 * rand.next());
  this.toString = ColorString;
  return this;
}
function LightColor () {
  this.red = Math.round (127 * rand.next()) + 128;
  this.green = Math.round (127 * rand.next()) + 128;
  this.blue = Math.round (127 * rand.next()) + 128;
  this.toString = ColorString;
  return this;
}
```

As you know, color component values can range from 0 to 255. The DarkColor() constructor generates a random color, each of the components of which has a value between 0 and 127. The LightColor() constructor generates a random color with component values between 128 and 255. When used together to create foreground and background colors, DarkColor and LightColor almost always produce a readable combination, though it may not always be an attractive combination.

The DarkColor and LightColor objects have an internal structure that is identical to that of the Color object, so they can be used anyplace a Color object can be used. Therefore, it is convenient to think of DarkColor and LightColor as simply being different constructors for a Color object.

Now you can modify the phrase() function to return a complete HTML page, including random foreground and background colors, font size, and format. The modified function is shown in listing 16.12. Note that in another application, placing the phrase-generation and page-generation code in separate functions might make sense; but for this example, a single function will do.

Listing 16.12   The Modified *phrase()* Function Returns a Complete Page

```
function phrase (adjs) {
  var size = "" + (Math.round(rand.next() * 3) + 4);
  var format = " ";
```

continues

Listing 16.12 Continued

```
if (rand.next() >= .5)
  format += "b";
if (rand.next() >= .5)
  format += "i";
if (rand.next() >= .5)
  format += "f";
var body;
if (rand.next() >= .5)
  body = new BodyColor (new DarkColor(), new LightColor());
else
  body = new BodyColor (new LightColor(), new DarkColor());
var plural = (rand.next() >= .5);
var vb = verb.toString();
var first = vb.charAt(0);
var vb = first.toUpperCase() + vb.substring(1,vb.length);
var art = article.toString();
var adj = new Object();
for (var i = 0; i < adjs; i++)
  adj[i] = adjective.toString();
var nn = (plural) ? pluralNoun.toString() : singularNoun.toString();
if (plural && art == "a")
  art = "some";
if (art == "a") {
  if (adjs > 0)
    first = adj[0].charAt(0);
  else
    first = nn.charAt(0);
  if (isVowel(first))
    art = "an";
}
var ph = vb + " " + art + " ";
for (i = 0; i < adjs; i++)
  ph += adj[i] + " ";
ph += nn;
var screen = new Static (body,center(new Text(ph,size,format)));
return screen.toString();
}
```

First, you generate a random font size from 4 to 7. Smaller fonts can be difficult to read, especially when shown in a fixed-width (<tt>) font or italics. Besides, the generated phrase is the only text in its frame, so you might as well make it big.

Next, you choose format specifiers. Note that you start with a string containing a single space. This is yet another Netscape 2.0 bug workaround—the indexOf() method call in the Text object generates an alert if it is called for an empty string. (It should simply return –1, indicating the substring was not found.)

For each format specifier, you generate a random number to determine whether it will be included. Testing for greater than or equal to .5 means you have a 50-50 chance that any specifier will be included.

You then decide whether to use a dark-on-light or light-on-dark color scheme, again by generating a random number and comparing it to .5. Note that you specify only the foreground and background colors in the BodyColor() constructor because you aren't using any links.

At the end of the phrase() function, you create a Static object, using the generated BodyColor object, and a centered Text object that includes the generated font size and format specifiers in addition to the generated phrase. You call the Static object's toString() method directly to return the completely formatted HTML page.

All that's left now is to provide a button so the user can request a new phrase and a selection list enabling the user to specify the number of adjectives to use in the phrase. You put these controls in a separate control frame, as shown in listing 16.13.

Listing 16.13   The Control Frame

```
function printPhrase () {
  var adj = self.control.document.cont.adj.selectedIndex;
  if (adj == 3)
    adj = Math.round (rand.next()*2);
  self.show.location = "javascript:parent.phrase(" + adj + ")";
}
var controlFrame =
  '<html><body bgcolor="#808080" text="#FFFFFF">' +
  '<form name="cont">' +
  '<table width=100% height=100% border=0 cellpadding=0 cellspacing=0>' +
  '<tr align="center">' +
  '<td colspan=2><b>Number of Adjectives</b> <select name="adj">' +
  '<option>None' +
  '<option>1' +
  '<option>2' +
  '<option selected>Random' +
  '</select></td>' +
  '<td colspan=2><input type="button" value="Generate Phrase!" ' +
  'onclick="parent.printPhrase()"></td>' +
  '</tr>' +
  '</table>' +
  '</form>' +
  '</body></html>';
```

When the user presses the Generate Phrase! button, the `printPhrase()` function is called. This function determines how many adjectives to use by examining the `selectedIndex` property of the selection list, `adj`. If the user has selected the fourth option, Random, a random value between 0 and 2 is calculated. Then the frame where you show the phrase, `show`, is updated by using a `javascript:` URL that calls the `phrase()` function.

The complete listing of the phrase generator is included on the CD in file 16exm01.htm. The word lists are beefed up a bit to generate a larger assortment of phrases. Figure 16.2 shows an example of the output.

FIG. 16.2
The random phrase generator.

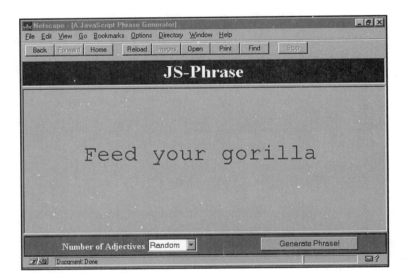

Adding and Sorting Words

The phrase generator can produce some pretty amusing results just as it is, but sooner or later users will want to get into the act and add some words of their own. They also will want to see which words are already defined. In this section, you extend the Word object so that it can accept additional words and produce a sorted (alphabetized) list of its contents. You also add some additional controls to the control frame so that the users can view and add words.

Start by taking a look at the sorting function. Many sorting algorithms are available. The simplest to comprehend and write is the *bubble sort*. The bubble sort algorithm makes $n - 1$ passes through a list of n items, comparing and, if necessary, exchanging adjacent pairs. After the last pass, the list is sorted.

Unfortunately, the bubble sort is also just about the slowest sorting algorithm available. If you're only sorting a handful of items, it doesn't make much difference which algorithm you use. But if you are sorting dozens or hundreds of items, or more, that difference becomes very significant. It could mean the difference between waiting a fraction of a second or a couple minutes for your sort to complete.

Fortunately, much faster algorithms are available, and although they're not as easy to comprehend, you can implement them using only a little more code than a bubble sort. One of the best is the *Quicksort* algorithm. I don't get into the details of its operation in this chapter, except to say that it takes a divide-and-conquer approach to its comparisons and exchanges.

The JavaScript Quicksort algorithm shown in listing 16.14 was written by Achille Hui of Stanford University.

Listing 16.14 A JavaScript Quicksort Implementation

```
function _pm_array_qsort(vec,lo,up,cmp_fun){
  var i, j, t;
  while(up > lo){
    i = lo;
    j = up;
    t = vec[lo];
    while(i < j){
      while(cmp_fun(vec[j],t) > 0)
        j -= 1;
      vec[i] = vec[j];
      while((i < j) && (cmp_fun(vec[i],t) <= 0))
        i++;
      vec[j] = vec[i];
    }
    vec[i] = t;
    if(i - lo < up - i){
      _pm_array_qsort(vec,lo,i-1,cmp_fun); lo = i+1;
    } else {
      _pm_array_qsort(vec,i+1,up,cmp_fun); up = i-1;
    }
  }
}
function _pm_array_defcmp(a,b){
  return (a == b) ? 0 : (a > b) ? 1 : -1;
}
```

continues

Listing 16.14   Continued

```
function pm_array_qsort(vec,lo,hi,cmp_fun){
  if(vec == null){
    return;
  } else if(cmp_fun == null){
    _pm_array_qsort(vec,lo,hi,_pm_array_defcmp);
  } else {
    _pm_array_qsort(vec,lo,hi,cmp_fun);
  }
}
```

To use this Quicksort, call the pm_array_qsort() function, passing it an array object (vec), the starting item number in the array (lo), the ending item number (hi), and optionally, a comparison function (cmp_fun).

The lo and hi parameters you use depend on how your array object is constructed. If you use the first entry (entry[0]) to contain the array length, for instance, then you should pass 1 as the lo parameter and the number of entries in the array as the hi parameter. If you use a zero-based array, then you should pass 0 as the lo parameter, and the number of entries minus one as the hi parameter.

Your Quicksort function includes a default comparison function, which is used to compare two items. The default comparison function can be used if your array consists of strings or numeric items. If you are sorting an array of objects, however, you need to supply a comparison function. The comparison function compares two items, a and b. If they are equal, it returns 0. If a is greater than b, then the function returns 1. If a is less than b, it returns –1.

Now you can beef up your Word object, as shown in listing 16.15. The improved Word object will let you add new words, sort the words in the object, produce a list of sorted words, and find a particular word.

Listing 16.15   An Improved *Word* Object Constructor

```
function Word () {
  var argv = Word.arguments;
  var argc = argv.length;
  this.list = new Object();
  for (var i = 0; i < argc; i++)
    this.list[i] = argv[i];
```

```
    this.count = argc;
    pm_array_qsort (this.list,0,this.count-1);
    this.add = AddWord;
    this.find = FindWord;
    this.print = PrintWords;
    this.toString = WordString;
    return this;
}
function AddWord (str) {
    this.list[this.count++] = str;
    pm_array_qsort(this.list,0,this.count-1);
}
function FindWord (str) {
    for (var i = 0; i < this.count; i++)
        if (this.list[i] == str)
            return i;
    return -1;
}
function PrintWords () {
    var str = "";
    for (var i = 0; i < this.count; i++)
        str += this.list[i] + '<br>';
    return str;
}
```

The Word() constructor calls the pm_array_qsort function to sort the original list of words supplied when the object is constructed. You could keep them unsorted instead, and sort them only when output is required. In this case, the design decision is arbitrary, but sometimes it is desirable to maintain an array in sorted form at all times.

The add() method, AddWord(), adds a new word to the end of the array and then sorts the array back into alphabetical sequence.

The find() method, FindWord(), searches the array to see whether a word is present. You use this method in conjunction with the add() method to prevent the user from adding duplicate words.

The print() method, PrintWords(), returns the sorted list of words, separated by HTML br tags.

In listing 16.16, you add some functions that prompt the user for a new word. You also add functions to list all the words for each type.

Listing 16.16   Functions to Prompt the User and List Words

```javascript
function addVerb () {
  var str = prompt ("Enter a verb (eat, kiss, bite, etc.):","");
  if (str == null || str == "")
    return;
  if (verb.find(str) != -1) {
    alert ("\nThat verb is already listed!");
    return;
  }
  verb.add(str);
  listVerbs();
}
function addAdjective () {
  var str = prompt ("Enter an adjective (pretty, smelly, nice,
  ➥etc.):","");
  if (str == null || str == "")
    return;
  if (adjective.find(str) != -1) {
    alert ("\nThat adjective is already listed!");
    return;
  }
  adjective.add(str);
  listAdjectives();
}
function addSingular () {
  var str = prompt ("Enter a singular noun (dog, cat, knife,
  ➥etc.):","");
  if (str == null || str == "")
    return;
  if (singularNoun.find(str) != -1) {
    alert ("\nThat noun is already listed!");
    return;
  }
  singularNoun.add(str);
  listSingular();
}
function addPlural () {
  var str = prompt ("Enter a plural noun (dogs, cats, knives, etc.):", "");
  if (str == null || str == "")
    return;
  if (pluralNoun.find(str) != -1) {
    alert ("\nThat noun is already listed!");
    return;
  }
  pluralNoun.add(str);
  listPlural();
}
function listVerbs () {
  self.show.location =
    "javascript:parent.showList('Verbs',parent.verb.print())";
}
```

```
function listAdjectives () {
  self.show.location =
    "javascript:parent.showList('Adjectives',parent.adjective.print())";
}
function listSingular () {
  self.show.location =
    "javascript:parent.showList('Singular
    ➥Nouns',parent.singularNoun.print())";
}
function listPlural () {
  self.show.location =
    "javascript:parent.showList('Plural
    ➥Nouns',parent.pluralNoun.print())";
}
function showList (title,str) {
  return '<html><body bgcolor="#FFFFFF" text="#0000FF">
  ➥<h1 align="center">' +
    title + '</h1><div align="center"><font size=5>' + str +
    '</font></div></body></html>';
}
```

The addVerb(), addAdjective(), addSingular(), and addPlural() functions prompt the user for a word. If the word is already present in the list, an error message is displayed. Otherwise, the word is added, and the updated list is displayed.

The listVerbs(), listAdjectives(), listSingular(), and listPlural() functions display the word lists by updating the show frame location using a javascript: URL. This URL includes a call to the showList() function, which returns a formatted HTML page listing the words for the given word type.

Finally, you update the control frame to include a set of buttons for adding and listing words, as shown in listing 16.17.

Listing 16.17   The Updated Control Frame

```
var controlFrame =
  '<html><body bgcolor="#808080" text="#FFFFFF">' +
  '<form name="cont">' +
  '<table width=100% height=100% border=0 cellpadding=0 cellspacing=0>' +
  '<tr align="center">' +
  '<td colspan=2><b>Number of Adjectives</b> <select name="adj">' +
  '<option>None' +
  '<option>1' +
  '<option>2' +
  '<option selected>Random' +
  '</select></td>' +
  '<td colspan=2><input type="button" value="Generate Phrase!" ' +
```

continues

Listing 16.17   Continued

```
'onclick="parent.printPhrase()"></td>' +
'</tr>' +
'<tr align="center">' +
'<td><input type="button" value="Add Verb" ' +
'onclick="parent.addVerb()"></td>' +
'<td><input type="button" value="Add Adjective" ' +
'onclick="parent.addAdjective()"></td>' +
'<td><input type="button" value="Add Singular Noun" ' +
'onclick="parent.addSingular()"></td>' +
'<td><input type="button" value="Add Plural Noun" ' +
'onclick="parent.addPlural()"></td>' +
'</tr>' +
'<tr align="center">' +
'<td><input type="button" value="List Verbs" ' +
'onclick="parent.listVerbs()"></td>' +
'<td><input type="button" value="List Adjectives" ' +
'onclick="parent.listAdjectives()"></td>' +
'<td><input type="button" value="List Singular Nouns" ' +
'onclick="parent.listSingular()"></td>' +
'<td><input type="button" value="List Plural Nouns" ' +
'onclick="parent.listPlural()"></td>' +
'</tr>' +
'</table>' +
'</form>' +
'</body></html>';
```

The complete listing of the improved phrase generator is included on the accompanying CD in file 16exm02.htm. One example result is shown in figure 16.3.

FIG. 16.3
The improved phrase generator includes controls to add and view words.

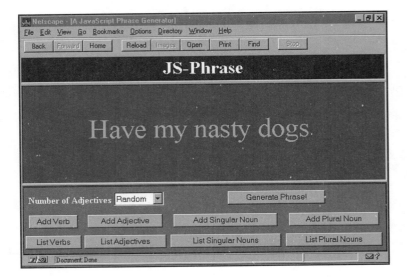

An Online Bookstore

In this section, you develop an online bookstore application. You create a small database of books and provide a way for the user to look up books by subject, author, or title. Along the way, you learn how to parse free-form user input and how to look up items in an indexed database.

Of course, in real life, you can't expect to keep the entire inventory of a bookstore in a single JavaScript document. But the techniques you develop here can be applied to many smaller databases or to results returned by a CGI program on the server.

Parsing Free-Form User Input

Usually, when you process input entered in a text field, the value is treated as a whole. If you are expecting a numeric value, you might check to ensure that the value is, indeed, numeric. You might also check to see that it falls within a certain range or ranges. If you expect an alphanumeric value, you might check it against a list of expected values.

But suppose you want to allow the user to enter a series of values in a single field but process the values individually? A good example is a database lookup or search function, where the user can enter a set of keywords. In that case, you need to *parse* the input field; that is, break it into a list of individual words or terms.

The process of parsing is fairly straightforward. The first step is to define the *whitespace* characters that can separate the terms in your input field. Whitespace is usually defined as blank, or space, characters, and tabs. It may also include carriage returns and linefeeds, as well as certain other nondisplaying characters.

The isWhitespace() function shown in listing 16.18 decides whether the input character is whitespace.

Listing 16.18 The *isWhitespace()* Function

```
function isWhitespace (ch) {
  if (ch == ' ' || ch == '\n' || ch == '\r' || ch == '\t' || ch == '\f' ||
      ch == '\v' || ch == '\b')
    return true;
  return false;
}
```

You may also want to test for certain *delimiter* characters. Common delimiters include commas, forward or backward slashes, periods, and so on. Delimiters can be a meaningful part of the input, or they can be nonessential characters that can be discarded.

The isDelimiter() function shown in listing 16.19 tests for delimiters.

Listing 16.19   The *isDelimiter()* Function

```
function isDelimiter (ch) {
  if (ch == ',' || ch == '?' || ch == '-' || ch == '.' ||
      ch == '\\' || ch == '/')
    return true;
  return false;
}
```

After you decide which whitespace and delimiter characters can separate your terms, you need a place to put the individual terms you extract from the input field. A simple array can do the trick. In this case, you can define a KeywordList object to hold them, shown in listing 16.20. This object will come in handy in the bookstore example.

Listing 16.20   The *KeywordList* Object Constructor

```
function KeywordList () {
  this.count = 0;
  this.word = new Object ();
  this.add = AddKeyword;
  return this;
}
function AddKeyword (word) {
  for (var i = 0; i < this.count; i++)
    if (this.word[i] == word)
      return;
  this.word[this.count++] = word;
}
```

In the bookstore example, you want to allow only unique keywords. Therefore, the add() method, AddKeyword(), prevents duplicate keywords from being added. However, this approach would not be appropriate in many applications. If you don't want to suppress duplicates in your application, then omit the first three lines in the body of the AddKeyword() function.

Now you're ready to write the parser itself, shown in listing 16.21.

Listing 16.21 The *parseKeywords()* Function

```
function parseKeywords (str) {
  var list = new KeywordList ();
  var inword = false;
  var word = "";
  var len = str.length;
  for (var i = 0; i < len; i++) {
    var ch = str.charAt(i);
    if (isWhitespace(ch) || isDelimiter(ch)) {
      if (inword) {
        list.add(word);
        word = "";
        inword = false;
      }
    }
    else {
      word += ch;
      inword = true;
    }
    if (i + 1 == len && inword)
      list.add(word);
  }
  return list;
}
```

The parseKeywords() function accepts a string, which can be the contents of an input field. It returns a KeywordList object, containing a list of the extracted terms.

The parseKeywords() function examines each character in the input string to decide if it is a whitespace or delimiter character. If it is not, the character is added to the current word. If so, the current word, if any, is added to the list, and preparation is made for a new word. You also add the current word to the list when you reach the last character of the input string.

The parseKeywords() function discards delimiter characters because they are not important to the bookstore application. However, delimiters can have special meaning to your application, in which case you might want to add them to the keyword list.

Building an Index

For the example, you want users of your online bookstore to be able to look up books by title, author, or subject. To do so, you must build some indexes for the book database. You use JavaScript's *associative array* feature to create the indexes.

Associative arrays enable you to associate a value with an array entry. You can then use that value to retrieve the desired entry. For example, suppose that you create a simple array named `animal` and associate a name with each entry, as follows:

```
var animal = new Object();
animal["dog"] = "Woof!";
animal["cat"] = "Meow!";
animal["pig"] = "Oink!";
```

The entries `"dog"`, `"cat"`, and `"pig"` correspond to items `0`, `1`, and `2` in the array. To retrieve an item, you can use either its number or the value associated with it, as follows:

```
document.write("A dog says " + animal[0] + "<br>");
document.write("A dog says " + animal["dog"] + "<br>");
```

To take advantage of this capability, you index each word in the book titles, subjects, and author names by creating an entry in an associative array.

The only hitch is that you can have only one entry per value. What if, as is very likely, more than one of the books uses that value in its title, subject, or author? The solution, as it turns out, is fairly simple. Instead of associating an individual book object with each entry in the array, you create a special object that contains a list of the items that match a given value and associate that object with the value.

Listing 16.22 shows the index object, along with its methods and the internal list object.

Listing 16.22   The *Index* and *IndexItemList* Object Constructors

```
function IndexItemList () {
  this.count = 0;
  this.item = new Object();
  this.add = AddIndexItem;
  return this;
```

```
  }
function AddIndexItem (object) {
  this.item[this.count++] = object;
}
function Index () {
  this.count = 0;
  this.item = new Object();
  this.add = AddToIndex;
  return this;
}
function AddToIndex (object, keywords) {
  for (var i = 0; i < keywords.count; i++) {
    var kw = keywords.word[i];
    var ilist = this.item[kw];
    if (ilist == null) {
      ilist = new IndexItemList();
      this.item[kw] = ilist;
    }
    ilist.add(object);
  }
}
```

The IndexItemList object is used internally to store a list of objects that contain a particular keyword value. In the bookstore example, it will contain references to one or more Book objects (which you define shortly) that share a given keyword. The IndexItemList object has a single method, AddIndexItem(). You don't need to access the IndexItemList object directly.

The Index object contains the associative array, item. This array contains a list of IndexItemList objects. Each entry in the array is associated with a value, in this case a keyword. The Index object includes a method to add items to the array. You will write another method to look up entries shortly.

The Index object's add() method, AddToIndex(), accepts an object to be indexed and a list of keywords in the form of a KeywordList object. For each keyword in the KeywordList, AddToIndex() first checks to see whether an IndexItemList object is associated with the keyword. Note that it uses the keyword value itself as an index into the array. If no IndexItemList object exists for the keyword, a new object is created and added to the array, again using the keyword as the index. Finally, the object to be indexed is added to the IndexItemList for that keyword value. This process is repeated for each keyword, so a given object can have several index entries.

Defining Book and Catalog Objects

Now you're ready to create the Book object. In listing 16.23, you also create a Catalog object that contains a list of all books, plus subject, title, and author indexes.

Listing 16.23   The *Book* and *Catalog* Object Constructors

```
function Book (author, title, subject, code, price) {
  this.author = author;
  this.title = title;
  this.subject = subject;
  this.code = code;
  this.price = price;
  return this;
}
function Catalog () {
  this.count = 0;
  this.book = new Object;
  this.author = new Index();
  this.title = new Index();
  this.subject = new Index();
  this.add = AddToCatalog;
  return this;
}
function AddToCatalog (book) {
  this.book[this.count++] = book;
  this.author.add(book,parseKeywords(book.author));
  this.title.add(book,parseKeywords(book.title));
  this.subject.add(book,parseKeywords(book.subject));
}
```

The Book() constructor simply creates an object containing each of the relevant pieces of information about the book.

The Catalog() constructor creates a simple array, book, which contains a single entry for each book. It also creates three Index objects: author, title, and subject.

The Catalog object's add() method, AddToCatalog(), does the really interesting work. First, it adds the book object to the book array. Next, it updates the author, title, and subject indexes. For each of the indexes, it calls the parseKeywords function to create a list of keywords from the value of the field. The Index object's add() method then creates an index entry for each of these values.

In listing 16.24, you create a catalog and add some books to it.

Listing 16.24   Creating a Catalog and Adding Books

```
var cat = new Catalog();
cat.add (new Book ("Kingsolver, Barbara", "Animal Dreams",
   "fiction animals dreams environment Native-American love",
   "ISBN 0-06-092114-5", 13.00));
cat.add (new Book ("Calasso, Roberto",
"The Marriage of Cadmus and Harmony",
   "fiction Greek myth mythology Zeus Athens",
   "ISBN 0-679-73348-5", 13.00));
cat.add (new Book ("Le Carre, John", "The Night Manager",
   "fiction suspense spy arms drugs",
   "ISBN 0-345-38576-4", 6.99));
cat.add (new Book ("Rice, Anne", "Interview with the Vampire",
   "fiction vampire New Orleans gothic horror",
   "ISBN 0-345-33766-2", 4.95));
cat.add (new Book ("Garcia Marquez, Gabriel",
"One Hundred Years of Solitude",
   "fiction South America magic dreams war love",
   "ISBN 0-06-091965-5", 13.00));
cat.add (new Book ("Barkakati, Naba",
"Object-Oriented Programming in C++",
   "nonfiction computer language programming object C",
   "ISBN 0-672-22800-9", 29.95));
cat.add (new Book ("Petzold, Charles", "Programming Windows",
   "nonfiction computer programming C windows",
   "ISBN 1-55615-264-7", 29.95));
```

Well, so far so good. You've got a catalog loaded up with books, and they're all cross-referenced by author, subject, and title. But how do you use this information?

What you need now is a search mechanism. You want the search to return multiple matches for a given set of keywords. Also, ideally, the results should be ranked by how well they match the keywords supplied.

To accomplish this task, you first create an object to hold a list of search results, as shown in listing 16.25.

Listing 16.25   The *Result* and *ResultList* Object Constructors

```
function Result (object, score) {
  this.object = object;
  this.score = score;
  return this;
}
```

continues

Listing 16.25   Continued

```
function ResultList () {
  this.count = 0;
  this.item = new Object();
  this.add = AddResult;
  this.sort = SortResults;
  return this;
}
function AddResult (object) {
  for (var i = 0; i < this.count; i++)
    if (this.item[i].object == object) {
      this.item[i].score++;
      return;
    }
  this.item[this.count++] = new Result (object,1);
}
function SortResults () {
  pm_array_qsort (this.item,0,this.count - 1,CompareResults);
}
function CompareResults (a,b) {
  return (a.score == b.score) ? 0 : (a.score <  b.score) ? 1 : -1;
}
```

The Result object holds an individual object—in this case, a Book object. It also contains a score field. This field indicates the number of "hits" the query gets for this particular object, that is, how many of the keywords specified in the query match this object.

The ResultList object contains a list of Result objects. It contains one Result for each object (book) that matches one or more of the specified keywords. The add() method, AddResult, searches the ResultList for a matching object. If it finds one, it increments the score by one. Otherwise, it creates a new Result entry for the object and sets the score to one.

The sort() method, SortResults(), sorts the Result objects in the ResultList in descending order according to score. That is, the objects with the highest score go to the top of the list. Because you are sorting objects rather than simple strings or numbers, you must supply a comparison function, CompareResults, to the pm_array_qsort() function.

Now you can add the search function. In listing 16.26, you update the Index object to make SearchIndex() the find() method.

Listing 16.26   Adding a *find()* Method to the *Index* Object

```
function Index () {
  this.count = 0;
  this.item = new Object();
  this.add = AddToIndex;
  this.find = SearchIndex;
  return this;
}
function SearchIndex (keywords) {
  var rlist = new ResultList();
  for (var i = 0; i < keywords.count; i++) {
    var kw = keywords.word[i];
    var ilist = this.item[kw];
    if (ilist != null)
      for (var j = 0; j < ilist.count; j++)
        rlist.add(ilist.item[j]);
  }
  rlist.sort();
  return rlist;
}
```

The find() method, SearchIndex(), takes a KeywordList object containing a list of words to search for. It first uses the keyword value to do an associative array lookup to retrieve the IndexItemList object, if any, for the given keyword. Then it calls the ResultList object's add() method to add each matching object to the result list, or increment the score for that object if it was already added to the list. This process is repeated for each search term specified. Finally, the ResultList is sorted by score and returned to the caller.

The Bookstore

You've got all the tricky pieces worked out, so you can build an interface and open your bookstore. You can make a control frame with a selection list for author, title, or subject, and a text field for keyword entry. A Search button starts the search. In listing 16.27, you write some functions to process this information and display the results.

Listing 16.27   Creating the Bookstore Interface

```
var controlFrame =
  '<html><body bgcolor="#808080" text="#FFFFFF">' +
```

continues

Listing 16.27 Continued

```
'<form name="cont">' +
'<table border=0 width=100% height=100% cellpadding=0 cellspacing=0>' +
'<tr align="center" valign="center">' +
'<td><b>Search by: </b><select name="stype">' +
'<option selected>Title' +
'<option>Author' +
'<option>Subject' +
'</select></td>' +
'<td><b>Keywords: </b><input size=30 name="keywords"></td>' +
'<td><input type="button" value="Search" ' +
'onclick="parent.doSearch()"></td>' +
'</tr></table>' +
'</form>' +
'</body></html>';

var results = null;

function doSearch () {
  var index = self.control.document.cont.stype.selectedIndex;
  var keywords = parseKeywords
    ➥(self.control.document.cont.keywords.value);
  if (index == 0)
    results = cat.title.find (keywords);
  else if (index == 1)
    results = cat.author.find (keywords);
  else
    results = cat.subject.find (keywords);
  self.show.location = "javascript:parent.showList()";
}

function showBook (item) {
  var book = results.item[item].object;
  var detail = book.author + '<br>' + book.title + '<br>' +
    book.subject + '<br>' + book.code + '<br>$' + book.price + '<br>' +
    '<h3><a href="javascript:parent.showList()">Return to list</h3>';
  return '<html><body bgcolor="#FFFFFF" text="#000000" link="#0000FF" ' +
    'alink="#FF0000"><div align="center"><table border=0><tr><td>' +
    detail + '</td></tr></table></body></html>';
}

function showList () {
  var list = "";
  for (var i = 0; i < results.count; i++)
    list += '<a href="javascript:parent.showBook(' + i + ')">' +
      '(' + results.item[i].score + ')  ' +
      results.item[i].object.author + ':  ' +
      results.item[i].object.title + '</a><br>';
  if (list.length == 0)
    list = '<h2 align="center">Sorry, no matches found</h2>';
  return '<html><body bgcolor="#FFFFFF" text="#000000" link="#0000FF" ' +
```

```
'alink="#FF0000"><div align="center"><table border=0><tr><td>' +
list + '</td></tr></table></body></html>';
}
```

Clicking the Search button calls the `doSearch()` function. This function examines the selection list and performs the appropriate search. The result list is placed in a global variable called `results`. The `doSearch()` function then loads the `show` frame with a `javascript:` URL that calls `showList()`.

The `showList()` function, in turn, reads the result list and creates a one-line entry for each book, consisting of the score (number of matching terms), along with the book's author and title. Each entry is enclosed in an `HREF` that calls the `showBook()` function to display details about the book.

The `showBook()` function displays each of the fields in the `Book` object. It also includes an `HREF` back to the `showList()` function so that the user can return to the result list of the current search.

That's it! Your bookstore is open for business. The complete listing is included on the accompanying CD in file 16exm03.htm.

Figure 16.4 shows the resulting list of titles based on a search of the keyword `love`, and figure 16.5 shows the complete author, title, and subject information for one book.

FIG. 16.4
Each book matching the search term is listed.

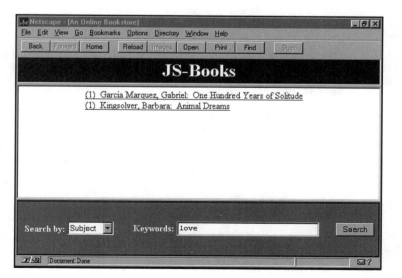

FIG. 16.5
Selecting a book shows a detailed listing.

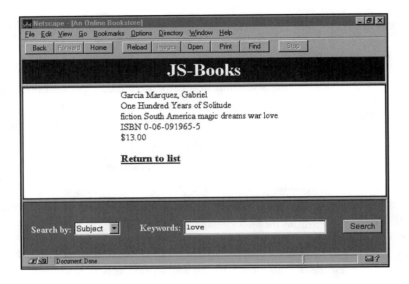

Improved Indexing and Searching

The indexing and searching algorithms do a good job of finding matching entries, but they suffer from a couple of drawbacks.

First, the user must enter keywords exactly as they were specified when the Book object was created. One obvious improvement is to store all keywords in lowercase and convert search words to lowercase before beginning the search.

But what if the user enters the plural or past tense version of a word? What if the user includes (or fails to include) apostrophes, quotation marks, or other punctuation symbols? The search engine will break down and fail to return any matching items.

You can address this problem to some extent by *normalizing* all keywords before adding them to the index or performing a lookup. Normalizing a word means reducing it to something akin to a root word. This process is not easy; volumes have been written and fortunes spent on developing effective indexing and searching algorithms. But you can use a few simple techniques to improve your search results dramatically.

First, create a function to normalize a word, as shown in listing 16.28.

Listing 16.28 The *normalizeWord()* Function

```javascript
function normalizeWord (keyword) {
  var esc = escape (keyword.toLowerCase());
  var kw = "";
  for (var i=0; i < esc.length; i++) {
    var ch = esc.charAt(i);
    if (ch == '%')
      i += 2;
    else
      kw += ch;
  }
  var len = kw.length;
  if (kw.charAt(len-1) == "s" && kw.charAt(len-2) != "s") {
    kw = kw.substring(0,len-1);
    len—;
  }
  if (kw.substring(len-2,len) == "ly") {
    kw = kw.substring(0,len-2);
    len -= 2;
  }
  if (kw.substring(len-2,len) == "ed") {
    kw = kw.substring(0,len-1);
    len—;
  }
  if (kw.substring(len-2,len) == "er") {
    kw = kw.substring(0,len-1);
    len—;
  }
  if (kw.substring(len-2,len) == "ie") {
    kw = kw.substring(0,len-2) + "y";
    len—;
  }
  if (kw.substring(len-3,len) == "ing" && len > 5) {
    kw = kw.substring(0,len-3);
    len -= 3;
    if (isVowel(kw.charAt(len-2)) && !isVowel(kw.charAt(len-3))) {
      kw += "e";
      len++;
    }
  }
  if (kw.charAt(len-1) == "e")
    if (!isVowel(kw.charAt(len-3))) {
      kw = kw.substring(0,len-1);
      len—;
    }
  if (len > 1 && (kw.charAt(len-1) == kw.charAt(len-2))) {
    kw = kw.substring(0,len-1);
    len—;
  }
  return kw;
}
```

The `normalizeWord()` function starts by converting the keyword to lowercase. Next, it strips out any punctuation marks or other unusual characters. To strip the characters, it calls JavaScript's `escape()` function, which converts all unusual characters to a percent sign (%) followed by two ASCII characters. These characters are then removed.

The `normalizeWord()` function then makes a series of transformations based on the word ending. Note that the order of these transformations is important. I won't go into detail on each transformation here. The goal is to reach a root version of the word. It isn't necessarily the true English root, but as long as you perform the same transformations on both the indexed words and the search words, you should improve chances of getting a match.

N O T E The transformations applied by the `normalizeWord()` function are useful only for English words. The call to `escape()` strips out accented letters, for instance, and the word ending transformations are meaningful only for English words. However, creating a similar function for other languages should be possible. ■

The other problem with this indexing scheme is that it indexes and searches for many words that are extraneous, such as "the," "and," "a," and so on. Most indexing and searching programs use a list of *stop words* to exclude extraneous words. These lists are often quite extensive, but you can write a simple function to deal with the worst offenders. Listing 16.29 shows a simple `isStopword()` function.

Listing 16.29   The *isStopword()* Function

```
function isStopword (word) {
  var wd = word.toLowerCase();
  if (wd == "a" || wd == "an" || wd == "and" ||
      wd == "or" || wd == "the")
    return true;
  return false;
}
```

Finally, you can modify the `parseKeywords()` function to call `normalizeWord()` and `isStopword()`, as shown in listing 16.30.

Listing 16.30   The Improved *parseKeywords()* Function

```
function parseKeywords (str) {
  var list = new KeywordList ();
  var inword = false;
  var word = "";
  var len = str.length;
  for (var i = 0; i < len; i++) {
    var ch = str.charAt(i);
    if (isWhitespace(ch) || isDelimiter(ch)) {
      if (inword) {
        if (!isStopword(word))
          list.add(normalizeWord(word));
        word = "";
        inword = false;
      }
    }
    else {
      word += ch;
      inword = true;
    }
    if (i + 1 == len && inword)
      if (!isStopword(word))
        list.add(normalizeWord(word));
  }
  return list;
}
```

The improvements made here are included in file 16exm03.htm on the CD. A number of additional improvements could be made, including better handling of symbols, and boolean *AND* and *OR* operations, to name a few. ●

CHAPTER 17

JavaScript on the Server

by Ray Daly

So far the focus in this book has been on using JavaScript on the client side. This chapter looks at how JavaScript is becoming an integral part of the other side—the server.

JavaScript extends the capabilities of the server. By providing a scripting language the software can do more without calling an external program. This makes it easier for Webmasters to add features to their sites that browsers can take advantage of. And it can reduce the load on the server by keeping the processing within the server software.

This chapter looks at the LiveWire environment from Netscape. LiveWire itself is not a server, but works with Netscape servers to create applications that make pages come alive. ■

How LiveWire uses JavaScript

With some experience using JavaScript on a browser, you might want to try your hand using JavaScript on the server side.

The LiveWire environment exposes four objects

The JavaScript you used on the browser uses objects. On the server, you have server objects available to you.

CGI scripts are replaced by JavaScript

With LiveWire, you can respond to server requests using JavaScript without having to call external routines.

Save data on the server hard drive

Contrary to what you may have heard, JavaScript can save data on a hard drive. However, the hard drive and the script must be on the server. (For security reasons, you cannot save it on the users' hard drive.)

An Overview of LiveWire

LiveWire from Netscape is an integrated, visual environment for building client-server applications for Internet or enterprise networks. These applications can be for the public to access or limited to a specific audience such as an intranet.

▶ **See** chapter 18, "Tools for JavaScript Development," for further discussion on LiveWire, **p. 629**.

LiveWire is actually a suite. It consists of the Netscape Navigator Gold, LiveWire Site Manager, LiveWire Server Extensions, LiveWire Server Front Panel, and JavaScript. LiveWire runs on the UNIX and Windows NT operating systems.

This chapter details the use of JavaScript in LiveWire. Given the nature of JavaScript, it is believed that other servers that incorporate JavaScript will work similarly.

N O T E JavaScript on the server is nearly identical to JavaScript on the browser including the syntax and the statements. There are also several shared objects: string, math, and date objects. However, most objects are specific to the application. This chapter covers the objects unique to LiveWire. ▣

Live Objects and Properties

LiveWire has four built-in objects: request, client, project, and server. Obviously these are related. Each server can run multiple projects. Any project can have multiple simultaneous clients using it. And most clients request more than one page. A graphical depiction of this relationship is shown in figure 17.1.

Request Object

Each time a browser wants more information it sends a request to a server. Data about these requests are available on the server from the request object in JavaScript. If you have written CGI scripts, you should be familiar with the properties that are built into the request object.

FIG. 17.1
While there can be only one
`server` object, there can
be several `project`
objects, more `client`
objects, and many more
`request` objects. However,
this picture is not static
since `request` and
`client` objects only exist
for short periods of time.

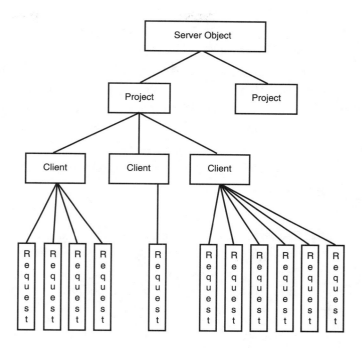

The Built-In Properties   The `request` object is initialized with four properties:
`agent`, `ip`, `method`, and `protocol`. A JavaScript function on the server can use this
information to determine its response to the request. The following list provides
details about each property:

- `agent`—This property tells the server about the client's software, usually a
  browser. This information is a line of text, but there is no standard format to
  this text. The same browser always presents the same information. For
  example, if you use Netscape Navigator 2.0 and your friend uses Netscape
  Navigator 2.0, the same information is sent by either of you when you access
  this server.

- `ip`—The `ip` property provides the IP address of the client. This tells the
  server from where on the Internet the request is sent and where to return a
  response. IP addresses are composed of a set of four numbers. Each is a
  value between 0 and 255. A sample IP number is 127.0.0.1.

  Usually the IP address you use when connecting with a host is unique, and
  no one else on the Net can use that address until you complete your session.

However, there are special cases of caches, proxies, and firewalls that require further study if you plan to use this property.

IP addresses can often be used to tell which domain is connecting to the server. By using what is called *reverse lookup*, the server can often determine the domain name of the client computer. You might use this to determine how many hits are coming from America Online or any other site.

■ method—This property provides the HTTP method associated with the request. There are three methods currently used: get, post, and head.

■ protocol—This is a standard text indicating the level of HTTP protocol used by the client. Currently this should be HTTP/1.0 in every case.

Other *Request* Properties A request may include additional information. Your browser's request may have resulted from submitting information from an HTML form. This information becomes a request property. It does not matter if the data is submitted with either the post or get method. The name of each element of the form becomes a property name.

For example, take a form with a text element with the name of answer. Complete the text box with a value of "59" and submit it to the server. The server receives the information in the form of "answer=59." The request object now has a property called request.answer which reflects the value of "59."

You can also store information in request properties. One property you might want to consider adding is a time and date stamp. Remember that the life of a request object is rather short, so values stored in these properties are not stored for long.

> **CAUTION**
>
> The request property in LiveWire reserves the names of ip, agent, method, and protocol for its own use. Therefore, if you plan to submit information from a form, make sure that your form does not use these names for its elements.

Application of *Request* Properties These built-in properties allow the server to vary the response to the request. The agent property is commonly used to supply different HTML documents to different types of browsers. For example, an HTML page with tables might only be served to a limited number of browsers while others receive a different version of the page.

Servers may limit access to certain information to specific IP addresses. Using the ip property, the server might only provide sensitive company information to clients requesting it from known company computers. Usually you want additional security, just screening IP addresses is not enough.

If a property is added for the date and time, it might be used to serve different responses. Perhaps certain parts of your site are only accessible after hours; or perhaps the graphics change depending on the time of day; or you could send a holiday greeting.

Obviously, form data sent to a server should generate a response. Perhaps a simple "thank you" and this form information is stored on the server's hard drive. Many sites have guestbooks that work this way. Other applications process the information and return a calculated response. For example, the information can be a message to append to an existing Web page. The response might acknowledge the submission but also display the updated page.

Part
IV
Ch
17

Client Object

Each time a new client accesses the server application, a new client object is created. However, there are no built-in properties for the client object. If you need information retained about the client, then you create a property.

***Client* Properties**   A very common use for a client property is a client identification number. When the client first accesses the server, he can receive a form. The server can then process this information and assign the client an identification number. This might be randomly generated or looked up from a list of previous customers.

As an example, a client can send a request. Part of the request can include a user supplied customer number in the text box named idnumber. You can then create a client property called custNo with the following line:

```
client.custNo = request.idnumber
```

***Client* Objects Expire**   The server overflows with client objects unless they are properly deleted. Since client objects are automatically created for each and every client to access, then there must be a mechanism for deleting them.

LiveWire automatically deletes any `client` object with no property values. So if you don't use a `client` object, you don't have to worry about deleting it. In other words, you only have to clean up after yourself.

The default expiration is ten minutes of inactivity. If the client does not send another request to the server within ten minutes of the previous request, the object expires.

Obviously, in many cases ten minutes is insufficient time and, therefore, you might want to manually control this. You can simply use the `expiration` statement

```
client.expiration(seconds)
```

where `seconds` is the number of seconds before the client expires.

Another manual control is `destroy`. If you no longer need the `client` object, simply use the statement

```
client.destroy()
```

LiveWire looks at the client that sent the request and destroys its `client` object. This eliminates all of the `client` object's properties as well.

Cookies Store Information Between Sessions Another technique for retaining client information is cookies. The browser must support the Netscape cookie protocol. If supported, the server sends the information to the client as name/value pairs. Obviously, this increases network traffic, but can offer substantial advantages to large access servers.

> **N O T E** For more information about cookies see **http://home.netscape.com/newsref/std/cookie_spec.html**. ■

There are several other techniques for maintaining this information. However, they all have limited application. Client URL encoding causes a large increase in network traffic. Using IP addresses on the server only works for clients using fixed IP addresses. This might work for some intranet applications; for general use, it is worthless. For more details, refer to the LiveWire documentation.

Project Objects

Each application, when started, creates project objects. This is global data for the entire application. Every client that accesses the application shares these objects.

Properties for *Project* Objects　The project object has no pre-defined properties. If you need to hold information for your project, you create the objects you need in the application.

Many projects need to store values. For example, in billing a customer you might need the next invoice number. This number is incremented when another invoice is generated.

Lock *Project* Objects　In any multi-user environment you must deal with cases of simultaneous access. On file servers, you lock a file while you are using it. You unlock it when you are finished with the operation. The other user must wait for you to finish.

If you do not lock files, the data can be corrupted. A simple example is with two people editing a document. If both are editing at the same time, then one saves his changes before the other. The problem is that the first set of changes are over written by the second.

Project objects should also be locked when in use. In your task, simply start with the line

```
project.lock();
```

Next, include your statements. For example,

```
invoiceno = invoiceno + 1
```

Then unlock the object with

```
project.unlock();
```

Server Objects

Global data for the entire server are in the server objects. These objects can be shared between applications. There are also a few objects that tell you about the server. Any request, client, or project can access these objects.

The Built-In *Server* Properties　The server object is initialized with the following two properties:

- agent—This provides name and version information about the server as a line of text. Netscape's Commerce Server is `Netscape-Commerce/1.12`.

- protocol—This is a standard text indicating the level of HTTP protocol used by the client. Currently this is `HTTP/1.0` for almost every case.

Adding *Server* Properties   As with most JavaScript objects, you can add properties to `server` objects. For example, you might want to add the time the server was last accessed. This might be read by a monitoring routine, as follows:

```
today = new Date()
server.accesstime = today.getTime()
```

As with `project` objects, `server` objects should be locked. Since you can have more than one process accessing the object at one time, you should use the same locking procedure as discussed for `project` objects.

External Process Communications: JavaScript and CGIs

Undoubtedly with your active interest in building Web sites, you have dealt with Common Gateway Interface (CGI) scripts. Prior to JavaScript, this was the primary means of creating interactive applications. Libraries of CGI scripts include counters, e-mailers, message boards, and many other functions.

LiveWire can replace CGI programming. Instead of calling external programs, the server software runs applications that are closely integrated to it. JavaScript is the language of these applications.

Applications are developed with three tools. You build these applications using LiveWire's Site Manager. The source files for the applications are developed using the same HTML editors used to build browser JavaScript pages. The applications run in response to requests from Netscape Navigator.

Steps to Building a LiveWire Application

Building a LiveWire application is not unlike other development procedures. The process can be done using either a command line compiler or a graphic interface.

The following are the steps to create a LiveWire application:

1. Create the source files (see the section "LiveWire Source Files" later in this chapter).

2. Using the graphic interface of Site Manager (see fig. 17.2), you must bring the files under site management. You do this by selecting the application directory on the screen and choosing Site, Manage. (For the command-line compiler, you can skip this step.)

FIG. 17.2
LiveWire's Site Manager displays your site directory in a tree structure where you specify which part of the site you want to manage. The directories managed by LiveWire are highlighted with a red marker.

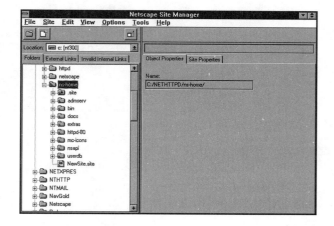

3. Build the application by creating a compiled *.web file.

4. Install the application using the LiveWire Application Manager (see fig. 17.3).

5. If you rebuild the application, restart it using the Application Manager.

6. Run the application by loading any of the pages with your browser.

Browsing into a LiveWire Application

Like any other Web site, a browser requests a Web page to access a LiveWire application. The browser can request any of the pages within an application. The server sees the request like any other request, though it is handled differently. In turn, the browser is not concerned if the HTML is a static page or from a dynamic LiveWire application. The form of the URL is as follows:

```
http://server.domain/application/page.html
```

FIG. 17.3
LiveWire's Application Manager installs the applications you develop. The Application Manager itself is a LiveWire application and is listed on the first line.

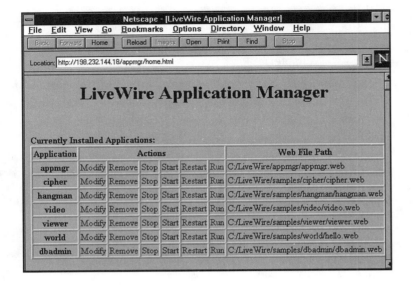

In this case the `domain` is the Internet domain and the server is the name of the HTTP server. The next element, `application`, is the name you define when the application is installed with the Application Manager. The final part, `page.html`, is simply the name of any page in the application. Each application has a default page. So if `page.html` is the default for this application, the `page.html` at the end of the URL would be optional.

In the following example,

```
http://home.myserver.com/callhome/phonebook.html
```

the page `phonebook.html` is severed from an application named `callhome`. This application resides on the server called `home` at the domain of `myserver.com`.

LiveWire Source Files

To build a LiveWire application, you construct one or more source files. The following are three types of files you can build:

- Standard HTML—These are your regular HTML pages. .html or .htm are the file extensions.

- HTML with JavaScript—These are HTML pages that have JavaScript embedded in them. The JavaScript is placed in the HTML document using either the SERVER tag or backquote (sometimes called back-tick). Again, .html or .htm are the file extensions for these documents.

- JavaScript functions—These are documents that consist solely of JavaScript code. A new file extension, .js, is used for these documents.

Using the *SERVER* Tag   The SERVER tag contains JavaScript that either executes a statement or produces HTML with the write function. A JavaScript statement can be a rather simple routine or a more complex set of functions.

Using the SERVER tag with JavaScript to produce HTML is very common. As a very simple example, you might create a document that returns the IP address to the browser, as follows:

```
<P>Your request came from ip address:
<SERVER> write(request.ip) </SERVER>
```

When using the SERVER tag, the result is sent in response to the request. The source code that contains the SERVER tag and your logic stays secure on the server. This is different than HTML pages that contain JavaScript where the browser gets all of the source code.

Using the Backquote   A shorthand method of putting JavaScript into the HTML document is to use the backquote ('). Using the backquote, the HTML is automatically generated without having to use the write statement.

Our preceding example would simply become

```
<P>Your request came from ip address:  'request.ip' </P>
```

The backquote is especially useful when the JavaScript produces an attribute value. Generally, HTML tags have the form of

```
<TAG ATTRIB="value" [...ATTRIB=VAL]>
```

where ATTRIB is the attribute and value is its value. Backquoted JavaScript can substitute for any attribute or value in this syntax.

CAUTION

Mixing backquotes with double quotes can confuse the compiler and you. The simple rule is that the backquote comes first. Everything inside the backquotes is treated as a JavaScript expression. If you place the backquote inside the double quote, then it is interpreted literally.

The JavaScript Balancing Act

When interactivity was only done with a CGI, all of the processing was done on the server. Because JavaScript can run on both the server and the browser, writing a successful application requires you to properly allocate the processing between the two.

Let the Browser Handle Much of the Work   Previous chapters detailed how JavaScript on the browser side can handle a great deal of processing. In general, let the browser code "polish" the information before sending it to the server. The following are several different tasks best handled by the browser:

- Validate user inputs
- Check that the values are within range
- Prompt for confirmations
- Verify inputs that are valid, but not usual
- Perform aggregate calculations (totals, averages, means, sales tax)
- Conditionalize HTML
- Perform other functions that require no server data

More Work for the Server   Though the browser code can take much of the burden off the server, the server still must perform. Given the increasingly interactive nature of Web applications, the demands on the server are increasing. The following types of tasks should be performed by the server:

- Direct the flow from one page to another
- Maintain data about the client from one request to the next
- Maintain the shared data among clients and applications
- Access various databases
- Access various files on the server (for example, multimedia)
- Call C libraries, as needed
- Dynamic customization of Java applets

Obviously, the server is a busy fellow. And this load is expected to grow dramatically as servers provide multimedia material and more interactivity.

Exchanging Information between the Browser and Server

In making your application come alive, the server and browser must exchange information. The client, or browser, typically sends user responses. These can first be "polished" by JavaScript routines on the browser side. The server in turn sends data back to the browser as HTML pages.

From Client to Server   User responses are submitted just as you currently handle forms. The user completes the form and clicks the submit button. The data from the radio buttons, checkboxes, textboxes, and textarea are sent to the server. The server then places this data into the `request` object. Each element of the form has a corresponding property.

> **N O T E**   Consider adding hidden files to your forms. Then, prior to submitting the data, have a JavaScript routine that processes the user input and puts the result into the hidden field's value property. Practical uses are totals, averages, word counts, and other mathematical results. This takes some of the load off the server. ■

From Server to Client   Usually a server only returns a static page in response to a browser request. In LiveWire, the response is still a page, but the contents of the page vary. User input can result in changes to default form values, new values of hidden form elements, or direct substitutions.

A server-side JavaScript can dynamically build in the HTML code for a form element that is part of the page. As an example, you can have the following statement in a source document:

```
<INPUT TYPE="text"  NAME="example" VALUE='request.agent'>
```

In this case the default value of the text is the browser `agent` information.

You use an identical procedure for hidden form elements. The only difference is that the type is `hidden` instead of `text`. Your client-side JavaScript can then use this value as part of any function.

Another means of making your pages come alive is to change part of the JavaScript code. When you send a page to the browser it can contain JavaScript code for the browser to execute as part of the page. There is no reason that this code has to be static.

Part
IV
Ch
17

The server can modify the page being sent to change the JavaScript code embedded in the page. The page on the server side might include

```
<SERVER>
write ("<SCRIPT>var luck = " + client.winnings + "</SCRIPT>")
</SERVER>
```

Assuming the value of `client.winnings` is 1000, the browser sees a line of

```
<SCRIPT>var luck =  1000 </SCRIPT>
```

External Files and Databases with JavaScript

In building a non-trivial application, you need to be able to read and write data from a file. It can be customer information, data about merchandise, or student grades. This is a basic procedure in almost every application.

LiveWire provides a `file` object. This allows your application to write to the server's file system. As a security measure, JavaScript on the browser does not permit saving data to the file system.

N O T E LiveWire Pro adds support for Structured Query Language (SQL) databases. It supports Informix, Oracle, Sybase, and Microsoft databases. ■

CAUTION

Don't give your users an open invitation to fill up your hard drive or otherwise abuse your system. Check the volume. Consider disallowing repetitive entries from the same IP address.

Create the New *File* Object

Like other JavaScript operations, file handling is also done using objects. LiveWire provides a `file` object and you create new objects for each file you want to use. If you need to use `file` files, then create a new `file` object for each one.

Use the standard syntax in creating `file` objects:

```
fileObjectName = new File("path")
```

In this case "path" is the file path relative to the application directory. This is not a URL, but uses the server's file system format—for example, /mydirectory/sample.txt.

Each `file` object has numerous methods that you can use. However, you must first open the file.

Open the File

After you create the `file` object, you then need to open the file before you can do anything else with it. To open the file, you use the `open` method, as follows:

```
result=fileObjectName.open ("mode")
```

The result is `true` if the file was opened successfully; otherwise it is `false`.

Part

IV

Ch

17

> **CAUTION**
>
> If the file is already opened, this operation fails. The original file object remains unchanged and open. You should test for this possibility since simultaneous requests can be sent to any LiveWire application.

A file is opened for reading and/or writing. You might want to create a new file, replace an old file, or just append to the end of an existing file. Using one of the following modes, you can open a file in any of these modes:

- r—Opens the file as a test file for reading, if it exists, and returns `true`. If the file does not exist, it returns `false`.

- w—Opens the file as a text file for writing. Creates a new (initially empty) text file whether the file exists or not.

- a—Opens the file as a text file for appending (writing at the end of the file). If the file does not already exist, it is created.

- r+—Opens the file as a text file for reading and writing. Reading and writing commence at the beginning of the file.

- w+—Opens the file as a text file for reading and writing. Creates a new (initially empty) file whether the file already exists or not.

- a+—Opens the file as a text file for reading and writing. Reading and writing commence at the end of the file. If the file does not exist, it is created.

You may have noticed that each of these methods deals only with text files. LiveWire provides you with an option to save the file in a binary format. Just append a b to any of these modes.

N O T E Forgot the filename? Simply use the write method to display it. For example, the following results in the display of the filename:

```
write ( fileObjectName )
```

File Positioning

When dealing with data stored in a file, you must consider where in the file the desired data is stored or where you intend to store it. You may not want to read the first three items, but you do want to read the next two items. The file object allows you to read the current position, change the position, or check if you are at the end of the file.

When you open a file, the current position depends on the mode you use to open it. Generally it starts at the beginning of a file, except for modes a+ and a where data is appended at the end of an existing file. For empty or new files, the end of the file and the beginning of the file are the same.

The current position in the file is available using the getPosition method. The first byte in a file is 0 and any other position is a positive number. An error is indicated by returning a -1. The syntax is

```
x =  fileObj.getPosition()
```

The setPosition method changes or sets the current position. You can change the position relative to the beginning of the file, relative to the end of the file, or relative to the current position. This is called the *reference*, and is an optional parameter. The default reference is the beginning of the file.

The syntax for the setPosition method is

```
fileObj.setPosition(position [,reference])
```

where reference is a numeric value—0 relative to the beginning of the file, 1 relative to the current position, and 2 relative to the end of the file. This method returns true if successful; otherwise, false.

For example, if the current position was 10 with the end file at 20, the following would be the results:

```
fileObject.setPosition ( 3)      /...new position is 3
fileObject.setPosition(2,0)      /...new position is 2
fileObject.setPosition(-2,1)     /...new position is 8
fileObject.setPosition(-2,2)     /...new position is 18
```

In reading a file you often want to read through the entire thing, but to do so you need to know when you have reached the end. So you test for the end of the file (eof). The `file` object has the `eof` method that returns a `true` after the first read operation that attempts to read past the end of the file.

```
fileObj.eof()
```

Writing with the *File* Object

The `file` object provides three methods of writing data to a file. These methods allow you to write a string, write a string followed by a `\n` (see the following note), or write a single byte to a file. Each method returns `true` if successful; otherwise it returns `false`.

The syntax is

```
fileObj.write(string)
fileObj.writeln(string)
fileObj.writeByte(number)
```

Like most languages, when data is sent to a file it is stored in a buffer to increase efficiencies. This internal buffer stores the data until the buffer is full, until the file is closed, or when flushed. (Flushed means the code forces the data in the buffer to write to the file.) Then it physically writes the data into the file.

To ensure that your data is properly saved, you can force a flush with the `flush` method. The syntax is

```
fileObj.flush()
```

Reading with the *File* Object

Just as there are three methods of writing to a file, so there are three methods to reading a file. You can read a specific number of bytes, read in the entire next line, or read in a single byte. Each method returns `true` if successful, otherwise it returns `false`. The syntax is

```
fileObj.read(count)
fileObj.readln()
fileObj.readByte()
```

N O T E On Windows systems, text files typically end a line of text with a carriage return and an end of line character (\r\n). On UNIX systems, the line ends with a single end of line character. To accommodate both formats, when using the `writeln` method, JavaScript adds one or both characters at the end of the line depending on the server platform. When reading a file, the line separator characters are not included when using the `readln` method. ▪

Converting Data

The data in any of your files is stored in either ASCII text format or binary. The `file` object has two methods for converting from one format to the other. Both methods, which follow, are static, so no object is required.

- ▪ The `stringToByte` method—Converts the first character of a string into a number. Characters after the first are ignored. The result is a numeric value to the first character or zero.

- ▪ The `byteToString` method—Converts a number into a one-character string. If the argument is not a string, the result is an empty string.

The syntax of these methods is

```
File.byteToString(number)
File.StringToByte(string)
```

Error Checking and Getting Information

Often you just want basic information about a file. Does the file exist? How long is the file?

The `exists` method returns a simple `true` if the file exists, otherwise it returns `false`. For example,

```
fileObj.exists()
```

The `getLength` method returns the number of bytes in a file. For a text file, it returns the number of characters. In case of an error, it returns a -1. For example,

```
fileObj.getLength()
```

LiveWire also allows you to check on the error status of a file or clear the error status. Since error status codes are platform dependent, you must check your operating system documentation for the actual codes. The syntax for these methods is

```
fileObj.error()
fileObj.clearError()
```

Example Using the *File* Object

Let's do a very simple example. Let's take an existing text file and copy it into a new file. The example in listing 17.1 does not include error checking. In a real application you would want to add this to the code. For example, you might want to check if anyone else is already using the file.

Listing 17.1   Copying a File on LiveWire

```
oldFile = new File ("oldtext.txt")      /...create object for existing
                                           text file
newFile = new File ("newtext.txt")      /...create object for new file

result1 = oldFile.open("r")             /...open file for reading only
result2 = newFile.open("w")
     /...open file, initially empty, for writing

until oldFile.eof() {
     /...until the end of the file is reached
     result3 = newFile.writeln(oldFile.readln())
     /...read a line from the old file and write it to the new file
}
result4 = oldFile.close()      /...close each file
result5 = newFile.close()
```

CHAPTER 18

Tools for JavaScript Development

by Scott J. Walter

Although JavaScript is still a "fledgling" language, its popularity among Web content developers is growing at an exponential rate. Providing an easy means to extend the capability of a site without having (necessarily) to write extensive Java applets (or learn the intimacies of object-oriented programming), JavaScript makes an effective "glue" to integrate Java, frames, and browser plug-ins into one seamless site.

Because of its newness, support tools that ease the creation of JavaScript documents are few. At the time this book was written, in fact, there was nothing available specifically to make it easier for developers to integrate JavaScript into their Web sites.

The best combination of tools to use in JavaScript development is Netscape Navigator and a plain-text editor (such as Windows

You will need a basic JavaScript Starter Kit

A toolset consisting of a browser, HTML editor, a graphics package, and a simple JavaScript framework.

Don't forget Netscape Navigator Gold

Use Netscape's integrated browser/editor to help build Web pages.

And then there's Netscape's LiveWire Pro

Implement server-side JavaScript.

Check out a "live" editing session

Put the Starter Kit to work by creating a simple electronic magazine framework driven by JavaScript.

Notepad), because it isn't easy to access SCRIPT tags in most HTML editors—in some, it isn't even possible yet. As more Java-oriented tools become available on the market or through the Internet, more will also support JavaScripting. ■

A JavaScript Starter Kit

Because a JavaScript editor is not currently available, it's necessary to build a collection of tools that make the process of scripting Web content as painless as possible. The following is a good basic collection of tools to have at your disposal:

- Navigator 2.0 or Navigator Gold 2.0 (in browser mode)
- A simple text editor (NotePad, WordPad, TextPad, etc.)
- A flexible graphics program (Paint Shop Pro, Lview Pro, etc.)
- A simple JavaScript template

Developing JavaScript-enabled content is not always a quick process. It takes some thought, some effort, and a lot of shifting from your editor to your browser... correcting some things and tweaking others. After you design a few pages, you will develop your own system for editing and testing. The quality of the tool you use is not important; that the tool works for you is.

Navigator and Navigator Gold 2.0

Netscape Navigator 2.0 is a standard on the Web; according to some surveys, it is used by 70 percent of all Web surfers. In an effort to make Web content development easier for the masses, Netscape has released a Gold version of Navigator. Navigator Gold merges the power of Navigator 2.0 with a WYSIWYG-based HTML editor.

Navigator Gold is primarily geared toward end-user creation of "straightforward" pages, with support limited to HTML 2.0. Rather than bombarding the user with HTML tags, Gold hides all but the end result. Formatting text, adding headings, creating links, and inserting graphics are all easily accomplished with the click of a mouse.

The integration between browser and editor is smooth and clean as well. Any page you load in the browser can be opened in the Editor by choosing File, Edit Document, or by choosing the Edit icon on the toolbar (see fig. 18.1).

FIG. 18.1
Choosing the Edit icon will switch to edit mode for the current document (closing the browser window). If you wish to open the editor in a separate window, choose Edit Document from the File menu.

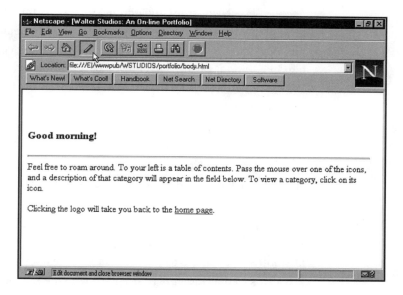

Part
IV

Ch
18

In edit mode, the visual display of the page changes (see fig. 18.2), the major difference being that any JavaScript instructions will be displayed in red.

FIG. 18.2
Editing the same page with Navigator Gold keeps the visual layout consistent with the display from the browser, but also shows JavaScript statements.

JavaScript coding

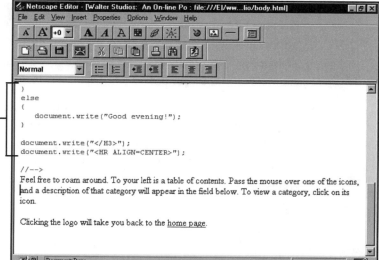

As previously stated, Gold is primarily designed for creation of simple end-user pages. It's a good editor for laying out the basic look and feel of a site. However, there are several things to be aware of:

- *Frames.* The Navigator Gold editor loads a document with FRAMESET tags as though it is a frame-disabled browser. Instead of being presented with a multiframe editing session, you are shown the text contained in a NOFRAME tag. In addition, saving a page with FRAMESET tags results in a "new" page being created with only the content of the NOFRAME tag. This effectively strips the frames from the document.

- SCRIPT *tags.* While the SCRIPT tag is not directly available from a pull-down menu, you can use Navigator Gold's capability to enter alternative HTML tags. However, there is no easy way to enter a terminating /SCRIPT tag. It's simpler to have the <SCRIPT> construction already embedded in your document.

- *Links.* Creating links with Navigator Gold is a snap, but there is no way (unless you edit the document with a text editor) to add the event handler attributes, such as onMouseOver, that give JavaScript so much power. Links are also saved as *absolute* references, which have the full path- and filename. So after you edit a document, you need to choose File, Publish (or choose the Publish icon) to resolve the absolute references (or, again, search the document with another text editor and make the changes yourself).

- *Event handlers.* If you have any links that have event handlers connected, the Navigator Gold editor tries to evaluate the handler's functions but, because JavaScript code is *not* evaluated from within the editor, an error will be generated. This means that certain handler combinations (onMouseOver, for example) could create documents that are difficult to edit.

Navigator Gold is a good basic editor that seamlessly integrates with the Navigator browser. For designing the initial look and feel of your pages, it's a good editor to use. But after you design the appearance of a page and want to *JavaScript-ize* it (or if you're planning on utilizing frames), you'll probably want to supplement your development with several other tools.

HTML Editing Tools

If you want to use an editor other than Navigator Gold, you can use one such as HoTMetaL, HotDog, or HTML Write. After you finish the basic layout of your page, however, switching between a simple editor such as NotePad or TextPad and your browser is a fast and efficient way to go. It's not much different from what most programmers go through: developing, editing, and compiling a program through an editor framework, then switching to another program to test, run, and debug it.

Graphics Tools

Paint Shop Pro is an excellent Windows-based graphics program that handles most image formats and can produce interlaced and transparent GIF files. Another program worth having on the Windows platform is the GIF Construction Set, by Alchemy Mindworks, which supports the easy creation of animated GIFs. If JPEG is more your style, you might find Lview Pro of some use.

 TIP If you're looking for suggestions for good tools to add to your own JavaScript Developer's Kit, read appendix A, "JavaScript Resources."

Part
IV

Ch
18

A Simple Template

One way to make creating JavaScript pages easier is to make a simple template page that contains the basic tags all HTML documents must have. Listing 18.1 shows a good starter template.

On the CD

Listing 18.1 template.htm A JavaScript Template Framework

```
<!-- template.htm:  A simple JavaScript template file -->
<HTML>
<BODY>
<SCRIPT LANGUAGE="JavaScript">
<!-- Hide from non-JavaScript browsers

document.write("<BR>Your JavaScript code goes here<BR>");
```

continues

Listing 18.1 Continued

```
// end hide from non-JavaScript browsers -->
</SCRIPT>

<CENTER>
<h1>JavaScript Template File</h1>
</CENTER>

Using this template gets you started!

</body>
</html>
```

The document.write() statement serves as a placeholder, and should be replaced with your own code. Make a copy of this file every time you need to create a new page and you'll have all the basic tags you need for JavaScripting.

LiveWire Pro

Netscape's LiveWire Pro is a collection of utilities that enable Web administrators to easily maintain a Web site. Working in conjunction with Netscape's FastTrack Server, LiveWire Pro provides a graphic interface to the Webmaster, enabling drag-and-drop site creation. You can edit individual Web pages using Navigator Gold 2.0, which is included with FastTrack.

There are some caveats—one is that LiveWire Pro only works with Netscape's Web servers (which restricts the usefulness of LiveWire Pro to those platforms that run Netscape's server software). If you're maintaining a Web site and want to incorporate server-side JavaScript, this is perfect—but it might be too much for an end-user working with his or her collection of pages.

Also, LiveWire Pro is currently available only for the Windows NT and Solaris platforms. LiveWire Pro NT can run under Windows 95—but without a Windows 95–native Netscape server, you're limited to using the Site Manager utility. This means you can maintain an existing site on another machine, but you can't create, edit, or maintain any applications of your own.

Basically, if you aren't running Windows NT and your own Web site (with a Netscape server), you're better off looking at some of the other tools the Internet has to offer.

It's a good idea to keep up with new tools, utilities, and helper programs as you embark into JavaScripting. The Internet is swelling with resources, many of which are free for the taking.

Now that you have a set of tools and a template, put them to work with an example: create an online, animated, JavaScript-powered eZine.

Building a JavaScript Site from Ground Up

The easiest way to get a feel for how to create a JavaScript-enabled Web site is to do it. For the sake of example, you're going to take a walk on the "e-publishing" side and create your own *eZine*, or online magazine.

Overall Structure

Before starting this project, it's a good idea to get an overall view of the layout, indicating how the pages interconnect. Your eZine will consist of the following parts:

- A cover page
- A table of contents
- Articles, articles, articles, and more articles

Using the FRAMESET and FRAME tags, you can make a seamless visual presentation. One possible layout (and the one used in this example) is shown in figure 18.3.

The browser has been divided into the following frames:

- A logo frame with an identifying graphic (perhaps a company logo or trademark). This is an excellent place to add an animated graphic file.
- A title frame to display the title of what is currently being read.

- The table of contents frame that lists the contents of the eZine.
- The body frame where the guts of the magazine will be displayed (such as the articles).

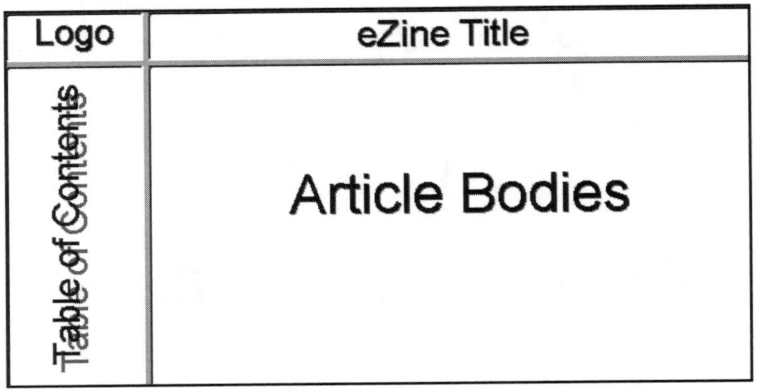

FIG. 18.3
A rough design layout for an online eZine, consisting of four frames: table of contents, eZine banner, title, and article body.

Logo	eZine Title
Table of Contents	Article Bodies

Taking full advantage of JavaScript, embellish the design with a few extra goodies:

- Basic <NOFRAME> support in the initial load page, so Web surfers who aren't using Navigator will be presented with a gentle "you really need to switch" reminder.
- When the user passes the mouse over a link in the table of contents, a caption providing further information on the link will be displayed in the browser's status bar—instead of the URL of the link.
- The cover page document takes advantage of JavaScript's access to the current date and time to provide different content at different times of the day.

As mentioned, Navigator Gold is great for formatting the visual content of a page, but currently lacks control over the underlying structure (the tags). Therefore, you'll use a combination of Navigator Gold and NotePad to create your pages in this example.

Creating the Frame Interface

The first thing you need is a document that sets up the frames. This is the document you want the user to load, so using Web conventions, this is called

INDEX.HTML (see listing 18.2). Because Gold doesn't handle this level well, you need to use NotePad to create this first page.

On the CD

Listing 18.2   index.htm   Frame Control Document That Sets Up the eZine Interface

```
<!-- index.htm:  JavaScript eZine driver -->
<HTML>

<HEAD>
<TITLE>A JavaScript-based eZine</TITLE>
</HEAD>

<FRAMESET COLS="125,*">
  <FRAMESET ROWS="50,*">
    <FRAME SRC="logo.htm" NAME="LOGO" NORESIZE BORDER=0
           MARGINHEIGHT=0 MARGINWIDTH=0 SCROLLING=NO>
    <FRAME SRC="toc.htm" NAME="TOC" NORESIZE BORDER=0
           MARGINHEIGHT=0 MARGINWIDTH=0 SCROLLING=AUTO>
  </FRAMESET>
  <FRAMESET ROWS="50,*">
    <FRAME SRC="title.htm" NAME="TITLE" NORESIZE BORDER=0
           MARGINHEIGHT=0 MARGINWIDTH=0 SCROLLING=NO>
    <FRAME SRC="coverpage.htm" NAME="BODY" NORESIZE
           MARGINHEIGHT=0 SCROLLING=AUTO>
  </FRAMESET>
</FRAMESET>

<NOFRAME>
<BODY BGCOLOR=#FFFFFF>

<CENTER><H1>A JavaScript-based eZine</H1></CENTER>

<HR>

Because this eZine takes advantage of JavaScript, you really ought to
get a browser that supports it, like
<A HREF="http://home.netscape.com/">Netscape Navigator 2.0</A>.

<HR>

Send your comments to the <A HREF="mailto: ">Editor</A>.

</BODY>
</NOFRAME>
</HTML>
```

This document divides the browser window into the four frames shown in figure 18.3. The additional code within the NOFRAME tag isn't necessary for JavaScript purposes, but allows surfers using a browser that can't handle frames to see at least a "teaser" of what's available.

With the frame structure laid out, you only need to create empty HTML files as placeholders for each of the frames. You can switch to Gold to continue the process of working with the individual documents, but remember not to use Gold for the frame page itself. Using the template file from listing 18.1, create the following files:

- LOGO.HTM
- TITLE.HTM
- TOC.HTM
- COVERPAGE.HTM

With those files in place, start Navigator and load INDEX.HTML. You should see something similar to figure 18.4.

FIG. 18.4
Using the previously defined template file to "stub out" the four frame documents may produce more text than you wish, but it is now easy to edit and watch as the pages work together.

You should be aware of the capabilities and side effects of the Gold editor. If you choose File, Edit Document, you are presented with Gold's editor mode and the file shown in figure 18.5.

FIG. 18.5
Editing INDEX.HTM with Navigator Gold. Notice that, from the editor's perspective, there are no FRAMESET tags. The two HTML tag icons at the top of the window define the COMMENT tag and NOFRAME tag.

NOFRAME tag —

COMMENT tag

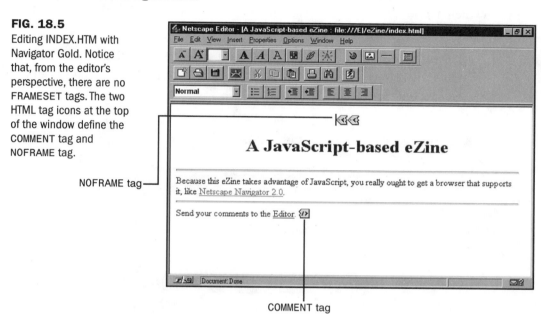

What you see is the part of the document in the NOFRAME tag. While this makes it easy to edit the final, user-end part of the document, you still have to do some basic tag editing. Using the JavaScript template file makes things a bit easier, as you will see when you piece together the next facet of the project: the table of contents.

N O T E Don't use Navigator Gold to edit a frame page *after* the FRAMESET and FRAME tags have been added. Because the editor doesn't display those tags, it also doesn't save them. Saving your document will cause all FRAMESET and FRAME tags to be deleted. ▪

The Table of Contents

The table of contents (located in the lower-left frame) serves as your control center. All article links are listed here. When the user passes the mouse over one of the links, a line of text describing that link appears in the browser's status bar. For your eZine, you'll have two "article" documents so you need to lay out the TOC.HTM file with two links to files ARTICLE1.HTM and ARTICLE2.HTM (which, for now, can be made using the JavaScript template). Creating a link with Gold is very easy if you follow these steps:

1. If you haven't typed in the anchor text yet, move the insertion cursor to the line where you want to display the link. If you want to turn existing text into a link, highlight the desired text.

2. Choose Insert, Link, or click the Make Link button.

3. Fill out the dialog box (see fig. 18.6).

FIG. 18.6
Create a link to an article from within the table of contents file by browsing to the file you want to link to, then clicking OK.

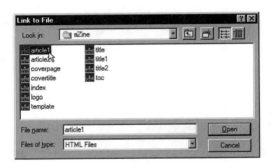

Adding a couple of horizontal lines to separate things and dropping the text size down to <H6> produces a tight, clean look. As they are now, however, the links will load the article documents into the table of contents frame. Edit the file from NotePad to add the TARGET attribute:

```
<A HREF="article1.htm" TARGET="MAIN">Article 1</A>
```

This directs the document load into the "body" frame (where the article bodies are displayed). Because you have to use NotePad to insert or edit your JavaScript code eventually, however, you might want to wait to make visual changes before you have to resort to a straight-text editor.

Status Bar Control

Now that you've finished the visual look of your table of contents, the last piece you need to implement is control of the status bar. Instead of displaying the URL of the link over which the mouse is positioned, display a one-line description of the article. Because this will be JavaScript coding, it will have to be done with NotePad.

> **N O T E** Gold doesn't handle the SCRIPT tag well. When you start adding JavaScript to a document, be careful when making changes in Gold. Specifically, event handlers can cause trouble as Gold tries to resolve them. ■

Use a simple array of strings and a little routine to change the status bar:

```
function MakeArray(size)
{
   this.length = size;
   for(i = 1; i <= size; i++)
   {
      this[i] = '';
   }

   return this;
}

msg = new MakeArray(2);

msg['story1'] = 'Article #1';
msg['story2'] = 'Article #2';
```

To make the prompt strings appear in the status bar, add the onMouseOver attribute to the link:

```
<A HREF="article1.htm" TARGET="BODY"
   ONMOUSEOVER="self.status=msg['story1'];return true;">Article 1</A>
```

Listing 18.3 finishes the TOC.HTM file.

Listing 18.3   toc.htm   Table of Contents Document File

On the CD

```
<!-- toc.htm:   eZine table of contents -->
<HTML>

<HEAD>
<TITLE>A JavaScript-enabled eZine</TITLE>
</HEAD>

<BODY>

<SCRIPT LANGUAGE="JavaScript">
<!-- Hide from non-JavaScript browsers
```

continues

Listing 18.3   Continued

```
function MakeArray(size)
{
   this.length = size;
   for(i = 1; i <= size; i++)
   {
      this[i] = '';
   }

   return this;
}


msg = new MakeArray(2);

msg['story1'] = 'Article #1';
msg['story2'] = 'Article #2';

// end hide -->
</SCRIPT>

<CENTER>


<H6>CONTENTS</H6>

<HR SIZE=4 ALIGN=CENTER>

<A HREF="article1.htm"
   TARGET="BODY"
   ONMOUSEOVER="self.status=msg['story1']; return true;">
Article 1</A>

<HR SIZE=2 WIDTH=25% ALIGN=CENTER>

<A HREF="article2.htm"
   TARGET="BODY"
   ONMOUSEOVER="self.status=msg['story2']; return true;">
Article 2</A>

<HR SIZE=4 ALIGN=CENTER>

</CENTER>

</BODY>
</HTML>
```

Articles

The ARTICLE1.HTM and ARTICLE2.HTM files are simply regular HTM files with one little twist. Listing 18.4 shows the basic framework for ARTICLE.HTM.

Listing 18.4   article.htm   Example Layout for an Article Document

```
<!-- article1.htm:  an example eZine story -->
<HTML>
<HEAD>
<TITLE>Article 1</TITLE>
</HEAD>
<BODY>

<SCRIPT LANGUAGE="JavaScript">
<!-- Hide from non-JavaScript browsers

window.parent.frames['TITLE'].location.assign("title1.htm");

// end hide from non-JavaScript browsers -->
</SCRIPT>

<H1>Article 1</H1>

<HR>

Article 1 goes here.

</BODY>
</HTML>
```

The built-in capabilities of Navigator Gold make editing these pages simple. In fact, it is exceptionally easy to handle text color changes, highlighting, and other character attributes—things that normally drive Web designers crazy—in addition to inserting graphics (see fig. 18.7).

The "twist" mentioned earlier is the JavaScript code snippet that causes a new title to load into the title frame:

```
window.parent.frames['TITLE'].location.assign("title1.htm");
```

This loads the title document for article 1 into the "title" frame each time the article is loaded. Remember, if you're using Navigator Gold, don't add this code until you finish editing your articles. Additional articles (ARTICLE2.HTM, ARTICLE3.HTM, and so on) would follow the same basic format , with the title document changed from TITLE1.HTM to TITLE2.HTM, TITLE3.HTM...you get the picture.

Part
IV
Ch
18

FIG. 18.7

Using Navigator Gold for text layout and color control is a straightforward process. Choose Properties, Document to open the dialog box that allows background, link, and text color setting.

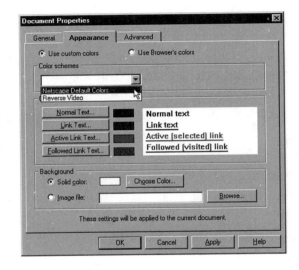

NOTE If you add any links to pages outside your eZine, use NotePad to add the `TARGET="-top"` attribute to the A tag; otherwise, the new page will load into the *current* frame instead of taking up the entire browser window. If what you're loading is itself made up of frames, a reduced version of that page will be displayed inside the current frame. A possible outcome of this kind of "nesting" is shown in figure 18.8. ■

FIG. 18.8

Not specifying that a document is to be loaded on "top" of any existing frames will cause that document (the INDEX.HTML file in this case) to be loaded into the frame where the link is located.

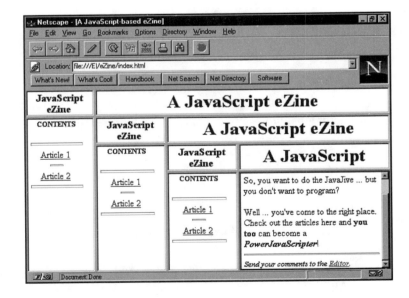

The HTML document that displays the title frame can be as simple as one line of displayed text as shown in listing 18.5.

On the CD

Listing 18.5   title1.htm   File to Load a Title Header into the Title Frame

```
<!-- title1.htm:  Title for Article 1 -->
<HTML>
<TITLE>Article 1</TITLE>
<BODY>
<H1>Article 1</H1>
</BODY>
</HTML>
```

The Cover Page

The cover page in listing 18.6 isn't incredibly fancy, but it does have a nice touch.

On the CD

Listing 18.6   coverpage.htm   The eZine Cover Page or First Document Displayed

```
<!-- coverpage.htm:  eZine coverpage -->
<HTML>

<TITLE>JavaScript:  The eZine!</TITLE>

<BODY>

<H1><CENTER>A JavaScript eZine</CENTER></H1>

<HR>

<SCRIPT LANGUAGE="JavaScript">
<!-- Hide from non-Javascript browsers

d = new Date();
hour = d.getHours();

if(hour < 5)
{
    document.write("Doing a little late-night surfing, eh?");
}
```

continues

Listing 18.6   Continued

```
else
if(hour < 6)
{
   document.write("Up early, I see!  Do you have your coffee?");
}
else
if(hour < 12)
{
   document.write("Good morning!");
}
else
if(hour < 18)
{
   document.write("Good afternoon!");
}
else
{
   document.write("Good evening!");
}

document.write("<P>");

//-->
</SCRIPT>

So, you want to do the JavaJive ... but you don't want to program?

<P>

Well ... you've come to the right place.  Check out the articles
here and <B>you too</B> can become a
<B><I>PowerJavaScripter</I></B>!

<HR>

<FONT SIZE=2>
<I>Send your comments to the <A HREF="mailto: ">Editor</A>.</I>
<FONT SIZE=>

</BODY>
</HTML>
```

In this example, the Date object is used to determine what time of day the user is reading your eZine. Depending on the hour, it displays a different message at the top of the page.

Figure 18.9 shows the presentation when you put it all together. While simple, this is a good start at creating your own publishing presence on the Web.

FIG. 18.9
Combining all the documents put together so far creates a JavaScript-enabled eZine framework.

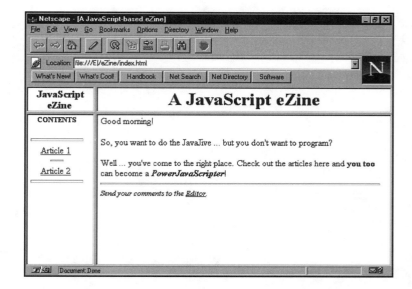

CHAPTER 19

Using Frames and Cookies in Advanced Applications

by Mona Everett with Mark C. Reynolds

One of the tremendous advantages of hypertext is its ability to link together many pieces of information in a nonlinear fashion. Rather than having to read a book one page at a time, you can leap from one link to the next as you explore different topics and their interconnections. However, sometimes this easy access to information can have unfortunate and cumbersome side effects.

One such side effect occurs when you find yourself moving back and forth between a small set of pages, over and over again. This happens because of a problem with *presentation*: the information you want is scattered over more than one page. If you are reading a tutorial, for example, you may find that you are revisiting the Table of Contents page with dreary repetitiveness. You can avoid this by having multiple browser windows open at the same time, but this often takes up too much of your display.

Store information in command-line parameters and cookies

Netscape's complex conventions for both types of storage are analyzed thoroughly.

Build framesets and communicate between them

While framesets are easy to build, it is more challenging to have them talk to one another. Document loading and frameset addressing are covered in detail.

Manage a JavaScript function library

Frames are an excellent place to store often-used JavaScript functions.

Create nested framesets

Framesets can be nested in a single document, or in more than one document.

Build a frame-based bug database

This industrial strength application ties together many JavaScript techniques, including dynamic document construction, nested framesets, aliasing, string parsing, and data storage.

This chapter focuses on the emerging HTML *frames* technology, which addresses this issue of presentation. Both the Netscape Navigator browser and Microsoft's Internet Explorer version 3.0 enable you to split a single browser window into multiple, independent subwindows, each containing its own URL. These sub-windows are known as frames. We will explore frames technology and its close relationship to JavaScript in some detail.

To do this we must first address the related topic of data storage. Sophisticated applications often require both data presentation and data storage/management capabilities. Unfortunately, information or parameter storage is particularly diffi-cult. In Netscape data may be temporarily saved between reloads using the location.search property, and also on the command line. In addition, both Netscape and Microsoft provide a persistent means of storage via cookies. We explore both methods in the first section of this chapter, and then subsequently illustrate how such data can then be used to format a page on the fly.   ■

Parameter Specification and Data Storage

Because Netscape is extremely security-conscious, it has made it difficult to store or load data—even between document reloads. Chapter 8 briefly described one method of storing simple data between document reloads via a string saved in location.search. This special location.search property is often referred to as the *command line*. A script can retrieve this string and redraw itself based on informa-tion in the string. We first examine this approach to data storage in more detail. This is followed by a discussion of the more permanent storage option offered by cookies.

▶ **See** the "JavaScript Object Hierarchy" section of chapter 8, which discusses the location object and its various properties, including the search property, **p. 258**.

Storing Parameters and Other Data

If you have a lot of data, you might appreciate having it accumulated and stored for you. You can use a submit widget or form.submit() to have the browser collect all of your data, encode it, and store it in the command line. As we will see in the next section, the output is very hard to read and looks like scrambled text.

Another possibility is to store data in dynamic arrays in a window or, better, in the frameset document. Unfortunately, this too is unstable. If you have database-like data, it must all be hand coded into the document that will host it, although you could use an HTML builder or other programming tool to automatically create the HTML document.

The only possibility that offers any permanence is *cookies*. Cookies are lines in a file that the browser enables you to write to disk. This file will be named `cookies.txt` on a Windows machine, or just `cookies` on a UNIX or Macintosh. Under Netscape Navigator this file will be in your Netscape directory or folder. Cookies are limited in size and number. Nevertheless, cookies are extremely useful. They are frequently used in the same way as a Windows .ini file, a Macintosh Preferences file, or a UNIX.rc file. The next two subsections examine both the command-line approach and the cookie approach.

Command-Line Parameters

Using the `submit()` routine to store form field values in the command line leads to a location that looks like listing 19.1.

Listing 19.1 A Typical Value for the *location.search* Property

```
?myname=Mona+M.+Everett%2C+Ph.D.&tc=navy&lc=blue&vc=orange
&aname=Mona+M.+Everett%2C+Ph.D.&myimage=DBLACE4.jpg&mytext
=navy&mylink=blue&myvlink=orange&myurl=http%3A%2F%2Fwww2.b
est.com%2F%7Edsiegel%2Ftips%2Ftips_home.html%22&cmmt=Welco
me+to+my+little+home+page+builder.++There%27s+no+tellin%27
+just+how+much+this+page+can+be+expanded.++What+do+you+thi
nk%3F%0D%0A&subbtn=Submit
```

Part
IV
Ch
19

If you examine this output, you may be able to discern some patterns. First of all, it begins with the characteristic question mark (?), which delineates the `location.search` string. Second, most of the information seems to occur in pairs with the field name as the left-hand member and the field value as the right-hand member. The pairs are separated by the character ampersand (&).

There are absolutely no spaces in this output. Every space has been replaced by a plus sign (+). Various escape sequences containing the percent sign (%) occur in this string. These sequences are used to encode non-alphanumeric characters in the input. In particular, any punctuation has been replaced by such a sequence.

▶ **See** the section "Global and Local Variables" in chapter 9, which discusses character escape sequences in more detail, **p. 300**.

JavaScript does not give you a lot of tools with which to dissect this sequence. Let's see how we can use the ones we have. First, there are a pair of built-in functions to handle the escape sequences. These are escape(), which takes a non-alphanumeric character and hands you back the coded sequence, and unescape(), which reverses the process. Second, we can use the substring method of the String object to "walk" through a string. A statement of the form

```
myString.substring(start,stop)
```

extracts all the characters starting from position start and ending at the last character just before the position stop. This enables us to examine each character in the string, one at a time, if we want. Based on the character encountered, we can replace it or take some action.

The file encdec.htm on the CD-ROM has two functions that use this approach. The first one, which decodes the command-line search string, provides the core of the page rewrite code. The second changes all of the < and > to < and >, respectively, so that you can write out HTML to the page. This function is not actively called in the page, but is used for debugging using document.write(). The latter function is also really useful if you want to write HTML dynamically to your page to show your user how to do something. Let's examine the function that decodes the command-line search string, arraySubParms(), shown in listing 19.2. Note that this function presupposes that an array named parms has been declared as a global variable, and also initialized.

On the CD

Listing 19.2   encdec.htm   A Function That Dissects the Command Line into its Component Parts

```
function arraySubParms(astr)
{
    k = astr.length
    astr = astr.substring(1,k)
    bstr = ''
    counter = 1
    for (i = 0 ; i <= k ; i++)
    {
```

```
ccStr =''
ccStr = astr.substring(i,i+1)

if (ccStr == '+') ccStr = ' '
if (ccStr == '%')
    {
       var xx = astr.substring(i,i+3)
       ccStr = unescape(xx)
       i += 3
    }
// car
if (ccStr == '=')
    {
            parms[counter] = bstr
            bstr = ''
            continue
    }
//right-hand member of pair
if (ccStr == '&')
    {
            parms[parms[counter]] = bstr
            counter++
            bstr = ''
            ccStr=''
            continue
    }

    bstr += ccStr
    }
}
```

When `arraySubParms(astr)` receives a string, it immediately finds the string's length and uses that value to chop off the first character, which is the question mark (?), that starts the `location.search` string. It then begins a loop that cycles through every character in the string with the statement `ccstr = astr.substring(i,i+1)`. The variable `ccstr` is then checked to see if it is equal to the plus sign (+). If it is, then that character is replaced with a space. If `ccstr` is a percent sign, the function uses the `substring` function again to grab three characters, starting from its current position. It then uses the built-in function, `unescape`, to turn these three characters back into an ASCII character.

Because three characters instead of one are used up, the pointer into the string, `i`, must be advanced by three with the statement `i+=3`. In either of these two cases (+ or &), the next two conditional tests will fail, and `ccstr`, which may have been modified, is added to `bstr`.

The browser places all of the form element names and their values into the command line as `name=value` pairs. Each pair is terminated by an ampersand (`&`). The next two conditional tests extract the left and right members of the pair and place them into the left and right members of the associative array `parms`. If the function finds that equal sign (`=`), it knows that `bstr`—which has steadily been accumulating characters—now holds the name of the element.

Another variable, `counter`, is used to keep track of the current index into the `parms` array. The left member is set with the statement, `parms[counter] = bstr`. The variable, `bstr`, is set to the empty string at this point so that it can start accumulating characters anew. The value of `counter` is *not* advanced. A `continue` statement is used to bypass the rest of the loop so that the equal sign (`=`), which was just seen, is not added into the new value of `bstr`.

> **N O T E** JavaScript associative arrays are one-dimensional arrays of pairs. The left and right members of a pair are set differently. Set the left member using a numerical index into the array, for example, `myArray[n]=lvar`. Set the right member with an index equal to the value that you placed into the left member, for example, `myArray[myArray[n]] = rvar`. You can also use `myArray[lvar] = rvar` if `lvar` has not changed between setting the left and right sides of the pair. ■

If the next test, for the ampersand (`&`), yields `true`, the function knows that it has now accumulated the right-hand member of the array in `bstr`. It sets the right-hand member with the statement, `parms[parms[counter]] = bstr`. Remember that you set the right-hand member with the index as the *name* of the left-hand member, *not* the index itself. The processing of the `name=value` pair is now complete. Again, `bstr` is set to the empty string in anticipation of the next loop iteration. In this particular case, however, `counter` is now incremented with the `counter++` statement.

When the function finally reaches the end of the `location.search` string, you will then have all of the variables in the global `parms` array. You can now use them anywhere within the current window or in any window that you create.

The second noteworthy function from the encdec.htm file is the `toprint()` function, which changes all occurrences of the < and > characters in any string into their corresponding control codes. This seemingly trivial operation is, in fact, very important. This is because the < and > characters are interpreted by HTML. If you want to write HTML to your document, you must somehow prevent them from being interpreted as HTML delimiters. Converting them to control codes does the trick. This function is very useful for debugging or to show HTML example code on your pages.

We will conclude this discussion of command-line parameters by examining the remaining code from file encdec.htm. It uses the global parms array that you have just prepared to rewrite your page according your specifications. Listing 19.3 shows the page rewrite code itself.

On the CD

Listing 19.3   encdec.htm   Rewriting a Web Page using Command-Line Data

```
var astr = location.search
if (astr != null && astr != ''){ // start conditional

var parms = new createArray(12)

arraySubParms(astr)

astr = '<BODY BGCOLOR="linen" '
astr += 'TEXT="'+ parms['mytext'] + '" '
astr += 'LINK="'+ parms['mylink'] + '" '
astr += 'VLINK="'+ parms['myvlink'] + '" '
astr += 'ALINK="red" '
astr += 'BACKGROUND = "NewImages/' + parms['myimage'] + '" '
astr += '><BR>'
document.write(astr)
//document.write(toprint(astr))
} // end conditional
else document.write('<BODY>')
document.write('<TABLE ALIGN=RIGHT WIDTH=350 BORDER=1>')
document.write('<TR><TD>')
document.write('<FONT SIZE=7 COLOR= "indianred">')
document.write('<CENTER>' +document.title + '</CENTER>')
document.write('</TD></TR></TABLE>')
document.write('<LEFT><B>')
document.write('This page is an example of dynamically revised by ¬
      a header script which acts on information stored in the ¬
      command line.  That information is based on user\' choices.')
document.write('</B></LEFT>')
document.write('<BR CLEAR ALL>')
document.write('<HR>')

var astr = location.search
if (astr != null && astr != ''){ // start conditional
```

continues

Part IV

Ch 19

Listing 19.3   Continued

```
astr ='<CENTER><FONT SIZE=7 COLOR="' + parms['link'] + '"><B> '
astr += parms['aname'] + '</B></FONT></CENTER>'
document.write(astr)
} // end conditional
document.write('<HR><BR>')
```

Let us examine the operation of this script in some detail. There are several points worth noting. First of all, the location.search property is examined to make sure that it is not null or the empty string. If location.search does not contain a valid string, then most of the script processing is skipped. Two if...else statements are used for this purpose.

After the search string has been obtained and the parms array filled in by the call to arraySubParms(), the script starts building the <BODY> statement. Note that it builds it into a string and does not write it immediately with document.write. Note, too, the commented-out call to printit(), which was used during debugging to see if the string was built correctly.

Once the string has been assembled, a <BODY...> statement, which sets the background image and colors, is written to the document. If there was no search string, a plain <BODY> statement is written.

The script then writes a nice header for the document. The script next uses a second conditional clause to write your name in large letters. It had to check for the existence of a search string in order to do so. If the search string is present, you get your name; if it is absent, you get brief directions on using the page. When the header script is complete, the HTML on the page is interpreted by the browser.

Because all the form elements can be cleared with a submit, this program is polite and restores all of them from the global parms array. Instead of writing each one separately, it iterates through the form.elements array. Remember that the array was created with the element name as the left-hand member of the array. This makes it easy to get the correct variable in the form element. This could have also been done using numerical indexing. The routine shown is particularly useful if you have a large number of elements to restore.

Notice that a couple of form elements were included that were not used to construct the page. They were included here in order to provide a lot of escaped characters and a longer string of text with which to test the script.

Storing Persistent Data in Cookies

The only method you can use to store variables between invocations of Netscape Navigator and Internet Explorer v3 is the cookie approach. This is also the only approach that works with windows in different hierarchies. Since the Internet Explorer release is still in beta testing at the time of this writing we will focus on the version of cookies used by Netscape Navigator.

Cookies were originally designed to enable a server to save information on the client's disk. When the client contacted that same host at a later time, the previously saved cookie would be sent back to the server. Cookies are therefore useful if a browser connection is interrupted and you want to pick up where you left off. They are also useful in the event the server crashes and later wants to pick up where it left off. Cookies are now available for general use in JavaScript.

Cookies have the following five parameters:

```
NAME=VALUE

expires=DATE

path=PATH

domain=DOMAIN_NAME

secure
```

Only the first one, which is a familiar NAME=VALUE pair, is required. All of the others are optional. However, if you do not save an expiration date, the cookie automatically expires when you close Netscape—not something you want to happen if you want to keep information from session to session. The various parameters are separated by semicolons. If you create a cookie with the same name and path as a cookie already in existence, the new one overwrites the existing one.

Although servers can write named cookies one at a time, JavaScript cannot. You can set an individual named cookie with the statement, document.cookie='cookiename=xxxx', but when you retrieve document.cookie, you get a string consisting of *all* of the cookies. Currently, the only way to retrieve an individual cookie is to search through the entire set of cookies obtained from `document.cookie`. Consequently, it helps to add a prefix or suffix to the names of your cookies with little-used characters. This makes them easy to find with `IndexOf()`.

Let's examine each of the cookie parameters in turn. As stated, the `NAME=VALUE` parameter is an associative pair. This means that it lends itself nicely to being stored in arrays and placed in form elements. This is the only required element of the cookie. The `expires=DATE` parameter is used to describe the expiration date for the cookie. As defined by Netscape, the date format must be `"Wdy, DD-Mon-YY HH:MM:SS GMT"` with the separators exactly as given. If you do not want persistent data between browser invocations, leave out this expiration date. If you want your cookie to never expire, give it a date several years in the future.

The `path=PATH` parameter is used to limit the search path of a server that can see your cookies. This is analogous to specifying a document `BASE` in an HTML document. If you use a slash (/), then everything in the domain can use your cookies.

The `domain=DOMAIN_NAME` parameter is only useful if the server is setting the cookie or, if for some reason, you want to generate a cookie that is available to the server. If the server generated the cookie, then the default domain is the domain name of the server that generated it. Finally, the parameter, `secure`, indicates that the cookie should only be sent if there is a secure client-server relationship.

Listing 19.4 shows the cookie versions of the routines for saving and restoring persistent information. This code can be found on the CD-ROM in the file c20-2.htm. In this case, the information goes to, and comes from, the document cookie rather than the command-line search string. These routines have been liberally modified from the original versions, which were written by Bill Dortch and placed in the public domain.

Listing 19.4   c20-2.htm   Saving and Restoring Document Cookie Information

```
function fixSep(what)
// escapes any semicolons you might have in your data
{
```

```
    n=0
    while ( n >= 0 )
        {
            n = what.indexOf(';',n)
            if (n < 0) return what
            else
                {
                    what = what.substring(0,n) + escape(';') ¬
                        + what.substring(n+1,what.length)
                    n++
                }
        }
    return what
}


function toCookie()
{
    document.cookie = ''
    nform = document.data
    for (i=0 ; i<nform.length; i++)
        {
            expr =makeYearExpDate(1)
            astr = fixSep(nform.elements[i].value)
            //astr = nform.elements[i].value
            astr= nform.elements[i].name + '=' + astr + ';expires=' ¬
                + expr + ';path=/'
            document.cookie=astr
        }
}

function makeYearExpDate(yr)
{
    var expire = new Date ();
    expire.setTime (expire.getTime() + ((yr *365) *24 * 60 * 60 * 1000));
    expire = expire.toGMTString()
    return expire
}

function getCookieAt(n)
{
  e = document.cookie.indexOf (";", n);
    if (e == -1)
        e = document.cookie.length
    rstr= unescape(document.cookie.substring(n,e))
    return rstr
}

function fromCookie()
```

continues

Listing 19.4 Continued

```
//restores summary fields from cookie
{
    nform = document.data
    astr = document.cookie
    alert(astr)
    cl = astr.length
    counter=0
    for (i = 0 ; i < nform.length ; i++)
{
                nstr = nform.elements[i].name + '='
                ll = nstr.length

                jx  = 0;
                  while (jx < cl)
                {
                    k = jx + ll;
                     xstr = astr.substring(jx,k);
if (xstr == nstr)
                    {
                            nform.elements[i].value = getCookieAt(k);
                            break ;
                        }
                    jx = document.cookie.indexOf(" ", jx) + 1;
                    if (jx == 0) break ;
                }

        }

}

function arrayFromCookie()
// fills global array from cookie
{
    astr = document.cookie
    cl = astr.length
    k=0
jx  = 0;
    for (i = 0 ; i < 6 ; i++)
        {
                jx=astr.indexOf(' ',jx)
                 k = astr.indexOf('=',jx);
                 xstr = astr.substring(jx+1,k);
parms[i]=xstr;
                 parms[parms[i]] = getCookieAt(k+1);
                 jx = astr.indexOf(";", jx) + 1;
                 if (jx <= 0 || i > 10) break ;

        }
```

The function `makeYearExpDate()` enables you to set the expiration date for several years in the future. It was designed for really persistent cookies. If you want a shorter time, you can easily modify this routine. Note that this function uses the `Date` object heavily. The static method, `Date.getTime()`, returns a neatly formatted date string, while the method, `Date.toGMTime()`, returns the date converted to Greenwich Mean Time, which is what the cookie expiration mechanism expects your cookies to contain.

The function `fixSep()` escapes any semicolons that your variables might have. It is highly undesirable to store semicolons in the cookie parameters because the semicolon is the parameter separator. You could, in fact, escape all the non-alphanumeric characters in the entire string. However, this would make it difficult to read, especially if you simply want to look at the cookie.

The function, `GetCookieAt(n)`, retrieves the cookie value starting at an offset of n characters into the cookie string. It replaces all escape sequences with their ASCII values. The function, `FromCookie()`, restores all of the summary forms variables from the cookie. It is really an undo function.

The final function, `arrayFromCookie()`, is called by the page rebuilding routines to build the global array, `parms`, from which the page is rewritten. Notice that we did not have to change the page rebuilding code from that of listing 19.3. We only changed the routine to build the `parms` array. Notice also that we can retrieve the value of a single cookie entry by indexing into the `parms` array.

Part
IV

Ch
19

Frames and JavaScript

Frames are one of the most important new features to be added to HTML. Frames allow multiple subwindows—or panes—in a single Web page. This gives you the opportunity to display several URLs at the same time, on the same Web page. It also allows you to keep part of the screen constant while other parts are updated. This is ideal for many Web applications that span multiple pages, but also have a constant portion (such as a Table of Contents). Before you learn about the implications of frames on JavaScript, a very brief tutorial on frames will be presented.

Specifying Frames in HTML

Frames in HTML are organized into sets which are known, appropriately enough, as *framesets*. In order to define a set of frames one must first allocate screen real estate to this frameset, and then place each of the individual frames within it. We will examine the syntax for the HTML FRAMESET and FRAME directives in order to understand how frames and framesets are organized.

One of the most important, and most confusing, aspects of frames is the parent/child relationships of frames, framesets, and the windows that contain them. The first frameset placed in a window has that window as its parent. A frameset also can host another frameset, in which case the initial frameset is the parent. Note that a top-level frameset itself is not named, but a frameset's child frames can be named. Frames can be referred to by name or as an index of the frames array. Figure 19.1 shows the overall hierarchy of frames, framesets, documents, and windows in Netscape Navigator.

FIG. 19.1
The hierarchy of windows, documents, and frames employs a complex, but consistent set of referencing rules.

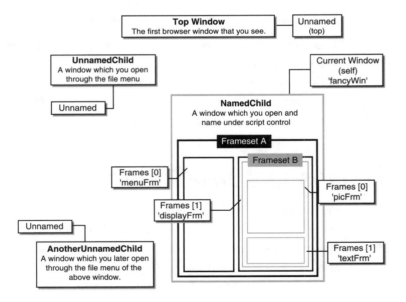

You can divide your window real estate with a statement of the form <frameset cols=40%,*>. This frameset statement divides the window horizontally into two frames. It tells the browser to give 40 percent of the window width to the left-hand frame, `frames[0]`, and anything remaining to the right-hand frame, `frames[1]`. You can explicitly give percentages or pixel widths for all frames, but it is more useful to use an asterisk (`*`), for at least one parameter. Use the wildcard character (`*`) for the widest frame, or for the frame that is least likely to be resized. This helps ensure that the entire frameset is displayed on a single screen. You can also divide the window vertically with a statement like `<frameset rows=20%,*,10%>`. This statement gives 20 percent of the available window height to the top frame, `frames[0]`, 10 percent to the bottom frame, `frames[2]`, and anything left to the middle frame, `frames[1]`.

> **CAUTION**
>
> You cannot divide a window both horizontally and vertically with one frameset. To do that, you must use nested framesets.

The subsequent `<FRAME...>` statements define the name, `source` (`URL`), and attributes of each frame in the frameset. For example,

```
<FRAME SRC='menu.htm' NAME='menuframe' MARGINWIDTH=2 MARGINHEIGHT=2
➥SCROLLING=YES>
```

defines a frame into which the `menu.htm` file will be loaded. This frame is named `menuframe`.

Unless you are designing a *ledge* (a frame that never changes) and you know it will always be displayed in the frame, make the frame scrollable. You can enter an explicit `SCROLLING` attribute, which should be the value `YES` or `NO`, but the frame will default to `SCROLLING=YES`. Scrolling is much kinder to your users. You might have a very high resolution display, but a lot of computers, particularly laptops, do not. The `MARGINWIDTH=`*xx* and `MARGINHEIGHT=`*xx* attributes also allow you some latitude in how you present your document within a frame.

N O T E Many browsers do not yet understand frames. Ideally, you should provide a version of your document that does not use frames for such browsers. At a minimum, you should warn the users about the presence of frames in your document using a `<NOFRAMES>...</NOFRAMES>` clause. ■

Make sure you have an initial URL to load into the frame, even if that URL is just a stub. Otherwise, you might find that the browser has loaded an index to the current directory. If you want to use a frame in the frameset to load other documents from a link, you must specify the target frame like this:

```
<A HREF='netcom.com/home' TARGET='menuframe'>Netscape</A>
```

Frames are a sophisticated way to build Web pages; you can keep your menu in one frame and display your content in another. However, it is easy to go overboard and have too many frames. If you present too much information in several different small frames, the user will probably be scrolling quite often. Since the whole purpose of frames is to present information in a pleasing manner, it is important not to try the user's patience. Frames can be a powerful tool, but they should be used judiciously.

Building a Frameset

Framesets are easy to build, although their hierarchy can become complex if they are nested. Listing 19.5 shows a simple frameset document. For it to display correctly, there must be HTML documents with the names given by the SRC attribute in each FRAME definition. When this code is loaded into Netscape Navigator, the page shown in figure 19.2 appears. This code appears in the file c20-3.htm on the CD-ROM.

On the CD

Listing 19.5   c20-3.htm   A Simple Frameset

```
<HTML>
<HEAD>
<TITLE><Simple Frame</TITLE>
<SCRIPT></SCRIPT>
</HEAD>
<FRAMESET cols=40%,*>
    <FRAME SRC="menu_2.htm" NAME="menuFrm" SCROLLING=YES
     MARGINWIDTH=3 MARGINHEIGHT=3>
    <FRAME SRC="display.htm" NAME="displayFrm" SCROLLING=YES
     MARGINWIDTH=3 MARGINHEIGHT=3>
    <NOFRAMES>
      You must have a frames-capable browser to
      <A HREF="noframes.htm">view this document</A> correctly.
    </NOFRAMES>
</FRAMESET>
</HTML>
```

FIG. 19.2
Framesets contain multiple frames and reference multiple URLs.

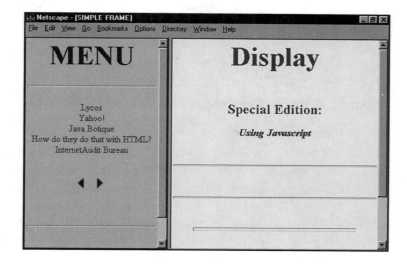

> **NOTE**
> When building a frameset, always remember the following rules:
>
> 1. The <FRAMESET>...</FRAMESET> block replaces the <BODY>...</BODY> block. It is incorrect to have both.
> 2. Always use a <NOFRAMES>...</NOFRAMES> clause for browsers that do not support frames.
> 3. Make all your frames scrollable except in exceptional circumstances.
> 4. Make sure the HTML documents referenced by the SRC attributes are "live" before the frameset is displayed. ■

One of the most difficult concepts about framesets and frames is how they are referenced. For the simple frameset previously shown, you can make a simple roadmap of the object references. When you want to reference the child frames from the frameset, you can use the following references:

- menu_2.htm   =   `frames[0]`   or   `menuFrm`
- display.htm   =   `frames[1]`   or   `displayFrm`

When one of the frames references its parent frameset, this object reference is used:

- Either frame   =   parent

The contents of each frame are referenced as properties of the frame. For example, the frameset can access the document object of menu_2.htm as `frames[0].document` or `menuFrm.document`.

Frames within Frames

Frames can be nested in two ways. We will illustrate both types of nesting by putting another frameset inside the `displayFrm` frame object defined in listing 19.5. To understand the first method, call the original frameset Frameset A. The frameset declaration shown in listing 19.6 nests a second frameset, referred to as Frameset B, within Frameset A. It does this by replacing `frames[1]` (the `displayFrm` frame) with another frameset. This code can be found in the c20-4.htm file on the CD-ROM. The auxiliary files menu_3.htm, pics.htm, and text.htm are also required.

On the CD

Listing 19.6   c20-4.htm   Example of Nested Frames in which a Frame is Replaced with Another Frameset

```
<HTML>
<HEAD>
<SCRIPT>
</SCRIPT>
</HEAD>
<frameset cols = 30%,*>
    <frame src = 'menu_3.htm' name='menuFrame' marginwidth=3 ¬
        marginheight=3>
        <frameset rows=66%,*>
            <frame src='pics.htm' name='picFrame' scrolling=yes
              marginwidth=3 ¬
                marginheight=3>
            <frame src='text.htm' name= 'textFrame' scrolling=yes ¬
                marginwidth=3 marginheight=3>
        </frameset>
    <noframes>
        You must have a frames-capable browser to ¬
            <a href=text.htm>view this document</a> correctly.
    </noframes>
</frameset>
</HTML>
```

Referencing in this type of nested frameset is no different than the type of object references described for a simple frameset. When a frameset references a child frame, the following object references are used:

- menu_3.htm = `frames[0]` or `menuFrame`
- pics.htm = `frames[1]` or `picFrame`
- text.htm = `frames[2]` or `textFrame`

When any of the component frames refers to the frameset that contains it, the following reference is used:

- Any frame increase = parent

The second method uses URLs to achieve nested framesets. We will set Frameset B's `displfrm` to a URL that contains a framed document. This URL will come from the file displfrm.htm and will create the frames `picFrame` and `textFrame`. In this case, the object references are somewhat more complex. When the parent refers to its child frames it uses the following:

- menu_4.htm = `frames[0]` or `menuFrm`
- displfrm.htm = `frames[1]` or `displayFrm`
- pics.htm = `frames[1].frames[0]` or `displayFrm.picFrame`
- text.htm = `frames[1].frames[1]` or `displayFrm.textFrame`

When the child frames refer to their frameset parent, these object references are used:

- menu_4.htm = parent
- displfrm.htm = parent
- pics.htm = parent.parent
- text.htm = parent.parent

> **CAUTION**
>
> Specifying an empty URL in a frame declaration can cause the index file in the server's current directory to be loaded into the frame. Anyone can then open any of the documents listed in that index file. This can be considerably detrimental if you do not want to give users unrestricted read access to that particular directory.

Examples of Interframe Communication

At this point, you know how to refer to parent framesets in frames, and also know the correct object references for child frames of a frameset. The next topic explores interframe communication. This example uses the CD-ROM files c20-3.htm, menu_2.htm (shown in listing 19.7), and display.htm. Make sure you place all these files in the same directory, and then load c20-3.htm into your browser. The file, menu_3.htm, that's loaded into the left frame provides a simple and useful example of interframe communication.

The menu3.htm file contains some links to well known sites. A TARGET that points to the displayFrm frame is given for each link. If you click a link, the URL loads into the displayFrm frame instead of into the menuFrm frame. Note that you cannot refer to the "parent" object when you use a TARGET. To experiment with the page, click several links. After you have done this a few times, try to go backwards using Netscape's Back button. Notice that the whole frameset disappears; it is replaced by the document you were looking at before you loaded the c20-3.htm frameset.

TIP

Netscape's Forward and Back buttons work on the entire document—not on individual frames.

This limitation can certainly make life difficult, especially if you follow several links in the displayFrm and now want to get back to an intermediate one. Fortunately, there is a way to do this, but you must specifically provide for it. Notice the two small image buttons below the links. If you click the left arrow, the displayFrm frame reverts to the previously visited URL. Similarly, the right arrow takes you forward in the frame.

Listing 19.7   menu_2.htm   Using URLs to Create Nested Framesets

```
<HTML>
<HEAD>
<TITLE>MENU.HTM</TITLE>
<SCRIPT>
function writetopic(what)
{
   aWin = self.parent.displayFrm
     //aWin = self.parent.frames[1]
     aWin.document.close()
```

```
       aWin.document.open()
       aWin.document.write('<CENTER><H2><B>' + what + '</B> </H2>
       ➥</CENTER>')
       aWin.document.close()
}
</SCRIPT>
</HEAD>
<BODY BGCOLOR='darkslateblue' TEXT='linen' LINK='corel' ¬
       VLINK='darkcorel' ALINK='yellow' >
<CENTER><FONT SIZE=7 COLOR="yellow"><B>MENU<B></FONT><CENTER>
<H3><HR></H3>
<FORM NAME="menuForm">
<INPUT TYPE='button' NAME="writeDisp" VALUE='Write to Display
       Frame' onClick='writetopic("Coming to you from ¬
       <BIG><I>menuFrm</I></BIG>..." )'>
</FORM>
<H3><BR><HR><BR></H3>
<H3><BR><HR SIZE=5 WIDTH=80%><BR></H3>
</BODY>
</HTML>
```

Another interesting aspect of frames is revealed if you attempt to use the View Source option of Netscape Navigator. Only the code for the frameset appears—the code for the frames contained in it does not. This is one approach to provide some simple protection for your source code. However, it only keeps novice users from seeing your code; experienced users can defeat this by loading the URLs referenced by the individual frames into a single browser window, and then using View, Source on that window.

Part
IV

Ch
19

> **CAUTION**
>
> The current release of Netscape Navigator does not reliably reload documents containing frames. This means that if you are editing a document and you press the Reload button, the most recent version of that document might not be reloaded.

Writing a New Document into a Frame

The examples in the files c20-4.htm and c20-5.htm do simple rewrites of documents into adjacent and foreign frames. We will now expand on that by taking the Text Object example from chapter 8 and writing it to a frame, rather than to a new window. The file c20-6.htm on the CD-ROM defines the frameset that loads the

subsidiary documents setnote.htm and note.htm into its frames. The file
setnote.htm contains a button that calls a `writeNote()` routine to write the new
HTML into the `frames[1]` frame. The file note.htm is just a stub so you don't have
to write an empty URL. Listing 19.8 shows the code for the `writeNote()` function.
Figure 19.3 shows what happens when the note is written into the frame.

Listing 19.8   c20-6.htm   The Code for the *writeNote()* Function

```
function writenote(topic)
{
     topic = 'This is a little note about rewriting adjacent frames."
     topic += " You do it the same way as you would to rewrite"
     topic += " or originally write a window."
       aWin = self.parent.displayFrm
     ndoc= aWin.document
     ndoc.close()
     ndoc.open()
     astr ='<HTML><HEAD><BR><TITLE>' + topic + '</TITLE>'
     astr +='</HEAD>'
     astr +='<SCRIPT>'
     astr +='function closeNote(aName){'
     astr +='self.close()'
     astr +='}'
     astr +='function saveNote(aName){'
     astr +='}'
     astr +='<\/SCRIPT>'
     astr +='<BODY>'
     astr +='<FORM>'
     astr +='<TABLE ALIGN=LEFT BORDER><TR ALIGN=CENTER><TD>'
     astr +='<INPUT TYPE=button NAME=saveBtn VALUE="Save"
ONCLICK="saveNote()" >'
     astr +='</TD>'
     astr +='<TD ROWSPAN=4>' + topic
     astr +='</TD>'
     astr +='</TR><TR ALIGN=CENTER><TD>'
     astr +='<INPUT TYPE=button NAME=closeBtn VALUE="Close"
ONCLICK="closeNote()" >'
     astr +='</TD></TR>'
     astr +='<TR><TD><BR></TD></TR>'
     astr +='<TR><TD><BR></TD></TR>'
     astr +='</TABLE>'
     astr +='</FORM>'
     astr +='<BR CLEAR=ALL><H3><BR></H3>'
     astr +='Note:  Save button is not active yet'
     astr +='</BODY></HTML>'
     ndoc.write(astr)
     ndoc.close()
}
```

FIG. 19.3
Documents can be
dynamically written into
frames.

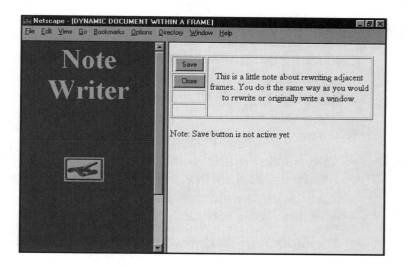

Building a JavaScript Function Library in a Frameholder

You have already learned that a frameset document cannot contain any HTML
other than frame definitions. It can, however, contain a script. In this script, you
can keep window global variables and functions. We will define a minimal string
manipulator in a frameset. With this tool you can do the following:

- Change a string to capital letters
- Change a string to lowercase
- Change all instances of a character
- Change HTML to an uninterpreted format that can be displayed by the
  browser as text

The first two operations merely require calls to string functions. The latter two can
be accomplished by routines that we have already written. You store these functions in the frameset of the file c20-7.htm on the CD-ROM. This frameset requires
the files funcs.htm and editor.htm to be in the same directory.

Part

IV

Ch

19

The frame named `menuFrm` will contain buttons to call your frameset functions. These functions must be able to refer to objects in their own frame as well as the adjacent frame `editFrm`. In addition, you must be able to call these functions from the parent frame. The true value of a frameset function library is its reusability. It is easy to copy the HTML file that defines the library and create a new document by changing a small amount of code—the code that builds the frameset itself. In this way, you can reuse your code.

Another way to reuse code is to have all the functions in a small or hidden frame. When you want to use those functions, you simply load that frame. If you take this approach, you don't have to change the frameset code. In both cases, however, it is more difficult to address an adjacent frame than it is to address a parent or child.

The `menuFrm` frame loads the document defined in the CD-ROM file funcs.htm. This file defines the buttons that access the frameset functions. Some of the object references are quite long, so this file makes liberal use of aliasing to shorten them. In fact, it does it so well that sometimes the whole procedure can be placed in the `onClick` event handler for the button. The file funcs.htm is loaded into the `frames[0]` object, while a simple editor window is placed in `frames[1]`. This editor is implemented as a `textarea`. When this frameset is loaded, the browser will display something like what is shown in figure 19.4.

FIG. 19.4
A frameset library can be used to implement a string processor.

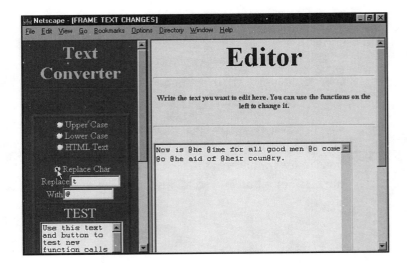

The file funcs.htm also has a test window and a button so you can try out the functions it provides. These functions act on objects in its document. The code is such that the button always calls a routine called `Testit`. The `Testit` function has calls to the four routines in the function library. You can easily adapt this code for your own purposes by replacing the `Testit` function.

The most complex part of using functions stored in the frameset is determining the appropriate name of the frameset window. This depends on the window from which the function call is made. The example previously shown offers a very simple solution: just use `self.parent.myfunc()`. The `self` portion of this expression can be omitted, but you might want it to discourage ambiguity.

A Bug Database in JavaScript

This section presents a working application written entirely in JavaScript. The bugs in this chapter are software bugs, not the kind that crawl. The database is limited to 30 bugs because, at present, the only way to store persistent data is in cookies, which are limited in size and number. You can easily modify the code in this database to use the `Image` objects or `Text` objects presented in chapter 9. Indeed, you can even make it a database to hold descriptions of the six-legged kind of bug.

The Top-Level Structure of the Bug Database

Bugs of any kind are usually considered objectionable. You're going to turn them into objects that can be dealt with in an organized fashion. When you design an object, you first ask what information needs to be stored with that object. In the case of a software bug, you might want to track the date the bug was reported, who reported the bug, what the bug is, a description or comments, and the current status of the bug.

This is the type of application you might expect to find written in Delphi or Visual Basic. In that case, you would have a great deal of work to do to port the application to other platforms. This application, however, runs in the Netscape Navigator browser window and, thus, will run on any of the platforms Netscape supports. The main shortcoming of this application is that it has no place to store its data except in Netscape cookies, which are limited.

You will need a number of files for this application, which consists of five frames. Make sure you have the following files from the CD-ROM: c20-8.htm, menu.htm, bugs.htm, function.htm, traymenu.htm, indicatr.htm, bmenu.htm, buginput.htm, and notepad.htm. The top level of this application is, of course, the framesets it uses. Listing 19.9 shows these framesets (from the CD-ROM file bugs.htm).

On the CD

Listing 19.9   bugs.htm   The Major Frameset for the Bugs Application

```
<HTML>
<HEAD>
<!- Created 12 Feb 1996 a6:59 PM 06:59 PM —>
<TITLE>Bugs Main Frameset</TITLE>
<SCRIPT>

//This function is a workaround to make sure that the table overlay is
➥drawn correctly.
function forceRewrite()
{
  blankWin=window.open('','blankWin','toobar=no,location=no,directories=no,
    status=yes,
    scrollbars=no,resizable=no,copyhistory=no,width=600,height=450')
    blankWin.close()
}
</SCRIPT>
</HEAD>
<FRAMESET ROWS= "80,*"  onLoad='forceRewrite()'>
     <FRAME SRC="menu.htm" NAME="menuFrm" MARGINHEIGHT=3 MARGINWIDTH=3>
     <FRAME SRC="bugs.htm" NAME="bugsFrm" SCROLLING=YES MARGINHEIGHT=3
     MARGINWIDTH=3>
     <NOFRAMES>
          You must have a frames-capable browser to
          <a href=noframes.htm>view this document</a> correctly.
     </NOFRAMES>
</FRAMESET>
<SCRIPT>
var func = self.frames[0].frames[0]
var tray = self.frames[0].frames[1]
var smenu = self.frames[1].frames[0]
var work = self.frames[1].frames[1]

function passDownEdit(which)
{
  smenu.toEditor(which)
}
</SCRIPT>
</HTML>
```

Before you examine this frameset definition, recall that Netscape draws images in an order that seems unpredictable. Its image drawing order is influenced by the state of your browser and by the size of the images.

One way around this is to force a screen refresh by forcing another window to obscure the screen. You can automate this approach by opening and closing another window rapidly above your application to force the redraw. You could use this seemingly worthless window creatively by making it a splash screen and closing it with a timer.

▶ **See** for more on the "Images as Objects" section of chapter 9 the problem of drawing images in Netscape, **p. 335**.

> **CAUTION**
>
> Script references to child frames or framesets cannot be made until after the framesets are declared. If you want to alias individual frames, do this in a footer script rather than in the header script.

We will now examine the structure of the frame declarations. The major frame holds three script items in addition to the frameset. A function called `forceRewrite` is defined in the header script. This function simply opens and closes a large window. This is done to overcome the image drawing limitation just mentioned. Notice that this function is called in the frameset tag via an `onLoad` handler. The `onLoad` handler executes after the page has been completely loaded. In this case, the point of this code is to allow all of the images to be loaded and then force a screen refresh so the table overlays are drawn correctly. Note that both `FRAMESET` and `BODY` statements may contain `onLoad` handlers.

The footer script contains aliases to all of the frames that will eventually be loaded. It has to be in the footer because the frameset does not know about its own child frames until you define them. The small footer function `passDownEdit` is used by the `NotePad` function to pass a command down to the child window `smenu`. Its purpose is to simplify window references.

The frameset itself defines two frames. Both of these hold other framesets. Table 19.1 lists the framesets, the frames they contain, the files loaded into those frames, their aliases, and their roles in the overall application. Figure 19.5 shows the page the bug database application creates.

Table 19.1   Definitions for Five Frames, Their Aliases, and Their Functions

Frameset	Frame	File	Alias	Function
menu.htm	0	functions.htm	func	Holds the function library.
	1	traymenu.htm	tray	Holds a table overlay with linked image buttons. Each button points to a predefined function name in the bottom-left frame.
	2	indicatr.htm	ind	Holds a dummy document that can have messages written to it.
bugs.htm	0	bmnue.htm	smenu	Holds all of the application code.
	1	buginput.htm	work	Input form for entering bug information.

FIG. 19.5
When the bug tracking application is loaded it produces this top-level display.

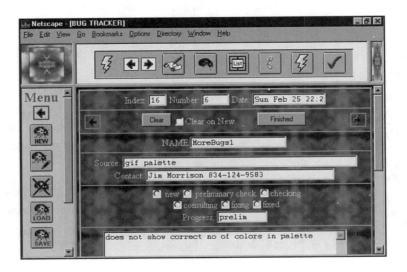

The Bug Object Defined

Because you're going to store bugs in your database, you must define a bug object. Because you can easily expect that there will be more than one bug in your database, you must further arrange for an array of bug objects to be created. Listing 19.10 shows the constructor for a single bug object.

On the CD

Listing 19.10 bmenu.htm Constructor Function for a Single Bug

```
function createBug(number,name,date,source,contact,progress,desc)
{
        this.length     = 11
        this.number     = number        // a sequential number
        this.bname      = name           // name of this bug
        this.index      = ''       // current index of this bug in dBugs
        this.date         = date           // date first reported
        this.source     = source        // what module is bug in
        this.contact    = contact       // who reported bug, telephone no
        this.prog         = progress     // how far along are you on
                                          ➥debugging
        this.desc         = desc           // description of bug
        this.show         = showBug  // method to make a display string
                                          ➥for bug

        return this

}
```

The array of bug objects will be called dBugs. It will be declared as a global variable. The constructor for this array is shown in listing 19.11. The dBugs object is an extended array. This means you have given the array properties in addition to the length property. You still want to use it as an array, however. As you learned in chapter 9, failure to initialize the entire array will lead to erratic results. Your constructor does initialize it, in fact. This extended array has a number of methods designed to maintain the array and give the user information about the array. Not every method will be used in this application.

▶ **See** the section "JavaScript's Associative Arrays" in chapter 9 for a more complete discussion of arrays, **p. 314**.

Part
IV

Ch
19

Listing 19.11 bmenu.htm The Constructor for the Bug Object Array dBugs

```
function createBugsArray(program)
{
     this.length       = 16
     this.index        = 16            // bug being looked at
                                       ➥NOW
     this.next           = 17            // next open slot
     this.program        = program      // program being
                                        ➥debugged
     this.seq            = 1            // next sequential
                                        ➥number
     this.corrected    = 1            // apparent index
     this.add            = addBug       // method to add a bug to
                                        ➥array
     this.remove         = delTheBug   // method to remove a bug to
                                        ➥array
     this.see            = seeABug       // method to display a
                                        ➥bug
     this.count          = countBugs   // method to return a count of
                                        ➥bugs
     this.list           = listBugs      // method to list all
                                        ➥bugs
     this.check          = checkName   // method to check for unique
                                        ➥name
     this.find           = findBug      // method to find a bug in
                                        ➥array
     this.pack           = packBugs    // method to clean up array
     this.seeMe          = seeMyself   // method to display the entire
                                        ➥array.
      this.start         = 16          // place where array really
                                        ➥begins

     this.length = this.start + 30
  var i
  for (i = this.start; i < this.start + 30; i++)
    this[i] = 'bug' + i
  for (i = this.start; i < this.start + 30; i++)
        this[this[i]] = 'temp ' + i

     return this
}
```

Entering a New Bug into the Database

The first task this application must do is solicit user input. It does this via an input screen in frame[1], which is aliased as work. All of the fields are in the same HTML form and would be accessed as work.document.forms[0]. Therefore, this latter object reference has also been aliased to wrkf, and declared as such in each of the other frames. An application menu (smenu) button calls newBug, which initializes some of the fields of the input form and then allows the user to fill out the form.

 Listing 19.12 shows the code for newBug. This function goes through a number of steps to do its work. It checks the flag newInProgress to see if you are already in the process of entering a new bug; if so, it warns the user that it is not allowed and exits. If this test fails, it sets the flag newInProgress to true. It examines a check-box on the form to see if the user wants the form elements cleared automatically with each new bug entry. It arranges that certain fields will have default values. The user will not be allowed to change the index, the date, or the sequence number fields.

Notice that this function does not make a new bug entry into the dBugs array. You do not do this until the user indicates that he is serious about the entry by clicking the Finished button on the input form.

On the CD

Listing 19.12   bmenu.htm   Setting Up for a New Bug Entry

```
function newBug()
{
    if (newInProgress)
            alert('You have not finished with the last new bug. Only one at ¬
                ↵a time, please!')
    else if (dBugs.next > dBugs.length)
        alert('You have reached your maximum of 30 bugs. You must fix some ¬
            ↵of the bugs which you have recorded before you can enter any
            ↵more!')
    else
            {
                newInProgress = true
                wrkf.notxt.value = dBugs.seq
                wrkf.seqtxt.value= dBugs.next
                var now = new Date;
```

continues

Listing 19.12   Continued

```
                    wrkf.datetxt.value= now.toLocaleString()
                    if (wrkf.autoclchk.checked) work.clearBug()
                    var thisbugname = dBugs.program + dBugs.seq
                    wrkf.nametxt.value= thisbugname
                    wrkf.progbtn[0].checked = true
                    wrkf.progtxt.value= 'new'
                    wrkf.destxt.value = 'New Bug'
                    wrkf.mystatus.value = 'new'
        }
}
```

 When the user does indicate that he is ready to enter the bug, the function
saveBug() is called by the input form's Finished button. Note that saveBug has not
been made a method of the bug object. However, you can make it into a method by
changing all references to dBugs into references to this. You would also have to
increase dBugs.start, dBugs.next, and the array length in this case. Listing 19.13
shows the code for the saveBug() function.

Listing 19.13   bmenu.htm   Function to Save a Bug into the *dBugs*
Array and Store it as a Cookie

```
function saveBug()
{
    readVar()
    var ii = dBugs.next
    var curbug =new createBug(''+ ii,'bugtemp' + ii,'','','','','')
    dBugs[ii] = nm
    dBugs[nm] = curbug
    dBugs[dBugs[ii]].contact      = ct
    dBugs[dBugs[ii]].source        = sr
    dBugs[dBugs[ii]].prog         = pr
    dBugs[dBugs[ii]].desc         = ds
    dBugs[dBugs[ii]].index         = dBugs.next
    dBugs[dBugs[ii]].number        = dBugs.seq
    dBugs[dBugs[ii]].bname        = nm
    var now = new Date
    dBugs[dBugs[ii]].date = now
    dataToCookie(nm,dBugs[dBugs[ii]],dBugs.index)
    saveSequential()
    dBugs.add()
    newInProgress = false
```

```
        updateStatus(ii,'......')
        flagDone()
    }
```

First, `saveBug` calls a function named `readVar()`, shown in listing 19.14. The `ReadVar()` function might seem a little peculiar to you. Why not just read the form values directly into a bug? Because of a Netscape bug (which might not apply to all platforms and might be fixed by the time you read this). Pulling the input data directly from the form appears to wreak havoc with the `dBugs` array. The form input value is concatenated with an empty string; this forces it to be interpreted as a string, thereby bypassing this bug. Note that the variables used in `readVar` are global variables.

On the CD

Listing 19.14   bmenu.htm   The Function *readVar()* Retrieves Input from the Form

```
function readVar()
{
    ct = '' + wrkf.contxt.value
    sr = '' + wrkf.srctxt.value
    pr = '' + wrkf.progtxt.value
    ds = '' + wrkf.destxt.value
    nm = '' + wrkf.nametxt.value
     st     = '' + wrkf.mystatus.value
    if (st == 'new')
    {
        var badname=true
        while (badname == true)
            {
                badname = dBugs.check(nm)
                if (badname == true ) {
            var prst = "This name has already been used."
            prst += " Please choose another"
            nm = prompt(prst, nm)
            }
            }
    }
}
```

Part
IV

Ch
19

`ReadVar()` has a second purpose: it makes sure new bugs have unique bug names. It checks the hidden field `mystatus` to be sure it is looking at a new bug, rather than an edited bug. In the bug database program, bugs are usually accessed by numerical indexes. The extended array has been set up so you can access a bug by name, as well. If the left side values of an associative array are not unique, this dual form of access is impossible. The code that does the checking calls the dBug.check method, which points to the function checkName(). The checkName() function simply cycles through the left side values of the associative array to see if the name passed to it appears there. If so, it returns true in a variable called badname; if not, it returns false. If badname is true, the user is asked to give it another name, which is again passed to checkName (see fig. 19.6). The cycle continues until a unique name has been found.

FIG. 19.6
Duplicate bug names are flagged by the input processing function.

When you have all of the information you need, you can create a new bug object (in the variable curbug). Where this bug should go in the dBugs array is dictated by the statement var ii = dBugs.next. The left side of that array element is filled with nm, the unique name of the bug. The right side of the array is filled with curbug. You could have filled various properties of curbug with information generated by the application or gleaned from the form by readVar() before you placed it into the dBugs array. Instead, we did it the hard way, by adding curbug to the array first and then filling it—just to demonstrate the double indirection into the bug object that is part of the dBugs array. This illustrates clearly that you are dealing with an array of arrays.

The final task is to add the date and then save the bug data in a cookie. The function `dataToCookie()` rolls up the bug information into a delimited string that can be saved in this manner, as shown in listing 19.15.

Listing 19.15   bmenu.htm   The Function dataToCookie Condenses a Bug into a Delimited String

```
function dataToCookie(bugname,bug,ndx)
{
    var astr = ''
    var aname = '@' + bugname
    var k = bug.length
        for (i = 1 ; i < k-1 ; i++)
        {
                astr += bug[i]  + '_'
        }
    astr += '$'
    func.saveOneCookie(aname,astr,'year')
}
```

To save `dataToCookie()` a little trouble, we pass it the bug name as a separate parameter, although it could be extracted from the `bug` object itself, which is passed in as the second parameter. The `DataToCookie()` function prefixes the cookie name with `'@'` because you probably want to store more than one kind of cookie, and you need a way to tell the various cookies apart. The routine then cycles through each of the `bug` object's elements (except the last one, which is a method), and concatenates all of the values with the underscore (_) character as the separator.

It ends the string using the dollar sign ($) character as a terminator, and then calls the library function `func.saveOneCookie(aname,astr,'year')`. Note that this `saveOneCookie` function is stored in the function library contained in the `frames[0]` object. `frames[0]` has been aliased to `func`. Any function in the function library can be accessed by preceding the method or value name with `func`. Listing 19.16 shows the code for the `saveOneCookie` function.

Listing 19.16   function.htm   The *saveOneCookie* Function from the Function Library

```
function saveOneCookie(name,what,how)
{
            var expr
             var cc = how.substring(0,1)
            cc = cc.toUpperCase()
            if (cc == 'Y')
                    expr =makeYearExpDate(1)
            if (cc== 'T')
                      expr = ''
            if (cc == 'D')
                    expr = makeDeleteExpDate()
            what = fixSep(what)
            var astr= name + '=' + what + ';expires=' + expr +
            ➡';path=/'
            document.cookie=astr
}
```

The function `saveOneCookie()` is important, so we will examine it closely. First, it extracts the first letter of the `how` parameter and converts it to uppercase. It then tests this value to determine the expiration date for the cookie. If the `how` parameter has the value `'year'`, the cookie expiration date is set to one year from the current date. If `how` is the string `'Temporary'`, no expiration date is attached to the cookie—the cookie expires at the end of the Netscape session. Finally, if `how` is `'Delete'`, the expiration date is set for a time before now. The cookie automatically expires and is removed.

The function `fixSep()` changes all semicolons (;) to escape codes. The `saveOneCookie` function arranges to separate all cookies with semicolons, so you don't want any in the cookie body. The bug database application uses its own special separator, but the `fixSep()` routine can be used generically.

Finally, the cookie is constructed from the value `name` and `what` parameters passed to the routine, the expiration date, and the path (which generally is `'/'`). The cookie is then stored. Remember that `document.cookie` stores cookies separately but retrieves them jointly.

Because you're assigning each bug an absolute sequential number that isn't dependent on the `dBugs` array, you need to be able to store this number between invocations of the program. The `saveSequential()` function simply prefixes the name with a caret (^) to distinguish this cookie from others, defines the cookie, and then calls `func.saveOneCookie()`.

At this point, the bug database application is finished storing the bug. It now has nothing left to do except clean up and notify the user that the bug has been saved. The flag `newInProgress` is reset to `false` so a new bug can be entered. A save message is placed in the status bar. However, this is not really an attention-getter, so another mechanism is used as well. You might have wondered about the odd frame in the upper-right corner of the bug database display. This frame is there only to provide the user visual cues. The `FlagDone()` function rewrites the document of `ind` to say `'DONE'` (vertically) and sets a timer to trigger a `'go back to original'` function. The code for this function is shown in listing 19.17. This could be made more elegant if you modified it so it plays a small animated sequence in its tiny window.

On the CD

Listing 19.17   bmenu.htm   A Function To Give User a Visual Cue that Something Has Happened

```
function flagDone()
{
                ind.document.open()
                ind.document.write('<FONT SIZE=2 COLOR="maroon"><B>')
                ind.document.write('D<BR>')
                ind.document.write('O<BR>')
                ind.document.write('N<BR>')
                ind.document.write('E<BR>')
                ind.document.write('</B></FONT>')
                ind.document.close()
                TimerID = setTimeout('ind.history.go(-0)',2000)
}
```

Part
IV

Ch
19

Retrieving a Bug

Now that you have successfully entered a bug, how do you retrieve it? A crude way is to have the user enter a number at a prompt or, perhaps, in an input field in the application menu. But users rarely remember what numbers are assigned to items, nor should they be required to do so. How about retrieval by name? That's better, but can the user remember the names? The most user-friendly solution is to present the user with a list of names.

The most obvious implementation of this list would be a select form element. Unfortunately, this element often misbehaves in current manifestations of Netscape, particularly if there are a large number of items on the list. A hotlist would also be nice. The bug database program produces two kinds of hotlists, in similar ways. The first is invoked by the System Menu List button. This is the first time you have used one of these buttons. Remember that the function of these buttons is to access a function in the resident application code. This function must have a standard name; in this case the function is alist(). The alist() function contains a single line of code:

```
showInWindow(dBugs.list('<BR>'),'Bugs')
```

The function showInWindow() puts the string argument given as its first parameter into a pop-up window whose name is given as the second parameter. The dbugs.list() method it calls cycles through the valid dBugs entries and calls the dBugs.see method for each. This method is actually a reference to the function seeABug(), shown in listing 19.18. The resulting hotlist is shown in figure 19.7.

Listing 19.18   bmenu.htm   The Function *seeABug()* Converts Bug Information into a String

```
function seeABug(which,trm,cit)
{
    var astr = ''
    var nstr = ''
        nstr = this[which]
        var abug = this[nstr]
        if (cit)
            astr = '<A HREF=JavaScript:self.creator.toEditor('
            astr +=       abug.index + ')>'
        astr += which + '      ' + nstr
    if (cit) astr += '</A>'
        astr += trm
        astr += 'Index:     ' + abug.index + trm
        astr += 'Name:      ' + abug.bname + trm
        astr += 'Number:    ' + abug.number + trm
        astr += 'Date:      ' + abug.date + trm
        astr += 'Source:    ' + abug.source + trm
```

```
astr += 'Contact:          ' + abug.contact + trm
astr += 'Progress:         ' + abug.progress + trm
astr += 'Description       ' + abug.desc + trm
return astr

}
```

FIG. 19.7
The System Menu List
button pops up a descrip-
tive hotlist of bugs.

Both the dBugs.list and the dBugs.see methods take a terminator parameter trm, so these functions can produce output that is properly formatted for HTML or for an alert. dBugs.list passes along the terminator to dBugs.see, along with the index of the bug and a variable called cit. If cit is true, dBugs.see will write the first line as a hotlink containing a JavaScript call to a function named toEditor(), along with its parameters. dbugs.list writes out most of the properties of each bug and presents it in a pop-up window for the user's perusal.

If the user clicks the hotlink, a call is made to the toEditor function, which retrieves the appropriate bug, unwraps it into the input window, and then sets dBugs.index to point to it. If the call came from a window and toEditor() finds that window open, toEditor() closes the window. The toEditor() function also sets the value of the input form's hidden field, mystatus, to 'edit' so saveBug() cannot insist that a new bug name be entered.

Part
IV

Ch
19

Editing a Bug

 The editBug button (a bug with a pencil beside it) on the Application menu performs a similar function, except in this case, the hotlist is composed only of bug names. Each name calls toEditor() if it is clicked. This hotlist is shown in figure 19.8.

FIG. 19.8
A simple hotlist is popped up by the Application menu Edit button.

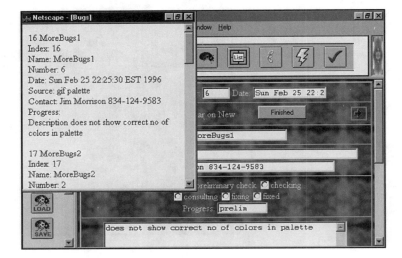

The bugs application lets you edit a bug as many times as you like, so you can update notes and report progress on the bug. It does not have a lot of error checking to ensure that the user enters data properly. You might want to build in the following mechanisms to improve the program:

- Prevent the user from changing the bug name.
- Go backwards on the progress list without an explanation.
- Present a list of bugs with a given progress classification.
- Have the cookies written specifically to the application cookie instead of the function library's cookie.

Deleting a Bug

What do you do when you delete a bug? This implementation of the bug database program does nothing automatically. Ideally, you would archive the bug and then delete it from the list of active bugs. At the moment, Netscape makes no provision for writing to files other than the document cookie, so there is no way to archive the bugs. The Application menu, though, does provide a Delete button so you can delete bugs. The function delTheBug() is used to delete bugs from the dBugs array (see listing 19.19).

Listing 19.19   bmenu.htm   The Function *delTheBug()* Deletes a Bug from the *dBugs* Array and the Document Cookie

```
function delTheBug(which)
{
    if (which < this.start |¦ which >= this.next)
    {
        alert('Cannot delete ' + which)
        return - 1
    }
    else
    {
        alert('deleting ' + which)
          var nstr = this[which]
        this[which] = '---'
        this['---'] = ''
        this.pack()
          func.saveOneCookie('@' + nstr,'','delete')
        return 1
    }
}
```

This function places '---' in the bug's name and wipes out the bug object referenced by it. It then calls the method dBug.pack(), which eliminates the first '---' it finds in the dBugs array (there should only be one) and moves everything below it up one slot. It then decrements the dBugs.next property. Finally, it calls the func.saveOneCookie() function with the cookie name, an empty string, and the delete flag. This final operation removes the bug from the document cookie.

Part

IV

Ch

19

Other Buttons

The Application menu, which is the vertical menu on the left side of the page, has some unexplained items on it. These include a Load button, a Save button, and a Back Arrow button. Most of the buttons on the System menu have not been explained, and not all are functional.

 Application Menu   The Load button loads all of the bugs from the document.cookie into the dBugs array. It calls a function named cookieToDBug() to do this. cookieToDBug() is also called in the document onLoad event handler so the application starts out with the array loaded.

 The Back Arrow button reloads smenu (from the file bmenu.htm). This is really a debugging function and you might want to remove it in a final application.

 System Menu   The System menu is the horizontal menu on the top of the page. The Forward and Backward Arrow buttons apply to the top window only. If you want to go backward and forward in a frame, you need to supply buttons to do so.

 These buttons act on the work frame that holds the input form. In the bug database application, this form does not change, so these buttons have no function in this application as it stands.

 The Notes button points to a function called aNote() in smenu. If you click the button, a plain little notepad pops up and enables you to save and load notes. Figure 19.9 shows this notepad.

FIG. 19.9
The System menu Notes button pops up a rudimentary notepad.

The Bugs button is meant for debugging purposes during development. It pops up a list of warnings or bugs when an application is finished. At the moment, it points to storeSequential, which often needs to be adjusted during debugging.

The List button, as you have seen, pops up a hotlist that gives information on each bug.

The Links button is meant to pop up a list of links related to what is in the application. It points to the function aLink() in smenu, which is not currently used in this application.

You typically use the Go button to execute an application-specific aGo() function in smenu. In this implementation, aGo pops up an alert with the contents of the document cookie.

The Done button closes the entire application.

Other HTML Elements The Input Screen is the large data entry area located at the center of the page. The Input screen Forward and Backward buttons scroll backward and forward in the dBugs array. When the user reaches the beginning or end of that portion of dBugs, the user notification area flashes NO.

The User Notification Area is in the upper-right frame; it usually has a picture in it. However, at the end of a load or when a scrolling record hits an end point, it displays a one-word message to the user. ●

Part
IV

Ch
19

Learning from the Pros

CHAPTER 20

Learning from the Pros: Site Outlines

— *by Rick Darnell*

One of the ways JavaScript has made navigating Web sites easier is through the use of multiple frames, typically implemented with a static list of links or a toolbar.

▶ **See** chapter 14, "Controlling Web Page Appearance," **p. 481**.

▶ **See** chapter 19, "Using Frames and Cookies in Advanced Applications," **p. 649**.

However, with JavaScript's capability to manipulate the contents of a window—including clearing and rewriting it—what would happen if the list of links was a dynamic object that could be expanded or collapsed? That's the idea Stefan Raab began to develop when he started to put together an indexing system for the Cue Systems'

Web site that would enable easy navigation and a visual key to its structure (see fig. 20.1).

FIG. 20.1
Implementing a navigation outline with JavaScript was easier than Stefan Raab of Cue Systems anticipated, requiring only a few days of coding and testing after learning the basics of scripting.

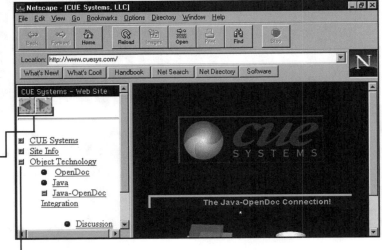

History buttons relate to the user's movement within the site.

Each heading includes a graphical button for expanding or collapsing that portion of the outline.

Stefan Raab of Cue Systems, LLC

Using JavaScript as part of a corporate Web site was practically an accident for Stefan Raab, Communications Development Manager for Cue Systems, located on the World Wide Web at **http://www.cuesys.com**.

The company's mission is to develop integration between Java and OpenDoc for universal document handling, regardless of the hardware platform. "We call it 'reinventing the wheel for the information age,'" he says.

Most of his time is spent on everything except Web site management, including documentation, system support, and patent registration. "This was strictly a spare time enterprise," Raab says. "As I found a few minutes, I started to put the pieces together."

With an original plan revolving around learning CGI and Perl, Raab had planned on spending up to a month getting familiar with the programming before tackling the Web outline project. As betas of Netscape 2.0 were released with working versions of JavaScript, he started working with the new tools for HTML to see what they were capable of.

When it comes to learning new tools, such as JavaScript, reinventing the wheel means sharing ideas and solutions with other programmers and developers by letting the flow of information on the Web help drive program development through shared source code.

"It really frustrates me when someone just lifts a section of code and doesn't try to do anything else with it," Raab says. He contends it defeats the purpose of making common items available and slows down the process that takes simple ideas and transforms them into powerful applications.

"I love just to watch stuff evolve," he says, adding that one of his favorite moments is when people modify his outline and make it work for applications he never thought of. "People take it and do something new, and that's the exciting part about this."

The Collapsing and Expanding Outline

"The outline is more than a menu," Raab explains. "It's a natural way to organize information," which applies to everything from books and magazines to shopping lists and lists of home improvement projects.

When developing Cue Systems' public Web site, he wanted to use an outline model to relay navigational information to the user. His plan was for an application to automatically track the pages and links and assemble the outline based on that information. Each time a user accessed his site, the server would search for folders and documents—using the information to build an outline, which in turn would be used as a hot-linked table of contents.

The initial plan involved CGI scripting to accomplish site searching and page creation to update the outline. In addition to assembling and testing CGI scripts, this option also meant increased traffic and loading on the server.

Using CGI meant increased difficulties on both sides of the development process. First, he had to learn Perl and then develop the script necessary to search a site and build pages. When a functioning script was in place, it would mean a decrease in server performance, as it spent time looking for Web documents and writing the outline.

As the plan for CGI began to fade, Raab still didn't want to abandon the idea. "The outline is the most powerful way to organize information," he says. "It's something people do automatically whether they know it or not."

Getting Up to Speed

"Getting this implemented was not a real priority," Raab says. The first thoughts of putting up a site for public consumption were in October 1995, but there was no serious development towards completion. Cue Systems maintains an intranet for its own use, but a site on the World Wide Web was not a pressing concern.

With the first usable version of JavaScript in a beta release of Netscape 2.0 in late fall 1995, Raab saw the possibilities for putting a site outline together without CGI. After trial-and-error experimentation and working with a JavaScript newsgroup, Raab picked up the fundamentals of implementing JavaScript in HTML.

For additional research, Raab and his colleagues went browsing for other pages that used outlines as a navigational tool. "We looked at other sites, but they just didn't use the function of an outline." Raab says other sites had an outline's appearance, but not the usability. In most cases, it was too simple with links to the top page of a general location, or too unwieldy with a list of links to an entire site.

Once Raab knew how his site shouldn't work, he put together an idea of how it could work and began assembling HTML and JavaScript code. With three days of work in January, a mock-up of the outline was completed.

Beginning his work with an immature language, such as JavaScript, and a beta version of Netscape meant sometimes working with an incomplete set of tools that didn't always perform as they should. "It took longer to work around bugs (in JavaScript)," he says. "It wasn't easy to update the page. There were a lot of un-documented things going on. We were spending a lot of time just finding out what was working."

The First Attempt: Forms

The first implementation of a dynamic outline used JavaScript's form manipulation features. This led to some unexpected behavior created by the way forms and form elements are implemented in JavaScript. Each level of the outline was represented by a form element, which worked well at first. The problems surfaced when adding or subtracting form checkbox elements as particular items were removed when the outline was collapsed.

Form elements are implemented in JavaScript as arrays and not true objects. As a form element was removed from the array, the other elements moved up in the array to occupy the vacant position. However, in addition to occupying the space by its neighbor, the checkbox element also assumed the value its neighbor left behind.

▶ **See** chapter 6, "Interactive HTML Objects," **p. 183**.

So, if a form element was changed from `false` (for expanded) to `true` (for collapsed), the following major topics assumed the checkbox values of the newly collapsed items sub-topics, resulting in bizarre behavior. Selecting or deselecting an outline item resulted in an almost random state of outline items below the affected form element.

onClicks and *anchors*

The next method for implementing was an outline that used the `onClick` method in conjunction with `anchors`. This option utilized a set of pages representing the different states of the outline with hashes to ensure the right portion was displayed when selected.

▶ **See** chapter 3, "Events and JavaScript," **p. 75**.

The problem was using hashes. To reference the top of a form, the URL included a hash with no `anchor`, which again resulted in unpredictable behavior and frequent crashes caused by referral to a "nonexistent" hash.

Those Persistent Objects

By continued experimentation with JavaScript, Raab learned about a quirk that held the key to the final solution: if a value is assigned to an object and the page is reloaded, the object will retain the value of its properties.

▶ **See** chapter 8, "Dynamic HTML and Browser Objects," **p. 257**.

The implications were immediately clear. The form of the outline could be stored as objects with properties relating to the current state. When the user changed the state, the page was reloaded and redrawn based on the new object information.

This was accomplished with another "hidden" feature of the language. JavaScript became a valid document type for URLs (see fig. 20.2). By selecting an item in the outline, a JavaScript command is invoked with an event handler using URL format.

FIG. 20.2
The URL displayed in the status line with the mouse over an outline item is a JavaScript command.

A JavaScript command used as a URL.

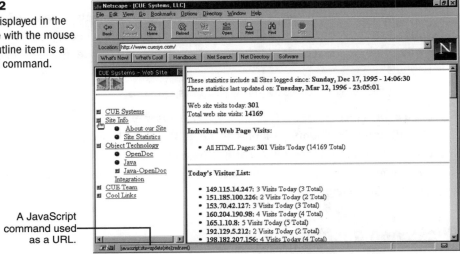

The key to implementing the outline lies in the persistent state of objects during page reloading and the capability to embed JavaScript commands in URLs. Note the URL reflected in the status bar, which displays the two functions that update the outline display.

Losing Automatic Outline Building

By choosing an HTML JavaScript solution over CGI scripting, Raab had to give up the option of an outline that automatically updated itself. That meant more up-front work implementing the idea because he now had to organize his site with pencil and paper to see how it would be implemented in JavaScript code.

"The worst part was building the outlines by hand," he says. Organizing the site on paper also led to organizing the site on the server. "It really took planning."

Like a lot of Web sites, most of Raab's pages were lumped together in a common content directory. By breaking out the pages into directories that reflected site organization, the site outline began to materialize. As the outline took shape, so did the site, and he was ready to implement the information into his script.

Raab insists it was a valuable exercise in the development of a coherent and usable site. Taking the time to "build a good plan straight from the beginning" has saved more time later when it has been necessary to update the site. It also leads to the one drawback of his implementation: when a page or a link changes on his site, it must be recorded in the outline HTML document. "Every time I add, change, or remove a link, I have to change the code," he says.

Although this can be an inconvenience, the majority of the links for the Cue Systems site only occur within the outline. If a link is changed, it's usually in the outline document where the outline data can be changed also. If the link is also contained on another page, Raab's organization and outline speed its identification and change.

Simple Idea—Broad Application

After he finished the code, he posted the results on a newsgroup with a "here's my simple outline" note. He didn't think he had accomplished much until the mail started to overflow in his electronic mail box.

"I was just overwhelmed. People were writing things like, 'This is the best use of JavaScript I've ever seen.' It was just message after message. I still get four or five messages a week like that as more people find it." The current version of the outline is included on the CD-ROM.

Some of the uses that have come back to Raab include a table of contents for an online book and an outline of graphics. Other possibilities he's considered, but hasn't yet seen, include personnel and corporate directories for both Internet and intranet sites, departments for electronic stores, and illustrating structures of hardware connections.

Listing 20.1 is the source code for Stefan Raab's dynamic outline menu. Each menu level is implemented with its own object, which can contain other objects for outline sub-topics. To work with the quirks of JavaScript's `write` method, the object properties are initialized, and the initial display is created using Raab's `draw()`

function. After a user changes the outline, the page is cleared and recreated using a redraw() function.

Listing 20.1   21list01.html   Cue Systems' Expanding and Collapsing Navigation Outline

```html
<!-- So, you think the outline is pretty cool huh? Yeah me too! -->
<!-- Well feel free to take it and use it to you hearts content -->
<!-- I just ask two things of you:                              -->
<!-- 1. Please send me the URL of the page that uses it! I want -->
<!--    to see what other people are doing with it! :)          -->
<!-- 2. Please keep this Comment attached. Feel free to add to  -->
<!--    it as you see fit!                                      -->
<!-- This is version 2.0                                        -->
<!-- Stefan Raab, cue Systems — stefan@cuesys.com              -->

<html>
<head>
    <title>Wheel</title>
</head>
<body>
<script>var cue = false
var site = false
var objects = true
var jod = true
var bul = false
var team = false
var links = false

function update(obj)
{
  if (obj)
    {
      obj = false;
    }
    else
    {
      obj = true;
    }

  return obj;
}

function redraw()
{
  document.clear()
  draw()
  document.close()
}
```

```
function clse()
{
  top.frames[0].history.go(1 - top.frames[0].history.length)
  var place= window.top.frames[1].location
  window.top.location.href = place.href
}

function draw()
{
  document.write('<A HREF="javascript:clse()">
  ➥<IMG SRC="http://www.cuesys.com/cueweb.gif" BORDER=0 WIDTH=195
  ➥Height=20></A><BR>')
  document.write('<A HREF="javascript:top.frames[1].history.go([nd]1)">
  ➥<IMG SRC="http://www.cuesys.com/icons/leftarr.gif" ALIGN="CENTER"
  ➥BORDER="0"></A>')
  document.write('<A HREF="javascript:top.frames[1].history.go(1)">
  ➥<IMG SRC="http://www.cuesys.com/icons/rightarr.gif"
  ➥ALIGN="CENTER" BORDER="0"></A>')
  document.write('<HR>')

  document.write('<DL>')
  if (cue)
   {
    document.write('<DT><A HREF="javascript:cue=update(cue);
    ➥redraw()">')
    document.write('<IMG SRC="http://www.cuesys.com/icons/minus.gif"
    ➥BORDER=0 HEIGHT=10 WIDTH=20></a>')
    document.write('<A HREF="http://cuesys.com/cue" Target="document">
    ➥CUE Systems</a>');
    document.write('<DL><DT><IMG SRC="http://www.cuesys.com/icons/
    ➥bul.gif" HEIGHT=10 WIDTH=20>')
    document.write('<A HREF="http://cuesys.com/cue/index.html"
    ➥TARGET="document">Mission Statement</A>')
    document.write('<DT><IMG SRC="http://www.cuesys.com/icons/bul.gif"
    ➥HEIGHT=10 WIDTH=20>')
    document.write('<A HREF="http://cuesys.com/cue/contact.html"
    ➥TARGET="document">Contact Information</A></DL>')
   }
  else
   {
    document.write('<DT><A HREF="javascript:cue = update(cue);
    ➥redraw()">')
    document.write('<IMG SRC="http://www.cuesys.com/icons/plus.gif"
    ➥HEIGHT=10 WIDTH=20 BORDER=0>')
    document.write('</a><A HREF="http://cuesys.com/cue"
    ➥Target="document">CUE Systems</a>');
   }
```

continues

Listing 20.1   Continued

```
if (site)
{
  document.write('<DT><A HREF="javascript:site=update(site);
➥redraw()"><IMG SRC="http://www.cuesys.com/icons/minus.gif"
➥BORDER=0 HEIGHT=10 WIDTH=20></a>')
  document.write('<A HREF="http://cuesys.com/site_info.html"
➥Target="document">Site Info</a>');
  document.write('<DL> <DT><IMG SRC="http://www.cuesys.com/icons/
➥bul.gif" HEIGHT=10 WIDTH=20>
     <A HREF="http://cuesys.com/site_info.html" TARGET="document"
     ➥>About our Site</A>')
  document.write('<DT><IMG SRC="http://www.cuesys.com/icons/bul.gif"
➥HEIGHT=10 WIDTH=20>
     <A HREF="http://cuesys.com/ps.html" TARGET="document"
     ➥>Site Statistics</A></DL>')
}
else
{
  document.write('<DT> <A HREF="javascript:site = update(site);
➥redraw()"><IMG SRC="http://www.cuesys.com/icons/plus.gif"
➥HEIGHT=10 WIDTH=20 BORDER=0></a>
     <A HREF="http://cuesys.com/site_info.html" Target="document"
     ➥>Site Info</a>');
}

if (objects)
 {
  document.write('<DT><A HREF="javascript:objects=update(objects);
➥redraw()"><IMG SRC="http://www.cuesys.com/icons/minus.gif"
➥BORDER=0 HEIGHT=10 WIDTH=20></a>')
  document.write('<A HREF="http://cuesys.com/objects"
➥Target="document">Object Technology</a>');
  document.write('<DL> <DT> <IMG SRC="http://www.cuesys.com/icons/
➥bul.gif" HEIGHT=10 WIDTH=20> <A HREF="http://cuesys.com/
➥objects/od" TARGET="document">OpenDoc</A>')
  document.write('<DT><IMG SRC="http://www.cuesys.com/icons/
➥bul.gif" HEIGHT=10 WIDTH=20>
     <A HREF="http://cuesys.com/objects/java" TARGET="document"
     ➥>Java</A>')
  if (jod)
   {
     document.write('<DT><A HREF="javascript:jod=update(jod);
➥redraw()"><IMG SRC="http://www.cuesys.com/icons/
➥minus.gif"  BORDER=0 HEIGHT=10 WIDTH=20></a>')
     document.write('<A HREF="http://cuesys.com/objects/jod"
➥Target="document">Java-OpenDoc Integration</a>');
     document.write('<DL><DT><BR CLEAR=ALL> <IMG
```

```
      ➥SRC="http://www.cuesys.com/icons/bul.gif" HEIGHT=10
      ➥WIDTH=20><A HREF="http://cuesys.com/lists/jod"
      ➥TARGET="document">Discussion List (ListServ)</A>')
      document.write('<DT>  <IMG SRC="http://www.cuesys.com/icons/
      ➥bul.gif" HEIGHT=10 WIDTH=20><A HREF="http://cuesys.com/
      ➥links/index.html#objects" TARGET="document">Other Links<
      ➥/A></DL>')
    }
    else
    {
      document.write('<DT>  <A HREF="javascript:jod = update(jod);
      ➥redraw()"><IMG SRC="http://www.cuesys.com/icons/plus.gif"
      ➥HEIGHT=10 WIDTH=20 BORDER=0></a>
      ➥<A HREF="http://cuesys.com/objects/jod"
      ➥Target="document">Java-OpenDoc Integration</a>');
    }
        document.write('</DL>')
  }
  else
  {
    document.write('<DT> <A HREF="javascript:objects =
    ➥update(objects);redraw()"><IMG SRC="http://www.cuesys.com/
    ➥icons/plus.gif" HEIGHT=10 WIDTH=20 BORDER=0></a>
    ➥<A HREF="http://cuesys.com/objects" Target="document"
    ➥>Object Technology</a>');
  }

if (team)
 {
   document.write('<DT><A HREF="javascript:team=update(team);
   ➥redraw()">')
   document.write('<IMG SRC="http://www.cuesys.com/icons/
   ➥minus.gif" BORDER=0 HEIGHT=10 WIDTH=20></a>')
   document.write('<A HREF="http://cuesys.com/people"
   ➥Target="document">CUE Team</a>');

   document.write('<DL><DT><IMG SRC="http://www.cuesys.com/icons/
   ➥bul.gif" HEIGHT=10 WIDTH=20>')
   document.write('<A HREF="http://cuesys.com/~rich" TARGET="document"
   ➥>Rich Kilmer</A>')
   document.write('<DT><IMG SRC="http://www.cuesys.com/icons/bul.gif"
   ➥HEIGHT=10 WIDTH=20>')
   document.write('<A HREF="http://cuesys.com/~dave" TARGET="document"
   ➥>Dave Craine</A>')
   document.write('<DT><IMG SRC="http://www.cuesys.com/icons/bul.gif"
   ➥HEIGHT=10 WIDTH=20>')
   document.write('<A HREF="http://cuesys.com/~stefan"
   ➥TARGET="document">Stefan Raab</A></DL>')
 }
```

continues

Listing 20.1 Continued

```
    else
    {
      document.write('<DT><A HREF="javascript:team =
update(team);redraw()">')
      document.write('<IMG SRC="http://www.cuesys.com/icons/plus.gif"
HEIGHT=10 WIDTH=20 BORDER=0>')
      document.write('</a><A HREF="http://cuesys.com/people"
Target="document">CUE Team</a>');
    }

  if (links)
    {
      document.write('<DT><A HREF="javascript:links=update(links);
      ➥redraw()">')
      document.write('<IMG SRC="http://www.cuesys.com/icons/minus.gif"
      ➥BORDER=0 HEIGHT=10 WIDTH=20></a>')
      document.write('<A HREF="http://cuesys.com/people"
      ➥Target="document">Cool Links</a>');

      document.write('<DL><DT><IMG SRC="http://www.cuesys.com/icons/
      ➥bul.gif" HEIGHT=10 WIDTH=20>')
      document.write('<A HREF="http://cuesys.com/links/
      ➥index.html#graphics" TARGET="document">Graphics</A>')
      document.write('<DT><IMG SRC="http://www.cuesys.com/icons/bul.gif"
      ➥HEIGHT=10 WIDTH=20>')
      document.write('<A HREF="http://cuesys.com/links/index.html#mac"
      ➥TARGET="document">Mac & Newton</A>')
      document.write('<DT><IMG SRC="http://www.cuesys.com/icons/bul.gif"
      ➥HEIGHT=10 WIDTH=20>')
      document.write('<A HREF="http://cuesys.com/links/index.html#random"
      ➥TARGET="document">Random</A>')
      document.write('<DT><IMG SRC="http://www.cuesys.com/icons/bul.gif"
      ➥HEIGHT=10 WIDTH=20>')
      document.write('<A HREF="http://cuesys.com/links/index.html#unix"
      ➥TARGET="document">UNIX etc</A></DL>')
    }
    else
    {
      document.write('<DT><A HREF="javascript:links = update(links);
      ➥redraw()">')
      document.write('<IMG SRC="http://www.cuesys.com/icons/plus.gif"
      ➥HEIGHT=10 WIDTH=20 BORDER=0>')
      document.write('</a><A HREF="http://cuesys.com/people"
      ➥Target="document">Cool Links</a>');
    }

  }
```

```
draw()</script>
</p>

</body>
</html>
```

"What you see (on our site) is a facade," Raab says. "It is a simple tool to aid navigation. But in its simplicity is its power. Like Java, JavaScript is making once-complicated programming applications easier to understand and implement in less space."

He doesn't view the current version of the script as a static product. He has more refinements and revisions planned, including making the code more modular and smaller still. And, there's always the question of what someone else is going to try with it. ●

CHAPTER 21

Learning from the Pros: Adding Frames and Controlling Navigation

— *by Rick Darnell*

Probably the most widely used new feature provided by JavaScript is the capability to use multiple frames to organize Web site content, especially when used in conjunction with navigation and toolbars. For many Web authors, this means converting existing pages and sites into a frame-based format. But it can be tricky. Although frames are a powerful new tool, if misplaced and misused they can be a hindrance to the user by eating up screen space and slowing down the browser.

Another key capability offered with JavaScript is control over browser behavior. New windows and new browsers are opened and closed using simple commands that also control the availability of the browser's tools.

Properly used, these two capabilities enable a Web developer to create a portal into the site and provide the tools he wants the user to have to navigate inside. Content presentation and access are controlled in one simple step (see fig. 21.1).

A button serves as the doorway into CyberExplorer's Web site.

FIG. 21.1
The Start Demo button on CyberExplorer's Web site opens a new browser without the traditional Netscape menu bar items. This enables the Web author to control entrance, exit, and navigation within the site.

Access to the right software is provided for users who need to upgrade before entering.

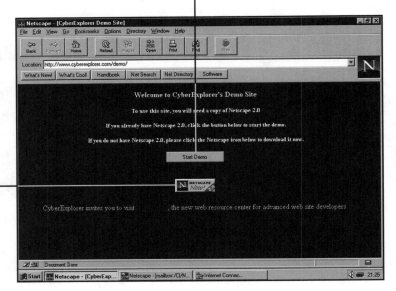

Matthew Fusfield of CyberExplorer

As an Internet consultant, Matthew Fusfield spends a lot of time keeping up with hardware and software advances that can be integrated into clients' Web sites. Because Web technology is changing on virtually a day-to-day basis, it has been a constant process, but one he has enjoyed watching.

"It's good to have new things to do," he says. If nothing new were developed, the capabilities would get old and stale. Emerging technologies enable him to continue providing new services and capabilities to his clients.

Unlike a lot of revisions and updates to software packages that don't add much capability, Fusfield has enjoyed working with the Internet products from Netscape and Microsoft. "I've always been impressed by them by how much their products continue to improve," he says, "and I've always been interested in being among the first to try them." Fusfield has been working with beta versions of Netscape since it was first released, so he learned about it from the ground up.

> **N O T E** CyberExplorer's home page, **http://www.cyberexplorer.com/demo/**, operates by opening a new browser to control the user's navigation options. ▨

The One-Way-Out Web Site

With JavaScript, it is possible to control the appearance and functionality of browser windows. Fusfield capitalizes on this with his Web site. Users are greeted by a button that is used to enter the site. This page also serves to help screen users who may not have the proper software to view the pages within.

When the Start Demo button is clicked, a new browser is loaded with a custom set of navigation buttons (see fig. 21.2).

FIG. 21.2
All pages of CyberExplorer's JavaScript demo include a navigation frame and a tool/navigation bar. An Exit button returns the user to the original browser window.

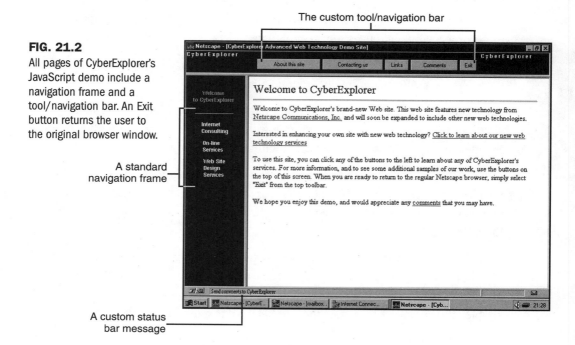

The custom tool/navigation bar

A standard navigation frame

A custom status bar message

As a reminder that users are not in an average Web site, a confirmation alert is used to let them know they're leaving CyberExplorer pages (see fig. 21.3). This is the preferred way to leave the site, although a user can always use the close button on the top-right corner of the screen.

FIG. 21.3
After pressing the Exit button, a confirmation box appears before closing the windows created by the CyberExplorer site and returning to the entrance shown in figure 21.1.

New Web Site Formats = Old-Fashioned Organization

Converting an old Web site into its new JavaScript format is a straightforward process involving refining the existing content, organizing it for frame presentation, and then creating new pages with JavaScript code with the new content pasted in—a process Fusfield uses for most of his projects.

"Generally, if it's a clean site with clean HTML, it takes a few hours over a few days," he says. "But planning is the important part."

After deciding how the site should work and what it should include, Fusfield sketches his ideas on paper, including flowcharts and screen layouts. After refining the idea on paper, he gets the HTML documents currently in use.

Any changes to the content or artwork are made in the old files. Then in separate files he creates the JavaScript code that controls navigation and other browser behavior. When scripts in the new files are complete, the content is inserted from the old files.

"I put it on a password-protected server to see how it behaves," Fusfield says. This says him a chance to use the site in its natural environment and decide what works and what doesn't. This is also a crucial step when working with a client because it enables the customer to review the site before it is generally available.

When the new site is running without a hitch, an important decision is left: what to do with the old files.

To Mirror or Replace

Fusfield says the decision to delete the old files in lieu of the JavaScript-enabled versions depends on the end user's alternatives. For a JavaScript-dependent site, such as CyberExplorer, it's "tough luck" for the user who's not using an up-to-date Netscape browser.

Another option is to provide access to a mirror site, which contains the same content but without JavaScript. This ensures that no users are left out, and is especially important for general-interest sites.

Creating Entrance to a Controlled Site

Creating a controlled environment, like Fusfield has created for CyberExplorer, is quite simple apart from the frames.

If the entrance page also provides access to a mirror site that doesn't require JavaScript, then a hot link can be embedded inside script comment markers, /* and */, to the alternative site. In this example, an all-or-nothing approach is used.

Listing 21.1 shows the HTML code used to create access to the CyberExplorer demo. Note the startdemo() function, which creates a new window without a toolbar or menu bar but provides for scrolling and a status bar. This enables the author to provide a unique set of tools and navigation aids while in the site.

Listing 21.1   Code for Creating First Page of the CyberExplorer Demo

```
<HTML>
<HEAD>
<TITLE>CyberExplorer Demo Site</TITLE>
<SCRIPT LANGUAGE="JavaScript">
<!--
function startdemo(){
    window.open('start.htm', 'CyberExplorer',
    ➥ 'toolbar=no,location=no,directories=no,
```

continues

Listing 21.1   Continued

```
    status=yes,menubar=no,scrollbars=yes,resizable=yes,copyhistory=no')
}
//-->
</SCRIPT>
</HEAD>

<BODY BGCOLOR="#000000" TEXT="#ffffff">
<center>
<P>
<P>
<P>
<P>
<P>
<h4>Welcome to CyberExplorer's Demo Site</h4>
<h5>To use this site, you will need a copy of Netscape 2.0</h5>
<h5>If you already have Netscape 2.0, click the button below to start
➥ the demo.</h5>
<h5>If you do not have Netscape 2.0, please click the Netscape icon
➥ below to download it now.</h5>
<FORM>
<input type="button" value=" Start Demo  " onClick="startdemo()">
</FORM>
```

When the button is clicked, a new window is created using the `window.open()` method. This directs the browser to create a new window and load it with the contents from start.htm—the file that creates the frames and loads the toolbars for the rest of the tour of the site.

With the tool definitions in the `window.open` method, Fusfield's site has captured the user's browser. "The ability to control how a browser behaves is very powerful. Basically, you can't leave until you hit the Exit button."

Finding a Use for Frames

"Frames can be clunky at times," Fusfield says, "At times, I think of ways the actual syntax would have been easier."

Learning how to effectively include frames in a site takes practice and a healthy dose of trial and error. "It's a little more difficult than other HTML tags." His starting point included documentation and examples available online, followed by a lot of experimentation.

Fusfield thinks it is worth the price, however. "They make sense in a lot of places," he said. "We're seeing the groundwork laid for complex interfaces," such as those available for America Online, Prodigy, and CompuServe. It's one of the good ideas that can actually make a page or Web site easier to view and navigate for the user, and serves as the basis for more sophisticated tools.

The problem is that frames require screen space. "With each frame, the screen (for content) is getting smaller." This is especially true when Web authors start creating frames for displaying advertising. "The spirit in which this capability was created was to help navigate…not advertise," he says. "Its best use is for navigation and toolbars."

Although advertising is a valid use for frames, it shouldn't interfere with or overpower the frame used for content. "Put it where it's not obtrusive." ●

CHAPTER 22

Learning from the Pros: Online Ordering System

— *by Rick Darnell*

One of the underutilized areas of JavaScript is client-side integration with CGI and server-side databases. With JavaScript's capability to validate information and keep a running total of items and prices, it can serve as a powerful tool to reduce the dependence on CGI scripts in generating catalog pages and order forms for users, thereby reducing the load on the server and the user's time spent on waiting for client-server communication.

Although Books Galore! is simple in structure and application, the fundamentals used illustrate what can be done, even with a simple CGI operation on a text-based data set (see fig. 22.1).

FIG. 22.1
The opening page of Books Galore! is a simple form that enables the user to choose which types of books to browse. The results of the form are used to parse a database and retrieve the product information.

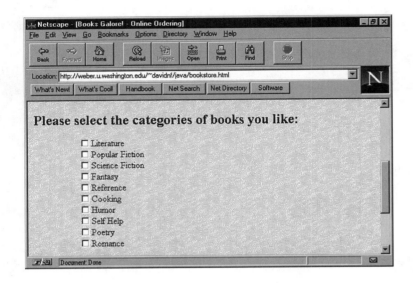

N O T E The Books Galore! ordering demo is found at **http://weber.u.washington.edu/ ~davidnf/java/bookstore.html**. As you try out the system, don't worry about the bill: it's only a demo, so no one is waiting on the other end of the line to take your money.

David Nagy-Farkas of LiveWeb

David Nagy-Farkas is a senior in computer engineering at the University of Washington in Seattle. With exposure to a wide variety of computer languages over the course of his studies, including C, C++, and SmallTalk, it was only natural that he trained his sights on two new entries in the programming fray: Java and JavaScript.

"I heard about them when they were released, and started checking them out," he says. After consulting online documentation from Netscape and other sources, he started to spend some of his spare time looking at how other people were using them, and generating applets and scripts of his own. Nagy-Farkas now spends a portion of his time creating HTML, Java, JavaScript, and CGI scripts on a freelance basis.

"Initially, I was just looking at what could be done," Nagy-Farkas says. He looked at a lot of other Web sites to see what other developers were doing with JavaScript. "What I found really wasn't that practical. There were a lot of calculators and stuff like that," but nothing that really indicated some of the more powerful client-side functions that are useful when dealing with data and a server.

NOTE David Nagy-Farkas's home page for Live Web Designs is found at **http://weber.u.washington.edu/~davidnf/java/bookstore.html**. The page includes examples of frames and Java applets. ■

Books Galore!

The product ordering system began as a simple project to keep a running total of items as a user selected or deselected items. "It was really pretty simple," Nagy-Farkas says. "I just worked with 'on-event' handlers. Anytime any field was changed that could affect the price, I recalculated the total."

Because he was still working with relatively undocumented beta releases from Netscape, his progress was hindered by a lack of information. "The running-total program was about as far as it could go with the state of the online documentation."

After more documentation was available, along with information about JavaScript's capability to write HTML, the rest of the project fell into place using arrays to keep track of items inserted into the page using the CGI script (see fig. 22.2). "All that I needed was a section of code to add the item to the array. The JavaScript functionality really made it pretty easy."

Because the project was for his own curiosity, Nagy-Farkas took his time to learn how JavaScript worked as he assembled each piece. The total time—including weeding out bugs that would pop up as each Netscape beta progressed—was about two weeks. "Wrapping it up in a book order" lasted three days, including developing the CGI scripts in Perl.

FIG. 22.2
This page is used for choosing which books to order and how many. Note the form fields at the bottom of the screen that contain the running totals. These are updated as soon as one of the fields above it is changed or clicked.

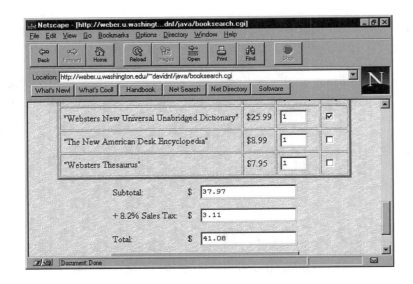

Portability by Design

The first version of the running total program wasn't very modular. When the idea evolved to turn it into an ordering system, Nagy-Farkas realized it would be a much simpler project if the JavaScript code was converted into a series of functions for each task.

As each section was converted into a JavaScript function, it was thoroughly tested. Nagy-Farkas learned his lessons about debugging JavaScript early. "Netscape's error messages aren't that helpful," he says, citing vague system responses when a piece of code fails compounded by a line numbering system that defies explanation.

"I only write a few lines at a time and then test them to make sure they work," he says. "When something goes wrong, it's a lot easier to track down where and what it is." The other result is robust code that the programmer knows works "every step of the way."

Listing 22.1 shows a sample section of code generated by the CGI script from the introductory page. The code can also be found in the file bookorder.html on the CD-ROM. The first section, including all of the JavaScript functions, is a standard header that never changes, regardless of which book categories the user chooses.

Information from the database is inserted into JavaScript templates containing HTML formatting, which is also written to the document and finally to the screen by utilizing document.write functions. The only items in the document that are considered "true" HTML content are the page title and directions. By creating a generic template for the products, it is a simple matter for the CGI script to parse the database and add the items to the page.

On the CD

Listing 22.1   bookorder.html   An HTML Page with JavaScript Generated by a CGI Script.

```
<!--     Copyright 1996 David Nagy-Farkas. All Rights Reserved    -->
<!--     David Nagy-Farkas reserves all rights regarding this     -->
<!--      code and any derived works. You may not reproduce       -->
<!--     this code without the explicit permission of the author. -->

<HTML>
<HEAD>
<BODY BACKGROUND="../chalk.jpg"></BODY>
<SCRIPT LANGUAGE="JavaScript">

<!-- hide the script's contents from feeble browsers

// Global Variables
var ForceSub = 0;
var subt = 0, addtax = 0, tot = 0; // subtotal, tax, and total
var tax = 0.082;                   // tax rate

/*****************
** Add a decimal point to a number
*/
function AddDecimal(number) {
  var withdecimal = "";
  var num = "" + number;
  if (num.length == 0) {
    withdecimal += "0";
  } else if (num.length == 1) {
    withdecimal += "0.0" + num;
  } else if (num.length == 2) {
    withdecimal += "0." + num;
  } else {
  withdecimal += num.substring(0, num.length - 2);
  withdecimal += "."
  withdecimal += num.substring(num.length - 2, num.length);
  }
  return withdecimal;
}
```

continues

Listing 22.1 Continued

```
/******************
** Creates a new array of length n
*/
function MakeArray(n) {
   for (var i = 0; i <= n; i++)
     this[i] = 0;
   this.length = n;
   return this;
}

/****************
** Creates a new Product object
*/
function Product(name, price) {
  this.name = name;
  this.quantity = 1;
  this.price = price;
  this.itemtot = 0;
}

/****************
** Outputs HTML for a product object
*/
function DisplayItem(item, number) {
  var result = "<TR><TD>";
  result += item.name + "</TD>";
  result += "<TD>$" + AddDecimal(item.price) + "</TD>";
  result += "<TD><INPUT TYPE='text' SIZE=5 VALUE=1 ";
  result += "name='" + item.name + "_quantity' ";
  result += "onFocus='reset(" + number + ")' onBlur='unreset(" + number + ")
  ➥'></TD>";
  result += "<TD><INPUT TYPE='checkbox' VALUE='off' ";
  result += "name='" + item.name + "_buy' ";
  result += "onClick='toggle(" + number + ")'></TD>";
  result += "<INPUT TYPE='hidden' name='" + item.name + "_itemprice' VALUE="
  ➥+ AddDecimal(item.price) +"></TR>";
  document.write(result);
}

/****************
** Outputs HTML for the top of a table column
*/
function PrintHead(header) {
  var result = "<CENTER><TABLE BORDER=4 CELLPADDING=5 CELLSPACING=2>";
  result += "<TR><TH COLSPAN=4><FONT SIZE=4 COLOR='maroon'>" + header +
  ➥"</FONT></TH></TR>"
```

```
    result += "<TR><TH>Item:</TH><TH>Cost:</TH><TH>Quantity:
    ➥</TH><TH>Buy?</TH></TR>";
    document.write(result);
}

/****************
** Ends a table column
*/
function PrintTail() {
    document.write("</TABLE></CENTER>");
}

/****************
** Executed when the quantity of a product is selected
*/
function reset(index) {
    if (document.forms[0].elements[3*index+1].value == "on") {
        ForceSub = 1;
        compute(index);
        ForceSub = 0;
    }
    document.forms[0].elements[3*index].value = "";
}

/***************
** Executed when done changing the quantity of a product
*/
function unreset(index) {
    if (document.forms[0].elements[3*index].value == "")
        document.forms[0].elements[3*index].value = inv[index].quantity;
    else
        inv[index].quantity = eval(document.forms[0].elements[3*index].value);
    if (document.forms[0].elements[3*index+1].value == "on")
        compute(index);
}

/***************
** Toggles the value of a checkbox
*/
function toggle(index) {
    if (document.forms[0].elements[3*index+1].value == "off") {
        document.forms[0].elements[3*index+1].value = "on"; }
    else if (document.forms[0].elements[3*index+1].value == "on") {
        document.forms[0].elements[3*index+1].value = "off"; }
    compute(index);
}

/***************
** Perform updates of totals and tax
*/
```

continues

Listing 22.1 Continued

```
function compute(index)
{
  if (document.forms[0].elements[3*index+1].value == "on" && !ForceSub) {
    inv[index].itemtot = eval(inv[index].itemtot) + (eval(inv[index].price) *
    ➥eval(inv[index].quantity));
    subt = (eval(subt) + (eval(inv[index].price) * </
    ➥eval(inv[index].quantity)));
  } else {
    inv[index].itemtot = eval(inv[index].itemtot) -
    ➥eval(inv[index].price) * eval(inv[index].quantity));
    subt = (eval(subt) - (eval(inv[index].price) *
    ➥eval(inv[index].quantity)));
  }
  addtax = Math.round(subt * tax);
  tot = (eval(subt) + eval(addtax));
  retotal();
}

/***************
**  Redisplay the totals
*/
function retotal() {
  document.forms[0].subtotal.value = AddDecimal(subt);
  document.forms[0].addedtax.value = AddDecimal(addtax);
  document.forms[0].total.value = AddDecimal(tot);
}

<!-- done hiding from old browsers -->

</SCRIPT>
</HEAD>

<CENTER><H1> Browse the Store! </H1></CENTER>
<HR>
<DL><DT><H3>Here are the available items you requested:</H3>
    <DD>Browse the selection of items and select the items you want by
checking the "buy" box next to your selection.  You may also specify the
quantity of items you wish to purchase.  At any time, you can check the
bottom of the page to see a running total of the items you have selected.
When you are finished, please <B>click on the "Finished" button</B> at
the bottom of the page.  Don't worry... there is no obligation to buy at
this point... this is just a demo.
```

LEARNING FROM THE PROS

```
</DL>
<HR>

<SCRIPT>
<!-- Hide the script from unworthy browsers
inv = new MakeArray(9);
inv[0] = new Product('"The Joy of Cooking" - Hardcover', 2000);
inv[1] = new Product('"The Frugal Gourmet and our Immigrant Ancestors"
➡by Jeff Smith', 795);
inv[2] = new Product('"Interview with the Vampire" by Anne Rice', 599);
inv[3] = new Product('"Patriot Games" by Tom Clancy', 699);
inv[4] = new Product('"The Firm" by John Grisham', 499);
inv[5] = new Product('"Jurassic Park" by Michael Crichton', 650);
inv[6] = new Product('"Websters New Universal Unabridged Dictionary"',
➡2599);
inv[7] = new Product('"The New American Desk Encyclopedia"', 899);
inv[8] = new Product('"Websters Thesaurus"', 795);
document.write("<FORM METHOD='POST'
➡ACTION='bookinvoice.cgi'>");PrintHead('Cooking');DisplayItem(inv[0],
➡0);DisplayItem(inv[1], 1);PrintTail();PrintHead('Popular Fiction');
➡DisplayItem(inv[2], 2);DisplayItem(inv[3], 3);DisplayItem(inv[4],
➡4);DisplayItem(inv[5], 5);PrintTail();PrintHead('Reference');
➡DisplayItem(inv[6],
➡6);DisplayItem(inv[7], 7);DisplayItem(inv[8],
➡8);PrintTail();document.write("<CENTER><TABLE CELLPADDING=4
➡CELLSPACING=4><TR>");
document.write("  <TD>Subtotal: </TD>");
document.write("  <TD>$</TD>");
document.write("  <TD><INPUT NAME='subtotal' VALUE=0.00
onBlur='retotal()'></TD></TR><TR>");
document.write("  <TD>+ 8.2% Sales Tax: </TD>");
document.write("  <TD>$</TD>");
document.write("  <TD><INPUT NAME='addedtax' VALUE=0.00
➡onBlur='retotal()'></TD></TR><TR>");
document.write("  <TD>Total: </TD>");
document.write("  <TD>$</TD>");
document.write("  <TD><INPUT NAME='total'
➡VALUE=0.00 onBlur='retotal()'></TD></TR>");
document.write("  </TABLE><INPUT TYPE='submit' VALUE='Done Browsing: Go
➡to Order Form'></CENTER></FORM>");
// stop hiding -->
        </SCRIPT>

<HR>
<A HREF="http://weber.u.washington.edu/~davidnf/java/bookstore.html">
<B>Head back to the starting page</A></B>
</HTML>
```

Working with Databases

If it was just a matter of hard wiring the JavaScript code with the product items, this would be a simple—albeit limited—project. But it is designed to work with a database that can change in content and size from day-to-day. This is where CGI becomes a necessary companion to JavaScript.

"The page is pretty standardized," Nagy-Farkas says. "The user submits a choice for book categories, and the CGI script returns with a brand new page." With the JavaScript functions in place, it becomes a matter of getting the right information into the document.

"The toughest part is parsing the database, especially if it's a large one," he says. Books Galore! is designed to take the extraneous parsing load off the server. Current CGI online ordering systems require parsing the database after each selection and then generating a new total with a new page to display it. "If you have a big list of items, redrawing is a pain."

With Books Galore!, the database is parsed once to get the information for the initial ordering screen and is not referenced again until the final invoice (see fig. 22.3). Any changes to a customer's order on the order form is handled by JavaScript.

FIG. 22.3
After the user submits an order, another CGI script generates the final invoice with information from the order screen, including a form at the bottom for entering name, address, and payment information.

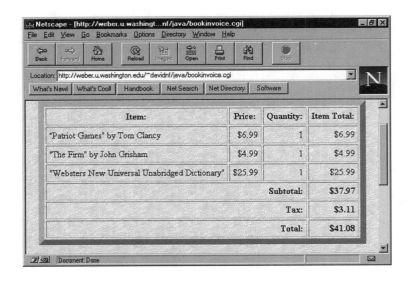

Item:	Price:	Quantity:	Item Total:
"Patriot Games" by Tom Clancy	$6.99	1	$6.99
"The Firm" by John Grisham	$4.99	1	$4.99
"Websters New Universal Unabridged Dictionary"	$25.99	1	$25.99
		Subtotal:	$37.97
		Tax:	$3.11
		Total:	$41.08

Determining Variable Types

One of the key items that slowed down the development process was the lack of variable typing in JavaScript. Depending on its use, a variable can be a string or a number. To make matters worse, there aren't effective methods in place to determine what a variable thinks it is at any given moment.

"It's really a nightmare keeping track of how things are typed," Nagy-Farkas says. A variable acts according to how it's being used—which affords a lot of flexibility, but also causes a lot of confusion, in passing parameters. "It takes a little time to figure out whether that integer you just passed into a function thinks it's an integer or a string."

When this snag started to become a bigger issue in application development, he also started to realize that JavaScript is more than just an extension of HTML. "You really have to have a basic feel for programming to get this to do anything," he says. Putting workable JavaScript pages together isn't "a ten-minute project … If you have a grasp of object-oriented programming structure, it helps a lot."

Will It Work for a Candy Store?

When Nagy-Farkas posted the first running total calculation application, no one seemed to be too interested. After adding the CGI script and the book order wrapping, "Feedback has been very positive" in spite of the fact the basic functionality of the page hasn't changed much—it still keeps a running total based on the most current user input.

"A lot of people have been asking for a 'vanilla' version of the Books Galore! program," Nagy-Farkas says. "It's really pretty portable right now."

By building the page at an early stage in modular components, the JavaScript code is virtually independent of the database that supplies its information. The section of the project that will change from application to application is the CGI script, which must be modified for each database. With portable code and the right CGI script, Books Galore! could be used for any virtual store-front operation. ●

Appendixes

JavaScript
Resources

by Scott J. Walter

Because JavaScript is designed for content presentation on the World Wide Web, it's only appropriate that the largest collection of resources for its implementation is found on the Internet. Because of JavaScript's very specific platform base (currently only recognized by Netscape Navigator), the number of "official" online resources that directly address it are few and far between. However, the "unofficial" resources (put up by experimenting souls who wish to share their discoveries of this new technology) are growing at a rapid rate.

Also, because JavaScript works well as a "glue" to bind Java applets, Netscape frames, and Navigator browser plug-ins together, it's well worth the effort to keep up-to-date on the latest plug-in technology.

In this appendix, I'll take you around the world and introduce you to the growing base of information available.

This list is by no means comprehensive—as new sites appear on the Web weekly—but it's a good place to start looking for information on JavaScript, Java, or other related technologies. ■

The World Wide Web

Because JavaScript is *for* the Web, it's only appropriate that the best sources of information on its use are found *on* the Web. As with most other Internet-based sources, the bulk of Java and JavaScript sites are primarily Java-oriented with JavaScript covered as a subsection. The following list is by no means comprehensive, and to keep up on new offerings on the Web, you're best bet is to take advantage of the Other Hot Links pages that many of the sites have.

JavaScript Index

http://www.c2.org/~andreww/javascript/

JavaScript Index is a solid compendium of JavaScript implementations and experimentation, including a growing list of personal home pages that show off a variety of JavaScript tricks. A subset of the site is the JavaScript Library, a small but expanding collection of source code from around the Web community.

The Unofficial JavaScript Resource Center

http://www.intercom.net/user/mecha/java/index.html

A new, well-produced site devoted to JavaScript, The Unofficial JavaScript Resource Center started out fairly limited, but promises to grow with more examples and techniques for a wide range of users. The idea is to provide a few examples and snippets of code to copy and drop into place. Its organization will make it a useful resource as the content expands.

Voodoo JavaScript Tutorial

http://ourworld.compuserve.com/homepages/vood/script.htm

Voodoo JavaScript Tutorial is an ongoing tutorial presented in easy-to-digest sections covering the basics of JavaScript. It includes examples built in to the page, along with descriptive text and code examples. It's a good place to get your feet wet.

Danny Goodman's JavaScript Pages

http://www/dannyg.com/javascript

This is a collection of examples covering more advanced concepts in JavaScript, including cookies. Danny Goodman is one of the *de facto* experts on JavaScript on the Web, and provides some good examples to learn and adapt other applications from.

Gordon McComb's JavaScript Pages

http://gmccomb.com/javascript/

Author and consultant Gordon McComb hosts this page, which is packed with information, examples, and JavaScript how-to's.

The Complete Idiot's Guide to JavaScript Homesite

http://www.winternet.com/~sjwalter/javascript/

This is the online companion to the book by the same name (also published by Que). Source code for the printed examples, links to other resources and sites, and regular tutorial sections on various parts of JavaScript are offered.

Gamelan

http://www.gamelan.com/

Called "*the* online Java index," EarthWeb's Gamelan has an extensive collection of links to other sites, examples, tools, utilities, and other interesting resources. Although primarily targeting Java, the JavaScript section is quite sizable as well.

Netscape

http://home.netscape.com/

Being the home of the only browser (currently) that supports JavaScript, Netscape's home site is a good place to check periodically, especially for updates and additions to the JavaScript language specification.

Netscape also has its own Development Partners Program, providing subscribers with extended technical and programming support, information on upcoming products, extensions and plug-ins, and access to pre-beta releases of new browser, server, and plug-in technology.

Netscape World

http://www.netscapeworld.com/

Another new online "eZine" dedicated to Netscape products. If you're interested in seeing just how powerful JavaScript can be, this is an excellent example of JavaScript in action. When you get here, notice the very thin frame on the right of your browser window—it's a tracking document that keeps various information consistent across the pages and frames of this site.

JavaWorld

http://www.javaworld.com/

IDG Communications (which also publishes *SunWorld Online*, *Macworld*, *PC World*, and *Computerworld*) has introduced this online version of its new magazine. While dedicated to Java programming and industry developments, it also has an ongoing column on JavaScript.

Borland's JavaWorld

http://www.borland.com/javaworld/

To support its endeavors to integrate Java development into *Latte*, Borland's host site for Java development promises to keep Java developers informed.

TeamJava

http://www.teamjava.com/

TeamJava is a group consisting of Web gurus, consultants, Internet programmers, Webwriters, and other such denizens of the Net. Their home page has links to other Java and JavaScript resources, as well as information on how to contact the consultants themselves.

Symantec

http://www.symantec.com/

Symantec led the pack when it came to providing a development platform for Java applet creation. With *Café*, the first publicly available Java development add-on to their popular C++ package, Symantec provided the Web community with the first GUI-based development environment for applet creation.

Dimension X

http://www.dnx.com/

Dimension X is the home of *Liquid Reality*, a Java applet development platform that merges the capabilities of a 3-D modeling package with a Java app builder.

The Java Developer

http://www.digitalfocus.com/faq/

Sponsored by Digital Focus, the Java Developer serves as the home site for The Java Developer FAQ and one of the more interesting implementations of frames to present search and question submission buttons as you browse the site.

Sun Microsystems

http://java.sun.com/

The place where it *all* started, Sun hosts the Java home site. Additionally, Sun maintains the Java Users Group (a subgroup inside the Sun Users Group) and several mailing and notification lists to keep developers informed of the latest events.

UseNet Newsgroups

Several UseNet newsgroups have sprung up to provide channels for developers looking for guidance with Java, JavaScript, and Web programming in general. They all have global distribution and should be available from your Internet provider.

comp.lang.javascript

As the only newsgroup specifically dedicated to JavaScript development, this one gets somewhat lively at times.

comp.lang.hotjava

Dedicated to discussion about Sun's HotJava browser (a Java browser *written* in Java), **comp.lang.hotjava** deals with problems that people are encountering with HotJava.

comp.lang.java

Although this group is focused on the discussion of Java programming tricks and tips, integrating JavaScript into Web content is also talked about.

comp.infosystems.www.authoring

The traditional collection of newsgroups for WWW-oriented discussion has been **comp.infosystems.www**. As the Web has expanded, so have they, covering everything from browsers to announcements of newly opened Web sites.

Even though there is no group specifically for JavaScript in the comp.infosystems hierarchy, the following groups—which cover various facets of Web authoring—are of interest:

- **comp.infosystems.www.authoring.cgi**
- **comp.infosystems.www.authoring.html**
- **comp.infosystems.www.authoring.images**
- **comp.infosystems.www.authoring.misc**

E-Mail Mailing Lists

For those who prefer the thrill of receiving tons of e-mail, there are mailing lists dedicated to Java and JavaScript that offer similar information to that found in UseNet newsgroups. Keep in mind, however, that mailing lists are a lot like a party line and can get rather chatty (the downside being you have to wade through all the flotsam in your inbox to figure out what you can use). If you plan to use mailing lists heavily, you might want to look into an e-mail program that supports *threading:* the linking together of messages that share the same subject. (It really helps organize the flood of information.)

N O T E   Although you post your questions and comments to the address of the list (for
broadcast to the rest of the list's readers), subscribing to and unsubscribing
from the list are done through *a separate e-mail address*, specifically the address of the
listserver.

The lists discussed in this section mention both the list address and the listserver
address, and sending subscribe requests to the list address (so everyone on the list
knows you don't know what you're doing) is a guaranteed way to get branded a *newbie*.

If you want more information on how to communicate with the listserver (or on other lists
a particular server might have), you can send a message to the listserver address with
"help" in the message body. ■

javascript-list@inquiry.com

Sponsored by the Obscure Organization (**http://www.obscure.org/**) and
TeleGlobal Media, Inc. (**http://www.tgm.com/**), the JavaScript Index is the only
mailing list at the time of this writing dedicated specifically to JavaScript. The discussion gets pretty varied and ranges from introductory questions to more involved discussions on how best to handle animation, framing, reloads, and so on.
To subscribe, send a message to **listmaster@inquiry.com** with `subscribe`
`javascript` in the message body.

java@borland.com

A companion newsletter that parallels the activity on Borland's JavaWorld site, the
Borland Java newsletter keeps you informed about Borland's work on integrating
Java technology into their development tools. To subscribe, send a message to
listserv@borland.com with `subscribe java [your first name] [your last`
`name]` in the message body.

java-announce@java.sun.com

Sun Microsystems, the home of Java, has its own collection of mailing lists.
The java-announce list is primarily for notifications of new Java-related tools.

To subscribe, send a message to **majordomo@java.sun.com** with `subscribe java-announce` in the message body.

Search Engines

There are several search engines available to JavaScript, including Alta Vista, Yahoo, Lycos, and WebCrawler.

Alta Vista

http://www.altavista.com/

A newcomer to the search engine world, Alta Vista sports over 13 *million* entries, making it the largest search site currently in cyberspace. This site attempts to catalog not only sites and pages but *words* within pages, making it very easy to generate thousands of matches for a particular search term (for example, searching on `JavaScript` will find not only sites that deal with JavaScript, but also sites that *use* it within their pages because that word is always part of the `SCRIPT` tag). To make the best use of this site, try to be as specific as possible, or be prepared to refine and narrow down your search parameters.

Yahoo!

http://www.yahoo.com/

Yahoo! is short for "You Always Have Other Options," and although this is most definitely true on the Net, you'd be hard pressed to find other search engines as broad.

Lycos

http://www.lycos.com/

One ofthe granddaddies of the search world, Lycos has a massive database, and a large collection of references to Java, JavaScript, and Web design in general.

WebCrawler

http://www.webcrawler.com/

Supported by America Online, WebCrawler is a broad-spectrum search system that's *fast* (one of the fastest reply systems on the Net).

General Web Sites

There are several sites on the Web that serve as a central clearing house for Internet-related applications (many of which are being developed as low-cost shareware by private individuals). Although these sites address a broader base than Java or JavaScript, they are expanding their coverage to include Java editors, extended HTML tools, and the like.

The Consummate Winsock Software List

http://cws.wilmington.net/

The Consummate Winsock Software (CWS) list is just as the name implies: a very complete collection of the best, the latest, the greatest, and the not so great. Combining a five-star rating system and a thorough collection of product reviews (including both pro and con analysis of all products), CWS is an excellent place to keep up with what's new and different.

TUCOWS

http://www.tucows.com/

The Ultimate Collection of Winsock Software (hence the acronym), TUCOWS rivals CWS for its completeness and variety in content. There is naturally some duplication between the two sites (the most popular pieces on the Net are found at both), but one complements the other quite nicely. (For the broadest picture of what's available, it's worth stopping by both.)

Similar to CWS, TUCOWS has a "cow" rating system, which highlights hot, "get it" titles.

Shareware.com

http://www.shareware.com/

What started as the Virtual Shareware Library (VSL), this site has been taken over by clnet central, an online/on-TV source for the latest breaking information on Internet technology. Although it doesn't attempt to rate software, it does provide a "top downloads" list to indicate what Netizens have deemed the hot products of the moment.

Unlike CWS and TUCOWS, which link one product to one download link, shareware.com's download section presents a list of sites (rated by reliability) around the world from which you can retrieve a particular file.

Netscape Navigator Plug-Ins: Live Object Support

Navigator 2.0 supports *live objects* (something embedded in an HTML file that is more than text or a simple graphic). Live objects extend the capabilities of the Web to encompass the world of multimedia, complete with sound, animation, and user interaction. Before live objects, non-HTML content (such as QuickTime movie files) that was embedded in a document had to be viewed through a *helper app*, an external program that was run once the object had been downloaded (producing an interface that was anything but seamless). With live objects, you can directly embed movies, sound, spreadsheets, and so on, into your Web pages.

Displaying live objects is handled by an extension to Navigator that's "plugged in to" the browser's framework (hence the term *plug-ins*). If you're familiar with the concept of object linking and embedding (OLE), you've already experienced the power of live objects (which can be thought of as OLE for the Web). Live object (plug-in) technology makes it possible for software publishers to take their own file formats and provide the means to integrate the formats directly into the browser interface.

The following plug-ins are just a few of those that are already available (or in development) for Navigator. For the most current list of plug-ins (and the companies developing them), check out Netscape's home page at **http://home.netscape. com/**.

Shockwave for Director by Macromedia

http://www.macromedia.com/

Macromedia Director is one of the most popular multimedia development environments available. The Shockwave plug-in enables developers to take their Director programs and "shock" them into compressed modules for transmission over the Web and playback through Navigator. Shockwave provides all the control a stand-alone Director program does and adds the capability to create live links to other Web sites *inside* the module.

Macromedia also maintains a gallery of shocked sites, providing a starting point for those interested in surfing the "shock wave."

RealAudio by Progressive Networks

http://www.realaudio.com/

Progressive Networks RealAudio plug-in integrates live and on-demand real-time audio into Web content. If your Web server is also running the RealAudio server, you can "stream" audio to users (enabling them to listen to the sound files before they have been completely downloaded). Users connected at 14.4kbps or faster experience real-time sound.

Live3D by Netscape

http://home.netscape.com/

Originally developed as WebFX by Paper Software, Live3D is a high-performance VRML platform that enables you to fly through VRML worlds on the Web and run interactive, multiuser VRML applications written in Java. Netscape Live3D features 3-D text, background images, texture animation, morphing, viewpoints, collision detection, gravity, and RealAudio streaming sound.

ToolVox by VoxWare

http://www.voxware.com/

What RealAudio does for general audio, ToolVox does for integrating speech into the Web. Because it's possible to compress speech to a greater extent than music (with little or no loss in quality), ToolVox can create very small sound files (with a compression ratio of 53:1).

OLE Control by NCompass

http://www.excite.sfu.ca/NCompass/

OLE technology allows for objects to be embedded into other documents. NCompass has brought that same technology to the Web with their OLE control. This plug-in, running under Windows 95, enables you to embed OLE controls as applets created using programming languages and development tools familiar to programmers: Visual C++, Visual Basic, the MS Windows Game SDK, and Borland C++, to name a few.

PreVU by InterVU

http://www.intervu.com/

Although RealAudio and ToolVox provide seamless integration of sound into Web content, PreVU makes it possible to stream MPEG video through Navigator. The PreVU plug-in makes MPEG playback possible without the need for special hardware or proprietary video servers. PreVU provides for first-frame viewing right in the Web page, streaming viewing while downloading, and full-speed cached playback off your hard drive.

VDOLive by VDOnet

http://www.vdolive.com/download/

Another entry into the "Web video on demand" segment, VDOLive compresses video images without compromising quality on the receiving end. The frame rate displayed to the user is controlled by the speed of the connection. (With a 28.8kbps connection, VDOLive runs in real time at 10 to 15 frames per second.)

ViewMovie by Iván Cavero Belaúnde

http://www.well.com/~ivanski/

ViewMovie allows for the embedding of QuickTime movie files in Web pages (enabling playback of videos without an external helper application). Embedded movies can also be used as link anchors and imagemaps.

Macintosh and PowerPC (Mac OS)

Because the vast majority of users on the Internet are connecting with Windows or UNIX machines, the bulk of the resources (especially the plug-ins) detailed in the preceding sections are for UNIX or Windows platforms, leaving Macintosh users out in the cold (a point that is periodically brought up in the online discussions about *whose system is better*). Such companies as Symantec are scheduled to provide Mac versions of their Java frameworks, but they aren't available yet. There are, however, several resources for Mac users that are well worth checking out.

Netscape Navigator 2.01

Although the Macintosh version of Netscape Navigator 2.0 *does* support JavaScript, it *does not* support Java. If you want to take advantage of Java technology, you'll need to stop by Netscape's home site (**http://home.netscape.com/**) and download a copy of the beta release of Navigator 2.01.

N O T E If you are a PowerPC user (or anyone else who's using Apple's Open Transport layer to handle your PPP connections), you *must* stop by Apple's home site (**http://www.apple.com/**) and download and install System 7.5 Update 2.0 (also called *System 7.5.3*). Navigator 2.01 is built around Open Transport 1.1, which is available only with Update 2.0. ■

Symantec Caffeine

http://www.symantec.com/

While Symantec's *Café* development platform for Windows 95 and Windows NT has become available through normal retail channels, the Macintosh version isn't out yet. However, Mac developers can get a free copy of *Caffeine* from Symantec's home site which adds Java applet development to the Macintosh version of the Symantec C++ compiler. You must already have Symantec C++ v8.0.4 in order to use this add-on.

Talker by MVP Solutions

http://www.mvpsolutions.com/

Talker is the Macintosh platform answer to ToolVox and integrates into the speech subsystem of the Mac OS. As with ToolVox, Talker objects are significantly smaller than recorded audio files. Unlike audio recorders, Talker "speaks" from a script file (making editing a breeze). Talker also enables Web pages to talk using many different voices (as chosen by the user).

Roaster

http://www.natural.com/

For Java applet developers, Roaster is the first Mac development environment that provides a GUI platform for the creation of Java applets.

CodeWarrior

http://www.metrowerks.com/

CodeWarrior is the most popular C++ development platform for Macintosh and PowerPC developers today, and Metrowerks is working on making a Java development add-on available. ●

JavaScript Glossary

by Rick Darnell

This appendix is an expanded discussion of JavaScript's language elements. This enhanced glossary not only defines common terms or lingo associated with JavaScript, but also lists the objects, methods, properties, and event handlers that make JavaScript such a growing, powerful language. ■

Terms

While not necessarily JavaScript objects or keywords, the following definitions can help in your understanding of JavaScript and how it works. These are the general terms that are used in most discussions about JavaScript and its implementation.

Cookie A special object containing state/status information about the client that can be accessed by the server. Included in that `state` object is a description of the range of URLs for which that state is valid. Future HTTP requests from the client falling within a range of URLs described within the `state` object will include transmission of the current value of the `state` object from the client back to the server.

This simple form of data storage allows the server to provide "personalized" service to the client. Online merchants can store information about items currently in an "electronic shopping basket," services can post registration information and automate functions such as typing a user-ID, and user preferences can be saved on the client and retrieved by the server when the site is contacted. For limited-use information, such as shopping services, it is also possible to set a time limit on the life of the cookie information.

CGI scripts are typically used to set and retrieve cookie values. To generate the cookie requires sending an HTTP header in the following format:

```
Set-Cookie: NAME=Value; [EXPIRES=date;] [PATH=pathname;]
➥[DOMAIN=domainname;] [SECURE]
```

When a request for cookie information is made, the list of cookie information is searched for all URLs that match the current URL. Any matches are returned in this format:

```
cookie: NAME1=string1; NAME2=string2; ...
```

Cookie was an arbitrarily assigned name. For more information about the cookie and its function, see **http://home.netscape.com/newsref/std/ cookie_spec.html**.

Event Handler Attributes of HTML tags embedded in documents. The attribute assigns a JavaScript command or function to execute when the event happens.

Function A user-defined or built-in set of statements that perform a task. It can also return a value when used with the `return` statement.

Hierarchy   Navigator objects exist in a set relation to each other that reflects the structure of an HTML page. This is referred to as *instance hierarchy* because it only works with specific instances of objects, rather than general classes.

The `window` object is the parent of all other Navigator objects. Underneath `window`, `location`, `history`, and `document` all share precedence. `Document` includes forms, links, and anchors.

Each object is a descendant of the higher object. A form called `orderForm` is an object, but is also a property of `document`. As such, it is referred to as `document.orderForm`.

Java   An object-oriented, platform-independent programming language developed by Sun Microsystems and used to add additional functionality to Web pages. Programming in Java requires a Java Development Kit with compiler and core classes.

JavaScript   A scripting language developed by Netscape for HTML documents. Scripts are performed after specific user-triggered events. Creating JavaScript Web documents requires a text editor and compatible browser.

Literal   An absolute value not assigned to a variable. Examples include 1, 3.1415927, "Bob", `true`.

Method   A function assigned to an object. For example, `bigString.toUpperCase()` returns an uppercase version of the string contained in `bigString`.

Object   A construct with properties that are JavaScript variables or other objects. Functions associated with an object are known as the *object's methods*. You access the properties of an object with a simple notation:

```
objectName.propertyName
```

Both object and property names are case-sensitive.

Operator   Performs a function on one or more operands or variables. Operators are divided into two classes: binary and unary. Binary operators need two operands, and unary operands can operate on a single operand.

For example, addition is a binary operand:

```
sum = 1 + 1
```

Part
VI

App
B

Unary operands are often used to update counters. The following example increases the variable by 1:

```
counter++
```

See appendix C, "JavaScript Commands and Grammar," for a list of operators and their precedence.

Property   Used to describe an object. A property is defined by assigning it a value. There are several properties in JavaScript that contain *constants:* values that never change.

Script   One or more JavaScript commands enclosed with a <SCRIPT> tag.

Objects

JavaScript is an object-oriented language, so at its heart is a predefined set of objects which relate to the various components of an HTML page and their relation to each other. To view or manipulate the state of an object requires the use of properties and methods, which are also covered in this appendix. If an object is also used as a property of another object, that relationship is listed following the definition. Related properties, methods, and event handlers for each object are listed following the definition.

anchors   A piece of text that can be the target of a hypertext link. This is a read-only object which is set in HTML with <A> tags. To determine how many anchors are included in a document, use the length property.

```
document.anchors.length
```

Unless the anchor name is an integer, the value of document.anchor[*index*] will return null.

Property of document. See link object; see anchor method.

button   An object that is a form element and must be defined within a <FORM> tag and can be used to perform an action.

Property of form. See objects reset and submit; see properties name and value; see click method; see onClick event handler.

checkbox   A form element that the user sets to *on* or *off* by clicking and that must be defined in a `<FORM>` tag. Using the `checkbox` object, you can see if the box is checked and review the name and value.

Property of `form`. See `radio` object; see properties `checked`, `defaultChecked`, `name`, `value`; see `click` method; see `onClick` event handler.

Date   Replaces a normal date type. Although it does not have any properties, it is equipped with a wide range of methods. In its current release, `Date` does not work with dates prior to 1/1/70.

Methods for getting and setting time and date information are divided into four classes: `set`, `get`, `to`, and `parse`/`UTC`.

Except for the date, all numerical representation of date components begin with zero. This should not present a problem except with months, which are represented by zero (January) through 11 (December).

The standard date syntax is `"Thu, 11 Jan 1996 06:20:00 GMT"`. U.S. time zone abbreviations are also understood; but for universal use, specify the time zone offset. For example, `"Thu, 11 Jan 1996 06:20:00 GMT+0530"` is a place five hours and 30 minutes west of the Greenwich meridian.

See methods `getDate`, `getDay`, `getHours`, `getMinutes`, `getMonth`, `getSeconds`, `getTime`, `getTimezoneOffset`, `getYear`, `parse`, `setDate`, `setHours`, `setMinutes`, `setMonth`, `setSeconds`, `setTime`, `setYear`, `toGMTString`, `toLocaleString`, `toString`.

document   An object created by Navigator when a page is loaded, containing information on the current document, such as title, background color, and forms. These properties are defined within `<BODY>` tags. It also provides methods for displaying HTML text to the user.

You can reference the anchors, forms, and links of a document by using the `anchors`, `forms`, and `links` arrays of the `document` object. These arrays contain an entry for each `anchor`, `form`, or `link` in a document.

Property of `window`. See `frame` object; see properties `alinkColor`, `anchors`, `bgColor`, `cookie`, `fgColor`, `forms`, `lastModified`, `linkColor`, `links`, `location`, `referrer`, `title`, `vlinkColor`; see methods `clear`, `close`, `open`, `write`, `writeln`; see event handlers `onLoad` and `onUnload`.

elements   An array of `form` elements in source order, including buttons, checkboxes, radio buttons, text, and textarea objects. The elements can be referred to by their index:

```
formName.elements[index]
```

Elements can also be referenced by the element name. For example, a password element called `newPassword` is the second form element on an HTML page. Its value is accessed in three ways:

```
formName.elements[1].value
formName.elements["newPassword"].value
formName.newPassword.value
```

Values cannot be set or changed using the read-only `elements` array.

Property of `form`. See `length` property.

form   A property of the `document` object. Each form in a document is a separate and distinct object that can be referenced using the `form` object. The `form` object is an array created as forms are defined through HTML tags. If the first `form` in a document is named `orderForm`, then it could be referenced as `document.orderForm` or `document.forms[0]`.

Property of `document`. See hidden object; see properties `action`, `elements`, `encoding`, `forms`, `method`, `name`, `target`; see `submit` method; see `onSubmit` event handler.

frame   A window that contains HTML sub-documents that are independently scrollable. `Frames` can point to different URLs and be targeted by other frames—all in the same window. Each `frame` is a `window` object defined using the `<FRAMESET>` tag to define the layout that makes up the page. The page is defined from a parent HTML document. All sub-documents are children of the parent.

If a `frame` contains definitions for `SRC` and `NAME` attributes, then the `frame` can be identified from a sibling by using the `parent` object as `parent.frameName` or `parent.frames[index]`.

Property of `window`. See objects `document` and `window`; see properties `defaultStatus`, `frames`, `parent`, `self`, `status`, `top`, `window`; see methods `setTimeout` and `clearTimeout`.

hidden A text object suppressed from appearing on an HTML form. Hidden objects can be used in addition to cookies to pass name/value pairs for client-server communication.

Property of form. See properties cookie, defaultValue, name, value.

history This object is derived from the Go menu and contains URL link information for previously visited pages.

Property of document. See location object; see length property; see methods back, forward, go.

link A location object. In addition to providing information about existing hypertext links, the link object can also be used to define new links.

Property of document. See anchor object; see properties hash, host, hostname, href, length, pathname, port, protocol, search, target; see link method; see event handlers onClick and onMouseOver.

location Contains complete URL information for the current document, while each property of location contains a different portion of the URL.

Property of document. See history object; see properties hash, host, hostname, href, location, pathname, port, protocol, search, target.

Math Includes properties for mathematical constants and methods for functions. For example, to access the value of *pi* in an equation, use:

```
Math.PI
```

Standard trigonometric, logarithmic, and exponential functions are also included. All arguments in trigonometric functions use radians.

See properties E, LN10, LN2, PI, SQRT1_2, SQRT2; see methods abs, acos, asin, atan, ceil, cos, exp, floor, log, max, min, pow, random, round, sin, sqrt, tan.

navigator Contains information on the current version of Navigator used by the client.

See objects link and anchors; see properties appName, appCodeName, appVersion, userAgent.

password Created by HTML password text fields and masked when entered by the user. It must be defined with an HTML <FORM> tag.

Part
VI

App
B

Property of `form`. See `text` object; see properties `defaultValue`, `name`, `value`; see methods `focus`, `blur`, `select`.

radio   Objects created within HTML `<FORM>` tags and representing radio buttons. A set of radio buttons enables the user to select one item from a list. When it is created, it takes the form of `document.formName.radioName[index]`, where the index is a number representing each button beginning with zero.

Property of `form`. See objects `checkbox`, `select`; see properties `checked`, `defaultChecked`, `index`, `length`, `name`, `value`; see `click` method; see `onClick` event handler.

reset   Correlates with an HTML reset button, which resets all `form` objects to their default values. A `reset` object must be created within a `<FORM>` tag.

Property of `form`. See objects `button` and `submit`; see properties `name` and `value`; see `click` method; see `onClick` event handler.

select   A selection list or scrolling list on an HTML form. A selection list enables the user to choose one item from a list, while a scrolling list enables the choice of one or more items from a list.

Property of `form`. See `radio` object; see properties `length`, `name`, `options`, `selectedIndex`; see methods `blur` and `focus`; see event handlers `onBlur`, `onChange`, `onFocus`.

For the `options` property of `select`, see `defaultSelected`, `index`, `selected`, `text`, `value`.

string   A series of characters defined by double or single quotes. For example:

```
myDog = "Brittany Spaniel"
```

returns a string object called `myDog` with the value `"Brittany Spaniel"`. Quotation marks are not a part of the string's value—they are only used to delimit the string. The object's value is manipulated using methods that return a variation on the string; for example `myDog.toUpperCase()` returns `"BRITTANY SPANIEL"`. It also includes methods that return HTML versions of the string, such as `bold` and `italics`.

See objects `text` and `textarea`; see `length` property; see methods `anchor`, `big`, `blink`, `bold`, `charAt`, `fixed`, `fontcolor`, `fontsize`, `indexOf`, `italics`, `lastIndexOf`, `link`, `small`, `strike`, `sub`, `substring`, `sup`, `toLowerCase`, `toUpperCase`.

submit   Causes the form to be submitted to the program specified by the action property. It is created within an HTML <FORM> tag. It always loads a new page, which may be the same as the current page if an action isn't specified.

Property of form. See objects button and reset; see properties name and value; see click method; see onClick event handler.

text   A one-line input field on an HTML form that accepts characters or numbers. Text objects can be updated by assigning new contents to its value.

Property of form. See objects password, string, textarea; see properties defaultValue, name, value; see methods focus, blur, select; see event handlers onBlur, onChange, onFocus, onSelect.

textarea   Similar to a text object, with the addition of multiple lines. A textarea object can also be updated by assigning new contents to its value.

Property of form. See objects password, string, text; see properties defaultValue, name, value; see methods focus, blur, select; see event handlers onBlur, onChange, onFocus, onSelect.

window   Created by Navigator when a page is loaded containing properties that apply to the whole window. It is the top-level object for each document, location, and history object. Because its existence is assumed, you do not have to reference the name of the window when referring to its objects, properties, or methods. For example, the following two lines have the same result (printing a message to the status line):

```
status("Go away from here.")
window.status("Go away from here.")
```

A new window is created using the open method:

```
aNewWindow = window.open("URL","Window_Name",["windowFeatures"])
```

The variable name is used to refer to the window's properties and methods. The window name is used in the target argument of a form or anchor tag.

See objects document and frame; see properties defaultStatus, frames, parent, self, status, top, window; see methods alert, close, confirm, open, prompt, setTimeout, clearTimeout; see event handlers onLoad and onUnload.

Part
VI

App

B

Properties

Properties are used to view or set the values of objects. An object is simply a vague generality until a property is used to define the values that make it specific.

action   The `action` property is a reflection of the `action` attribute in an HTML `<FORM>` tag, consisting of a destination URL for the submitted data. This value can be set or changed before or after the document has been loaded and formatted.

In this example, the `action` for a form called `outlineForm` is set to the URL contained in the variable `outlineURL`.

```
outlineForm.action=outlineURL
```

Property of `form`. See properties `encoding`, `method`, `target`.

alinkColor   The color of a link after the mouse button is pressed—but before it's released—and expressed as a hexadecimal RGB triplet or string literal. It cannot be changed after the HTML source is processed. Both of these examples set the color to alice blue:

```
document.alinkColor="aliceblue"
document.alinkColor="F0F8FF"
```

Property of `document`. See properties `bgColor`, `fgColor`, `linkColor`, `vlinkColor`.

anchors   An array of all defined anchors in the current document. If the length of an anchor array in a document is 5, then the anchors array is represented as `document.anchors[0]` through `document.anchors[4]`.

Property of `document`. See anchor object; see properties `length` and `links`.

appCodeName   Returns a read-only string with the code name of the browser.

```
document.write("The code name of your browser is " +
➥navigator.appCodeName)
```

For most Netscape Navigator 2.0 users, this returns:

```
The code name of your browser is Mozilla
```

Property of `navigator`. See properties `appName`, `appVersion`, `userAgent`.

appName   Returns a read-only string with the name of the browser.

Property of `navigator`. See properties `appCodeName`, `appVersion`, `userAgent`.

appVersion Returns a string with the version information of the browser in the format "releaseNumber (platform; country)". For a release of Netscape 2.0,

```
document.write(navigator.appVersion)
```

returns

```
2.0 (Win95; I)
```

This specifies Navigator 2.0 running on Windows 95 with an international release. The U country code specifies a U.S. release, while an I indicates an international release.

Property of `navigator`. See properties `appName`, `appCodeName`, `userAgent`.

bgColor The document background color expressed as a hexadecimal RGB triplet or string literal. It can be reset at any time. Both of these examples set the background to alice blue:

```
document.bgColor = "aliceblue"
document.bgColor = "F0F8FF"
```

Property of `document`. See properties `alinkColor`, `fgColor`, `linkColor`, `vlinkColor`.

checked A Boolean value (`true` or `false`), indicating whether a checkbox or radio button is selected. The value is updated immediately when an item is checked. It's used in the following form:

```
formName.checkboxName.checked
formName.radioButtonName[index].checked
```

Property of `checkbox` and `radio`. See `defaultChecked` property.

cookie String value of a small piece of information stored by Navigator in a client-side cookies.txt file. The value stored in the `cookie` is found using substring `charAt`, `IndexOf`, and `lastIndexOf`.

For more information, see the discussion in the "Terms" section.

Property of `document`. See `hidden` object.

defaultChecked A Boolean value (`true` or `false`) indicating whether a checkbox or radio button is checked by default. Setting a value to `defaultChecked` can override the checked attribute of a form element. The following section of code will reset a group of radio buttons to its original state by finding and setting the default button:

```
for (var i in menuForm.choices) {
    if (menuForm.choices[i].defaultChecked) {
        menuForm.choice[i].defaultChecked = true
    }
}
```

Property of checkbox and radio. See form object; see checked property.

defaultSelected   A Boolean value (true or false) representing the default state of an item in a form select element. Setting a value with this property can override the selected attribute of an <OPTION> tag. The syntax is identical to defaultChecked.

Property of options. See properties index, selected, selectedIndex.

defaultStatus   The default message displayed in the status bar at the bottom of a Navigator window when nothing else is displayed. This is preempted by a priority or transient message, such as a mouseOver event with an anchor. For example,

```
window.defaultStatus = "Welcome to my home page"
```

displays the welcome message while the mouse is not over a link, or Netscape is not performing an action that it needs to notify the user about.

Property of window. See status property.

defaultValue   The initial contents of hidden, password, text, textarea, and string form elements. For password elements, it is initially set to null for security reasons, regardless of any set value.

Property of hidden, password, text, textarea. See value property.

E   The base of natural logarithms, also known as Euler's constant. The value is approximately 2.718.

Property of Math. See properties LN2, LN10, LOG2E, LOG10E, PI, SQRT1_2, SQRT2.

elements   An array of objects containing form elements in HTML source order. The array index begins with zero and ends with the number of form elements –1.

Property of form. See elements object.

encoding Returns a string reflecting the MIME encoding type, which is set in the enctype attribute of an HTML <FORM> tag.

Property of form. See properties action, method, target.

fgColor The color of foreground text represented as a hexadecimal RGB triplet or a string literal. This value cannot be changed after a document is processed. It can take two forms:

```
document.fgColor="aliceblue"
document.fgColor="F0F8FF"
```

Property of document. See properties alinkColor, bgColor, linkColor, vlinkColor; see fontcolor method.

forms An array of objects corresponding to named forms in HTML source order and containing an entry for each form object in a document.

Property of document. See form object; see length property.

frames An array of objects corresponding to child frame windows created using the <FRAMESET> tag. To obtain the number of child frames in a window, use the length property.

Property of window. See frame object; see length property.

hash Returns a string with the portion of a URL beginning with a hash mark (#), which denotes an anchor name fragment. It can be used to set a hash property, although it is safest to set the entire URL as an href property. An error is returned if the hash isn't found in the current location.

Property of link and location. See anchor object; see properties host, hostname, href, pathname, port, protocol, search properties.

host Returns a string formed by combining the hostname and port properties of a URL, and provides a method for changing it.

```
location.host = "www.montna.com:80"
```

Property of link and location. See properties hash, hostname, href, pathname, port, protocol, search.

hostname Returns or changes a string with the domain name or IP address of a URL.

Property of link and location. See properties hash, host, href, pathname, port, protocol, search.

href   Returns a string with the entire URL. All other location and link properties are substrings of href, which can be changed at any time.

Property of link and location. See properties hash, host, hostname, pathname, port, protocol, search.

index   Returns the index of an option in a select element with zero being the first item.

Property of options. See properties defaultSelected, selected, selectedIndex.

lastModified   A read-only string containing the date that the current document was last changed, based on the file attributes. The string is formatted in the standard form used by JavaScript (see Date object). A common usage is:

```
document.write("This page last modified on " + document.lastModified)
```

Property of document.

length   An integer reflecting a length- or size-related property of an object.

Object	Property Measured
history	Length of the history list
string	Integer length of the string; zero for a null string
radio	Number of radio buttons
anchors, forms, frames, links, options	Number of elements in the array

Property of anchors, elements, forms, frame, frames, history, links, options, radio, string, window.

linkColor   The hyperlink color displayed in the document, expressed as a hexadecimal RGB triplet or as a string literal. It corresponds to the link attribute in the HTML <BODY> tag, and cannot be changed after the document is processed.

Property of document. See properties alinkColor, bgColor, fgColor, vlinkColor.

links   An array representing `link` objects defined in HTML using `<A HREF=URL>` tags with the first `link` identified as `document.links[0]`.

See `link` object. See properties `anchors` and `length`.

LN2   A constant representing the natural logarithm of 2 (approximately 0.693).

Property of `Math`. See properties `E`, `LN10`, `LOG2E`, `LOG10E`, `PI`, `SQRT1_2`, `SQRT2`.

LN10   A constant representing the natural logarithm of 10 (approximately 2.302).

Property of `Math`. See properties `E`, `LN2`, `LOG2E`, `LOG10E`, `PI`, `SQRT1_2`, `SQRT2`.

location   Returns a string with the URL of the current document. This read-only property (`document.location`) is different from the location `objects` properties (`window.location.propertyName`), which can be changed.

Property of `document`. See `location` object.

LOG2E   A constant representing the base 2 logarithm of `e` (approximately 1.442).

Property of `Math`. See properties `E`, `LN2`, `LN10`, `LOG10E`, `PI`, `SQRT1_2`, `SQRT2`.

LOG10E   A constant representing the base 10 logarithm of `e` (approximately .434).

Property of `Math`. See properties `E`, `LN2`, `LN10`, `LOG2E`, `SQRT1_2`, `SQRT2`.

method   Reflects the method attribute of an HTML `<FORM>` tag: either `<GET>` or `<POST>`. It can be set at any time. The first function returns the current value of the form object, while the second function sets the method to the contents of `newMethod`.

```
function getMethod(formObj) {
   return formObj.method
}
function setMethod(formObj,newMethod) {
   formObj.method = newMethod
}
```

Property of `form`. See properties `action`, `encoding`, `target`.

name   Returns a string with the `name` attribute of the object. This is the internal name for `button`, `reset` and `submit` objects, not the on-screen label.

For example, after opening a new window with `indexOutline = window.open("http://www.wossamatta.com/outline.html","MenuPage")` and issuing the command `document.write(indexOutline.name)`, JavaScript returns "MenuPage", which was specified as the name attribute.

Property of `button`, `checkbox`, `frame`, `password`, `radio`, `reset`, `select`, `submit`, `text`, `textarea`, `window`. See `value` property.

options   An array of `option` objects created by a `select` form element. The first option's index is zero, the second is 1, and so on.

See `select` object.

parent   Refers to the calling document in the current frame created by a `<FRAMESET>` tag. Using `parent` allows access to other frames created by the same `<FRAMESET>` tag. For example, two frames invoked are called "index" and "contents." The "index" frame can write to the "contents" frame using the syntax:

```
parent.contents.document.write("Kilroy was here.")
```

Property of `frame` and `window`.

pathname   Returns the path portion from a URL. Although the `pathname` can be changed at any time, it is always safer to change the entire URL at once using the `href` property.

Property of `link` and `location`. See properties `hash`, `host`, `hostname`, `href`, `port`, `protocol`, `search`.

PI   Returns the value of *pi* (approximately 3.1415927). This is the ratio of the circumference of a circle to its diameter.

Property of `Math`. See properties `E`, `LN2`, `LN10`, `LOG2E`, `LOG10E`, `SQRT1_2`, `SQRT2`.

port   Returns the port number of a URL address, which is a substring of the `host` property in `href`.

Property of `link` and `location`. See properties `hash`, `host`, `hostname`, `href`, `pathname`, `protocol`, `search`.

protocol   Returns a string with the initial portion of the URL, up to and including the colon, which indicates the access method (`http`, `ftp`, `mailto`, etc.).

Property of `link` and `location`. See properties `hash`, `host`, `hostname`, `href`, `pathname`, `port`, `search`.

referrer   Returns a read-only URL of the document that called the current document. In conjunction with a CGI script, it can be used to keep track of how users are linked to a page.

```
document.write("You came here from a page at " + document.referrer)
```

Property of `document`.

search   Returns a string containing any query information appended to a URL.

Property of `link` and `location`. See properties `hash`, `host`, `hostname`, `href`, `pathname`, `port`, `protocol`.

selected   Returns a Boolean value (`true` or `false`) indicating the current state of an option in a `select` object. The selected property can be changed at any time, and the display will immediately update to reflect the new value. The selected property is useful for `select` elements that are created using the `multiple` attribute. Using this property, you can view or change the value of any element in an `options` array without changing the value of any other element in the array.

Property of `options`. See properties `defaultSelected`, `index`, `selectedIndex`.

selectedIndex   Returns an integer specifying the index of a selected item. The `selectedIndex` property is useful for `select` elements that are created without using the `multiple` attribute. If `selectedIndex` is evaluated when the `multiple` option is selected, the property returns the index of the first option only. Setting the property clears any other options that are selected in the element.

Property of `select`, `options`. See properties `defaultSelected`, `index`, `selected`.

self   Refers to the current window or form, and is useful for removing ambiguity when dealing with `window` and `form` properties with the same name.

Property of `frame` and `window`. See `window` property.

SQRT1_2   The square root of 1/2, also expressed as the inverse of the square root of 2 (approximately 0.707).

Property of `Math`. See properties `E`, `LN2`, `LN10`, `LOG2E`, `LOG10E`, `PI`, `SQRT2`.

SQRT2   The square root of 2 (approximately 1.414).

Property of `Math`. See properties `E`, `LN2`, `LN10`, `LOG2E`, `LOG10E`, `PI`, `SQRT1_2`.

status Specifies a priority or transient message to display in the status bar at the bottom of the window, usually triggered by a `mouseOver` event from an `anchor`. To display when the mouse pointer is placed over a link, the usage is:

```
<A anchor definition onMouseOver="window.dstatus='Your message.';
➥return true">link</A>
```

Note the use of nested quotes and the required `return true` required for operation.

Property of `window`. See `defaultStatus` property.

target A string specifying the name of a window for responses to be posted to after a form is submitted. For a link, `target` returns a string specifying the name of the window that displays the content of a selected hypertext link.

```
homePage.target = "http://www.wossamatta.com/"
```

A literal must be used to set the `target` property. JavaScript expressions and variables are invalid entries.

Property of `form`, `link`, `location`. See properties `action`, `encoding`, `method`.

text Returns the value of text following the `<OPTION>` tag in a `select` object. It can also be used to change the value of the option, with an important limitation—while the value is changed, its appearance on-screen is not.

Property of `options`.

title Returns the read-only value set within HTML `<TITLE>` tags. If a document doesn't include a title, the value is `null`.

Property of `document`.

top The topmost window, called an ancestor or Web browser window, that contains `frames` or nested `framesets`.

Property of `window`.

userAgent Header sent as part of HTTP protocol from client to server to identify the type of client. The syntax of the returned value is the same as `appVersion`.

Property of `navigator`. See properties `appName`, `appVersion`, `appCodeName`.

value The value of an object depends on the type of object it is applied to.

Object	Value Attribute
`button`, `reset`, `submit`	Value attribute that appears on-screen, not the button name
`checkbox`	*On* if item is selected, *off* if not
`radio`	String reflection of value
`hidden`, `text`, `textarea`	Contents of the field
`select`	Reflection of option value
`password`	Returns a valid default value, but an encrypted version if modified by the user

Changing the value of a `text` or `textarea` object results in an immediate update to the screen. All other `form` objects are not graphically updated when changed.

Property of `button`, `checkbox`, `hidden`, `options`, `password`, `radio`, `reset`, `submit`, `text`, `textarea`. For `password`, `text`, and `textarea`, see `defaultValue` property; for `button`, `reset`, and `submit`, see `name` property; for `options`, see properties `defaultSelected`, `selected`, `selectedIndex`, `text`; for `checkbox` and `radio`, see properties `checked` and `defaultChecked`.

vlinkColor Returns or sets the color of visited links using hexadecimal RGB triplets or a string literal. The property cannot be set after the document has been formatted. To override the browser defaults, color settings are used with the `onLoad` event handler in the `<BODY>` tag:

```
<BODY onLoad="document.vlinkColor='aliceblue'">
```

Property of `document`. See properties `alinkColor`, `bgColor`, `fgColor`, `linkColor`.

window A synonym for the current window to remove ambiguity between a `window` and `form` object of the same name. While it also applies to the current frame, it is less ambiguous to use the `self` property.

Property of `frame` and `window`. See `self` property.

Part

VI

App

B

Methods

Methods are functions and procedures used to perform an operation on an object, variable, or constant. With the exception of built-in functions, methods must be used with an object:

```
object.method()
```

Even if the method does not require any arguments, the parentheses are still required.

The object which utilizes the method is listed after the definition and is followed by any cross-references to other methods. Stand-alone functions that are not used with objects are indicated with an asterisk (*).

abs   Returns the absolute (unsigned) value of its argument.

```
document.write(Math.abs(-10));
document.write(Math.abs(12))
```

The above examples return 10 and 12, respectively.

Method of Math.

acos   Returns the arc cosine (from zero to *pi* radians) of its argument. The argument should be a number between –1 and 1. If the value is outside the valid range, a zero is returned.

Method of Math. See methods asin, atan, cos, sin, tan.

alert   Displays a JavaScript Alert dialog box with an OK button and a user-defined message. Before the user can continue, he must press the OK button.

Method of window. See methods confirm and prompt.

anchor   Used with write or writeln methods, anchor creates and displays an HTML hypertext target. The syntax is:

```
textString.anchor(anchorName)
```

where textString is what the user sees, and anchorName is equivalent to the name attribute of an HTML <ANCHOR> tag.

Method of string. See link method.

asin   Returns the arc sine (between *–pi/2* and *pi/2* radians) of a number between
–1 and 1. If the number is outside the range, a zero is returned.

Method of `Math`. See methods `acos`, `atan`, `cos`, `sin`, `tan`.

atan   Returns the arc tangent (between *–pi/2* and *pi/2* radians) of a number
between –1 and 1. If the number is outside the range, a zero is returned.

Method of `Math`. See methods `acos`, `asin`, `cos`, `sin`, `tan`.

back   Recalls the previous URL from the history list. This method is the same as
`history.go(-1)`.

Method of `history`. See methods `forward` and `go`.

big   Formats a string object as a big font by encasing it with HTML `<BIG>` tags.
Both of the following examples result in the same output—displaying the message
"Welcome to my home page" in a big font:

```
var welcomeMessage = "Welcome to my home page."
document.write(welcomeMessage.big())

<BIG> Welcome to my home page.</BIG>
```

Method of `string`. See methods `fontsize`, `small`.

blink   Formats a `string` object as a blinking line by encasing it with HTML
`<BLINK>` tags. Both of the following examples produce a flashing line that says
"Notice":

```
var attentionMessage = "Notice"
document.write(attentionMessage.blink())

<BLINK>Notice</BLINK>
```

Method of `string`. See methods `bold`, `italics`, `strike`.

blur   Removes focus from the specified `form` element. For example, the following
line removes focus from `feedback`:

```
feedback.blur()
```

assuming that `feedback` is defined as:

```
<input type="text" name="feedback">
```

Method of `password`, `select`, `text`, `textarea`. See methods `focus` and `select`.

bold Formats a `string` object in bold text by encasing it with HTML `<B>` tags.

Method of `string`. See methods `blink`, `italics`, `strike`.

ceil Returns the smallest integer greater than, or equal to, its argument. For example,

```
Math.ceil(1.01)
```

returns a 2.

Method of `Math`. See `floor` method.

charAt Returns the character from a string at the specified index. The first character is at position zero and the last at length –1.

```
var userName = "Bobba Louie"
document.write(userName.charAt(4)
```

returns an "a."

Method of `string`. See methods `indexOf` and `lastIndexOf`.

clear Clears the contents of a window, regardless of how the window is filled.

Method of `document`. See methods `close`, `open`, `write`, `writeln`.

clearTimeout Cancels a `timeout` set with the `setTimeout` method. A timeout is set using a unique timeout ID, which must be used to clear it:

```
clearTimeout(waitTime)
```

Method of `frame` and `window`. See `setTimeout` method.

click Simulates a mouse click on the calling `form` element with the effect dependent on the type of element.

Form Element	Action
`Button`, `reset`, and `submit`	Same as clicking button
`Radio`	Selects radio button
`Checkbox`	Marks checkbox and sets value to *on*

Method of `button`, `checkbox`, `radio`, `reset`, `submit`.

close For a `document` object, closes the current stream of output and forces its display. It also stops the browser Winsock animation and displays "Document: Done" in the status bar.

For a `window` object, closes the current window. As with all window commands, the `window` object is assumed. For example,

```
window.close()
close()
self.close()
```

all close the current window.

Method of `document` and `window`. See methods `clear`, `open`, `write`, `writeln`.

confirm   Displays a JavaScript confirmation dialog box with a message and buttons for OK and Cancel. Confirm returns a `true` if the user selects OK and `false` for Cancel. The following example loads a new window if the user presses OK:

```
if (confirm("Are you sure you want to enter.") {
    tourWindow = window.open("http:\\www.haunted.com\","hauntedhouse")
}
```

Method of `window`. See methods `alert` and `prompt`.

cos   Returns the cosine of the argument. The angle's size must be expressed in radians.

Method of `Math`. See methods `acos`, `asin`, `atan`, `sin`, `tan`.

escape*   Returns ASCII code of its argument based on the ISO Latin–1 character set in the form %*xx*, where *xx* is the ASCII code. It is not associated with any other object, but is actually part of the JavaScript language.

See `unescape` method.

eval*   This built-in function takes a string or numeric expression as its argument. If a string, it attempts to convert it to a numeric expression. `Eval` then evaluates the expression and returns the value.

```
var x = 10
var y = 20
document.write(eval("x + y"))
```

This method can also be used to perform JavaScript commands included as part of a string.

```
var doThis = "if (x==10) { alert("Your maximum has been reached") }
function checkMax () {
   x++;
   eval(doThis)
}
```

This can be useful when converting a date from a form (always a string) into a numerical expression or number.

exp Returns e (Euler's constant) to the power of the argument to compute a natural logarithm.

Method of Math. See methods log and pow.

fixed Formats the calling string into a fixed-pitch font by encasing it in HTML <TT> tags.

Method of string.

floor Returns the integer less than, or equal to, its argument. For example,

```
Math.floor(2.99)
```

returns a 2.

Method of Math. See ceil method.

focus Navigates to a specific form element and gives it focus. From that point, a value can be entered by JavaScript commands or the user can complete the entry.

Method of password, select, text, textarea. See methods blur and select.

fontcolor Formats the string object to a specific color expressed as a hexadecimal RGB triplet or a string literal, similar to using <FONT COLOR=COLOR>.

Method of string.

fontsize Formats the string object to a specific font size: one of the seven defined sizes using an integer through the <FONTSIZE=SIZE> tag. If a string is passed, then the size is changed relative to the value set in the <BASEFONT> tag.

Method of string. See methods big and small.

forward Loads the next document on the URL history list. This method is the same as history.go(1).

Method of history. See methods back and go.

getDate Returns the day of the month as an integer between 1 and 31.

Method of Date. See setDate method.

getDay Returns the day of the week as an integer from zero (Sunday) to six (Saturday). There is not a corresponding `setDay` command because the day is automatically computed when the date value is assigned.

Method of `Date`.

getHours Returns the hour of the day in 24-hour format, from zero (midnight) to 23 (11 PM).

Method of `Date`. See `setHours` method.

getMinutes Returns the minutes with an integer from zero to 59.

Method of `Date`. See `setMinutes` method.

getMonth Returns the month of the year as an integer between zero (January) and 11 (December).

Method of `Date`. See `setMonth` method.

getSeconds Returns the seconds in an integer from zero to 59.

Method of `Date`. See `setSeconds` method.

getTime Returns an integer representing the current value of the `date` object. The value is the number of milliseconds since midnight, January 1, 1970. This value can be used to compare the length of time between two date values.

For functions involving computation of dates, it is useful to define variables defining the minutes, hours, and days in milliseconds:

```
var dayMillisec = 1000 * 60 * 60 * 24 //1,000 milliseconds x 60 sec x 60 min x
➥24 hrs
var hourMillisec = 1000 * 60 * 60 //1,000 milliseconds x 60 sec x 60 min
var minuteMillisec = 1000 * 60 //1,000 milliseconds x 60 sec
```

Method of `Date`. See `setTime` method.

getTimezoneOffset Returns the difference in minutes between the client machine and Greenwich Mean Time. This value is a constant except for daylight savings time.

Method of `Date`.

getYear   Returns the year of the `date` object minus 1900. For example, 1996 is returned as `96`.

Method of `Date`. See `setYear` method.

go   Loads a document specified in the history list by its URL or relative to the current position on the list. If the URL is incomplete, then the closest match is used. The search is not case-sensitive.

Method of `history`. See methods `back` and `forward`.

indexOf   Returns the location of a specific character or string, starting the search from a specific location. The first character of the string is specified as zero and the last is the string's length–1. The syntax is:

```
stringName.indexOf([character¦string], [startingPoint])
```

The `startingPoint` is zero by default.

Method of `string`. See methods `charAt` and `lastIndexof`.

isNaN**   For UNIX platforms only, this stand-alone function returns `true` if the argument is not a number. On all platforms except Windows, the `parseFloat` and `parseInt` return `NaN` when the argument is not a number.

See methodS `parseFloat` and `parseInt`.

italics   Formats a `string` object into italics by encasing it an HTML `<I>` tag.

Method of `string`. See methods `blink`, `bold`, `strike`.

lastIndexOf   Returns the index of a character or string in a `string` object by looking backwards from the end of the string or a user-specified index.

Method of `string`. See methods `charAt` and `indexOf`.

link   Creates a hypertext link to another URL by defining the `<HREF>` attribute and the text representing the link to the user.

Method of `string`. See `anchor` method.

log   Returns the natural logarithm (base e) of a positive numeric expression greater than zero. An out-of-range number always returns $-1.797693134862316e+308$.

Method of `Math`. See methods `exp` and `pow`.

max Returns the greater of its two arguments. For example,

```
Math.max(1,100)
```

returns `100`.

Method of `Math`. See `min` method.

min Returns the lesser of its two arguments.

Method of `Math`. See `max` method.

open For a document, opens a stream to collect the output of `write` or `writeln` methods. If a document already exists in the target window, then the open method clears it. The stream is ended by using the `document.close()` method.

For a window, it opens a new browser window in a similar fashion to choosing File, New Web Browser from the Netscape menu. Using the URL argument, it loads a document into the new window; otherwise, the new window is blank. When used as part of an event handler, the form must include the window object; otherwise, the document is assumed. Window features are defined by a comma-separated list of options with `=1` or `=yes` to enable and `=0` or `=no` to disable. Window features include toolbar, location, directories, status, menubar, scrollbars, resizable, copyhistory, width, and height.

Method of `document` and `window`. See methods `clear`, `close`, `write`, `writeln`.

parse Takes a date string, such as `"Jan 11, 1996"`, and returns the number of milliseconds since midnight, Jan. 1, 1970. This function can be used to set date values based on string values. When passed a string with a time, it returns the time value.

Because `parse` is a static function of `Date`, it is always used as `Date.parse()` rather than as a method of a created `date` object.

Method of `Date`. See `UTC` method.

parseFloat* Parses a string argument and returns a floating-point number if the first character is a plus sign, minus sign, decimal point, exponent, or a numeral. If it encounters a character other than one of the valid choices after that point, it returns the value up to that location and ignores all succeeding characters. If the first character is not a valid character, `parseFloat` returns one of two values based on the platform:

Windows   0

Non-Windows   NaN

See isNaN method.

parseInt* Parses a string argument and returns an integer based on a specified radix or base. A radix of 10 converts the value to a decimal, while eight converts to octal, and 16 to hexadecimal. Values greater than 10 for bases above 10 are represented with letters (A through F) in place of numbers.

Floating-point values are converted to integers. The rules for evaluating the string are identical to parseFloat.

See isNaN and parseFloat methods.

pow Returns a base raised to an exponent.

Method of Math. See exp and log methods.

prompt Displays a prompt dialog box that accepts user input. If an initial value is not specified for inputDefault, the dialog box displays the value <undefined>.

Method of window. See alert and confirm methods.

random On UNIX machines only, returns a pseudo-random number between zero and 1.

Method of Math.

round Returns the value of a floating-point argument rounded to the next highest integer if the decimal portion is greater than or equal to .5, or the next lowest integer if less than .5.

Method of Math.

select Selects the input area of a specified form element. Used in conjunction with the focus method, JavaScript can highlight a field and position the cursor for user input.

Method of password, text, textarea. See methods blur and focus.

setDate Sets the day of the month.

Method of Date. See getDate method.

setHours   Sets the hour for the current time.

Method of `Date`. See `getHours` method.

setMinutes   Sets the minutes for the current time.

Method of `Date`. See `getMinutes` method.

setMonth   Sets the month with an integer from zero (January) to 11 (December).

Method of `Date`. See `getMonth` method.

setSeconds   Sets the seconds for the current time.

Method of `Date`. See `getSeconds` method.

setTime   Sets the value of a `date` object.

Method of `Date`. See `getTime` method.

setTimeout   Evaluates an expression after a specified amount of time, expressed in milliseconds. This is not repeated indefinitely. For example, setting a timeout to three seconds will evaluate the expression once after three seconds—not every three seconds. To call `setTimeout` recursively, reset the timeout as part of the function invoked by the method. Calling the function `startclock` in the following example sets a loop in motion that clears the timeout, displays the current time, and sets the timeout to redisplay the time in one second.

```
var timerID = null;
var timerRunning = false;
function stopclock () {
  if(timerRunning) cleartimeout(timerID);
  timerRunning=false;
}
function startclock () {
  stopclock();
  showtime();
}
function showtime () {
  var now = new Date();
  ...
  document.clock.face.value =   timeValue;
  timerID = setTimeout("showtime()",1000);
  timerRunning = true;
}
```

Method of `window`. See `clearTimeout` method.

setYear   Sets the year in the current date using an integer representing the year minus 1900.

Method of Date. See getYear method.

sin   Returns the sine of an argument. The argument is the size of an angle expressed in radians, and the returned value is from –1 to 1.

Method of Math. See methods acos, asin, atan, cos, tan.

small   Formats a string object into a small font using the HTML <SMALL> tags.

Method of string. See methods big and fontsize.

sqrt   Returns the square root of a positive numeric expression. If the argument's value is outside the range, the returned value is zero.

strike   Formats a string object as strikeout text using the HTML <STRIKE> tags.

Method of string. See methods blink, bold, italics.

sub   Formats a string object into subscript text using the HTML <SUB> tags.

Method of string. See sup method.

submit   Performs the same action as clicking a submit button.

Method of form. See submit object; see onSubmit event handler.

substring   Returns a subset of a string object based on two indexes. If the indexes are equal, an empty string is returned. Regardless of order, the substring is built from the smallest index to the largest.

Method of string.

sup   Formats a string object into superscript text using the HTML <SUP> tags.

Method of string. See sub method.

tan   Returns the tangent of an argument. The argument is the size of an angle expressed in radians.

Method of Math. See methods acos, asin, atan, cos, sin.

toGMTString   Converts a date object to a string using Internet Greenwich Mean Time (GMT) conventions. For example, if today is a date object:

```
today.toGMTString()
```

then the string "Mon, 18 Dec 1995 17:28:35 GMT" is returned. Actual formatting may vary from platform to platform. The time and date is based on the client machine.

Method of `Date`. See `toLocaleString` method.

toLocaleString   Converts a `date` object to a string using the local conventions, such as *mm/dd/yy hh:mm:ss*.

Method of `Date`. See `toGMTString` method.

toLowerCase   Converts all characters in a string to lowercase.

Method of `string`. See `toUpperCase` method.

toString   Converts a `date` or `location` object to a string.

Method of `Date`, `location`.

toUpperCase   Converts all characters in a string to uppercase.

Method of `string`. See `toLowerCase` method.

unEscape*   Returns a character based on its ASCII value expressed as a string in the format %*xxx* where *xxx* is a decimal number between zero and 255, or 0×0 to $0 \times FF$ in hex.

See `escape` method.

UTC   Returns the number of milliseconds for a date in Universal Coordinated Time (UTC) since midnight, January 1, 1970.

UTC is a constant, and is always used as `Date.UTC()`, not with a created `date` object.

Method of `Date`. See `parse` method.

write   Writes one or more lines to a document window, and can include HTML tags and JavaScript expressions, including numeric, string, and logical values. The `write` method does not add a new line (`<BR>` or `/N`) character to the end of the output. If called from an event handler, the current document is cleared if a new window is not created for the output.

Part

VI

App

B

Method of `document`. See methods `close`, `clear`, `open`, `writeln`.

writeln   Writes one or more lines to a document window followed by a new line character, and can include HTML tags and JavaScript expressions, including numeric, string, and logical values. If called from an event handler, the current document is cleared if a new window is not created for the output.

Method of `document`. See methods `close`, `clear`, `open`, `write`.

Event Handlers

Event handlers are where JavaScript gets its power. By looking for specific user actions, JavaScript can confirm or act on input immediately, without waiting for server introduction.

onBlur   Blurs occur when a `select`, `text`, or `textarea` field on a form loses focus.

Event handler of `select`, `text`, `textarea`. See event handlers `onChange` and `onFocus`.

onChange   A change event happens when a `select`, `text`, or `textarea` element on a form is modified before losing focus.

Event handler of `select`, `text`, `textarea`. See event handlers `onBlur`, `onFocus`.

onClick   Occurs when an object, such as a button or checkbox, is clicked.

Event handler of `button`, `checkbox`, `radio`, `link`, `reset`, `submit`.

onFocus   A form element receives focus by tabbing to or clicking the input area with the mouse. Selecting within a field results in a `select` event.

Event handler of `select`, `text`, `textarea`. See event handlers `onBlur` and `onChange`.

onLoad   A load event is created when Navigator finishes loading a window or all frames within a `<FRAMESET>` tag.

Event handler of `window`. See `onUnload` event handler.

onMouseOver Occurs when the mouse pointer is placed over a `link` object. To function with the `status` or `defaultStatus` properties, the event handler must return `true`.

Event handler of `link`.

onSelect A select event is triggered by selecting some or all of the text in a `text` or `textarea` field.

Event handler of `text`, `textarea`.

onSubmit Triggered by the user submitting a form. The event handler must return `true` to allow the form to be submitted to the server. Conversely, it returns `false` to block the form's submission.

Event handler of `form`. See `submit` object and method.

onUnload Occurs when exiting a document. For proper operation, place the `onUnload` handler in the `<BODY>` or `<FRAMESET>` tags.

Event handler of `window`. See `onLoad` event handler. ●

JavaScript Commands and Grammar

by Rick Darnell

Finding information on programming in JavaScript can be a bit like looking for the Holy Grail. Between Netscape's site, online tutorials, and examples, information seems to be everywhere but at your fingertips. So here is the information you're looking for in one place, including statements, operators, and color values. ■

JavaScript Statements

The statements used to control program flow in JavaScript are similar to Java and C. A statement can span several lines if needed, or several statements can be placed on the same line. The key to remember is that a semicolon must be placed between all statements. Since JavaScript is not strict in its formatting, you must provide the line breaks and indentation to make sure the code is readable and easy to understand later.

break Terminates the current `for` or `while` loop and passes control to the first statement after the loop.

comment Notes from the script author that are ignored by the interpreter. Single line comments are preceded by `//`. Multiple line comments begin with `/*` and end with `*/`.

continue Passes control to the condition in a `while` loop and to the `update` expression in a `for` loop.

for Creates a loop with three optional expressions enclosed in parentheses and separated by semicolons, followed by a set of statements to be executed during the loop:

```
for( initialExpression; condition; updateExpression) {
statements...
}
```

The `initial` expression is used to initialize the counter variable, which can be a new variable declared with `var`. The `condition` expression is evaluated on each pass through the loop. If the condition is `true`, the loop statements are executed. The `update` expression is used to increment the counter variable.

for...in Iterates a variable for all of properties of an object:

```
for (variable in object) {
statements...
}
```

For each property, it executes the statement block.

function Declares a JavaScript function with a name and parameters. To return a value, the function must include a `return` statement. A function definition cannot be nested within another function.

```
function name ([parameter] [...,parameter]) {
statements...
}
```

if...else   A conditional statement that executes the first set of statements if the condition is `true`, and the statements following `else` if `false`. If...else statements can be nested to any level.

```
if (condition) {
statements...
} [else {
 statements...
}]
```

return   Specifies a value to be returned by a function.

```
return expression;
```

var   Declares a variable and optionally initializes it to a value. The scope of a variable is the current function or, when declared outside a function, the current document.

```
var variableName [=value] [..., variableName [=value]]
```

while   Repeats a loop while an expression is `true`.

```
while (condition) {
statements...
}
```

with   Establishes a default object for a set of statements. Any property references without an object are assumed to use the default object.

```
with (object) {
statements...
}
```

This statement is especially useful when applied to the `Math` object for a set of calculations. For example,

```
with (Math) {
var Value1 = cos(angle);
var Value2 = sin(angle);
}
```

replaces

```
{
var Value1 = Math.cos(angle);
var Value2 = Math.sin(angle);
}
```

Operator Precedence

Precedence refers to the order in which compound operations are computed. Operators on the same level have equal precedence. Calculations are computed from left to right on all binary operations beginning with the operators at the top of the list and working down.

call, member	.	[]	()		
negation/increment	++	—	!	~	-
multiply/divide	*	/	%		
addition/subtraction	+	-			
shift	<<	>>	>>>		
relational	<	>	<=	>=	
equality	==	!=			
bitwise AND	&				
bitwise XOR	^				
bitwise OR						
logical AND	&&				
logical OR	||				
conditional	?:				
assignment	=	*op*=			
comma	,				

JavaScript Objects

JavaScript is an object-oriented language, and as such, includes a set of built-in objects to represent the HTML document, especially form elements. Built-in objects can be accessed by both the client and server.

String Contains a string of characters.

Math Provides numerical constants and mathematical functions.

Date   Stores a date in the number of milliseconds since 1/1/1970, 00:00:00, and returns a date string in the format "Thu, 11 Jan 1996 06:20:00 GMT".

Document   The foundation object created with an HTML <BODY> tag and used to write other information to the page.

Form   An object for gathering and echoing data, created by HTML <FORM> tags.

Window   The highest precedence object accessible by JavaScript relating to the current open Navigator window. New windows and frames can also be created.

Reserved Words

Part
VI

App
C

The following words cannot be used as user objects or variables in coding JavaScript. Not all are currently in use by JavaScript—they are reserved for future use.

abstract

boolean

break

byte

case

catch

char

class

const

continue

default

do

double

else

extends

false

final

finally

float

for

function

goto

if

implements

import

in

instanceof

int

interface

long

native

new

null

package

private

protected

public

return

short

static

super

switch

synchronized

this

throw

throws

transient

true

try

var

void

while

with

Color Values

Colors can be referenced in a variety of properties in two ways: by using the string literal or a RGB hexadecimal triplet formed by combining the three color values. For example, `aliceblue` is represented as `F0F8FF`.

Color/string literal	Red	Green	Blue
aliceblue	F0	F8	FF
antiquewhite	FA	EB	D7
aqua	00	FF	FF
aquamarine	7F	FF	D4
azure	F0	FF	FF
beige	F5	F5	DC
bisque	FF	E4	C4
black	00	00	00
blanchedalmond	FF	EB	CD
blue	00	00	FF
blueviolet	8A	2B	E2
brown	A5	2A	2A
burlywood	DE	B8	87
cadetblue	5F	9E	A0

Part
VI

App
C

chartreuse	7F	FF	A0
chocolate	D2	69	1E
coral	FF	7F	50
cornflowerblue	64	95	ED
cornsilk	FF	F8	DC
crimson	DC	14	3C
cyan	00	FF	FF
darkblue	00	00	8B
darkcyan	00	8B	8B
darkgoldenrod	B8	86	0B
darkgray	A9	A9	A9
darkgreen	00	64	00
darkkhaki	BD	B7	6B
darkmagenta	8B	00	8B
darkolivegreen	55	6B	2F
darkorange	FF	8C	00
darkorchid	99	32	CC
darkred	8B	00	00
darksalmon	E9	96	7A
darkseagreen	8F	BC	8F
darkslateblue	48	3D	8B
darkslategray	2F	4F	4F
darkturquoise	00	CE	D1
darkviolet	94	00	D3
deeppink	FF	14	93
deepskyblue	00	BF	FF
dimgray	69	69	69
dodgerblue	1E	90	FF
firebrick	B2	22	22

floralwhite	FF	FA	F0
forestgreen	22	8B	22
fuchsia	FF	00	FF
gainsboro	DC	DC	DC
ghostwhite	F8	F8	FF
gold	FF	D7	00
goldenrod	DA	A5	20
gray	80	80	80
green	00	80	00
greenyellow	AD	FF	2F
honeydew	F0	FF	F0
hotpink	FF	69	B4
indianred	CD	5C	5C
indigo	4B	00	82
ivory	FF	FF	F0
khaki	F0	E6	8C
lavender	E6	E6	FA
lavenderblush	FF	F0	F5
lawngreen	7C	FC	00
lemonchiffon	FF	FA	CD
lightblue	AD	D8	E6
lightcoral	F0	80	80
lightcyan	E0	FF	FF
lightgoldenrodyellow	FA	FA	D2
lightgreen	90	EE	90
lightgrey	D3	D3	D3
lightpink	FF	B6	C1
lightsalmon	FF	A0	7A
lightseagreen	20	B2	AA

lightskyblue	87	CE	FA
lightslategray	77	88	99
lightsteelblue	B0	C4	DE
lightyellow	FF	FF	E0
lime	00	FF	00
limegreen	32	CD	32
linen	FA	F0	E6
magenta	FF	00	FF
maroon	80	00	00
mediumaquamarine	66	CD	AA
mediumblue	00	00	CD
mediumorchid	BA	55	D3
mediumpurple	93	70	DB
mediumseagreen	3C	B3	71
mediumslateblue	7B	68	EE
mediumspringgreen	00	FA	9A
mediumturquoise	48	D1	CC
mediumvioletred	C7	15	85
midnightblue	19	19	70
mintcream	F5	FF	FA
mistyrose	FF	E4	E1
moccasin	FF	E4	B5
navajowhite	FF	DE	AD
navy	00	00	80
oldlace	FD	F5	E6
olive	80	80	00
olivedrab	6B	8E	23
orange	FF	A5	00
orangered	FF	45	00

orchid	DA	70	D6
palgoldenrod	EE	E8	AA
palegreen	98	FB	98
paleturquoise	AF	EE	EE
palevioletred	DB	70	93
papayawhip	FF	EF	D5
peachpuff	FF	DA	B9
peru	CD	85	3F
pink	FF	C0	CB
plum	DD	A0	DD
powderblue	B0	E0	E6
purple	80	00	80
red	FF	00	00
rosybrown	BC	8F	8F
royalblue	41	69	E1
saddlebrown	8B	45	13
salmon	FA	80	72
sandybrown	F4	A4	60
seagreen	2E	8B	57
seashell	FF	F5	EE
sienna	A0	52	2D
silver	C0	C0	C0
skyblue	87	CE	EB
slateblue	6A	5A	CD
slategray	70	80	90
snow	FF	FA	FA
springgreen	00	FF	7F
steelblue	46	82	B4
tan	D2	B4	8C

teal	00	80	80
thistle	D8	BF	D8
tomato	FF	63	47
turquoise	40	E0	D0
violet	EE	82	EE
wheat	F5	DE	B3
white	FF	FF	FF
whitesmoke	F5	F5	F5
yellow	FF	FF	00
yellowgreen	9A	CD	32

Current Bugs and Future Enhancements

by Andrew Wooldridge

This appendix summarizes some of the current "bugs" in JavaScript that you should be aware of and lists a few of the new features hinted at by Netscape in future releases of Netscape Navigator. By the time you have this book in your hands many of these bugs may indeed be fixed (as well as new ones discovered), but you will be able to gain some insight into why JavaScript behaves as it does in your version.

Bugs in JavaScript

Before addressing the new features targeted for release in Netscape Navigator 2.1 and 3.0, lets look at some of the items that represent current bugs in Netscape's JavaScript. These are presented here to help you avoid hours of head scratching and recoding, only to find out that it's not really your fault. To find out if these have been fixed in your version of Netscape, go to the Release Notes section in Navigator. In Windows, select Release Notes from the Help menu; in Macintosh, select Release Notes from the Balloon Help menu. The following items are a few of the current bugs in Netscape's 2.01 version of JavaScript, and ways to avoid them:

- `onLoad` event handler loads prematurely—The `onLoad` event handler may get called before it is supposed to when you use pages without frames. To work around this, use `window.setTimeout()` to test for the existence of form elements in your page before running the script you intended for the `onLoad` event.

- `Unterminated String Literal` error message—This occurs when you try to assign a very long string to a text value (see listing D.1).

Listing D.1   Long Strings Literals in JavaScript

```
var thisString="Wow this is a long string of code which will not work in
current versions of Netscape! Especially Windows 3.1. Wow this is a long
string of code which will not work in current versions of Netscape!
Especially Windows 3.1. Wow this is a long string of code which will not
work in current versions of Netscape! Especially Windows 3.1. Wow this
is a long string of code which will not work in current versions of
Netscape! Especially Windows 3.1."
```

To fix this, break the string into smaller pieces and concatenate them together using the plus operator (+).

- `Eval()` crashes Navigator in Windows 3.11—This is a known bug and the next version should take care of this. In the mean time, avoid using `eval()` or check the `appVersion` (for example, `navigator.appVersion`) of the client machine and direct them around this code if it is being run on Windows 3.11.

- `window.open()` only opens an empty window—In Macintosh and X versions of Navigator you have to send the `window.open()` message twice for the information to be passed to the window. If you only send it once, you get a blank open window. This bug should be fixed in 2.1.

- Opening a new window in some X platforms ignores Boolean options—When you open a window you can specify items such as `toolbar=yes`, and so on. Some versions of Navigator for X ignore this. You should always specify the options for the `window.open()` method to avoid this problem. Look for a fix in 2.1.

- Height and width in IMAGE tags—You should always include `HEIGHT` and `WIDTH` attributes on all your images to avoid this bug where event handlers might be ignored on form elements below the images. Another less elegant work-around is to add an empty `<SCRIPT>...</SCRIPT>` tag to the bottom of that page.

- `lastIndexOf` searching—Normally, the `lastIndexOf` method should start searching right to left based on the position you specified in the `fromIndex` value. As of now, it starts one character to the right of that position.

- `method` property of a `form` object—Right now this property is read-only (in 2.01) but you should be able to reset the value of this property in your scripts. Look for a fix in 2.1.

- `document.close()`—If you call `document.close()` while a document you opened is still loading, it causes Navigator to crash. Check to make sure the document has completely loaded before you call `document.close()`.

- `name` property of object and order of creation—When you give the same name to multiple objects in a form, JavaScript is supposed to create an array with each of those objects in order of creation. If you don't specify an event handler with this object, the indexing will be in reverse of the creation order. This bug shows up most often when you use radio buttons in a form. You should add an event handler to each element (even if the event handler does nothing) in order for them to be indexed correctly.

- `window.status` property—If you check the `window.status` property, it is always the value of `window.defaultStatus`. What it should actually be is the current value of this window's status bar instead of a constant value. This will be fixed in an upcoming version to reflect the current status instead.

Part
VI

App
D

- `window.open()` and spaces in names—Calling a `window.open` with a name containing spaces doesn't work, but doesn't call an error message. For example,

  ```
  window.open("", "Hi There")
  ```

  simply does not work, nor does it give you an error message. Always check that you don't use spaces. The fix in 2.1 will give you an error message.

- `SCRIPT` tags inside table cells—`SCRIPT` tags inside table cells that write some HTML don't work in 2.0—the HTML is written twice, and the first output is misinterpreted as if it were JavaScript within the `SCRIPT` tag, during the second pass. To work around this, invert things so your `SCRIPT` tag writes the table cell markup and the generated HTML (`document.lastModified`), as follows:

  ```
  <TABLE WIDTH=100%><TR>
  <SCRIPT LANGUAGE="JavaScript">
    document.write("<TD>", document.lastModified, "</TD>")
  </SCRIPT>
  </TR></TABLE>
  ```

- `Math.random()`—Currently, this only works on some X platforms. It is to be fixed in 2.1.

- `onMouseOver` in Navigator Gold in Windows—Currently this feature is not working. Look for a fix in the next release of Navigator Gold.

- Inter-frame and inter-window string and object references—When you reference a string or an object across frames or windows, the value can get corrupted. You should instead assign the "remote" value (the one in the other frame or window) to a new "local" variable. Also, in the instance of strings, you should pre-append a " " to the new value to make sure JavaScript reads the value as a string. For example:

  ```
  var mystr = "" + parent.otherFrame.stringProperty
  ```

  You should also avoid passing objects between frames and windows until Netscape version 3.0, which should correct this corruption problem.

Permanent Limitations

JavaScript has certain limitations built in that most likely will not change over time. These limitations are tied closely with the issues of security. Although JavaScript will execute small "programs" on your machine, you do not want it to send or receive information that you do not explicitly request.

JavaScript will most likely never be able to directly write to a file (although recently a script was developed that allows JavaScript to prompt you to save some data in a file of your choice—much like when you download an unknown file type). It hopefully will not be able to access your personal history files (as in sending them to others). It will not access your e-mail address (again, as in sending it to another site).

Also, it will probably, in the future, check a site against some list you develop (or via some RSA security key) and mark a site as "trusted" or "not trusted" and treat that script accordingly. Scripts from trusted sites will probably have greater freedom to manipulate information for you, as well as perform tasks that untrusted sites would be banned from. There is also a new concept called information *tainting* that will allow scripts to access more sensitive information from your browser.

New Features in JavaScript

Brendan Eich, the engineer at Netscape in charge of JavaScript, has been working to improve JavaScript with each version of Netscape that is released. Because of time constraints, many features originally targeted for the first release have been delayed. The following section represents some of the features that will be included in future releases of JavaScript.

Netscape Navigator 2.1

Netscape Navigator 2.1 is the next release of the browser to include new features and bug fixes. This release is expected some time in the summer of '96 (as of this writing). This release represents mainly a set of minor changes and improvements over 2.01.

If you read the bug listings earlier in this appendix, you know much about what will be fixed in 2.1. There are a number of items, though, that are not considered bugs, which are also intended to be added to the next version of JavaScript (via the next version of Navigator—since there is no distinction in terms of versioning). The following lists some of these features:

- onMouseOver for imagemaps—Currently you cannot use the onMouseOver event handler to control different actions using a client-side imagemap. If you place onMouseOver events in each tag that specifies an area, the Navigator ignores the tag. In 2.1, you should be able to trigger events using a client-side imagemap. For example, listing D.2 shows the original map.

Listing D.2   Client-Side Imagemap—Before JavaScript

```
<MAP NAME=bottom>
<AREA SHAPE=rect COORDS="0,0, 46,31" HREF=/search/index.html>
<AREA SHAPE=rect COORDS="47,0, 106,31" HREF=/ads/index.html>
<AREA SHAPE=rect COORDS="107,0, 163,31" HREF=/misc/contact_info.html>
<AREA SHAPE=rect COORDS= "164,0, 223,31"
➥HREF="http://merchant.netscape.com/netstore/index.html">
<AREA SHAPE=rect COORDS= "224,0, 285,31" HREF=/toc.html>
<AREA SHAPE=rect COORDS= "286,0, 354,31" HREF=/comprod/mirror/index.html>
<AREA SHAPE=rect COORDS= "355,0, 418,31" HREF=/escapes/galleria.html>
<AREA SHAPE=rect COORDS= "419,0, 468,31"  HREF=/feedback/index.html>
<AREA SHAPE=default  HREF=/index.html>
</MAP>
```

Using onMouseOver you can add to an area an event to be triggered when a user passes his mouse over that area specified, as follows:

```
<AREA SHAPE=rect COORDS="0,0, 46,31" HREF=/search/index.html
onMouseOver="alert('hi!')">
```

Currently, if you want events to be triggered by an imagemap, you must use the javascript: URL tag in an HREF link. For example, the preceding line would read as follows:

```
<AREA SHAPE=rect COORDS="0,0, 46,31" HREF="javascript:alert('hi!')">
```

The limitation to this is that the user must click that area in order for the script to be executed.

- Security fixes—There are many security issues that will be addressed in the next version of Navigator. In 2.1, JavaScript will have much of the same limitations that Java currently has in terms of writing to the user's local machine, or getting personal information from the client back to the server—such as mail addresses or listings of files.

■ Overall stability—You may notice that JavaScript crashes your machine, or brings up an `Out of memory` error on a page using a clock or some other constantly running script. This is primarily due to the machine not freeing up memory as it becomes available (especially with recursive calls to `setTimeout()`), and will be fixed in 2.1.

Netscape Navigator 3.0

The 3.0 release of Netscape Navigator will include a host of new features in addition to improvements of JavaScript. For instance, it will use Collabra Share, video and audio streaming, Live3D (VRML), and a second generation Java engine. The following is a short listing of the expected changes to JavaScript that have been announced through various channels via the Internet:

■ Regular expressions—Many scripting languages use a feature called *regular expressions*. Regular expressions are a set of characters that follow certain rules to match characters in a string. What this means to the JavaScript programmer is that you will be able to search for text based on rules like "Find all five character strings that begin with C and end with ch."

Languages like Perl take great advantage of this ability to parse through submissions of forms via the Web. There will probably be a whole new set of statements for this capability, such as a `find()` method or a `regex()` method.

■ Printing—When a user retrieves a Web page containing JavaScript that generates HTML on-the-fly in some way (such as saying "Good Evening" at night using the `Date` object), he currently cannot print the page in the same way that it is displayed on the browser. Instead, the page is printed with blank areas where the generated HTML should have been, or the source code appears (if the page programmer did not use the comment tags to hide the code). This is because of the way the Navigator stores the information that it uses to create the page. Essentially, when a page is printed, it is reread by the browser and converted to the correct code to be sent to the printer. Unfortunately, this interpreter does not recognize JavaScript code. It's as if your browser is of two minds—the new browser, which understands the JavaScript elements, and the older browser, which ignores the commands. In this release, you should be able to print source pages as "generated source" or just "source."

■ SRC tag—When JavaScript was originally released, it listed the SCRIPT tag as having an attribute called SRC. For example,

```
<SCRIPT SRC="http://www.mysite.com/foo/scripts/hello.js">
</SCRIPT>
```

In the 3.0 release, you will be able to hide the source code of your scripts using this SRC tag. It operates much like it would for the IMG tag. Your JavaScript code is written in a file that has a .js extension, which you then can reference from anywhere on your pages without having to relist the code over and over again across pages. What is interesting about this new attribute is that it not only will allow you to modularize your JavaScript code, but *all* of your HTML code. For instance, take a look at a simple example in listing D.3.

Listing D.3 Simple HTML Example

```
<HTML>
<HEAD>
<TITLE>Welcome to my Site!</TITLE>
</HEAD>
<BODY>
<H1>Today's Date is July 14, 1996!</H1>
Welcome.....blah blah
<address>my@address.com</address>
</BODY>
</HTML>
```

Using the new SRC attribute in the SCRIPT tag, you can pull out all of the parts of a page that are reused across your Web site and just point to them from inside a <SCRIPT SCR="">. Listing D.4 is the small page converted to a series of scripts.

Listing D.4 Alternative Code Using JavaScript SRC Attribute

```
<HTML>
<HEAD>
```

```
<SCRIPT SRC="mytitle.js"><SCRIPT>
</HEAD>
<BODY>
<SCRIPT SRC="todaysdate.js"></SCRIPT>
<SCRIPT SRC="myintromessage.js"></SCRIPT>
<SCRIPT SRC="myaddress.js"></SCRIPT>
</BODY>
</HTML>
```

This might not seem to save much space at first, but imagine that you have 200 Web pages, and all of them have your address at the bottom. Today you get a new e-mail address. You now have to change your address on 200 pages. Perhaps you know enough UNIX to globally change your pages, or perhaps you have a script that might do that as well, but if you don't, you will be editing your pages for a long time.

With JavaScript, all you will have to do is change the myaddress.js file and all of the pages will reflect this new change. In addition, you can edit your myaddress.js file to point itself to myname.js, which appends your name to the end of your address. What this really means is that you will be able to dramatically modularize your pages.

Communicating with Other Elements in the Navigator

As with the SRC tag, the JavaScript documentation originally talked about using JavaScript to read and write properties of plug-ins and Java applets from within the JavaScript script. This specification has yet to be completely hashed out, but you will soon be able to see the properties of applets and plug-ins. There will be two new Navigator properties: navigator.plugins (an array of plug-ins that specify all of the currently registered plug-ins) and navigator.mimeTypes (which specify information about all of the MIME types supported by that Navigator). Later there will also be document.plugins, which reflect the information listed in all of the EMBED tags of a given page.

It's expected that you will also have something like navigator.applets that will correspond to the APPLET tag listings. To get or change attributes of these new properties you will use navigator.plugins[0].propertys[0], or something similar.

The Future

JavaScript has a bright future if it can keep up with the rapid pace of change that has been the norm for the past few years in the software and Internet development world. JavaScript is relatively robust and useful, and adds a new dimension of interactivity to the Web. There has been a general trend in the computer industry to pass more work off to the client machine, which now has the processing power to handle it. JavaScript continues this trend by allowing you to avoid using CGIs for many tasks. And with the development of server-side JavaScript, Web sites will probably become more like full blown applications—instead of their current relatively static nature. ●

Index

QUE® has the right choice for every computer user

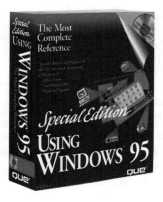

From the new computer user to the advanced programmer, we've got the right computer book for you. Our user-friendly *Using* series offers just the information you need to perform specific tasks quickly and move onto other things. And, for computer users ready to advance to new levels, QUE *Special Edition Using* books, the perfect all-in-one resource—and recognized authority on detailed reference information.

The *Using* series for casual users

Who should use this book?

Everyday users who:
- Work with computers in the office or at home
- Are familiar with computers but not in love with technology
- Just want to "get the job done"
- Don't want to read a lot of material

The user-friendly reference

- The fastest access to the one best way to get things done
- Bite-sized information for quick and easy reference
- Nontechnical approach in plain English
- Real-world analogies to explain new concepts
- Troubleshooting tips to help solve problems
- Visual elements and screen pictures that reinforce topics
- Expert authors who are experienced in training and instruction

Special Edition Using for accomplished users

Who should use this book?

Proficient computer users who:
- Have a more technical understanding of computers
- Are interested in technological trends
- Want in-depth reference information
- Prefer more detailed explanations and examples

The most complete reference

- Thorough explanations of various ways to perform tasks
- In-depth coverage of all topics
- Technical information cross-referenced for easy access
- Professional tips, tricks, and shortcuts for experienced users
- Advanced troubleshooting information with alternative approaches
- Visual elements and screen pictures that reinforce topics
- Technically qualified authors who are experts in their fields
- "Techniques form the Pros" sections with advice from well-known computer professionals

Complete and Return this Card for a *FREE* Computer Book Catalog

Thank you for purchasing this book! You have purchased a superior computer book written expressly for your needs. To continue to provide the kind of up-to-date, pertinent coverage you've come to expect from us, we need to hear from you. Please take a minute to complete and return this self-addressed, postage-paid form. In return, we'll send you a free catalog of all our computer books on topics ranging from word processing to programming and the internet.

Mr. ☐ Mrs. ☐ Ms. ☐ Dr. ☐

Name (first) ☐☐☐☐☐☐☐☐☐☐☐ (M.I.) ☐ (last) ☐☐☐☐☐☐☐☐☐☐☐☐☐☐☐☐☐☐

Address ☐☐☐☐☐☐☐☐☐☐☐☐☐☐☐☐☐☐☐☐☐☐☐☐☐☐☐☐☐☐

☐☐☐☐☐☐☐☐☐☐☐☐☐☐☐☐☐☐☐☐☐☐☐☐☐☐☐☐☐☐

City ☐☐☐☐☐☐☐☐☐☐☐☐☐☐☐☐☐☐ State ☐☐ Zip ☐☐☐☐☐ ☐☐☐☐

Phone ☐☐☐ ☐☐☐ ☐☐☐☐ Fax ☐☐☐ ☐☐☐ ☐☐☐☐

Company Name ☐☐☐☐☐☐☐☐☐☐☐☐☐☐☐☐☐☐☐☐☐☐☐☐☐☐

E-mail address ☐☐☐☐☐☐☐☐☐☐☐☐☐☐☐☐☐☐☐☐☐☐☐☐☐☐

1. Please check at least (3) influencing factors for purchasing this book.

Front or back cover information on book .... ☐
Special approach to the content .... ☐
Completeness of content .... ☐
Author's reputation .... ☐
Publisher's reputation .... ☐
Book cover design or layout .... ☐
Index or table of contents of book .... ☐
Price of book .... ☐
Special effects, graphics, illustrations .... ☐
Other (Please specify): _____ ☐

2. How did you first learn about this book?

Saw in Macmillan Computer Publishing catalog .... ☐
Recommended by store personnel .... ☐
Saw the book on bookshelf at store .... ☐
Recommended by a friend .... ☐
Received advertisement in the mail .... ☐
Saw an advertisement in: _____ ☐
Read book review in: _____ ☐
Other (Please specify): _____ ☐

3. How many computer books have you purchased in the last six months?

This book only .... ☐   3 to 5 books .... ☐
2 books .... ☐   More than 5 .... ☐

4. Where did you purchase this book?

Bookstore .... ☐
Computer Store .... ☐
Consumer Electronics Store .... ☐
Department Store .... ☐
Office Club .... ☐
Warehouse Club .... ☐
Mail Order .... ☐
Direct from Publisher .... ☐
Internet site .... ☐
Other (Please specify): _____ ☐

5. How long have you been using a computer?

☐ Less than 6 months   ☐ 6 months to a year
☐ 1 to 3 years   ☐ More than 3 years

6. What is your level of experience with personal computers and with the subject of this book?

	With PCs	With subject of book
New	☐	☐
Casual	☐	☐
Accomplished	☐	☐
Expert	☐	☐

Source Code ISBN: 0-7897-0789-6

7. Which of the following best describes your job title?

Administrative Assistant .... ☐
Coordinator .... ☐
Manager/Supervisor .... ☐
Director .... ☐
Vice President .... ☐
President/CEO/COO .... ☐
Lawyer/Doctor/Medical Professional ...... ☐
Teacher/Educator/Trainer .... ☐
Engineer/Technician .... ☐
Consultant .... ☐
Not employed/Student/Retired .... ☐
Other (Please specify): _____ ☐

8. Which of the following best describes the area of the company your job title falls under?

Accounting .... ☐
Engineering .... ☐
Manufacturing .... ☐
Operations .... ☐
Marketing .... ☐
Sales .... ☐
Other (Please specify): _____ ☐

9. What is your age?

Under 20 .... ☐
21-29 .... ☐
30-39 .... ☐
40-49 .... ☐
50-59 .... ☐
60-over .... ☐

10. Are you:

Male .... ☐
Female .... ☐

11. Which computer publications do you read regularly? (Please list)

_____
_____
_____
_____
_____
_____
_____
_____
_____
_____

Comments: _____
_____
_____

Fold here and scotch-tape to mail.